Edwin Wilbur Rice

People's Dictionary of the Bible

Describing persons, places, countries, customs, birds, animals, trees, plants, books,

events, and many other things in Holy Scripture

Edwin Wilbur Rice

People's Dictionary of the Bible
Describing persons, places, countries, customs, birds, animals, trees, plants, books, events, and many other things in Holy Scripture

ISBN/EAN: 9783337241117

Printed in Europe, USA, Canada, Australia, Japan

Cover: Foto ©Lupo / pixelio.de

More available books at **www.hansebooks.com**

PEOPLE'S

DICTIONARY OF THE BIBLE

DESCRIBING

PERSONS, PLACES, COUNTRIES, CUSTOMS, BIRDS, ANIMALS, TREES, PLANTS, BOOKS, EVENTS, AND MANY OTHER THINGS IN HOLY SCRIPTURE.

EDITED BY

EDWIN W. RICE, D. D.,

Author of "People's Commentaries" on Matthew, Mark, Luke and John, "Our Sixty-Six Sacred Books," etc., etc.

PHILADELPHIA:
THE AMERICAN SUNDAY-SCHOOL UNION,
1122 CHESTNUT STREET.
NEW YORK: 8 AND 10 BIBLE HOUSE.
1893.

Price, Single Copy, 25 cents; Postage, 8 cents. By the Hundred, $20.

[Copyright by THE AMERICAN SUNDAY-SCHOOL UNION, 1893.]

PREFACE.

This work has been prepared for the multitude who want a comprehensive, concise, handy Dictionary of the Bible for Twenty-five cents.

Bulky, learned, expensive, denominational, controversial, and theological dictionaries are abundant. But Bible readers, lay missionaries, members of Christian Endeavor Societies, guilds, leagues, King's Daughters, Sunday-schools and other organizations helpful to the young are often at a loss in their labors, from the lack of an inexpensive Bible Dictionary *fairly abreast of present Biblical Scholarship*, and free from denominational bias, technical theological terms, unsound teachings, and lengthy discussions—a dictionary for handy and quick reference.

This work is for them.

Some Christian friends who felt the need of such a work, urged the Editor to prepare it, and generously provided the funds to pay the cost of its preparation and donated the plates to the American Sunday-School Union, so that this Dictionary might be sold at a price that would encourage a large distribution of it, and put it within the reach of all.

The following principles have guided in the preparation of the work:

1. To present the results of the best scholarly information in respect to persons, places, customs, and subjects mentioned in the Bible, in alphabetical order and in a simple and concise style.

2. To define such words and topics only as are found in the English Bible, and to give an explanation of any peculiar use or meaning of them.

3. To admit no name or word, about which nothing is known except the mere mention of it in the Bible.

4. Carefully to exclude whatever would be regarded as sectarian or denominational by any body of Evangelical Christians. It is needless to add that this did not exclude any Bible terms.

5. To give the pronunciation and meaning of names and titles.

Special attention has been given to some marked fulfilments of prophecy.

The Appendix contains a list of parables and miracles in the Bible, tables of time, weights, measures, distances, and moneys, a list of obsolete words found in the Authorized Version, and of the titles and names of Christ, a list of stations in the Journeyings of Israel, and valuable Chronological tables.

The Editor has made free use especially of the geographical articles which he contributed to Schaff's "Dictionary of the Bible." Moreover, the standard works of Ayre, Bastow, Cassell, Fairbairn, Fausset, Kitto and Smith, the latest Cyclopædias, and the recent voluminous reports and works on Palestinian, Egyptian and Assyrian exploration, have all been drawn upon for material, to bring the information in this work up to date.

The Rev. Edward K. Tullidge aided in gathering the material, and in fixing the proportionate length of the articles; Samuel B. Schieffelin also prepared several of the articles; Martin P. Rice, of the University of Pennsylvania, verified the references to Scripture, and the pronunciation of proper names; the Rev. Moseley H. Williams made valuable suggestions while the work was in preparation; Mr. William H. Hirst carefully read the proofs, and the entire material was thoroughly revised by the Editor, so that the latest and best results of sound Biblical knowledge might be included for the use of the ordinary reader.

This is the seventh work in the "People's Series" of new, scholarly and handy helps for Bible study.*

The Dictionary is sent forth in the Divine Master's name, with the earnest hope that it may be found useful to the millions of English-speaking peoples who love and accept the Holy Scriptures as the authoritative word of God.

May, 1893.   EDWIN W. RICE.

---

* The list of the "People's Series" is as follows. Prices exclusive of postage. Discount made on quantities.

1. INDEX TO THE BIBLE.................. 15 cts.   4. COMMENTARY ON MARK............... 50 cts.
                                                     By Edwin W. Rice, D. D.
2. PEOPLE'S HYMN BOOK................ 20 cts.   5. COMMENTARY ON LUKE............... 85 cts.
   By S. B. Schieffelin.   By Edwin W. Rice, D. D.
3. COMMENTARY ON MATTHEW........ 85 cts.   6. COMMENTARY ON JOHN................ 85 cts.
   By Edwin W. Rice, D. D.   By Edwin W. Rice, D. D.

PEOPLE'S DICTIONARY OF THE BIBLE.

Explanations:—A. V.—Authorized Version; R. V.—Revised Version; Sept.—Septuagint, or Greek Version of the Old Testament; ä, as in *fär;* ā, as in *cáre;* ē, as in *thēre;* ĕ, as in *tĕrm;* ĭ, as in *pīque;* ŏ, as in *fŏr;* ōō, as in *fōōd;* ŏŏ, as in *fŏŏt;* ŭ, as in *fŭrl;* the other abbreviations are self-explanatory.

A

Aaron (âr'on or ā'ron). The name, if of Hebrew origin, means *enlightened.* According to Jerome, it means *mountain of strength.* The son of Amram and Jochebed, of the tribe of Levi. He was three years older than his brother Moses. Ex. 6:20; 7:7. Aaron was noted for his eloquence, and was appointed by Jehovah to speak for Moses in the court of Pharaoh. Ex. 4:14-16. He aided Moses in leading the Hebrews out of Egypt; and was consecrated the first high priest of the Hebrew nation. Ex. 7:1-10; 28:1-43; Lev. 8:1-36. He was a man of great devotion; but, from want of firmness, he sometimes fell into grievous sins. While Moses was absent in Mount Sinai receiving the law, Aaron weakly yielded to the people's demand to have some image of a deity for them to worship. The image he made was a golden calf, after the form of the Egyptian Apis or Mnevis. Ex. 32:1-35; Ps. 106:19, 20. Aaron joined Miriam, his sister, in sedition against Moses, Num. 12:1-12, and, with Moses, neglected to acknowledge the power of God at Kadesh. For this sin he was denied the privilege of entering the promised land. Num. 20:12-24. While the Hebrews were encamped at Moserah, in the fortieth year after leaving Egypt, Aaron, at the divine command, ascended Mount Hor and died, at the age of 123 years. Num. 20:25-29; Deut. 10:6. The sons and descendants of Aaron served as priests at the sanctuary; while the other families of the tribe of Levi performed those religious duties which were of an inferior kind. Num. 4:15, 16, 24. Aaron is called the "saint of the Lord" with reference to his official character, Ps. 106:16, but, as the most superficial study of his life shows, he had many faults. Yet the people loved him, and the mourning over his death, which lasted 30 days, Num. 20:28, was sincere. One of the fasts of later Judaism was held in his memory, on the first day of the fifth month, Ab, our July or August.

Aaron married Elisheba, daughter of Amminadab, probably a prince of the tribe of Judah, and had four sons, Nadab, Abihu, Eleazar and Ithamar. Ex. 6:23; Num. 1:7. The Jewish priesthood began in the family of Aaron and remained in its possession, though not uninterruptedly, in the line of Eleazar; it passed into the family of Ithamar, the brother of Eleazar, in the person of Eli; but, in consequence of the wickedness of Eli's sons, God declared that it should be taken from his family, 1 Sam. 2:30, and this prophecy was fulfilled in the time of Solomon, who took the priesthood from Abiathar and restored it to Zadok, of the line of Eleazar. 1 Kings 2:27.

Aaronites (âr'on-îtes or ā'ron-ītes). 1 Chron. 12:27. Levites of the family of Aaron: the priests who served the sanctuary. Eleazar, Aaron's son, was their chief. Num. 4:16.

Abaddon, or Apollyon (a-băd'dŏn or a-pŏl'yŏn). The former name is Hebrew and the latter Greek, and both signify *the destroyer.* Job 31:12; Rev. 9:11. He is the same as the "angel of the abyss," that is, the angel of death, or the destroying angel. Ps. 78:49. Abaddon frequently occurs in the Hebrew, and is translated "destruction," meaning often the world of the dead. Job 26:6; 28:22; Ps. 88:11; Prov. 15:11.

Abana (ăb'a-nah or a-bä'nah), *stony.* The Hebrew and English marginal reading is "Amanah," meaning "perennial;" this may be the correct form. It is the same as the Greek "*Chrysorrhoas,*" or "golden river," and the modern "Barada," meaning "cold." A river of Damascus, one of those which Naaman, in his pride, preferred to the waters of Israel. 2 Kings 5:12. It rises in the beautiful plain of Zebedâny, issuing from a little lake, and receiving in its course the waters of two or three fountains. Quitting this plain, the river dashes over a cliff, 30 feet high, runs through a magnificent ravine, and is afterwards joined by the stream from 'Ain Fijeh, one of the largest springs in Syria. Having emerged from the mountains into the plains of Damascus, it flows through orchards and meadows till it enters the city, and passing through it, falls finally into a marshy lake, 15 or 20 miles below. At its rise the river is 3343 feet above the sea, and 1149 above Damascus, which is distant from the source about 22 miles. The Abana waters about 800 square miles of territory, and it is calculated that 14 villages and 150,000 souls depend on it for their water supply. Damascus is thus made, though on the edge of a desert, one of the loveliest spots in the world. The streams of Israel, on the other hand, with the exception of the Jordan, are nearly dry the greater part of the year, and, running in deep and rocky channels, give but partial fertility to the land through which they flow. This may well account for the question of Naaman the Syrian: "Are not Abana and Pharphar, rivers of Damascus, better than all the waters of Israel?" 2 Kings 5:12.

Abarim (ăb'a-rĭm or a-bä'rĭm), *mountains beyond,* or *of the fords,* a range of mountains east of the river Jordan, in the land of Moab, opposite Jericho. Num. 27:12; 33:47; Deut. 32:49. Nebo, Peor, and Pisgah belong to this range. In Jer. 22:20 the word is translated "passages" in the Authorized Version, but the Revised Version reads Abarim.

Ije-abarim in Num. 21:11 means *heaps*

9

or *ruins of Abarim*, and was near the same range.

Abba (ăb'bah), a Chaldee word signifying *father* (Hebrew ab), easily pronounced by infant children, and expressing the peculiar tenderness, familiarity, and confidence of the love between parent and child. Mark 14:36; Rom. 8:15; Gal. 4:6. Luther translated *Abba, Pater*, "Abba, dear Father."

Abdon (ăb'dŏn), *servile*. 1. A Levitical city in Asher. Josh. 21:30; 1 Chron. 6:74. 2. The tenth judge of Israel, Judg. 12:13,15, probably the same as Bedan, 1 Sam. 12:11, son of Hillel, of the tribe of Ephraim. He succeeded Elon, and judged Israel eight years. His rule was a peaceful one, as no oppression of Israel during his time is mentioned. The record that he had 40 sons and 30 nephews (or rather grandsons) who rode on young asses, implies their high dignity and consequence: comp. Judg. 5:9, 10, 3. Also two Benjamites. 1 Chron. 8:23, 30; 9:36. 4. A son of Micah. 2 Chron. 34:20. See **Achbor**.

Abednego (a-bĕd'ne-gō), *servant of Nego* or *Nebo*, a Chaldee name given to Azariah, one of the three captive young princes of Judah, who were Daniel's companions at the court of the king of Babylon. Dan. 1:7. Their virtue, wisdom, and piety secured their promotion at court, Dan. 1:3–19; 2:17–49; and their firmness in witnessing for God among idolaters, with their deliverance from the fiery furnace by Jehovah, led many to acknowledge the true God, and rendered these pious youths forever illustrious. Dan. 3; Heb. 11:34.

Abel (ā'bel), *vapor*, Gen. 4:2, was the second son of Adam and Eve, so called perhaps from the shortness of his life, as he was murdered by Cain. Hence to Eve the life of Abel seemed but "a vapour, that appeareth for a little time, and then vanisheth away." Jas. 4:14. Abel was occupied as a keeper or feeder of sheep; and in process of time brought of the firstlings, or first-fruits of his flock, au offering unto the Lord. It is supposed that besides a thank-offering, Abel brought a sin-offering, and thus showed his sense of sin, as well as his faith in a promised Saviour. He did it by faith, Heb. 11:4, founded no doubt upon some revelation from God. His offering was a type of Christ, the "Lamb slain from the foundation of the world." Rev. 13:8; 5:6, 12; 1:5: John 1:29. "The Lord had respect unto Abel and his offering." Gen. 4:4, and accepted it. Heb. 11:4. Not so with Cain. Either his sacrifice, or the manner of presenting it, was offensive to God, and the offering was rejected. 1 John 3:12. Cain was angry, and filled with envy, and when he and his brother were in the field together, he took his brother's life. Gen. 4:3–8. Our Saviour distinguishes Abel by the title *righteous*. Matt. 23:35. He is also one of the faithful "elders" mentioned in the epistle to the Hebrews, ch. 11:4, and is justly called the first martyr.

Abel, *meadow, grassy plain*, as below. A name prefixed to several places. Instead of *"the great stone of* Abel," in 1 Sam. 6:18, the Septuagint, and Chaldee versions, and some Hebrew manuscripts, read "the great stone;" as in the margin, and the 14th and 15th verses. Most likely this "great stone" was a boundary mark, or an ancient monument, in Bethshemesh, on the confines of Judah, Dan, and Philistia.

Abel-beth-Maachah (ā'bĕl-bĕth-mā'a-kah), *meadow of the house of oppression*, 2 Kings 15:29, a town in the north of Palestine near Cæsarea-Philippi. It was attacked by Joab, 2 Sam. 20:14, 15; by Benhadad, 1 Kings 15:20; and by Tiglath-Pileser, 2 Kings 15:29.

Abel-Maim (ā'bel-may'im), *meadow of waters*. 2 Chron. 16:4. Another name for Abel-beth-Maachah.

Abel-Meholah (ā'bel-me-hō'lah), *meadow of the dance*. Judg. 7:22. A town in the plain of Jordan, distinguished as the home of Elisha. 1 Kings 4:12; 19:16.

Abel-Mizraim (ā'bel-miz-ray'im), *meadow of Egypt*. Gen. 50:10, 11. The place where Joseph and his company halted seven days in passing from Egypt to Canaan to bury Jacob. It was "beyond"—that is, west of, the Jordan, as the writer was on the east side. Some think it was near Hebron.

Abel-Shittim, or **Shittim** (ā'bel-shit-tim), *meadow of the acacias*. Num. 33:49; 25:1. A town six or seven miles distant from the east bank of the Jordan, opposite to Jericho. It was the last encampment of the Israelites on that side of the river. It was at this place that the Israelites fell into the grossest idolatry, for which they were visited with a desolating plague which destroyed 24,000 people. Num. 25:1; Micah 6:5. The spies whom Joshua sent to Jericho went from Shittim. Josh. 2:1.

Abi (ā'bī), *father, progenitor*, mother of King Hezekiah, 2 Kings 18:2; written Abijah in 2 Chron. 29:1.

Abia, Abiah, or **Abijah** (ā-bī'ah or ā-bī'jah), *whose father is Jehovah*. 1. Son of Becher, the son of Benjamin. 1 Chron. 7:8. 2. Wife of Hezron. 1 Chron. 2:24. 3. Second son of Samuel. 1 Sam. 8:2. 4. The son of Rehoboam. 1 Chron. 3:10; Matt. 1:7. See **Abijah**, 2. 5. Mother of King Hezekiah. **Abi**. 6. Same as Abijah, 3.

Abia, course of. Luke 1:5. In 1 Chron. 24 we have an account of the division of the priests into twenty-four classes, courses, or orders, who ministered at the altar in rotation. The courses were distinguished by the name of the most prominent member of the family from which the course was taken. The eighth of these courses fell to the family of Abia or Abijah; and to this course belonged Zacharias, the father of John the Baptist.

Abiathar (a-bī'a-thar), *father of abundance, i. e., liberal*. Tenth high priest and descendant of Levi through Eli. Abiathar was the only one of all the sons of Ahimelech the high priest who escaped the slaughter inflicted upon his father's house by Saul, in revenge for his having inquired of the Lord for David and given him the shewbread to eat. 1 Sam. 22:21-23. Abiathar having become high priest fled to

David, and was thus enabled to inquire of the Lord for him. 1 Sam. 23:9; 30:7; 2 Sam. 2:1; 5:19, etc. He adhered to David in his wanderings while pursued by Saul; he was with him while he reigned in Hebron, and afterwards in Jerusalem. 2 Sam. 2:1-3. He continued faithful to him in Absalom's rebellion. 2 Sam. 15:24, 29, 35, 36; 17:15-17; 19:11. When, however, Adonijah set himself up for David's successor on the throne, in opposition to Solomon, Abiathar sided with him, while Zadok was on Solomon's side. For this Abiathar was deprived of the high priesthood. Zadok had joined David at Hebron, 1 Chron. 12:28, so that there were henceforth two high priests in the reign of David, and till the deposition of Abiathar by Solomon, when Zadok became the sole high priest, thus fulfilling the prophecy of 1 Sam. 2:30. Ahimelech, or Abimelech, son of Abiathar, is substituted for Abiathar, son of Ahimelech. 2 Sam. 8:17; 1 Chron. 18:16; 24:3, 6, 31. The Lord Jesus, Mark 2:26, names Abiathar as the high priest in whose time David ate the shewbread. Probably the sense is: "In the days of Abiathar, *who was afterwards* high priest," and *under whom the record of the fact* would be made. Perhaps too the loaves, being his perquisite, Lev. 24:9, were actually handed by Abiathar to David. Both father and son, moreover, it seems from the quotations above, bore both names, and were indifferently called by either.

Abib (ă′bĭb), *budding*, Ex. 13:4. See **Month**.

Abiezer (ă-bĭ-ē′zer), *the father of help*. Eldest son of Gilead, and descendant of Manasseh, Josh. 17:2; 1 Chron. 7:18; Num. 26:30, where the name is given in the contracted form Jeezer. He was the ancestor of the great judge Gideon. 2. A native of Anathoth. 2 Sam. 23:27. The name also occurs in Judg. 6:34; 8:2; and in an adjectival form, "the Abiezrite," in Judg. 6:11, 24; 8:32.

Abigail (ăb′ĭ-gāil or gĕl), *father, i. e., source, of joy*. 1. The beautiful wife of Nabal, a wealthy owner of goats and sheep in Carmel. When David's messengers were slighted by Nabal, Abigail supplied David and his followers with provisions, and succeeded in appeasing his anger. Ten days after this Nabal died, and David sent for Abigail and made her his wife. 1 Sam. 25:14, etc. By her he had a son, called Chileab in 2 Sam. 3:3, but Daniel in 1 Chron. 3:1. 2. A sister of David, married to Jether the *Ishmaelite*, and mother, by him, of Amasa. 1 Chron. 2:17. In 2 Sam. 17:25, for *Israelite* read *Ishmaelite*.

Abihu (a-bī′hew), *whose father is He, i. e., God*. One of the sons of Aaron, who, together with his brothers, Nadab, Eleazar, and Ithamar, were set apart by God to the office of the priesthood. Soon after they entered upon their sacred duties, Nadab and Abihu were guilty of a violation of God's commands, respecting the manner of offering incense, and they were suddenly destroyed by fire from heaven. They used strange, or common, fire, instead of the sacred fire which they were required to use from the altar of burnt offering. Lev. 10:1, 2. As the prohibition of wine and strong drink, especially when entering into the sanctuary, immediately follows, we may infer that Nadab and Abihu were intoxicated when they fell into this presumptuous sin.

Abijah (a-bī′jah), *whose father is Jehovah*. 1. A son of Jeroboam I., king of Israel, who died under interesting circumstances in early life. 1 Kings 14:1. See **Jeroboam**. 2. Abijah or Abijam, 2 Chron. 13:1, the son of Rehoboam and Michaiah, succeeded his father as king of Judah, B. C. 959. He made war against Jeroboam, king of Israel, for the purpose of getting back the kingship of the ten tribes, and defeated him, with a loss of 500,000 men. These figures are probably through a copyist's mistake made too large; the loss, it is likely, was not greater than 50,000. He began to reign in the eighteenth year of Jeroboam, and was succeeded by his son Asa in the twentieth year of Jeroboam, so that he reigned only a part of three years. The apparent contradiction in respect to the parentage of this person, as it is given in 1 Kings 15:2 and 2 Chron. 13:2, may be explained by supposing that his mother Maachah (or Michaiah) was the daughter of Uriel and the granddaughter of Absalom, who is called Abishalom. 1 Kings 15:2. The term "daughter" is given in the Bible to other relatives than one's own child; *e. g.*, to a niece, granddaughter, or great-granddaughter. 3. The head of one of the courses of priests, 1 Chron. 24:10; Neh. 12:17; termed Abia in Luke 1:5. 4. The mother of Hezekiah, 2 Chron. 29:1; also called Abi in 2 Kings 18:2. 5. One of the priests who "sealed the covenant;" *i. e.*, appended their seals unto it to signify that they were parties to it. Neh. 10:7. 6. A priest who returned with Zerubbabel from Babylon. Neh. 12:4, 17.

Abijam (a-bī′jam), *father of the sea, i. e., a maritime person*. 1 Kings 15:1, 7, 8. See **Abijah** (2).

Abilene (ăb′ĭ-lē′ne), from *Abila*, a small district of Palestine on the eastern slopes of Anti-Libanus, of which Abila on the river Barada was the capital. It was governed by Lysanias in the time of John the Baptist. Luke 3:1.

Abimelech (a-bĭm′e-lĕk), *father of the king*, or *royal father*. This seems to have been the common title of several of the Philistine kings. 1. A king of Gerar, and contemporary with Abraham, who took Sarah into his harem, and thought to make her his wife; but being warned of God in a dream of Sarah's relationship to Abraham, that she was not his sister, but his wife, he restored her to her husband, with a present of a thousand pieces of silver, as "a covering of the eyes" for Sarah; that is, as an atoning present, and to be a testimony of her innocence in the eyes of all. Gen. 20:1-18. 2. Another king of Gerar, probably son of the former, who rebuked Isaac for his dissimulation, in calling his wife his sister, and afterwards made a league with him at Beersheba. Gen. 26:6, 31. 3. A son of Gideon, by his concubine, who, after the

11

death of his father, persuaded the men of Shechem to make him king. He slew his father's 70 sons on one stone, leaving only Jotham, the youngest, alive, who hid himself. Three years afterwards the men of Shechem rose against Abimelech; he defeated them and destroyed their city, and sowed it with salt. While attacking Thebez, he was mortally wounded by a piece of a millstone thrown upon his head by a woman from the top of the tower. That it might not be said, "a woman slew him," he called to his armor-bearer to thrust him through with his sword, and thus he died. This was the first attempt to establish a monarchy in Israel. Judg. 9:5, 54. 4. The name given in the title of Ps. 34 to Achish, king of Gath. 5. The name of "Ahimelech" is thus written in 1 Chron. 18:16.

Abinadab (*a-bĭn'a-dăb*), *father of nobleness*, *i. e.*, *noble*. 1. 1 Sam. 16:8. One of the eight sons of Jesse, and one of the three of his sons who followed Saul in battle. 2. 1 Sam. 31:2. One of Saul's sons who was slain at the battle of Gilboa. 3. 1 Sam. 7:1 and 1 Chron. 13:7. A Levite of Kirjath-jearim, with whom the ark of the Lord was deposited when it was brought back from the Philistines. 4. 1 Kings 4:11. One of the twelve officers appointed by Solomon to provide alternately, month by month, food for the king and his household.

Abiram (*a-bī'ram*), *father of height*, *i. e.*, *renowned*. 1. Num. 16:1. One of the sons of Eliab, the Reubenite, who were destroyed with Korah for a conspiracy against Moses. See **Korah**. 2. 1 Kings 16:34. The first-born of Hiel, the Bethelite.

Abishag (*ăb'ĭ-shăg* or *a-bī'shăg*), *father of error*, a beautiful virgin of Shunem, in Issachar, chosen to cherish David in his old age. After his death, Adonijah sought her hand to promote his treasonable schemes, and was punished by death. 1 Kings 1:2.

Abishai (*a-bĭsh'a-ī* or *a-bī-shā'ī*), *father of a gift*, eldest son of Zeruiah, David's sister, brother of Joab and Asahel, one of the bravest of David's "mighty men," 1 Chron. 2:16, always faithful to his royal uncle, and usually a personal attendant. He went with him alone to the tent of Saul, 1 Sam. 26:5-12, and was a leader in the war with Ish-bosheth, 2 Sam. 2:18, 24, in the war with the Edomites, 1 Chron. 18:12, 13, and with the Syrians and Ammonites. 2 Sam. 10:10, 14. In a battle with the Philistines he rescued David, and slew Ishbi-benob the giant, 2 Sam. 21:16, 17. He broke through their host around Bethlehem, and lifted up his spear against 300, and slew them, 2 Sam. 23:14-18; and was with David in the matters of Shimei, Absalom, and Sheba. 2 Sam. 16:9; 18:2; 19:21; 20:6, 7.

Abishua (*a-bĭsh'ŭ-ah* or *ăb'ĭ-shū'ah*), *father of welfare*. 1. The son of Phineas, the high priest. 1 Chron. 6:4, 5, 50; Ezra 7:5. 2. The son of Bela. 1 Chron. 8:4.

Abner (*ăb'ner*), *father of light*. 1. Son of Ner, who was the brother of Kish, 1 Chron. 9:36, the father of Saul. (B. C. 1063.) Abner, therefore, was Saul's first cousin, and was made by him commander-in-chief of his army. 1 Sam. 14:51; 17:57; 26:5-14. After the death of Saul David was proclaimed king of Judah; and some time subsequently Abner proclaimed Ish-bosheth, Saul's son, king of Israel. War soon broke out between the two rival kings, and a "very sore battle" was fought at Gibeon between the men of Israel under Abner and the men of Judah under Joab. 1 Sam. 2:15-32. In this engagement he killed, in self-defence, Asahel, the brother of Joab and Abishai. Perhaps he now had some idea of seizing the Israelitish throne for himself; for he appropriated a woman of Saul's harem, which Ish-bosheth interpreted as an overt act of rebellion. Abner, incensed at his ingratitude, opened negotiations with David, by whom he was most favorably received at Hebron. He then undertook to procure David's recognition throughout Israel; but after leaving his presence for the purpose was enticed back by Joab, and treacherously murdered by him and his brother Abishai, at the gate of the city, ostensibly in retaliation for the death of Asahel; really, we may suppose, through jealousy, as he would have at least rivalled Joab in position. David, though unable to punish the powerful brothers, solemnized Abner's funeral with great respect and general mourning, and poured forth a simple dirge over the slain hero. 2 Sam. 3:33, 34. 2. The father of Jaasiel, chief of the Benjamites in David's reign, 1 Chron. 27:21; probably the same as the preceding.

Abominable, Abomination. 1. An abomination, or an abominable thing, is a thing hateful or detestable, as the employment or calling of shepherds was to the Egyptians. Gen. 46:34. 2. Under the Mosaic law those animals and acts are called abominable the use or doing of which was prohibited. Lev. 11:13 and Deut. 23:18. 3. Idolatry of every kind is especially denoted by this term. Jer. 44:4 and 2 Kings 23:13. 4. So of sins in general. Isa. 66:3. THE ABOMINATION OF DESOLATION, literally *the abomination of the desolator*. This was Daniel's prediction of the pollution of the temple at Jerusalem, by Antiochus Epiphanes, who set up in it the altar and the statue of Jupiter Olympus: the daily sacrifice was taken away, and the abomination that maketh desolate drove all the true worshippers of God from the temple. Dan. 11:31; 12:11. But the prophecy had, to say the least, a further reference. For our Lord appeals to it, Matt. 24:15-18; Mark 13:14-16, and declares that its fulfillment was to be the warning for his disciples to flee from the doomed city. This would be simultaneous with the investment of Jerusalem. Luke 21:20, 21. Some have believed the investment (when Cestius Gallus first encamped around Jerusalem, 66 A. D., and then withdrew) the abomination of desolation itself; the Roman standards (objects of worship to the soldiers) being then planted on holy ground. But these standards had been there before; and so it is more likely that the abominable thing was something done by the Jews themselves. Now Josephus mentions a profanation by the Zealots who had got possession of the

12

temple; and to this or some similar deed our Lord, we may suppose, referred. The Christians, it may be added, took the warning, the opportunity being afforded by the retirement of Gallus, and fled to Pella.

Abram (*ā'bram*), *high father*, afterwards named **Abraham** (*ā'bra-ham*), *father of a multitude*, Gen. 17:4, 5, the great founder of the Jewish nation, as well as of the Ishmaelites and other Arabian tribes. Gen. 25. He was a son of Terah, a descendant of Shem, and a brother of Nahor and Haran, and was born in Ur, a city of Chaldea. Gen. 11:27, 28. Here he lived 70 years, when at the call of God he left his idolatrous kindred, Josh. 24:2, 14, and removed to Haran, in Mesopotamia, Acts 7:2-4, accompanied by his father, his wife Sarai, his brother Nahor, and his nephew Lot. Here, a few years after, Terah died. Abram's proper history now begins. He was commanded to go into Canaan, receiving at the time a two-fold promise, that his seed should become a vast multitude, and that through them all the families of the earth should be blessed. Abram was become a wealthy chief, and, with the servants and the substance that belonged to him, accompanied by his wife Sarai and his nephew Lot, he entered Canaan. 12:1-5. The country was already occupied by descendants of Ham. He passed through the heart of the country by the great highway to Shechem, and pitched his tent by the oak of Moreh. Gen. 12:6. Here he received in vision from Jehovah the further revelation that this was the land which his descendants should inherit. Removing from Moreh he pitched on a mount to the east of Bethel, and journeying south he went down into Egypt (famine then afflicting Canaan), establishing there the first link of that mysterious chain which so long, through almost all their history, bound the chosen people for discipline and for warning to the Egyptians. But here, alas! Abram's faith wavered. Fearing that the great beauty of Sarai might tempt the powerful monarch of Egypt and expose his own life to peril, he arranged that Sarai should represent herself as his sister, which her actual relationship to him, as probably the daughter of his brother Haran, allowed her to do with some semblance of truth. But her beauty was reported to the king, and she was taken into the royal harem. He was rescued by God's providence from the false position in which he had placed himself, and enriched by Pharaoh he returned to Canaan. Gen. 12:10-20. Abram was wealthy; and Lot was wealthy too. Had the land been empty, they might very well have extended their encampments in it. But the Canaanites and Perizzites were there too; and therefore uncle and nephew must separate. From a hill near Bethel, which it is said may still be identified, Abram and Lot surveyed the country; and Lot, having his choice allowed him, selected the rich valley of the Jordan for his abode, careless what kind of associates he would thus meet with; while Abram, with the renewed assurance that Canaan should be given to his seed, went southward to Mamre and dwelt there. Lot was soon involved in the disasters of the neighborhood he had chosen. He was made prisoner in the irruption of an eastern monarch, of whom something, it is said, is yet to be dimly traced in the deciphered Assyrian inscriptions (see **Chedor-laomer**); and Abram resolved to attempt his nephew's rescue. On his victorious return he received the blessing of Melchizedek. But Abram's faith began to be sorely tried. The promise was to him in his seed; and as yet he had no child. Years rolled on; and the likelihood of his having offspring grew less and less. The promise was therefore repeated: Abram believed it. And now, because his faith held on, not only when accomplishment seemed easy, but when it was delayed and seemed most difficult, well-nigh impossible, now, when there was the word alone, the bare promise, with no outward confirmation, and Abram still believed, God "counted it to him for righteousness." The trial of his faith was very, very precious, "much more precious than of gold that perisheth." 1 Pet. 1:7. And then there was a symbol vouchsafed him, and larger promise that his posterity should possess the whole extent of country between the river of Egypt and the Euphrates. Sarai's faith, however, faltered; and, as the promise was not yet announced that the holy seed should come from Sarai's womb, she gave her husband her Egyptian maid, intending to adopt her child. Abram then had a son, Ishmael; but *he* was not the heir of promise. Thirteen years passed on, perhaps spent at Mamre; and the purposes of God were ripening. The covenant was now made more definite: Sarai was included in the promise; the names of the pair were changed to Abraham and Sarah; and the sign of circumcision was added, to be a token throughout all generations that God had been with and was blessing Abraham his friend. But there must be delay and trial still. The Lord held again mysterious conference with Abraham, before Sodom was destroyed, and Abraham, perhaps in consequence of that catastrophe, journeyed south-west into the land of the Philistines at Gerar; and there the evil step in Egypt was repeated. At length God's time was come; and Sarah bare Abraham a son (probably at Gerar) in his old age. And then indeed there was joy; the promise long waited for being now fulfilled. The name given to the child, Isaac (*laughter* or *sporting*), indicated this. Once Sarah had laughed incredulously at the idea of her having a son, and Abraham had laughed too, his faith, strong as it was, being then inclined to fix on Ishmael as the heir of his name and blessing. Gen. chaps. 13-20. But now the happy parents laughed with thankful joy; and all their friends that heard the tidings laughed and rejoiced with them. Gen. 21:1-7. There was a feast made when Isaac was weaned; yet the mirth of that feast was dashed with heaviness. The son of the bondwoman, jealous perhaps of

Isaac's happier lot, was discovered mocking; and Sarah insisted that he and his mother Hagar should be banished from the encampment. It was very grievous to Abraham; but God commanded him to yield; and Hagar and Ishmael went forth, a sign of the call of the Gentiles, and proving the best means of fulfilling the promise that Ishmael should become a great nation. Gen. 21:8-21; Gal. 4:22-31. There were some petty troubles from Abimelech in the patriarch's life, but with this exception nothing is recorded of the space of perhaps 25 years. His residence was now at Beer-sheba. And then came a strange and crushing trial. To comprehend it, we must bear in mind that Abraham lived among idolaters, who ruthlessly made their children pass through the fire. Lev. 18:21, 24, 25; Deut. 18:9, 10. Many a time must Abraham have seen from afar the smoke of sacrifices, and known that human victims were offered there. And his heart must have glowed when he remembered that *his* God required no such homage; and perhaps he had to stand the scoff of those around, that he had chosen a very easy religion, demanding not the self-denying obedience which theirs did. For, surely, though they practiced these cruel abominations, many hearts among them must have bled as their dearest were taken as victims; and though they yielded to the stern law it must have been with grief and bitter tears. Their obedience, then, they would say, was far deeper and more meritorious than Abraham's easy service. But then came the command, "Take now thy son, thine only son Isaac whom thou lovest . . . and offer him for a burnt-offering." It was not merely the laceration of domestic ties, not only the apparent blight of the promise so long waited for and then fulfilled—the whole basis of his trust seemed overturned, the character of the God he worshipped changed, his religion no better than that of the surrounding tribes. Imagination cannot conceive a harder trial. But his faith, hitherto unshaken, supported him in this final trial, "accounting that God was able to raise up his son, even from the dead, from whence also he received him in a figure." Heb. 11:19. The sacrifice was stayed by the angel of Jehovah, the promises were again confirmed to him, the spiritual blessings in them being prominently exhibited; and, with gratitude which even the sacred historian does not attempt to describe, Abraham returned to Beer-sheba. This great event was the most wonderful in the patriarch's life. Then it was, no doubt, that his eye was opened to perceive in the dim future another sacrifice, of a dearer Son yielded by a higher Father (and probably on or near that very spot), a sacrifice actually consummated, by the virtue of which a propitiation of world-wide virtue was effected. The rest of Abraham's history is comparatively scanty. He seems to have removed from Beer-sheba to Kirjath-arba or Hebron; and there Sarah died when he was 137. He purchased for her sepulchre the field and cave of Machpelah from the princes of the land, for the exorbitant price of 400 shekels of silver. The bargain with Ephron is very characteristic of eastern manners to the present day. Some, misled by Ephron's courteous speech, have fancied that he really intended to offer his field to Abraham for a gift. But this is from sheer ignorance of Oriental habits. Ephron was a shrewd man, who well knew how to drive a bargain; and a good one he made for himself. Gen. 23. Abraham then took care that his son Isaac should not marry into the idolatrous families around. And next there is the strange record that he had another wife, and children by her; and even "concubines" are mentioned. Keturah was a secondary or inferior wife, not given to the patriarch by Sarah, as Hagar was. It may be, therefore, that, though the fact is noted so late, the children had been born much earlier. But we can hardly arrive at certainty on this matter. Be it as it may, Abraham sent away his other sons with gifts into the east, that they might not interfere with Isaac, to whom his great inheritance belonged. And then he died. 175 years old, having seen Isaac's sons, and was buried by Isaac and Ishmael in the cave of Machpelah, where perchance his bones may still be lying. Such briefly is the story of this father of the faithful, from whom the precious seed descended, and into whose bosom the faithful dead are said to have been conveyed. Luke 16:22. His faith we are to follow: his good example we should diligently imitate.

Absalom (*ăb'sa-lom*), *father of peace.* The third son of David, by Maachah, the daughter of Talmai, king of Geshur, born at Hebron. 2 Sam. 3:3; 1 Chron. 3:2. Absalom revenged the dishonor done to Tamar, his sister, by Amnon, his half-brother, by killing him at a feast, and then fled to his father-in-law, Talmai. 2 Sam. 13. After three years, by means of Joab, he was enabled to return to Jerusalem, and in two years more fully restored to David's favor. Absalom was now nourishing the ambitious scheme of supplanting his father. He was very beautiful and had extraordinary hair, which when cut every year weighed 200 shekels, the exact equivalent to which in our weights it is not easy to ascertain; or, possibly, the hair was of 200 shekels' value. He took great pains to acquire popularity, and after four years (so we may read, 2 Sam. 15:7) he raised the standard of revolt at Hebron. The history of this rebellion, its first success—there being evidently some ill-feeling in his own tribe of Judah towards David—with the iniquitous conduct of Absalom, and his final defeat, is in 2 Sam., chap. 15-18. David wished to spare his unhappy son's life; but, in the rout, his mule carrying him under the thick boughs of an oak, his head was caught; and Joab, being made aware of this, dispatched him. Absalom had three sons and a daughter, but it would seem that his sons died before him, as he erected a pillar to keep his name in remembrance. 2 Sam. 18:18. A monument outside the walls of Jerusalem now bears his name, but it is a structure of comparatively modern date.

Accad (ăk'kad), *fortress*, one of the four cities in the kingdom of Nimrod. Gen. 10:10. It was in the land of Shinar, and George Smith locates it at *Agadi*, on the Euphrates, north of Babylon. Rawlinson places it at *Aker-Kuf*, ten miles west by north of Bagdad. Others had regarded it as identical with *Ctesiphon*.

Accho (ăk'ko), *heated sand*, now Acca or Acre, Judg. 1:31, or Ptolemais (so called after the first Ptolemy, king of Egypt, into whose hands it fell about 100 years before Christ), was a seaport town on the bay of Acre, over against Carmel, about 30 miles south of Tyre. It was in the territory assigned to the tribe of Asher, and one of the cities from which they were unable to expel the Canaanites; and it is even now considered the strongest place in Palestine. It is mentioned in Acts 21:7. It now has about 6000 inhabitants. The place has been noted in modern times for the successful resistance it made, under Sir Sydney Smith, to the French army in 1799. It has an old cathedral, and a bishop of the Greek Church. The Romish monks have an inn, which serves them instead of a convent.

Accursed, Cursed. The Greek word anathema, and the Hebrew word answering to it, signify things accursed, set apart or devoted to destruction. But the phrase is variously rendered: 1. Josh. 6:17, devoted to destruction. 2. 1 Cor. 12:3, a deceiver. 3. Gal. 1:8, 9, separated from the church.

Aceldama (a-sĕl'da-mah), *field of blood*. Acts 1:19. A field said to have been intended for the burial of strangers, which the chief priests bought with the money returned by Judas, as the price of the Saviour's blood. Matt. 27:6-8. It was just without the wall of Jerusalem, south of Mount Zion, and is supposed to have been originally called the Potter's Field, because it furnished a sort of clay suitable for potter's ware. The "field of blood" is now shown on the steep southern face of the valley or ravine of Hinnom. It was believed in the middle ages that the soil of this place had the power of rapidly consuming bodies buried in it, and in consequence of this, or of the sanctity of the spot, great quantities of the earth were taken away.

Achaia (a-kā'yah or a-kä'yah). This was the original name of a district in the northwest of the Peloponnesus: in New Testament times it had a wider signification; for the Roman provinces of Achaia and Macedonia comprehended the whole of Greece. It is in this larger sense that Achaia must be understood. Acts 18:12, 27; 19:21; Rom. 15:26; 16:5; 1 Cor. 16:15; 2 Cor. 1:1; 9:2; 11:10; 1 Thess. 1:7, 8. Achaia was first a senatorial province, and had proconsuls. Tiberius changed it into a province imperial under procurators; and Claudius restored it to the senate. Hence Gallio, before whom Paul appeared, was proconsul. Corinth was the capital city.

Achan (ā'kan), *troubler*. A man of the tribe of Judah, who at the sacking of Jericho took, contrary to God's express command, a portion of the spoil. Hence the repulse before Ai. Achan's guilt being discovered, he was carried with his family and all his property into the valley of Achor, and there stoned and afterwards burned. It would seem that Achan's family shared his punishment—how far they were involved in his crime we know not—and that his possessions were destroyed. Josh. 7. He is also called Achar (ā'kar).

Achish (ā'kish), *angry* or *serpent charmer*. A Philistine king at Gath. David fled twice to him. The first time he was in some danger, from being recognized as one who had distinguished himself against the Philistines; he therefore feigned madness. 1 Sam. 21:10-15. The second time Achish treated David kindly, gave him Ziklag, and took him to the campaign against Saul, but was persuaded by his officers to send him home again. 1 Sam. 27; 28:1, 2; 29. At a later period Shimei went to Achish in pursuit of his servants; but it is doubtful whether this was the same king. 1 Kings 2:39, 40. In the title of Ps. 34 he is called Abimelech.

Achmetha (ăk'me-thah), *strong box* or *press*. Ezra 6:2. The Ecbatana of ancient Media, and the place where the records of the kingdom were preserved. The place is occupied, as it is supposed, by the modern city of Hamadan, in Persia. It was surrounded by seven walls, and at one period was considered the strongest and most beautiful city of the east, except Nineveh and Babylon.

Achor (ā'kor), *trouble*. A valley near Jericho, where Achan was stoned; and from the trouble Achan brought upon Israel it had its name. Josh. 7:24, 26. Yet from that trouble sanctified a new career of victory began. With this idea we find the place and the circumstance afterwards adverted to. Hos. 2:15. The valley of trouble was the door through which Israel entered Canaan first; and again through the valley of trouble would the Lord lead his ransomed people to peace and rest. The boundary line of Judah ran by Achor. Josh. 15:7. It is also mentioned in Isa. 65:10.

Achsa, Achsah (ăk'sah), *anklet*. The daughter of Caleb. Caleb promised her in marriage to any one who should take Kirjath-sepher, or Debir. Judg. 1:11. Othniel, son of Kenaz, Caleb's younger brother, took the city and gained the hand of Achsah, to whom her father gave an inheritance. Josh. 15:16-19; Judg. 1:12-15.

Achshaph (ăk'shaf), *enchantment*. Josh. 12:20. A city conquered by Joshua, and afterwards assigned to the tribe of Asher. It was not far from Accho. Josh. 19:25.

Achzib (ăk'zib), *deceit*. 1. Josh. 19:29. A city of the tribe of Asher. Judg. 1:31. Its present name is Zib. It is found near the sea coast, ten or twelve miles north of Ptolemais, and was visited by Buckingham in 1816. 2. Josh. 15:44, and Micah. 1:14. A town of Judah.

Acrabbim (*ak-krăb'bim*). Josh. 15:3, margin. See **Maaleh-acrabbim**.

Acts of the Apostles. The book so called is the fifth and last of the historical books of the New Testament; it connects the Gospels with the Epistles, being a fitting supplement to the former and a valuable introduction to the latter. There can be no reasonable question that Luke was the writer of this book. Its date is pretty well determined by the time at which its narrative closes—two years after Paul's being brought a prisoner to Rome. We may, therefore, with much probability assign it to 63 A.D. The title "Acts of the Apostles," by which this book is commonly known, would seem to be a later addition. It does not describe accurately the contents. For the object of the evangelist was neither to give a complete history of the church during the period comprised, nor to record the labors of all the apostles: it was rather to exhibit the fulfillment of promise in the descent of the Holy Spirit, and the consequent planting and growth of the Christian church among Jews and Gentiles by the establishment of centres of influence in various provinces of the empire, beginning at Jerusalem and ending at Rome. Keeping this idea steadily in view, we shall see that all the events recorded fall naturally into their places, and that any seeming abruptness is sufficiently accounted for. This book divides itself into two main parts; each being grouped around a central figure. —1. The planting and extension of the church among the Jews by the ministry of Peter. Chs. I–12. Subdivisions are (1) the organization of the church in Jerusalem, 1–7; (2) the branching forth of the gospel in various directions from the mother church. 8–12. 2. The planting and extension of the church among the Gentiles by the ministry of Paul. 13–28. Subdivisions are (1) Paul's ministry at large, 13–22:26; (2) his ministry in bonds. 22:27; 28. It must be carefully observed that these two parts are closely connected as belonging to one great system. For it is Peter who first introduces a Gentile convert into the church; and Paul, during the whole of his administrations, is careful to proclaim the gospel, in every place where he has opportunity, first to the Jews and afterwards to the Gentiles. There is on the face of it a truthfulness in this book which strongly commends itself to the reader. Thus the speeches attributed to different individuals are in full accordance with their respective characters and the circumstances in which they stood. The author was himself present at several of the events which he narrates—and this he carefully notes by change of person and in the verbs and pronouns he uses; he had, moreover, as a companion of the apostles, the best opportunities of knowing accurately the things he did not personally witness. The book of Acts has sometimes been called the "first missionary report, but with no financial account." The personal presence of the Lord Jesus Christ with his church adding to its numbers, calling Paul, speaking with him, and also of the Holy Ghost directing the church, are especially noticeable in the Acts of the Apostles. Acts 2:4, 47; 4:31; 8:39; 9:5, 6, 10; 10:19; 13:2; 16:6; 18:9.

Adam (*ăd'am*), *red, red earth.* The name appropriated to the first man, the father of the inhabitants of the world; used, however, sometimes more generally, as in Gen. 5:1, 2, where the woman is included. This name was probably chosen to remind the man of his earthly nature, seeing that out of the ground his body was taken, though his soul, the breath of life, was breathed into his nostrils by God's immediate act. This history of his creation is narrated in Gen. 1:26–30; 2:7, 15–25, a single pair being formed, to whom the earth was given for a possession, to replenish it with their children, to enjoy the fruits of it, and to have dominion over the inferior animals. We are told that "God created man in his own image" and after his "likeness;" not with respect to bodily shape, but with a likeness to God in moral attributes. This is implied by the expressions of St. Paul, who plainly considers righteousness and holiness the likeness of God. Eph. 4:24; Col. 3:10. The phrase must also denote the possession of dominion and authority; for immediately it is subjoined "let them have dominion," Gen. 1:26, explanatory, it would seem, of the term "image." And so St. Paul calls the man "the image and glory of God," on the ground of his being "the head of the woman." 1 Cor. 11:3, 7. The high intellectual power with which man was endowed is illustrated by his giving appropriate names to the lower animals. Gen. 2:19, 20. He was indeed a glorious creature, and would have been uninterruptedly and increasingly happy had he continued in his first estate of innocence. Adam's lamentable fall is next related. How long it was after his creation, ingenious men have puzzled themselves to discover, but in vain. By sin Adam lost his best prerogative. He had suffered spiritual death, and he was to suffer bodily death: dust as he was, to dust he should return. To his posterity he transmitted, therefore, a corrupted nature, which could be restored and recovered only by the power of the second Adam, a head of life and blessedness to all that believe in him. Rom. 5:15, 16; 1 Cor. 15:21, 22, 45, 47, 48. Of Adam's subsequent history we know little. We are expressly told that he had "sons and daughters," though the names of but three of his sons are recorded. He lived 930 years, Gen. 4:1, 2, 25, 26; 5:3–5; 1 Chron. 1:1; Luke 3:38, and was probably contemporary with Methusalah about 240 years. Methusalah lived 600 years with Noah; Shem lived 150 years with Abram, and 50 years with Isaac, according to the Ussher Chronology, so that the history of the world before the flood might have been carried through three or four persons to the time of Moses. 2. A city near the Jordan, by which the waters were cut off when Israel passed over. Josh. 3:16.

Adamant. This word is found twice in our version, Ezek. 3:9 Zech. 7:12, in both cases used metaphorically to signify firmness of character and purpose. The original word occurs again in Jer. 17:1, where it is translated "diamond," with which the writer's pen is said to be pointed. The term must signify some exceedingly hard stone; and diamond is the hardest we know.

Adar (ā'dar). 1. A place on the south boundary of Judah. Josh. 15:3. 2. The 12th month of the Jewish sacred year. See **Month**.

Adder. Four different Hebrew words are so rendered in the A. V. That occurring Gen. 49:17 (arrowsnake, marg.), implies a gliding motion. It is a small and very venomous snake, with two antennæ like horns, well known in Egypt, accustomed to lie in wait in the sand and near paths. "Adder" occurs also, Ps. 58:4; 91:13, as the translation of another word, perhaps embodying the idea of twisting or twining. It is described as deaf to the charmer, and, as the same word is generally rendered "asp," e. g., Deut. 32:33, it must have been venomous. It is probably the Egyptian cobra. We find another Hebrew word, Ps. 140:3, which is compound, including the two ideas of coiling and lying in wait. It also was poisonous. There is one more word which implies hissing. It occurs several times, Prov. 23:32; Isa. 11:8, 14:29; 59:5; Jer. 8:17, but is rendered "adder" in the text only in the first-named place, elsewhere "cockatrice." It seems to have lived in holes, to have been oviparous, and venomous.

Admah (ăd'mah), *earth* or *fortress*, one of the five cities in the vale of Siddim, Gen. 10:19; 14:2, destroyed with Sodom.

Adonibezek (a-dŏ'nĭ-bē'zek or a-dŏn'ĭ-bē'zek), *lord of Bezek.* The king of Bezek, conquered by the tribe of Judah. He had his thumbs and great toes cut off, having himself inflicted the same punishment on 70 chiefs. Judg. 1:4-7.

Adonijah (ăd'o-nī'jah), *my lord is Jehovah.* 1. The fourth son of David, by Haggith, born at Hebron. 2 Sam. 3:4; 1 Chron. 3:2. When his father was old, he, being a man of fine person and probably popular, aspired to the crown, in order to exclude Solomon. He was joined by Joab and Abiathar, and seems to have had the countenance of his brothers. But David, being informed by Bath-sheba and Nathan, immediately ordered Solomon to be anointed king; and the intelligence of this broke up the conspiracy. Solomon promised, if Adonijah remained quiet, that this offence should be overlooked. 1 Kings 1. He did not remain quiet, but, after David's death, persuaded Bath-sheba to ask for him Abishag, a woman of his father's harem. Solomon, regarding this as a renewal of his attempt upon the crown, commanded him to be executed. 1 Kings 2:13-25. 2. A Levite in Jehoshaphat's time. 2 Chron. 17:8. 3. One who sealed the covenant. Neh. 10:16.

Adoniram (ăd'o-nī'ram). See **Adoram**.

Adonizedek (a-dŏ'nĭ-zē'dek or a-dŏn-ĭ-zē'dek), *lord of justice.* The Amorite king of Jerusalem who organized a league with four other Amorite princes against Joshua. These confederate kings having laid siege to Gibeon, Joshua marched to the relief of his new allies and put the besiegers to flight. The five kings took refuge in a cave at Makkedah, whence they were taken and slain, their bodies hung on trees, and then buried in the place of their concealment. Josh. 10:1-27.

Adoption, Gal. 4:5, is an act by which one is received into a man's family as his own child, and becomes entitled to the peculiar privileges of that connection, as fully and completely as a child by birth. Ex. 2:10 and Esth. 2:7. In the figurative use of the term by the sacred writers it implies that relation which we sustain to God, when, by his grace, we are converted from sin to holiness. The spirit of adoption is received, and we are made the children (or *sons*) and heirs of God, and joint-heirs with Christ.

Adoram (a-dō'ram), *lord of height.* 1 Kings 12:18. By an unusual contraction from Adoniram, 2 Sam. 20:24, and 1 Kings 4:6, and also Hadoram, 2 Chron. 10:18, chief receiver of the tribute during the reigns of David, 2 Sam. 20:24; Solomon, 1 Kings 4:6, and Rehoboam, 1 Kings 12:18. This last monarch sent him to collect the tribute from the rebellious Israelites, by whom he was stoned to death.

Adrammelech (a-drăm'me-lĕk), *splendor of the king,* or *fire king.* 1. One of the idols adored by the Sepharvaim, who were settled in Samaria. They made their children pass through the fire in honor of this deity, and of another called Anammelech, "image of the king." Rawlinson supposes the sun and his wife Anunit—perhaps the moon—to be referred to. 2 Kings 17:31. 2. A son of Sennacherib, who aided in slaying his father. 2 Kings 19:37; Isa. 37:38.

Adramyttium (ăd-ra-mĭt'tĭ-ŭm). A seaport town of Mysia: it was an Athenian colony, and is now but a village, retaining the name *Adramyt,* with some trade. It was in a ship of Adramyttium that Paul on his voyage to Italy sailed from Cæsarea to Myra. Acts 27:2-5.

Adria (ā'drĭ-ah), Acts 27:27, is now the gulf which lies between Italy on one side, and the coast of Dalmatia on the other. It is called the Gulf of Venice. In the apostle's time it is supposed to have denoted the whole breadth of the Mediterranean sea, from Crete to Sicily.

Adriel. 1 Sam. 18:19. See **Merab.**

Adullam (a-dŭl'lam), *justice of the people.* Josh. 15:35. An ancient and royal city in Judah, 15 or 20 miles southwest of Jerusalem. The king of the place was slain by Joshua. It was fortified by Rehoboam, and, probably on account of its strength, was called the glory of Israel. Mic. 1:15. Near this city was a cave, where David secreted himself when he fled from Achish. The cave is described by a modern traveller as uneven, intricate, and very capacious; he says it is perfectly plain that 400 men might conceal themselves in the sides of the cave, as David's men did, and escape observation. 1 Sam. 22:1.

Adultery. Strictly denotes uncleanness between a man and a woman, either of whom is married. Broadly, it includes all manner of unchastity in heart, speech, or behavior. Matt. 5:27, 28. According to the law of God, given by Moses, the adulterer and the adulteress shall surely be put to death. Lev. 20:10. The mode of testing a charge made by a man accusing his wife of adultery is given, Num. 5:12-31. Christ says that whosoever looketh on a woman to lust after her hath committed adultery with her already in his heart. Matt. 5:28. In many parts of the Scripture the church is called an adulteress when she forsakes the worship of God and practices idolatry. Isa. 57:3-12; Jer. 3:1, 2, 9; 13:27; Ezek. 23:27; Matt. 12:39, etc. By our Saviour adultery was made the only ground for divorce.

Adummim (a-dŭm'mim), *bloody.* The name of a dangerous or mountainous part of the road between Jerusalem and Jericho, about four miles from the latter place. This lonely road is said to be still much infested by robbers, and the scene of many sanguinary murders. It is supposed that the scene of the parable of the Good Samaritan was laid here. Josh. 15:7; 18:17; Luke 10:30-36.

Advocate. 1 John 2:1. See **Comforter.**

Ænon. John 3:23. See **Enon.**

Agabus (ăg'a-bŭs), *locust.* The only New Testament prophet mentioned by name. He predicted a great famine, which occurred in the reign of Claudius, A. D. 44. Acts 11:28. He also predicted the imprisonment of Paul. Acts 21:10, 11.

Agag (ā'găg), *flame.* 1. The name or title of a powerful king of the Amalekites, who was contemporary with Moses. Num. 24:7. 2. An Amalekite king, who was conquered by Saul, and put to death by Samuel for his cruelty. 1 Sam. 15:8-33. The term "Agagite" signifies an Amalekite. Esth. 3:1, 10; 8:3, 5.

Agar (ā-gar). Gal. 4:24. See **Hagar.**

Agrippa (a-grĭp'pah). See **Herod.**

Ahab (ā'hăb), *father's brother.* 1. The sixth king of Israel, the son and successor of Omri. His reign lasted 22 years, 918-897 B.C.. He was the weakest and one of the most impious of all the Israelitish monarchs. He has the miserable character given him of doing "evil in the sight of the Lord above all that were before him." He not only maintained the worship of the calves set up by Jeroboam, but, having married Jezebel, daughter of Eth-baal, king of the Zidonians, he yielded himself to her evil influence, and introduced the worship of Baal into Samaria. A persecution of the prophets of the Lord followed—many of them being destroyed by Jezebel. As a judgment, a drought was sent upon the land; and then came the solemn vindication of Jehovah's authority by the prophet Elijah before Ahab and the assembled people, and the punishment, according to the law of Moses, of the idolatrous prophets. 1 Kings 17:18. Jezebel was irritated to madness at the news of this catastrophe, and resolved to sacrifice Elijah; while Ahab was either unable or unwilling to interfere. Afterwards his wicked queen led him into one of his worst crimes. He seems to have had a cultivated taste. He built cities, and erected an ivory palace, 1 Kings 22:39, the walls being probably inlaid with ivory, and had pleasure grounds by his house in Jezreel, which he wished to enlarge by the addition of a vineyard belonging to Naboth. Naboth, however, refused either to sell or to exchange his hereditary property; and Ahab, disappointed, manifested the temper of a spoiled child. The unscrupulous Jezebel then put him in possession of the coveted plot of ground by the judicial murder of Naboth; and Ahab went to view it, but was met by Elijah, who denounced on him a fearful judgment. On his repentance, superficial though it was, this sentence was partially revoked, and delayed till the days of Ahab's son. In two wars with Syria this prince was successful, but he improperly spared Ben-hadad, the Syrian king. In a third campaign, having attempted, in alliance with Jehoshaphat, to retake Ramoth-gilead, still occupied by the Syrians, Ahab, though he disguised himself, was mortally wounded; and the dogs licked up the blood washed from his chariot in the pool of Samaria. Weak and unstable, Ahab let himself be made the tool of his wife; and his history is an instructive warning against such subserviency to a dangerous influence. 1 Kings 21. 2. A false prophet in Babylon. Jer. 29:20-23.

Ahasuerus (a-hăs-u-ē'rus), *lion-king,* the name of one Median and two Persian kings mentioned in the Old Testament. 1. In Dan. 9:1 Ahasuerus is said to be the father of Darius the Mede. The first Ahasuerus is Cyaxares, the conqueror of Nineveh, B.C. 634. 2. The Ahasuerus, king of Persia, referred to in Ezra 4:6, must be Cambyses, thought to be Cyrus' successor, and perhaps his son. B.C. 529. 3. The third is the Ahasuerus of the Book of Esther. This Ahasuerus is probably Xerxes of history, Esther 1:1, B.C. 485, and this conclusion is favored by the resemblance of character and by certain chronological indications, the accounts of his life and character agreeing with the book of Esther. In the third year of Ahasuerus was held a great feast and assembly in Shushan the palace, Esther 1:3, following a council held to consider the invasion of Greece. He divorced his queen Vashti for refusing to appear in public at this banquet, and married, four years afterwards, the Jewess Esther, cousin and ward of Mordecai. Five years after this, Haman, one of his counsellors, having been slighted by Mordecai, prevailed upon the king to order the destruction of all the Jews in the empire. But before the day appointed for the massacre, Esther and Mordecai induced the king to put Haman to death, and to give the Jews the right of self-defence.

Ahava (a-hā'vah or a'ha-vah), *water.* A river probably in Babylonia, near where Ezra collected the returning exiles. Ezra 8:21, 31.

Ahaz (ā'hăz), *seizer* or *possessor.* 1. The eleventh king of Judah; he was contemporary with the prophets Isaiah, Hosea, and

Micah. He reigned 16 years. If, as it is stated in 2 Kings 16:2, A. V., Ahaz was 20 years old when he ascended the throne, he must have been the father of Hezekiah when eleven years of age. 2 Kings 18:2. Here, however, the Septuagint and the Syriac read "twenty-five years old." 2 Chron. 28:1. He was distinguished for his idolatry and contempt of the true God; and against him many of the prophecies of Isaiah are directed. He died B.C. 726; and such was his impiety, that he was not allowed burial in the sepulchre of the kings. 2 Kings 16:1, 2, 20; 2 Chron. 28:1-27; Isa. 7:1, 25. 2. A descendant of Jonathan. 1 Chron. 8:35; 9:42.

Ahaziah (*ă-ha-zī'ah*), *whom Jehovah holds*. 1. The eighth king of Israel; he was the son and successor of Ahab. He reigned two years, alone and with his father, who associated him in the kingdom the year before his death. In the second year of his reign he fell through the lattice of an upper apartment of his palace, and died soon after, as Elijah had foretold, B.C. 895. Ahaziah imitated the impiety of his father and mother in the worship of Baal and Ashteroth. 1 Kings 22:40-51; 2 Kings 1; 2 Chron. 20:35, 37. 2. The sixth king of Judah; he succeeded his father, and reigned only one year. 2 Kings 8:26. In 2 Chron. 22:2, he is said, by an error of the scribes, to have been "forty-two years old" when he began to reign, which would make him two years older than his father. The correct age is "twenty-two," as stated in 2 Kings 8:16-26. Ahaziah was governed by his idolatrous mother Athaliah; he received his mortal wound by the command of Jehu, and died at Megiddo, B.C. 883. 2 Kings 9:27. In 2 Chron. 22:9, the circumstances of the death of Ahaziah appear to be stated differently: but the account is only more full, and follows the order of events. Ahaziah is also called "Jehoahaz," 2 Chron. 21:17; 25:23; and "Azariah," 2 Chron. 22:6.

Ahiah (*a-hī'ah*), *friend of Jehovah*. 1. Supposed by some to be the same with Ahimelech, 1 Sam. 21:1, was the son of Ahitub, and his successor in the priest's office. 1 Sam. 14:3, 18. See **Ahimelech** and **Ahitub**. 2. Ahiah (A. V.), or, Ahijah (R. V.), son of Shisha, one of Solomon's scribes. 1 Kings 4:3. 3. A descendant of Benjamin. 1 Chron. 8:7.

Ahijah (*a-hī'jah*), *brother* or *friend of Jehovah*. 1. A prophet who dwelt in Shiloh, in the reign of the first Jeroboam. He is thought to be the person who spoke twice to Solomon from God. 1 Kings 6:11; 11:11, 29; 14:6; 2 Chron. 9:29. 2. The father of Baasha. 1 Kings 15:27, 33. 3. One of the sons of Jerahmeel. 1 Chron. 2:25. 4. One of David's distinguished officers. 1 Chron. 11:36. 5. One of the Levites. 1 Chron. 26:20. 6. One who sealed the covenant. Neh. 10:26.

Ahikam (*a-hī'kam*), *brother of the enemy*. A person who rescued Jeremiah, when it was proposed to give him into the hands of the people, to be put to death. 2 Kings 22:12-14; 25:22; Jer. 26:24; 39:14.

Ahimaaz (*a-hĭm'a-ăz*), *brother of anger*. 1. The father of Ahinoam, Saul's wife. 1 Sam. 14:50. 2. The son of Zadok the priest. He, with Jonathan, Abiathar's son, contrived to bring David intelligence, during Absalom's rebellion, of Ahithophel's counsel, and Hushai's endeavor to counteract it. They were hid in a well and escaped capture. 2 Sam. 15:27, 36; 17:15-22. When the royal forces had gained the victory, he offered to convey the news to David; but his request was refused by Joab because of Absalom's death. After Cushi had been despatched, Ahimaaz again solicited permission to run, and, having overcome Joab's reluctance, he started, outran Cushi, and apprised the king of the success achieved. In answer, however, to the inquiry respecting Absalom, he, not quite truthfully, replied that he had seen a tumult, but "knew not what it was." 2 Sam. 18:19-30. We hear nothing more of Ahimaaz, and, comparing 1 Kings 4:2; 1 Chron. 6:8, 9, 53, it seems probable that he died before his father, and was never high priest. 3. One of Solomon's commissariat officers. 1 Kings 4:15. We cannot suppose this person identical with No. 2.

Ahimelech (*a-hĭm'el-ĕk*), *brother of the king*. The ninth high priest of the Hebrews. He dwelt at Nob, and was the intimate friend of David; on this account he was put to death by Saul, together with all the priests that were with him, except his son Abiathar, who fled to David. By an error of the scribes he is called "Abimelech," 1 Chron. 18:16; also "Ahiah," 1 Sam. 14:3; and he is sometimes confounded with Abiathar. 1 Sam. 21:1, 2; 22:9.

Ahinoam (*a-hĭn'o-ăm*, or *ă-hi-nō'am*), *brother of pleasantness*. 1. The wife of Saul. 1 Sam. 14:50. 2. One of David's wives. 25:43; 27:3; 30:5; 2 Sam. 2:2; 3:2.

Ahio (*a-hī'o*), *brotherly*. 1. Son of Abinadab. 2 Sam. 6:3, 4. 2. A descendant of Benjamin. 1 Chron. 8:14. 3. A son of Jehiel. 1 Chron. 8:31; 9:37.

Ahithophel (*a-hĭth'o-fĕl*), *brother of folly*. A native of Giloh, a city of Judah, David's trusted counsellor, 1 Chron. 27:33, 34, who was induced to join the party of Absalom. 2 Sam. 15:12, 31, 34. His advice was intended to make the breach irreparable betwixt the father and the son; and, had his counsel immediately to pursue David been followed, it is possible that the king would have been cut off before he reached the Jordan. But by God's providence Hushai's counterplan was preferred by Absalom; and Ahithophel, foreseeing the defeat of the rebellion, retired to his own city and hanged himself. 2 Sam. 16:15; 17:23. Some have endeavored to account for Ahithophel's treason by the supposition that, as it seems likely he was Bath-sheba's grandfather, he wished to revenge on David the evil done to her. But this is not reasonable. The success of Absalom would probably have been fatal to Bath-sheba; it would certainly have barred Solomon, Ahithophel's great-grandson, from the throne. Perhaps there may be a reference in Ps. 41:9; 55:12-14, to Ahithophel, and possibly through him to a yet worse traitor, Judas.

Ahitub (a-hī'tub), *brother, i. e., friend, of goodness.* 1. The grandson of Eli, and father of Ahiah or Ahimelech. 1 Sam. 14:3; 22: 9, 11, 12, 20. We do not know whether he ever exercised the functions of high priest. 2. The father, or, possibly, grandfather of Zadok. 2 Sam. 8:17; 1 Chron. 6:7, 8, 52; 9:11; 18:16; Ezra 7:2; Neh. 11:11. It is probable from Neh. 11:11 that he was actually high priest.

Aholah (a-hō'lah), she has *her own tent*. A symbolical name for Samaria. Ezek. 23: 4, 5, 36, 44.

Aholiab (a-hō'li-ăb), *tent of his father*. An artificer of the tribe of Dan employed with Bezaleel in the construction of the tabernacle. Exod. 31:6; 35:34; 36:1, 2; 38:23.

Aholibah (a-hŏl'i-bah or a-hō'li-bah), *my tabernacle is in her*. A symbolical name for Judah. Ezek. 23:4, 11, 22, 36, 44.

Ahuzzath (a-huz'zath), *possession*. A friend of Abimelech, king of Gerar. Gen. 26:26.

Ai (ā'ī), *heap of ruins*. 1. A city of the Canaanites, Gen. 13:3, where it is "Hai" in the Authorized Version, but Ai in the Revised Version. Taken by Joshua. Josh. 7:2-5; 8:1-29. Also called Aiath, Isa. 10: 28, and Aija in the A. V. and R. V., Neh. 11: 31. Abraham pitched his tent between Hai and Bethel. Gen. 12:8. The city of Ai was east of Bethel, and about nine miles north of Jerusalem. It is named 38 times in the Bible. 2. A city of the Ammonites, not far from Heshbon. Jer. 49:3.

Ain (ā'in), *eye, spring*. 1. A place, or probably a fountain, and one of the landmarks on the eastern boundary of Canaan. Num. 34:11. It is now known as *Ain el-Azy*, a remarkable spring, one of the sources of the Orontes, and about ten miles west of Riblah. 2. A city of southern Palestine, first given to Judah, Josh. 15:32; afterward assigned to Simeon, Josh. 19:7; and then to the Levites, Josh. 21:16; 1 Chron. 4:32. The same place as Ashan, 1 Chron. 6:59; and possibly as En-rimmon, Neh. 11:29.

Ajalon (ăj-a-lon), or **Aijalon** (āi'ja-lŏn), *place of gazelles*. 1. A town in the tribe of Dan, assigned to the Levites, sons of Kohath, Josh. 19:42; 21:24; Judg. 1:35, and a city of refuge. It was not far from Timnath, and was taken by the Philistines from Ahaz. 2 Chron. 28:18. It lay on the south side of a fine valley, not far from the valley of Gibeon, and is recognized in the modern village of Yalo, near the road to Jaffa, some 14 miles from Jerusalem. The valley is the place where Joshua commanded the sun and moon to stand still, and they obeyed him. Josh. 10:12; see also 1 Sam. 14:31. 2. A town in Benjamin, some three miles east of Bethel. It was fortified by Rehoboam. 2 Chron. 11:10. Some regard this as the same place as the above, in possession of different tribes at different times. 1 Chron. 6:66, 69. 3. In the tribe of Zebulun, the place of Elon's burial. Judg. 12:12.

Akrabbim (a-krăb'bim), *scorpions*. A range of hills on the south border of Judah towards the southern extremity of the Dead Sea; which seems to have been infested with scorpions and serpents. Deut. 8:15; Num. 34:4; Judg. 1:36. Instead of "the ascent of Akrabbim," we have in the Hebrew the name "Maaleh-Acrabbim," scorpion heights, in Josh. 15:3.

Alabaster. What is usually called alabaster is a kind of soft gypsum, properly sulphate of lime. But the alabaster of which jars and vases were usually made was finer grained, opaque, and usually white, but frequently shaded with other soft colors; hence sometimes called onyx marble, which is properly a carbonate of lime. Several vases of alabaster have been found in Egypt, varying in form and size; one of which, bearing the name and title of the queen of Thothmes II., had ointment in it, which had retained its odor for several centuries. In Mark 14:3 the phrase "she brake the box," is simply, "she brake the alabaster," *i. e.*, the vase so called; and merely refers to the breaking of the seal which closed the vase, and kept the perfume from evaporation. Matt. 26:7; Luke 7:37.

Alexander (ăl-egz-ăn'der), *strong man*, or *helper of men*. 1. The son of Simon. Mark 15:21. 2. A member of the council. Acts 4:6. 3. A Jew of Ephesus. Acts 19: 34. 4. A coppersmith, and an apostate from Christianity. 1 Tim. 1:19, 20; 2 Tim. 4: 14.

Alexandria (ăl-egz-ăn'dri-a). The Grecian capital of Egypt, founded by and named after Alexander the Great, B. C. 332. It was a noted seaport of Lower Egypt, and was situated on a low, narrow tract of land which divides Lake Mareotis from the Mediterranean, and near the western mouth of the Nile, about 120 miles from the present city of Cairo. Soon after its foundation by Alexander, it became the capital of the Ptolemies and the Grecian kings reigning in Egypt, and one of the most populous and prosperous cities of the East. Its harbor could accommodate vast navies, fitting it to become the commercial metropolis of the entire Eastern world. In front of the city, on the island of Pharos, stood a famous lighthouse, named after the island and noted as one of the seven wonders of the world. Alexandria numbered, in the days of its ancient prosperity, 600,000 inhabitants, half of them slaves, and ranked next to Athens in literature. It had the greatest library of ancient times, which contained upward of 700,000 rolls or volumes. The portion in the museum, consisting of 400,000 volumes, was burnt in B. C. 47. The additional or "new library" in the Serapeum, afterward increased to about 500,000 volumes, including the original 300,000 volumes, was destroyed by the fanatical vandalism of the Saracens in A. D. 640. At Alexandria the Old Testament was translated into the Greek by 70 learned Jews—hence called the "Septuagint"—in the third century before the Christian era. The Alexandrian Greek dialect, known as Hellenistic Greek, was the language used by the early Christian fathers, and is still the study of the biblical scholar in the pages of the New Testament. Alexandria was the birthplace of Apollos, Acts 18:24, and in the apostle Paul's time it carried on an extensive commerce with the countries on the Mediterranean. Acts 6:9; 27:6; 28:11. In Alexandria originated the Arian heresy denying that Jesus Christ was divine, and there Athanasius, the "father of orthodoxy," firmly opposed the false and defended the true doctrine of the deity of our Lord. From A. D. 300 to 600 the city was second only to Rome in size and importance, and was the chief seat of Christian theology. It was conquered by the Saracens under Caliph Omar about A. D. 640, when it began to decline. The rising importance of Constantinople, and the discovery of an ocean passage to India by way of Cape Good Hope, contributed to its further ruin, until it was reduced from a prosperous city of 500,000 to a poor village of only 5000 to 6000 inhabitants. It is now an important city of 240,000 inhabitants—including 50,000 Franks—and is connected with Cairo by a railway, and also with Suez, on the Red Sea. Among the ancient monuments to be seen are the Catacombs, the Column of Diocletian, 94 feet high and named "Pompey's Pillar"—not from the famous Pompey, but from a Roman prefect who erected the column in honor of the emperor Diocletian—and one of the two obelisks or "Needles of Cleopatra," which, however, belong to the time of the Pharaohs and were brought from Heliopolis. The obelisk on the embankment of the Thames, London, and the one in Central Park, New York, once stood at Alexandria.

Alexandrians (*Al-egz-ăn'dri-anz*). A synagogue of these is mentioned. Acts 6:9. There are said to have been 460 or 480 synagogues in Jerusalem. It was reasonable, therefore, to expect that Alexandria, where so many Jews dwelt, would have a special synagogue for their worship in Jerusalem.

Algum. 2 Chron. 2:8. See **Almug.**

Alleluia. Rev. 19:1. See **Halleluiah.**

Almond Tree. Gen. 43:11. This tree resembles a peach tree, but is larger. In Palestine it blossoms in January, and in March has fruit. Its blossoms are pinkish-white. Its Hebrew name signifies to watch and hasten, and to this there is an allusion in Jer. 1:11, 12. Aaron's rod was from an almond. Num. 17:8. In Eccl. 12:5 the hoary head is beautifully compared with the almond tree, either on account of its whiteness, beauty and winter blossoming, or the hastening on of decay. The golden bowls of the sacred candlestick were made "like almonds, with their knops and their flowers." Exod. 25:33, 34.

Alms, Alms Deeds. The word is not found in the Authorized Version of the Old Testament, but is frequent in the New Testament. The duty was, however, enjoined very strictly upon the Jews, who by law were required always to leave gleanings in the fields that the poor might be fed. Lev. 19:9, 10; 23:22; Deut. 15:11; 24:19; 26:2-13; Ruth 2:2. Every third year the tithe of the produce of the farmers was to be shared with the Levite, the fatherless, the stranger, and the widow. Deut. 14:28. Alms-giving is a subject of praise in the Old Testament—*e. g.,* Job 31:17; Ps. 41:1, and 112:9. In the temple there was one box for the reception of alms to be dedicated to the education of the poor children of good family. Alms-giving was a part of Pharisaic practice. Our Lord did not rebuke them for it, but for their self-satisfaction in the performance. Matt. 6:2. In Acts 10:31; Rom. 15:25-27; 1 Cor. 16:1-4 the Christian mode of relieving the wants of others is set forth.

Almug Trees, 1 Kings 10:11; or **Algum Trees.** 2 Chron. 2:8. Two forms of the same word. One of the kinds of timber which Solomon ordered from Tyre for the building of the temple. Jewish historians describe it as a fine, white, glossy wood, and it was used for musical instruments, and the ornamental work of the temple. Sandal wood answers best to the description in the passage cited. Dr. Shaw supposes it to have been what we call the cypress, which is still used for harpsichords and other stringed instruments.

Aloe. An odoriferous tree, called also "lign aloe." Num. 24:6; Ps. 45:8; Prov. 7:17; Song of Sol. 4:14. The aroma of the tree proceeds from its resin, especially when decaying. Aloe wood is useful for perfuming rooms and clothing. We find it also mixed with myrrh, used in burial. John 19:39.

Alpha (*ăl'phah*). The first letter of the Greek alphabet, corresponding to Aleph, the first Hebrew letter. These letters were used as numerals. Alpha therefore denotes one, the first. And, as Omega is the last Greek letter, our Lord calls himself Alpha and Omega, the first and the last, implying his divine eternity. Rev. 1:8, 11; 21:6; 22:13; comp. Isa. 44:6.

Altar. Noah built an altar when he left the ark. Gen. 8:20. In the early times altars were usually built in certain spots hallowed by religious associations, *e. g.,* where God appeared. Gen. 12:7; 13:18; 26:25; 35:1. Though generally erected for the offering of sacrifice, in some instances they appear to have been only memorials. Gen. 12:7; Ex. 17:15, 16. Altars were most probably originally made of earth. The law of Moses allowed them to be made of either earth or unhewn stones. Exod. 20:24, 25. I. The altar of burnt offering. It differed in construction at different times. In the tabernacle, Ex. 27:1 ff.; 38:1 ff., it was comparatively small and portable. In shape it was square. It was five cubits in length, the same in breadth, and three cubits high. It was made of planks of shittim or acacia wood overlaid with brass. The interior was hollow. Ex. 27:8. At the four corners were four projections called horns, made, like the altar itself, of shittim wood overlaid with brass, Ex. 27:2, and to them the victim was bound when about to be sacrificed. Ps. 118 : 27. Round the altar, midway between the top and bottom, ran a projecting ledge, on which perhaps the priest stood when officiating. To the outer edge of this, again, a grating or network of brass was affixed, and reached to the bottom of the altar. At the four corners of the network were four brazen rings, into which were inserted the staves by which the altar was carried. These staves were of the same materials as the altar itself. As the priests were forbidden to ascend the altar by steps, Ex. 20 : 26, it has been conjectured that a slope of earth led gradually up to the ledge from which they officiated. The place of the altar was at "the door of the tabernacle of the congregation." Ex. 40 : 29. In Solomon's temple the altar was considerably larger in its dimensions. It differed too in the material of which it was made, being entirely of brass. 1 Kings 8 : 64 ; 2 Chron. 7 : 7. It had no grating, and instead of a single, gradual slope, the ascent to it was probably made by three successive platforms, to each of which it has been supposed that steps led. The altar erected by Herod in front of the temple was 15 cubits in height and 50 cubits in length and breadth. According to Lev. 6 : 12, 13, a perpetual fire was to be kept burning on the altar. II. The altar of incense, called also the golden altar to distinguish it from the altar of burnt offering, which was called the brazen altar. Ex. 38 : 30. That in the tabernacle was made of acacia wood, overlaid with pure gold. In shape it was square, being a cubit in length and breadth and two cubits in height. Like the altar of burnt offering it had horns at the four corners, which were of one piece with the rest of the altar. This altar stood in the holy place, "before the vail that is by the ark of the testimony." Ex. 30 : 6 ; 40 : 5. The altar of Solomon's temple was similar, 1 Kings 7 : 48 ; 1 Chron. 28 : 18, but was made of cedar overlaid with gold. In Acts 17 : 23 reference is made to an altar to an unknown god. There were several altars in Athens with this inscription, erected during the time of a plague, since they knew not what god was offended and required to be propitiated. In the New Testament the word altar does not occur in connection with Christian worship. Altar, sacrifice, priest, and temple, being typical of Christ and the Christian dispensation, have passed away. Their work was done when the offering of the body of Jesus Christ once was made. For, by one offering, he hath perfected forever them that are sanctified. Heb. 10 : 9, 10, 14.

Amalek (ăm'a-lĕk), *people of prey, booty.* The son of Eliphaz, and grandson of Esau. Gen. 36 : 16 ; 1 Chron. 1 : 36. He was probably the father of the Amalekites, an ancient and powerful people, Gen. 14 : 7 ; Num. 24 : 20, who inhabited the regions on the south of Palestine, between Idumea and Egypt, and also to the eastward of the Dead Sea and Mount Seir. Judg. 5 : 14 ; 12 : 15 ; 1 Sam. 15 : 5. The Hebrews had scarcely passed the Red Sea, when the Amalekites attacked them; they were defeated by Joshua. Ex. 17 : 8. Saul destroyed them as a nation, 1 Sam. 15 : 2-33, and David utterly routed them. 1 Sam. 30 : 17. A small remnant seems to have escaped, till at last the word of the Lord was fulfilled, and their name was blotted from the earth, in their utter destruction. Num. 24 : 20 ; 1 Chron. 4 : 43. The "Agagite," in Esth. 3 : 1, 10 ; 8 : 3, 5, was probably an Amalekite, whose ancestor had escaped from the general carnage.

Amana (ăm'a-nah, or a-mā'nah), *perennial.* 1. Margin, same as Abana or Abanah (R. V.) 2 Kings 5 : 12. See **Abana**. 2. A ridge or peak of the Lebanon range, in which the river Amana or Abana has its source. Song of Sol. 4 : 8.

Amasa (ăm'a-sah), *burden.* 1. A kinsman of David, and chief captain in Absalom's rebel army. David pardoned Amasa, but he was assassinated by Joab. 2 Sam. 17 : 25 ; 19 : 13 ; 20 : 9, 10 ; 1 Chron. 2 : 17. 2. A descendant of Ephraim. 2 Chron. 28 : 12.

Amasai (a-mās'a-ī or ăm'a-sā-ī), *burdensome.* 1. A Levite, one of the sons of Elkanah. 1 Chron. 6 : 25. 2. A chief of the captains who joined David in the desert. 1 Chron. 12 : 18. 3. One of the Levites. 1 Chron. 15 : 24. 4. The father of Mahath. 2 Chron. 29 : 12.

Amaziah (ăm-a-zī'ah), *whom Jehovah strengthens.* 1. The son and successor of Jehoash, or Joash, king of Judah. He was 25 years old at his accession, and he reigned 29 years, 838–809 B. C. His conduct was, at first, unexceptionable; but he afterwards declined from God's law, and brought misfortune and judgment upon himself and his kingdom. The history does not tell us that he repented; for the consequences of his idolatry still pursued him. His own subjects conspired against him, and, when he fled to Lachish, slew him there. He was succeeded by his son Azariah, or Uzziah. 2 Kings 14 : 1-21 ; 2 Chron. 25. 2. A Simeonite. 1 Chron. 4 : 34. 3. A Levite. 1 Chron. 6 : 45. 4. An idolatrous priest of the golden calf at Bethel, in the reign of Jeroboam II. Amos 7 : 10-17.

Amber. Ezek. 1 : 4, 27 ; 8 : 2. Most likely the substance called "amber" in our versions is not that which is now known by that name. It is rather a metal. Some have believed it a mixture of brass (or copper) and gold, or brass with a gold-like brilliancy.

Amen (ā-měn'), *firm, faithful, verily.* The proper signification of this word is that one person confirms the words of another, and expresses his wish for the success and accomplishment of the other's vows and declarations. Thus it is used in Num. 5 : 22 ; Deut. 27 : 15-26 ; 1 Kings 1 : 36 ; Jer. 28 : 6. Also after ascriptions of praise, Ps. 106 : 48 ; and in A. V. of Matt. 6 : 12, but omitted in R. V. Again, we find it at the beginning of a sentence, to signify the firm certainty of what was about to be said, as very frequently in our Lord's addresses (Matt. 25 : 40 ; John 3 : 3, 5, 11, and in other places), where it is usually rendered "verily." The

Amethyst. One of the precious stones in the high priest's sacred breast-plate. Ex. 28:19; 39:12. The oriental amethyst is a gem of great hardness and lustre, violet, and occasionally red; the occidental amethyst is a variety of quartz, of much beauty, but not difficult to cut. This stone had its Hebrew name, *ahlâmah*, from its supposed property of inducing dreams. Its Greek name, from which the English word comes, implied that it was a charm against drunkenness. The amethyst is mentioned as one of the foundations of the New Jerusalem. Rev. 21:20.

Amminadab (am-mĭn'a-dăb), *kindred of the prince.* 1. The son of Ram or Aram, who was great-grandson of Judah. His daughter, Elisheba, was the wife of Aaron; and his son Naashon, or Nahshon, prince of Judah in the wilderness. Ex. 6:23; Num. 1:7; 2:3; 7:12,17; 10:14; Ruth 4:19, 20; 1 Chron. 2:10. 2. A son of Kohath. 1 Chron. 6:22. This is possibly a transcriber's error, as elsewhere generally, Ex. 6:18; 1 Chron. 6:2, 18, he is called Izhar. 3. The chief in David's time of the sons of Uzziel, a Levite, son of Kohath. 1 Chron. 15:10, 11.

Amminadib, *companions of the prince.* This occurs in Song of Sol. 6:12. But in the margin it is *my willing people,* A. V.; *my princely people,* R. V., and probably the word should not be taken as a proper name.

Ammon, Ammonites, Children of Ammon (ăm'mon, ăm'mon-ītes), *strong people,* or, perhaps, the same as Ben-ammi, *son of my kindred.* A people descended from Ben-ammi, the son of Lot by his younger daughter, Gen. 19:38; comp. Ps. 83:7, 8, as Moab was by the elder; and dating from the destruction of Sodom. The near relation between the two peoples indicated in the story of their origin continued throughout their existence. Comp. Judg. 10:6; 2 Chron. 20:1; Zeph. 2:8, etc. Indeed, so close was their union, and so near their identity, that each would appear to be occasionally spoken of under the name of the other. Unlike Moab, the precise position of the territory of the Ammonites is not ascertainable. In the earliest mention of them, Deut. 2:20, they are said to have destroyed the Rephaim, whom they called the Zamzummim, and to have dwelt in their place, Jabbok being their border. Num. 21:24; Deut. 2:37; 3:16. "Land," or "country," is, however, but rarely ascribed to them, nor is there any reference to those habits and circumstances of civilization, which so constantly recur in the allusions to Moab. Isa. 15, 16; Jer. 48. On the contrary, we find everywhere traces of the fierce habits of marauders in their incursions. 1 Sam. 11:2; Amos 1:13. It appears that Moab was the settled and civilized half of the nation of Lot, and that Ammon formed its predatory and Bedouin section. On the west of Jordan they never obtained a footing. The hatred in which the Ammonites were held by Israel is stated to have arisen partly from their opposition, or, rather, their denial of assistance, Deut. 23:4, 5, to the Israelites on their approach to Canaan. But whatever its origin the animosity continued in force to the latest date. The tribe was governed by a king, Judg. 11:12, etc.; 1 Sam. 12:12; 2 Sam. 10:1; Jer. 40:14; and by "princes," 2 Sam. 10:3; 1 Chron. 19:3. It has been conjectured that Nahash, 1 Sam. 11:1; 2 Sam. 10:2, was the official title of the king as Pharaoh was of the Egyptian monarchs; but this is without any sure foundation. The divinity of the tribe was Molech, generally named in the Old Testament under the altered form of Milcom—"the abomination of the children of Ammon;" and Malcham. Zeph. 1:5. In more than one passage under the word rendered "their king" in the A. V. an allusion is intended to this idol.

Amnon (ăm'non), *faithful.* The eldest son of David, by Ahinoam of Jezreel. 2 Sam. 3:2. He is known only by his guilt in violating his half-sister Tamar; for which Absalom, two years after, caused him to be assassinated, 2 Sam. 13, thus also getting an elder brother out of his way to the throne.

Amon (ā'mon), an Egyptian divinity, whose name occurs in that of No-amon, Nah. 3:8 R. V., but in A. V. "populous No," or Thebes, also called No. The Greeks called this divinity Ammon. The ancient Egyptian name is Amen. Amen was one of the eight gods of the first order, and chief of the triad of Thebes. He was worshiped at that city as Amen-ra, or "Amen the sun."

Amon (ā'mon), *builder.* King of Judah, son and successor of Manasseh, reigned two years from B. C. 642 to 640. Following his father's example, Amon devoted himself wholly to the service of false gods, but was killed in a conspiracy. The people avenged him by putting all the conspirators to death, and secured the succession to his son Josiah. To Amon's reign we must refer the terrible picture which the prophet Zephaniah gives of the moral and religious state of Jerusalem. 2. A governor of Samaria. 1 Kings 22:26. 3. A person also called Ami.

Amorites (ăm'o-rītes), *mountaineers.* Gen. 10:16. A Syrian tribe descended from Canaan, and among the most formidable of the tribes with whom the Israelites contended. They were of gigantic stature and great courage, Amos 2:9, and inhabited one of the most fertile districts of the country, being bounded on three sides by the rivers Arnon, Jabbok, and Jordan. The Israelites asked permission of the king to travel through their territory, promising to injure nothing, not even to draw water from their wells; but the request was refused. The Amorites collected and attempted to oppose their progress, but were totally defeated, and their territory taken and divided between the tribes of Reuben and Gad.

Amos (ā'mos), *burden.* 1. The third of the minor prophets was a shepherd of Tekoa, a small town of Judah. He prophesied concerning Israel, in the days of Uzziah, king of Judah, and Jeroboam the Second, king of Israel, about B. C. 790. The book of Amos takes a high rank among the writings of the prophets. The writer must have been a man of some education, as is evident from his observations relating to geography, history, and astronomy. He is full of fancy and imagery, concise, and yet simple and perspicuous. Amos 1:1, 7, 10-17. 2. A son of Nahum, R. V., or Naum, A. V., of Luke 3:25.

Amphipolis (am-fip'o-lis), *around the city.* A chief city of the southern portion of Macedonia under the Romans. The river Strymon flowed on both sides of the city, hence its name. It was 33 miles southwest of Philippi, and three miles from the sea. Paul and Silas passed through it. Acts 17:1. Neo-khorio, or Newtown, a village of about 100 houses, now occupies a portion of the site of Amphipolis.

Amraphel (ăm'ra-fĕl), *keeper,* or *highest of the gods.* Perhaps a Hamite king of Shinar or Babylonia, who joined the victorious incursion of the Elamite Chedorlaomer against the kings of Sodom and Gomorrah and the cities of the plain. Gen. 14:1.

Anakim (ăn'a-kĭm), *long-necked, i. e., men of tall stature.* Anak, the son of Arba, had three sons, who were giants, and were founders of a Canaanitish tribe, famous for their stature and fierceness. The seat of the tribe before the invasion by the Hebrews was in the vicinity of Hebron. They were nearly extirpated by the Hebrews so that only a few remained afterwards in the cities of the Philistines, Num. 13:22; Deut. 9:2; Josh. 11:21, 22; 14:15; and Jer. 47:5, which in the Septuagint reads: "O remnant of the Anakim" that is cut off.

Anammelech. See Adrammalech.

Ananias (ăn-a-nī'as), *whom Jehovah covers, i. e., protects.* 1. A high priest in Acts 23:2-5; 24:1. He was the son of Nebedaeus, succeeded Joseph son of Camydus, and preceded Ismael son of Phabi. He was nominated to the office by Herod king of Chalcis, in A. D. 48; was deposed shortly before Felix left the province, and assassinated by the sicarii at the beginning of the last Jewish war. 2. A false disciple at Jerusalem, husband of Sapphira. Acts 5:1-11. Having sold his goods for the benefit of the church, he kept back a part of the price, bringing to the apostles the remainder, as if it were the whole, his wife also being privy to the scheme. Peter denounced the fraud, and Ananias fell down and expired. 3. A Jewish disciple at Damascus, Acts 9:10-17, of high repute, Acts 22:12, who sought out Saul during the period of blindness and dejection which followed his conversion, and announced to him his future commission as a preacher of the gospel. Tradition makes him to have been afterwards bishop of Damascus, and to have died by martyrdom.

Anathema (a-năth'ē-mah), *set apart, separated, devoted.* This Greek word represents a Hebrew phrase which generally denoted among the Jews the absolute, irrevocable and entire separation of a person from the communion of the faithful, or from the privileges of society, or from the number of the living; or the devoting of any man, animal, city or thing, to be extirpated, destroyed, consumed, and, as it were, annihilated. Josh. 6:17-21; 7:1-26. Another kind of anathema, very peculiarly expressed, occurs in 1 Cor. 16:22: "If any man love not the Lord Jesus Christ, let him be *anathema. Maran atha.*" This last word is made up of two Syro-Chaldaic words, signifying "The Lord cometh;" that is, the Lord will surely come, and will execute this curse by condemning those who love him not.

Anathoth (ăn'a-thŏth), *answers* or *echoes.* A Levitical city in Benjamin, Josh. 21:18; 1 Chron. 6:60; the birthplace of Jeremiah, Jer. 1:1; 11:21, 23; 32:7-9; on the route of the Assyrians, Isa. 10:30; some of its people returned with Zerubbabel, Ezra 2:23; Neh. 7:27.

Andrew (ăn'drū), *manly.* One of the apostles, the brother—whether older or younger is not known—of Simon Peter, with whom it would seem he lived. Mark 1:29. He was of Bethsaida, and became one of the disciples of John the Baptist, at whose word he followed Jesus, and afterwards brought his brother Simon. John 1:40-44. The order in which Andrew is named varies in different places; but generally he stands next after the three chiefs, and is associated with Philip. There are but a few scattered notices of him in the evangelic history. Mark 13:3; John 6:8, 9; 12:22. After the resurrection he is enumerated with the rest of the eleven (Acts 1:13); and then we hear no more of him. Tradition has been busy with his later history; and he is said to have been crucified at Patræ in Achaia, on a cross formed like the letter X, which has hence been called "St. Andrew's Cross."

Angel. Gen. 24:7. The word for angel, both in the Greek and Hebrew languages, signifies a *messenger,* and in this sense is often applied to men. 2 Sam. 2:5; Luke 7:24 and 9:52. When the term is used, as it generally is, to designate spiritual beings, it denotes the office they sustain as the agents by whom God makes known his will and executes his government. Our knowledge of such beings is derived wholly from revelation, and that rather incidentally. We know, from their residence and employment, that they must possess knowledge and purity far beyond our present conceptions, and the titles applied to them denote the exalted place they hold among created intelligences. Christ did not come to the rescue of angels, but of men. Comp. Heb. 2:16. The angels are represented as ministering spirits sent forth to do service to the heirs of salvation. Heb. 1:14. They appear at every important stage in the history of revelation, especially at the birth of Christ, Luke 2:9-13; in his agony in Gethsemane, Luke 22:43; at his resurrection, Matt. 28:2; Mark 16:5; Luke 24:4, and at the final judgment, Matt. 13:41. Of their appearance and employment we may form some idea from the following passages, viz., Gen. 16:7-11. Compare Gen. 18:2; 19:1, with Heb. 13:2; Judg. 13:6; Ezek. 10; Dan. 3:28 and 6:22; Matt. 4:11; 18:10 and 28:2-7; Luke 1:19; 16:22 and 22:43; Acts 6:15; 12:7; Heb. 1:14; 2:16; 2 Thess. 1:7; Rev. 10:1, 2, 6. Of their number some idea may be inferred from 1 Kings 22:19; Ps. 68:17; Dan. 7:10; Matt. 26:53; Luke 2:9-14; 1 Cor. 4:9; Heb. 12:22. Of their strength we may judge from Ps. 103:20; 2 Pet. 2:11; Rev. 5:2; 18:21; 19:17. And we learn their inconceivable activity from Judg. 13:20; Isa. 6:2-6; Matt. 13:49; 26:53; Acts 27:23; Rev. 8:12, 13; but the R. V. reads "eagle" in verse 13. There is also an order of evil spirits ministering to the will of the prince of darkness, and both active and powerful in their opposition to God. Matt. 25:41. Though Scripture does not warrant us to affirm that each individual has his particular guardian angel, it teaches very explicitly that angels minister to every Christian. Matt. 18:10; Ps. 91:11, 12; Luke 15:10; Acts 12:15; Heb. 1:14. They are the companions of the saved. Heb. 12:22, 23; Rev. 5:11. They are to sustain an important office in the future and final administration of God's government on earth. Matt. 13:39; 25:31-33; 1 Thess. 4:16. But they are not proper objects of adoration. Col. 2:18; Rev. 19:10. Augel of his Presence, Isa. 63:9, by some is supposed to denote the highest angel in heaven, as Gabriel, who stands "in the presence of God," Luke 1:19; but others believe it refers to the incarnate Word. Angel of the Lord, Gen. 16:7, is considered, by some, one of the common titles of Christ in the Old Testament. Ex. 23:20. Compare Acts 7:30-32 and 37, 38. Angel of the church. Rev. 2:1. The only true interpretation of this phrase is the one which makes the angels the rulers and teachers of the congregation, so called because they were the ambassadors of God to the churches, and on them devolved the pastoral care and government.

Anise, a well-known annual herb, resembling caraway, etc., but more fragrant. The plant mentioned in Matt. 23:23 was no doubt the *dill,* which grows in Palestine, and was tithed by scrupulous Jews.

Anna (*ăn'nah*), *grace,* a prophetess, daughter of Phanuel, of the tribe of Asher. Luke 2:36. Her husband having died after she had been married seven years, she devoted herself to the Lord, and was very constant in her attendance on the services of the temple. She did not, however, live in the temple itself. At 84 years of age she listened to the prophetic blessing which Simeon uttered when he held the infant Redeemer in his arms, and joined in it with great fervor.

Annas (*ăn'nas*), *answer, response.* The son of Seth, and a high priest of the Jews. He was appointed by Quirinus, governor of Syria, A. D. 7, and was removed by Valerius Gratus, procurator of Judæa, A. D. 23. The office was originally held for life, but in Judæa's degenerate and dependent position it was one of the spoils of office, to be given to the ruler's favorite, and to be taken away upon the loss of favor. After his deposition Annas continued to hold the title; and although Caiaphas, his son-in-law, was the actual high priest, he was the ruling power. This explains the reference in Luke 3:2. This power he retained for nearly fifty years, having had five sons in succession in the high priest's office. Our Lord was brought first before Annas on the night of his seizure. John 18:13, 24. The guilt of Christ's crucifixion rests most upon Annas, since Pilate tried to shield him, and Caiaphas was but Annas' tool. Annas is mentioned as the president of the Sanhedrin, before whom Peter and John were brought. Acts 4:6.

Anointing in Holy Scripture is either: I., with oil; or II., with the Holy Ghost. I. *With oil.* 1. Anointing the body or head with oil was a common practice with the Jews, as with other oriental nations. Deut. 28:40; Ruth 3:3; Micah 6:15. Abstinence from it was a sign of mourning. 2 Sam. 14:2; Dan. 10:3; Matt. 6:17. Anointing the head with oil or ointment seems also to have been a mark of respect sometimes paid by a host to his guests. Luke 7:46 and Ps. 23:5. The bodies of the dead were often anointed, not with a view to preserve them from corruption, but to impart a fragrancy to the linen in which the corpse was wrapped. Mark 14:8; 16:1; Luke 23:56; John 19:39, 40. 2. Anointing with oil was a rite of inauguration into each of the three typical offices of the Jewish commonwealth. (*a*) Prophets were occasionally anointed to their office, 1 Kings 19:16, and are called messiahs, or anointed. 1 Chron. 16:22; Ps. 105:15. (*b*) Priests, at the first institution of the Levitical priesthood, were all anointed to their offices, the sons of Aaron as well as Aaron himself, Ex. 40:15; Num. 3:3; but afterwards, anointing seems not to have been repeated at the consecration of ordinary priests, but to have been especially reserved for the high priest, Ex. 29:29; Lev. 16:32; so that "the priest that is anointed," Lev. 4:3, is generally thought to mean the high priest. (*c*) Kings. Anointing was the principal and divinely appointed ceremony in the inauguration of the Jewish kings. 1 Sam. 9:16; 10:1; 1 Kings 1:34, 39. The rite was sometimes performed more than once. David was thrice anointed to be king. After the separation into two kingdoms, the kings both of Judah and of Israel seem still to have been anointed. 2 Kings 9:3; 11:12 (*d*) Inanimate objects also were anointed with oil in token of their being set apart for religious service. Thus Jacob anointed a pillar at Bethel, Gen. 31:13; and at the introduction of the Mosaic economy, the tabernacle and all its furniture were consecrated by anointing. Ex. 30:26-28. 3. Ecclesiastical. Anointing with oil in the name of the Lord is prescribed by James to be used together with prayer, by the elders of the church, for the recovery of the sick. Jas. 5:14. Analogous to this is the anointing with oil practised by the twelve. Mark 6:13. II. *With the Holy Ghost.* 1. In the Old Testament a Deliverer is promised under the title of Messiah, or Anointed, Ps. 2:2; Dan. 9:24-26; and the nature of his anointing is described to be spiritual, with the Holy Ghost. Isa. 61:1; see Luke 4:18. In the New Testament Jesus of Nazareth is shown to be the Messiah or Christ, or anointed of the Old Testament, John 1:41; Acts 9:22; 17:2, 3; 18:4, 5, 28; and the historical fact of his being anointed with the Holy Ghost is asserted and recorded. Acts 10:38; 4:27; John 1:32, 33. 2. Spiritual anointing with the Holy Ghost is conferred also upon Christians by God, 2 Cor. 1:21, and they are described as having an unction from the Holy One, by which they know all things. 1 John 2:20, 27.

Antichrist. This term is employed by the apostle John alone, who defines it in a manner which leaves no doubt as to its meaning. Its application is less certain. In the first passage—1 John 2:18—in which it occurs, the apostle makes direct reference to the false Christs whose coming, it had been foretold, should mark the last days. In verse 22 we find, "he is antichrist, that denieth the Father and the Son;" and still more positively, "every spirit that confesseth not that Jesus Christ is come in the flesh is of antichrist." Comp. 2 John 7. From these definitions it has been supposed that the object of the apostle in his first epistle was to combat the errors of Cerinthus, the Docetæ and the Gnostics, who denied the union of the divine and human nature in Christ. The coming of Antichrist was believed to be foretold in the "vile person" of Daniel's prophecy, Dan. 11:21, which received its first accomplishment in Antiochus Epiphanes, but of which the complete fulfillment was reserved for the last times. He is identified with "the man of sin, the son of perdition." 2 Thess. 2:3. This interpretation brings Antichrist into close connection with the gigantic power of evil, symbolized by the "beast," Rev. 13, who received his power from the dragon (*i. e.*, the devil, the serpent of Genesis), who was invested with the kingdom of the ten kings. Rev. 17:12, 17. The destruction of Babylon is to be followed by the rule of Antichrist for a short period, Rev. 17:10, to be in his turn overthrown in "the battle of that great day of God Almighty," Rev. 16:14, with the false prophet and all his followers. Rev. 19. The personality of Antichrist is to be inferred as well from the personality of his historical precursor, as from that of him to whom he stands opposed. Such an interpretation is to be preferred to that which regards Antichrist as the embodiment and personification of all powers and agencies inimical to Christ, or of the Antichristian might of the world. But the language of the apostles is obscure, and this obscurity has been deepened by the conflicting interpretations of expositors. All that the dark hints of the apostles teach us is, that they regarded Antichrist as a power whose influence was beginning to be felt even in their time, but whose full development was reserved till the passing away of the principle which hindered it, and the destruction of the power symbolized by the mystical Babylon. The word antichrist does not always mean openly opposed to Christ, but putting something in the place of Christ. Any person teaching any way to God, excepting through Christ, is Antichrist. Any person teaching any way of salvation, excepting through the blood of Christ, is Antichrist. John says that in his day, "Now are there many antichrists." 1 John 2:18. The papal church, putting its traditions in the place of the Scriptures, putting the Virgin Mary, the saints, the Pope, the priest, good works, the mass, purgatory, etc., as the way of salvation, in place of salvation by faith in the Lord Jesus Christ, is pre-eminently Antichrist.

Antioch (*ăn'ti-ŏk*), *place that withstands* (from *Antiochus*). The name of two cities in New Testament times. 1. Antioch in Syria, Acts 11:19, 22, founded by Seleucus Nicator, about 300 B. C., and enlarged by Antiochus Epiphanes. This city was about 300 miles north of Jerusalem, on the left bank of the river Orontes, 16½ miles from the Mediterranean, in a deep pass between the Lebanon and the Taurus ranges of mountains. At Antioch the disciples were first called Christians, Acts 11:26; it was an important centre for the spread of the gospel, Acts 13; from it Paul started on his missionary journeys, Acts 15:35, 36; 18:22, 23; important principles of Christian faith and practice were raised and settled through the church at Antioch. Acts 14:26, 27; 15:2-30; Gal. 2:11-14. It was made a "free" city by Pompey, was beautified by the emperors with aqueducts, baths, and public buildings; and in Paul's time it ranked third in population, wealth and commercial activity among the cities of the Roman empire. Christianity gained such strength there, that in the time of Chrysostom, who was born at Antioch, one-half of the 200,000 inhabitants of the city were Christians. The old town, which was five miles long, is now represented by a mean, shrunken-looking place of about 6000 population, called *Antakieh*. 2. Antioch in or near Pisidia was also founded or rebuilt by Seleucus Nicator. It was situated on a ridge—Strabo calls it a "height"—near the foot of the mountain-range, and by the northern shore of Lake *Eyerdir*. Paul preached there, Acts 13:14; 14:21, and was persecuted by the people. 2 Tim. 3:11. There were at least sixteen cities of the name of Antioch in Syria and Asia Minor.

Antipatris (*ăn-tĭp'a-trĭs*), *for the father.* A city of Palestine, situated in the midst of a fertile and well-watered plain, between Cæsarea and Lydda, called by Josephus, "the plain of Caphar Saba." It was rebuilt by Herod the Great, and called "Antipatris," in honor of his father, Antipater. Its ancient splendor has passed away; it is now marked by the ruins called *Ras-el Ain.* Acts 23:31.

Apharsathchites, Apharsites, A-

pharsachites (*a-fär′sath-kīles, a-fär′sītes, a-fär′sak-ītes*). Colonists from Assyria to Samaria. Ezra 4:9; 5:6; 6:6.

Aphek (*ā′fek*), *strength*. The name of several towns. 1. A royal city of the Canaanites whose king was slain by Joshua, Josh. 12:18. It was near Hebron, and probably the same as Aphekah. Josh. 15:53. 2. A city of Asher, Josh. 19:30, in the north of Palestine, near Sidon, Josh. 13:4; supposed to be the same as Aphik, Judg. 1:31, and the classical Aphaca, noted in later history for its temple of Venus; now Afka, near Lebanon. 3. A place where the Philistines encamped before the ark was taken, 1 Sam. 4:1, northwest of Jerusalem and near Shocho, now Belled el-Foka. 4. A place near Jezreel, in Issachar, where the Philistines were, before defeating Saul, 1 Sam. 29:1, and cannot be identified with No. 3, as some have suggested. 5. A walled city in the plains of Syria, on the road to Damascus. 1 Kings 20:26, 30; 2 Kings 13:17. It was about six miles east of the Sea of Galilee; now called Fik.

Apocrypha. The name given generally to certain ancient books and parts of books often appended to the scriptures of the Old Testament, some of which are held by the Roman Catholic church to be of canonical and divine authority. The Westminster Confession and the Church of England allow the books to be read for example of life and instruction of manners; but yet doth not apply them to establish any doctrine. They are regarded as human writings, not inspired. They are:

The third book of Esdras } [Esdras
The fourth book of Esdras } 1 and 2.]
The book of Tobias [Tobit].
The book of Judith.
The Rest of the book of Esther.
The book of Wisdom.
Jesus the son of Sirach [Ecclesiasticus].
Baruch the Prophet.
The Song of the Three Children.
The Story of Susanna.
Of Bel and the Dragon.
The Prayer of Manasses.
The first book of Maccabees.
The second book of Maccabees.

There are also some apocryphal writings claiming a place among the books of the New Testament; but, as these have never been recognized in the Christian church, they require no notice here.

Apollonia (*ap-pol-lō′ni-a*), *belonging to Apollo*. The name of several places in Europe and Asia, of which Apollonia in Illyria was the most celebrated. But the Apollonia through which Paul passed, Acts 17:1, was a city of Macedonia, about 36 miles east of Thessalonica, and 30 miles southwest of Amphipolis.

Apollos (*a-pol′los*), probably abbreviated from Apollonios, *given by Apollo*. A Jew from Alexandria, eloquent (which may also mean learned) and mighty in the Scriptures: one instructed in the way of the Lord, as taught by the disciples of John the Baptist. Acts 18:25. On his coming to Ephesus during a temporary absence of Paul, Apollos was more perfectly taught by Aquila and Priscilla. After this he preached the gospel, first in Achaia and then in Corinth, Acts 18:27; 19:1; where he watered that which Paul had planted. 1 Cor. 3:6. When Paul wrote his first Epistle to the Corinthians, Apollos was with or near him, 1 Cor. 16:12, probably at Ephesus in A. D. 57. He is mentioned once more in the New Testament. Tit. 3:13. Some suppose Apollos wrote the Epistle to the Hebrews.

Apollyon. Rev. 9:11. See **Abaddon**.

Apostle. The official title, implying messenger, of the twelve disciples whom our Lord chose, "that they should be with him, and that he might send them forth to preach." These twelve were arranged in three groups, Simon Peter and his brother Andrew, with James and John, the two sons of Zebedee; then Philip, Bartholomew, Thomas, and Matthew; and, lastly, James, the son of Alpheus, Lebbeus (called Thaddeus, Judas, and Jude), Simon Zelotes or the Canaanite, and Judas Iscariot. Matt. 10:1-4; Mark 3:13-19; Luke 6:12-16; comp. Acts 1:13. While Matthew narrates the sending forth of the apostles to preach, Mark and Luke describe the choice of them; and this choice, it appears, was made upon a mountain, not improbably that well-known horned hill of Hattin where also the notable sermon on the mount was probably delivered. Some time after their appointment the apostles were sent forth to preach and perform miracles, a special charge being given them. Matt. 10:1, 5-42; Mark 6:7-13; Luke 9:1-6. They generally, however, accompanied their Master, witnessed his mighty works, heard the explanation of his parables, and were the selected company at the institution of the last supper. One, however, Judas, betrayed him; and when Jesus was seized they all forsook him. Matt. 26:47-56. One or two had courage to attend his examination, John 18:15, 16, and one was present at his execution. John 19:26. But, so far as appears, they took no part in the Lord's burial, and could hardly be persuaded that he was risen. After his resurrection, the eleven, the traitor having hung himself, had frequent interviews with him, and witnessed his ascension. Luke 24:50, 51. According to their Master's command, they continued at Jerusalem, waiting for the promised gift of the Holy Ghost. One was appointed to fill the place of Judas. The Scripture account is as follows: "His bishopric let another take. Wherefore of these men which have companied with us all the time that the Lord Jesus went in and out among us, beginning from the baptism of John, unto that same day that he was taken up from us, must one be ordained to be a witness with us of his resurrection." Matthias was chosen by lot to fill the place of Judas. Acts 1:20-26. After the day of Pentecost the apostles were no longer fearful and temporizing; they preached boldly in the name of Jesus. They took the lead, as the acknowledged heads of the movement, verses 12, 13, devoted themselves to ministerial labor, Acts

6:2-4, exercised peculiar powers, 8:14-18, and had primary authority in the church. Acts 9:27; 15:2; 1 Cor. 9:1; 12:28; 2 Cor. 10:8; 12:12; Gal. 1:17; 2:8, 9. Two centres and two departments of apostolic working are described in the Acts of the Apostles; from Jerusalem among the Jews by Peter, from Antioch by Paul among the Gentiles. For Paul was extraordinarily appointed to the apostleship by Christ, Gal. 1:1; and others seem to have been added, as Barnabas, Acts 14:14; and according to the belief of some writers many more. Scripture says but little of the personal history of most of the apostles; but what is known of each will be found under their respective names. The title is once given to our Lord. Heb. 3:1.

Appii Forum (*ăp'py-ĭ-fō'rum*), *forum*, or *market-place of Appius*. A well-known station on the Appian road, which led from Rome to Capua. It doubtless derived its name from Appius Claudius, who constructed the road. It was about 43 Roman miles from Rome, and its site is marked by some ruins near Treponti. A body of Christians from Rome met Paul at this place. Acts 28:15.

Apple Tree, Apple (Heb. *tappûach*). Apple tree is named in the English Versions in Song of Sol. 2:3; 8:5, and Joel 1:12. The fruit of this tree is alluded to in Prov. 25:11 and Song of Sol. 2:5; 7:8. It is difficult to say what tree is intended by the Hebrew word *tappûach*. The apple proper is rare in Syria, and its fruit poor. Some writers say the Hebrew word means either the quince or the citron; others speak of the apricot, which is abundant and deliciously perfumed. On the other hand, Dr. Royle says, "The rich color, fragrant odor and handsome appearance of the citron, whether in flower or in fruit, are particularly suited to the passages of Scripture mentioned above." Neither the quince nor the citron nor the apple appears fully to answer all the scriptural allusions. The orange would answer all the requirements of the scriptural passages, and orange trees are found in Palestine; but it is not certain that this tree was known in the earlier times to the inhabitants of Palestine. The question of identification, therefore, must still be counted unsettled.

Apples of Sodom. Found on the shores of the Dead Sea; like a cluster of oranges, yellow to the eye, and soft to the touch; but on pressure they explode with a puff, leaving only shreds of the rind and fibres. The Arabs twist the silk into matches for their guns. Compare "vine of Sodom" and "grapes of gall" in Deut. 32:32.

Aquila (*ăk'wĭ-lah*), *an eagle*. A Jew of Pontus whom Paul found at Corinth on his arrival from Athens. Acts 18:2. He had fled, with his wife Priscilla, from Rome, in consequence of an order of Claudius commanding all Jews to leave the city. He became acquainted with Paul, and they abode together, and wrought at their common trade of making the Cilician tent or hair cloth. On the departure of the apostle from Corinth, a year and six months after, Priscilla and Aquila accompanied him to Ephesus. There they remained, and there they taught Apollos. Acts 18:18, 19, 24-26. At what time they became Christians is uncertain, but they appear to have specially helped Paul, and to have labored in Rome. Rom. 16:3-5.

Ar (*ar*) **and Ar of Moab.** Num. 21:28. The chief city of Moab, on the east of the Salt Sea; called also Aroer, Deut. 2:36; sometimes used for the whole land of Moab, Deut. 2:29; burned by Sihon. Num. 21: 26-30.

Arabia (*a-rā'biah*), *arid, sterile*. A peninsula in the southwestern part of Asia, between the Red Sea, the Indian Ocean, and the Persian Gulf. Its extreme length from north to south is about 1300 miles, its greatest breadth about 1500 miles, though from the northern point of the Red Sea to the Persian Gulf is only about 900 miles. It has the sea on all sides except the north. Its area is estimated at 1,030,000 square miles; and of the three ancient divisions of the country, that known as Arabia Felix was by far the largest and most important. Its main features are a coast range of low mountains or table land, seldom rising over 2000 feet, broken on the eastern coast by sandy plains; this plateau is backed up by a second loftier range of mountains in the east and south. The Sinaitic peninsula is a small triangular region in the northwestern part, or corner, of Arabia. See **Sinai.** The ancients divided it into Petræa, Deserta, and Felix; or the stony, the desert, and the happy or fertile. The principal animals are the horse, famed for its form, beauty, and endurance; camels, sheep, asses, dogs, the gazelle, tiger, lynx, and monkey; quails, peacocks, parrots, ostriches; vipers, scorpions, and locusts. Of fruits and grains, dates, wheat, millet, rice, beans, and pulse are common. It is also rich in minerals, especially in lead. Arabia in early Israelitish history meant a small tract of country south and east of Palestine, probably the same as that called Kedem, or "the east." Gen. 10:30; 25:6; 29:1. Arabia in New Testament times appears to have been scarcely more extensive. Gal. 1:17; 4:25. The chief inhabitants were known as Ishmaelites, Arabians, Idumeans, Horites, and Edomites. The allusions in the Scripture to the country and its people are very numerous. Job is supposed to have dwelt in Arabia. The forty years of wandering by the Israelites under Moses was in this land. See **Sinai.** Solomon received gold from it, 1 Kings 10:15; 2 Chron. 9:14; Jehoshaphat flocks, 2 Chron. 17:11; some of its people were at Jerusalem at the Pentecost, Acts 2:11; Paul visited it, Gal. 1:17; the prophecies of Isaiah and Jeremiah frequently refer to it. Isa. 21:11-13; 42:11; 60:7; Jer. 25:24; 49: 28, 29. The Minnaean country to which Moses fled, according to recent discoveries, was among the most cultured of ancient times, having alphabetic writing and literary works earlier than the Phœnicians. It has been said, that if any people in the world afford in their history an instance of high antiquity and great simplicity of manners, the Arabs surely do. Of all peoples, the Arabs have spread farthest over the globe, and in all their wanderings have preserved their language, manners, and peculiar customs more perfectly than any other nation.

Arad (ā'rād), *to flee, to be wild, untamed.* 1. A Canaanitish city in the south of Judah. The site of this ancient city is a barren-looking eminence rising above the surrounding country, now called Tel Arad. In Num. 21:1; 33:40, "king Arad," A. V., is incorrect for "king of Arad." Josh. 12:14; Judg. 1:16. 2. A descendant of Benjamin. 1 Chron. 8:15.

Aram (ā'ram), *high region* 1. A son of Shem. Gen. 10:22, 23; 1 Chron. 1:17. 2. A descendant of Nahor, Abraham's brother. Gen. 22:21. 3. An Asherite. 1 Chron. 7:34. 4. The son of Esrom, elsewhere called Ram. Matt. 1:3, 4; Luke 3:33, A. V., but the R. V. reads Arni.

Aram, *highlands.* The elevated region northeast of Palestine, toward the Euphrates river. Num. 23:7; 1 Chron. 1:17; 2:23. It was nearly identical with Syria. Aram-naharaim of Gen. 24:10 is translated Mesopotamia in the English Version, and refers to the region between the Euphrates and Tigris rivers. There were probably several petty kingdoms included under Aram, as Aram-zobah, Aram Beth-rehob, Aram Damascus, Padan-aram; all these were gradually absorbed by that of Damascus, which became the capital of all "Aram," or Syria.

Ararat (ăr'a-răt), *holy land,* or *high land.* A mountainous region of Asia which borders on the plain of the Araxes, and is mentioned (1) as the resting-place of Noah's ark, Gen. 8:4; (2) as the refuge of the sons of Sennacherib, 2 Kings 19:37, R. V., or margin, A. V.; Isa. 37, 38, R. V., or margin, A. V.; (3) as a kingdom with Minni and Ashchenaz. Jer. 51:27. The mountains of Ararat, Gen. 8:4, properly refer to the entire range of elevated table land in that portion of Armenia; and upon some lower part of this range, rather than upon the high peaks popularly called Ararat, the ark more probably rested. For (1) this plateau or range is about 6000 to 7000 feet high; (2) it is about equally distant from the Euxine and the Caspian Seas, and between the Persian Gulf and the Mediterranean, and hence a central point for the dispersion of the race; (3) the region is volcanic in its origin; it does not rise into sharp crests, but has broad plains separated by subordinate ranges of mountains; (4) the climate is temperate, grass and grain are abundant, the harvests quick to mature. All these facts illustrate the biblical narrative. George Smith, however, places Ararat in the southern part of the mountains east of Assyria. *Chaldean Account of Genesis,* p. 289.

Araunah (a-rau'nah), *ark! a large ash* or *pine.* A Jebusite, it has been supposed of royal race, from whom David purchased a threshing-floor as a site for an altar to the Lord. 2 Sam. 24:18-25. In 1 Chron. 21:18-28, and 2 Chron. 3:1, the name is Ornan. There is an apparent discrepancy in the two accounts in respect to the price paid by David. According to the author of Samuel it was 50 shekels of silver; whereas in Chronicles we find the sum stated to be 600 shekels of gold. But we may suppose the floor, oxen, and instruments purchased for the 50 shekels; the larger area, in which the temple was subsequently built, for 600. Or, the first-named sum was the price of the oxen, the last of the ground.

Arba. Gen. 35:27. See Hebron.

Archangel, *a chief angel,* only twice used in the Bible. 1 Thess. 4:16; Jude 9. In this last passage it is applied to Michael, who, in Dan. 10:13, 21; 12:1, is described as "one of the chief princes," having a special charge of the Jewish nation, and in Rev. 12:7-9 as the leader of an angelic army.

Archelaus (är-ke-lā'us), *chief,* or *prince of the people.* A son of Herod the Great, by Malthace his Samaritan wife. Herod bequeathed to him his kingdom, but Augustus confirmed him in the possession of only half of it—Idumea, Judea, and Samaria, with the title of ethnarch, or chief of the nation. After about ten years, on account of his cruelties, he was banished to Vienne in Gaul; and his territories were reduced to the form of a Roman province under the procurator Coponius. In Matt. 2:22, he is said to be king, referring to the interval immediately after the death of Herod, when he assumed the title of king.

Archi (är'ki). Josh. 16:2 A. V., but R. V. reads "border of the Archites," a people living near Bethel, and to which Hushai belonged. 2 Sam. 15:32.

Arcturus (ark-tū'rus). Job 9:9; 38:32, in A. V., but the R. V. correctly reads "bear" in both passages. Arcturus is the name of a fixed star of the first magnitude in the constellation Boötes; but the Hebrew word in Job refers to the constellation Ursa Major, or Great Bear. The "sons" are probably the three stars in the tail of the bear.

Areopagus (ăr-e-ŏp'a-gŭs, or ărc-ŏp'a-gŭs), *Mars' Hill.* A narrow naked ridge of limestone rock at Athens, sloping upwards from the north, and terminating in an abrupt precipice on the south, 50 or 60 feet above a valley which divides it from the west end of the Acropolis. It had its name from the legend that Mars (Ares), the god of war, was tried here by the other gods on a charge of murder. Here sat the court or council of the Areopagus, a most ancient and venerable tribunal, celebrated through Greece. It examined criminal charges, as murder, arson, wounding; but the lawgiver Solon gave it also political powers. Those who had held the office of archon were members of this court, and they sat for life, unless guilty of some crime. The Areopagus was respected under the Roman dominion, and existed in the empire. Here it was that Paul made his memorable address, Acts 17:19-34; one of the council, persuaded by it or more fully instructed afterwards, becoming

29

a Christian. But it does not appear that the apostle was, properly speaking, tried; rather he was placed on this spot in order that what he had to say might be more readily heard by the multitude. Sixteen stone steps from the agora (market) yet exist, and the stone seats forming three sides of a quadrangle looking southwards, also two blocks, appropriated, it is believed, to the accuser and the criminal.

Aretas (*är'e-tas*), *virtuous*. 2 Cor. 11:32. The king of Arabia Petræa at the time the governor of Damascus attempted to apprehend Paul. Acts 9:24, 25. His daughter married Herod Antipas, but was afterward divorced to allow him to marry Herodias. In consequence of this insult, Aretas made war upon Antipas and defeated him. Antipas was soon after banished and his kingdom given to Agrippa. It is likely that Aretas was restored to the good graces of the Romans, and that Caligula granted him Damascus, which had already formed part of his predecessor's kingdom. In this way we can account for the fact in Paul's life stated above.

Argob (*är'gŏb*), *stony*, a small district of Bashan, east of the Jordan; named only four times in the Bible. It is about 30 miles long by 20 miles wide, chiefly a field of basalt (black rock), elevated about 30 feet above the surrounding plain, and bordered by a rocky rampart of broken cliffs. It once contained 60 strong and fortified cities, the ruins of many of them being still to be seen. It is now called the Lejah.

Ariel (*ā'ri-el* or *a-ri'el*), *lion of God*. One of Ezra's chief men who directed the caravan which Ezra led from Babylon to Jerusalem. Ezra 8:16. Jerusalem being the chief city of Judah, whose emblem was a lion, Gen. 49:9, the word Ariel is applied to that city. Isa. 29:1.

Arimathea (*ăr-ĭ-ma-thē'ah*), *the heights*. A city of Palestine, whence came Joseph the counsellor, mentioned in Luke 23:51. Trelawney Saunders places it east of Bethlehem.

Aristarchus (*ăr-is-tär'kus*), *best ruler*. A Macedonian of Thessalonica who accompanied Paul upon his third missionary journey. Acts 20:4; 27:2. He was nearly killed in the tumult which Demetrius excited in Ephesus, Acts 19:29, and it is said that he was finally beheaded in Rome. Paul alludes to him both as his fellow-laborer and fellow-prisoner. Col. 4:10; Phile. 24.

Ark. The vessel constructed by Noah at God's command, for the preservation of himself and family, and a stock of the various animals, when the waters of the flood overflowed the inhabited earth. If the cubit be reckoned at 21 inches, the dimensions of the ark were 525 feet in length, 87 feet 6 inches in breadth, 52 feet 6 inches in height. The proportions are those of the human body; and they are admirably adapted for a vessel required, like the ark, to float steadily with abundant stowage. This is proved by modern experiments. The ark was made of "gopher-wood," probably cypress; and it was to be divided into "rooms" or "nests," that is, furnished with a vast number of separate compartments, placed one above another in three tiers. Light was to be admitted by a window, not improbably a sky-light, a cubit broad, extending the whole length of the ark. If so, however, there must have been some protection from the rain. A "covering" is spoken of, Gen. 8:13; but several writers have believed that some transparent or translucent substance was employed, excluding the weather and admitting the light. It is observable that the "window" which Noah is said to have opened, Gen. 8:6, is not in the original the same word with that occurring in 6:16. Perhaps one or more divisions of the long sky-light were made to open. There was a door also, through which the persons and the animals would enter and pass out. Many questions have been raised, and discussed at great length by skeptics and others, respecting the form and dimensions of the ark; the number of animals saved in it—whether including all species then existing in the world, except such as live in water or lie dormant, or only the species living in the parts of the world then peopled by man; and as to the possibility of their being all lodged in the ark, and their food during the year. Some of these questions the Bible clearly settles. Others it is vain to discuss, since we have no means of deciding them. It was by miracle that he was forewarned and directed to prepare for the flood; and the same miraculous power accomplished all that Noah was unable to do in designing, building, and filling the ark, and preserving and guiding it through the deluge. 2. *Moses's ark* was made of the bulrush or papyrus, which grows in marshy places in Egypt. It was daubed with slime, which was probably the mud of which their bricks were made, and with pitch or bitumen. Ex. 2:3. 3. *Ark of the covenant.* The most important piece of the tabernacle's furniture. It appears to have been an oblong chest of shittim (acacia) wood, two and a half cubits long, by one and a half broad and deep. Within and without gold was overlaid on the wood; and on the upper side or lid, which was edged round about with gold, the mercy seat was placed. The ark was fitted with rings, one at each of the four corners, and through these were passed staves of the same wood similarly overlaid, by which it was carried by the Kohathites. Num. 7:9; 10:21. The ends of the staves were visible without the veil in the holy place of the temple of Solomon. 1 Kings 8:8. The ark, when transported, was covered with the "veil" of the dismantled tabernacle, in the curtain of badgers' skins, and in a blue cloth over all, and was therefore not seen. Num. 4:5, 20. The chief facts in the earlier history of the ark, see Josh. 3 and 6, need not be recited. Before David's time its abode was frequently changed. It sojourned among several, probably Levitical, families, 1 Sam. 7:1; 2 Sam. 6:3, 11; 1 Chron. 13:13, 15, 24, 25, in the border villages of eastern Judah, and did not take its place in the tabernacle, but dwelt in curtains, *i. e.*, in a separate tent pitched for it in Jerusalem by David. When idolatry became more shameless in the kingdom of Judah, Manasseh placed a "carved image" in the "house of God," and probably removed the ark to make way for it. This may account for the subsequent statement that it was reinstated by Josiah. 2 Chron. 33:7; 35:3. It was probably taken captive or destroyed by Nebuchadnezzar.

Armageddon (är-ma-gĕd'don), *the hill*, or, perhaps, *the city of Megiddo*. A symbolical name for the place where a final struggle between the hosts of good and evil must take place. Rev. 16:16. Spelled Har-Magedon in R. V. For an exposition of the apostle's meaning, the reader must be referred to commentaries; it will be sufficient here to say that there is an allusion to that great battle-field where Barak and Gideon conquered, Judges 4; 5:19; 6:33; 7; where Saul and Josiah fell, 1 Sam. 29:1; 31; 2 Sam. 4:4; 2 Chron. 35:20-24; the plain of Esdraelon, on the southern border of which Megiddo stood.

Armenia (ar-mē'ni-ä), *mountains of Minni(?)* The English name for a country called Ararat in the Hebrew, 2 Kings 19:37; Isa. 37:38, A. V., but the R. V. has Ararat in both of these places; hence "Armenia" does not occur in the Revised English Version. Armenia is in western Asia, between the Caspian and the Black Seas, and the Caucasus and Taurus ranges of mountains. Three districts, probably included in Armenia, are mentioned in the Bible—Ararat, Minni and Ashchenaz, and Togarmah. 1. Ararat was a central region near the range of mountains of the same name. 2. Minni and Ashchenaz, Jer. 51:27, districts in the upper valley of a branch of the Euphrates. 3. Togarmah, Ezek. 27:14; 38:6, was apparently the name by which the most, or perhaps the whole, of the land was known to the Hebrews. The present number of Armenians is estimated to be from 2,500,000 to 3,000,000, of whom about 1,000,000 live in Armenia. Its chief modern towns are Erzeroum, Erivan, and Van. See Ararat.

Arms, Armor. There were: I. *Offensive Weapons:* arms. II. *Defensive weapons:* armor. I. Offensive weapons. 1. Apparently the earliest and most widely used was the *Chereb* or sword, a lighter and a shorter weapon than the modern sword. It was carried in a sheath, 1 Sam. 17:51; 2 Sam. 20:8; 1 Chron. 21:27, slung by a girdle, 1 Sam. 25:13, and resting upon the thigh, Ps. 45:3; Judg. 3:16, or upon the hips, 2 Sam. 20:8. 2. The spear; at least three distinct kinds. (*a*) The *Chanith*, a "spear" of the largest kind. It was the weapon of Goliath, 1 Sam. 17:7, 45; 2 Sam. 21:19; 1 Chron. 20:5, and also of other giants, 2 Sam. 23:21; 1 Chron. 11:23, and mighty warriors, 2 Sam. 2:23; 23:18; 1 Chron. 11:11, 20. (*b*) Apparently lighter than the preceding was the *Cidôn* or "javelin." When not in action the *Cidôn* was carried on the back of the warrior, 1 Sam. 17:6, A. V. "target." (*c*) Another kind of spear was the *Rômach*, mentioned in Num. 25:7 and 1 Kings 18:28, and frequently in the later books, as in 1 Chron. 12:8 ("buckler"); 2 Chron. 11:12. It varied much in length, weight and size. (*d*) The *Shelach*, probably a lighter missile or "dart." See 2 Chron. 23:10; 32:5 ("darts"); some suppose darts are meant by the reading in the margin of A. V. of Neh. 4:17, 23; but the R. V. reads "weapon" in both cases, which makes it uncertain what kind of armor is meant. Job 33:18; 36:12; Joel 2:8. (*e*) *Shebet*, means a rod or staff, used once only to denote a weapon. 2 Sam. 18:14. 3. Of missile weapons of offence the chief was undoubtedly the *bow* (Hebrew, *Kesheth*). The *arrows* were carried in a quiver. Gen. 27:3; Isa. 22:6; 49:2; Ps. 127:5. From an allusion in Job 6:4 they would seem to have been sometimes poisoned; and Ps. 120:4 may point to a practice of using arrows with some burning material attached to them. 4. The *sling* is mentioned in Judg. 20:16. This simple weapon, with which David killed the giant Philistine, was the natural attendant of a shepherd. Later in the monarchy, slingers formed part of the regular army. 2 Kings 3:25. 5. The *battle-axe*, Jer. 51:20, was a powerful weapon; its exact form is unknown. II. *Armor.* 1. The *breastplate* noticed in the arms of Goliath, a "*coat of mail*," literally a "*breastplate* of scales." 1 Sam. 17:5. 2. The *habergeon* is mentioned twice—in reference to the gown of the high priest. Translated coat of mail in R. V. Ex. 28:32; 39:23. It was probably a quilted shirt or doublet. 3. The *helmet* was a protection for the head. 1 Sam. 17:5; 2 Chron. 26:14; Ezek. 27:10. 4. *Greaves* were coverings for the feet, made of brass, named in 1 Sam. 17:6 only. 5. Two kinds of *shield* are distinguishable. (*a*) The large shield, encompassing the whole person. Ps. 5:12. It was carried before the warrior. 1 Sam. 17:7. (*b*) Of smaller size was the *buckler* or *target*, probably for use in hand-to-hand fight. 1 Kings 10:16; 2 Chron. 9:15, 16.

Army. I. *Jewish army.* Every able-bodied man over 20 years of age was a soldier, Num. 1:3; each tribe formed a division, with its own banner and its own leader, Num. 2:2; 10:14; their positions in the camp and on the march were fixed, Num. 2; the whole army started and stopped at a given signal, Num. 10:5, 6; so they came up out of Egypt. Ex. 13:18. On the approach of an enemy a selection was made from the general body, Deut. 20:5; 2 Kings 25:19; and officers were appointed, Deut. 20:9. The army was then divided into thousands and hundreds under captains. Num. 2:34; 31:14; 2 Chron. 25:5; 26:12. With the kings arose the custom of a body-guard and a standing army. David's band of 600, 1 Sam. 23:13; 25:13, he retained after he became king, and added the Cherethites and Pelethites. 2 Sam. 15:18; 20:7. David organized a national militia, divided into twelve divisions, under their respective officers, each of which was called out for one month in the year. 1 Chron. 27. The maintenance and equipment of the soldiers at the public expense date from the establishment of a standing army. II. *Roman army*. The Roman army was divided into legions. The number in a legion varied from 3000 to 6000, each under "chief captains," Acts 21:31, who commanded by turns. The legion was subdivided into ten cohorts ("band,"), Acts 10:1; the cohort into three maniples, and the maniple into two centuries, containing originally 100 men, as the name implies: but subsequently from 50 to 100 men, according to the strength of the legion. There were thus sixty centuries in a legion, each under the command of a centurion. Acts 10:1, 22; Matt. 8:5; 27:54. In addition to the legionary cohorts, independent cohorts of volunteers served under the Roman standards. One of these cohorts was named the Italian, Acts 10:1, because the soldiers in it were from Italy.

Arnon (är'non), *noisy*. A stream running into the Dead Sea from the east, and which divided Moab from the Amorites. Num. 21:13; Judg. 11:8. The Arnon is about 50 miles long, 90 feet wide, and from four to ten feet deep at its mouth; full in winter, but nearly dry in summer; had several fords, Isa. 16:2, and "high places," Num. 21:28; is referred to 24 times in the Bible. The reference to "high places" in Isa. 15:2, some Jewish scholars regard as the name of a place and read, "Beth-bamoth and Dibon are gone up to weep." Its modern name is el-Mojib. It runs through a deep ravine with precipitous limestone cliffs on either side, in some places over 2000 feet high. Ruins of forts, bridges, and buildings abound on its banks, and fish in its waters.

Aroer (ăr'o-er, or a-rō'er), *ruins*, or *juniper*. 1. A city on the northern bank of the Arnon. Its ruins are still called Ara'ir. If Aroer be meant by "the city in the midst of the river," Josh. 13:9, it may have originated in the circumstance that the city stood partly on the bank, and partly extending into the river. Deut. 2:36; 3:12; 4:48; Josh. 12:2; 13:16; Judg. 11:26; Jer. 48:19. 2. Another city, situated farther north, over against Rabbah of Ammon, on a brook of Gad, a branch of the Jabbok. The site is still called Ayra, Num. 32:34; Josh. 13:25; 2 Sam. 24:5; Isa. 17:2; but possibly another city near Damascus. 3. A city of the south of Judah; the inhabitants were called "Aroerites." The ruins are still called Ar'arah. 1 Sam. 30:28; 1 Chron. 11:44.

Arpad (är'păd), or **Arphad** (är'făd), *strong city*. A town or region in Syria, near Hamath, 2 Kings 18:34; Isa. 10:9, dependent on Damascus, Jer. 49:23.

Artaxerxes (är'tăg-zĕrk'sēz), *the great warrior*. The name of two kings of Persia mentioned in the Bible: 1. Ezra 4:7-24, the king who stopped the rebuilding of the temple because he listened to the malicious report of the enemies of the Jews. He is supposed to have been Smerdis, the Magian, the pretended brother of Cambyses, who seized the throne B.C. 522, and was murdered after eight months. 2. Ezra 7:7, and Neh. 2:1, both speak of a second Artaxerxes, who is generally regarded as the same with Artaxerxes Longimanus, *i. e.*, the Long-handed, son of Xerxes, who reigned B.C. 464-425. In the seventh year of his reign he permitted Ezra to return into Judæa, with such of his countrymen as chose to follow him; and 14 years afterwards he allowed Nehemiah to return and build up Jerusalem.

Arvad (är'văd), *wandering*. A small island, two or three miles off the coast of Phœnicia, related closely to Tyre, Ezek. 27:8:11. See also Gen. 10:18; 1 Chron. 1:16. Ruins of a huge wall are still found, and Greek inscriptions graven on black basaltic columns. The stones are so large that the best engineers are puzzled to know how they were moved. The place is now called Ruad, and has about 3000 population. It is probably the same as Arpad and Arphad.

Asa (ā'săh), *physician*. 1. The third king of Judah; he succeeded his father Abijam, about B.C. 955, and reigned 41 years at Jerusalem. He was distinguished for his success in war, and his zeal for the worship of Jehovah. He purified Jerusalem from the infamous practices attending the worship of idols; and deprived his mother of her office and dignity of queen, because she erected an idol to Astarte. In the latter part of his life he became diseased in his feet; and Scripture reproaches him with having had recourse to the physicians, rather than to the Lord. 1 Kings 15:8, 9; 2 Chron. 16:2. 2. A Levite. 1 Chron. 9:16.

Asahel (ā'sa-hĕl, or ăs'a-hĕl), *whom God made*. 1. The nephew of David, son of his sister Zeruiah, and brother of Joab and Abishai. He was fleet of foot, and pursued Abner so keenly after a skirmish, that that warrior was reluctantly compelled, in self-defence, to kill him. 2 Sam. 2:18-32; 3:27, 30; 23:24; 1 Chron. 11:26; 27:7. 2. A Levite. 2 Chron. 17:8. 3. Another Levite. 2 Chron. 31:13. 4. Father of a person employed with Ezra. Ezra 10:15.

Asaph (ā'sǎf), *collector*. 1. The father of Joah, recorder to King Hezekiah. 2 Kings 18:18, 37; Isa. 36:3, 22. 2. A Levite musician, one of the leaders of the singers in the reign of David. 1 Chron. 6:39. He is called a "seer," and is said to have composed several of the Psalms; of which 50, 73, 83 are in the titles attributed to him; several of these must, however, be of later date than the times of David. His descendants, or a school of musicians founded by him, are called sons of Asaph; and some of these returned from captivity with Zerubbabel. Ezra 2:41; Neh. 7:44. We often find Asaph spoken of in later ages with distinction. 2 Chron. 29:30; Neh. 12; 46. 3. The keeper of the king's forest to Artaxerxes. Neh. 2:8. 4. A Levite. Neh. 11:17.

Ashdod (ăsh'dŏd), *stronghold, castle*. One of the five confederate cities of the Philistines, allotted to Judah, Josh. 15:46, 47: the chief seat of Dagon-worship, 1 Sam. 5. It was three miles from the Mediterranean, and midway between Gaza and Joppa.

The place is called Azotus in the New Testament. Acts 8:40. It is now a mean village called Esdud; near it are extensive ruins.

Ashdoth (ăsh'doth), *outpouring* of torrents, *a ravine*. A district situated near Mount Pisgah, called also "Ashdoth-Pisgah" or "slopes of Pisgah," R. V. In the margin, "The springs of Pisgah." Deut. 3:17; 4:49; Josh. 12:3.

Asher (ăsh'er), *happy*. 1. The eighth son of Jacob. 2. One of the twelve tribes (see **Tribes**). 3. A territory extending from Carmel to Lebanon, about 60 miles long and ten to twelve wide, having 22 cities with their villages. The Phœnicians held the plain by the sea, and Asher the mountains. Josh. 19:24-31; Judg. 1:31, 32. This territory contained some of the richest soil in all Palestine; and to this fact, as well as to its proximity to the Phœnicians, the degeneracy of the tribe may be attributed. 4. A place on the boundary between Ephraim and Manasseh. Josh. 17:7.

Asherah (a-shē'rah, and plural *Asherim*). 2 Kings 23:14, R. V. The Greek and Latin name of a Phœnician goddess or idol, A. V. "grove." Asherah is closely connected with Ashtoreth, or Asheroth, R. V., and her worship. Elijah asked that 400 prophets of Asherah that ate at Jezebel's table be gathered at Carmel. Judg. 3:7; comp. 2: 3; Judg. 6:25; 1 Kings 18:19. Ashtoreth was the Hebrew name of the goddess; Asherah mistranslated "grove" in the A. V., is retained as Asherah in the R. V. It means an image or statue of the goddess, made of wood. See Judg. 6:25-30; 2 Kings 23:14. See **Ashtaroth**.

Ashes. The ashes on the altar of burnt-offering were gathered into a cavity in its surface. On the days of the three solemn festivals the ashes were not removed, but the accumulation was taken away afterwards in the morning, the priests casting lots for the office. The ashes of a red heifer burnt entire, according to regulations prescribed in Num. 19, had the ceremonial efficacy of purifying the unclean, Heb. 9:13, but of polluting the clean. Ashes about the person, especially on the head, were used as a sign of sorrow.

Ashkelon (ăsh'ke-lŏn), and **Askelon** (ăs'ke-lŏn), *migration*. One of the five cities of the Philistines, a seaport town ten miles north of Gaza; taken by Judah, Judg. 1: 18; visited by Samson, Judg. 14:19; and its destruction predicted in Jer. 47:5, 7; Amos 1:8; Zech. 9:5; Zeph. 2:7. Ashkelon was the seat of worship of the Philistine goddess Astarte, whose temple was plundered by the Scythians, B. C. 625; was the birthplace of Herod the Great. Near the ruins of the old city is Jûrah, a village of about 300 population.

Ashkenaz (ăsh'ke-năz), *strong, fortified*. 1. A district, probably in Armenia, the home of a tribe of the same name. In 1 Chron. 1:6; Jer. 51:27 it is called Ashchenaz. See **Armenia**. 2. Son of Gomer, Gen. 10:3, of the family of Japhet, and the probable ancestor of those who inhabited the country of the same name, Jer. 51: 27, lying along the eastern and southeastern shore of the Black Sea. The precise district is unknown.

Ashtaroth (ăsh'ta-rŏth), **Astaroth** (ăs'-ta-rŏth). 1. A city of Bashan, east of the Jordan, Deut. 1:4; Josh. 9:10; 13:31; the same as Beesh-terah, Josh. 21:27; probably Tell-Ashterah, in Jaulan. 2. Ashtoreth, sing.; Ashtaroth, plur. and more usual. An idol called the goddess of the Sidonians, Judg. 2:13, much worshipped in Syria and Phœnicia. Solomon introduced the worship of it. 1 Kings 11:33. The Greeks and Romans called it Astarte. The 400 prophets of the Asherah which ate at Jezebel's table, mentioned 1 Kings 18:19, R. V., were probably employed in the service of Asherah, the female deity. The worship of Ashtoreth was suppressed by Josiah. The goddess was called the "queen of heaven," and the worship was said to be paid to the "host of heaven." Her name is usually mentioned in connection with Baal. Baal and Ashtoreth are taken by many scholars as standing for the sun and the moon respectively.

Asia (ā'shi-ah). This word in scripture never means the continent, as with us. In the Old Testament it is not found; in the New Testament it means a small Roman province, in Asia Minor, in the northwest corner of Asia. Its boundaries were often changed; but generally it may be said to have comprised Phrygia, Mysia, Lydia, and Caria, in Asia Minor, and thus it must be understood in Acts 6:9; 19:10. Sometimes, however, the name is used in a more restricted sense; and Phrygia is distinguished from Asia. Acts 2:9, 10; 16:6. Asia was made by Augustus one of the senatorial provinces, and was governed, therefore, by a proconsul. It prospered under the emperors; and the gospel was preached there by Paul. Acts 19:10; 1 Cor. 16:19. The "seven churches" to which messages were sent, in Rev. 1:4, were in Asia.

Asp. Deut. 32:33. See **Serpent**.

Ass. Five Hebrew names of the animals of this family occur in the Old Testament. 1. Chamôr denotes the male domestic ass. 2. Athôn, the common domestic she-ass. 3. Aîr, the name of a wild ass, which occurs Gen. 32:15; 49:11. 4. Pere, a species of wild ass mentioned Gen. 12:16. 5. Arôd occurs only in Job 39:5; but in what respect it differs from the former is uncertain. The ass in eastern countries is a very different animal from what he is in western Europe. The most noble and honorable amongst the Jews were wont to be mounted on asses. The ass to us is a symbol of stubbornness and stupidity, while in the East it is remarkable for its patience, gentleness, intelligence, and great power of endurance. The color is usually a reddish brown, but there are white asses, much prized. The ass was used in peace as the horse was in war; hence the appropriateness of Christ in his triumphal entry riding on an ass. Mr. Layard remarks that in fleetness the wild ass equals the gazelle.

Asshur. Gen. 10:11. See **Assyria**.

Assos (ăs'ŏs). A Greek city of Mysia in "Asia," 19 miles southeast of Troas, and on the Mediterranean Sea. Extensive ruins of buildings, citadel, tombs, and a gateway still exist there. Paul visited it. Acts 20:13.

Assyria (as-syr'i-ah). A great empire of western Asia, founded at a very early date, though Babylonia is probably older, and is traced to Asshur, Gen. 10:10, 11, who built Nineveh, Rehoboth (?), Calah, and Resen. Assyria proper, the northern (Babylonia the southern portion), had about the same territory as Kurdistan. The empire at times covered a far larger extent of territory, and in its prosperity nearly all of western Asia and portions of Africa were subject to its power. According to Prof. F. Brown, "the Babylonio-Assyrian territory was about 500 miles from northwest to southeast, and in the widest part 300 miles from east to west, including Mesopotamia." The Persian Gulf formerly extended about 130 miles further to the northwest than it does now, the gulf having been filled up by mud borne down by the Tigris and Euphrates rivers. There are immense level tracts of the country, now almost a wilderness, which bear marks of having been cultivated and thickly populated in early times. Among its products, besides the common cereals, were dates, olives, cotton, mulberries, gum-arabic, madder, and castor-oil. Of animals, the bear, deer, wolf, lynx, hyena, antelope, lion, tiger, beaver, and camel were common. The fertility of the country is frequently noted by ancient writers.

History. Of the early history of Assyria little can be said. Profane historians differ; and scripture gives but scanty information. The deciphered inscriptions are revealing more, but are not yet fully examined; new ones are coming to light every year. Babylon is older than Nineveh; it was the beginning of Nimrod's empire, but not content with the settlements he had acquired, he invaded the country called Asshur from the son of Shem, and there founded cities afterwards most famous. Gen. 10:8-12. So far the sacred record would seem to teach us. But that it mentions an early Assyrian kingdom is not certain. Certain eastern monarchs are named, Gen. 14:1, 9, as pushing their conquests westwards, but there is a record of a Chaldean but not of an Assyrian king among them. Says Prof. Brown: "We find mention in the inscriptions of Persia (Parsua), Elam (Elamtu) with Susa (Shushan, cf. Neh. 1:1, etc.), its capital, and Media (Mada), with Ecbatana (Agamtanu = Achmetha, Ezra 6:2), its capital, and Armenia (Urartu = Ararat, 2 Kings 19:37), and the land of the Hittites (Chatti), who, we thus learn, as well as from the Egyptian inscriptions, had their chief seat far to the north of Damascus—Carchemish (Gargamish), their capital, being on the Euphrates, not far from the latitude of Nineveh (modern Jerabis). The river Habor (Chabur), of 2 Kings 17:6, is a river often named that flows into the middle Euphrates from the northeast, and Gozan (Guzanu) (ib.) is a city and district in the immediate vicinity. These are but a few of the important identifications." At first the Assyrian empire was confined within narrow limits; it became at length, by the addition of neighboring districts, a formidable state. Left partially under the sway of their own chiefs, who were reduced to vassalage, they continually had or took occasion for revolt. This led to the deportations of captives, to break the independent spirit of feudatory states, and render rebellion more difficult and hopeless. The Assyrian empire, at its widest extent, seems to have reached from the Mediterranean Sea and the river Halys in the west, to the Caspian and the Great Desert in the east, and from the northern frontier of Armenia south to the Persian Gulf. Abraham came from Ur Kasdim (Ur of the Chaldees), according to Gen. 11: 28, 31; 15:7; Neh. 9:7. "The only known Ur situated in the territory of the Chaldeans is the city of Uru, lying on the right bank of the Euphrates, far below Babylon, whose site now bears the name Muqayyar (*Mugheir*). The identification of this with the biblical Ur Kasdim has been disputed, but the arguments against it are not conclusive, and no other satisfactory identification has been proposed. We are therefore entitled to hold that the Hebrews were, from the beginning of their history, under the influence not only of the common stock of Shemitic endowments, customs, and beliefs, but also of those that were specifically Babylonian." After Abraham, for nearly 1200 years, we have no record of the contact of Hebrews with Assyrian or Babylonian peoples. In the ninth century, B. C., Nineveh and Assyria push into Hebrew territory. Shalmanezer II. encounters Benhadad of Damascus, and probably Ahab of Israel. The dark cloud threatening Israel and Judah from Assyria for their unfaithfulness to God is described in strains of solemn warning. Sometimes "the nations from far" are spoken of; and their terrific might and mode of warfare are detailed without naming them. Isa. 5: 26-30. Sometimes in express words the king of Assyria is said to be summoned as the Lord's executioner, and the desolation he should cause is vividly depicted. Isa. 8: 17-25. Samaria would fall; and her fall might well admonish Judah. Judah should deeply suffer. The invader should march through her territory; but the Lord would effectually defend Jerusalem. Isa. 10:5-34. The Assyrian king, in the might of his power, subjected the ten tribes, and carried multitudes of them into the far east; he passed also like a flood over the country of Judah, taking many of the cities throughout her territory; and in his presumptuous boldness he conceived that no earthly power could resist him, and even defied Jehovah, the God of Jacob. But the firm purpose of the Lord was to defend that city to save it. The catastrophe is related with awful brevity: "Then the angel of the Lord went forth, and smote in the camp of the Assyrians an hundred and four score and five thousand; and, when they arose early in the morning, behold they were all dead corpses." Isa. 37. The Assyrian empire attained afterwards probably its greatest power and widest extent. But it was doomed.

In later Persian times "the Ahashwerosh (Ahasuerus) of Ezra 4:6 and the book of Esther is Xerxes, the son of Darius, B. C. 486–464; and the Artachshashta (Artaxerxes) of Ezra 4:7, 8, 11, 23, etc., Neh. 2:1; 5:14, etc., is the son of Xerxes, Artaxerxes Longimanus, B. C. 464-425. Ezra 4:7, 8, etc., is thought by many to refer to the false Smerdis, the pretended brother of Cambyses, who in B. C. 522 reigned eight months; but the difficulty in supposing both that he had the name Artaxerxes and that Artaxerxes in the different passages does not refer to the same persons is too great." Finally, in "Darius the Persian," Neh. 12:22, we have a reference to Darius Codomannus, B. C. 336–330. He who rules justly in the world would destroy Assyria (which had been long before warned by Jonah), as Assyria had destroyed other kingdoms. Accordingly, in the prophecies of Nahum and Zephaniah, we find denunciations predicting the entire downfall of this haughty power. The language is fearfully precise. Nah. 1; 2; 3; Zeph. 2:13-15. The work of destruction seems to have been effected by the Medes and Babylonians. Assyria fell, and was never again reckoned among the nations; the very places being for long centuries unknown where her proudest cities had stood. *The people.*—The excavations which have been so successfully prosecuted have supplied a fund of information as to the manners and habits of the Assyrians. The sovereign was the despotic ruler and the pontiff, and the palaces contained also the temples. With no limitation of the monarch's power, the people were kept in a servile condition and in moral degradation. The conquered provinces being placed under the authority of dependent princes, insurrections were frequent; and the sovereign was almost always engaged in putting down some struggle for independence. War was waged with ruthless ferocity. Cities were attacked by raising artificial mounds; the besieging armies sheltered themselves behind shields of wicker-work, and battered the defences with rams. In the field they had formidable war chariots. And the sculptures exhibit the modes of cruelty practiced upon those that were subdued. They were flayed, they were impaled; their eyes and tongues were cut out; rings were placed in their lips; and their brains were beaten out with maces. Comp. Ezek. 26:7-12. The Assyrians worshipped a multitude of gods. Asshur (probably the Nisroch of the Scriptures, and the eagle-headed deity of the sculptures), was the chief. But there were 4000 others, presiding over the phenomena of nature and the events of life. The architecture of the Assyrians was of a vast and imposing character. In the fine arts they made considerable proficiency. Their sculptures are diversified, spirited, and faithful. They had, however, little knowledge of perspective, and did not properly distinguish between the front and the side views of an object. Animals, therefore, were represented with five legs; and sometimes two horses had but two fore-legs. The later sculptures are found to be better than the earlier. The Assyrians were skilled in engraving even the hardest substances. They were familiar with metallurgy, and manufactured glass and enamels; they carved ivory, and varnished and painted pottery. They indulged in the luxuries of life. Men wore bracelets, chains, and ear-rings, flowing robes ornamented with emblematic devices wrought in gold and silver; they had long-fringed scarfs and embroidered girdles. The vestments of officials were generally symbolical; the head-dress was characteristic; and the king alone wore the pointed tiara. The beard and hair were carefully arranged in artificial curls; and the eyebrows and eye-lashes were stained black. Of the women there are few representations. The weapons of war were richly ornamented, especially the swords, shields and quivers. The helmets were of brass, inlaid with copper. The chariots were embellished, and the horses sumptuously caparisoned. Their literature was extensive—grammars, dictionaries, geographies, sciences, annals, panegyrics on conquerors, and invocations of the gods. Little, however, can be expected from a series of inscriptions, dictated by the ruling powers, who did not hesitate sometimes to falsify the records of their predecessors. The wealth of Assyria was derived from conquest, from agriculture, for which their country was favorably circumstanced, and from commerce, for which they had peculiar facilities. But these advantages, as they contributed to wealth, fostered luxury, and that corruption, under a grinding tyranny, which is the sure precursor of an empire's ruin. The ruins are a splendid monument in testimony of the truth of prophecy and of Scripture.

Athaliah (*Ath-a-li'ah*), *whom Jehovah afflicts.* 1. The daughter of Ahab by Jezebel. She was married to Jehoram, king of Judah; and, when her son Ahaziah was slain by Jehu, she destroyed the rest of the royal family except Joash, an infant, who was concealed in the temple by his aunt Jebosheba (most likely not Athaliah's daughter), the wife of Jehoiada the high priest. Athaliah usurped the throne for six years, 884–878 B. C. In the seventh year, Jehoiada brought out the young prince. Athaliah, probably engaged in her idolatrous worship in the house of Baal, heard the shouts of the people, rushed into the temple, and saw the young king standing by, or perhaps on a pillar or platform; but her cry of "treason" only caused her own arrest and deserved execution. 2 Kings 8:18, 26; 11; 2 Chron. 22:2, 10–23;21; 24:7. 2. A Benjamite. 1 Chron. 8:26. 3. One whose son, with many of the same family, returned from Babylon with Ezra. Ezra 8:7.

Athens (*Ath'enz*). The chief town of Attica (now Greece); was visited by Paul on his second missionary journey, after he had been sent away, for safety, from Berea. Acts 17:13-15. Athens, in the time of the apostle, was included in the Roman province of Achaia, but was a free city, retaining some of the forms which had belonged to it in its palmy days. The Athenians, curious and inquisitive, as they had ever been, mockingly desired Paul to give them some account of the new doctrine he was setting forth. For both in the Jews' synagogue, and also in the agora or market-place, he had disputed with those who came to him, and had preached the gospel of Jesus, raised by God's mighty power from the dead. Within the city were four notable hills, three northward, forming almost a semicircle. The Acropolis, or citadel, was the most easterly of these: it was a rock about 150 feet high. Next, westward, was a lower eminence, the Areopagus or Mars' Hill, and then the Pnyx, where the assemblies of the people were held. To the south of these three hills was a fourth, the Museum. The agora lay in the valley between the four. It has been supposed that there were two market-places, but it is now satisfactorily proved that there was but one. The localities, therefore, which Paul frequented, are readily understood. He was taken from the agora, and brought up to the Areopagus, where he delivered his wonderful address. Acts 17:18-31. His preaching made no great impression: the philosophers despised it. Some, however, clave to him; and a Christian community was formed of whom were Dionysius the Areopagite, Acts 17:32-34, Damaris and others. Modern Athens, situated about five miles from the sea, its port being the Piræus, has been made the capital of the present kingdom of Greece.

Atonement. (Literally, a setting *at one*.) Satisfaction or reparation made for an injury, by doing or suffering that which will be received in satisfaction for an offence or injury. Specifically, in the Bible: The expiation of sin made by the obedience, personal sufferings, and death of Christ. Human language is imperfect, and human conceptions are often defective, when applied to the Most High. He is not touched with anger, resentment, etc., in the gross sense in which we commonly use the terms. We have, therefore, to take care that we do not represent him as hard to be mollified, with a thirst of vengeance to be slaked by the suffering of a victim. Nowhere does Scripture assert that the Father had a purpose of burning wrath against the world, which was changed by the interposition of the Son, on whom it lighted, so that, satiated by his punishment, he spared mankind. The Scripture rather teaches that "God so loved the world, that he gave his only-begotten Son, that whosoever believeth in him should not perish, but have eternal life." John 3:16. "God is love." 1 John 4:16. But God cannot "behold evil" with complacency. Hab. 1:13. It is consequently impossible that he can pass over it. Hence he threatens to visit it with a penalty: "the soul that sinneth it shall die." Ezek. 18:4. His infinite holiness and justice, and the intrinsic demerit of sin, require this. The proper idea of an atonement is that which brings the forgiveness of transgressors into harmony with all the perfections of the Godhead. One of these perfections must not be exalted to the depression of another: all must be equally and fully honored. Redemption, devised in the counsels of the eternal Three, was carried forward by the Son of God, who became man, that in the nature that had sinned he might make satisfaction for sin. He made this satisfaction by his obedience unto death, perfectly fulfilling the divine law, for he "did no sin;" and enduring the penalty of it, for "his own self bare our sins in his own body on the tree." 1 Peter 2:22, 24. In such a sacrifice, God's judgment against the evil and desert of sin was most illustriously displayed. As no other sacrifice of like value could be found, proof was given to the universe that sin was the most disastrous evil, and that its "punishment was not the arbitrary act of an inexorable judge, but the unavoidable result of perfect holiness and justice, even in a Being of infinite mercy." The objections urged against the doctrine of the atonement, as if a vicarious sacrifice for sin were irrational, or placed the character of the Deity in an unamiable light, are not, when sifted, found to be very cogent. It must always be remembered that Christ's atonement was not to induce God to show mercy, but to make the exercise of his love to sinners consistent with the honor of his law and the pure glory of his name. Sin is therein especially branded; and God's wisdom, righteousness, holiness, faithfulness, and mercy, are most eminently displayed. And, whereas it is said that he must forgive freely without requiring satisfaction, because he commands his creatures freely to forgive, it is forgotten that the cases are not parallel. Private offences are to be forgiven freely. But a ruler must execute his just laws. And so God is a great King, and as a king he administers public justice and will not arbitrarily clear the guilty. Doubtless there is much in his purposes and plans which we are incapable of rightly estimating. Enough is revealed to show us that "God was in Christ, reconciling the world unto himself, not imputing their trespasses unto them." 2 Cor. 5:19. But we should recollect that, "as the heavens are higher than the earth, so are" his "ways higher than" our "ways and" his "thoughts than" our "thoughts." Isa. 55:9.

The day of expiation, or atonement, was a yearly solemnity, observed with rest and fasting on the tenth day of Tishri, five days before the Feast of Tabernacles. Lev. 23:27; 25:9; Num. 29:7. This would now be in the early part of October. The ceremonies of this day are described in Lev. 16. On this day alone the high priest entered the Most Holy Place. Heb. 9:7. The various rites required him to enter several times on this day robed in white: first with a golden censer and a vessel filled with incense; then with the blood of the bullock, which he had offered for his own sins and those of all the priests. The third time he entered with the blood of the ram which he had offered for the sins of the nation. The fourth time he entered to bring out the censer and vessel of incense; and having returned, he washed his hands and performed the other services of the day. The ceremony of the scapegoat also took place on this day. Two goats were set apart, one of which was sacrificed to the Lord, while the other, the goat for complete separation, was chosen by lot to be set at liberty. Lev. 16:20-22. These solemn rites pointed to Christ. Heb. 9:11-15. As this day of expiation was the great fast-day of the Jewish church, so godly sorrow for sin characterizes the Christian's looking unto the Lamb of God, and "the rapture of pardon" is mingled with "penitent tears."

Attalia (āt-ta-lī'ah). A seaport town of Pamphylia, Acts 14:25, named from its founder, Attalus; later it was called Satalia, and now Adalia.

Augustus (au-gŭs'tus), *venerable.* A title given to the Cæsars by the Roman Senate, first applied in B. C. 27 to C. J. C. Octavianus. This was four years after the battle of Actium. Augustus was the emperor who appointed the enrollment, Luke 2:1, causing Joseph and Mary to go to Bethlehem, the place where Jesus was born. He also closed the temple of Janus, in token of the rare occurrence, a universal peace; thus unconsciously celebrating the coming of the Prince of Peace. He died A. D. 14, having two years before admitted Tiberius Cæsar to a share in the government. In Acts 25:21, 25, the title (translated the emperor in R. V.) refers to Nero.

Aven (ā'ven), *nothingness.* 1. The name applied to the city elsewhere called On, or Heliopolis. Ezek. 30:17. 2. A contracted form, Hos. 10:8, of Beth-aven, *i. e.*, Bethel. 3. A place mentioned by Amos, 1:5, called Bikath-aven, in the margin of A. V. It seems to be a "plain" or valley in Lebanon, where Baalbek is situated, still called el Buka'a.

Avenger of Blood. It was, and even still is, a common practice among nations of patriarchal habits, that the nearest of kin should, as a matter of duty, avenge the death of a murdered relative. The law of Moses was very precise in its directions on the subject of retaliation. 1. The wilful murderer was to be put to death without the right of redemption. The nearest relative of the deceased became the authorized avenger of blood. Num. 35:19. 2. The law of retaliation was not to extend beyond the immediate offender. Deut. 24:16; 2 Kings 14:6; 2 Chron. 25:4; Jer. 31:29, 30; Ezek. 18:20. 3. The shedder of blood could fly to one of six Levitical cities, appointed as cities of refuge, and be safe, until proved guilty of wilful murder. Num. 35:22-25; Deut. 19:4-6.

Azariah (ăz-a-rī'ah), *whom Jehovah helps.* 2 Kings 14:21. There are 24 persons of this name mentioned in the Old Testament. The most distinguished of them was Azariah (called also Uzziah), the son and successor of Amaziah, on the throne of Judah. He was, in many respects, an excellent king; but, being elated by his prosperity, he aspired to execute the office of a priest, and to offer incense in the temple. In this he was resisted by the priests, and while enraged by their interference, the leprosy broke out upon his forehead, and remained upon him until the day of his death; so that he was obliged to spend the latter part of his life in solitude. 2 Chron. 26:21.

Azekah (a-zē'kah), *dug over, broken up.* A place to which Joshua's pursuit of the Amorites extended after the battle for the relief of Gibeon. Josh. 10:10, 11. It stood in the plain country of Judah, to which tribe it was allotted. Josh. 15:35. In later times we find the Philistines pitching near it, 1 Sam. 17:1; it was fortified by Rehoboam, 2 Chron. 11:9, and was one of the last towns taken by Nebuchadnezzar in Zedekiah's reign before Jerusalem fell. Jer. 34:7. It was again inhabited after the return from captivity. Neh. 11:30.

B

Baal (bā'al), *lord.* 1. A Reubenite. 1 Chron. 5:5. 2. The son of Jehiel, and grandfather of Saul. 1 Chron. 8:30; 9:36.

Baal. The chief male divinity of the Phœnician and Canaanitish nations, as Ashtoreth was their chief female divinity. There can be no doubt of the great antiquity of the worship of Baal. It prevailed in the time of Moses among the Moabites and Midianites, Num. 22:41, and through them spread to the Israelites. Num. 25:3-18; Deut. 4:3. In the times of the kings it became the religion of the court and people of the ten tribes, 1 Kings 16:31-33; 18:19, 22, and appears never to have been wholly abolished among them. 2 Kings 17:16. Temples were erected to Baal in Judah, 1 Kings 16:32, and he was worshipped with much ceremony. 1 Kings 18:19, 26-28; 2 Kings 10:22. The religion of the ancient British islands resembled this ancient worship of Baal. The Babylonian Bel, Isa. 46:1, or Belus, is supposed to be identical with Baal, though perhaps under some modified form. The plural, Baalim, is found frequently, and the singular, Baal, in different compounds, among which appear—

1. BAAL-BERITH (bā'al-bē'rith), *the covenant Baal.* Judg. 8:33; 9:4. The God who comes into covenant with the worshippers.

2. BAAL-HANAN (bā'al-hā'nan). 1. The name of one of the early kings of Edom. Gen. 36:38, 39; 1 Chron. 1:49, 50. 2. The name of one of David's officers, who had the superintendence of his olive and sycamore plantations. 1 Chron. 27:28.

3. BAAL-PEOR (bā'al-pē'or), *lord of the opening, i. e.*, for others to join in the worship. The narrative, Num. 25, seems clearly to show that this form of Baal-worship was connected with licentious rites.

4. BAAL-ZEBUB (bā'al-zē'bub), *lord of the fly,* and worshipped at Ekron. 2 Kings 1:2, 3, 16.

Baal also occurs as the prefix or suffix to the names of several places in Palestine. Some of them are—

1. BAAL, a town of Simeon, named only in 1 Chron. 4:33, which from the parallel list in Josh. 19:8 seems to have been identical with BAALATH-BEER.

2. BAALAH (bā'al-ah), *mistress.* 1. Another name for KIRJATH-JEARIM, or KIRJATH-BAAL, perhaps now Kuriet el Enab(?). Josh. 15:9, 10; 1 Chron. 13:6. 2. A town in the south of Judah, Josh. 15:29, which in 19:3 is called BALAH, and in the parallel list, 1 Chron. 4:29, BILHAH.

3. BAALATH (bā'al-āth), *mistress*, a town of Dan named with Gibbethon, Gath-rimmon and other Philistine places. Josh. 19:44.

4. BAALATH-BEER (bā'al-āth-bē'er), *lord of the well.* A town in the south part of Judah, given to Simeon, which also bore the name of RAMATH-NEGEB, or "the height of the south." Josh. 19:8.

5. BAAL-GAD (bā'al-gād), *lord of fortune*, used to denote the most northern, Josh. 11:17; 12:7, or perhaps northwestern, 13:5, point to which Joshua's victories extended. Possibly it was a Phœnician or Canaanite sanctuary of Baal under the aspect of Gad, or Fortune.

6. BAAL-HAMON (bā'al-hā'mon), *lord of a multitude.* A place at which Solomon had a vineyard, evidently of great extent. Song of Sol. 8:11.

7. BAAL-HAZOR (bā'al-hā'zor), *village of Baal.* A place where Absalom appears to have had a sheep-farm, and where Amnon was murdered. 2 Sam. 13:23.

8. MOUNT BAAL-HERMON (bā'al-hēr'mon), *lord of Hermon*, Judg. 3:3, and simply Baal-hermon, 1 Chron. 5:23. This is usually considered as a distinct place from Mount Hermon; but we know that this mountain had at least three names, Deut. 3:9, and Baal-hermon may have been a fourth in use among the Phœnician worshippers of Baal.

9. BAAL-MEON (bā'al-mē'on), *lord of the house.* One of the towns built by the Reubenites. Num. 32:38. It also occurs in 1 Chron. 5:8, and on each occasion with Nebo. In the time of Ezekiel it was Moabite, one of the cities which were the "glory of the country." Ezek. 25:9.

10. BAAL-PERAZIM (bā'al-pĕr'a-zĭm, or pĕ-rā'zim), *lord of divisions.* The scene of a victory of David over the Philistines, and of a great destruction of their images. 2 Sam. 5:20; 1 Chron. 14:11. See Isa. 28:21, where it is called MOUNT PERAZIM.

11. BAAL-SHALISHA (bā'al-shăl'i-shah), *lord of Shalisha.* A place named only in 2 Kings 4:42, apparently not far from Gilgal; Comp. 4:38.

12. BAAL-TAMAR (bā'al-tā'mar), *lord of the palm tree.* A place named only in Judges 20:33, as near Gibeah of Benjamin. The palm tree (tāmár) of Deborah, Judg. 4, 5, was situated somewhere in the locality.

13. BAAL-ZEPHON (bā'al-zē'phŏn), *lord of the north.* A place in Egypt near where the Israelites crossed the Red Sea, Num. 33:7; Ex. 14:2, 9, probably on the western shore of the Gulf of Suez, a little below its head.

Baana or **Baanah** (bā'a-nah), *son of affliction.* 1. A Benjamite, one of the murderers of Ish-bosheth. 2 Sam. 4:2, 5, 6, 9. 2. The father of one of David's warriors. 2 Sam. 23:29; 1 Chron. 11:30. 3, 4. Two officers under Solomon. 1 Kings 4:12, 16. 5. One who returned with Zerubbabel. Ezra 2:2; Neh. 7:7. 6. A person whose son took part in rebuilding the wall of Jerusalem. Neh. 3:4. He may be identical with the one who sealed the covenant. Neh. 10:27.

Baasha (bā'a-shah), *wickedness*, or, as some suppose, *in the work.* Son of Ahijah, of the tribe of Issachar. He was probably of mean origin. At the siege of Gibbethon, he conspired against Nadab, king of Israel, killed him and all his family, and possessed himself of the throne. He attempted to fortify Ramah, with a view, it would seem, of preventing the access of the Israelites into Judah, 1 Kings 15:17, but his design was frustrated by a Syrian invasion, instigated by Asa, king of Judah. Baasha's evil conduct provoked the denunciation of God's judgments upon his house, as predicted by Jehu the prophet. He reigned 24 years, 953–930 B.C., and was buried in Tirzah, his capital. 1 Kings 15:16–22; 16:1–7; 21:22; 2 Chron. 16:1–6; Jer. 41:9.

Babel, Tower of (bā'bel). An incomplete building, named only once in the Bible. Gen. 11:4, 5. It was in the plain of Shinar, and made of burnt bricks, with "slime" (probably bitumen) for mortar. Jewish tradition and early profane writers say that the tower was destroyed. The captive Jews at Babylon imagined they recognized it, however, in the famous temple of Belus, which some identify with the temple of Nebo at Borsippa, the modern Birs Nimrúd. Rawlinson thinks that Birs Nimrúd cannot be identical with either the temple of Belus or the tower of Babel, but concedes that it may be used to show the probable form of the Babel tower. The Birs Nimrúd is one of the most striking ruins on the plain, and is six miles southwest of Hillah, on the Euphrates. This immense mound is about 2300 feet in circumference and 235 to 250 feet high. It was built of burnt bricks, each brick being twelve inches square and four inches thick. Several of them bear an inscription of Nebuchadnezzar. The tower is represented as in the form of a pyramid, built in seven receding stories, each placed upon the southwestern side of the one below, and each of the first three being 26 feet high, each of the last four being 15 feet high. On the seventh story was a temple, containing, perhaps, a statue of the god Belus.

Babylon (băb'by-lon), Greek form of *Babel.* The noted capital of the Chaldæan and Babylonian empires, situated on both sides of the Euphrates river, about 200 miles above its junction with the Tigris, 300 miles from the Persian Gulf. The valley is broad, and the river Euphrates is now about 600 feet wide and 18 feet deep at this place. Babylon, according to Herodotus, was a vast square on both sides of the Euphrates, enclosed by a double line of walls, about 56 miles in circuit and including about 200 square miles. Ctesias and others make the circuit about 42 miles, enclosing about 106 square miles. The walls, according to Herodotus, were about 335 feet high and 75 feet broad. Ctesias, quoted by Diodorus, states that they were 200 feet high and built by 2,000,000 men. Later writers, regarding these measurements as incredible, give the circuit of the walls at about 40 miles, their height at 75 to 100 feet, and their width at 32 feet, or wide enough to allow four chariots to drive abreast on the top. M. Oppert and Rawlinson, as explorers, hold that the ruins warrant the statement of Herodotus as to the extent of Babylon. The wall of Babylon was surmounted by 250 towers, and it had 100 gates of brass. Jer. 51:58; Isa. 45:2. Babylon is described as cut into squares—some say 676—by straight streets crossing each other at right angles, those at the river being closed by brazen gates, as the banks of the river were fortified by high walls; the river was crossed by drawbridges and lined with quays; the two palaces on opposite sides of the river were connected by a bridge, and also by a tunnel under the river. Among the wonderful buildings were: 1. Nebuchadnezzar's palace, an immense pile of buildings, believed to be nearly six miles in circumference. 2. The hanging-gardens, one of the seven wonders of the world, built by Nebuchadnezzar to please his Median queen, Amytis, who longed for her native mountains. These gardens were 75 feet high and covered three and a half acres, enclosed in an area of larger extent, some say 1000 feet on each side. Upon this mountain was soil of depth to support the largest trees, and the water was drawn up from the river by means of a screw. 3. The temple of Belus, a vast pyramid or tower, 600 feet square, having eight stages or stories, and according to Rawlinson 480 feet high, with a winding ascent passing around it, and a chapel of a god at the top. Babylon is named over 250 times in the Bible. It was founded by Nimrod, Gen. 10:10; its builders were dispersed, Gen. 11:9. Then, except some allusion to Shinar, Gen. 14:1, the Chaldæans, Job. 1:17, and the Babylonish garment (R. V. "mantle"), Josh. 7:21, it drops out of Scripture history until the era of the captivity. It was often subject to Assyria, 2 Chron. 33:11, and was the residence of at least one Assyrian king. After the fall of Nineveh, B.C. 625, it became an independent kingdom, and under Nebuchadnezzar was enlarged, beautified, and reached the height of its magnificence. In Isa. 13:19; 14:4, it is called "the glory of kingdoms," "the golden city," and in Jer. 51:41 "the praise of the whole earth," etc. It was the home of the chief of the captive Jews. Dan. 1:1-4. Its desolation was frequently foretold. Isa. 13:4-22; Jer. 25:12; 50:2,3; 51; Dan. 2:31-38; Hab. 1:5-10. Even before Babylon reached the summit of its glory, Isaiah prophesied: "Babylon, the glory of kingdoms, the beauty of the Chaldees' excellency, shall be as when God overthrew Sodom and Gomorrah. It shall never be inhabited, neither shall it be dwelt in from generation to generation; neither shall the Arabian pitch tent there; neither shall the shepherds make their fold there; but wild beasts of the desert shall lie there." Isa. 13:19-22; 14:22; 23:47. This prophecy has been literally fulfilled. It describes Babylon as it has been for many centuries and is now. Cyrus took it; Darius afterwards rifled it; Xerxes stripped its temples; and Alexander died in attempting its restoration. The modern town of Hillah now occupies a portion of the space covered by the ruins of ancient Babylon, and a telegraph connects it with the city of Bagdad. See **Chaldæa** and **Assyria.**

Babylon, in Rev. 14:8; 16:19; 17:5; 18:2, 21, is a symbolical name for heathen Rome, which took the place of ancient Babylon as a persecuting power. This is also the sense given to Babylon in 1 Pet. 5:13 by the fathers and many commentators; but others refer it to Babylon in Asia, since it is quite possible that Peter labored for a while in that city, where there was at that time a large Jewish colony; still others maintain that Babylon in Egypt, now called Old Cairo, is meant.

Babylon, Province or Kingdom of. The country of which Babylon was the capital. Dan. 2:49; 3:1, 12, 30; 4:29. Its boundaries and history are involved in much obscurity. It was originally known as the "land of Shinar" and the "land of Nimrod." Gen. 10:10; Micah 5:6. It was chiefly between the Euphrates and Tigris rivers. Asshur or Assyria and Mesopotamia were on the north, Elam and Media on the east, Chaldæa on the south. As Chaldæa gained in power its name was applied to the whole country, including Babylon. See **Chaldæa.** The early kingdom of Babylon is generally regarded as covering an extent of about 27,000 square miles, rich of soil and abundant in resources, the home of one of the earliest civilized nations. After the time of Nimrod Babel or Babylon appears to be displaced in Scripture history by Chaldæa until the time of Joshua, Josh. 7:21; after this both again disappear, until about the time of the captivity. At the fall of Nineveh, B.C. 625, Babylonia speedily extended its sway over most of western Asia and Egypt, and under Nebuchadnezzar became a vast empire, lasting, however, less than a century, and fell before the Medians under Cyrus and Darius, B.C. 538, and soon after dropped out of history as a separate country. In architecture, sculpture, science, philosophy, astronomical and mathematical knowledge, and in learning, the Babylonians made original investigations and discoveries not surpassed by any other ancient people. "To Babylonia," says G. Rawlinson, "far more than to Egypt, we owe the art and learning of the Greeks."—Five Ancient Monarchies, iii. 76. In religion the Babylonians differed little from the early Chaldæans. Their chief deities were Bel, Merodach, and Nebo. The names of these gods frequently appear in the names of noted princes, as Bel-shazzar, Nabo-polassar, Merodach-baladan, Evil-merodach, Abed-nebo or -nego. Their gods were worshipped with great pomp and magnificence. The temples erected in honor of the gods and devoted to their worship were celebrated for their vastness, and for the massiveness and finish of their sculptures. Of the precise mode of their worship little is known. It was conducted by priests, through whom the worshippers made offerings, often of great value, and sacrifices of oxen and goats. Images of the gods were exhibited, probably on frames or sacred vehicles, and, as some suppose, were sometimes set up in a public place, as on the plain of Dura, Dan. 3:1; but late investigations indicate that the image there set up was a statue of Nebuchadnezzar.—*Schaff's Dict.* The empire began with the accession of Nabo-polassar, B. C. 625; was in its greatest prosperity during the reign of Nebuchadnezzar, lasting 44 years, to B. C. 561. See **Nebuchadnezzar**. Under the less able rulers who followed, the power of the empire declined, and it fell a comparatively easy prey to the Medo-Persians under Cyrus, B. C. 538.

Baca (*bā'ca*), *weeping, lamentation.* A valley in Palestine, probably sterile. Ps. 84:6 A. V.; but the R. V. translates it "weeping." The pilgrim-journeys to Jerusalem are here described. Those who so go up, "passing through the valley of weeping, make it a spring," *i. e.*, the sterile land becomes to them a watered valley. The plural of this word is rendered "mulberry trees" in 2 Sam. 5:23, 24; 1 Chron. 14:14, 15.

Badgers' Skins. Ex. 25:5; Ezek. 16:10 A. V.; but the R. V. reads "seal-skins" ("porpoise-skin," in the margin) in both cases. The true badger is rare, if known, in Arabia. It is believed that the skins meant were those of such marine animals as the dolphin, dugong, porpoise, and seal.

Bag. Deut. 25:13, and Luke 12:33, where the R. V. reads "purses." Eastern money was often sealed up in bags containing a certain sum, for which they passed current while the seal remained unbroken. 2 Kings 12:10. The same custom continues at this day.

Bahurim (*ba-hū'rim*), *young men.* A town of Benjamin, near Jerusalem, on the road to the Jordan. It is several times mentioned in the history of David. 2 Sam. 3:16; 16:5; 17:18.

Balaam (*bā'lam*, or *bā'la-am*), *not of the people, i. e., a foreigner.* The son of Beor or Bosor, and a native of Pethor, on the Euphrates. Num. 22:5. Evidently he was an unrighteous man, but was selected for a special mission, as in some other cases. See 1 Sam. 10:10; 1 Kings 13:18-20; Matt. 7:22; John 11:51. He had the reputation of a famous diviner. When the Hebrews were journeying to Canaan, Balak king of Moab, sent for Balaam, to curse the Hebrew armies. Balaam ultimately accepted the tempting offer, and returned with the messengers to Moab. On his way he was miraculously informed that his course was wicked and perverse; and he was effectually restrained by the beast on which he rode from doing what Balak had sent for him to do. So far from cursing, he was led to pronounce a prophetic blessing on the Hebrews, in language which, for eloquence and force, is hardly surpassed in the whole range of Hebrew poetry. Balaam, however, seems to have suggested to Balak a much more certain method of destroying them. This was by causing the young women of Moab to inveigle the Hebrews into the impure and idolatrous worship of Baal-Peor. The stratagem was successful, and 24,000 Hebrews were slain. Num. 31:16; 2 Pet. 2:15; Jude 11; Rev. 2:14. Balaam himself fell shortly afterwards in an engagement between the Hebrews and the Midianites. Num. 31:8; Josh. 13:22.

Balak. See **Balaam**.

Balm (from *balsam*, Heb. *tzŏrī, tzrī*), occurs in Gen. 37:25; 43:11; Jer. 8:22; 46:11; 51:8; Ezek. 27:17. It is an aromatic plant, or the resinous odoriferous sap or gum which exudes from such plants. It is impossible to identify it with any certainty. Hasselquist has given a description of the true balsam tree of Mecca. He says that the exudation from the plant "is of a yellow color, and pellucid. It has a fragrant smell, which is resinous, balsamic, and very agreeable. It is very tenacious or glutinous, sticking to the fingers, and may be drawn into long threads."

Bamah (*bā'mah*), *high place.* The name applied to idolatrous places of worship. Ezek 20:29.

Band. A band of Roman soldiers consisted of the tenth part of a legion, called a "cohort;" it varied, according to the size of the legion, from 400 to 600 soldiers. Matt. 27:27; Acts 21:31, and elsewhere.

Baptism. A religious rite which was in use before Christ's ministry began, but which he approved and which was continued by his disciples as a Christian ordinance. Matt. 28:19, 20; Mark 16:16. In this rite, the use of water in the name of the Holy Trinity becomes the sign or emblem of purification from sin and uncleanness, and of becoming a member of the church of Christ. Baptism in the New Testament, like circumcision in the Old Testament, is a sign and seal of the covenant of grace whereby God promises forgiveness of sin and salvation, and man vows obedience and devotion to his service. See Acts 2:41; Rom. 6:3, 4; Gal. 3:27; 1 Pet. 3:21. Christ himself did not baptize, John 4:2, 5: the apostles received the baptism of fire and of the Holy Ghost. Acts 2. In the case of Cornelius the *gift* of the Holy Spirit preceded water baptism, Acts 10:44-48; while, on the other hand, in the case of Simon Magus, water baptism was not accompanied or followed by that gift on him. Acts 8:13, 21-23. The difference between Baptists and Pædobaptists refers to the subjects and to the mode of baptism. The former hold that adult believers only are to be baptized, and that immersion is the only valid mode of baptism; the latter maintain that children of believing parents may and ought to be baptized, and that baptism may be administered by sprinkling and pouring as well as by immersion. They hold that the covenants of God, from the beginning of the world, have been with his people and their children; and that special blessings are promised, if parents were faithful and the children kept the covenant with Adam, Gen. 2:17; 1 Cor. 15:22; with Noah, Gen. 9:9; with Abraham, Gen. 17:7; 18:19; with the Jews, Rom. 3:1; 9:4; with Christians, 1 Cor. 7:14; Eph. 6:4; Acts 2:39. They refer to the baptism of Lydia and her household, Acts 16:15; of the jailer and all his, Acts 16:33; and the household of Stephanus, 1 Cor. 1:16. The baptism of repentance was preached by John the Baptist before Jesus began his ministry. Baptism with the Holy Ghost and with fire, Matt. 3:11; Luke 3:16, is a strong expression to signify the outpouring of the Holy Spirit upon believers, as on the day of Pentecost especially, but often since in the history of the church. The baptism of the Holy Ghost, promised, Acts 1:5, is described as "poured out upon them," Acts 2:4, 17, 18; 10:45; and "fell upon them," Acts 8:16; 10:44; 11:15.

Barabbas (bär-ăb'bas), *son of Abba.* A noted criminal at Jerusalem who was in prison for sedition and murder when Christ was condemned. Matt. 27:16. It was a custom of the Romans to release one prisoner at the time of the Jewish Passover. The Jews were permitted to name any prisoner whose release they desired; and when the choice lay between Barabbas and Christ, they chose the robber. Matt. 27:21; Mark 15:6-11; Luke 23:18; John 18:40; Acts 3:14. Pilate was anxious to save Christ, but at last released Barabbas.

Barachias, or Barachiah, R. V. (băr'a-kī'as), *whom Jehovah hath blessed.* The father of Zacharias, or "Zachariah," R. V., Matt. 23:35; Luke 11:51. See **Zacharias**.

Barak (bā'rak), *lightning.* The son of Abinoam, who was appointed by Deborah commander of the Hebrew forces. He so completely routed the Canaanitish forces, that they never recovered from the blow. As judge of the Hebrews, he was probably the colleague, or successor of Deborah. Judg. 4:4-24; 5:9; Heb. 11:32.

Barbarian. This term is used to denote any one who was not a Greek. In its scriptural use it does not imply any rudeness or savageness of nature or manners. Acts 28:2, 4 and Rom. 1:14.

Bar-Jesus (bär-jē'sus), *son of Jesus.* A Jewish magician in Crete, who opposed Paul and Barnabas, endeavoring to prevent Sergius Paulus from embracing Christianity, and was struck blind, "not seeing the sun for a season." This affliction, as the Greek *achlus* implies, was rather an obscuration than a total extinction of sight. He is also called "Elymas" — *a magician, a sorcerer.* Acts 13:6-12.

Bar-jo'na, *son of Jonah.* Matt. 16:17. See **Peter.**

Barnabas (bär'na-bas), *son of exhortation,* or *of prophecy.* The surname of Joses, a Levite; a native of the isle of Cyprus, and an early convert to the Christian faith. He was a companion of the apostle Paul, and had a large share in the labors and sufferings which attended the early spread of Christianity. Acts 4:36, 37; 9:26, 27.

Barsabas (bär'sa-bas), *son of Saba.* 1. The surname of Joseph, also surnamed Justus, one of the first disciples of Christ. He was one of the candidates for the vacancy in the apostleship, occasioned by the fall of Judas Iscariot. Acts 1:23. 2. The surname of Judas, a Christian teacher, and one of the "chief men among the brethren." Acts 15:22, 27, 32.

Bartholomew (bär-thŏl'o-mew), *son of Tolmai.* One of the twelve apostles. Matt. 10:3; Mark 3:18; Luke 6:14; Acts 1:13. He is named in connection with Philip, and seems to have been the same person whom John calls Nathanael, John 1:45-51, and mentions among the other apostles, John 21:2.

Bartimaeus or Bartimeus (bär'ti-mē'us), *son of Timeus.* A blind man whose sight was restored by our Lord, when in the neighborhood of Jericho. Mark 10:46-52. If this narrative be compared with Matt. 20:29-34; Luke 18:35-43, some differences appear. For Matthew speaks of two blind men. According to some writers, our Lord healed one of these (as in Luke) on entering Jericho, and another (Bartimeus, as in Mark) on leaving it; and Matthew has, with characteristic brevity in recording miracles, combined both these in one.

Baruch (bā'rook), *blessed.* 1. The secretary of the prophet Jeremiah, and who was of a distinguished Jewish family. Jer. 32:12. His friendship for Jeremiah was strong and constant. At his dictation Baruch wrote Jeremiah's prophecies. These he read before the princes, who rehearsed them to Jehoiakim, the king, having previously placed the writing in one of the offices of the temple. The king ordered the writing to be read in his presence, and he became so angry that he destroyed the manuscripts and gave orders to arrest both the prophet and his secretary, but they had concealed themselves. Jehovah, however, repeated the prophecies to Jeremiah, with some additions, and Baruch wrote them a second time. Baruch was falsely accused of influencing Jeremiah in favor of the Chaldæans, and they were both imprisoned until the capture of Jerusalem, B. C. 586. They were afterward forced to go down to Egypt. Jer. 43:6, 7. 2. The name of three other persons, otherwise unknown. Neh. 3:20; 10:6; 11:5.

Barzillai (bär-zĭl'la-ī or lāī), *iron, of iron.* 1. A Gileadite, distinguished for his hospitality and liberality towards David during the revolt of Absalom. 2 Sam. 17:27; 19:31-39; 1 Kings 2:7. 2. The father of Adriel, 1 Sam. 18:19; 2 Sam. 21:8. 3. One of the priests. Ezra 2:61; Neh. 7:63.

Bashan (bā'shan), *light sandy soil.* A district reaching from Hermon to Gilead at the river Arnon, and from the Jordan valley eastward to Salcah. It is referred to about 60 times in the Bible. Bashan has two ranges of mountains, one along the Jordan valley, about 3000 feet high, another irregular range on the east side of the district; between them are plains or undulating tableland watered by springs. The rock of basalt on the west is broken into deep chasms and jagged projections; the hills are covered with oak forests, as in former times. Isa. 2:13; Ezek. 27:6; Zech. 11:2. The plain of the Jaulan (Golan of Scripture) is a vast field of powdered lava and basalt, a fertile pasture to this day. The northeastern portion of Bashan, including the Argob of Scripture, is a wild mass of basaltic rock. The centre of Bashan was mostly a fertile plain, and was regarded as the richest in Syria. The early people of Bashan were the giants Rephaim. Gen. 14:5. Og, its king, was defeated and slain by Israel, Num. 21:33; 32:33, and the country divided. Its pastures, cattle, sheep, oaks, and forests were famous. Deut. 32:14; Ps. 22:12; Isa. 2:13; Jer. 50:19; Ezek. 39:18. After the captivity it was divided into four provinces. The country is now nominally under Turkish rule, but is really held by tribes of Arabs, dangerous, warlike, and unsubdued. Bashan is almost literally crowded with cities and villages, now in ruins, some supposed to date back to Joshua's conquest, corroborating the account in Scripture. Josh. 13:30.

Bath. 1 Kings 7:26. See **Measures.**

Bath-sheba (bǎth-shē'bah or bath'she-bah), *daughter of the oath*. The wife of Uriah the Hittite, an officer in David's army. She is called Bath-shua in 1 Chron. 3:5. David first committed adultery with her, then caused her husband to be slain, and afterwards took her to wife. Bath-sheba was the mother of Solomon, whose succession to the throne she took pains to secure, 1 Kings 1:15-31, and of three other sons, 1 Chron. 3:5. She is afterwards mentioned in the history of Adonijah, 1 Kings 2:13, in the title of Psa. 51, and among the ancestors of Christ. Matt. 1:6.

Battering Ram. Ezek. 4:2. The engines of Ezek. 26:9 were most likely battering-rams, mentioned under the name of rams. Ezek. 4:2; 21:22. Those used by the Assyrians appear to have consisted of a strong frame-work on wheels, so covered as to protect the soldiers working it, and armed with one, or sometimes two, pointed weapons. It differed considerably from the more familiarly known ram employed by the Romans. "Engines of shot" are mentioned in Jer. 6:6, marg., 32:24, marg.; Ezek. 26:8, marg., but incorrectly.

Battlement. Deut. 22:8. See **Dwelling.**

Bdellium (dĕl'yŭm). A substance said to be found in the land of Havilah. Gen. 2:12. It is also said that the manna, like the hoar-frost, Ex. 16:14, or coriander-seed in size, was like bdellium in color. Num. 11:7. Some believe this bdellium was a precious stone; some think it of vegetable origin, a kind of gum exuding from a tree. And this, indeed, is the ordinary meaning of that which ancient writers commonly call bdellium.

Bear. Prov. 17:12. The Syrian bear seems but a variety of the brown bear of Europe and Asia, though it is much lighter in color. Its food is seeds, fruits, and roots, to which it occasionally adds a goat or sheep.

Beard. The nations of western Asia paid great attention to their beard. In this respect they differed from the Egyptians, who shaved, except when mourning, Gen. 41:14; though they had the custom of wearing false beards, made of plaited hair, and graduated according to rank. For private persons these were small, about two inches long; for kings, much longer and square at the bottom; while gods had beards of which the lower part curled up. The Hebrews probably allowed their beards to grow when in Egypt; and we find in their subsequent history that neglect of them was a proof of slovenliness, and allowable only in seasons of distress. 2 Sam. 19:24. They were carefully trimmed and perfumed. Ps. 133:2. They were not to be touched by others, except by intimate friends, with the right hand, in a way of affectionate reverence, or to be respectfully kissed, 2 Sam. 20:9; and any indignity offered to them by pulling, spitting, or the like, was highly resented. Hence there could have been no greater insult than that shown by Hanun to David's ambassadors, 2 Sam. 10:4. Shaving the beard, or cutting it off, was a sign of the deepest degradation, Isa. 15:2; Jer. 41:5, hence the threatening in Isa. 7:20 was full of significance. There are some notices of the beard in the Hebrew ritual. Thus, the recovered leper was to shave off his beard on the last day of his cleansing, Lev. 14:9; but generally the corners of the beard were not to be marred. Lev. 19:27; 21:5. This prohibition is supposed to be directed against shaving the beard where it joins the hair. Some Arabian tribes, it seems, did this in devoting themselves to an idol-god. See Jer. 9:26; 25:23; 49:32.

Beaten Oil. Lev. 24:2. See **Olive.**

Bed. Among the ancient Egyptians, the bed was a kind of low sofa or divan, ornamented with ivory, and of such a length as to answer for a sofa by day and a bed by night. Ps. 41:3; 132:3; Amos 6:4; 2 Kings 1:4, 6, 16; Prov. 7:16. The poorer people slept upon thick, coarse mattresses, or skins, which were thrown down at night upon the divan, or upon the floor. Sometimes they had but a simple cloak, or a blanket, which also answered to wrap themselves in by day. Ex. 22:26, 27; Deut. 24:12, 13. Hence it was easy for the persons whom Jesus healed "to take up their beds and walk." Matt. 9:6; Mark 2:9; John 5:8. In the East, most people only take off the outer garment, and often use it for a covering on retiring to bed.

Bedan (bē'dan), *servile*. 1. In 1 Sam. 12:11 the name of this judge stands between Jerubbaal, or Gideon, and Jephthah, but probably it is a copyist's error for Barak. See Revised Version, margin. The difference in Hebrew is not great. 2. A Manassite. 1 Chron. 7:17.

Beelzebub (be-ĕl'ze-bŭb), *lord of filth, or of flies*. A name of contempt applied to Satan, the prince of the evil angels. Beelzebub, in the original Greek, is, in every instance, "Beelzebul." See margin of Revised Version. This name is not so much a contemptuous corruption of Baalzebub, the god of Ekron, as it is a designation *of idols*; hence Beelzebul = the idol of idols, *i. e.*, the chief abomination, was used as an appellation of the prince of devils. Matt. 10:25; 12:24, 27; Mark 3:22; Luke 11:15-27.

Beer-lahai-roi (bē'er-la-hāi'roy), *well of the living*. A fountain in the wilderness, southwest of Beersheba, Gen. 16:7, 14; 24:62; 25:11; perhaps *Muweileh;* not the same as that in Gen. 21:19.

Beer-sheba (bē'er-shē'bah, or be-er'shebah) *well of the oath*. An old place in Palestine which formed the southern limit of the country. There are two accounts of the origin of the name. According to the first, the well was dug by Abraham, and the name given, Gen. 21:31; the other narrative ascribes the origin of the name to Isaac instead of Abraham. Gen. 26:31-33. Beersheba was given to Judah, Josh. 15:28, and then to Simeon, Josh. 19:2; 1 Chron. 4:28. In the often-quoted "from Dan even to Beersheba," Judg. 2:1, it represents the southern boundary of Canaan, as Dan the northern. In the time of Jerome it was still a considerable place. There are at present on the spot two principal wells and five smaller ones. One well is twelve feet in diameter and 44 feet deep to the water; the other well is five feet in diameter, and was 42 feet to the water. The curbstones around the mouths of both wells are worn into deep grooves by the action of the ropes used in drawing the water for many centuries. These wells are in constant use to-day.

Behemoth (bē'he-mŏth, or be-hē'moth), *the great beast;* or, if it be supposed an Egyptian word, it may mean *the water-ox*. A mammoth animal, described in Job 40:15-24, where the explanation is added in the margin of the R. V., "that is, the hippopotamus." The identification of behemoth has puzzled critics, and the strangest conjectures have been propounded. The mammoth, or other extinct quadruped, has been thought behemoth by some; while others maintain it is the elephant; and some would take the word as having a symbolical meaning. The weight of evidence is in favor of the hippopotamus. As leviathan is most likely the crocodile, it is not unreasonable to suppose that behemoth is, like the crocodile, an inhabitant of the Nile; and that, as leviathan is amphibious, behemoth must be amphibious too, and hence the hippopotamus, a conclusion which is strengthened by the comparison of verses 15, 21, 22 with 24.

Bel. Isa. 46:1. See **Baal**.

Belial (bē'li-al), *worthlessness*, hence *lawlessness*, *wickedness*. This word is properly applied by the sacred writers to such lewd, profligate, and vile persons, as seem to regard neither God nor man. Deut. 13:13, A. V., but "base fellows," R. V. Judg. 19:22; 1 Sam. 2:12. In the New Testament, "Belial" is used as an appellation of Satan, the power or lord of evil: "What concord hath Christ with Belial," the prince of licentiousness and corruption? 2 Cor. 6:15.

Belshazzar (bel-shăz'zar), *Bel's prince*, or *may Bel protect the king*, was the son or grandson of Nebuchadnezzar, and the last Assyrian king of Babylon. Dan. 5:1, 18. During the siege of the city of Babylon he gave a sumptuous entertainment to his courtiers, and impiously made use of the temple furniture (of which Nebuchadnezzar had plundered the temple at Jerusalem) as drinking-vessels. In the midst of the festivities, to the terror of the king, a hand miraculously appeared to be writing upon the wall: *Mene, Mene, Tekel, Upharsin*. Daniel was called in to explain the mystery, which, interpreted, proved to be a prophecy of the king's death and the kingdom's overthrow, which took place in the course of the succeeding night, when Darius the Median captured the city. Dan. 5:25-31.

Belteshazzar (bĕl'te-shăz'zar), *Bel's prince*, or *Bel protect his life*. The name given to the prophet Daniel at the court of Nebuchadnezzar. Dan. 1:7. See **Daniel**.

Benaiah (be-nā'yah), *whom Jehovah has built*. One of David's distinguished officers, who succeeded, after Joab's death, to the command of the Hebrew army. 2 Sam. 8:18; 23:20-23. There are twelve persons of this name mentioned in the Bible.

Benhadad (bĕn'hā'dad or bĕn'hā-dad), *son of Hadad*. The name of three kings of Damascus. 1. Benhadad I. was either son or grandson of Rezon, and in his time Damascus was supreme in Syria. He made an alliance with Asa, and conquered a great part of the north of Israel. From 1 Kings 20:34 it would appear that he continued to make war upon Israel in Omri's time, and forced him to make "streets" in Samaria for Syrian residents. 2. Benhadad II., son of the preceding, and also king of Damascus. Long wars with Israel characterized his reign. Some time after the death of Ahab, Benhadad renewed the war with Israel, attacked Samaria a second time, and pressed the siege so closely that there was a terrible famine in the city. But the Syrians broke up in the night in consequence of a sudden panic. Soon after Benhadad II. fell sick, and sent Hazael to consult Elisha as to the issue of his malady. On the day after Hazael's return Benhadad was murdered, probably by some of his own servants. 2 Kings 8:7-15. He must have reigned some 30 years. 3. Benhadad III., son of Hazael, and his successor on the throne of Syria. When he succeeded to the throne, Jehoash recovered the cities which Jehoahaz had lost to the Syrians, and beat him in Aphek. 2 Kings 13:17, 25. Jehoash gained two more victories, but did not restore the dominion of Israel on the east of Jordan. The approximate dates of these three persons are 950, 890 and 840 B. C.

43

Benjamin (bĕn'ja-mĭn), *son of the right hand.* 1. The youngest son of Jacob, born in Palestine, not far from Bethlehem, after the return from Padan-aram. Rachel, his mother, died in giving him birth, and named him Ben-oni, *son of my sorrow,* but the father called him Benjamin. Of Benjamin's personal character and history little is recorded. His brothers, touched perhaps with some sense of their cruel wrong to Joseph, seem to have treated him with tenderness; and, when they first went down to Egypt to buy corn, he was left at home. Gen. 42:3, 4, 13. Joseph, however, required that he should be brought, and, to insure the return of the brethren, kept Simeon as a hostage. Verses 14-20, 33, 34. A prophetic blessing was pronounced by Jacob upon Benjamin. Gen. 49:27. The blessing of Moses, Deut. 33:12, was significant of the location of the tribe between Ephraim and Judah, on the hills where "the joy of the whole earth," "the city of the great King," was afterwards established, a safe and happy dwelling-place "between his shoulders." The territory allotted to the Benjamites extended from the Jordan eastward to the frontier of Dan in the west. The Benjamites excelled as archers, 2 Chron. 17:17; while among the rest of Israel archery was (at least it has been so supposed) at one time neglected, 2 Sam. 1:18; and their skill in slinging with either hand is particularly noted. 1 Chron. 12:2; Judges 20:16. The greatest misfortune that ever befel the tribe occurred not very long after the settlement in Canaan. Their cities were burnt; and there survived of the whole tribe but 600 men, for whom the oath of the Israelites rendered it difficult to provide wives when the angry passions of the nation had settled down. Judg. 19:21. Restored to their inheritance this remnant must have been wealthy proprietors; three of the families are mentioned as supplying a large force of soldiers. 1 Chron. 7:6-11. The first monarch of Israel was a Benjamite; and no doubt his own tribe would be specially favored. 1 Sam. 22:7. But the Benjamites never showed much attachment to Saul or his family. Indeed, many of them joined David while yet an outlaw. 1 Chron. 12:1-7. We thus see the drawings of Benjamin towards Judah, which issued in the firm union of both the tribes when the kingdom was divided. Thenceforward the history of the two is identical: both went into captivity, and both returned. Neh. 11:31-36. The name reappears with Saul of Tarsus, whose glory was that he belonged to "the tribe of Benjamin." Rom. 11:1; Phil. 3:5. Thus Benjamin had the distinction of producing one of Israel's first judges, Ehud, Judg. 3:15, her first king, and the great apostle to the Gentiles. 2. A Benjamite chief. 1 Chron. 7:10. 3. One who married a foreign wife. Ezra 10:32. 4. Benjamin is mentioned as taking part in the dedication of the wall of Jerusalem. Neh. 12:34. It would seem as if an individual were intended.

Berea (be-rē'ah). A city of Macedonia, Acts 17:10-13 (Berœa in R. V.), on the eastern side of the Olympian mountains; now Verria, with a population of about 6000.

Bernice (ber-nī'se). The eldest daughter of Herod Agrippa I., and sister to Herod Agrippa II., Acts 25:13, 23; 26:30, married first to her uncle Herod, king of Chalcis, after whose death she lived under suspicious circumstances with her brother. She then became the wife of Polemo, king of Cilicia. This marriage was soon dissolved; and she returned to Agrippa, and was subsequently the mistress first of Vespasian, then of Titus.

Berodach-Baladan. See **Merodach-Baladan.**

Besor (bē'sôr), *cool, cold.* The name of a torrent emptying itself into the Mediterranean, near Gaza. 1 Sam. 30:9, 10, 21.

Beth-abara (bĕth'ăb'a-rah, or bĕth'ah-bā'rah), *house of the ford,* a place beyond Jordan. John 1:28. The R. V. and some of the best manuscripts read Bethany for Beth-abara; possibly it was at Beth-nimrah, or Nimrin; or, as Conder thinks, at 'Abarah, a leading ford of the Jordan on the road to Gilead.

Bethany (bĕth'a-ny), *house of dates,* or, *of misery.* A village on the eastern slope of Mount Olivet, about one and a half to two miles ("15 furlongs") east of Jerusalem, John 11:18, toward Jericho; the home of Mary and Martha, whither Jesus often went. Matt. 21:17; Mark 11:11, 12. It was the home of Simon, Mark 14:3, the place where Lazarus was raised from the dead, John 11:18-44; and near it Jesus ascended to heaven, Luke 24:50; named in the Gospels eleven times only. See **Beth-abara.**

Beth-aven (bĕth'ā'ven), *house of vanity,* or *idols.* A place and desert near Bethel on the east, Josh. 7:2; 18:12; 1 Sam. 13:5; 14:23; a name reproachfully used at times for Bethel itself, after the golden calves were there set up, Hos. 4:15; 10:5; Bethel meaning the "house of God."

Bethel (bĕth'ĕl), *house of God.* Josh. 18:13. 1. A town about twelve miles north of Jerusalem. It was visited by Abraham, Gen. 12:8; 13:3; marked by Jacob after his vision of the ladder, Gen. 28:11-19; 31:13; dwelling-place of Jacob, Gen. 35:1-8; name applied to Luz, Judg. 1:22, 23. See Josh. 16:2; Gen. 28:19; Samuel judged there, 1 Sam. 7:16; a place of calf-worship, 1 Kings 12:29; 2 Kings 10:29; called Beth-aven—*i. e.,* "house of idols," Hos. 10:5 (in verse 8 simply Aven); taken by Judah, 2 Chron. 13:19; home of prophets, 2 Kings 2:2, 3; of a priest, 2 Kings 17:28; 23:15, 19; was desolate, Amos 3:14; 5:5, 6; settled by Benjamites after the captivity, Neh. 11:31; named about seventy times in the Old Testament; not noticed in the New Testament; now called Beitin (nine miles south of Shiloh), a village of about 25 Moslem hovels, standing amid ruins which cover about four acres.

Bether, the Mountains of (bē'ther). Song of Sol. 2:17. Probably near the Lebanon range.

Bethesda (be-thĕs-dah), *house of mercy,* or *flowing water.* A pool in Jerusalem near the sheep-gate or market, John 5:2-9; tradition has identified it with the modern pool Birket-Israil, 360 feet long, 120 feet wide, and 80 feet deep, half filled with rubbish, but Schick recently discovered two pools about 100 feet northwest of and beneath the church of St. Anne (noticed in the tenth to fourteenth centuries), which answer better the Scripture description of Bethesda.

Beth-horon (bĕth'hō'ron), *house of the cave.* The name of two places, the "Upper" and "Nether" Beth-horon, Josh. 16:3, 5, about three miles apart, on the opposite sides of a ravine or steep pass—the Thermopylæ of Palestine—on the road from Jerusalem to the sea-coast.

Bethlehem (bĕth'le-hem), *house of bread.* 1. A town in the "hill-country," about six miles south of Jerusalem, situated on a narrow ridge running eastward, which breaks down in abrupt terraced slopes to the deep valleys below. The town is 2527 feet above the sea. It is one of the oldest in Palestine. Near by was Rachel's burialplace (still marked by a white mosque near the town), and called Ephrath, Gen. 35:19; the home of Naomi, Boaz, and Ruth, Ruth 1:19; birthplace of David, 1 Sam. 17:12; burial-place of Joab's family, 2 Sam. 2:32; taken by the Philistines, and had a noted well, 2 Sam. 23:14, 15; fortified by Rehoboam, 2 Chron. 11:6; foretold as the birthplace of Christ, Micah 5:2; the birthplace of Jesus, Matt. 2:1; was visited by the shepherds, Luke 2:15-17, and by the Magi, Matt. 2. It is noticed over 40 times in the Bible. It has existed as a town for over 4000 years. It was a small place until after the time of Christ; was improved and its wall rebuilt by Justinian; now has about 5000 inhabitants, nearly all nominally Christians, mostly of the Greek church. It is now called Beit-lahm. It is surrounded by nicely-kept terraces covered with vine, olive, and fig trees. The church of the Nativity, the oldest in Christendom, built in A. D. 330 by the empress Helena, stands over the grotto reputed to be the place of our Lord's birth, and is the joint property of the Greeks, Latins, and Armenians, who have separate convents adjoining it. The "plain of the Shepherds" is about a mile from the town.

Beth-peor (bĕth'pē'or), *temple of Peor.* A place where the worship of Baal-peor had prevailed, in the district allotted to Reuben. Deut. 3:29; 4:46; Josh. 13:20. It was in a ravine over against Beth-peor that Moses was buried. Deut. 34:6.

Bethphage (bĕth'fa-jee; Eng. bĕth'fāj), *house of green figs.* A place near Bethany, Matt. 21:1; Mark 11:1; Luke 19:29, and possibly west of that place.

Bethsaida (bĕth'sā'i-dah), *house of fishing.* A city of Galilee, near Capernaum. John 12:21; Matt. 11:21. Some writers urge that there were two Bethsaidas, since the desert place where the 5000 were fed belonged to "the city called Bethsaida," Luke 9:10, while after the miracle the disciples were to go before him unto the other side to Bethsaida, Mark 6:45, which it is said could not refer to the same town. If there were two towns of this name, the first one was in Galilee on the west side of the lake, and 2. Bethsaida Julias, in Gaulanitis, on the eastern bank of the Jordan, near its entrance into the lake. Others think it unlikely that two cities in such close neighborhood should have borne the same name. Hence Dr. W. M. Thomson supposes that there was but one Bethsaida, which was built on both sides of the Jordan, and places the site at Abu-Zany, where the Jordan empties into the Lake of Galilee. The Sinaitic manuscript omits "belonging to a city called Bethsaida" in Luke 9:10; hence, Wilson agrees that there is no necessity for two Bethsaidas. The eastern city was beautified by Philip the tetrarch, and called Bethsaida Julias (in honor of a daughter of the emperor Augustus), perhaps to distinguish it from the western Bethsaida, in Galilee.

Beth-shean (bĕth'shē'an), *house of quiet.* Bethsan (bĕth'san), or Bethshan (bĕth'shan). A city five miles west of the Jordan, first in Issachar, but later in Manasseh. Josh. 17:11; 1 Chron. 7:29. Saul's body was fastened to its walls, 1 Sam. 31:10, 12; after the captivity it was called Scythopolis, and was a chief city of Decapolis; now Beisan, having ruins of temples, colonnades, hippodrome, theatre, and city walls.

Beth-shemesh (bĕth-shē'mesh, or bĕth'shĕ-mĕsh), *house of the sun.* 1. A city on the north of Judah belonging to the priests, Josh. 15:10; 21:16; perhaps Ir-shemesh and Mount Heres, Josh. 19:41; Judg. 1:35; noted as the place to which the ark was returned, 1 Sam. 6:9-20; now a heap of ruins near 'Ain Shems, about 14 miles west of Jerusalem. 2. A fenced city of Naphtali, Josh. 19:38. 3. A city on the border of Issachar, Josh. 19:22; perhaps the same as No. 2. 4. A place in Egypt, Jer. 43:13; same as Heliopolis, or On. See On.

Betroth. See **Marriage.**

Beulah (beū'lah, or be-ū'lah), *married.* This word is used metaphorically of Judea, as of a land which, though desolated, Jehovah would again delight in, and it should be filled with inhabitants. Isa. 62:4.

Bezaleel (be-zăl'e-el), *in the shadow of God, i. e., in his protection.* **Bezalel** (bez'ah-lĕl), R. V. 1. An artificer endued by God with special skill for constructing and adorning the tabernacle. Ex. 31:2; 35:30. 2. One who put away his strange wife, after the exile. Ezra 10:30.

Bezek (bē'zek), *lightning.* 1. A city in the allotment of Judah, where Adoni-bezek lived, whom the Israelites, having defeated the Canaanites and Perizzites, took prisoner. Judg. 1:3-5. 2. A place where Saul reviewed his troops previously to the relief of Jabesh-gilead, 1 Sam. 11:8; it was within a day's march of Jabesh (9).

Bible. See **Scriptures.**

Bier. Luke 7:14. See **Burial.**

Bildad (bĭl'dăd), *son of contention, i. e., quarreller.* One of Job's friends, called the Shuhite. Job 2:11; 8:1; 18:1; 25:1; 42:9. He is abrupt, almost unfeeling in the part he takes in the discussion with Job;

45

and his arguments are not always to the point. See Job.

Birthright. Gen. 25:31. The first-born son among the Jews enjoyed special privileges above his brethren, and these privileges were hence called his birthright, or his right by birth. Among these privileges were: great dignity, Gen. 49:3; a double portion of his father's estate, Deut. 21:17; and, in the royal families, usually succession to the kingdom, 2 Chron. 21:3; consecration to the Lord, Ex. 22:29. In consequence of this fact—that God had taken the Levites from among the children of Israel, instead of all the first-born, to serve him as priests—the first-born of the other tribes were to be redeemed at a valuation made by the priest, not exceeding five shekels, from serving God in that capacity. Num. 18:15, 16; comp. Luke 2:22 ff.—*Horne's Introduction.* The eldest son seems to have been regarded, in the father's absence, as in some respects his representative. A father might direct how his property should be distributed after his death, hough it interfered with ordinary customs; but we hear nothing of the will in a technical sense in the Bible, until we come to the epistle to the Galatians. Daughters were generally left portionless, it being expected that they would be provided for by the eldest brother or by their husbands. When there were no sons, however, they became joint heirs of their father's estate, providing they did not marry outside the family line. Even then they might claim their portion if the husband took the family name of his wife. In cases where there were only daughters in the family, and they unmarried, their names were entered in the registers of families as representatives of the father's house. See *Bissell's Biblical Antiquities*. The paternal blessing was also in a peculiar sense the right of the first-born, though the right itself and all the blessings of it might be forfeited or transferred, as in the case of Jacob and Esau, Gen. 25:33; Reuben and Joseph, 1 Chron. 5:1. But by whomsoever enjoyed, it was regarded as invested with great dignity and superiority. The Jews attached a sacred import to the title "first-born." Hence the peculiar force and appropriateness of the titles "first-born," "first-begotten," given to the divine Redeemer. Rom. 8:29; Col. 1:18; Heb. 1:2, 4, 6.

Bishop. 1 Tim. 3:2. The original word means "overseer," such as Joseph was in Potiphar's house, Gen. 39:4, or as the 3600 men were in Solomon's temple, 2 Chron. 2:18, or as Uzzi was of the Levites, Neh. 11:22. In the New Testament the term is synonymous with presbyter or elder, with this difference—that bishop is borrowed from the Greek and signifies the function; presbyter is derived from an office in the synagogue and signifies the dignity of the same office. Comp. Acts 20:17, 28; Phil. 1:1; 1 Tim. 3:1 ff.; Tit. 1:5 ff. These presbyters or bishops of the apostolic period were the regular teachers and pastors, preachers and leaders, of the congregations. We may imagine, however, that among themselves there would be a division made according to individual fitness. Each congregation of Christians, as gathered by the apostles, was organized into a church, having a number of elders, or bishops, ordained over it, Acts 15:23; 20:17, 28; Phil. 1:1; Titus 1:5, 7, indicating that the office was the same. See **Elder.**

Bithynia (bĭ′thĭn′ĭ-ah). A rich Roman province of Asia Minor, on the Black Sea; named only twice in scripture. Acts 16:7; 1 Pet. 1:1.

Bitter Herbs. Ex. 12:8. The Jews were commanded to eat the Passover with a salad of bitter herbs; and the Rabbins tell us that such plants as wild lettuce, endives, and chicory were employed for that purpose, as they still are by the Arabs in those regions. The use of them on that occasion was intended to call to their remembrance the severe and cruel bondage from which God delivered them when they were brought out of Egypt.

Blains. Ex. 9:9. Pustules rising in the skin. There was first an ulcer and boil inflamed; then the pustules, or blains, broke out on it. This was one of the most fearful of the ten plagues inflicted upon the Egyptians. We may conceive its intensity, when we find that it utterly disabled the magicians who were afflicted with it from meeting Moses. Ex. 9:8-11. It has been thought to be the black leprosy, a virulent kind of elephantiasis, "the botch of Egypt," "a sore botch that cannot be healed," Deut. 28:27, 35; that same disease which afflicted Job. Job 2:7.

Blasphemy. Irreverent or insulting language in regard to God. Ps. 74:18; Rom. 2:24, and elsewhere. But the original words in scripture had often a wider signification, and meant evil-speaking, slander, reviling generally. Matt. 15:19; Luke 22:65, and elsewhere. The punishment prescribed by the Mosaic law for the crime of actual blasphemy was death by stoning. This we find executed on the son of Shelomith, Lev. 24:10-16; and it was on this charge, though a false one, that our Lord and Stephen were condemned. Matt. 26:65, 66; Acts 6:11. If Jesus had not been the Son of God, his assumption of equality with the Father *would have been* blasphemous. That assumption was true; but the Jews accused him of blasphemy because they knew not who he was. In regard to blasphemy against the Holy Ghost, the essence of this fearful sin seems to have been that the Jews, shutting their eyes to the proof of miracles which Christ gave, daringly attributed those good works to an unclean spirit. Mark 3:28-30. So a desperate resistance to the gracious influence of the Holy Spirit shuts up the soul to irretrievable ruin. It is not that the blood of Jesus Christ could not cleanse such a sinner, but that the man defeats the kind purpose that would lead him to it. He never applies to the fountain of unlimited virtue; and so he remains uncleansed forever.

Blessing. Gen. 12:2. This word is variously used in Scripture. God is said to bless his creatures. This is not merely the expression of a wish for their welfare, but the actual bestowal of some good, or the means towards a good. Gen. 1:22; 32:29; Job 42:12; Acts 3:26; and elsewhere. Sometimes creatures are said to bless their Creator, when they acknowledge his kindnesses and seek to show forth his praise. Ps. 103:1, 2; 134:1, 2. Sometimes men bless their fellow-creatures, when they express their gratitude for favors received, pray for a blessing upon them, or predict their prosperity. Gen. 14:19–20; 28:1–4; 47:7–10; Num. 24:10; Job 29:13. And, as thus to bless is the expression of gratitude or kindness, so a token of gratitude or kindness, that is, a gift, is sometimes called a blessing. 2 Kings 5:15.

Blood. The blood of an animal is declared to be "the life" of it. Gen. 9:4; Lev. 17:11. And hence God may be said to have reserved it to himself; it was not to be eaten; it was that by which sacrificial atonement was made; all the cleansings of the law being by the shedding and sprinkling of blood. Heb. 9:18–22. In this respect it had a typical meaning. The blood-shedding of the Mosaic victims prefigured that greater and more efficacious blood-shedding, when Christ gave his life for mankind, Matt. 20:28; 1 John 3:16; so that his blood "cleanseth from all sin." 1 John 1:7. Further, when blood was shed wantonly, a curse was incurred. The blood of a bird or animal was to be poured upon the ground and covered up, Lev. 17:13; and the blood of a man cried for vengeance against the murderer. Gen. 4:10,11. Hence the command to Noah that a murderer must be put to death, Gen. 9:6, a command sanctioned in the Mosaic legislation, Num. 35:30, 31, 33, a command which it would be hard to prove not intended to be binding as an universal law upon the world. And, if any one was slain, and the slayer could not be found, the nearest city was to make an atonement. Deut. 21:1–9. In the earlier law it is written, "Surely your blood of your lives will I require . . . At the hand of every man's brother will I require the life of man. Whoso sheddeth man's blood, by man shall his blood be shed." Gen. 9:5,6. In the Lord's Supper we are reminded of Christ's giving his life for us. He said: "This cup is the New Testament in my blood, which is shed for you." Luke 22:20; Mark 14:24. Our ascription of praise is: "Unto him that loved us, and washed us from our sins in his own blood." See **Sacrifice.**

Boanerges (bō'a-ner'jēs), *sons of thunder.* The name Christ gave to James and John, probably because of their fiery zeal; for proof of which see Luke 9:54; Mark 9:38; comp. Matt. 20:20.

Boaz (bō'az), or **Booz** (bō'oz), *lovely.* 1. Was a descendant of Judah, Ruth 2:1, and through him is traced the regular succession of Jewish kings and of Christ. Matt. 1:5. Boaz was a man of wealth and of great respectability. He married Ruth and begat Obed, the father of Jesse, the father of David. 2. One of the brazen pillars erected by Solomon before the portico of the temple. Its companion was Jachin. They were named for their givers or makers, or else had a symbolical meaning. 1 Kings 7:21; 2 Chron. 3:17; Jer. 52:21.

Book. 1 Chron. 29:29; Rev. 10:2. Books in the form we have them were unknown to the ancients. The materials employed by them to write upon, and sometimes now called books, were of various kinds. Plates of lead or copper or of wood, coated with wax, were in common use, the inscriptions being made with a stylus. Tablets of this latter kind were in use in England as late as 1300. Leaves and the bark of trees were also used, such as the Egyptian papyrus, from which our word paper is derived. The skins of animals were also in use, the books being prepared in the form of long rolls, twelve or fourteen inches wide, and fastened at each end to sticks, not unlike the rollers to which maps are attached. A very good idea may be formed of an ancient roll by supposing a common newspaper to have rods or rollers at the right and left sides. The reader takes hold of the rods, and unrolls the sheet until he comes to the desired column. Thus, in Luke 4:17, the phrase "opened the book," should probably read "unrolled the scroll," and in verse 20, for "closed the book," read "rolled up the volume," or "scroll." This shows the force of the figure. Isa. 34:4, where the heavens are represented as rolled together as suddenly as the opposite ends of an unrolled scroll fly to meet each other when the hand of the reader is withdrawn from it. Thus a book means one complete "roll;" so we read of the "book of the law;" the "book of life," Rev. 21:27; see Ps. 69:28; "books of judgment," Dan. 7:10; "book of Jasher" (or righteous), Josh. 10:13; "book of the Chronicles of," etc., R. V., "the kings of Judah," 1 Kings 14:19, 29; "book of the generation," or the genealogical records, Gen. 5:1; Matt. 1:1. A kind of paper was made from the stalk of an Egyptian vegetable called papyrus, or paper reed, which is still found in various parts of India. The stalk was slit with a needle into plates or layers as broad and thin as possible. Some of them were ten or fifteen inches broad. These strips were laid side by side upon a flat horizontal surface, and then immersed in the water of the Nile, which not only served as a kind of sizing, but also caused the edges of the strips to adhere together as if glued. The sheets thus formed were dried in the sun, and then covered with a fine wash, which made them smooth and flexible. They were finally beaten with hammers, and polished. Twenty or more of these sheets were sometimes connected in one roll. In ancient times, writings that were to be sealed were first wrapped round with thread or flax, to which the wax and seal were applied. These seals must be broken before the book could be read. In Assyria, the ancient writings were upon tablets, and cylinders made of clay. Large libraries of this character have been found in the ruins of Nineveh, Babylon, and adjacent cities. The pen was either a stylus made of some hard substance, Jer. 17:1, or a reed pen similar to that now in use in the East. See Jer. 36:23. The ink was carried in a hollow horn fastened to the girdle. Ezek. 9:2. See **Bulrush.**

Booth. Gen. 33:17. See **Dwelling.**

Bottle. Several words are used in Scripture which our translators have rendered "bottle." The skins of kids and goats, and sometimes of oxen, are used for the purpose of holding liquids. When the animal is killed, the head and feet are cut off, and the body drawn out without any further incision. The skin is tanned with acacia bark; the legs then serve for handles, and the neck as the mouth of the "bottle," being tied up when the wine or water, as the case may be, has been poured in. The hairy side is outward. These bottles are still in constant use in Syria and the adjacent countries, and are very common also in Spain.

Bow. Gen. 27:3. See **Arms.**

Box Tree. Isa. 41:19. A small evergreen tree, either the same with or closely resembling the shrubby box of our gardens.

Bozrah (*boz'rah*), *fortress*. Two cities. 1. Bozrah in Edom, Isa. 34:6; 63:1, which was to become a perpetual waste, Jer. 49: 13; Amos 1:12; Micah 2:12; modern Buseireh, in the mountains of Petra, 20 miles southeast of the Dead Sea. 2. Bozrah in Moab, Jer. 48:24. Judgment has surely fallen upon it. Porter thinks it is the same as modern Buzrah, where are the ruins of a magnificent city nearly five miles in circuit, once having 100,000 inhabitants, but now only 20 families. It is near the Hauran, 60 miles south of Damascus. Portions of its massive walls and towers, theatre, temples, stone doors and roofs, some of the ruins of the work of the early inhabitants, perhaps the giants Rephaim, but more likely of the later Roman builders, are still to be seen in good state of preservation.

Bracelet. Gen. 24:30. See **Garments.**

Branch. This word is often used figuratively in Scripture. A branch is a descendant from a tree the parent, Isa. 11:1; or it signifies one united to or dependent upon another. Thus, Christ is the vine; and his disciples are the branches. John 15:5. Hence Paul's metaphor, Rom. 11: 17-24, is easily understood. Beside the more general symbolical meaning, the term "branch" is sometimes specifically applied to the Messiah, as in Jer. 23:5; 33:15, where the promise runs that, from David's royal stock, a branch of righteousness, a righteous descendant, shall spring. And the same exalted personage is again predicted, Zech. 3:8; 6:12, the branch that shall grow and flourish, and become glorious, and endure for ever.

Brass. The "brass" frequently spoken of in Scripture is not that compound metal to which we give the name of brass; for it is described as dug from the mine. Deut. 8:9; Job 28:2. Very frequently copper is meant; and, no doubt, also bronze, which is a composition of copper and tin, while brass is copper and zinc.

Brazen Sea. 2 Kings 25:13. See **Laver.**

Bread (*bred*). Gen. 14:18. The bread of the better class of Jews was generally made of wheat; barley and other grains were sometimes used. Judg. 7:13. The materials were prepared as in modern times in the East. The process of kneading it was performed in kneading-troughs, Gen. 18:6; Ex. 12:34; Jer. 7:18, or wooden bowls, such as the Arabians use at this day for a like purpose. It has been supposed by some that the kneading was done upon a circular piece of leather, such as is now used in Persia, and which would be more properly called a kneading-bag, as it draws up like a knapsack. Either of the utensils would be easily transported. Very simple leaven was used in the dough. The loaves were shaped like a plate, and, when leavened, were ordinarily of the thickness of one's little finger. The unleavened bread was very thin, and was broken, not cut. Lam. 4:4; Matt. 14:19; 15:36; 26:26. It has been said that the thickness or thinness of the loaves was regulated by the time they were to be kept; that which was to be kept longest being made thick, that it might retain its moisture. This is contrary to modern philosophy on this subject, as we see in the manufacture of ship bread. For the mode of baking see **Oven.** The term bread is often used for food or provisions in general.

Breastplate. The name of a part of the official dress of the Jewish high priest. Ex. 28:15. It was a piece of embroidered work, about ten inches square and made double, with a front and lining, so as to answer for a pouch or bag. It was adorned with twelve precious stones. See **High Priest.** The two upper corners were fastened to the ephod, from which it was not to be loosed, Ex. 28:28, and the two lower corners to the girdle. The rings, chains, and other fastenings were of gold or rich lace. It was called the *memorial*, Ex. 28: 12, 29, inasmuch as it reminded the priest of his representative character in relation to the twelve tribes; and it is also called the breastplate of judgment, Ex. 28:15, perhaps because it was worn by him who was instrumentally the fountain of justice and judgment to the Jewish church. Others think it is because the Urim and Thummim were annexed to it.

Brick. In Scripture bricks are frequently and early mentioned, as well as the material with which they were cemented. Gen. 11:3. Both the "slime" or bitumen, and the clay of which the bricks were formed, were abundant in the Mesopotamian plain. Bricks appear to have been, in Egypt and at Nineveh, very generally sun-dried; for the Babylonian buildings they were more commonly burnt in kilns. The clay was sometimes mixed with chopped straw to increase the tenacity and compactness of the bricks; and this was the more needful when the material was the Nile mud. Ex. 1:14; 5:6-19. Egyptian bricks, with dates upon them, are still preserved as fit for use as when they were first made. They are of a large size, varying from 14¼ to 20 inches in length; 6½ to 8¾ inches in breadth; and in thickness 4½ to 7 inches.

Bride and Bridegroom. Isa. 62:5. See **Marriage**.

Brigandine. Jer. 46:4, A. V. It is translated "coat of mail" in R. V. See **Armor**.

Buckler. Ps. 18:2. See **Armor**.

Building. Ezra 5:4. See **Dwellings**.

Bul. 1 Kings 6:38. See **Month**.

Bulrush. Isa. 18:2, A. V.; "papyrus" in R. V. A species of reed found on the marshes of the Nile, and grows to the height of twelve or fifteen feet. The stalks are pliable, and capable of being interwoven very closely, as is evident from its being used in the construction of the "ark" or boat-cradle in which Moses was hid by his mother. Ex. 2:3, 5. It was from this vegetable that the papyrus was derived, which was used for writing. It was made of the inside bark, which was cut into strips, and the edges cemented together, and dried in the sun. The fact that the papyrus was used for food when prepared in one way, and for writing when prepared in another way, explains the passages in which the eating of books, etc., is mentioned. Jer. 15:16; Ezek. 3:1, 3; Rev. 10:8-10.

Burden. Is often used figuratively, to denote afflictions, failings, sins, Ps. 38:4; 55:22; Gal. 6:2; services under the law, Matt. 23:4; official responsibilities, Ex. 18:22; Deut. 1:12; and especially prophetic messages, not always of a threatening character. Isa. 19:1. In this last sense the Hebrew word may be rendered "oracle," "divine declaration," or "prophecy," as in Prov. 30:1; 31:1. See Jer. 23:33-40.

Burial. The Hebrews did not burn, but buried their dead, usually in caves and artificial tombs. Gen. 25:9; 35:29. To be deprived of burial was thought one of the greatest marks of dishonor. Eccl. 6:3; Jer. 22:18, 19. It was denied to none, seldom even to enemies. Deut. 21:23; 1 Kings 11:15. Good men made it a part of their piety to inter the dead. Unburied corpses polluted their land if the dead were exposed to view. 2 Sam. 21:14. The touch of a dead body, or of anything that had touched a dead body, was esteemed a defilement, and required a ceremonial cleansing. Num. 19:11-22. Only three cases of burning the bodies of the dead occur in Scripture: the family of Achan, after they were stoned, Josh. 7:24, 25, the mangled remains of Saul and his sons, 1 Sam. 31:12, and perhaps the victims of some plague, Amos 6:10. The nearest relatives usually closed the eyes of the dying, gave them the parting kiss, and then began the wailing for the dead. Gen. 46:4; 50:1. The loud and shrill lamentations referred to in Mark 5:38, John 11:19, were by hired mourners, see also Jer. 9:17, 18; Amos 5:16, who praised the deceased, Acts 9:39, and by doleful cries and frantic gestures, aided at times by melancholy tones of music, Matt. 9:23, strove to express the deepest grief, Ezek. 24:17, 18. Immediately after death the body was washed, and laid out in a convenient room, Acts 9:37-39, and sometimes anointed, Matt. 26:12. It was wrapped in many folds of linen, with spices, and the head bound about with a napkin, as the body of Jesus was, Matt. 27:59; sometimes each limb and finger wrapped separately, John 11:44, as the mummies of Egypt are found to have been. But among the Jews the body was not embalmed, and the burial took place very soon, on account both of the heat of the climate and of the ceremonial uncleanness incurred. Rarely did 24 hours elapse between death and burial, Acts 5:6, 10; and in Jerusalem now burial, as a general rule, is not delayed more than three or four hours. The body was wrapped in the garments worn when living, or linen cloths thrown over it, and it was placed upon a bier—a board borne by men—to be conveyed to the tomb. 2 Sam. 3:31; Luke 7:14. Sometimes a more costly bier or bed was used, 2 Chron. 16:14; and the bodies of kings and some others may have been laid in stone sarcophagi. Gen. 50:26; 2 Kings 13:21. The tomb was usually without the city, and spices and aromatic woods were often burned at the burial. 2 Chron. 16:14. A banquet sometimes followed the funeral, Jer. 16:7, 8; and the bereaved friends were wont to go to the grave from time to time, to weep, John 11:31; a custom observed even at this day.

Burnt Offering. Gen. 8:20. See **Sacrifice**.

Bushel. Matt. 5:15. See **Measures**.

Butler. Gen. 40:1. See **Cup-bearer**.

Butter. The word so rendered in our version very frequently means curds, curdled or sour milk, which has fermented. Gen. 18:8; Judg. 5:25; 2 Sam. 17:29; Isa. 7:22. In some places it is put for milk in general. Deut. 32:14; Job 20:17; 29:6. It is used to illustrate the smooth deceit of an enemy. Ps. 55:21. In Prov. 30:33 some would read cheese. Butter, indeed, as we understand and use it, is not known in Syria; it would soon become rancid and unfit for food. But there is a process of churning which Dr. Thomson describes. A bottle is made by stripping off entire the skin of a young buffalo. This is filled with milk, kneaded, wrung, and shaken, till, such as it is, the butter comes. This butter is then taken out, boiled or melted, and put into bottles made of goats' skins. In winter it resembles candied honey; in summer it is mere oil. Probably it is this substance, and this mode of churning, that is alluded to in Prov. 30:33.

C

Cab. 2 Kings 6:25. See **Measures**.

Cabin. Jer. 37:16. A prison cell.

Cæsar, R. V., but Cesar, A. V. (aē'zar), cut or gash. The official title of the Roman emperors. It comes from the famous Julius Cæsar. It occurs about 30 times in the N. T., and is applied to Augustus, Luke 2:1; Tiberius, Luke 3:1; Claudius, Acts 11:28; and Nero, Acts 25:8. Such Jews as were Roman citizens had the right of appeal to Cæsar, Acts 25:11, who was their ruler.

For an account of these, see Augustus, Tiberius, Claudius, and Nero.

Cæsarea (*sĕs-a-rē'ah*). The chief Roman city of Palestine in New Testament times. It was on the Mediterranean, about 47 miles northwest of Jerusalem. It was first called "Strato's Tower." Herod the Great built a city there, B. C. 10, and named it in honor of Augustus Cæsar. Herod Agrippa I. died there, Acts 12 : 19–23. Philip the evangelist lived there, Acts 8 : 40 ; 21 : 8 ; and Cornelius, 10 : 1–24. Paul frequently visited it, 9 : 30 ; 18 : 22 ; 21 : 8 ; 23 : 33 ; was in bonds there two years, 24 : 27 ; it was the official residence of Festus and of Felix. It is now in ruins, and is called Kaisarieh.

Cæsarea-Philippi (*sĕs-a-rē'ah-fĭ-lĭp'pī*), now called Banias by the Arabs, is a town at the base of Mount Hermon, about 20 miles north of the Sea of Galilee and 45 miles southwest of Damascus. It was the northern limit of our Lord's journeys, Matt. 16 : 13 ; Mark 8 : 27, and was probably Baalgad of Old Testament history. It was here that Peter, in the name of all the other apostles, made that confession of faith in Christ as the Son of God, and that Christ uttered the prophecy concerning the indestructible character of his church. Matt. 16 : 16 ff. The town is remarkable for its physical and historical associations. It was near two important sources of the Jordan ; its ancient classical name was Paneas, in commemoration of the sanctuary of the god Pan ; it was enlarged by Philip the tetrarch, and named Cæsarea-Philippi to distinguish it from the other Cæsarea, on the Mediterranean ; later on it was called Neronias by Herod Agrippa II. ; it became the seat of a bishopric : it was repeatedly taken during the Crusades.

Caiaphas (*kā'ya-fas*), *depression*. A high priest of the Jews, A. D. 27–36, and presided over the Sanhedrin at the time of our Saviour's trial. John 11 : 49, 51. The office was formerly held for life, but at this time the high priest was appointed at the pleasure of the Roman government. The raising of Lazarus angered the Sanhedrin, and Caiaphas turned their thoughts toward the execution of the hated and feared teacher Jesus by deliberately advising his death on the plea of expediency. His language was unconscious prophecy. John 11 : 49–52. Caiaphas was deposed by the proconsul Vitellius, 36 A. D.

Cain (*kāin*), *possession*. Gen. 4. 1. The eldest son of Adam and Eve ; he tilled the ground as a farmer. In a fit of jealousy, roused by the rejection of his own sacrifice and the acceptance of Abel's, he slew his brother, and became an exile from God's presence, but received a promise of protection from the avenger of blood. He settled in the land of Nod, and built a city, which he named after his son Enoch. His descendants are enumerated, together with the inventions for which they were remarkable. 2. A city, called "Kain" in R. V., in the mountains of Judah. Josh. 15 : 57.

Calamus, Song of Sol. 4 : 14 ; Ezek. 27 : 19, or **Sweet Calamus**, Ex. 30 : 23, or **Sweet Cane**, Isa. 43 : 24 ; Jer. 6 : 20. These are probably names for the same plant. It seems to have been an aromatic reed brought "from a far country." Lemongrass is "a plant of remarkable fragrance and a native of Central India, where it is used to mix with ointments, on account of the delicacy of its odor." Calamus may have been a species of this.

Caleb, Gen. 10 : 11, *age*. See **Assyria**.

Caleb (*kā'ŭb*), *capable*. 1. According to 1 Chron. 2 : 9, where he is called **Chelubai** (*kĕ-lū'bāī*), 18, 19, 42, 50, the son of Hezron, the son of Pharez, the son of Judah, and the father of Hur, and consequently grandfather of Caleb, one of the twelve spies. 2. The son of Jephunneh, one of the twelve spies sent by Moses to Canaan. Num. 13 : 6. He and Oshea, or Joshua the son of Nun, were the only two who brought a favorable report and encouraged the people boldly to take possession of the land. Forty-five years afterwards Caleb came to Joshua and claimed possession of the land of the Anakim, Kirjath-arba or Hebron, and the neighboring hill country. Josh. 14. This was immediately granted to him, and the following chapter relates how he took possession of Hebron, driving out the three sons of Anak ; and how he offered Achsah his daughter in marriage to whoever would take Kirjath-sepher, *i. e.*, Debir, and when Othniel, his brother or nephew, had performed the feat, he not only gave him his daughter to wife, but with her the upper and nether springs of water which she desired. Josh. 15 : 16–19.

Calf. The young of cattle, much used in sacrifice, often stall-fed, and regarded as choice food. Gen. 18 : 7 ; 1 Sam. 28 : 24 ; Amos 6 : 4 ; Luke 15 : 23, 27, 30. Some of the Egyptian deities, as Apis and Mnevis, were honored under the symbol of a calf. There were two notable occasions on which calf-like images were set up by the Ismelites for worship. The first was when Aaron, at the demand of the people, made of their golden ear-rings a molten calf, hollow probably, or of gold plating upon wood. After the metal was cast it was fashioned, finished or ornamented, with a graving tool. Moses, when he saw it, burnt and reduced this image to powder, cast it into the water and made the Hebrews drink it. Ex. 32. Some centuries later Jeroboam set up golden calves at Dan and Bethel, which thus became and long continued to be centres of unhallowed worship. 1 Kings 12 : 28–30. Some suppose it was intended to honor Jehovah by these visible symbols, or at least to mix his worship with that of idols. For example, Aaron proclaimed "a feast to the Lord," Ex. 32 : 5 ; and Jeroboam, we may fairly believe, never hoped to keep his subjects from resorting to Jerusalem, by at once setting up a god in downright opposition to Jehovah. His object was to persuade them that their worship would be as acceptable by means of his symbols as by the ceremonials of the temple. The passing between the divided parts of a calf, Jer. 34 : 18, 19, has reference to an ancient mode of ratifying a covenant. Comp. Gen. 15 :

10, 17. The "calves of our lips," Hos. 14:2, reads in the R. V., "So will we render *as* bullocks, *the offerings of* our lips," that is, we will offer praise, as animals are offered in sacrifice. Heb. 13:15. See **Lamb.**

Calneh (kăl′neh), *fortified dwelling,* or *fort of the god Ana,* or *Anu.* One of the original cities of Nimrod's empire, Gen. 10:10; Amos 6:2, apparently the same with Calno, Isa. 10:9, and Canneh, Ezek. 27:23. It is probably the modern Niffer, about 60 miles south-southeast of Babylon, on the eastern bank of the Euphrates.

Calvary. This word occurs but once in the New Testament, Luke 23:33, A. V., to indicate the place of our Lord's execution. It is the adoption into English of the Latin word for "skull," answering to the Greek *kranion,* which is itself the translation of the Hebrew *Golgotha.* The R. V. reads, "the place which is called the skull." Some suppose it to be so named from the fact that, executions being performed there, skulls were found there. It is more probable that it was a bare round spot, in shape something like a skull; hence, perhaps, the notion that it was a hill. There is no topographical question more keenly disputed than whether the spot now venerated as the site of the holy sepulchre is really the ancient Golgotha or Calvary: the latest explorations do not support the tradition, but point to a site outside the walls of Jerusalem, near the so-called Grotto of Jeremiah.

Camel. Gen. 12:16. There are two species: the Bactrian and the Arabian camel. The latter was used by the Israelites, and is the one commonly referred to in Scripture. It was used both for riding and for carrying loads, as at present. Gen. 24:64; 2 Kings 8:9. Camel's furniture is mentioned, Gen. 31:34, perhaps a kind of litter or canopied seat; and it is not improbable that the panniers or baskets, which are suspended on both sides of the animal, were employed anciently as now. The dromedary, Isa. 60:6, was the same species, but of a finer breed. The camel is ill-tempered, vindictive, and obstinate; but its value to man may be estimated by what has been said. The ordinary strong working animal will go 24 miles a day, while the higher-bred and better-trained, or dromedary, will, it is said, travel 200 miles in 24 hours. This quadruped was forbidden as food to the Hebrews, Lev. 11:4; Deut. 14:7; the flesh, however, especially the hump, is now liked by the Arabs; the milk is considered a cooling, nutritious drink, and the dung is much used for fuel. The camel was well known in early ages. Gen. 12:16; 24:64; 37:25. It was used in war, at least by predatory bands, Judg. 6:5; 1 Sam. 30:17; and coarse garments were made of its hair. Matt. 3:4; Mark 1:6. The word occurs in various proverbial expressions, as in Matt. 19:24; similar to which are some used in the Talmud: also in 23:24, where the early English versions and the R. V. have very properly "strain out."

Camp and **Encamp.** Ex. 14:19. The order in which the Israelites camped in the wilderness was specially prescribed by divine command. The tabernacle was placed in the centre; and round it were the tents of the house of Levi, in four divisions; Moses and Aaron, with the priests, on the east side, the Gershonites westward, Num. 3, the Kohathites southward, and the Merarites northward. The great host, also in four divisions, encircled these. Three tribes lay to the east, Judah the chief, and Issachar and Zebulun. Num. 2:2-9. On the south were three other tribes—Reuben, Simeon, and Gad. The tribes of Joseph's house lay to the west —Ephraim, Manasseh, and Benjamin. And on the north side was the camp of Dan, in the order of Dan, Asher, and Naphtali. We read of gates to the camp, Ex. 32:26, 27; the dead were buried outside these, Num. 10:4, 5; also lepers, and various unclean persons, and captives, at least for a while, were to be there. Lev. 13:46; 14:3; Num. 5:1-4; 12:14, 15; 31:19, 24; Josh. 6:23. The skins, etc., of victims were burnt there, and ashes poured out and uncleanness removed thither, and criminals executed there. Lev. 4:11, 12; 6:11; 8:17; 24:14; Num. 15:35, 36; Deut. 23:10-12.

Cana of Galilee (kā′nah). A town noted as the scene of Christ's first miracle, John 2:1-11, and of another miracle, 4:46-54, and as the home of Nathanael. 21:2. Tradition places it at Kefr-Kenna, about four English miles northeast of Nazareth, and the traveller is now shown an earthen jar, which is claimed to be one of the waterjars used at the wedding. Robinson and others, with less probability, identify Cana with Kâna-el-Jelil, about nine miles north of Nazareth. It has a fine situation, and the ruins indicate the existence in former times of a considerable village.

Canaan, *low region, merchant, servant?* The fourth son of Ham. Gen. 9:18; 1 Chron. 1:8. On occasion of his irreverent conduct, a prophetic curse was denounced by Noah on Ham's posterity through Canaan. Gen. 9:25-27. We know not how far this took effect on Canaan personally: it had its fulfillment in his descendants, only because it was deserved and drawn down upon them by their sins. Canaan was the father of the nations who peopled Palestine, west of the Jordan. Gen. 10:6, 15-18; 1 Chron. 1:13-16.

Canaan, land of (kā′nan or kā′na-an). Gen. 12:5. The country inhabited by the posterity of Canaan (a son of Ham and grandson of Noah), who were hence called Canaanites. God promised this land to the children of Israel, the posterity of Abraham, as their possession. Ex. 6:4; Lev. 25:38. The boundaries of Canaan were Mount Lebanon on the north, the wilderness of Arabia on the south, and the Arabian desert on the east. On the west their possessions extended at some points to the margin of the Mediterranean. Their boundaries on this side were partially restricted by the Philistines, who held the low lands and strong cities along the shore. Gen. 10:19. Besides the possessions of the Israelites, the land of Canaan embraced Phœnicia on the north and Philistia on the southwest. Zeph. 2:5. The land of Canaan was called the land of Israel, 1 Sam. 13:19, because it was occupied by the descendants of Jacob or Israel; the holy land, Zech. 2:12; the land of promise, Heb. 11:9, because it was promised to Abraham and his posterity as their possession; the land of Judah, Jer. 39:10, because Judah was the leading tribe; the land of the Hebrews, Gen. 40:15, or the descendants of Eber, an ancestor of Abraham. The modern name of Palestine, or the land of the Philistines, was originally applied to the region lying along the coast of the Mediterranean, southwest of the Land of Promise, but in its present usage denotes the whole country bounded by the Jordan on the east, the Mediterranean on the west, Arabia on the south, and Lebanon on the north. Previous to its conquest by Joshua, Canaan was peopled by several tribes, as Hittites, Jebusites, Amorites, Girgasites, Hivites, Perizzites, and four others, all early known as Canaanites. Gen. 10:15-19. Later, "Canaanites" appears to designate a separate tribe, and the land was inhabited by them and six other tribes. Canaan was the country for which Terah started, Gen. 11:31; Abram dwelt in it; it was promised to him for a possession, Gen. 12:5, 8, etc.; Isaac, Jacob, and the patriarchs made their home there. Gen. 26-35. It was left by Jacob because of the famine; searched by the twelve spies, Num. 13:2; viewed by Moses, Deut. 32:49; conquered by Joshua, Josh. 11:23; divided by lot among the twelve tribes, Josh. 13:7; a king of the country was slain by Deborah and Barak, Judg. 4:24. In the temple at Karnak, in Egypt, a triple list of 118 or 119 towns of Canaan has lately been discovered, which is believed to be a record of an Egyptian conquest of the land by Thothmes III. previous to that by Joshua. It is the oldest known record of Canaanite cities before the time of Joshua. For later history see **Palestine.**

Candace (kăn'da-sē or kan-dā'sē, Eng., kan'dăs), *sovereign of slaves!* The name is a title of Ethiopian queens. Acts 8:27. Her chamberlain or treasurer, a eunuch, was met by Philip the evangelist on the road between Jerusalem and Gaza, and converted. Her kingdom was Upper Nubia.

Candlestick. In the tabernacle the golden "candlestick"—or lamp-stand—stood on the left hand as one entered the Holy Place, opposite the table of shewbread. It consisted of a pedestal; an upright shaft; six arms, three on one side, and three on the opposite side of the shaft; and seven lamps surmounting the shaft and arms. The arms were adorned with three kinds of carved ornaments, called cups, globes and blossoms. Its lamps were supplied with pure olive oil, and lighted every evening. Ex. 25:31-40; 30:7, 8; 37:17-24; Lev. 24:1-3; 1 Sam. 3:3; 2 Chron. 13:11. In the first temple there were ten candelabra of pure gold, half of them standing on the north, and half on the south side, within the Holy Place. 1 Kings 7:49, 50; 2 Chron. 4:7; Jer. 52:19. In the second temple there was but one, resembling that of the tabernacle. This was carried to Rome, on the destruction of Jerusalem, and copied on the triumphal arch of Titus, where its mutilated image is yet to be seen.

Cankerworm. Joel 1:4; 2:25; Nah. 3:15, 16. The same original word is rendered "caterpillar" in Ps. 105:34; Jer. 51:14, 27. But the Revised Version reads cankerworm in all these passages. It may perhaps designate the locust when it is in its larva state. See **Locust.**

Canticles, *song.* A name for Song of Sol.

Capernaum (ka-per'na-um), *village of Nahum.* A city on the western shore of the Sea of Galilee, Matt. 4:13; comp. John 6:24, but not named in the Old Testament. It was in the "land of Gennesaret." Matt. 14:34; comp. John 6:17, 21, 24. It was of sufficient size to be called a "city," Matt. 9:1; Mark 1:33; had its own synagogue, in which our Lord frequently taught, Mark 1:21; Luke 4:33, 38; John 6:59; and it had also a station where the taxes or customs were gathered both by stationary and by itinerant officers. Matt. 9:9; 17:24; Mark 2:14; Luke 5:27. Capernaum is of interest as the residence of our Lord and his apostles, the scene of many miracles and teachings. The spots which lay claim to its site are: 1. Khan Minieh, a mound of ruins which takes its name from an old khan hard by. This mound is situated close upon the seashore at the northwestern extremity of the plain (now El Ghuweir). 2. Three miles north of Khan Minieh is Tell Hûm, where are ruins of walls and foundations covering a space of half a mile long by a quarter wide, on a point of the shore projecting into the lake and backed by a very gently rising ground. It is impossible to locate Capernaum with certainty, but the probability is in favor of Tell Hûm. It was joined with Chorazin and Bethsaida, in the fearful prediction of our Lord, the ruin of the cities giving a striking fulfillment of it. See Matt. 11:21-23.

Caphtor. Deut. 2:23. See **Crete.**

Cappadocia (kăp'pa-dō'shĭ-ah). The largest and most easterly province of Asia Minor. It was high table-land, intersected by ranges of mountains, sparsely wooded, but good for grain or grazing. Cappadocia was conquered by Cyrus, ruled by Alexander the Great, tributary to the Seleucidæ, and became a Roman province, A. D. 17. Some of its people were in Jerusalem on the day of Pentecost, Acts 2:9, and afterward Christians of the province were addressed by Peter. 1 Pet. 1:1.

Captain. In the Old Testament the rendering of a Hebrew word generally signifying a military officer. There were various ranks, from the captains of 50 to the captain of the host (or commander-in-chief). 1 Sam. 17:18; 2 Sam. 19:13; 2 Kings 1:9; 11:15. Captains of the guard are also mentioned. Gen. 37:36; 2 Kings 25:8. These were military officers, charged, it would seem, with the defence of the royal person, and with the execution of sentences pronounced by the king: comp. 1 Kings 2: 29-34, 46. The officer in the New Testament, called a captain in Acts 28:16, was probably the commander of the prætorian troops at Rome, but the R.V. omits the clause containing the word. There is another Hebrew word translated sometimes "captain," Josh. 10:24, A. V. ("chiefs" in the R.V.), sometimes "ruler," Isa. 3:6, which denotes both a military and a civil officer. The captain of the temple, Luke 22:4; Acts 4:1; 5:24, was not a military man, but the chief of the priests and Levites that watched in the temple at night. Comp. Ps. 134:1. The word "captain" applied to our Lord, Heb. 2:10, has not a military signification.

Captivity. A word used to designate the subjugation of God's people. God often punished the sins of the Jews by captivities or servitudes. Deut. 28. Their first captivity or bondage from which Moses delivered them was rather a permission of Providence than a punishment for sin. There were six subjugations of the 12 tribes during the period of the Judges. But the most remarkable captivities, or rather expatriations of the Hebrews, were those of Israel and Judah under their kings. Israel was first carried away in part about 740 B. C. by Tiglath-pileser. 2 Kings 15:29. The tribes east of the Jordan, with parts of Zebulun and Naphtali, 1 Chron. 5:26; Isa. 9:1, were the first sufferers. Twenty years later, Shalmaneser carried away the rest of Israel, the northern kingdom, 2 Kings 17:6, and located them in distant cities, many of them probably not far from the Caspian Sea; and their place was supplied by colonies from Babylon and Persia. 2 Kings 17:6-24. This is sometimes known as the Assyrian captivity. Aside from certain prophecies, Isa. 11:12, 13; Jer. 31:7-9, 16-20; 49:2; Ezek. 37:16; Hos. 11:11; Amos 9:14; Ob. 18: 19, etc., which are variously interpreted to mean a past or a future return, a physical or a spiritual restoration, there is no evidence that the ten tribes as a body ever returned to Palestine. Of Judah are generally reckoned three deportations, occurring during the Babylonian or great captivity: 1. Under Jehoiakim, in his third year, B. C. 606, when Daniel and others were carried to Babylon. 2 Kings 24:1, 2; Dan. 1:1. 2. In the last year of Jehoiakim, when Nebuchadnezzar carried 3023 Jews to Babylon; or rather, under Jehoiachin, when this prince also was sent to Babylon, in the reign of Nebuchadnezzar, B. C. 598. 2 Kings 24:12; 2 Chron 36:6-8, 10; Jer. 52:28. 3. Under Zedekiah, B. C. 588, when Jerusalem and the temple were destroyed, and all the better class of the people and their treasures were carried to Babylon. 2 Kings 25; 2 Chron. 36. This was 132 years after the final captivity of Israel. The 70 years during which they were to remain in captivity, Jer. 25:11; 29:10, are reckoned from the date of the first captivity, B. C. 606. Besides these, several other invasions and partial captivities are alluded to in 2 Kings 15:19; 17:3-6; 18:13; 25:11. While in Babylonia, the Jews were treated more like colonists than slaves. They had judges and elders who governed them, and decided matters in dispute. The books of Nehemiah and Daniel describe Jews in high positions at court, and the book of Esther celebrates their numbers and power in the Persian empire. There were priests among them, Jer. 29:1, and they preserved their genealogical records and many of their religious rites and customs. When the 70 years were fulfilled, Cyrus, in the first year of his reign at Babylon, B. C. 536, made a proclamation permitting the people of God to return to their own country and rebuild the temple. Ezra 1:11. Nearly 50,000 accepted the invitation, though a large proportion preferred to remain. Ezra 2:2; Neh. 7:7. This company laid the foundation of the second temple, which was completed in the sixth year of Darius. Fifty-eight years after, Ezra led a small company of 7000 from Babylon to Judæa. He was succeeded as governor by Nehemiah, who labored faithfully and successfully to reform the people. The Jewish character and language were changed by their sojourn for so long a time among foreigners, Neh. 8:8; and it is noteworthy that we hear little of idols or idolatry among them after the captivity. About 40 years after the crucifixion of Christ, Jerusalem was destroyed by the Romans. According to Josephus, 1,100,000 perished at the siege of Jerusalem by Titus, and nearly 100,000 captives were scattered among the provinces and slain in gladiatorial shows, doomed to toil as public slaves, or sold into private bondage. Under the emperor Hadrian, A. D. 133, a similar crushing blow fell on the Jews who had again assembled in Judæa. They are scattered over the world, suffering under the woe which unbelief brought upon their fathers and themselves. See **Jews**.

Carbuncle. One of the gems in the high priest's breast-plate, Ex. 28:17; 39:10; it is also mentioned in Ezek. 28:13. It must, from the derivation of the Hebrew word, have been a bright flushing gem. Some have supposed it the emerald. Carbuncle occurs again as the rendering of another term in Isa. 54:12. The original words here may mean "sparkling stones;" perhaps the Oriental garnet is intended.

Carchemish, or **Charchemish** (kär'-ke-mish), *citadel of Chemosh*. A chief city of northern Syria, on the Euphrates, where a great and decisive battle was fought, in which Nebuchadnezzar defeated Pharaoh-necho, 2 Chron. 35:20; 2 Kings 23:29; Jer. 46:2, in B. C. 605.

Carmel (kär'mel), *fruitful place* or *park*. 1. A long mountain which forms a striking feature of Palestine. It is a noble ridge, the only headland of lower and central Palestine, jutting out with a bold bluff or promontory, nearly 600 feet high, almost into the Mediterranean. It extends southeast for a little more than twelve miles, where it terminates suddenly in a bluff somewhat corresponding to its western end. That which has made Carmel most familiar to us is its intimate connection with the history of the two great prophets of Israel—Elijah and Elisha. 2 Kings

2:25; 4:25; 1 Kings 18:20-42. It is now commonly called Mar Elyas; *Kŭrmel* being occasionally, but only seldom, heard. 2. A town in the mountainous country of Judah, Josh. 15:55, familiar to us as the residence of Nabal. 1 Sam. 25:2-5, 7, 40.

Carriages. Acts 21:15, A. V., but the R. V. reads "baggage" here and in Isa. 10:28; 1 Sam. 17:22. The load or burden of man or beast; baggage, Isa. 10:28; or mat on which anything is carried, 1 Sam. 17:22. In Isa. 46:1, "carriages," A. V., is rendered "things that ye carried about" in R. V. "They took up their carriages," *i. e.*, they packed up their things and commenced their journey. Acts 21:15. See R. V.

Cassia. Ex. 30:24. The bark of a tree like the cinnamon, and one of the ingredients of the holy anointing oil. It was brought from India by the Tyrians. The Hebrew refers, in Ps. 45:8, to another kind of spice, remarkable for its fragrance, but not yet identified.

Castor (*kăs'tor*), and **Pollux** (*pŏl'lux*). Acts 28:11, A. V.; R. V. reads "The Twin Brothers." In heathen mythology, "Castor" and "Pollux" were the names of twin sons of Jupiter, who presided over the destinies of sailors. Hence an image representing them was often seen on the prow of ancient ships, like the figure-heads of modern days. In the case of Paul's ship, the name was Castor and Pollux.

Caterpillar (*the consumer*). Probably another word for locusts in their immature or wingless state, appearing in vast numbers and of most destructive voracity. 1 Kings 8:37.

Caul. Lev. 3:4, 10; 5:4, 9. A lobe of the liver. In Hos. 13:8, the membrane inclosing the heart. In Isa. 3:18, network for the hair.

Cedar. Several cone-bearing, evergreen trees appear to be included under this title. But ordinarily, the cedar of Lebanon (the still famous tree of that name, *Cedrus Libani*) is meant. The Scriptures give its characteristics. Comp. Ps. 92:12; Ezek. 31:3-6; 1 Kings 7:2; 10:27; Song of Sol. 4:11; Hos. 14:6; Isa. 2:13; 10:19. It grows to the height of 70 or 80 feet. The branches are thick and long, spreading out almost horizontally from the trunk, which is sometimes 30 or 40 feet in circumference. Ezek. 31:3, 6, 8. Maundrell measured one which was 36 feet and 6 inches in the girth, and 111 feet in the spread of its boughs. The wood is of a red color and bitter taste, which is offensive to insects, and hence it is very durable and admirably adapted for building. Cedar was used for the most noble and costly edifices, as the palace of Persepolis, the palace of Solomon, and the temple at Jerusalem. This timber served not only for beams for the frame and boards for covering buildings, but was also wrought into the walls. 2 Sam. 7:2; 1 Kings 6:36, and 7:12. The gum which exudes from the trunk and the cones is as soft and fragrant as the balsam of Mecca. This tree, there is reason to believe, once quite covered the mountains of Lebanon between the heights of 3000 and 7000 feet. Rev. H. H. Jessup has visited and described eleven distinct groves of cedars on those mountains, including, altogether, several thousand trees. The wood of the cedar is notable for toughness, durability, and adaptedness to the climate and circumstances of Syria. There is no such thing as a rotten cedar. The name of Lamartine, carved on one of the giant trees 109 years ago, is fresh and legible to-day. All other woods indigenous to Syria are liable to the attacks of insects or a kind of dry rot. Cedar beams are unchangeable. The cedar is a desirable wood for carving. Isa. 44:14. It is hard, fragrant, takes a high polish, which develops a beautiful grain, and it grows darker and richer by time.

Cedron. John 18:1. See **Kidron**.

Cenchrea (*sĕn'kre-ah*, accurately **Cenchreæ**, as it is spelt in the R. V.). The eastern harbor of Corinth, on the Saronic Gulf, and the emporium of its trade with the Asiatic shores of the Mediterranean, about nine miles east of that city; the western harbor was Lechæum. A church was formed at Cenchrea, of which Phebe was a deaconess. Rom. 16:1. Paul sailed from thence to Ephesus. Acts 18:18. The town was full of idolatrous monuments and shrines. It is now called Kikries.

Censer. There are two Hebrew words so translated, mahbtah and miktereth; the latter occurring only in the later books. 2 Chron. 26:19; Ezek. 8:11. It was a vessel or metal fire-pan to take up coals on which the incense could be placed. It was portable, and probably had a long handle. Censers are described among the furniture of the altar—the brazen altar, not the altar of incense, Num. 4:14; and a special charge is given for the use of the censer on the day of atonement. Lev. 16:12. Probably those of the ordinary kind were of brass or copper, comp. Ex. 27:3; but the Jews suppose that the one used by the high priest was of gold; and this supposition is to a certain extent corroborated by the fact that Aaron is bidden to use some particular censer—the definite article being prefixed to the word. Lev. 16:12; Num. 16:46. Korah and his company had censers, Num. 16:6, 17, 37, 38, 39; but they were doubtless of the common sort. Solomon made golden censers. 1 Kings 7:50; 2 Chron. 4:22. A golden censer is mentioned in the New Testament. Heb. 9:4. It is questioned, however, whether the golden altar is not rather meant. The R. V. frequently reads "fire-pans" for censers. The Greek word rendered "censer" in Rev. 8:3, 5, is derived from frankincense, implying that frankincense was burnt therein. The "vials," 5:8, have been thought to mean similar vessels.

Centurion. The commander of a century or military company, of which there were 60 in a Roman legion. At first there were, as the name implies, 100 men in each century; subsequently the number varied according to the strength of the legion. Matt. 8:5; 27:54; Acts 10:1; 22:25; 23:23; 27:1.

Cephas (*sē'fas*), *rock*. A Syriac surname

54

given to Simon, which in the Greek is rendered Petros, and in the Latin Petrus, both signifying "a rock." John 1:42. See **Peter.**

Chalcedony. One of the stones described as forming the foundation of the new Jerusalem. Rev. 21:19. Chalcedony is ordinarily understood to be a species of agate, milky white or pale yellow, often with a wavy internal structure. Some liken it in color and want of transparency to skimmed milk. Another description represents it as of the color of a pale flame, shining out of doors, obscure in a house, not easily cut, and attributes to it the power of attracting light substances. Also it has been supposed to be turquoise, carbuncle, or ruby, or an inferior kind of emerald.

Chaldæa (*kal-dē'ah*). An ancient country on both sides of the river Euphrates, and bordering on the Persian Gulf. It had an estimated area of 23,000 square miles. In later times it included a territory about 450 miles long by 100 to 130 miles wide. It occupied the southern portion of the great Mesopotamian plain, the most fertile part of that country. It was divided into Northern and Southern Chaldæa, each having four important cities. In later times the "land of the Chaldæans" was applied to all Babylonia, and to the whole of the empire over which the Chaldæans ruled. The chief features of the country were the rivers, for on all sides it is a dead level, broken now only by solitary mounds, old ruins, marshes, and streams. The summers are hot, the winters rainy, and seldom colder than 30° F. Wheat, millet, barley, dates and fruits of all kinds were abundant. Its fertility and productions were proverbial in ancient times. Chaldæa is noticed in Scripture as the native country of Abram, Gen. 11:31; its people attacked Job, Job 1:17, and it was the term by which the empire of Nebuchadnezzar was sometimes called. Originally it was the district in the south of the "land of Shinar" where Nimrod built four cities. Gen. 10:10. Among the four great kingdoms or empires on the Euphrates, secular historians usually place the Chaldæan as the first in order or earliest, lasting for about ten centuries, from B. C. 2300 to about B. C. 1300; the Assyrian empire next, lasting about six and a half centuries, from B. C. 1270 to B. C. 625; the Babylonian empire third in order, continuing from about B. C. 625 to B. C. 538; and the Medo-Persian fourth. After its subjugation, in B. C. 1300, Chaldæa held an insignificant place in history for over six centuries, but recovered in B. C. 625, and established a new kingdom, known as the Babylonian empire. For the later history see **Babylon, Assyria,** and **Nineveh.**

Chalkstones. Isa. 27:9. A soft mineral substance resembling what we call limestone. To make the stones of the Jewish altars like chalkstones is to crumble and destroy them.

Chamber. Gen. 43:30. Usually, the private apartments of a house are called chambers. 2 Sam. 18:33; Ps. 19:5; Dan. 6:10. Particular rooms of this class in Eastern houses were designated by significant terms.

GUEST-CHAMBER. Mark 14:14. This we may suppose to have been a spacious unoccupied room, usually in the upper part of the house, and furnished suitably for the reception and entertainment of guests and for social meetings. The proverbial hospitality of the Jews would make such provision necessary, and especially at Jerusalem, in festival seasons, when every house in the city was the stranger's home. Mark 14:15; Luke 22:12; Acts 1:13.

INNER CHAMBER. 2 Kings 9:2. A chamber within another chamber.

LITTLE CHAMBER. 2 Kings 4:10. An apartment built upon and projecting from the walls of the main house, and communicating by a private door with the house, and by a private stairway with the street.

UPPER CHAMBER, or LOFT, Acts 9:37, occupied the front part of the building, over the gate or outer entrance, and was used to lodge strangers. Comp. 1 Kings 17:19 and 23 with 2 Kings 4:10.

Chamberlain. 2 Kings 23:11. An officer who had charge of the royal chambers, or the king's lodgings, wardrobes, etc. Esth. 1:10, 12, 15 A. V. The R. V. reads "chamberlains," but has "or eunuchs" in the margin. The word occurs twice in A. V. of N. T., but entirely different offices are meant in the Greek. Blastus, "the king's chamberlain," mentioned in Acts 12:20, "held a post of honor which involved great intimacy and influence with the king." Erastus, "the chamberlain of the city of Corinth," Rom. 16:23, was the treasurer of the city; the R. V. reads "treasurer."

Chameleon. Lev. 11:30. A kind of lizard, of singular habits and appearance. Its body is about six inches long; its feet have five toes each, arranged like two thumbs opposite to three fingers; its eyes turn backwards or forwards independently of each other. It feeds upon flies, which it catches by darting out its long, viscous tongue. It has the faculty of inflating itself at pleasure with air, and thus changing its color from its ordinary gray to green, purple, and even black when enraged. The eyes project out of the head, and can be moved in any direction, and each eye can be moved independently of the other, so that the animal can see ahead with one eye, and at the same instant see behind with the other eye.

Chamois (*sham'my*). Deut. 14:5. A species of wild sheep.

Chapiter. There are three Hebrew words translated "chapiter," the first signifying something which surrounds; the second an ornament; the third is the ordinary word for head or top. It is the upper part of a pillar, answering to what is now called the capital, or a kind of moulding round the top of a column or utensil, probably carved into the representation of flowers or fruits. Ex. 36:38; 38:17, 19, 28; 1 Kings 7:16-20; 2 Kings 25:17; 2 Chron. 3:15; 4:12, 13. The "pommels" of the chapiters were convex projections or mouldings.

Chapman. 2 Chron. 9:14. A travelling merchant.

Charger. A shallow vessel for receiving water or blood, also for presenting offerings of fine flour with oil. Num. 7:79. The daughter of Herodias brought the head of John the Baptist in a charger, Matt. 14:11; probably a trencher or platter.

Chariots. Scripture speaks of two kinds of chariots, two-wheeled, and both drawn by horses: one for princes and generals to ride in, Gen. 41:43; 46:29; 2 Kings 5:9; Acts 8:28; or dedicated to idols, 2 Kings 23:11; the other "chariots of iron," armed with iron scythes or hooks, projecting from the ends of the axletrees. The Canaanites whom Joshua engaged at the waters of Merom had horsemen, and a multitude of chariots. Josh. 11:4; Judg. 1:19. Sisera, general of Jabin, king of Hazor, had 900 chariots of iron, Judg. 4:3; and Solomon raised 1400, 1 Kings 10:26, in spite of the prohibition in Deut. 17:16; 1 Sam. 8:11, 12. The later kings also used this form of military defense. Isa. 31:1. Elijah went up to heaven in a chariot of fire. 2 Kings 2:12. R. V. reads "chariots." In Song of Sol. 3:9, chariot seems to mean a portable sedan or palanquin, as it is translated in the R. V.

Chebar ($k\bar{e}'bar$). A river in Chaldæa, Ezek. 1:1, 3; 3:15, etc.; probably the same as Habor, and perhaps the royal canal which connected the Tigris with the Euphrates, 30 miles above Babylon.

Cheese. The cheese of the East is made of cows' milk, though that of sheep and of goats and of camels is sometimes used. Instead of rennet, the milk is coagulated either with buttermilk or a decoction of the flowers of the wild artichoke; and putting the curds into small baskets made with rushes, or with the dwarf-palm, they bind them up close and press them. These cheeses are rarely above two or three pounds weight: and are about the size of a tea saucer. Oriental cheese when new is comparatively soft, but it soon turns hard and dry; and is excessively salt. 1 Sam. 17:18; 2 Sam. 17:29.

Chemarim ($k\check{e}m'a\text{-}r\bar{\imath}m$). *those who go about in black.* Occurs once only in the English version, Zeph. 1:4, but frequently in the Hebrew, and is translated "idolatrous priests," as in 2 Kings 23:5; Hos. 10:5 (priests).

Chemosh ($k\bar{e}'m\check{o}sh$). *subduer.* The national deity of the Moabites. Num. 21:29; Jer. 48:7, 13, 46. In Judg. 11:24 he also appears as the god of the Ammonites. Solomon introduced, and Josiah abolished, the worship of Chemosh at Jerusalem. 1 Kings 11:7; 2 Kings 23:13. Also related to Baal-peor, Baal-zebub, Mars, and Saturn.

Chephirah ($ke\text{-}f\bar{\imath}'rah$), *village.* One of the Gibeonite towns, Josh. 9:17, which was afterwards assigned to Benjamin. Josh. 18:26; see Ezra 2:25; Neh. 7:29. It is identical with the modern Kefir.

Cherethites ($k\check{e}r'e\text{-}th\bar{\imath}tes$), *executioners,* and **Pelethites** ($p\check{e}l'e\text{-}th\bar{\imath}tes$ or $p\check{e}'leth\text{-}\bar{\imath}tes$), *couriers.* The life-guards of King David. 2 Sam. 8:18; 15:18; 20:7, 23; 1 Kings 1:38, 44; 1 Chron. 18:17; 2 Kings 11:4, R. V. "Carites." But it has been conjectured that they may have been foreign mercenaries, and therefore probably Philistines.

Cherith ($k\bar{e}'rith$), *gorge,* **The Brook,** a brook or torrent "before Jordan" where the prophet Elijah was hid. 1 Kings 17:5. Robinson and several others identify it with Wady Kelt, a swift, brawling stream, 20 yards wide and three feet deep, running into the Jordan from the west, a little south of Jericho. Some identify it with Wady Fusail, a little farther north, and yet others think it was some stream on the other, or eastern, side of the Jordan.

Cherub (plural **Cherubim**). An order of celestial beings or symbolical representations quite distinct from angels, and often referred to in the Old Testament and in the book of Revelation. Angels are often sent on messages, but cherubim are not so described. The cherubim are variously represented as living creatures, Gen. 3:24; Ezek. 1; Rev. 4; or as images wrought in tapestry, gold, or wood, Ex. 36:35; 37:7; Ezek. 41:25; as having one, two, or four faces, Ex. 25:20; Ezek. 41:18; 10:14, as having two, four, or six wings, 1 Kings 6:27; Ezek. 1:6; Rev. 4:8; in the simplest form, as in the golden figures above the ark of the covenant; or in the most complex and sublime form, as in Ezekiel's wonderful visions of the glory of God—discerning and ruling all things, and executing irresistibly and with the speed of thought all his wise and just decrees. Ezek. 1:10. The fullest of these descriptions represents the cherub as a winged figure, like a man in form, full of eyes, and with a four-fold head—of a man, a lion, an ox, and an eagle, with wheels turning every way, and speed like the lightning: presenting the highest earthly forms and powers of creation in harmonious and perfect union. Ezek. 1; 10; 41; Rev. 4. Usually also the cherubim stand in a special nearness to God; they are engaged in the loftiest adoration and service. moving in instant accordance with his will, Ps. 18:10; Ezek. 1:26; 10:20; Rev. 4; they are seen in the temple inseparably associated with the mercy-seat, "the cherubim of glory," Heb. 9:5—made of the same mass of pure gold, Ez. 25:19. bending reverently over the place of God's presence. Ps. 99:1, where he met his people, Num. 7:89. accepting the blood of atonement, Lev. 16:14–16; they shone forth as their Saviour. Ps. 80:1; Isa. 37:16. 2. A place in Babylonia. Ezra 2:59; Neh. 7:61.

Chestnut Tree. Gen. 30:37; Ezek. 31:8, A. V., but the R. V. reads plane-tree in both places. The tree grows to a large size, with a mass of rich foliage. The stem is lofty, covered with a smooth bark, which annually falls off. The flowers are small, and come out a little before the leaves. This tree is a native of western Asia, but is found as far east as Cashmere.

Chief Priest. See Priest.

Chimham ($k\bar{\imath}m'h\check{a}m$), *longing.* A follower, and probably a son, of Barzillai the Gileadite, who returned from beyond Jordan with David. 2 Sam. 19:37, 38, 40 (B. C. 1023). David appears to have bestowed on him a possession at Bethlehem, on which, in later times, an inn or khan was standing. Jer. 41:17.

Chinnereth or Chinneroth (kĭn'ne-rĕth or kĭn'ne-rŏth), *harps.* Josh. 11:2. A fenced city of Naphtali, on the lake, or sea, of the same name; afterward called Gennesar, or Gennesaret, and about three miles northwest of Tiberias, according to Fuerst.

Chios (kī'os). An island of the Ægean Sea, five miles from the coast of Ionia, in Asia Minor. It is 32 miles long and from 8 to 18 miles wide, and noted for its wines. Paul passed by it. Acts 20:14, 15. Its modern name is Scio or Khio.

Chisleu. Neh. 1:1. See **Month.**

Chittim or Kittim (kĭt'tĭm). Num. 24:24; Isa. 23:1, 12; Jer. 2:10; Ezek. 27:6; Dan. 11:30. R. V. always reads Kittim. In these passages the "Isles," "ships," "products," and "people" of Kittim are mentioned or alluded to; hence the name has generally been supposed to mean the island of Cyprus, though Kitto thinks it a general term applied to islands and coasts west of Palestine.

Chiun. Amos 5:26. An idol. See **Remphan.**

Chorazin (ko-rā'zĭn). A city named with Capernaum and Bethsaida in the woes pronounced by Christ. Matt. 11:20-23; Luke 10:13. The identification of Chorazin depends largely, though not wholly, upon that of Capernaum. Robinson places it at Tell Hum, but others, with greater probability, fix its site at Kerazeh, two and a half miles northwest of Tell Hum, and west of the valley of the Jordan.

Christ. See **Jesus.**

Chronicles, books of. Among the ancient Jews these formed but one book, though they are now divided in Hebrew Bibles, as well as in our own, into two. They were called The Words of Days, *i. e.*, Diaries or Journals. The Septuagint translators denominated them Paraleipomena, Things omitted; and from Jerome we have derived the name "Chronicles." They are an abridgment of the whole of the sacred history, more especially tracing the Hebrew nation from its origin, and detailing the principal events of the reigns of David and Solomon, and of the succeeding kings of Judah down to the return from Babylon. The writer goes over much the same ground as the author of the books of Kings, with whose work he was probably acquainted. He does not, however, merely produce a supplement, but works out his narrative independently after his own manner. The composition of the books is ascribed to Ezra by Jewish and Christian tradition, and in language and style they resemble the book of Ezra. The date of Chronicles cannot be fixed earlier than the return from exile; and as the history ends with the decree of Cyrus, that may be assumed as the time of their composition.

Chrysolite, *golden stone.* A precious stone of the quartz kind, whose prevailing color is yellow with a golden lustre. It is supposed to be the modern topaz. Rev. 21:20.

Chrysoprasus, *golden green.* A precious stone probably allied to the beryl, usually of a greenish-golden color. Rev. 21:20. R. V., Chrysoprase.

Chub (kŭb), R. V., **Cub** (kŭb), *a people.* Probably in north Africa, and of a land near Egypt. Ezek. 30:5.

Chun (kŭn), R. V., **Cun** (kŭn). 1 Chron. 18:8. Same as Berothai. 2 Sam. 8:8.

Church. The terms which this word represents are variously used by the sacred writers. Matt. 16:18. It may be sufficient to notice two uses of the term. In the New Testament it is applied particularly to Christians as a body or community. Acts 16:5. It is also applied to the people of God in all ages of the world, whether Jews or Christians, Acts 7:38; 12:1; Eph. 3:21; 5:25; for although there have been two dispensations, viz., that of the law by Moses, and that of the gospel by Jesus Christ, yet the religion of the Bible is one religion: whether before or after the coming of Christ, true believers are all one in Christ Jesus. Gal. 3:28. Of this church or company of the redeemed, the Lord Jesus Christ is now the Head, and the Church is therefore called *the body,* Col. 1:18, 24, and comprises the redeemed who are gone to heaven, as well as those who are, or will be, on the earth. Heb. 12:23. Particular portions of the whole body of Christians are also called the church, as the church at Jerusalem, at Corinth, etc. Acts 8:1; 1 Cor. 1:2; 4:17. As the great work wrought on earth and the reigning of Christ in heaven constitute him the Founder and Head of the Church, as it now exists, he is compared to "the chief corner-stone" in the building, Eph. 2:20, on whom the whole structure is dependent. For this purpose God "hath put all things under his feet." Eph. 1:22. The figurative language which is employed by Christ himself, as well as by his apostles, to denote the nature of his relations to the church (as composed of all true believers), and its relations to him, is of the most significant character. Some of these have been intimated above; others are that of husband and wife, Eph. 5:30-32, a vine and its branches, John 15:1-6, and a shepherd and his flock, John 10:11. And it is by many supposed that the Song of Solomon is a highly figurative and poetical illustration of the mutual love of Christ and the people of his church in all ages. In modern times the word is applied to various associations of Christians, united by a common mode of faith or form of government; as the Episcopal Church, the Baptist Church, the Moravian Church, etc. The word church is but once (then doubtfully) applied in Scriptures to a building. 1 Tim. 3:15. The visible Israelitish church was divided into twelve tribes separated, yet to be united as the people of God: having one Scripture, one sacrifice, one Jehovah. Christ told his apostles, "Ye shall sit on twelve thrones, judging the twelve tribes of Israel." Matt. 19:28. James addresses his epistle, "To the twelve tribes which are scattered abroad" ("which are of the dispersion," R. V.). Jas. 1:1. In the progress of the church "there were sealed one hundred and forty-four thousand of all the tribes of Israel," Rev. 7:4, showing that the visible church will continue to be divided into tribes, with one Scripture and one Saviour. The world seldom was in greater darkness than when for 1260 years it was controlled by one visible church, the Church of Rome. And the clamor of many to make a united visible church by attacking all creeds and confessions holding the great doctrines of the Scriptures, and in their place to adopt the assumptions of idolatrous churches, will never be realized. The church had in New Testament times, elders, overseers or bishops, in each congregation. Matt. 26:3; Acts 14:23; Titus 1:5, 7; Acts 20:17, 28; 1 Pet. 5:1, 3. Compare Ex. 3:16; 4:29. The various tribes of the ancient visible church were constantly adopting the idolatries of the surrounding nations, and were brought into subjection by them, and at last were scattered and the most of them lost on that account. The most of the prophets were sent to the church to upbraid them for their idolatries and for forsaking God. Christ came to the visible church and was rejected. The epistles speak of errors in the churches founded by the apostles. And as was predicted in the second and third chapters of Revelation, the candlestick of nearly every one of them has been removed.

Chushan-Rishathaim (*kū'shan-rĭsh'a-thā'ĭm*), *most wicked Cushite*, or otherwise, *lord of the land of the two rivers*. A king of Mesopotamia, of whom nothing more is known than that he subjugated Israel shortly after the time of Joshua. His power was broken after eight years by Othniel, the son of Kenaz. Judges 3:8-11.

Cilicia (*sĭ-lĭsh'ī-ah*), the southeasterly province of Asia Minor, having Cappadocia on the north, Syria on the east, the Mediterranean Sea on the south, and Pamphylia and Pisidia (?) on the west. Eastern Cilicia was a rich plain; western Cilicia was rough and mountainous, lying on the Taurus range. Its capital was Tarsus, and many of its people were Jews. It is frequently mentioned in the book of Acts. 6:9; 15: 23, 41; 21:39; 22:3; 23:34; 27:5; and Gal. 1:21. See Tarsus.

Circumcision. A Jewish rite which Jehovah enjoined upon Abraham, the father of the Israelites, as the token of the covenant, which assured to him the promise of the Messiah. Gen. 17. It was thus made a necessary condition of Jewish citizenship. Every male child was to be circumcised when eight days old, Lev. 12:3, on pain of death. The biblical notice of the rite describes it as distinctively Jewish; so that in the New Testament "the circumcision" and "the uncircumcision" are frequently used as synonyms for the Jews and the Gentiles. The rite has been found to prevail extensively in both ancient and modern times. Some of the Jews in the time of Antiochus Epiphanes, wishing to assimilate themselves to the heathen around them, "made themselves uncircumcised." Against having recourse to this practice, from an excessive anti-Judaistic tendency, Paul cautioned the Corinthians. 1 Cor. 7:18.

Cistern. A vessel to hold water; also reservoirs. During nearly half the year no rain falls in Palestine, and never-failing streams and springs are rare. The chief dependence of a large portion of the population was upon the water which fell in the rainy season and which they gathered in cisterns. Isa. 36:16; Jer. 2:13. The water is conducted into them during the rainy season, and with proper care remains pure and sweet during the whole summer and autumn. When dry, they might be used as a prison, Gen. 37:22; Jer. 38:6; the "pit" was doubtless a cistern, or a granary, as at this day; and to drink water only from one's own domestic cistern means, to content one's self with the lawful enjoyments of his own home. Prov. 5:15.

Cities. The distinction of villages from towns, and of towns from cities is not very clearly marked in Scripture. The earliest notice of city building is of Enoch by Cain, in the land of his exile. Gen. 4:17. After the confusion of tongues the descendants of Nimrod founded Babel, Erech, Accad and Calneh, in the land of Shinar, and Asshur, a branch from the same stock, built Nineveh, Rehoboth-by-the-river, Calah and Resen, the last being "a great city." The earliest description of a city, properly so called, is that of Sodom. Gen. 19:1-22. Even before the time of Abraham there were cities in Egypt, Gen. 12:14, 15; Num. 13:22, and the Israelites, during their sojourn there, were employed in building or fortifying the "treasure cities" of Pithom and Raamses. Ex. 1:11. Fenced cities, fortified with high walls, Deut. 3:5, were occupied and perhaps partly rebuilt after the conquest, by the settled inhabitants of Syria on both sides of the Jordan.

Cities of Refuge. Were six Levitical cities specially chosen for refuge to the involuntary homicide until released from banishment by the death of the high priest. Num. 35:6, 13, 15; Josh. 20:2, 7, 9. There were three on each side of Jordan. 1. Kedesh, in Galilee, 1 Chron. 6:76. 2. Shechem, in Ephraim, Josh. 21:21; 1 Chron. 6:67; 2 Chron. 10:1. 3. Hebron, in Judah, Josh. 21:13; 2 Sam. 5:5; 1 Chron. 6:55; 29:27; 2 Chron. 11:10. 4. On the east side of Jordan—Bezer, in the tribe of Reuben, in the plains of Moab, Deut. 4:43; Josh. 20: 8; 21:36. 5. Ramoth-gilead, in the tribe of Gad, Deut. 4:43; Josh. 21:38; 1 Kings 22:3. 6. Golan, in Bashan, in the half-tribe of Manasseh, Deut. 4:43; Josh. 21:27; 1 Chron. 6:71.

Citizenship. The Jew had no citizenship: he belonged to Jehovah. The use of this term in Scripture refers to the usages of the Roman empire. The privilege of Roman citizenship was originally acquired in various ways, as by purchase, Acts 22: 28, by military services, by favor or by manumission. The right once obtained descended to a man's children. Acts 22:28. A citizen could not be bound or imprisoned without a formal trial, Acts 22:29, still less be scourged, Acts 16:37. Another privilege attaching to citizenship was the appeal from a provincial tribunal to the emperor at Rome. Acts 25:11.

Claudius Lysias (*klaw′di-ŭs lĭsh′ĭ-as* or *lĭs′ĭ-as*). A Roman tribune, commanding in Jerusalem. His conduct on two occasions, in reference to Paul, is creditable to his efficiency and humanity. Acts 21:31–40; 22 and 23.

Claudius (*klaw′di-ŭs*). Tiberius Claudius Nero Drusus Germanicus, the son of Nero Drusus, born at Lyons 9 or 10 B. C.; became fourth Roman emperor on the assassination of Caius Caligula, and reigned 41–54 A. D. He was a weak and indolent man, and was poisoned by his fourth wife, Agrippina. Several famines occurred in the reign of Claudius, one of which extended to Palestine and Syria. Acts 11:28–30. And there was an edict of his which, in consequence of a tumult, expelled the Jews from Rome. Acts 18:2. It is not agreed when this edict was issued. It is variously assigned to years between 49 and 53 A. D.

Clean and Unclean. A distinction, most probably with reference to sacrifice, was made between clean and unclean animals before the flood. Gen. 7:2, 8; 8:20. Under the Mosaic law the distinction was extended to food. Thus in Lev. 11 and Deut. 14 there are lists of animals, birds, and fishes, which the Hebrews might and might not eat. The regulations thus made were doubtless promotive of health. But, besides, they, as well as the purifications prescribed for uncleanness in men, Lev. 11:15; Num. 19, had a symbolical meaning, which is illustrated in Heb. 9:9–14. Eating with Gentiles was regarded as a greater offence against the traditional law than being in company with them, and was one of the charges against our Lord. Matt. 9:10, 11; 11:19; Luke 5:30. This view of the law was distinctly annulled by the vision to Peter, before he preached to Cornelius. Acts 10:9–16.

Clothes. Gen. 37:29. See Garments.

Clouted. Josh. 9:5. Worn out and patched clothes.

Cnidus (*nī′dus*). A Greek city at the extreme southwestern corner of Asia Minor, now in ruins, on Cape Crio.

Coast. Judg. 11:20, 22. "Border" and "borders."

Cockatrice. Isa. 11:8; 14:29; 59:5, A. V. The R. V. reads in all cases "basilisk" or "adder," margin. The word, in the Scriptures, evidently denotes a very venomous reptile. The original signifies a creature that "hisses," doubtless some species of serpent. Tristram proposes the great yellow viper, the largest of its kind found in Palestine, and one of the most dangerous.

Cock-crowing. This word occurs in the New Testament to designate the third watch in the night, about equidistant from midnight and dawn. Matt. 26:34; Mark 13:35. This watch was called by the Romans *gallicinium*. They divided the night into four watches of three hours each, that is, from six in the evening to nine; from nine to twelve; from twelve to three; and from three to six. The last two watches were both of them called "cock-crowings," because cocks usually crowed in that space of time. We have no evidence in support of the Rabbinical opinion that cocks were not permitted to be kept in Jerusalem on account of the holiness of the place.

Cockle, *stinking like carrion*. This word may denote troublesome or offensive weeds in general. Job 31:40.

Coffer. 1 Sam. 6:8. A box or chest hanging from the side of a cart.

College. 2 Kings 22:14; 2 Chron. 34:22, A. V., but the R. V. reads "the second quarter," meaning the lower part of the city.

Collops, Fat. Job 15:27. Thick pieces.

Colors. Gen. 37:3. The art of coloring cloth was brought to great perfection among the Jews, and by the Phœnicians and Egyptians. Four artificial colors are spoken of in the Bible: 1. Purple, which was derived from a shellfish native to the Mediterranean Sea. Purple was the royal and noble color, indicative of wealth and station. Judg. 8:26; Esth. 8:15; Luke 16:19; Rev. 17:4. 2. Blue, produced from a similar source, used in the same way, and for the same purposes. Ex. 25:4; Esth. 1:6. 3. Scarlet and crimson appear to express the same color. 4. Vermilion was used in fresco-painting, Ezek. 23:14, for coloring the idols themselves, and for decorating the walls and beams of houses. Jer. 22:14. The natural colors noticed in the Bible are white, black, red, yellow, and green, yet only three colors are sharply defined—white, black, and red. To show the vagueness of the use of the others, the tint green (translated "yellow" in the A. V.), is applied in the Hebrew to gold, Ps. 68:13, and to the leprous spot. Lev. 13:49.

Colosse, or **Colossæ** (*ko-lŏs′sē*). A city of Phrygia, on the Lycus, a branch of the Mæander, and twelve miles above Laodicea. Paul wrote to the church there, Col. 1:2, and possibly visited it on his third missionary journey. See Acts 18:23; 19:10. The town is now in ruins; there is a little village called Chronos three miles south of the site of Colosse.

Colossians (*ko-lŏsh′ĭ-anz*, or *ko-lŏsh′anz*), **the Epistle to the.** Was written by the apostle Paul while he was a prisoner at Rome, Acts 28:16, and apparently, Col. 4:3, 4, before his imprisonment had assumed the more severe character which seems to be reflected in the epistle to the Philippians, Phil. 1:20, 21, 30; 2:27, and which not improbably succeeded the death of Burrus in A. D. 62, and the decline of the influence of Seneca. The epistle was addressed to the Christians of the city of Colossæ, and was delivered to them by Tychicus, whom the apostle had sent both to them, Col. 4:7, 8, and to the church of Ephesus, Eph. 6:21, to inquire into their state and to give exhortation and comfort. The epistle seems to have been called forth by the information Paul had received from Epaphras, Col. 4:12; Phile. 23, and from Onesimus, both of whom appear to have been natives of Colossæ. The main object of the epistle is to warn the Colossians against a spirit of semi-Judaism and a philosophy which was corrupting the simplicity of their belief, and was noticeably tending to obscure the glory and dignity of Christ. The shorter epistle to the Colossians seems to have been first written, and to have suggested the more comprehensive epistle to the Ephesians.

Comforter. The rendering of the Greek *paracletos*, which strictly means "one called to another;" hence a "helper." The Greek term is applied to Christ: "We have an advocate with the Father, Jesus Christ the righteous." 1 John 2:1. Usually it designates the Holy Spirit. He is the "other Comforter," or "Helper," succeeding Christ, the great promised blessing of the Christian church. John 14:16, 17, 26; 15:26; Luke 24:49; Acts 1:4. The English word Comforter does not adequately represent the Greek word *paracletos*, nor fully describe the office of the Holy Spirit. The disciples found the promise fulfilled to them. The Spirit aided them when called before councils; guided them into all truth respecting the plan of salvation; brought to their remembrance the words and deeds of Christ; and revealed to them things to come. His presence was accompanied by signal triumphs of grace, and made amends for the absence of Christ. He is therefore not only a Comforter, but is also a Teacher, Witness, Reprover, and Guide. John 14:26; 15:26; 16:8, 13, 14. He is "another Comforter," not in the sense of a different kind of a Comforter or Helper, but of an additional one. The church is still under the guidance of the Comforter. The Holy Spirit still convinces the world of sin, of righteousness, and of judgment.

Compass. 2 Kings 3:9. "To fetch a compass" there, Acts 28:13, and elsewhere means "to go around," or "to make a circuit." R. V.

Concision. A term used sarcastically of Judaizers who insisted on circumcision as necessary for Gentile Christians. Phil. 3:2.

Concubine. A secondary wife. The practice of having concubines probably grew out of a desire for numerous offspring, and this also was one support of polygamy: when there was a plurality of wives, some were placed in an inferior grade. Concubines are mentioned very early in Scripture, as in the history of Abraham, Gen. 16, of Nahor, 22:24, of Jacob, 30. Sometimes wives, as in the cases of Sarah, Rachel and Leah, gave their servants to their husbands for concubines, in order to obtain children, and the children so born were then reckoned as belonging to the wife whose servant the mother was. Keturah is said to have been Abraham's wife, Gen. 25:1; and yet, 5, 6, all Abraham's sons save Isaac are called the sons of concubines. We must, then, conclude that the concubines had a recognized position, and that the children were legitimate, though more dependent, perhaps, upon the father's will for any share in his inheritance than the sons of the actual or chosen wives. The law of Moses did not stop the practice of having concubines, but modified it. Ex. 21:7-9; Deut. 21:10-17. Concubines were often servants or captives, Ex. 21:7-11; Deut 21:10-14; but this was not always the case. The Levite's concubine, Judg. 19, was neither; and it is observable that her father is called the Levite's father-in-law. After the establishment of the Israelitish monarchy, the kings increased the number of concubines; and the right over those of one monarch, accrued to his successor; so that to seize on any of them was regarded as an overt act of rebellion. 2 Sam. 3:7; 12:8; 1 Kings 2:22; 11:3. The New Testament teaching restores marriage to its original character, requiring a man to be the husband of one wife. Gen. 2:24; Matt. 19:5; 1 Cor. 7:2.

Conduit. 2 Kings 18:17; 20:20; Isa. 7:3; 36:2. Used to signify some mode for conveying water, as a "water course" (R. V. channel), Job 38:25, or a "trench." It probably included an aqueduct, such as must have been used to convey the water from the Pool of Solomon to Jerusalem.

Coney is the Syrian hyrax, a small animal, resembling in size and form the rabbit, and of a brownish color. It is, however, much heavier than the hare or rabbit, almost without a tail, and has long bristly hairs scattered through the fur. The feet are naked below, and the nails flat and rounded, except those on the inner toe of the hind feet, which are long and awl-shaped. The coney cannot dig, but resides in the clefts of rocks. It is called by Solomon "wise," and "a feeble folk;" is quiet and gregarious in habit, and so timid that it starts at the shadow of a passing bird. It is described as chewing its cud, Lev. 11:5; Deut. 14:7; for it has a peculiar movement of the jaw as if chewing. It is a very nimble, active animal.

Conversation. Phil. 3:20, A. V., but the R. V. reads more accurately "citizenship."

Corban (*Kor'ban*), *offering*, a word implying that the thing to which it applied was consecrated to God. Mark 7:11.

Corinth (*Kŏr'inth*), the capital of Achaia and a noted city of Greece. It had two seaports, Cenchrea and Lechæum. On the south a rocky mountain called Acrocorinthus rises abruptly to the height of 2000 feet, upon the summit of which was a temple of Venus. Paul preached at Corinth, about A.D. 53, a year and six months, Acts 18:11; paid it, A.D. 54-57, a short second visit ("by the way"), not mentioned in the Acts, but implied in 1 Cor. 16:7; 2 Cor. 12:13, 14; 13:1, where he speaks of an intended *third* journey to Corinth, which coincides with that in Acts 20:2; and spent there the three winter months, from 57 to 58, during which he wrote the Epistle to the Romans. Acts 20:2, 3; comp. 1 Cor. 16:6; Rom. 16:1. He wrote two letters to the Christians in that city, rebuking their sins, and refers to the Isthmian games celebrated at Corinth every Olympiad. The city is now desolate, the little miserable village of *Gortho* occupying its site.

Corinthians (*Ko-rĭn'thĭ-anz*), The Epistles to. These two epistles discuss questions arising out of the application of the gospel to the ordinary affairs of life. I. The first epistle was written by Paul at Ephesus, about A. D. 57, when the apostle received intelligence respecting the Corinthian church, through the family of Chloe, 1 Cor. 1:11, and a letter requesting advice, 7:1, probably brought by Stephanas, 16:17. Factions had risen in the church, some using Paul's name and some those of Peter, Apollos, and of Christ, in bitter contentions. Paul endeavors to restore harmony among them. He directs them as to the best method of Christian beneficence, and closes with friendly greetings. II. The second epistle was called forth by intelligence received through Titus, at Philippi. Paul learned of the favorable reception of his former letter, and the good effects produced, but that a party remained opposed to him—accusing him of fickleness in not fulfilling his promise to visit them; blaming his severity toward the incestuous person; and charged him with an assumption of unwarranted authority. In his reply he answers all these objections; enlarges upon the excellence of the new covenant, and the duties and rewards of its ministers, and on the duty of the Corinthian Christians in charitable collections. He then vindicates his dignity and authority as an apostle. He closes by urging them to penitence, peace, and brotherly love. The second epistle probably was written a few months after the first.

Cormorant, *the plunger*, Lev. 11:17; Deut. 14:17, an unclean bird, like the cormorant—which is a water-bird about the size of a goose. Another Hebrew word, translated "cormorant" in Isa. 34:11; Zeph. 2:14, A. V., should rather be translated as it is in the R. V., and in other passages of the A. V., "pelican."

Corn. A general name for grain. The most common kinds were wheat, barley, spelt, R. V., Ex. 9:32 and Isa. 28:25, "rye;" Ezek. 4:9, "fitches" and millet; oats are mentioned only by rabbinical writers. Our Indian corn was unknown in Bible times. The Jewish law permitted any one in passing through a field of standing corn to pluck and eat. Deut. 23:25; see also Matt. 12:1. From Solomon's time, 2 Chron. 2:10, 15, as agriculture became developed under a settled government, Palestine was a corn-exporting country, and her grain was largely taken by her commercial neighbor Tyre. Ezek. 27:17; comp. Amos 8:5.

Cornelius (*Kor-nēʹli-ŭs*, Eng. *Kŏr-nēlʹyŭs*). A Roman centurion of the Italian cohort stationed in Cæsarea, Acts 10:1, etc., a man full of good works and almsdeeds. With his household he was baptized by Peter, and thus Cornelius became the first-fruits of the Gentile world to Christ.

Corner. According to the Mosaic law, it was forbidden to reap the corners of the field, so that there might be gleanings for the poor. Lev. 19:9; 23:22. The "corner of the house-top," Prov. 21:9, is a narrow place exposed to sun and rain, contrasted with the wide room or house below. The word "corner" in the phrase "corners of Moab," or of any other country, Num. 24:17; Jer. 48:45, means the length and breadth of the country, and also of the world. "Corner of a bed," Amos 3:12, the corner of a room; was on the elevated part (used by night for a bed or couch), and contained the most honorable seat. In the passage last cited it figuratively denotes the most proud and luxurious of the Israelites in Samaria. In Zech. 10:4 the word "corner" is used to denote either the corner-stone or the most conspicuous part of a building, and evidently refers to Christ, Matt. 21:42.

Corner-stone. Job 38:6. Christ is called "the corner-stone of the Church," because he gives strength and unity to the whole structure of God's house. Comp. Eph. 2:20; 1 Pet. 2:6; Matt. 21:42; Rom. 9:32, 33; 1 Cor. 1:23.

Cornet (Heb. *shôphâr*). A loud-sounding instrument, made of the horn of a ram or of a chamois (sometimes of an ox), and used by the ancient Hebrews for signals, Lev. 25:9, R. V. "trumpet," and much used by the priests. 1 Chron. 15:28.

Cos (*Kŏs*) or **Coos** (*Kō-os*). A small island in the Ægean sea off the coast of Caria, the birthplace of Hippocrates, with a chief town of the same name, in which was a famous temple of Æsculapius. The island was celebrated for its wines, beautiful stuffs, and ointments. Paul passed a night here on his voyage from Miletus to Judea. Acts 21:1.

Council. There are three legal bodies called "councils" in the English N. T.: 1. The Sanhedrin, the supreme court of the Jews, the fountain of their government, which sat at Jerusalem. By this body Jesus was tried. Matt. 26:59. 2. The lesser courts. Matt. 10:17; Mark 13:9. One was in each town, but two in the capital. Josephus states that each court consisted of seven judges, with two Levites as assessors. The "judgment," Matt 5:21, probably applies to them. 3. The "council" spoken of in Acts 25:12 was a kind of jury "composed of councillors appointed to assist and advise the Roman governors."

Covenant. An agreement or mutual contract made with great solemnity. The Hebrew word *bireth*, for covenant, means "a cutting," having reference to the custom of cutting or dividing animals in two and passing between the parts in ratifying a covenant. Gen. 15; Jer. 34:18, 19. In the New Testament the corresponding word is *diathēkē*, which is frequently translated testament in the Authorized Version. In the Bible the word is used: 1. Of a covenant between God and man; as God's covenant with Noah, after the flood. The Old Covenant, from which we name the first part of the Bible the Old Testament, is the covenant of works; the New Covenant, or New Testament, is that of grace. 2. Covenant between tribes, Josh. 9:6, 15; 1 Sam. 11:1, or between individuals, Gen. 31:44. In making such a covenant God was solemnly invoked as witness, Gen. 31:50, and an oath was taken. Gen. 21:31. A sign or witness of the covenant was sometimes framed, such as a gift, Gen. 21:30, or a pillar or heap of stones erected. Gen. 31:52. God's covenants, from the beginning, have been with his people and their seed—with Adam, Gen. 2:17; Rom. 5:12; 1 Cor. 15: 22; with Noah, Gen. 9:9; with Abraham, Gen. 17:7; 22:18; with the Jews, Ex. 6:4; 19:5; 20:6; 34:27; Lev. 26:9,42,45; Deut. 4:9, 37; with Christians, Acts 2:39; Eph. 6:2. A covenant of salt, Num. 18:19; 2 Chron. 13:5, was a compact in which salt was used in its ratification.

Cracknels. 1 Kings 14:3. Small dry cakes.

Crane. A large bird measuring four feet in height and seven feet from tip to tip of its extended wings. When upon the wing it is usually hoarse, and its cry is hoarse and melancholy; hence the allusion of Isa. 38:14. These birds return in the spring with great regularity from their migrations, and flocks of thousands pass over Palestine. Jer. 8:7. But the two Hebrew words *sus* and *agur*, rendered "crane" and "swallow," may signify the "swallow twittering" or "chattering."

Crete (*kreet*), now *Candia*. A large island in the Mediterranean sea, midway between Syria and Italy. It is about 140 miles long by 35 miles wide. The people were proverbially liars, Tit. 1:12—a character they are said still to bear. "Homer dates all the fictions of Ulysses from Crete, as if he meant to pass a similar censure on the Cretans." Cretans were at Jerusalem on the day of Pentecost, Acts 2:11; Paul was shipwrecked near the island, and he left Titus there as the first pastor and superintendent, who was "to ordain elders in every city" of the island. Tit. 1:5. It is now under the tyranny of the Turks.

Crimson. Jer. 4:30. See **Colors**.

Crisping-pins, Isa. 3:22, A.V., "satchels" R.V. Probably some small ornamented reticule.

Cross. The frightful mode of punishment by the cross appears to have been practised from the earliest periods well known to history. Crosses were made of two beams of wood, crossing each other either at right angles, or obliquely in the shape of the letter X; with various modifications of form. There was sometimes also a kind of bracket attached near the bottom of the upright piece, as a partial support to the sufferer. Crucifixion was inflicted among the ancient Persians, Assyrians, Egyptians, Carthaginians, Indians, Scythians, Greeks, and Macedonians. Among the Romans, it prevailed from very early times down to the reign of Constantine the Great, by whom it was abolished; and from the Romans it most probably passed to the Jews; though some have imagined that they could trace the punishment in such passages as Deut. 21:22, 23. The mode of execution by the cross may be thus described. Sometimes the sufferer was fastened to the cross as it lay on the ground; it was then lifted, with the body attached, and dropped into the hole, so prepared that the feet were not more than about half a yard from the earth. But sometimes the cross was first set up; and then the criminal was attached to it. Tying and nailing were both in use. Our Lord was nailed. A medicated draught was offered to stupefy the senses: this Jesus refused. Mark 15:23. It was merciful to break the legs: death would come the sooner. The cross on which our Lord suffered was, if we may credit a legend, made of the aspen; which is said hence to be continually trembling. More reasonably, it may be believed to have been of oak, which was plentiful in Judea. The cross of Christ was honored by his disciples. It was Christ crucified whom the apostles preached; the divine Redeemer stooping so low as to endure this shocking death, in order to make a sufficient sacrifice, satisfaction, and oblation, for the sins of the world. 1 Cor. 1:23, 24; 2:2. Hence they gloried in the cross of Christ, Gal. 6:14, and willingly, for love of him, took up the cross (a figurative expression) and followed him, suffering for his sake persecution even to the death. 2 Tim. 2:11, 12. Some centuries elapsed before the symbol was turned into an image, the cross into the figure of Christ suspended on it. It may be added that though among other nations bodies were generally suffered to rot upon the cross, the rites of sepulture being denied, the Jews observed the precept of Deut. 21:23, and took down the corpse before sunset. When the Roman empire became Christian, the cross, heretofore so shameful, was adopted as a symbol of honor; it glittered on the helmets of the soldiery, was engraven on their shields, and interwoven into their banners.

Crown. "Many crowns" is an expression occurring in Scripture, Rev. 19:12; it being customary for those who claimed authority over more than one country to wear double or united crowns. We have a familiar illustration of this in the papal tiara, or triple crown. Crowns of laurel, etc., were given to victors in the ancient games; hence the Christian's final prize is represented as a crown, the symbol of successful contest, the appropriate ornament of the royal dignity conferred upon him. 1 Cor. 9:25; 2 Tim. 2:5; 4:8; Rev. 3:11. The term is also used figuratively elsewhere, as in Prov. 12:4; 14:24; 16:31. There were ancient coins called "crowns."

Crown of Thorns. Our Lord was crowned in mockery by the Roman soldiers. Matt. 27:29; Mark 15:17; John 19:2. It is questioned whether this was only mockery, or whether it was specially intended for additional torture. Such a crown, it is clear, must have been made of some plant that would readily twist into a wreath. The large-leaved acanthus would not: hardly would the *Spina Christi*, as it is called, with strong sharp thorns. Hasselquist imagines the thorn in question the Arabian *nubk*, a very common plant, "with many small and sharp spines, soft, round, and pliant branches; leaves much resembling ivy, of a very deep green, as if in designed mockery of a victor's wreath."

Cruse. This word appears as the translation of three Hebrew words: one of these occurs in 1 Sam. 26:11, 12, 16; 1 Kings 17:12, 14, 16; 19:6, to denote a vessel used for water or oil. Again, we have a "cruse of honey." 1 Kings 14:3. The same word is also rendered "bottle." Jer. 19:1, 10. This must have been of earthenware, and had its Hebrew name from the gurgling sound caused when any liquid was poured from it. The only other place in which our version has "cruse" is 2 Kings 2:20. The original word is translated "dish" in 2 Kings 21:13, "pans" in 2 Chron. 35:13, and "bosom" in Prov. 19:24; 26:15, A. V., but dish in the R. V. It was probably a metal platter or dish.

Crystal. This word occurs in the Common English Version of Job 28:17. The R. V. reads "glass." The original term signifies something of exceeding purity. The Egyptians had the secret of introducing gold between two surfaces of glass, together with various colors. They could also enamel upon gold. It is very likely that a reference to some such work of art is intended. The word rendered "crystal" in Ezek. 1:22, is elsewhere "ice" or "frost." The margin of the R. V. reads "ice" here also. It is probably called "terrible" because of the bright shining of such a substance in the rays of the sun, dazzling and blinding the eye that looks on it. We further find "crystal," the rock crystal, in Rev. 4:6; 22:1; also the epithet crystal-clear is given to jasper. Rev. 21:11.

Cubit. Gen. 6:15. See **Measures.**

Cuckoo. Lev. 11:16; Deut. 14:15, A. V. A bird whose flesh was not to be eaten. The cuckoo is known in Palestine; but more likely some of the lesser kinds of sea-fowl are meant. The R. V. reads "seamew" in both the above places.

Cummin. Matt. 23:23. A low herb of the fennel kind, which produces aromatic seeds and is found in Syria. In Isa. 28:25, 27, reference is made to the manner of sowing and threshing it.

Cup-bearer. An officer of high dignity at Eastern courts, as the butler of Pharaoh. Gen. 40; 41:9. Cup-bearers are mentioned in the description of Solomon's court, 1 Kings 10:5; and Rabshakeh, as his name indicates, was cup-bearer to the king of Assyria. 2 Kings 18:17. Nehemiah held the same post under Artaxerxes. Neh. 1:11; 2:1. And it was not only an honorable appointment, but must have been a source of great emolument, for Nehemiah was evidently a man of wealth. Neh. 5:14-19. The cup was washed in the king's presence, and when filled, after the officer had tasted a little of the wine, which he poured into his left hand, was presented on three fingers. So no modern Eastern attendant ever grasps any vessel he offers to his master, but places it on his left hand, and steadies it with his right.

Cush (*kŭsh*). 1. A country near the Gihon, Gen. 2:13 (margin A. V., and the text of the R. V.), north of Assyria. 2. The country peopled by Cush or the Ethiopians, Gen. 10:6, lying to the south of Egypt, on the upper Nile, and possibly extending its rule into southern Arabia. See **Ethiopia.**

Cymbals. There are two kinds of cymbals, both of which we find mentioned in Ps. 150:5. The first kind, called the loud cymbals, like castanets, consisted of small round plates, two of which are held in each band, one upon the thumb and the other upon the middle finger, and being struck together skilfully make an agreeable sound. The second kind, called the high-sounding cymbals, were two broad convex plates of brass, the concussion of which produced a shrill, piercing sound, like clattering rather than tinkling. 1 Cor. 13:1. Both kinds are in common use to-day in the East.

Cypress. R. V. holm tree. Isa. 44:14. The Hebrew word indicates a tree with hard-grained wood, not the cypress, but probably the Syrian juniper which grows wild upon Lebanon, is meant, as the cypress never does in the Holy Land. The latter tree is a tall evergreen, the wood of which is heavy, aromatic, and remarkably durable. Its foliage is dark and gloomy, its form close and pyramidal, and it is usually planted in the cemeteries of the East. Coffins were made of it in the East, and the mummy-cases of Egypt are found at this day of the cypress wood. The timber has been known to suffer no decay by the lapse of 1100 years.

Cyprus (*sī'prŭs*). A large fertile island of the Mediterranean Sea, triangular in form, 150 miles long, and from 50 to 60 miles broad. Venus was its chief goddess—hence her name Cypria. It contained two prominent cities, Salamis and Paphos, and 17 towns. Salamis was at the east and Paphos at the west end of the island. Acts 13:4, 5. Barnabas was a native of Cyprus, and its people are noticed in apostolic history. Acts 4:36; 13:4; 15:39. Sergius Paulus, proconsul of Cyprus, was converted by Paul on his first missionary tour, Acts 13:7 ff., and thus became the first Christian ruler on record. Cyprus was colonized by the Phœnicians at a very early date. It was the Chittim, or Kittim, of the Old Testament. Num. 24:24. Copper mining and the production of swords, armor, and other articles in bronze were its principal industries. There was also an extensive commerce. In literature, Cyprus boasted of very early distinction. After belonging to Egypt, Persia, and Greece, it became a Roman possession 58 B.C., and is now under the English government.

Cyrene (*sī-rē'nē*). The chief city of Libya, in northern Africa. Simon, who bore our Saviour's cross, was of that city, Matt. 27:32; its people were at Jerusalem during the Pentecost, and they had a synagogue there, Acts 2:10; 6:9, and some of them became preachers of the gospel. Acts 11:20; 13:1. Cyrene was destroyed by the Saracens in the fourth century, and is now desolate.

Cyrenius (*sī-rē'nĭ-ŭs*). Luke 2:2, A. V., but Quirinius in R. V. The transliteration of a Greek name, which is itself the Greek form of the Roman name of Quirinius. The full name is Publius Sulpicius Quirinius.

He was consul B. C. 12, and made governor of Syria after the banishment of Archelaus in A. D. 6. He was sent to make an enrolment of property in Syria, and made accordingly, both there and in Judea, a census. But the census in Luke 2:2 seems to be identified with one which took place at the time of the birth of Christ. There is good reason for believing that Quirinius was twice governor of Syria, and that his first governorship extended from B. C. 4—the year of Christ's birth—to B. C. 1, when he was succeeded by M. Lollius.

Cyrus (*si'rus*), *the sun*. In Hebrew *Koresh*, founder of the Persian empire; used by Jehovah in the execution of his designs of mercy towards the Jews, as foretold by Isaiah 44:28; 45:1-7; comp. 2 Chron. 36: 22, 23; Ezra 1:1-4; Dan. 6:28. Some suppose Cyrus to be a title of a ruler, as Cæsar or Pharaoh; in that case Isaiah would not necessarily designate a particular king, but only the chief ruler of Persia. This Cyrus was the son of Cambyses, king of Persia, and a nephew of Darius the Mede (Cyaxares), and united the crowns of Persia and Media. He ordered a return of the Jews, who had been seventy years in captivity, to their own land, and furnished them very liberally with the means of rebuilding their temple. Daniel lived at his court, and was his favorite minister and adviser. Dan. 6:28. The captivity of the Jews, which was ended by the decree of Cyrus, B. C. 536, ended also the sin of idolatry in the nation.

D

Daberath (*dăb'e-răth*), *the subduer*. A town on the borders of Issachar and Zebulun. Josh. 19:12; 1 Chron. 6:72.

Dagon (*dā'gon*), *fish*. The national deity of the Philistines. There was a temple of Dagon at Gaza, Judg. 16:23, and one at Ashdod, 1 Sam. 5:1, 7; the latter was destroyed by Jonathan Maccabæus. Probably the worship of the male (Dagon) and female (Derceto) deities was conjoined in the same sanctuary. 1 Sam. 31:10; 1 Chron. 10:10. There are places called Bethdagon, where doubtless this idolatrous worship prevailed. Josh. 15:41; 19:27. Dagon was represented with the face and hands of a human being, and with a fishy tail. Some representations of a fish-god have been discovered among the Assyrian sculptures.

Dalmanutha (*dăl-mă'nŭ'thah*). A town on the sea of Galilee, near Magdala, in R. V. Magadan, Mark 8:10; Matt. 15:39; probably at 'Ain-el-Bârideh, on the west side of the sea, two miles from Tiberias, where are ruins.

Dalmatia (*dal-mā'shĭ-ah*). A mountainous district on the east of the Adriatic Sea; visited by Titus. 2 Tim. 4:10.

Damascus (*da-măs'kus*). The ancient city of Syria, 133 miles northeast of Jerusalem. It is on a fertile plain, 30 miles in diameter, with mountains on three sides. The plain is well watered by the Barada, the Chrysorrhoas (or "Golden Stream" of the Greeks, the Abana of Scripture; now El A'waj, "the Crooked"), and the Pharpar of Scripture. 2 Kings 5:12. The climate is delightful; the nights are cool and the dews heavy; yet the people sleep on the flat roofs of their houses. Damascus is called by the Arabs "the Eye of the Desert" and the "Pearl of the East." It is to the Mohammedan the earthly reflection of Paradise. Travellers have vied with each other in describing the beauty of Damascus. "From the edge of the mountain range," says Stanley, "you look down on the plain.... The river Abana (the Barada), with its green banks, is seen at the bottom rushing through the cleft: it bursts forth, and as if in a moment scatters over the plain, through a circle of 30 miles, the same verdure which had hitherto been confined to its single channel.... Far and wide in front extends the level plain, its horizon bare, its lines of surrounding hills bare, all bare far away on the road to Palmyra and Bagdad. In the midst of this plain lies at your feet the vast lake or island of deep verdure, walnuts and apricots waving above, corn and grass below; and in the midst of this mass of foliage rises, striking out its wide arms of streets hither and thither, and its white minarets above the trees which embosom them, the city of Damascus. On the right towers the snowy height of Hermon, overlooking the whole scene. Close behind are the sterile limestone mountains; so that you can stand literally between the living and the dead." *Sinai and Palestine*, p. 410. Damascus has been called the oldest city in the world. Josephus says it was founded by Uz, a grandson of Shem; Abraham visited it, Gen. 14:15; 15:2, A. V., but the R. V. reads "Dammesek Eliezer;" it was conquered by David, 2 Sam. 8:5, 6; was allied with Israel and against Israel, 1 Kings 15:18, 20; 2 Chron. 16:3; was taken by Tiglath-pileser; denounced by Jeremiah, Jer. 49:27; and afterward seldom noticed in Old Testament history. It was surrendered to Alexander the Great after the battle of Issus, B. C. 333. In the New Testament it is noticed as the place of the scene of Paul's conversion, Acts 9:1-25; later it became the residence of a Christian bishop; was conquered by the Arabs A. D. 635; became a provincial capital of the Turkish empire, 1516; and is now the residence of a Turkish governor. It is the hot-bed of Mohammedan fanaticism. In 1860, 6000 Christians were massacred by the Moslems in cold blood, in the city and adjoining districts. It has a population of from 110,000 to 150,-000. The principal street, known as Sultany, or Queen's street, runs in nearly a straight line from east to west, and is supposed to be the same as the street called "Straight" in Acts 9:11.

Dan (*dăn*), *judge*. 1. A son of Jacob by his concubine Bilhah, Rachel's handmaid. Gen. 30:6; 35:25; Ex. 1:4; 1 Chron. 2:2. Of Dan's personal history we know nothing, except that he had one son, Hushim or Shuham. Gen. 46:23; Num. 26:42. He shared with his brethren the prophetic blessing of Jacob, Gen. 49:16, 17, fulfilled, perhaps, in the administration of Samson, and in the craft and stratagem which his descendants used against their enemies. Other explanations, however, have been given. Those descendants multiplied largely; for at the first census after quitting Egypt the tribe numbered 62,700 males above 20 years of age; and, when numbered again on their coming to Jordan, they were 64,400. Num. 1:38, 39; 26:42, 43. Moses ere his death, like Jacob, pronounced a prophetic blessing on the tribe: "Dan is a lion's whelp: he shall leap from Bashan," Deut. 33:22, fulfilled in the predatory expeditions of which one at least is recorded in their subsequent history. 2. The territory in Canaan allotted to Dan was on the seacoast, west of Benjamin and between Ephraim and Judah. It embraced a broad plain, 14 miles long, near the sea. The Amorites kept them from the plain and forced them into the mountains. Hence they had another portion granted them, near Mount Hermon, Judg. 18, where they set up a graven image stolen from Micah. 3. Dan, city of, the chief city of the northern district held by this tribe. Judg. 20:1. It was originally called Laish, Judg. 18:29; noted for idolatry, Judg. 18:30; now called Tel-el-Kâdy, or "Mound of the Judge," three miles from Banias, north of the waters of Merom. 4. The Dan of Ezek. 27:19, R. V. "Vedan," is possibly the same as No. 2, but some identify it with Dedar, others with Aden, in Arabia.

Dance, Dancing. In Eastern nations the mingling of the sexes in the dance is seldom if ever known, although dancing was common, as a religious act, and also as a voluptuous entertainment. Just as impassioned language became "poetry," and song broke forth from the lips, so among Oriental peoples the limbs partook of the excitement, Ps. 35:10, and joy was exhibited in dancing. We read of dances among the Hebrews at solemn religious festivals. Thus David danced before the Lord at the bringing up of the ark into Jerusalem. 2 Sam. 6:14. His wife Michal reproached him for dancing. 2 Sam. 16:20-22. There were also dances of Hebrew women. We have an example of this after the passage of the Red Sea. There was a responsive song of triumph; the men, however, are not said to have danced, but the women did. Ex. 15:20. Similar were the dances that celebrated David's victory over Goliath, 1 Sam. 18:6; see also Ps. 68:25; the "timbrels" being musical instruments invariably accompanied with dancing. The sexes were not mixed in social dances. Thus it is evident that the daughters of Shiloh were not accompanied by even their male relatives. Judg. 21:21. Theirs would seem to have been a religious festival. There were also dances of mere pleasure and revelry. 1 Sam. 30:16, R. V. reads "feasting" instead of "dancing;" Job 21:11; Jer. 31:4, 13; Luke 15:25. Of the modes or figures of the Hebrew dance we know little; whether it was in a ring, or whether the performers were arranged in more than one row. In the East at present a female leads the dance; and others follow, imitating exactly her movements. Possibly, double rows, something similar to the country-dance, may be alluded to in Sol. Song 6:13; where Ginsberg translates "Like a dance to double choirs." The daughter of Herodias danced alone. Matt. 14:6. It may be observed that a Hebrew word, *mahhol*, rendered "dance" in our version, Ps. 150:4, and elsewhere, is supposed by some to mean a musical instrument.

Daniel (dăn′i-el, or dăn′yel), *judgment of God.* 1. A son of David by Abigail the Carmelitess. 1 Chron. 3:1. In 2 Sam. 3:3 he is called Chileab. 2. The name of one of "the greater prophets." Nothing is certainly known of his parentage or family. He appears, however, to have been of royal or noble descent, Dan. 1:3, and to have possessed great natural talents. Dan. 1:4. He was taken to Babylon in "the third year of Jehoiakim," and trained for the king's service. He and his companions resolved to abstain from the "king's meat" for fear of defilement. Dan. 1:8-16. At the close of his three years' discipline, Dan. 1:5, 18, Daniel had an opportunity of exercising his peculiar gift, Dan. 1:17, of interpreting dreams, on the occasion of Nebuchadnezzar's decree against the Magi. Dan. 2:14 ff. In consequence of his ability, by divine assistance, to reveal the dream to the king, he was made "ruler of the whole province of Babylon." Dan. 2:48. He afterwards interpreted a second dream of Nebuchadnezzar, Dan. 4:8-27, and the handwriting on the wall which disturbed the feast of Belshazzar. Dan. 5:10-28. At the accession of Darius he was made "first," according to the A. V., but the R. V. reads "one" of the "three presidents" of the empire, Dan. 6:2, and was delivered from the lion's den, into which he had been cast for his faithfulness in the worship of Jehovah. Dan. 6:10-23. At the accession of Cyrus he still retained his prosperity. Dan. 6:28, compare; Dan. 1:21, though he does not appear to have remained at Babylon, and in "the third year of Cyrus" he saw his last recorded vision, on the banks of the Tigris. Dan. 10:1, 4. In the prophecies of Ezekiel mention is made of Daniel as a pattern of righteousness, Ezek. 14:14, 20, and wisdom, Ezek. 28:3. The narrative implies that Daniel was distinguished for purity and knowledge at a very early age. Dan. 1:19. 3. A descendant of Ithamar, who returned with Ezra. Ezra 8:2. 4. A priest who sealed the covenant drawn up by Nehemiah. Neh. 10:6. He is perhaps the same as No. 3.

Daniel, book of. The book of Daniel was not placed among the prophetical books in the Hebrew Bible, but in the third division (writings) and after the Psalms. It is written partly in Chaldaic or Aramaic, and partly in the sacred Hebrew. The introduction, Dan. 1 to 2:4 *a*, is written in Hebrew. At the answer of the Chaldæans, which the A. V. says was made in "Syriac," the language changes to Aramaic, and this is retained till the close of the seventh chapter or 2:4 *b* to 7. The personal introduction of Daniel as the writer of the text, 8:1, is marked by a change of the language again back to the Hebrew, which continues to the close of the book. Chs. 8 to 12. The book may be divided into three parts. The first chapter forms an introduction. The next six chapters, 2–7, give a general view of the progressive history of the powers of the world, and of the principles of the divine government as seen in the events of the life of Daniel. The remainder of the book, chs. 8–12, traces in minuter detail the fortunes of the people of God, as typical of the fortunes of the Church in all ages. In the first seven chapters Daniel is spoken of historically; in the last five he appears personally as the writer. The cause of the difference of person is commonly supposed to lie in the nature of the case. The New Testament incidentally acknowledges each of the characteristic elements of the book, its miracles, Heb. 11:33, 34, its predictions, Matt. 24:15, and its appearance of the angel Gabriel, Luke 1:19, 26. Statements in the book itself imply that it was written by Daniel, and this is confirmed by references to it in the New Testament and in first book of Maccabees. 1:54; 2:59, 60. Josephus also reports that it was written by Daniel, "one of the greatest of the prophets." *Antiq.* 10:11. Some historical difficulties in the book have been removed by late discoveries, and as more light is gained respecting the history of this period, the external evidence tends to support the historical claims of the book.

Darius *(da-ri'us), restrainer.* The name of several kings of Media and Persia mentioned in the Bible. 1. Darius the Median, Dan. 5:31, was the son of Ahasuerus; he took Babylon from Belshazzar the Chaldæan, being at that time about 62 years old. The best identification is that which makes him Astyages, the last king of the Medes. "Only one year of the reign of Darius is mentioned, Dan. 9:1; 11:1; and if, as seems probable, Darius (Astyages) occupied the throne of Babylon as supreme sovereign, with Nerigalsarasser as vassal-prince, after the murder of Evil-merodach (Belshazzar), B.C. 559, one year only remains for this Median supremacy before its overthrow by Cyrus, B.C. 558, in exact accordance with the notices in Daniel." Under him Daniel was advanced to the highest dignity, which exposed him to the malice of enemies and led to his being cast into the den of lions, but by a miracle he escaped injury. 2. Darius, the son of Hystaspes, the founder of the Perso-Aryan dynasty, and ruler, B.C. 521–486. Ezra 4:5, 24; Hag. 1:1, 15; Zech. 1:1, 7; 7:1. He found in the palace at Achmetha or Ecbatana, the capital of Cyrus, a decree of that king concerning the temple in Jerusalem. This he confirmed, and the temple was finished in four years, B.C. 516. Ezra 6:15. It may, however, have been used before it was entirely completed, as is inferred from Zech. 7:2, 3. 3. Darius the Persian, mentioned in Neh. 12:22, is generally identified with Darius Codomannus, the antagonist of Alexander the Great, who ascended the throne B.C. 336, and reigned until B.C. 330. He was the last Persian monarch, and was killed by his own generals. Alexander defeated him, and thus the prophecy of Daniel, Dan. 8, was fulfilled.

Dathan *(dā'than).* See **Korah**.

David *(dā'vid), beloved.* The great king of Israel. He was the eighth and youngest son of Jesse, of Bethlehem and of the tribe of Judah. Six of his brothers are named in Scripture, 1 Chron. 2:13–15; of the other, we know only the fact of his existence, 1 Sam. 17:12; and it is needless to mention the conjectures which have been formed of him. David had also two sisters. 1 Chron. 2:16, 17. His mother's name is not recorded, unless, as some have believed, she was the Nahash of 2 Sam. 17:25. When the Lord, because of the ungodly conduct of Saul, had determined to choose another king, Samuel was directed to go to Bethlehem; and from the sons of Jesse anoint another as king over Israel. Dean Stanley thus describes David's appearance and physique as he stood before Samuel: "He was short of stature, had red hair and bright eyes. He was remarkable for the grace of his figure and countenance, well made, and of immense strength and agility. In swiftness and activity he could only be compared to a wild gazelle, with feet like harts' feet, with arms strong enough to break a bow of steel or bend a bow of brass." R.V. Ps. 18:33, 34. Samuel anointed David "in the midst of his brethren," 1 Sam. 16:13; and the Spirit of God was from that day specially upon him. David returned to the care of his flocks. Such education as the times afforded he doubtless had, and God's law was his study. He had poetic genius, too; and music was his delight. When Saul, afflicted now with that black spirit of melancholy which his sins had justly brought upon him, might, it was thought, be soothed by a minstrel's music, David took his harp to the palace; and his music calmed Saul's distemper; and Saul was gratified and became attached to his skilful attendant. David was not indeed altogether removed from home. He went backwards and forwards, as the king's dark hour was upon him, and his services were needed. In 1 Sam. 16:21 it is said that Saul made David his armor-bearer. And this has puzzled commentators exceedingly. For it then would have been strange if neither Saul nor any one about his person had recognized David when he came, as we find in the next chapter, to accept Goliath's challenge. And so all sorts of devices have been contrived to get the history into chronological order; some imagining that the fight with the Philistine was before David was attached to Saul as the minstrel. David offers to engage Goliath: but Saul doubts whether the young man was equal to such a perilous encounter; and David of course makes no allusion to his having previously stood before the king. Had it come out then that he was but the minstrel, the discovery would have been enough to prevent his being allowed the combat: he tells, therefore, how he killed the lion and the bear; and his evident enthusiasm wrings a consent from Saul that he shall go to battle. Saul accordingly arms him—not with his own personal armor, as some have not very wisely supposed: the stalwart king would have known better than to encumber the stripling with his own coat of mail—but with weapons—plenty were no doubt in the royal tent—more suited to his size. With these, however, unaccustomed as he was to such harness (an additional proof that he had never yet been Saul's armor-bearer), David refuses to go. He will rather take his shepherd's sling, and choose him out pebbles from the brook. David was successful; the huge Philistine fell; and the Israelitish troops pealed out their shouts of victory. Then Abner was willing to appear as a patron, and took the conqueror to Saul. And, in answer to the king's query, David replies, "I am the son of thy servant Jesse the Bethlehemite, 1 Sam. 17:58, adopting the style by which he was first named to the king. 1 Sam. 16:18. He is now fully recognized, found both a skilful musician and a valiant soldier, and attains the position mentioned before, 1 Sam. 16:21. Saul loves him, and makes him his armor-bearer, and sends a second message to Jesse, 1 Sam. 16:22, which, if not explained in this way, would seem unnecessary. See 1 Sam. 16:19. David is now established in the king's favor: he is specially beloved by Jonathan; he is set over the men of war, 1 Sam. 18:5, perhaps made captain of the body-guard, and employed in various services the rest of the campaign; by which his popularity was increased. But the king's mind began ere long to change. The rejoicings at the reestablishment of peace provoked his jealousy. For the chief praise in the songs of the women was given to David. 1 Sam. 18:6-9. And speedily the evil spirit resumed his sway. David did not then refuse to take up again his harp; though once or twice the maddened king strove to kill him with his javelin, and, because he could no longer bear his constant presence, removed him from the body-guard to a separate command. 1 Sam. 18:13. After he had married Saul's younger daughter Michal, instead of the elder Merab, who had been promised him, Saul, further enraged by David's increasing credit with the nation, and understanding, it is likely, by this time, that the young Bethlehemite was the chosen of the Lord, to whom the kingdom was to be transferred, sent to arrest him in his house. By Michal's stratagem he escaped, and fled to Samuel at Naioth in Ramah. Hither, however, he was followed, 1 Sam. 19, and again he fled; his stay with Samuel, whom he had perhaps not seen since the anointing, being in all probability not longer than a day or two. Convinced by an interview with Jonathan that Saul's enmity was no mere transient passion, 1 Sam. 20, David went to Nob, where his duplicity cost the high priest his life, and thence to Achish, king of Gath, where, to escape the jealousy of the Philistines, he simulated madness. 1 Sam. 21. Returning into Judah, he gathered a band of men, and maintained himself sometimes in the wilderness, sometimes hiding in caves, sometimes occupying a town, as Keilah. His father and mother he had placed with the king of Moab, 1 Sam. 22:3; and he had now the presence of the prophet Gad. 1 Sam. 22:5. At Keilah, too, Abiathar, become high priest on his father's murder, joined him, 1 Sam. 22:20; 23:4, and various warriors: eleven Gadite chiefs are particularly specified, and some of Judah and Benjamin. 1 Chron. 12:8-18. To this period belong the circumstances narrated in the concluding chapters of the first book of Samuel—the adventure with Nabal, and David's marriage with Abigail; his twice sparing Saul's life; perhaps the battle for the water of the well of Bethlehem, 1 Chron. 11:15-19; and also the residence with Achish, who gave him Ziklag. David's conduct at this time cannot be justified. He laid waste the country of Philistine allies, and pretended that he had destroyed only the tribes dependent upon Judah; and he joined Achish's army when marching to the battle of Gilboa. Here he was reinforced by some Manassites, 1 Chron. 12:19, 20, but was dismissed from the expedition through the renewed jealousy of the Philistine lords. He returned, therefore, to Ziklag, to find it plundered and burnt. However, he recovered what was lost, and obtained greater spoil, which he politicly sent to his friends in Judah, and, on the news of Saul's defeat and death just after, he repaired, by God's direction, to Hebron, and was anointed king. 2 Sam. 2:2-4. But reigned as yet over only a part of the nation; for Abner established Ish-bosheth, Saul's son, on the west of the Jordan, and over Israel generally. But gradually the tribes were flocking to David, 1 Chron. 12:23-40; and Saul's house was weakening as he was strengthened; till at length Abner himself came with a proposal to transfer to him the whole kingdom. 2 Sam. 3. But Abner was murdered by Joab, David's nephew and commander-in-chief, a man too powerful to be punished; and shortly after Ish-bosheth was assassinated by two of his officers; and then the nation was reunited; and David reigned over the kingdom of Israel: seven years and six months having elapsed since he had taken the crown of Judah. 2 Sam. 4:5. He was now "one of the great men of the earth." 2 Sam. 7:9. He consolidated his power at home, took Jerusalem and made it his capital, removing thither the ark of God, 2 Sam. 6, organized his army, 1 Chron. 11, and regulated the services of the sanctuary, 15:16, enlarged his harem, 2 Sam. 3:2-5; 5:13-16, opened commercial intercourse with the king of Tyre, 2 Sam. 5:11, and also extended his power abroad, subduing the Philistines, Syrians, Moabites, and Ammonites. His dominion was an empire, extending far as the large promise made originally to Abraham, and repeated again and again to the chosen people. Gen. 15:18-21; Ex. 23:31; Deut. 11:24. He had lingered at Jerusalem, while Joab was besieging Rabbah of the children of Ammon. And then occurred those shameful deeds, the adultery with Bath-sheba, and the murder of Uriah, which at first, it seems, did not touch his conscience, but which, when charged home upon him by the prophet Nathan, humbled the guilty monarch in the dust. 2 Sam. 11; 12. He repented deeply, see Ps. 51, which is ascribed to this period, and he obtained pardon by God's mercy. But he was not again the David of former days. The sword was never to depart from his house. 2 Sam. 12:10. And it never did. There was the defilement of Tamar, and the murder of his first-born Amnon, 2 Sam. 13; and then Absalom's unnatural rebellion and death, 2 Sam. 15; 18; and Sheba's insurrection, 2 Sam. 20; and the plague for the numbering of the people, 2 Sam. 24; and Adonijah's seizure of the government, when the most long-tried counsellors of David deserted him, a movement that could be crushed only by the aged monarch's devolving his crown upon Solomon, 1 Kings 1; with various other griefs. He transmitted a magnificent heritage to Solomon, to whom he left the carrying out of that purpose he had long before conceived. 2 Sam. 7; 1 Chron. 28; 29, of erecting a temple. David's character is clearly shown in the events of his life—whose strains of inspired song intertwine with all the devotional and joyful feelings of God's people in every age. The Psalms are a rich heritage to the church. Very many were from David's pen. And, though we cannot with precision point out all he wrote, or describe the times and circumstances under which those were penned that we know did come from him, yet we delight to couple particular compositions with various crises of David's life—as Ps. 42 with his flight across the Jordan in Absalom's rebellion; Ps. 24 with the bringing up of the ark to Jerusalem; Ps. 18 with David's deliverance from his enemies, and to see his emotions of praise, and hope, and repentance, and gratitude, and faith, at the wonderful dealings of God with him. Of the children of David many are mentioned in Scripture; and there were probably more; twenty-one sons are enumerated and one daughter. 2 Sam. 3:2-5; 5:13-16; 12:15, 24; 1 Chron. 3:1-9; 14:3-7; 2 Chron. 11:18.

Day. The Hebrews, probably, from the narrative of creation, Gen. 1:5; see Dan. 8:14, marg., began their day at sunset. Lev. 23:32. Their divisions of the day appear to have been in early times very inartificial. Thus we read of a distribution into three parts—evening, morning, and noon. Ps. 55:17. The first mention of an hour is by the prophet Daniel, Dan. 3:6, 15; 4:19, "for a while," R. V.; 5:5; probably, then, the reckoning of the twelve hours of the day was borrowed from the Chaldeans. In New Testament times it was a well understood distribution of time. John 11:9. These twelve hours, extending from sunrise to sunset, were, of course, of variable length. The variation is not, however, so much as it would be in our latitude; and, the sixth hour being noon, the third may be roughly said to be our nine in the morning, the ninth three in the afternoon. The nights were divided into watches, at first three, afterwards four. The word "day" is used in various senses, sometimes for a festal or birthday, Job 3:1; sometimes for the great day of God's judgment, Acts 17:31; 2 Tim. 1:18. The meaning is sometimes indefinite, as it is with us, Gen. 2:4; and according to some the "days" of creation, Gen. 1:5, 8, 13, 19, 23, 31, indicate not natural days, but long periods of time. Day is also used symbolically, Num. 14:34; and sharp contests there are among interpreters of prophecy whether the days of Dan. 12:11, 12; Rev. 11:3, 9 do not mean years.

Deacon. The name of an office-bearer in the Christian church. It is generally connected with the appointment of the seven who were to relieve the apostles in the "daily ministration," the distribution of the funds, and of provision for the members of the early church. Acts 6:1-6. The special name of deacon is not, however, given to the seven; the order called deacons was subsequently established, and founded upon or in imitation of the office committed to the seven. See Alford, *The Greek Test.*, note on Acts 6:5. It has indeed been suggested that there was already a class called "the young men," which was the prototype of the diaconate. Acts 5:6, 10. Different Greek words are used, however, in the two verses just referred to, and the specific duties of the two classes do not closely resemble each other. The Greek word for deacon often is used to indicate any person ministering in God's service. Thus it designates our Lord himself, Rom. 15:8; and Paul describes by it his own position, 2 Cor. 6:4; Eph. 3:7; Col. 1:23; in all which places it is translated "minister." Then it began to be used of a particular order in the church. Phil. 1:1; 1 Tim. 3, 8-10, 12, 13. The qualifications of deacons are described; from which in some measure their duties may be deduced. They were to hold a certain authority, and to show themselves patterns to believers. They were to be pure in faith; but it is not required, as it is of the bishop or overseer, that they should be "apt to teach." The inference undoubtedly is that, even if there were exceptions, teaching was not an ordinary part of the deacon's duties. Some of the seven, however, certainly joined teaching with the more secular "daily ministration." And though Paul does not affirm that it was part of a deacon's duty, his words constitute no proof that it was not. It has been questioned whether the diaconate was originally a step to a higher ecclesiastical office; and different interpretations have been given of 1 Tim. 3:13. It seems natural to understand that the honor there mentioned was gained in the position of deacon, and not in promotion to another office. Generally speaking, too, permanence in the diaconate seems to have been the rule in primitive times.

Deaconess. Mention is made, Rom. 16:1, of a "servant" (Greek *diakona*) of the church of Cenchrea; and notices are scattered through several of Paul's epistles of women who were engaged in Christian ministrations. Rom. 16:3, 12; Phil. 4:2, 3; 1 Tim. 3:11; 5:9, 10; Tit. 2:3, 4. If these texts do not refer to a distinct class, they seem to indicate the beginnings of such a class. And it is certain that, a few years later, deaconesses were a recognized body. Pliny, in his famous letter to Trajan, lib. 10, ep. 97, speaks of two whom he put to the torture, in order to extract information from them respecting the Christians; and ecclesiastical writers from a very early date frequently refer to them.

Debir (*dĕ'bir*), *a sanctuary*. The name of three places in Palestine. 1. A town in the mountains of Judah, Josh. 15:49, one of a group of eleven cities to the west of Hebron. The earlier name of Debir was Kirjath-sepher, "city of book," Josh. 15:15; Judg. 1:11, and Kirjath-sannah, "city of palm," Josh. 15:49. It was one of the cities given with their "suburbs" to the priests. Josh. 21:15; 1 Chron. 6:58. Debir has not been discovered with certainty in modern times. 2. A town east of the Jordan, on the northern border of Gad, and not far from Mahanaim. Josh. 13:26. Some suppose it to be the same with Lodebar. 3. A place on the northern border of Judah, behind Jericho. Some connect it with the *wady Dabor*, which falls into the northwest corner of the Dead Sea. Josh. 15:7. 4. One of the five kings hanged by Joshua. Josh. 10:3, 23, 26.

Deborah (*dĕb'o-rah*), *a bee*. 1. The nurse of Rebekah, and her companion into Canaan. Gen. 24:59. She was buried at Bethel, under the "oak of weeping." Gen. 35:8. Nurses held an honorable place in early times in the East, where they were important members of the family. 2 Kings 11:2; 2 Chron. 22:11. 2. A prophetess, the wife of Lapidoth, who judged Israel. She dwelt under, *i. e.*, had a tent pitched beneath, a noted tree; a palm tree it is called, and may have been at Baal-tamar, Judg. 20:33, or not far distant from the tree under which the first Deborah was buried. Deborah incited Barak to deliver his people from the oppression of Jabin; at his desire accompanied him, though with a rebuke, and after the victory uttered a triumphal song of praise. Judg. 4:5.

Decapolis (*de-kăp'o-lĭs*), *ten cities*. A region noticed three times in the Bible. Matt. 4:25; Mark 5:20; 7:31. It lay near the Sea of Galilee, probably on both sides of the Jordan. The cities were rebuilt by the Romans about B. C. 65; but as other cities grew up, writers are not agreed as to the names of the ten cities. Pliny gives them as follows: Scythopolis, Hippos, Gadara, Pella, Philadelphia, Gerasa, Dion, Canatha, Raphana, Damascus. Six are deserted, and none have many inhabitants except Damascus.

Dedan (*dĕ'dan*). 1. A grandson of Cush, Gen. 10:7, and the name of a people, with a region of like name. 1 Chron. 1:9. Dedan is thought to be the same as Daden, an island of the Persian Gulf; the inhabitants were noted merchants. Ezek. 27:15; 38:13. 2. A people of northern Arabia, descended from Dedan, a descendant of Abraham and Keturah. Gen. 25:3; 1 Chron. 1:32; Jer. 49:8; 25:23; Ezek. 25:13. The descendants of this Dedan lived near Idumæa. Jer. 49:8. It is not certain, but probable that the Cushite tribe engaged more extensively in trade. The "travelling companies" of Dedanim, A. V. plural of Dedan, R. V. "Dedanites," are noticed in Isa. 21:13. They are also named with the merchants of Tarshish by Ezekiel, 38:13, and were celebrated from their trade with the Phœnicians.

Degrees, Songs of. Fifteen psalms, 120-134, are so entitled. A variety of reasons has been suggested to account for this. The Jews believe that they were sung by the Levites on the fifteen steps which separated the men's court from the women's in the temple. Gesenius suggested that there was a progression in the thought and phraseology: the last member of a verse or part of it being taken up, repeated, and amplified in the next verse, thus:

"I will lift up mine eyes unto the hills,
From whence cometh *my help*.
My help cometh from the Lord,
Which made heaven and earth."
—Ps. 121:1, 2.

But this structure cannot be detected in all of them. Hengstenberg and others believe that they were "pilgrim-songs," chanted by those who went up to Jerusalem at the solemn feasts.

Delilah (*de-lī'lah*, or *dĕl'i-lah*), *pining with desire*. A harlot of the valley of Sorek, in the tribe of Judah, and near the borders of the Philistines, with whom Samson associated and who betrayed him. Judg. 16:4-18. See Samson.

Demas (*dē'mas*). Probably contracted from Demetrius. A companion of Paul during his first imprisonment at Rome. Col. 4:14; Philem. 24. The mournful note is subsequently made that he had forsaken the apostle, "having loved this present world." 2 Tim. 4:10. Whether this meant actual apostasy we know not.

Demetrius (*de-mē'tri-ŭs*), *belonging to Demeter or Ceres*. 1. A maker of silver shrines —models of the great temple—of Diana or Artemis at Ephesus. Acts 19:24. 2. A Christian mentioned with commendation by John. 3 John 12.

Derbe (*der'be*). A city of Lycaonia, Acts 14:6, 20; 16:1, about 20 miles from Lystra. Kiepert places it near Lake Ak-Ghieul, but some modern missionaries place it at Divlé, several miles farther south.

Desert. In the Scriptures this term does not mean an utterly barren waste, but an uninhabited region. The Hebrew words translated in the English Versions by "desert" often denote definite localities. 1. *Arabah*. This refers to that very depressed region—the deepest valley in the world—the sunken valley north and south of the Dead Sea, but more particularly the former. Arabah in the sense of the Jordan valley is translated by the word "desert" only in Ezek. 47 : 8 A. V. The R. V. reads Arabah. 2. *Midbar.* This Hebrew word, frequently rendered "desert," R. V. "wilderness," is accurately "the pasture ground." It is most frequently used for those tracts of waste land which lie beyond the cultivated ground in the immediate neighborhood of the towns and villages of Palestine. Ex. 3 : 1; 5 : 3; 19 : 2. 3. *Charbah* appears to mean dryness, and thence desolation. It is rendered "desert" in Ps. 102 : 6, R. V. "waste places," Isa. 48 : 21; Ezek. 13 : 4, R. V. "waste places." The term commonly employed for it in the Authorized Version is "waste places" or "desolation." 4. *Jeshimon,* with the definite article, apparently denotes the waste regions on both sides of the Dead Sea. In all these cases it is treated as a proper name in the Authorized Version. Without the article it occurs in a few passages of poetry, in the following of which it is rendered "desert:" Ps. 78 : 40; 106 : 14; Isa. 43 : 19, 20.

Deuteronomy (*deū'ter-ŏn'o-my*), or *the Second Law* (so called from its repeating the law), is the fifth book of the Bible, and, except the last chapter, was probably written by Moses. Deut. 1 : 5, comp. with Deut. 31 : 1; 2 Chron. 25 : 4; Dan. 9 : 13; Mark 12 : 19; Acts 3 : 22. This book contains three addresses of Moses to the Israelites in the plain of Moab in the 11th month of the 40th year of their journeyings. The *first* address, 1 : 1—4 : 40, is a brief rehearsal of the history of the "Wandering," and plea to obedience. The *second* address, 5 : 1—26 : 19, contains a recapitulation, with a few additions and alterations, of the law given on Sinai. The *third* part of Deuteronomy, 27 : 1—30 : 20, opens with the joint command of Moses and the elders to keep all the commandments, and, when they had crossed the Jordan, to write them upon the great plastered stones they were ordered to set up with appropriate ceremonies. Then follows the third address, 27 : 11—30 : 20, whose topic is, "The blessing and the curse." After these three addresses, in chapter 31 there follows the delivery of the law to Joshua and Moses' speech on the occasion, containing a command to read the law every seven years. In chapter 32 we have the song of Moses; in chapter 33 Moses' blessing of the twelve tribes. These were the last written words of Moses, and most beautifully do they set forth the majesty of God and the excellency of Israel. The final verses of the book give an account of the death of Moses, and were, of course, written by another hand.

Devil, *slanderer.* A name given to the greatest of evil spirits. He is so called 34 times in the Scriptures. He is called Satan 39 times; Beelzebub, the prince of the demons, 7 times. Matt. 12 : 24. He is called the angel of the bottomless pit, Abaddon, in Hebrew; Apollyon, in Greek; that is, destroyer, Rev. 9 : 11; adversary, 1 Pet. 5 : 8; accuser, Rev. 12 : 10; Belial, Judg. 19 : 22; 2 Cor. 6 : 15; deceiver, Rev. 12 : 9, R. V.; dragon, Rev. 12 : 7; 20 : 2; the god of this world, 2 Cor. 4 : 4; the evil one, from whom, in the Lord's prayer, we are to pray to be delivered, Matt. 6 : 13; 13 : 19, 38; Luke 11 : 4, A. V.; Eph. 6 : 16; 1 John 2 : 13, 14; 3 : 10, 12; liar, John 8 : 44; Lucifer, Isa. 14 : 12, A. V., but R. V. reads day star; murderer, John 8 : 44; prince of the power of the air, Eph. 2 : 2; prince of this world, John 12 : 31; serpent, Gen. 3 : 1–4; Rev. 12 : 9; 20 : 2; a sinner from the beginning, 1 John 3 : 8. From the beginning of the world the devil has had a hand, and sometimes a controlling one, in the most important events in the history of man. He tempted Eve, Gen. 3 : 1; he tried Job, Job 1 : 7; provoked David to number Israel, 1 Chron. 21 : 1; he tempted our Lord in the wilderness, Matt. 4 : 1; he "entered into Judas," Luke 22 : 3; he is the deceiver which deceiveth the whole world, Rev. 12 : 9, etc. "He that committeth sin is of the devil; for the devil sinneth from the beginning. For this purpose was the Son of God manifested, that he might destroy the works of the devil." 1 John 3 : 8. The time is coming, and may be near at hand, when "the dragon, that old serpent, which is the devil and Satan," shall be bound for a thousand years, "that he should deceive the nations no more till the thousand years should be fulfilled; and after that he must be loosed a little season." Rev. 20 : 2. "And when the thousand years are expired, Satan shall be loosed out of his prison and shall go out to deceive the nations." Rev. 20 : 7. The fall and punishment of the devil is recorded. Matt. 25 : 41; Luke 10 : 18; John 8 : 44; 2 Pet. 2 : 4; 1 John 3 : 8; Jude 6; Rev. 20 : 10. The word devil is sometimes applied to a very wicked man or woman. John 6 : 70; Acts 13 : 10; and in the Greek of 2 Tim. 3 : 3; Tit. 2 : 3, where the A. V. reads "false accusers."

Devils, Demons. Although there is only one being known as the devil, the English version of the Scriptures often uses the words devil and devils, where it should read demon and demons. The words in the original Greek are different from the word used when the devil is referred to. Frequent accounts are given of persons possessed by demons, and of our Lord casting out demons. They are evil spirits plainly distinguished from the persons whom they possess, sometimes a number of them entering into a person. Luke 8 : 2; 8 : 30. They can go out of persons and can enter into swine. Matt. 8 : 31; Mark 5 : 11–13. They have a separate consciousness; they know the Lord Jesus Christ, Luke 4 : 41; 8 : 28, and are addressed by Christ as personal beings, Mark 1 : 24; 5 : 9; and they are looking forward to the day of judgment, to them the day of torment. Matt. 8 : 29; James 2 : 19. As frequent accounts are given, in the Old Testament and in the New, of the devil and of demons entering into persons, there is no reason to doubt that they do so now.

Dial. It was on the "dial of Ahaz" that the miraculous sign given to Hezekiah for his recovery from sickness showed itself. 2

Kings 20:8-11; Isa. 38:7, 8. It is uncertain what the "dial" of Ahaz was. The word so translated is elsewhere rendered "degrees," "steps," e. g., Ex. 20:26. Some have imagined it a hemispherical cavity in a horizontal square stone, provided with a gnomon or index in the middle, the shadow of which fell on different lines cut in the hollow surface; some think that it was a vertical index surrounded by twelve concentric circles; while some, with perhaps greater probability, believe it an obelisk-like pillar, set up in an open elevated place, with encircling steps, on which the shadow fell. Ahaz appears to have had a taste for curious things, 2 Kings 16:10, and might have borrowed this dial from Assyria. The inquiry from Babylon in regard to it would seem to imply that the miracle was heard of, but not witnessed there. 2 Chron. 32:31.

Diamond. One of the gems in the high priest's breastplate is so called in our version. Ex. 28:18; 39:11. The same word also occurs in reference to the king of Tyre. Ezek. 28:13. It was doubtless some hard stone; for the original Hebrew term implies striking. But it is questionable whether, in the early ages of the world, the art of cutting and engraving the diamond was understood. It is, therefore, more generally supposed that an onyx or some other hard crystal is here meant.

Diana (dī-ā′nah, or dī-ăn′ah); Greek, Artemis. A heathen goddess of the Romans and Greeks, of great renown. The Diana of Ephesus was a different deity from the chaste huntress of the Greeks. She was like the Sidonian goddess Ashtoreth, and appears to have been worshipped with impure rites and magical mysteries. Acts 19:19. Her image, which was reputed to have fallen down from Jupiter, seems to have been a block of wood shaped into a female bust above covered with many breasts, the head crowned with turrets, and each hand resting on a staff. The temple of this goddess was the pride and glory of Ephesus, and one of the seven wonders of the world. It was 425 feet long, and 220 broad, and had 127 graceful Ionic columns of white marble, each 60 feet high, and the temple was 220 years in building. When Alexander the Great was born, B. C. 356, an earlier temple was burned down by one Herostratus, in order to immortalize his name: the splendid one above described had been rebuilt in its place. Compare 1 Cor. 3:9-17, written in Ephesus; and Eph. 2:19-22. The "silver shrines for Diana," made by Demetrius and others, were probably little models of the temple sold for amulets and household use. Ancient coins of Ephesus represent the shrine and statue of Diana, with a Greek inscription, "of the Ephesians." Acts 19:28, 34, 35. Others bear the words which Luke employs, translated "deputy" and "worshipper" of Diana. In her temple at Ephesus were stored immense treasures, and any preaching that tended to lower the shrine in the minds of the people, as Paul's did, would naturally arouse a great tumult.

Dibon (dī′bon), wasting. The name of two towns. 1. Dibon in Moab. Num. 21:30; Isa. 15:2. It was built by Gad, Num. 32:34, and hence called Dibon-gad; was assigned to Reuben, Josh. 13:9, 17; was also called Dimon. Isa. 15:9. It afterward returned to Moab, Isa. 15:2; Jer. 48:18, 22; now called Dhibân, about 12 miles east of the Dead Sea and 3 miles north of the Arnon. Its ruins are extensive, covering the tops of two adjacent hills. See **Moab**. 2. A town in the south of Judah, Neh. 11:25; the same as Dimonah, Josh. 15:22, and probably modern ed-Dheib.

Dinah (dī′nah), judged, acquitted, or avenged. The daughter of Jacob and Leah. Gen. 30:21. The history of her visiting the daughters of the heathen inhabitants of the land, of her defilement by Shechem, and of the treacherous and bloody revenge taken by her brothers Simeon and Levi, are recorded in Gen. 34. Nothing more is certainly known of her; she probably accompanied her family into Egypt. Gen. 46:15.

Dionysius (dī′o-nĭsh′ĭ-ŭs), belonging to Dionysus, or Bacchus. An eminent Athenian, converted by means of Paul's preaching. Acts 17:34. Tradition reports him to have been bishop of Athens, and to have suffered martyrdom there.

Diotrephes (dī-ŏt′re-fēz), Jove-nourished. A professed Christian, who resisted the authority of John. 3 John 9. His place of residence is unknown.

Dispersion, Jews of the. The "dispersed," or the "dispersion," was the term applied to those Jews who continued in other countries after the return from Babylon. Babylon thus became a centre from which offshoots spread; and colonies of Jews established themselves in Persia, Media, and other neighboring countries. The result of Greek conquest was to draw off Jewish settlers to the west. Hence they were found in the cities of Asia Minor, enjoying privileges from the Syrian kings. Settlements were also formed in Egypt, extending themselves along the northern coasts, and possibly also into the interior. See Jas. 1:1; 1 Pet. 1:1. And, after the capture of Jerusalem by Pompey, Jews were introduced at Rome. The dispersed, however, all looked to Jerusalem as the metropolis of their faith; they paid the legal half-shekel towards the temple services; they had with them everywhere their sacred book, which thus became known to the Gentiles, Acts 15:21; while a wholesome influence was perceptible on themselves.

Divination is the profession of foretelling future events. Deut. 18:10. Various modes of doing this have been resorted to in different nations. Thus Joseph's cup was used in this art. Gen. 44:5. The Egyptian magicians used to practise divination: so did the Chaldæans at Babylon. Divination was practised among the Greeks. The appearance of the sky and of the heavenly signs, the flight and song of birds, the phenomena presented by the entrails of victims, etc., were supposed to prognosticate events; and, according to these prognostications, public as well as private actions were regulated. The Romans were equally zealous in divining. The hold that such practices had upon the public mind was very strong. We need the less wonder at it when we notice the eagerness with which, even now, persons will resort to a specious fortune-teller. There is frequent mention of diviners in Scripture; and the Hebrews are repeatedly warned against the pretensions of those who affected to foretell events.

Divorce. A dissolution of the marriage relation. The law on this subject is found in Deut. 24:1-4, and the cases in which the right of a husband to divorce his wife was lost are stated in Deut. 22:19, 29. The ground of divorce is a point on which the Jewish doctors of the New Testament era differed widely; the school of Shammai seeming to limit it to a moral delinquency in the woman, whilst that of Hillel extended it to trifling causes, *e. g.*, if the wife burnt the food she was cooking for her husband. The Pharisees wished perhaps to entangle our Saviour with these questions in their rival schools, Matt. 19:3; but by his answer to them, as well as by his previous maxim, Matt. 5:31, 32, he declares that he regarded all the lesser causes than "fornication" as standing on too weak ground, and set forth adultery as the proper ground of divorce, Matt. 5:32; 19:9; Mark 10:11, 12; Luke 16:18.

Doctor. See **Lawyer, Teacher.**

Doeg (*dō'eg*), *fearful*. An Edomite, the chief of Saul's herdsmen, "detained before the Lord," probably by a vow, or because it was the sabbath, when David fled to Nob. 1 Sam. 21:7. Doeg afterwards falsely accused Ahimelech, the high priest, to Saul; and, when none of the king's guard would execute the ferocious sentence to slay the priests of the Lord, he fell upon them and killed 80 persons, sacking also their city. 1 Sam. 22:9-19; Ps. 52, title.

Dog. This well-known animal is frequently mentioned in the Bible. But, though it was employed to watch the flocks, Job 30:1, and to guard the house, Isa. 56:10, it was by no means regarded as we regard it, the companion and friend of man, but was an unclean animal under Jewish law and regarded with contempt. Ex. 22:31; Deut. 23:18; 1 Sam. 17:43; 24:14. Dogs were scavengers, half wild, prowling about the fields and the towns, devouring offal and dead bodies, and disturbing the night with their howlings. This is the case now in the east; troops of dogs abounding, recognized in a degree by food and water being occasionally given them, and, according to the instincts of their nature, guarding the place where they congregate, but deemed impure and unclean, just as among the ancient Hebrews. Hence we can understand the comparison of savage and cruel men to dogs, Ps. 22:16; Phil. 3:2, and the contempt and dislike attached to the name of a dog. 1 Sam. 24:14; 2 Sam. 3:8; 9:8. Solomon contrasts a living dog with a dead lion, Eccl. 9:4, and Abner exclaims: "Am I a dog's head?" 2 Sam. 3:8, implying that a dog is the meanest thing alive. The same contempt is implied in the charge: "He that sacrifices a lamb, .. *as if* he cut off a dog's neck." Isa. 66:3. In the New Testament it is used to designate vile persons who are shut out of heaven, Rev. 22:15, and foolish persons devoted to their folly. 2 Pet. 2:22. To the present day the word is applied by Jews to Gentiles, and by Mohammedans to Christians, as a term of reproach.

Dor (*dōr*), *dwelling*. A royal city of the Canaanites, Josh. 11:2; 12:23, within the territory of Asher, but allotted to Manasseh, Josh. 17:11; Judg. 1:27; 1 Chron. 7:29, and it was one of Solomon's provision-districts, 1 Kings 4:11; now Tantûra, eight miles north of Cæsarea, where there are considerable ruins.

Dorcas (*dōr'kas*), *gazelle*. See **Tabitha.**

Dothan (*dō'than*), *two cisterns*. Where Joseph found his brethren, Gen. 37:17, and Elisha resided. 2 Kings 6:13. It was on the south side of the plain of Jezreel, 12 miles north of Samaria; now called Tel-Dothân, five miles southwest of Jenin. Numerous bottled-shaped cisterns hewn in the rock are still found, which are supposed to resemble the "pit" of Gen. 37:24. Caravans still pass this place, as of old, on their way from Damascus to Egypt.

Dove. A clean bird in the Mosaic law sent out by Noah. Gen. 8:8, 12. The Hebrew word *yonah* includes the various varieties of doves and pigeons found in Palestine, excepting turtle-doves, called *tór*. There are very many allusions to this bird, for its beauty of plumage, Ps. 68:13, its simpleness, Hos. 7:11, its harmlessness, Matt. 10:16, etc., so that it even symbolizes the Holy Spirit, the meekness, purity, and splendor of righteousness. Matt. 3:16; Mark 1:10; Luke 3:22; John 1:32. Doves are frequently domesticated in the east. Pigeons and turtle-doves might, alone of birds, be offered in sacrifice; full-grown turtle-doves in pairs, but only the young of pigeons. Lev. 1:14; 5:7, 11; 12:6-8. They were the offering of the poorer classes; hence made by Mary. Luke 2:24. And on this account it was that those who sold doves established themselves in the precincts of the temple. Matt. 21:12; Mark 11:15; John 2:14-16.

Dove's Dung. In the siege of Samaria by Ben-hadad, a fourth part of a cab of dove's dung was sold for five shekels. 2 Kings 6:25. Bochart supposes chick-peas here meant; Keil, without deciding the question, produces testimony that excrement has been used for food in famine, and that the literal meaning is not impossible. Dr. Thomson considers dove's dung a coarse kind of bean. The seeds of millet are called "doves' seed" by the Hebrews, which favors the bulb or seed of some plant.

Dowry. See **Marriage.**

Dragon. The original word for this in the Bible has three meanings. Very commonly, where it occurs in connection with ostriches, owls, deserts, and ruins, it denotes the jackal, whose characteristics are unmistakably indicated, such as his "wailing" and "snuffing up the wind." So in Job 30:29, the R. V. reads "jackals," and also in Ps. 44:19 and Jer. 9:11, in which passages solitude and desolation are illustrated. The same idea is in Micah 1:8. In some passages it denotes monsters of the deep or huge land-reptiles, as in Ps. 91:13; R. V. reads "serpent." In Deut. 32:33 it refers to some poisonous reptile, being used in connection with the asp, a poisonous snake. The figurative use of this term, as in Ps. 74:13; Ezek. 29:3; Rev. 12:3 and 20:2, is quite obvious.

Dream. One mode of divine communication to the mind of man has been by dreams. Num. 12:6. While bodily organs were asleep and yet the perception active, God has sometimes spoken, sometimes in the way of direct message, occasionally by symbolic representation, for which afterwards an interpreter was needed. The prophetic dream must be distinguished from the prophetic vision. The latter might be in the night, Acts 18:9; 23:11; 27:23; but the senses were not wrapped up in sleep. It was by means of dreams that God communicated with those who were not of his covenant people. Gen. 20:3-7; 31:24; 40:5; 41:1-8; Judg. 7:13; Dan. 2:1; 4:5, 10-18; Matt. 2:12; 27:19. Often, indeed, it was by a dream that God spoke to his most favored servants. Gen. 15:12-16; 37:5-10; Matt. 1:20, 21. God communicated by a dream with Solomon, not only while he was young, 1 Kings 3:5-15, but also in his mature life. 1 Kings 9:2-9. We can only say that the Lord acts herein according to his good pleasure. The false dreaming of a dreamer of dreams, it may be added, was censured and to be punished. Deut. 13:1-5.

Drink, Strong. See **Wine**.

Dromedary. Isa. 60:6. A breed of the camel, remarkable for its speed. Jer. 2:23. It can travel from 60 to 90 miles or more in a day. The dromedary is taller and has longer limbs than other varieties of camel, and cannot as well bear heat or cold.

Drusilla (*dru-sil'lah*). Acts 24:24. The young daughter of Herod Agrippa I., and sister of Agrippa II. She was first betrothed to Antiochus Epiphanes, prince of Commagene; but, as he refused to become a Jew, she was married to Azizus, prince of Emesa. Soon after, Felix, the Roman procurator, persuaded her, by means of the Cyprian sorcerer Simon, to leave her husband and marry him. Acts 24:24. She bore him a son, Agrippa, who perished in the eruption of Vesuvius in the reign of Titus.

Dulcimer. A musical instrument similar to a bag-pipe like that in use at the present day among the peasants of northwestern Asia and southern Europe. Dan. 3:5, 10, 15. It was composed of two pipes with a leathern sack, and produced a harsh, screaming sound. It has no resemblance at all to the modern dulcimer.

Dumah (*dū'mah*), *silence*. 1. A son of Ishmael. Gen. 25:14; 1 Chron. 1:30. 2. A town in Judah, near Hebron, Josh. 15:52; now *ed-Dômeh*, ten miles southwest of Hebron. 3. A region, perhaps near Mount Seir. Isa. 21:11.

Dung. In many countries of the East wood is so scarce and dear as to be sold by weight. Hence animal excrements are used as fuel. Ezek. 4:12. It is a very common material for heating ovens, even among people of comfortable circumstances. The odor arising from the use of it is offensive, and penetrates the food.

Dura (*dū'rah*), *circle*. The place where Nebuchadnezzar set up his golden image. Dan. 3:1. Layard identifies it with *Dur*, below Tekrit, on the east bank of the Tigris; but Oppert would place it, with more probability, to the southeast of Babylon, near a mound called *Dûair*, where he found the pedestal of a colossal statue.

Dust. To lick the dust, Ps. 72:9, signifies abject submission. To shake the dust from the feet, Matt. 10:14; Luke 10:11, implies the renouncing of all contact. The Pharisees entering Judea from a Gentile country were accustomed to shake the dust from their feet, as a renunciation of Gentile communion. But there was a further meaning; as Paul's shaking his garments, Acts 18:6, so shaking off the dust was a declaration of being free from the blood of those who rejected the gospel-message. The casting of dust on or against a person was a form of bitter execration. 2 Sam. 16:13; Acts 22:23.

Dwelling. The dwellings of the poor in oriental lands are generally mere huts of mud or sun-burnt bricks. The earliest form of human habitation was probably a booth, though Cain built a city. Gen. 4:17. The patriarchs were chiefly dwellers in tents, a form of habitation invented or adopted by Jabal. Gen. 4:17-20. Of the various forms of dwellings common in early times, and alluded to in Scriptures, we may mention: 1. The booth. 2. The tent. 3. The cave dwellings. 4. The house of varied materials—wood, dried mud, brick, stone, etc. The fathers of the Israelitish nation for the most part dwelt in tents. They were, in the providence of God, pilgrims in a land which should be given as a settled home to their posterity; wholesome lessons being thus taught them, and their example being to be afterwards quoted for the confirmation of the faith of the church. Acts 7:4, 5; Heb. 11:8-10. Jacob indeed is said to have "built him a house at Succoth," Gen. 33:17; but the original word so rendered is of vague signification, and comprises almost every kind of erection, from the humblest hut or even tent to the gorgeous palace or sacred temple. After leaving Egypt, the Israelites inhabited tents in the wilderness; so that it was not till they occupied Canaan that they were domiciled in houses properly so called. In the cities which they took—the few excepted which they were commanded to destroy—they found houses ready to their hand. Deut. 6:10, 11; Josh. 24:13. Some of the material of these houses may be still existing in the massive dwellings of Bashan, altered from what they were when the victorious tribes took possession of them.

73

The Plan. Probably the houses of the ancient Israelites differed little from those inhabited by modern Syrians. We may well, therefore, derive our illustrations of such as are mentioned in the Bible from usages of the present day. In some parts of Palestine and Arabia stone is used, and in certain districts caves in the rocks are used as dwellings. Amos 5:11. The houses are usually of one story only, viz., the ground floor, and often contain only one apartment. Sometimes a small court for the cattle is attached; and in some cases the cattle are housed in the same building, or the people live on a raised platform, and the cattle round them on the ground. 1 Sam. 28:24. The windows are small apertures high up in the walls, sometimes grated with wood. The roofs are commonly, but not always flat, and are usually formed of a plaster of mud and straw laid upon boughs or rafters, or of tiles or flat stones, supported by beams of wood. Upon the flat roofs, tents or "booths" of boughs or rushes are often raised to be used as sleeping-places in summer. The difference between the poorest houses and those of the class next above them is greater than between these and the houses of the first rank. The materials of the better class of houses were stone, marble, and other costly kinds, perhaps, porphyry, basalt, etc., 1 Chron. 29:2, carefully squared, panelled, and fitted, Amos 5:11, cemented in Babylonia with bitumen, Gen. 11:3, with clay, or mortar composed of lime, ashes, and sand, straw being sometimes added. Inferior materials, and want of proper mixing, would make this mortar liable to crumble, Ezek. 13:10-15, in rainy weather. Sometimes stones were fastened together with iron clamps or lead. Bricks, kiln-burnt, were probably also used. Other materials were timber, such as cedar, shittim (acacia), sycamore, olive, and in palaces algum and cypress. Ex. 26:15; 1 Kings 6:15, 16, 32-34; 7:8, 12; 10:12; Isa. 9:10. The precious metals and ivory were also employed for overlaying woodwork, etc., 1 Kings 6:35; 22:39; Amos 3:15.

A modern eastern house of the better class presents a dead wall to the street, with an interior court. There is a low entrance door with an inscription from the Koran, and over it a latticed window, or kiosk, sometimes projecting like our antique bay-windows; there may be also a few other small latticed windows high up in the wall. A passage from the outer door, which is attended to by the porter, John 18:16, 17; Acts 12:13, 14, leads into the first or outer court, but is so contrived that the entrance to the court is not exactly opposite to the external door; so that no view of the court is obtained from the street, nor any of the street from the court. The principal apartment looks into this court, and some of them are open to it. The court is occasionally shaded by an awning; and on the floor or pavement of it, rugs are spread on festive occasions; while in the centre there is often a fountain. Around the court, or part of it, a veranda runs, and over this, when the house has more than one story, there is often another balustraded gallery. In the corner of the court are the stairs to the upper apartments. Immediately opposite the side of entrance is the principal reception room, open to the court. It has a raised terrace or platform, and is richly fitted up with sofas (the *diván*) round three sides, and probably with a fountain in the centre. Here the master of the house receives his visitors, his place being the corner of the diván, and each person taking off his shoes before he steps upon the raised portion of the apartment. When there is no second floor, but more than one court, the women's apartments—*háreem, harem* or *haram*—are usually in the second court; otherwise they form a separate building within the general enclosure, or are above on the first floor. When there is an upper story, the most important apartment answers to the upper room, which was often the guest chamber. Luke 22:12; Acts 1:13; 9:37; 20:8.

The windows of the upper rooms often project one or two feet, and form a latticed chamber. See "the chamber in the wall." 2 Kings 4:10, 11. The "lattice" through which Ahaziah fell perhaps belonged to an upper chamber of this kind, 2 Kings 1:2, as also the "third story," from which Eutychus fell. Acts 20:9; comp. Jer. 22:13. Paul preached in such a room on account of its superior size and retired position. The outer circle in an audience in such a room sat upon a dais, or upon cushions elevated so as to be as high as the window-sill. From such a position Eutychus could easily fall. There are usually no rooms specially for sleeping in eastern houses. The outer doors are closed with a wooden lock, but in some cases the apartments are divided from each other by curtains only. There are no chimneys, but fire is made when required with charcoal in a brazier, or a fire of wood might be kindled in the open court of the house. Luke 22:55. It was in a house built after this manner, probably, that our Lord was arraigned before the high priest at the time when the denial of him by Peter took place. He "turned and looked" on Peter as he stood by the fire in the court, Luke 22:56, 61; whilst he himself was in the "hall of judgment."

In oriental dwellings, *the roof* is an important part. Its flat surface is made useful for various household purposes, as drying corn, hanging up linen and preparing figs and raisins. In forming the roof, twigs, matting, and earth are laid upon the rafters, trodden down and covered with a compost, hard when it is dry. But it is necessary carefully to roll it after rain. On such roofs weeds often grow, but are speedily dried up and wither. Ps. 129:6, 7; Isa. 37:27. These roofs were to be carefully protected by a battlement or parapet, lest accidents should occur. Deut. 22:8. This towards the street is a wall, towards the interior court usually a balustrade. It may have been through this that Ahaziah fell. 2 Kings 1:2. The roof is reached by an external staircase, so that it is not necessary to go through any of the rooms in ascending or descending. Matt. 24:17. Many uses were and are made of these roof platforms. Linen and other articles were spread there to dry. Josh. 2:6. They were places of private conference, of recreation, and for sleeping. 1 Sam. 9:25, 26; 2 Sam. 11:2; 16:22; Job 27:18; Prov. 21:9; booths were erected there at the feast of tabernacles, Neh. 8:16, and tents, 2 Sam. 16:22. In times of public calamity, lamentations were uttered there. Isa. 15:3; 22:1; Jer. 48:38. There, too, was private prayer made, and sometimes idolatrous rites performed. 2 Kings 23:12; Jer. 19:13; 32:29; Zeph. 1:5; Acts 10:9.

Added particulars. Ceilings were made of cedar, and artistically colored. Jer. 22:14, 15; Hag. 1:4. There were no chimneys; that so called, Hos. 13:3, was but a hole; indeed there were ordinarily no fires except in a kitchen, where, on a kind of brick platform, places were provided for cooking. Apartments were warmed when needed by fire-pans, Jer. 36:22; or fires were kindled in the court, Mark 14:54; Luke 22:55; John 18:18. Different rooms, too, as already mentioned in modern practice, were used in summer-time and in winter-time, Amos 3:15; and, whereas those for use in warm weather were open to the court, those for colder seasons were closed in with lattice-work, and curtains, and, probably for want of glass in the windows, with shutters. There were no rooms specially appropriated as bedrooms; just as it is common at the present day to sleep on the diván in the ordinary apartments. Hence the assassins would have easier access to Ish-bosheth. 2 Sam. 4:5-7. The various notices we meet with in Scripture will be easily understood if the previous descriptions be borne in mind. The chamber on the wall designed for Elisha, 2 Kings 4:10, was probably the room over the gate, with the projecting window. Perhaps, also, the summer parlor where Ehud found Eglon, Judg. 3:20, was the same. The "guest chamber," where our Lord commanded his disciples to prepare for the last supper, Luke 22:11, 12, was one of the large reception rooms in an upper story. The "upper room," where the disciples assembled after the ascension, Acts 1:13, was similar to the "guest chamber" mentioned above. The circumstances attending the cure of the paralytic, Mark 2:2-4; Luke 5:18, 19, may thus be explained. Our Lord was perhaps in the veranda; while the people crowded the court and impeded the passage from the street. The bearers, therefore, went to the roof, and taking away part of the covering of the veranda, let the sick man down.

There were also houses constructed with particular reference to the seasons. Summer houses were built partly under ground, and paved with marble. The fountains which gush out in the courts, and the methods used for excluding heat, and securing currents of fresh air render modern eastern houses very refreshing in the torrid heat of summer. The ivory house of Ahab was probably a palace largely ornamented with inlaid ivory. The circumstance of Samson's pulling down the house by means of the pillars may be explained by the fact of the company being assembled on tiers of balconies above each other, supported by central pillars on the basement; when these were pulled down the whole of the upper floors would fall also. Judg. 16:26. It may be added that, when a man had built a house and had not dedicated it, he was free from military service. Deut. 20:5. The use of the word in such passages as Ex. 2:21; 1 Sam. 3:12; 2 Sam. 3:1; 7:11; Ezek. 2:5, is easily understood.

Dyeing. The art of coloring fabrics, and the threads forming them, was known in early times. The ancient Egyptians excelled in the brilliancy of their dyed fabrics; and from them the Hebrews, while dwelling among them, probably learnt the art of dyeing. The Phœnicians, Greeks and Romans had much skill in this art also. We read of the *scarlet* thread at the birth of Zarah, Gen. 38:28, 30, and of the colored or dyed curtains of the tabernacle and the sacerdotal robes which were manufactured in the desert. Ex. 26:1, 14; 28:5-8. The chemical skill of the Egyptian linen manufacturers in employing the metallic oxides and acids or mordants, is placed beyond dispute by ocular proof. The various processes of dyeing and printing, or imparting the pattern, by blocks—the origin of calico printing—are exhibited on the monuments in all their minute details. Even the printing blocks, engraved with phonetic letters, and with the dye upon them, may be now seen in the British Museum. The purple dyes were highly valued and in great repute. Lydia was a seller of this famous purple, Acts 16:14, made probably from a dye procured from a shellfish of the sea. It still abounds in the Red Sea.

E

Eagle (Heb. *nesher; a tearer with the beak*). There can be little doubt that the eagle of Scripture is the griffon (*Gyps fulvus*), or great vulture, see margin of the R. V., Lev. 11:13, a bird very abundant in Palestine and adjacent countries. In spite of its name, it is a much nobler bird than a common vulture, and is scarcely more of a carrion-feeder than are all eagles. Indeed, the griffon is used by the orientals as the type of the lordly and the great. This well-known bird of prey was unclean by the Levitical law. Lev. 11:13; Deut. 14:12. It is called the "great vulture" in the margin of the R. V. The habits of the eagle are described in Num. 24:21; Job 9:26; 39:27-30; Prov. 23:5; 30:17, 19; Jer. 49:16; Ezek. 17:3; Ob. 4; Hab. 1:8; 2:9; Matt. 24:28; Luke 17:37.

Earing, Earing-time. Gen. 45:6; Ex. 34:21. R. V., "plowing." Earing is an old English word for plowing. The same word is used, Ps. 129:3, and is translated plowed. What we call arable land is sometimes called "earable" land; R. V., "plowed." Deut. 21:4; 1 Sam. 8:12; and Isa. 30:24, where the R. V. reads "till."

Earnest. Something given as a pledge for the performance of a specified bargain. Gen. 38:17; R. V., "pledge." It must be observed that the earnest, properly speaking, is a part of the whole to be granted; what remains, therefore, and is expected, is similar in kind to that already received. Thus, the earnest of the Spirit (the Spirit itself being the earnest) is that measure of grace vouchsafed here which shall be augmented and ripened into the fulness of grace hereafter. 2 Cor. 1:22; 5:5; Eph. 1:13, 14.

Earring. Earrings were usually worn by the Hebrew women, and by the children of both sexes, Ex. 32:2; more rarely by the men. Asiatic males have, in both ancient and modern times, worn earrings; and the presumption is that the male Hebrews would observe the same custom. The original word generally translated "earring" is ambiguous, and may signify an ornament for the ear or for the nose. In Gen. 35:4; Ex. 32:2, it is so qualified as to mean clearly an earring. In Gen. 24:47; Prov. 11:22; Isa. 3:21; Ezek. 16:12, it is as clearly a nose-jewel; while in Judg. 8:24, 25; Job 42:11; Prov. 25:12; Hos. 2:13, it is uncertain.

Earth. Ps. 24:1. Besides the ordinary acceptation of the word, as in the passage cited, it is used by the sacred writers to denote only a particular country. Thus, the phrase, Ezra 1:2, "all the kingdoms of the earth," means only Chaldea and Assyria; and it is often restricted to Judæa only.

Easter, Acts 12:4 (originally the festival of the Anglo-Saxon goddess Eastre), is a mistranslation. It should be, as in the Greek, translated, Passover; the Jewish feast. It is so translated in the R. V.

Eat, Eating. See **Meals**.

Ebal (*ē'bal*), *stone, stony*. One of the two mountains by which Israel stood receiving blessings and cursings. Deut. 11:29; 27:4; Josh. 8:30-35. Ebal and Gerizim are opposite each other, nearly meeting at their bases, but are a mile and a half apart at their summits. Mount Ebal, the northern peak, is rocky and bare; it rises 3077 feet above the sea and 1200 feet above the level of the valley, which forms a natural amphitheatre. From repeated experiments it has been found that the voice can be heard distinctly from the top of one mountain to the other and in the valley between. In the valley lay ancient Shechem, now Nablus.

Ebed-melech (*ē'bed-mē'lek*), *a king's servant*, an Ethiopian eunuch in the service of King Zedekiah, through whose interference Jeremiah was released from prison. Jer. 38:7 ff.; 39:15, 16.

Eben-ezer (*ĭb'en-ē'zer*), *stone of help*. A stone set up by Samuel after a signal defeat of the Philistines, as a memorial of the "help" received from Jehovah. 1 Sam. 7:12. Its position is carefully defined as between Mizpeh and Shen.

Eber (*ē'ber*), *beyond*. 1. The great-grandson of Shem, Gen. 10:21, 24; 11:14-17; 1 Chron. 1:19, and the ancestor of Abraham in the seventh generation. See **Hebrews, Heber**.

Ecclesiastes (*ek-klē'sĭ-ăs-tēs*), *the preacher*. It is the seventh book after the Psalms in the Hebrew Scriptures (but the second after the Psalms in the A. V.), and its title in Hebrew is *Koheleth*, signifying one who speaks publicly in an assembly. *Koheleth* is the name by which Solomon, probably the author, speaks of himself throughout the book. The book teaches that to obey God is the highest good. It is the confession of a man of wide experience looking back upon his past life and looking out upon the disorders and calamities which surround him. The writer is a man who has sinned in giving way to selfishness and sensuality, who has suffered for his sin in satiety and weariness of life, but who has through all this been under the discipline of a divine education, and has learned from it the lesson which God meant to teach him.

Eden (*ē'den*), *pleasantness*. 1. The home of Adam and Eve before their fall. Gen. 2:15. Its site has not been fixed. Two of its rivers are identified, the Euphrates, and the Hiddekel or Tigris; the others are disputed. Some say Gihon was the Nile and Pison the Indus. The best authorities agree that the "garden of Eden eastward" was somewhere in the highlands of Armenia, or in the valley of the Euphrates, but its precise location cannot be determined. The Bible begins with a beautiful picture of Eden, the paradise of innocence on earth, and closes with an equally beautiful picture of the more glorious paradise of the future, with its river of life and tree of life. Rev. 22:2. 2. A region conquered by the Assyrians, 2 Kings 19:12; Isa. 37:12; probably in Mesopotamia, near modern Balis, and same as the Eden of Ezek. 27:23. 3. The house of Eden. Amos 1:5. See **Beth-eden**.

Edom (*ē'dom*), *red*. Called also Idumæa and Mount Seir. Gen. 32:3; 36:8; 19:21. The country extended from the Dead Sea southward to the Gulf of Akabah, and from the valley of the Arabah eastward to the desert of Arabia, being about 125 miles long and 30 miles wide. It was given to Esau, and called the field or land of Edom. Gen. 32:3; 36:16; Num. 33:37. The country is well watered, rich in pasturage, abounding with trees and flowers, reminding us of Isaac's prophecy: "Thy dwellings shall be the fatness of the earth." Gen. 27:39. Its principal towns were Bozrah, Elath, Maon, Ezion-geber, Selah or Petra. Its destruction was proclaimed. Isa. 34:5-8; 63:1-4; Jer. 49:17; Ezek. 25:12-14; Amos 1:10, 11. See **Esau and Idumæa**.

Edrei (*ĕd're-ī*) *strength, stronghold*. 1. A capital city of Bashan. Num. 21:33; Deut. 1:4; 3:1-10; Josh. 12:4. It was in the territory of Manasseh beyond (east of) Jordan. Num. 32:33. It is not noticed in later Bible history, although it was an important city until the seventh century of the Christian era. Its ruins, called Edhra, cover a circuit of three miles. Among the ruins are remains of churches, temples, and mosques. The place has now about 500 population. 2. A town of Naphtali. Josh. 19:37. Porter identifies it with Tel Khuraibeh, near Kedesh; Conder, with *Ydter*.

Eglon (*ĕg'lon*), *calf-like*. 1. King of the Moabites, who held the Israelites in bondage eighteen years. Judg. 3:14. He formed an alliance with the Ammonites and Amalekites, and took possession of Jericho, where he resided, and where he was afterward assassinated by Ehud. See Ehud. 2. An Amorite town in Judah. Josh. 10:3-5; 15:39; now 'Ajlan, a hill of ruins, ten miles northeast of Gaza.

Egypt (*ē'jĭpt*). This is one of the oldest and most remarkable countries in ancient history, famous for its pyramids, sphinxes, obelisks, and ruins of temples and tombs. In early times it reached a high state of culture in art and literature, and is of great interest to Jew and Christian as the early home of the Israelites and of their great lawgiver Moses. Our notice of it must be confined to its relations to Bible events, and to those facts in its history that throw light on the Scripture. In Hebrew, Egypt is called *Mizraim*, a dual form of the word, indicating the two divisions—Upper and Lower Egypt, or (as Tayler Lewis suggests), the two strips on the two sides of the Nile. It is also known as the Land of Ham, Ps. 105:23, 27, and *Rahab*, "the proud one." Ps. 87:4; 89:10; Isa. 51:9. The Coptic and older title is *Kemi*, or *Chemi*, meaning black, from the dark color of the soil. The name Egypt first occurs in its Greek form in Homer, and is applied to the Nile and to the country, but afterward it is used for the country only. Egypt is in the northeastern part of Africa and lies on both sides of the Nile. In ancient times it included the land watered by the Nile as far as the First Cataract, the deserts on either side being included in Arabia and Libya. Ezekiel indicates that Egypt reached from Migdol, east of the Suez Canal, to Syene, now Assouan, on the border of Nubia, near the First Cataract of the Nile. Ezek. 29:10, margin. The length of the country in a straight line from the Mediterranean to the First Cataract is about 520 miles; its breadth is from 300 to 450 miles, and its entire area is about 212,000 square miles. Nubia, Ethiopia, and other smaller districts bordering on the Nile to the south of Egypt, were, at times, under its sway. The country has three great natural divisions: 1. The Delta. 2. The Nile Valley. 3. The sandy and rocky wastes. The Delta is one vast triangular plain, chiefly formed by the washing down of mud and loose earth by the great river Nile and watered by its several mouths, and by numerous canals. The Delta extends along the Mediterranean for about 200 miles and up the Nile for 100 miles. The Tanitic branch of the Nile is on the east of the Delta, and the Canopic branch on the west, though the Delta is now limited chiefly to the space between the Rosetta and the Damietta branches, which is about 90 miles in extent.

Climate.—The summers are hot and sultry, the winters mild; rain, except along the Mediterranean, is very rare, the fertility of the land depending almost entirely upon the annual overflow of the Nile, or upon artificial irrigation by canals, waterwheels, and the shadoof. Winds are strong, those from a northerly source being the most prevalent, while the simoon, a violent whirlwind and hurricane of sand, is not infrequent. The soil, when watered, is fertile, and fruits, vegetables, plants, and nuts are abundant. The papyrus reed was that from which paper was made. The reeds have disappeared, as Isaiah predicted. Isa. 19:6, 7. Domestic and wild animals were numerous, including the crocodile and hippopotamus, and vulture, hawk, hoopoe (a sacred bird), and ostrich were common. Flies and locusts were sometimes a scourge. Joel 2:1-11.

Inscriptions.—The hieroglyphic signs on the monuments are partly ideographic or pictorial, partly phonetic. The hieroglyphic, the shorter hieratic, and the demotic alphabets were deciphered by Champollion and Young by means of the famous trilingual Rosetta Stone, discovered in 1799, and the Coptic language, which is essentially the same with the old Egyptian. For a summary of the respective merits of Young and Champollion with regard to the interpretation of Egyptian hieroglyphics, see Allibone's *Dictionary of Authors*, vol. 3, p. 2002. The process of decipherment was, briefly, as follows: the Rosetta Stone had an inscription in three characters, hieroglyphic, demotic, and Greek. The Greek, which was easily read, declared that there were two translations—one in the sacred, the other in the popular language of the Egyptians, adjacent to it. The demotic part was next scrutinized, and the groups determined which contained the word Ptolemy. These were compared with other framed symbols on an obelisk found at Philæ, and after a time the true interpretation of these signs discovered, so that scholars can now read most of these hieroglyphic signs with great accuracy.

History.—The ancient history of Egypt has been divided into three periods by leading writers: the old monarchy, extending from the foundation of the kingdom to the invasion of the Hyksos; the middle, from the entrance to the expulsion of the Hyksos; and the new, from the re-establishment of the native monarchy by Amasis to the Persian conquest. Manetho enumerates 30 dynasties as having ruled in Egypt before Alexander the Great, probably several of them at the same time, but over separate parts of the country. Manetho was an Egyptian priest who lived in the era of the Ptolemies in the third century B. C. His work (a history of Egypt, written in Greek) is lost, but his list of dynasties has been preserved in later writers. The beginning of the first dynasty in his list is fixed by Lepsius in 3892 B. C., but by Böckh in 5702 B. C. 1. The old monarchy: Memphis was the most ancient capital, the foundation of which is ascribed to Menes, the first historic king of Egypt. The most memorable epoch in the history of the old monarchy is that of the Pyramid kings, placed in Manetho's fourth dynasty. Their names are found upon these monuments: the builder of the great pyramid is called Suphis by Manetho, Cheops by Herodotus, and *Khufu* or *Shufu* in an inscription upon the pyramid. The erection of the second pyramid is attributed by Herodotus and Diodorus to Chephren; and upon the neighboring tombs has been read the name of *Khafra* or *Shafre*. The builder of the third pyramid is named Mycerinus by Herodotus and Diodorus; and in this very pyramid a coffin has been found bearing the name *Menkura*. The most powerful kings of the old monarchy were those of Manetho's twelfth dynasty; to this period is assigned the construction of the Lake of Moeris and the Labyrinth. 2. The middle monarchy. In this period the nomadic horde called Hyksos for several centuries occupied and made Egypt tributary; their capital was Memphis; they constructed an immense earth-camp, which they called Abaris; two independent kingdoms were formed in Egypt, one in the Thebaid, which held intimate relations with Ethiopia; another at Xois, among the marshes of the Nile; but finally the Egyptians regained their independence, and expelled the Hyksos; Manetho supposes they were called *hyksos*, from *hyk*, a king, and *sos*, a shepherd. The Hyksos form the fifteenth, sixteenth and seventeenth dynasties. Manetho says they were Arabs, but he calls the six kings of the fifteenth dynasty Phœnicians. 3. The new monarchy covers the eighteenth to the end of the thirtieth dynasty. The kingdom was consolidated by Amosis, who succeeded in expelling the Hyksos. The glorious era of Egyptian history was under the nineteenth dynasty, when Sethi I., B. C. 1322, and his grandson, Rameses the Great, B. C. 1311, both of whom represent the Sesostris of the Greek historians, carried their arms over the whole of western Asia and southward into Soudân, and amassed vast treasures, which were expended on public works. Under the later kings of the nineteenth dynasty the power of Egypt faded: but with the twenty-second we again enter upon a period that is interesting from its associations with biblical history. The first of this dynasty, Sheshonk I., B. C. 990, was the Shishak who invaded Judea in Rehoboam's reign and pillaged the temple. 1 Kings 14: 25. Probably his successor, Osorkon I., is the Zerah of Scripture, defeated by Asa. The chronology and dates in Egyptian history are very unsettled and indefinite. The two noted authorities on this subject—M. Mariette and Prof. Lepsius—differ over 1100 years in their tables as to the length of dynasties I.,—XVII. and others vary in their computations about 3000 years as to the length of the empire. Some have conjectured that Menes, the founder of Egypt, was identical with Mizraim, a grandson of Noah. Gen. 10: 6. So probably the same with Shebek II., who made an alliance with Hoshea, the last king of Israel. Tehrak or Tirhakah fought Sennacherib in support of Hezekiah. After this a native dynasty—the twenty-sixth—of Saite kings again occupied the throne. Psametek I. or Psammetichus I., B. C. 664, warred in Palestine, and took Ashdod (Azotus) after a siege of 29 years. Neku or Necho, the son of Psammetichus, continued the war in the east, and marched along the coast of Palestine to attack the king of Assyria. At Megiddo Josiah encountered him, B. C. 608-7. 2 Chron. 35:21. The army of Necho was after a short space routed at Carchemish by Nebuchadnezzar, B. C. 605-4. Jer. 46:2. The second successor of Necho, Apries, or Pharaoh-hophra, sent his army into Palestine to the aid of Zedekiah, Jer. 37:5, 7, 11, so that the siege of Jerusalem was raised for a time. There is, however, no certain account of a complete subjugation of Egypt by the king of Babylon. Amosis, the successor of Apries, had a long and prosperous reign, and somewhat restored the weight of Egypt in the East. But Persia proved more terrible than Babylon to the house of Psammetichus, and the son of Amosis had reigned but six months when Cambyses reduced the country to the condition of a province of his empire, B. C. 525.

Egypt and the Bible.—To the Bible-reader the chief points of interest in Egyptian history are those periods when that country came in contact with the patriarchs and the Israelites. The visit of Abraham to Egypt. Gen. 12:10-20. This visit took place, according to the Hebrew (or short) chronology, about B. C. 1920, which would bring it, according to some, at the date of the Hyksos, or Shepherd-kings; others regard this as too late a date, and put it in the beginning of the twelfth dynasty; and his favorable reception is supposed to be illustrated by a picture in the tombs at Beni Hassan (where are many remarkable sculptures), representing the arrival of a distinguished nomad chief with his family, seeking protection under Osirtasen II. Next is the notice of Joseph in Egypt. Gen. 37:36. This beautiful and natural story has been shown to be thoroughly in accord with what is known of Egyptian customs of that age. Inscriptions on the monuments speak of the dreams of Pharaoh; the butler's and baker's duties are indicated in pictures; one of the oldest papyri relates the story that a foreigner was raised to the highest rank in the court of Pharaoh; and Dr. Brugsch believes an inscription on a tomb at el-Kab to contain an unmistakable allusion to the seven years of famine in Joseph's time, as follows: "I gathered grain, a friend of the god of harvest. I was watchful at the seed-time. And when a famine arose *through many years*, I distributed the grain through the town in every famine." The greatest point of interest is, perhaps, the period of oppression of the Israelites in Egypt, and the Exodus. Ex. 1: 8-22; 12:41. Who was the Pharaoh of the oppression, and who the Pharaoh of the Exodus? To this two answers are given by different scholars: 1. Amosis or Aahmes I., the first ruler of the eighteenth dynasty, is identified with the Pharaoh of the oppression, and Thothmes II., about 100 years later, as the Pharaoh of the Exodus, by Canon Cook. 2. That Rameses II., the third sovereign of the nineteenth dynasty, is the Pharaoh of the oppression, and Menephthah the Pharaoh of the Exodus, is the view now held by a majority of Egyptologists. Rameses II. is the Sesostris of the Greeks, who blended him with his father, Sethi I., or Sethos. He ruled 67 years and was the great conqueror and builder, covering his empire with monuments in glory of himself. "His name," says Dr. Ebers, "may be read to-day on a hundred monuments in Goshen." Among his many structures noted on monuments and in papyri are fortifications along the canal from Goshen to the Red Sea, and particularly at Pi-tum and Pi-rameses or Pi-ramessu; these must be the same as the treasure-cities Pithom and Rameses, built or enlarged by the Israelites for Pharaoh. Ex. 1:11. Herodotus tells us that a son and successor of Sesostris undertook no warlike expeditions and was smitten with blindness for ten years because he "impiously hurled his spear into the overflowing waves of the river, which a sudden wind caused to rise to an extraordinary height." Schaff says: "This reads like a confused reminiscence of the disaster at the Red Sea." The chief objection to this view is that it allows less than 315 years between the Exodus and the building of Solomon's temple; but the present uncertainties of the Hebrew and Egyptian chronologies deprive the objection of great weight. After the Exodus the Israelites frequently came into contact with Egypt at various periods in their history. Through an Egyptian, David recovered the spoil from the Amalekites, 1 Sam. 30:11, etc.; Solomon made a treaty with king Pharaoh and married his daughter, 1 Kings 3:1; Gezer was spoiled by Pharaoh and given to Solomon's wife, 1 Kings 9:16; Solomon brought horses from Egypt; Hadad fled thither for refuge, as did also Jeroboam, 1 Kings 10:28; 11:17; 12:2; Shishak plundered Jerusalem and made Judæa tributary, 1 Kings 14:25, and a record of this invasion and conquest has been deciphered on the walls of the great temple at Karnak, or el-Karnak. In this inscription is a figure with a strong resemblance to Jewish features, which bears Egyptian characters that have been translated "the king of Judah." Pharaoh-necho was met on his expedition against the Assyrians by Josiah, who was slain. 2 Kings 23:29, 30. Pharaoh-hophra aided Zedekiah, Jer. 37:5-11, so that the siege of Jerusalem was raised, but he appears to have been afterward attacked by Nebuchadnezzar. The sway of Egypt was checked and finally overcome by the superior power of Babylonia, and its entire territory in Asia was taken away. 2 Kings 24:7; Jer. 46:2. The books of the prophets contain many declarations concerning the wane and destruction of the Egyptian power, which have been remarkably fulfilled in its subsequent history. See Isa. 19; 20; 30:3; 31:3; 36:6; Jer. 2:36; 9:25, 26; 43:11-13; 44:30; 46; Ezek. 29; 30; 31; 32; Dan. 11:42; Joel 3:19; and "the sceptre of Egypt shall depart away." Zech. 10:11. In the New Testament there are several references to the relations of the Israelites to Egypt as they existed in Old Testament times; see Acts 2:10; 7:9-40; Heb. 3:16; 11:26, 27; but the interesting fact in the New Testament period was the flight of the holy family into Egypt, where the infant Jesus and his parents found a refuge from the cruel order of Herod the Great. Matt. 2:13-19. Among the various other allusions to Egypt in the Bible are those to its fertility and productions, Gen. 13:10; Ex. 16:3; Num. 11:5; to its mode of irrigation as compared with the greater advantages of Canaan, which had rain and was watered by natural streams, Deut. 11:10; its commerce with Israel and the people of western Asia, Gen. 37:25, 36; 1 Kings 10:28, 29; Ezek. 27:7; its armies equipped with chariots and horses, Ex. 14:7; Isa. 31:1; its learned men and its priests, Gen. 41:8; 47:22; Ex. 7:11; 1 Kings 4:30; its practice of embalming the dead, Gen. 50:3; its aversion to shepherds, and its sacrifices of cattle, Gen. 46:34; Ex. 8:26; how its people should be admitted into the Jewish Church, Deut. 23:7, 8; the warnings to Israel against any alliance with the Egyptians, Isa. 30:2; 36:6; Ezek. 17:15; 29:6; and to the towns of the country. Ezek. 30:13-18. The records on existing monuments have been found to confirm the accuracy of all these allusions to the customs of the people.

Ruins.—"Egypt is the monumental land of the earth," says Bunsen, "as the Egyptians are the monumental people of history." Among the most interesting ancient cities are: (*a*) On or Heliopolis, "the city of the sun," ten miles northeast of Cairo, where there was an obelisk of red granite 68 feet high, and erected previous to the visit of Abraham and Sarah to the land of the Pharaohs. Formerly the obelisks of Cleopatra stood here also, but were removed to Alexandria during the reign of Tiberius; and one of them now stands on the banks of the Thames, London, and another in Central Park, New York. Joseph was married at Heliopolis, Gen. 41:45, and there, according to Josephus, Jacob made his home; it was probably the place where Moses received his education, where Herodotus acquired most of his skill in writing history, and where Plato, the Greek philosopher, studied. (*b*) Thebes "of the hundred gates," one of the most famous cities of antiquity, is identified with No or No-Ammon of Scripture. Jer. 46:25; Ezek. 30:14-16; Nah. 3:8. The ruins are very extensive, and the city in its glory stretched over thirty miles along the banks of the Nile, covering the places now known as Luxor, Karnak, and Thebes. (*c*) Memphis, the Noph of Scripture. Jer. 46:19. "Nothing is left of its temples and monuments but a colossal statue of Rameses II., lying mutilated on the face in the mud." The temples at Karnak and Luxor are the most interesting, the grandest among them all being the magnificent temple of Rameses

II. There are ruins of temples at Denderah, Abydos, Philæ, Heliopolis, and at Ipsamboul, 170 miles south of Philæ, in Nubia. Among the noted tombs are those at Thebes, Beni-Hassan, and Osiout, and among the obelisks are those at Luxor, Karnak, Heliopolis, and Alexandria. In a cave near Thebes 39 royal mummies and various other objects were discovered in 1881. Among the mummies was that of Rameses II., the Pharaoh of the oppression, which has been fully described by Maspero. These wonderful ruins attest the magnificence and grandeur, but also the absolute despotism and slavery, of this land in the earliest ages and as far back as before the days of Abraham, and they also attest in the most impressive manner the fulfillment of prophecy. Over 2000 years it has been without "a prince of the land of Egypt," Ezek. 30:13; and "the basest of the kingdoms." Ezek. 29:15.

Ehud (*ĕ'hud*), *union*. 1. The second judge or judicial ruler of the Hebrews, who assassinated Eglon, and delivered them from the oppression which they had suffered for eighteen years under the Moabites. He was a Benjamite, strong, and left-handed. Judg. 3:12-30; 4:1. 2. A descendant of Benjamin. 1 Chron. 7:10; 8:6.

Ekron (*ĕk'ron*), *emigration*. The most northerly of the five cities of the Philistines, Josh. 13:3; in the lowlands of Judah, Josh. 15:11; conquered by Judah, Josh. 15:45; allotted to Dan, Josh. 19:43; reconquered by Samuel, 1 Sam. 5:10; 7:14; again a Philistine city, 1 Sam. 17:52; 2 Kings 1:2; Jer. 25:20; Amos 1:8; Zech. 9:5; now called *Akir*, on a hill 12 miles southeast of Joppa, a wretched village of about 50 mud hovels. The prophecy has been fulfilled, "Ekron shall be rooted up." Zeph. 2:4.

Elah (*ē'lah*), *terebinth*, **valley of**. 1. Where David slew Goliath. 1 Sam. 17:2, 19; 21:9. It is now called *Wady es-Sunt*, or "Acacia Valley," 14 miles southwest of Jerusalem. The valley is about a quarter of a mile wide, and has steep sides rising to a height of about 500 feet. The torrent or brook has a deep channel in the middle of the valley, and its course is strewn with smooth white stones. Terebinth trees, which gave the original title to the valley, are still found there. 2. The name of six persons in early biblical history.

Elam (*ē'lam*). 1. A country peopled by the descendants of Shem, and called, after his son, Elam. Gen. 10:22. It lay south of Assyria and west of Persia proper, and reached to the Persian Gulf. Herodotus called it Cissia. It was a province of Persia, of which Susa was capital. Ezra 4:9; Dan. 8:2. Elam was a strong power in Abram's time. Gen. 14:9. Its people aided in the destruction of Babylon, Isa. 21:2; invaded Israel, 22:6. Its destruction was foretold. Jer. 49:34-39; 25:25; Ezek. 32:24, 25. A remarkable statement illustrating the truth of the Scriptures in respect to Elam has been deciphered from Assyrian cylinders in the British Museum. 2. The name of six persons in the Old Testament.

Elath (*ē'lath*), *trees, a grove*, perhaps *terebinth-grove*. A city of Idumea, on the extremity of the eastern Gulf of the Red Sea, which is called from it *Sinus Elaniticus*—Elanitic Gulf, or the Gulf of Akabah. Deut. 2:8; 2 Kings 14:22; 16:6. The Edomites being subdued, 2 Sam. 8:14, David took possession of Elath or Eloth; and after him Solomon, whose fleet sailed from the neighboring town Ezion-geber to Ophir. 1 Kings 9:26; 2 Chron. 8:17, 18. It was again recovered by the Idumeans; and once more subdued by Uzziah, king of Judah; but Rezin, king of Syria, took it at length from the Jews, who seem never again to have recovered it. The site of Elath, the Ailah and Ælana of the Greeks and Romans, now consists of nothing but extensive mounds of rubbish, near the castle and village of *Akabah*.

Eldad (*ĕl'dăd*), *whom God loves*, meaning same as *Theophilus*. One of the 70 to whom the prophetical spirit of Moses was communicated. He with Medad did not go with the rest to the tabernacle, but prophesied in the camp. Joshua therefore begged Moses to forbid them. Num. 11:24-29.

Elder. We find the "eldest servant" of Abraham's house "ruling over all that he had," Gen. 24:2; we have also mention of "the elders of Joseph's house," and the "elders of the land of Egypt," Gen. 50:7, obviously indicating the chiefs of Joseph's establishment, and high Egyptian officers. Moses was desired to convey the divine message to "the elders of Israel," Ex. 3:16; and they were both to accompany him when he demanded freedom from Pharaoh, and also to be the means of communication between Moses and the mass of the people. Ex. 3:18; 4:29; 12:21. We are not told who these elders were, probably the leading persons in each tribe. We find them after the departure from Egypt, Ex. 17:6; 19:7; and from these, 70 were selected for special worship with Moses, Aaron, Nadab, and Abihu. Ex. 24:1, 2, 9-11. Moses had, at the suggestion of Jethro, appointed officers to administer justice, Ex. 18:26, but he seems to have required, further, a body of (if they may be so called) political advisers. Accordingly 70 out of the general class of elders were chosen, approved men; and on these the divine Spirit was especially poured. Num. 11:10-30. Possibly it was from this example that the Sanhedrin was afterwards constituted. There were "elders" of neighboring nations, synonymous with "princes," as of Moab and Midian, Num. 22:7, 13, and of the Hivites. Josh. 9:11. And we find the institution remaining in Israel through the whole history, under every change of government, and a certain authority exercised by them to which the people submitted. Sometimes they are mentioned as local magistrates, presiding over separate tribes or districts, and sometimes as the superior class, it is likely, acting generally for the nation. Deut. 19:12; 21:2, 3, 6; 31:28; Josh. 9:15, 18-21; 24:1; Judg. 2:7; 8:14; 11:5; 1 Sam. 4:3; 8:4; 16:4; 30:26; 2 Sam. 17:4; 19:11; 1 Kings 12:6; 20:8; 21:11; 2 Kings

10:1,5; 1 Chron. 21:16; Ezra 5:5; 6:7, 14; 10:8, 14; Jer. 29:1; Ezek. 8:1, 12. Those who locally administered justice are said to have been termed "elders of the gate," Prov. 31:23; Lam. 5:14; because that was the place where a court was often held. Ruth 4:2, 4, 9, 11. Elders are mentioned in Maccabean times, apparently distinct from the Sanhedrin, 1 Macc. 7:33; 12:6. In the New Testament history they are associated with the chief priests and scribes, but yet not to be confounded with them. Matt. 16:21; 21:23; 26:59; 27:41. And an analogous class yet subsists among Arab tribes, viz., their *sheikhs*, a word implying "old men." Officers of the Christian church are designated by elders, Acts 14:23; 20:17; and regulations are given in regard to them, 1 Tim. 5:1, 17, 19; the Greek word for elder being *presbuteros*. In every congregation of believers, as gathered by the apostles, a number of elders were ordained. Acts 14:23; 20:17; Titus 1:5. Their duty was to feed, oversee and look after the flock. They were called elders, overseers, or bishops, Acts 20:28; 1 Tim. 3:5; 1 Pet. 5:1, 3; Heb. 13:17, showing that their duties were similar. Titus 1:5, 7; Acts 20:28; Phil. 1:1. The injunction, "Let the elders that rule well be counted worthy of double honor, especially they who labor in the word and doctrine," shows, that the office, as ruler and teacher, is united. 1 Tim. 3:2; 5:17, Rom. 12:8; 1 Thess. 5:12, 13; 1 Pet. 5:2; Titus 1:9. They were local officers of congregations, sometimes called bishops or overseers. See Acts 20:17, 28; Titus 1:5 ff.; 1 Pet. 5:1. The distinction in Scripture between the teaching and the ruling elder is not very clear, unless it can be found in 1 Tim. 5:17.

Elealeh (*ē-le-ā'leh*), *whither God ascends*. A city east of Jordan; given to the Reubenites, Num. 32:3, 37; afterward possessed by Moab, Isa. 15:4; 16:9; Jer. 48:34; now *el-A'al*, "the high," one mile northeast of Heshbon.

Eleazar (*ē'le-ā'zar* or *e-lē'a-zar*), *whom God helps*. 1. The third son of Aaron. Ex. 6:23-25; 28:1. After the death of his brothers Nadab and Abihu, he was placed at the head of the Levites, Num. 3:32, and subsequently succeeded his father as high priest. Num. 20:28. He was then united with Moses in the divine communications, Num. 26:1, and with Joshua, who was solemnly inaugurated before him. Num. 27:18-23. Eleazar entered Canaan, and, in conjunction with Joshua, divided it among the tribes. Josh. 14:1; 17:4; 21:1. His death is mentioned, Josh. 24:33, but not the time of it; perhaps it was near that of Joshua. He was succeeded as high priest by his son Phinehas. 2. The son of Abinadab of Kirjath-jearim, "sanctified" or appointed to take charge of the ark after its restoration by the Philistines. 1 Sam. 7:1. 3. A son of Dodo, and one of David's chief warriors. 2 Sam. 23:9; 1 Chron. 11:12. 4. A Levite of the family of Merari, who had no sons, only daughters. 1 Chron. 23:21, 22; 24:28. 5. A Levite who helped to weigh the vessels that Ezra brought to Jerusalem. Ezra 8:33. 6. One who had married a foreign wife. Ezra 10:25. 7. A priest who took part in the dedication of the wall of Jerusalem. Neh. 12:42. 8. A person named among our Lord's ancestry. Matt. 1:15.

El-Elohe-Israel (*ĕl'e-lō'he-ĭz-ra-el*), *God, the God of Israel*. The name bestowed by Jacob on the altar which he erected facing the city of Shechem. Gen. 33:19, 20.

Eli (*ē'li*), *summit, the highest*, according to some, *adopted of the Lord*. A noted high priest and judge of Israel. He was of the family of Ithamar, Aaron's youngest son; for his descendant Ahimelech or Abiathar, 1 Sam. 14:3; 22:20; 2 Sam. 8:17, is expressly said to be of that house. 1 Chron. 24:3. We do not know how or when the high priesthood passed from Eleazar's family to that of Ithamar; but because of Eli's sin in not restraining his ungodly sons, it reverted again to the elder line. 1 Sam. 2; 22-25; 1 Kings 2:35. With the exception of this great fault, of which he was repeatedly warned, Eli appears to have been a holy man. To him was committed the charge of Samuel the prophet when a child. And his anxiety for the ark of God, carried with the Israelitish army to battle, is graphically depicted in the sacred history. He sat watching for news in the open road; and when he heard the disastrous intelligence, the death of his two sons, and, worst of all, the capture of the ark by the Philistines, he who could have borne the desolation of his own house sank down in grief, and his neck brake, and he died. He was 98 years old, and had judged Israel 40 years; some of these years probably including the time of Samuel. 1 Sam. 1-4. Part of the fulfillment of the threatening against Eli's house is noted in 1 Kings 2:27.

Eliab (*e-lī'ab*), *to whom God is father*. The eldest son of Jesse, 1 Sam. 17:13, and a man of angry and envious temper, as appears from his treatment of his brother David. There are in all six persons of this name mentioned in the Bible.

Eliakim (*e-lī'a-kim*), *whom God establishes*. 1. The master of the household of Hezekiah, and one of the commissioners appointed to treat with the king of Assyria. 2 Kings 18:18, 26, 37; 19:2; Isa. 22:20; 36:3, 11, 22; 37:2. 2. The son and successor of Josiah, king of Judah. His name was changed to Jehoiakim. 2 Kings 23:34; 2 Chron. 36:4. There are five persons of this name mentioned in the Bible.

Eliezer (*ē'li-ē'zer*). To whom God is help. Gen. 15:2. A name which occurs 11 times in the Old Testament. The most distinguished person who bore it was Abraham's steward and confidential servant. Compare Gen. 24:2.

Elihu (*e-lī'hu* or *ĕl'i-hū*), *whose God is He*, i. e., *Jehovah*. 1. The Buzite, a friend of Job, and, perhaps, the arbitrator between him and his three acquaintances who had come to sympathize with him in his calamities. The soothing, yet faithful and honest, discourse of Elihu is finely contrasted with the sharp and severe language of the other three; and especially are his wisdom, piety, and benevolence admirable, when we consider his youth, and the character and standing of those whom he addressed. Job 32-37. Four other persons of the same name are mentioned in the old Testament.

Elijah (*e-lī'jah*), *my God is Jehovah*. 1. That most renowned prophet of Israel who, with no introduction as to his birth or parentage, or even account of the divine commission given to him, bursts forth in sacred story as the stern denouncer of judgment on apostate Israel, and who, after his marvelous course of miracle and bold vindication of God's authority, is translated without tasting death. He first appears as a messenger from God to Ahab, the wicked king of Israel, probably in the tenth year of his reign. He was sent to prophesy three years' drought in the land of Israel. After delivering this startling and distressing prophecy, he was directed to flee to the brook Cherith, where he was miraculously fed by ravens. When the brook had dried up he was sent to a widow woman of Zarephath, and again the hand of the Lord supplied his wants and those of his friends. He raised the widow's son to life. 1 Kings 17. After the famine had lasted the predicted period, Elijah encountered Ahab, and then ensued the magnificent display of divine power and of human trust upon the ridge of Carmel. 1 Kings 18. See **Ahab**. The reaction from such a mental strain left the prophet in a weak, nervous condition, and in a fit of despondency he fled from Jezebel into the "wilderness" and desired death. In Mount Sinai the downcast man of God was witness of Jehovah's strength and experienced Jehovah's tenderness in a very remarkable vision. 1 Kings 19:9-18. He anointed Elisha to be prophet in his room. 1 Kings 19. He then retired into privacy, but after the dastardly murder of Naboth he suddenly appeared before the guilty king and announced the judgment of Jehovah against the royal pair. 1 Kings 21. Several years after occurred the prophecy of Ahaziah's death. 2 Kings 1:1-4. See **Ahaziah**. The slaughter by fire of the two companies of troops sent to take Elijah must have greatly increased the popular awe of the prophet. Elijah was translated to heaven in a miraculous manner. 2 Kings 2. The character of Elijah made a deep impression upon the Jews. He was expected to return to earth as the forerunner of Messiah; an expectation encouraged by the remarkable prophecy, Mal. 4:5, 6, already referred to. The prophecy was indeed fulfilled, but not in the way they imagined. John Baptist, though not personally Elijah, John 1:21, was to go before the Messiah in the spirit and power of the ancient prophet, Luke 1:17; and thus our Lord himself explained the matter to his disciples, Matt. 17:10-13. There was, it is true, a personal appearance of Elijah with Moses, when the two in glory stood beside the transfigured Saviour on the holy mount, and talked with him of his coming death— a proof how both the law and the prophets pointed to a Redeemer suffering ere he was triumphant. Matt. 17:1-8; Mark 9:2-8; Luke 9:28-36. There are those who believe that the prediction of Elijah's coming has not yet had its full accomplishment; and they expect, before the second appearing of the Lord, that the old stern prophet of Gilead, who never died, will tread the earth again. Such a question, however, cannot be discussed here.

Elisabeth (*e-liz'a-beth*), *God her oath*, that is, *worshipper of God*. The wife of Zacharias, and mother of John the Baptist. She was of a priestly family, and also the cousin of the Virgin Mary. She is described as being, with her husband, a person of piety, "walking in all the commandments and ordinances of the Lord blameless." Luke 1:5-66.

Elisha (*e-lī'shah*), *God his salvation*. A distinguished prophet of Israel and successor of Elijah. The acts of his earlier ministry are related at considerable length. He is first mentioned as the son of Shaphat, the agriculturist of Abel-meholah in the valley of the Jordan. While occupied in guiding the plow he received the call of Elijah, and appears ever after to have attended on him. 1 Kings 19:16, 19-21; 2 Kings 3:11. How deep the affection was with which he regarded his master, the narrative of Elijah's last days on earth sufficiently testifies. At his translation Elisha asked a double portion of the departing prophet's spirit, secured his falling mantle, and had speedily full proof that the Lord God of Elijah was with him. 2 Kings 2:1-15. Elisha, though a young man, was bald. The young persons mocked at the great miracle just performed. Why should not the bald head go up after his master? the world would be well rid of both. Such profanity must have an instant significant punishment. And at the word of the prophet, speaking in God's name, she-bears destroyed a number of these mockers. 2 Kings 2:23-25. Many would hear and fear, and learn to reverence God's ambassador. He was the counsellor and friend of successive kings. He was the opposite to Elijah in most things. He lived in the city or with his students, honored and sought for, a welcome guest in the homes he graced by his presence. And yet he was filled with a "double"—*i. e.*, an elder brother's—portion of Elijah's spirit, both to work miracles and to give counsel for present and future emergencies. He multiplied the widow's oil, 2 Kings 4:5-8, and when the son of the good Shunammite—God's reward to her for her kindness to his prophet—died, he raised him to life. 2 Kings 4:8-37. He cured Naaman, smote Gehazi with leprosy, misled the Syrians, foretold abundant food, and when dying gave the king the promise of victory. 2 Kings 5 to 8. But God would still put honor on his servant. He was buried, and afterwards, when Moabite bands were ravaging the country, and some one was to be carried to the tomb, the attendants, surprised by the spoilers, hastily thrust the corpse into Elisha's sepulchre. But no sooner had it touched the great prophet's bones than the dead man lived again. 2 Kings 13:20, 21. Truly, by all these wondrous works it was abundantly proved that there was a God in Israel.

Embalming. A process by which dead bodies are preserved from decay. When Jacob died in Egypt, "Joseph commanded his servants, the physicians, to embalm his father, for burial in Canaan." The process occupied forty days. Joseph also was himself embalmed, that his body might be carried with the children of Israel when they left Egypt for Palestine. Gen. 50:2, 3, 26. It does not appear that the Hebrews practiced the mode of embalming of the Egyptians. Still some partial process was employed, tending to soothe the surviving friends by arresting or delaying natural corruption. Thus Asa was laid in a bed "filled with sweet odors and divers kinds of spices prepared by the apothecaries' art." 2 Chron. 16:14. Also the women who had followed Jesus "bought sweet spices, that they might come and anoint him," Mark 16:1; Luke 23:56; and Nicodemus "brought a mixture of myrrh and aloes," and "wound" the body "in linen clothes with the spices, as the manner of the Jews is to bury." John 19:39, 40. In some instances, too, the later Jews embalmed a body in honey, after having covered it with wax. See *Bissell, Bib. Antiq.*

Emerald. Perhaps the glowing. A very precious gem of a pure green color, to which it owes its chief value, as the deepest colors are the most esteemed. Ex. 28:18; Ezek. 27:16; 28:13. The emerald was anciently obtained from Egypt. Probably it corresponds to the carbuncle.

Emerods. 1 Sam. 5:6, 9. R. V. "tumours." The name of a painful disease sent upon the Philistines; probably it resembled the modern disease of the bleeding piles. It was customary with the heathens to offer to their gods figures of wax or metal representing the parts which had been cured of disease, whence it is inferred, in connection with 1 Sam. 6:5, that the priests and diviners of the Philistines recommended a similar course.

Emims (ĕ'mimz), R. V. "the Emim" (ĕ'mim), *terrors.* A race of giants living east of the Dead Sea; related to the Anakim. Gen. 14:5; Deut. 2:10, 11.

Emmanuel. See **Immanuel.**

Emmaus (em-mā'us or ĕm'ma-ŭs), *hot springs.* A village near Jerusalem, where two disciples entertained Jesus after his resurrection. Luke 24:13. Its site has been disputed; among the places suggested are: 1. *'Amwâs,* on the plain of Philistia, 22 miles from Jerusalem and 10 miles from Lydda. 2. *Kuryet el 'Enab,* by Robinson, 3 hours from Jerusalem, on the road to Jaffa. 3. *Kŭlônieh,* 2 leagues or 4½ miles west of Jerusalem. 4. *Urtâs,* a poor village about 2 miles southwest of Bethlehem. 5. In the fourteenth century Emmaus was placed at *Kubeibeh,* a little over 7 miles northwest of Jerusalem.

Endor (ĕn'dôr or ĕn'dor), *spring of Dor.* A place in Issachar, possessed by Manasseh, Josh. 17:11, where Sisera and Jabin were slain, Ps. 83:9, 10, and where Saul consulted the witch. 1 Sam. 28:7. It is now a miserable village called *Endôr,* about 6½ miles from Jezreel.

Engedi (ĕn-gĕ'dĭ or ĕn'ge-dī), *fountain of the kid.* A place in Judah, on the west side of the Dead Sea, Josh. 15:62; Ezek. 47:10, about midway between its northern and southern ends. En-gedi was first called Hazazon-tamar, Gen. 14:7; 2 Chron. 20:2; it was David's hiding-place from Saul, 1 Sam. 23:29; 24:1; and where David cut off the skirt of Saul's robe, 24:4; its vineyards are mentioned, Song of Sol. 1:14; now called 'Ain Jidy.

Enoch (ē'nok), *initiating* or *initiated, i. e., dedicated.* 1. A son of Cain. Gen. 4:17, 18. 2. One of the most eminent of the antediluvian patriarchs, the son of Jared and father of Methuselah. He has this remarkable testimony, "that he walked with God;" an expression denoting near communion with the Lord, and conformity to his will. And "he was not; for God took him," that is, like Elijah in subsequent times, "he was translated that he should not see death." His life was, for the period in which he lived, a short one upon earth, 365 years; but it was a life of faith, pleasing in the eye of his Maker. Gen. 4:18-24; Luke 3:37; Heb. 11:5. Jude cites a prophecy of Enoch. Heb. 14. In 1 Chron. 1:3, Enoch is called Hanoch.

Enon, or **Ænon** (ē'non), *springs.* A place near Salim where John was baptizing. John 3:23. Three sites have been proposed for it: 1. The traditional one, by Jerome, about 8 miles south of Beisan; not confirmed by later authorities. 2. In Wady Fârah, 5 miles northeast of Jerusalem. 3. The more probable site is east of Nablûs, near the village Sâlim, where there are copious springs.

En-rogel (ĕn'rō'gel), *fountain of the fuller.* A spring near Jerusalem. Josh. 15:7; 18:16; 2 Sam. 17:17, 21; 1 Kings 1:9. Some place it at the "well of Job," in the valley of Hinnom. M. Ganneau would identify it with the Fountain of the Virgin.

Epaphroditus (e-păf'ro-dī'tus), *Venus-like, beautiful.* A Christian who was sent from Philippi with contributions for Paul, while prisoner at Rome. There he was sick; and a delightful view is afforded of the apostle's tenderness of spirit by the way in which he speaks of one so dear to himself, and to the Philippian believers. Phil. 2:25-30; 4:18. He was the bearer of the epistle to Philippi. Some have imagined that he was identical with Epaphras, because the one name is a contracted form of the other; but we have no sufficient grounds for such a conclusion.

Ephah. See **Measures.**

Ephesians (e-fē'zhanz). The citizens of Ephesus. Acts 19:28. The Epistle to the Ephesians was written by Paul to the Christians at Ephesus. The church in that renowned city was established and built up under Paul's ministry, Acts 18:19, 21; 19, during the years 54-57 A. D. This letter was written by the apostle about A. D. 62, while he was in prison at Rome, and forwarded by Tychicus, a beloved brother and faithful minister. Eph. 6: 21. While other epistles of Paul were evidently called forth by the circumstances of the church to which they were addressed, this epistle is of a general character, and was intended for a number of congregations in Asia Minor. The main doctrinal thought of the epistle is the church in Christ Jesus, the eternal principles of her life, her unity of many members, her warfare and her victory, her steady growth and her glorious end. Hence, in the hortatory portion or last three chapters, he urges the duty of preserving unity, and makes the relation of Christ to his church and of the church to Christ the ideal standard of the domestic relation between man and wife and parents and children.

Ephesus (*ĕf'e-sŭs*). The commercial city of Asia Minor, "one of the eyes of Asia." It stood upon the south side of a plain, with mountains on three sides and the sea on the west. The river Cayster ran across the plain. Paul visited Ephesus on his second tour, Acts 18:19–21; Apollos was instructed there by Aquila and Priscilla, Acts 18:24–26; Paul dwelt there three years, Acts 19; charged the elders of the church, Acts 20: 16–28; the angel of the church of Ephesus is named in Rev. 2:1-7. The city is now desolate: the ruins of the stadium and theatre remain.

Ephod. A vestment appropriated to the high priest. Ex. 28:4–35. See **High Priest**. An ephod is said to have been worn by Samuel, 1 Sam. 2:18, by the ordinary priests, 1 Sam. 22:18, and by David, 2 Sam. 6:14; 1 Chron. 15:27; but this vesture differed from the high priest's, both in the extraordinary ornaments of the latter, and also in the material. The linen of the high priest's ephod is described by another and peculiar word. When idolatrous worship was set up, ephods were sometimes made for it. Judg. 8:27; 17:5; 18:14, 17, 18, 20.

Ephraim (*ē'fra-ĭm*), *double land, two-fold increase, very fruitful*. The second son of Joseph, born in Egypt before the famine, Gen. 41:50-52, and therefore upwards of 20 at Jacob's death. Joseph, when he was apprised of his father's sickness, was anxious to obtain the recognition of his sons Manasseh and Ephraim. Jacob adopted them as patriarchs, or heads of tribes, equally with his own sons. But he placed the younger, Ephraim, before the elder, Manasseh, "guiding his hands wittingly," in spite of Joseph's remonstrance, and prophetically declaring that the posterity of Ephraim should be far greater and more powerful than the posterity of Manasseh. Gen. 48. The territory of Ephraim lay in the centre of Canaan, south of Manasseh and north of Benjamin and Dan, extending from the Jordan to the Mediterranean Sea. It was about 55 miles long, and about 30 miles in its greatest breadth. It was well watered and fertile, fulfilling the blessing of Moses in Deut. 33:13–16.

Ephraim, Gate of. One of the gates of ancient Jerusalem, 2 Kings 14:13; 2 Chron. 25:23; Neh. 8:16; 12:39; probably on the north side, as the present Damascus gate is.

Ephraim, Mount. A name applied to the hill-country of Ephraim, extending from Bethel to the plain of Jezreel; called also the "mountains of Israel," R. V. "hill country of Israel," Josh. 11:21, and "mountains of Samaria." Jer. 31:5, 6; Amos 3:9.

Ephraim, Wood of. A forest in which the great battle was fought when Absalom was killed. 2 Sam. 18:6. It lay east of the Jordan, in Gilead, near Mahanaim. Thick woods of oaks and terebinths still exist in that region.

Ephratah (*ĕf'ra-tah*, or *e-frā'tah*), or **Ephrath** (*ĕf'rath*, or *ē'frath*), *fruitful*. 1. Second wife of Caleb, the son of Hezron, mother of Hur and grandmother of Caleb, the spy, according to 1 Chron. 2:19, 50, and probably 24, and 4:4. B. C. 1695. 2. The ancient name of Bethlehem-judah. Gen. 35:16, 19; 48:7.

Epicureans (*ĭp'ĭ-kū-rē'anz*, or *ĭp'ĭ-kū're-anz*). A sect of philosophers which derived its origin from Epicurus, of Athenian descent, but born in Samos 341 B. C. He lived much in Athens, where he had a garden in which he delivered his lessons to his disciples; he died 270 B. C. In his ethics Epicurus denied that there was a creator of the world; still he believed that there were gods, to be worshipped for the excellence of their nature: they lived in quiet, and did not interfere with the government of the universe. He made good and evil depend on the increasing of pleasure and diminishing of pain, or the reverse; esteeming the pleasures and pains of the mind superior to those of the body, so that a happy life must be a virtuous life. The soul, he taught, was indissolubly connected with the body. Hence it will be seen that the dogmas of Epicureanism were strongly in opposition to the truths of the gospel. Consequently the Epicureans at Athens, though differing from the Stoics in the rejection of absolute destiny, and on other points, yet equally with them ridiculed the doctrines of Paul. Acts 17:18.

Erastus (*e-răs'tus*), *amiable*. A Christian chamberlain or treasurer of Corinth. Acts 19:22; Rom. 16:23; 2 Tim. 4:20. It is impossible to say whether these references all belong to the same person.

Erech (*ē'rek*), *enduring*. A city of Nimrod. Gen. 10:10. Its people are called Archevites and noticed in connection with the Babylonians. Ezra 4:9. Jerome identifies Erech with Edessa, in Mesopotamia; others identify it with Orchoe or Orech of the Greek and Roman geographers. It corresponded to modern Warka, about 120 miles southeast of Babylon.

Esar-haddon (*ē'sar-hăd'don*), son and successor of Sennacherib, king of Assyria, and one of the greatest of her kings. 2 Kings 19:37. He was the builder of magnificent structures, including three palaces and thirty temples. His reign extended from B.C. 680 to 667, and during it Manasseh, the king of Judah, was taken prisoner by his captains and carried before him at Babylon, and kept a captive for some time. 2 Chron. 33:11.

Esau (*ē'saw*), or **Edom** (*ē'dom*), Son of

Isaac and Rebecca, and twin brother of Jacob. Gen. 25:25; 36:1. The most important events of his life are intimately connected with the life of Jacob. See **Jacob**. His family settled on Mount Seir, east of Jordan, which was hence called Edom, and his descendants were the Edomites, one of the most powerful and formidable nations of that age. The prophecies concerning Esau and Edom have been literally fulfilled. His family has become extinct, "cut off forever," so that there is none "remaining of the house of Esau," Obad. 18; Jer. 49:17; Ezek. 25:13, and "the things of Esau" have been "so searched out and his hidden things sought up," Obad. 6, "that not a relic can be found in their ancient dwellings." See **Edom**.

Eshcol (*ĕsh'kŏl*), *bunch*, or *cluster*, **Valley of**. A valley in the land of Canaan. Num. 13:23, 24; 32:9; Deut. 1:24. It was in the southern part of this land where Van Lennep found clusters of grapes 19 inches in length, and it is said that bunches weighing from 12 to 20 pounds are still found in southern Palestine.

Esther (*ĕs'tẽr*), *a star, the planet Venus*. A Hebrew maiden, the daughter of Abihail, of the tribe of Benjamin. At the death of her father and mother she was adopted by her cousin Mordecai, the descendant of a Jew who had been carried away captive with Jehoiachin. Mordecai resided at Shushan, or Susa. See **Mordecai**. On the repudiation of Vashti, Ahasuerus, king of Persia, ordered a large number of young virgins to be collected throughout his realm, and brought into his harem. Esther (her Persian name was Hadassah) was distinguished among these, and was chosen to bear the title of queen. By her influence the plot of Haman to destroy the Jews was frustrated. Haman was hanged. The Jews revenged themselves on their foes, and Mordecai was advanced to a high place in the empire. It was common with Persian kings to have many wives, and Esther was one of these.

Esther, the Book of. This book is so termed because Esther is the principal character in it, and not from any notion that she wrote it. It has generally been held in high estimation among the Jews, who class it with Ruth, Ecclesiastes, Solomon's Song, and the Lamentations, as the five megilloth or rolls, and solemnly read it at the feast of Purim. Its literary character is fully equal to the best of the other historical books of the Bible. The style is lively and almost dramatic. But the peculiarity of the book is that the name of God does not occur in any form. The omission was probably intentional, and in order to permit the reading of Esther at the joyous, even hilarious, festival of Purim, without irreverence. The language of the book contains several Persian words, translated "satrap," "post," "edict," "royal" (not "camel;" 8:10, and 14 read "swift steeds that were used in the king's service, bred of the stud," R. V.), "cotton," "crown," "nobles," "a copy," and "lot." The circumstantial minuteness of detail, the vividness of the portraits, the Persian words, and the whole tone of the book indicate that the author was a Jew who lived about the time of the events recorded, at the court of Persia, where he had access to the official documents of the kingdom. Rawlinson assigns the book to a period from 20 to 30 years after Xerxes's death, B.C. 444-434.

Etam (*ē'tam*), **the Rock**. The place of Samson's retreat after the slaughter of the Philistines. Judg. 15:8, 11. Conder locates it at Beit 'Atâb, a little north of Eshu'a (Eshtaol), which he thinks fully meets all the requisites of the case. It has clefts, caves, and a rock tunnel which would so effectually conceal one that those not acquainted with the place might not find him, nor even the entrance to the tunnel, except by accident.

Ethiopia (*ē'thi-ō'pi-ah*), *burnt-faces*. Called Cush by the Hebrews, a country south of Egypt. Ezek. 29:10. In the Scriptures "Ethiopia" usually refers to the region extending from Egypt southward beyond the junction of the White and Blue Nile. This was Seba, Isa. 43:3, and known to the Romans as the kingdom of Meroe. The country is rolling and mountainous, the elevation increasing toward the south, until it reaches a height of about 8000 feet in Abyssinia. Frequent notices of this country and its people are found in the Bible. It was settled by the children of Ham, Gen. 10:6, dark-skinned men of stature. Jer. 13:23; Isa. 45:14. They were selected as members of royal households. Jer. 38:7-13. The treasurer of its queen, Candace, was baptized by Philip. Acts 8:27-38. It is noticed in connection with Egypt, Isa. 20:4; 43:3; 45:14; with Libya (Phut), Jer. 46:9; Lydia and Chub (Lub and Lud), Ezek. 30:5, and the Sukkiim. 2 Chron. 12:3. Moses married an Ethiopian, Num. 12:1; Ethiopians were in Shishak's army, 2 Chron. 12:3; Zerah, an Ethiopian king, had an army of a million soldiers, 2 Chron. 14:9-12; Job mentioned the precious stones of Ethiopia, Job 28:19; the Israelites were familiar with the merchandise of that country, Isa. 45:14; and Isaiah foretold the subjugation of Ethiopia by the Assyrians. Isa. 20:4, 5. Among the Assyrian inscriptions of Assurbanipal, now in the British Museum, George Smith deciphered several which especially illustrate and confirm the fulfillment of this prophecy. Among other prophecies in respect to Ethiopia are Ps. 68:31; 87:4; Isa. 45:14; Ezek. 30:4-9; Dan. 11:43; Hab. 3:7; Zeph. 2:12; Nah. 3:8-10. The Romans in the reign of Augustus Cæsar, B.C. 22, defeated Candace, queen of Ethiopia, and made the country tributary to Rome. Candace was an official title of the queens, one of whom is named in Acts 8:27.

Eunuch. 2 Kings 9:32; Esther 2:3; Acts 8:27. In the strict and proper sense eunuchs were the persons who had charge of the bed-chambers in palaces and larger houses. But as the jealous and dissolute temperament of the East required this charge to be in the hands of persons who had been deprived of their virility, the word eunuch came naturally to denote persons in that condition. But as some of these rose to be confidential advisers of their royal masters or mistresses, the word was occasionally employed to denote persons in such a position, without indicating anything respecting their manhood. The word "eunuch" is employed by Christ, Matt. 19:12, in various senses to designate: 1. Those who are naturally incapacitated; 2. Those who have been mutilated; 3. Those who voluntarily abstain from marriage in order to devote themselves more exclusively to the interests of the kingdom of God.

Euphrates (*eū-frā'tēz*), *the abounding*. A noted river, the largest in western Asia; rises in Armenia in two sources. Its whole length is 1780 miles. It is navigable for large ships to Bassora, 70 miles above its mouth; a steamer drawing four feet of water has ascended to Bir, 1197 miles. It flows in a broad, deep current, filled to the level of its banks, and at Babylon is considerably less than a mile in width. For the last 800 miles of its course it does not receive a single tributary. The Tigris flows in a narrower channel, with deeper banks and a less rapid current. The country between the two rivers slopes toward the Tigris, and thus greatly favors the draining off of the superfluous waters of the Euphrates. In Scripture the Euphrates is named as one of the rivers of Eden, Gen. 2:14; called "the great river," Gen. 15:18; Deut. 1:7; noted as the eastern boundary of the Promised Land, Deut. 11:24; Josh. 1:4; 1 Chron. 5:9; and of David's conquests, 2 Sam. 8:3; 1 Chron. 18:3; of those of Babylon from Egypt, 2 Kings 24:7; is referred to in prophecy, Jer. 13:4-7; 46:2-10; 51:63; and in Rev. 9:14; 16:12. In upward of 26 other passages it is spoken of as "the river." By this stream the captive Jews wept. Ps. 137:1. It is now called the Frat by the natives.

Euroclydon (*eū-rŏk'ly-dŏn*), R. V. "Euraquilo." Acts 27:14. A very tempestuous wind on the Mediterranean, now known under the name of a "Levanter." It blows from all points, and its danger results from its violence and the uncertainty of its course.

Evangelist. One who brings good tidings. One who travels as a missionary everywhere and from house to house to teach and preach Jesus Christ. Eph. 4:11; Acts 21:8; 2 Tim. 4:5; Acts 5:42; 8:4, 35, 40, etc. The "work of an evangelist," 2 Tim. 4:5, seems to have been specially the carrying of the gospel-message to persons and places previously unacquainted with it. Hence, one bearing another office might be an evangelist. Thus Philip, "one of the seven," is called an "evangelist." Acts 21:8. Evangelists are distinguished from "pastors and teachers," and placed before them in Eph. 4:11, as being itinerant; whereas pastors and teachers belonged more to a settled church: they are omitted in the list of 1 Cor. 12:28; because no reference was there made to missionary extension of the church, but rather to its internal organization. Eusebius speaks of evangelists as both preaching Christ and circulating the record of the holy gospels. Hence, probably, the ordinary usage of the word evangelists to denote the writers of the four Gospels.

Eve (*ēve*), *life*. The wife of Adam, and mother of mankind. Her formation, her yielding to the tempter, and inducing Adam to join her in disobedience to the divine command, the promise in respect to her seed, and the names she imposed on three of her sons, indicating her expectations and feeling in regard to them, are narrated in Gen. 2, 3, 4. See also 2 Cor. 11:3; 1 Tim. 2:13, 14.

Evening, Ps. 55:17, **Even-tide,** Gen. 24:63. The Hebrews reckoned two evenings, one commencing at sunset and embracing the period of twilight, and the other commencing at dark. Some suppose that the first evening commenced as early as 3 o'clock in the afternoon, and the second at sunset. It was in the interval between the two evenings, at whichever of these periods it occurred, that the passover was to be killed and the daily sacrifice offered. See marginal reading of Ex. 12:6; Num. 9:3; 28:4. "Even-tide" is the same with "evening-time."

Evil-merodach (*ē'vil-me-rō'dak*), *Merodach's fool*. But perhaps some name of Persian or Assyrian origin underlies this. The son and successor of Nebuchadnezzar. He reigned two years, 561-559 B.C., and was murdered by Nergal-sharezer or Neriglissar, who had married his sister, and who seized his crown. He treated Jehoiachin with kindness; and possibly his mildness of rule may have given opportunity to the treason which cut him off. 2 Kings 25:27-30; Jer. 52:31-34. But some authorities report him to have been luxurious and intemperate.

Exodus (*ĕx'o-dŭs*), *going out* [of Egypt]. The second book in the Old Testament. Its author was Moses. It was written probably during the forty years' wanderings in the wilderness. The first part of the book gives an account of the great increase of Jacob's posterity in the land of Egypt, and their oppression under a new dynasty, which occupied the throne after the death of Joseph; the birth, education, flight and return of Moses; the attempts to prevail upon Pharaoh to let the Israelites go; the signs and wonders, ending in the death of the first-born, by means of which the deliverance of Israel from the land of bondage is at length accomplished, the institution of the passover, and the departure out of Egypt and the journey of the Israelites to Mount Sinai. The second part gives a sketch of the early history of Israel as a nation, set apart, and in its religious and political life consecrated to the service of God.

Exodus, the. The departure of the Israelites from Egypt. The Exodus was the execution of a divine plan. God sent ten plagues upon Egypt in punishment for enslaving the Israelites. "And Pharaoh rose up in the night, he and all his servants, and all the Egyptians; and there was a great cry in Egypt, for there was not a house where there was not one dead." Then followed the midnight call of Pharaoh for Moses and Aaron, the command to depart, and the actual leaving of the house of bondage. There are two prominent theories about the locality and mode of the miraculous passage of the Israelites through the Red Sea: 1. The usual theory, which locates the passage several miles south of Suez, where the sea is about ten miles broad. This theory fits in best with the literal meaning of the narrative, for in this case the waters must have been actually divided for several miles, and have flowed back on either hand. But the difficulties the view raises are more numerous than those it solves. 2. The second theory puts the crossing at the head of the gulf, near or some distance north of Suez. In Moses's time the gulf may have extended as a reedy marsh as far as the Bitter Lakes. The crossing was made possible by a special providence and a miraculous adaptation of the laws of nature. The east or rather northeast wind drove off the waters from the small arm of the sea which runs up by Suez; this would leave the water on the more northern part of the arm, so that there would be water on both sides to serve as an entrenchment. This would meet the exigences of the narrative. Ex. 14:22. But even in this case the passage of two millions of people, with all their cattle, was a great miracle. It has its counterpart in the crossing of the river Jordan at the end of the journey through the wilderness.

Eye, Eyes. The practice of putting out the eyes as a mode of punishment has been in both ancient and modern times very common in the East. Captives in war, and those who might be supposed likely to head rebellions against the sovereign were frequently thus treated. Judg. 16:21; 1 Sam. 11:2; 2 Kings 25:7. The painting of the eye was and is usual among Eastern women. This was what Jezebel did, 2 Kings 9; 30, marg., R. V. "painted her eyes;" comp. Jer. 4:30; Ezek. 23:40. A peculiar brilliancy is imparted to the eye, and a languishing, amorous cast given to the whole countenance. The eyelids and eyebrows are thus painted with what is called *kôhl.* "The powder from which kôhl is made is collected from burning almond-shells, or frankincense, and is intensely black. Antimony and various ores of lead are also employed. The powder is kept in vials or pots, which are often disposed in a handsomely worked cover or case; and it is applied to the eye by a small probe of wood, ivory or silver, which is called *meel,* while the whole apparatus is named *mik-hûly.*"

Ezekiel (*e-zē'ki-el*), *the strength of God.* A prophet who was taken captive eleven years before the destruction of Jerusalem. He was a member of a community of Jewish exiles who settled on the banks of the Chebar, a "river" of Babylonia. He began to prophesy B. C. 595, and continued until B. C. 573, a period of more than 22 years. He was married and had a house, Ezek. 8: 1; 24:18, in his place of exile, and lost his wife by a sudden and unforeseen stroke. He was esteemed by his companions in exile, and their elders consulted him on all occasions. He is reputed to have been murdered in Babylon, and his tomb, said to have been built by Jehoiachin, is shown, a few days' journey from Bagdad. Ezekiel was noted for his stern and inflexible energy of will and character and his devoted adherence to the rites and ceremonies of his national religion.

The Book of Ezekiel.—The book of his prophecy is divided into parts, of which the destruction of Jerusalem is the turning-point. Chapters 1-24 contain predictions delivered before that event, and chaps. 25-48 after it, as we see from chap. 26:2. Again chaps. 1-32 are mainly occupied with correction, denunciation and reproof, while the remainder deal chiefly in consolation and promise. A parenthetical section in the middle of the book, chaps. 25-32, contains a group of prophecies against *seven* foreign nations, the septenary arrangement being apparently intentional. There are no direct quotations from Ezekiel in the New Testament, but in the Apocalypse there are many parallels and obvious allusions to the later chapters.

Ezion-gaber (*ē'zi-on-gā'ber*), or **geber** (*gē-ber*), *giant's backbone.* A city on the Red Sea, the last station of the Israelites before they came to the wilderness of Zin, Num. 33:35; Deut. 2:8; the station of Solomon's navy, 1 Kings 9:26; 2 Chron. 8:17, and of Jehoshaphat's navy. 1 Kings 22:48. Probably it was at 'Ain el-Ghudyán, about ten miles up what is now the dry bed of the Arabah. Kiepert and Robinson suppose that the northern end of the gulf anciently flowed up to this point.

Ezra (*ĕz'rah*), *help.* 1. A descendant of Judah. 1 Chron. 4:17. 2. A Jewish priest and scholar who lived in Babylon during the reign of Artaxerxes Longimanus, over whom he had such influence that in his seventh year he obtained permission to lead a large company of persons and go to Jerusalem, B.C. 457. Ezra 7. In Jerusalem he carried through the reforms he had intended, particularly the separation of the "strange wives." Ezra 10. With an account of this important measure the book of Ezra ends. The next notice of him is in Neh. 8:1. Nehemiah was governor when Ezra entered Jerusalem the second time; accordingly, Ezra attended only to priestly duties, such as teaching. Neh. 8: 1. It is unknown when he died. Jewish tradition makes him the founder of the great synagogue, the collector of the books of the Bible, the introducer of the Chaldee character instead of the old Hebrew, the author of Chronicles, Ezra, and Nehemiah, and lastly, the originator of synagogue worship. And it is very likely that he was the author of these changes, or at all events that they occurred in his time. The book of Ezra covers about 79 years, and should be read in connection with the prophecies of Haggai and Zechariah. It contains (1) chaps. 1-6, an account of the return of

50,000 Jews under Zerubbabel in the first year of Cyrus, the rebuilding of the temple, and the interference of the Samaritans; (2) chaps. 7-10, the history of Ezra's immigration and his reforms, particularly in regard to the strange wives. The book of Ezra is written in Chaldee from chap. 4:8 to 6:19, narrating the attempt of the Samaritans to hinder the building of the temple, and from the beginning of chap. 7 to the 27th verse. The people recently returned from the captivity were more conversant with the Chaldee than even with the Hebrew tongue. Ezra is the author of at least the greater part of the book. The date may be given as B. C. 456.

F

Face. Most of the combinations into which this word enters are intelligible enough. It may be observed that, as to seek any one's face is to seek his favor, or admission to his presence, Ps. 27:8; Prov. 7:15, so to see his face is to see him in person, Gen. 48:11, to have entrance to his court, if he be of high rank, as a king, Gen. 43:3, 5; 2 Sam. 14:24, 28, 32; hence this phrase denoted the royal favor, dignity or privilege. Esth. 1:14. So to see God's face is to find him propitious, to have nearness of access to him, Job 23:26; Ps. 17:15; and this is specially said to be the privilege of the holy angels that they see God's face. Matt. 18:10; Luke 1:19.

Fair Havens. A harbor on the southern shore of the island of Crete. Acts 27:8-10, 21. It is about midway between the eastern and western ends of the island, and is still known as Kalous Limionas, or "Fair Havens." It is a fair winter harbor, though not as good as Phœnice, or Phœnix, 40 miles westward.

Faith. Heb. 11:7. Faith is distinguished from credulity in that it does not accept anything as true which is not based on sufficient evidence; it is contrasted with unbelief in that it accepts whatever is proposed to it when the testimony thereof is adequate. Faith may be dead, if it be merely in the understanding, admitting facts as true, but not realizing their bearing upon ourselves. Such a faith is that historical faith, which credits the narrative of our Lord's passion and death, but seeks not, through them, remission of personal guilt. The faith of devils goes farther than this; for they "believe and tremble," Jas. 2:19; but they find no means of release from their apprehended doom. True "faith is the substance (or realizing) of things hoped for, the evidence (or sure persuasion) of things not seen." Heb. 11:1. With such a faith "Abraham believed God; and it was counted unto him for righteousness." Gen. 15:6; Rom. 4:3; Gal. 3:6. So those who believe in Christ, accepting his offered mercy, relying on his never-forfeited word, are for his sake regarded as God's children. Hence men are said to be "justified by faith," Rom. 3:23-26; 5:1. Faith, if genuine, will work by love, Gal. 5:6, yielding the fruits of a holy life and conversation. Matt. 7:20; Jas. 2:26. There are various shades of meaning belonging to the word "faith" in Scripture; sometimes it means the gospel revelation. Acts 6:7; Rom. 10:8. The precious gift of faith and the increase thereof should be earnestly sought in humble prayer. Luke 17:5; Phil. 1:29.

Famine. Several famines are noted in the Scripture history. Two are mentioned as occurring in Canaan in the days of Abraham and Isaac, compelling those patriarchs to remove to Egypt and to Gerar. Gen. 12:10; 26:1. Then succeeded that remarkable famine which Joseph was enabled to predict, and which extended widely over Egypt and various other regions. Gen. 41:53-57. A scarcity in Palestine was once occasioned, Judg. 6:4-6, by the invasion of the Midianites, and another (or the same) is referred to in Ruth 1:1. Others are noted, sometimes caused by war or by locusts. 2 Sam. 21:1; 1 Kings 17:1, 7; 18:2; 2 Kings 4:38; 8:1, 2; Lam. 5:10; Joel 1:10-12, 17, 18. We read in the New Testament, Acts 11:28, of a famine predicted by a Christian prophet named Agabus. Famine is sometimes used in a figurative sense; as when a worse destitution is described than that of bread, a sorer thirst than that for water—even a famine of the divine word, a thirst because the living streams of mercy flow out no more. Amos 8:11-14.

Fan. An instrument used to separate the chaff from the grain. Isa. 30:24; Jer. 15:7; Matt. 3:12; Luke 3:17. The shovel in Isaiah is probably something used to separate the grain from the straw. It was perhaps a broad scoop by which the corn was thrown against the wind, often, doubtless, during the evening breeze, Ruth 3:2, in order that the chaff might be blown away. The word translated "fan" in the first place above referred to has been thought to mean something of a similar kind, as a fork, which is still used in Palestine. It was possibly a measure or basket, in which to receive the grain. "Very little use," says Dr. Thomson, "is now made of the fan; but I have seen it employed to *purge the floor* of the refuse dust, which the owner throws away as useless."

Farthing. Two Greek words are translated "farthing" in the New Testament: *kodrantes;* Roman, *quadrans*—worth about three-eighths of a cent; Matt. 5:26; Mark 12:42; and *assarion;* Roman, *æs* or *as*—the tenth of a denarius, worth about a cent to 1½ cents.

Fasts. Abstinence from food for religious or spiritual good. Fasts are often mentioned in Scripture. The following account is condensed from Smith's larger Dictionary: 1. One fast only was appointed by the Mosaic law, that on the day of atonement. There is no mention of any other periodical fast in the Old Testament except in Zech. 7:1-7; 8:19. From these passages it appears that the Jews, during their captivity, observed four annual fasts—in the fourth, fifth, seventh and tenth months. 2.

Public fasts were occasionally proclaimed to express national humiliation and to supplicate divine favor. In the case of public danger the proclamation appears to have been accompanied with the blowing of trumpets. Joel 1:14; 2:15. See 1 Sam. 7:6; 2 Chron. 20:3; Jer. 36:6-10. After the feast of tabernacles, when the second temple was completed, "the children of Israel were assembled with fasting, and with sackcloth and earth upon them," to hear the law read and to confess their sins. Neh. 9:1. 3. Private occasional fasts are recognized in one passage of the law—Num. 30:13. The instances given of individuals fasting under the influence of grief, vexation or anxiety are numerous. 4. In the New Testament the only references to the Jewish fasts are the mention of "the fast" in Acts 27:9 (generally understood to denote the day of atonement), and the allusions to the weekly fasts. Matt. 9:14; Mark 2:18; Luke 5:33; 18:12. These fasts originated some time after the captivity. 5. The Jewish fasts were observed with various degrees of strictness. Sometimes there was entire abstinence from food. Esth. 4:16, etc. On other occasions there appears to have been only a restriction to a very plain diet. Dan. 10:3. Those who fasted frequently dressed in sackcloth or rent their clothes, put ashes on their head and went barefoot. 1 Kings 21:27; Neh. 9:1; Ps. 35:13. 6. The sacrifice of the personal will, which gives to fasting all its value, is expressed in the old term used in the law, *afflicting the soul.*

Feasts. Special thanksgivings and periods of rejoicing. The religious feasts mentioned in Scripture fall under three heads: (*A*) Those properly connected with the institution of the Sabbath; (*B*) the historical or great festivals; (*C*) the day of atonement. (*A*) Immediately connected with the Sabbath are: 1. The weekly Sabbath itself. 2. The seventh new moon, or feast of trumpets. 3. The sabbatical year. 4. The year of jubilee. (*B*) The great feasts are—1. The passover. 2. The feast of pentecost, or weeks, of wheat harvest, or of the first-fruits. 3. The feast of tabernacles or of ingathering. On each of these occasions every male Israelite was commanded to "appear before the Lord," that is, to attend in the court of the tabernacle or the temple, and to make his offering with a joyful heart. Deut. 27:7; Neh. 8:9-12. On all the days of holy convocation there was to be an entire suspension of ordinary labor of all kinds, Ex. 12:16; Lev. 16:29; 23:21, 24, 25, 35; but on the intervening days of the longer festivals work might be carried on. The significance of the three great festivals is stated in the account of the Jewish sacred year. Lev. 23. The times of the festivals were evidently appointed so as to interfere as little as possible with the industry of the people. The religious festivals preserved the religious faith of the nation and religious unity among the people. They promoted friendly intercourse, distributed information through the country at a time when the transmission of news was slow and imperfect; and imported into remote provincial districts a practical knowledge of all improvements in arts and sciences. After the captivity the feast of purim, Esth. 9:20 ff. *seq.*, and that of the dedication, 1 Macc. 4:56, were instituted. Jesus went up to Jerusalem at the latter feast. John 10:22.

Felix (*fē'lix*), *happy.* A Roman procurator of Judea appointed by the emperor Claudius in A. D. 53. His period of office was full of troubles and seditions. Paul was brought before Felix in Cæsarea. Paul was remanded to prison, and kept there two years in hopes of extorting money from him. Acts 24:26, 27. At the end of that time Porcius Festus superseded Felix, who, on his return to Rome, was accused by the Jews in Cæsarea, and would have suffered for his crimes had not his brother Pallas prevailed with the emperor Nero to spare him. This was probably about A. D. 60. The wife of Felix was Drusilla, a daughter of Herod Agrippa I., who was his third wife and whom he persuaded to leave her husband and marry him.

Ferret. Lev. 11:30. The animal referred to was probably of the lizard tribe; the *gecko*, R. V. The rabbinical writers seem to have identified this animal with the hedgehog.

Festus (*fĕs'tus*). Acts 24:27. Porcius Festus was appointed by Nero to succeed Felix as procurator of Judea, about 60 or 61 A. D. Before him Paul had to defend himself, but removed his cause from the provincial tribunal by appeal to Cæsar. Acts 24:27; 25; 26. Festus administered his government less than two years, and died in Judea.

Fig, Fig Tree. This, *Ficus carica*, was a tree very common in Palestine. Deut. 8:8. Mount Olivet was famous anciently for fig trees; and still some are to be found there. The first notice we have of this tree is when Adam and Eve endeavored to clothe themselves with leaves. Gen. 3:7. Whether the leaves they used were those of the ordinary fig tree may be questioned; but the practice of fastening leaves together for various utensils, as baskets, etc., is common in the East to the present day. Not only was the fresh fruit of the fig tree valued, but also cakes of figs are mentioned in Scripture; *e. g.*, 1 Sam. 25:18; 30:12. These were made either by simple compression, or by pounding them into a mass, sometimes together with dates. They were then cut into cakes, often similar to bricks, and hardened by keeping. Twice the fig tree is mentioned in the New Testament. Our Lord, shortly before his crucifixion, being hungry, sought fruit from a fig tree, and, finding none, condemned it. Matt. 21:18-20; Mark 11:12-14, 20. It was early in the season, not the ordinary time for figs; but yet, as the fruit precedes the leaves, and there were leaves on this tree, figs might naturally have been expected on it; and, as there were then none, there was proof enough that the pretentious tree was worthless. The parable of the fig tree spared at the intercession of the dresser of the garden, Luke 13:6-9, is full of instruction. There is, it may be added, an expressive phrase in which the fig tree is introduced; when men are said to sit under their own vine and their own fig tree, 1 Kings 4:25; Zech. 3:10, a state of general peace and prosperity is indicated.

Firmament. In Scripture the Hebrew word denotes an expanse, a wide extent; the great arch or expanse over our heads, in which are placed the atmosphere and the clouds, and in which the stars *appear* to be placed, and are *really* seen.

First-born. Under the law, in a Hebrew family, the eldest son was regarded as devoted to God, and was in every case to be redeemed by an offering not exceeding five shekels, within one month from birth. If he died before the expiration of 30 days, the Jewish doctors held the father excused, but liable to the payment if he outlived that time. Ex. 13:12-15; 22:29; Num. 8:17; 18:15, 16; Lev. 27:6. The eldest son received a double portion of the father's inheritance, Deut. 21:17, but not of the mother's. Under the monarchy the eldest son usually, but not always, as appears in the case of Solomon, succeeded his father in the kingdom. 1 Kings 1:30; 2:22. The male first-born of animals was also devoted to God. Ex. 13:2, 12, 13; 22:29; 34:19, 20. Unclean animals were to be redeemed with the addition of one-fifth of the value, or else put to death; or, if not redeemed, to be sold, and the price given to the priests. Lev. 27:13, 27, 28.

First-fruits. As the first-born of men and firstlings of beasts, so the first-fruits of the increase of the land were regarded as holy to the Lord. Rom. 8:23; 11:16; 1 Cor. 15:20, 23; 16:15; Jas. 1:18; Rev. 14:4. One remarkable provision of the law was that the Hebrews must not for three years touch the produce of any fruit-tree they planted. The fourth year of bearing it was consecrated as the first-fruits to the Lord, Lev. 19:23-25; in the fifth year it was free for the owner's use. This rule is not supposed to have applied to the trees the people found on entering Palestine. There were general commands as to the offering of the first fruits, Ex. 22:29; 23:19; 34:26, and also specified times when such offerings were to be publicly made. The first-fruits of the harvest in the sheaf were to be presented at the feast of the passover, on the morrow after the sabbath. Lev. 23:9-14. Till this was done, no harvest-work was to be proceeded with. At the feast of pentecost the first-fruits of the completed harvest in the shape of two loaves made of the new flour were to be presented. Ex. 34:22; Lev. 23:15-17; Num. 28:26. Besides these public and national oblations, there were others of a more private and individual kind. Such were the first-fruits of the dough, Num. 15:20, 21; and of the threshing-floor, which Jewish writers distinguish into two kinds, the first including wheat, barley, grapes, figs, pomegranates, olives, and figs; the second oil, wine, and other produce which supported human life, also the first of the fleece and the hair of goats. No rule was laid down in scripture as to the proportion the offered first-fruits ought to bear to the whole produce; but one-sixtieth is said to be the least; sometimes one-fortieth or one-thirtieth part was presented. The address which the offerer was to make to God is prescribed in Deut. 26:1-11. Doubtless in times of national declension less regard would be paid to the law of the first-fruits; but we find that during the various reforms they flowed in abundantly. 2 Chron. 31:5; Neh. 10:35, 37; comp. Ezek. 20:40; 48:14. The first-fruits generally became the portion of the priests and Levites, to be eaten by them and their families. Num. 18:12; Deut. 18:4; Ezek. 44:30. In Israel after the schism they were sometimes offered to the prophets. 2 Kings 4:42.

Fir Tree. Probably the Aleppo pine (*Pinus halepensis*), which is almost as large as the cedar, is now found on Lebanon, and was formerly doubtless abundant through Palestine. Hos. 14:8. Sometimes the cypress and juniper may have been included under this name, as well as other pines found here.

Fitches. This word occurs in Isa. 28:25, 27. It would seem to be the black cummin, *Nigella sativa*, used for both food and medicine. The seed is aromatic, and of a sharp taste. This plant was beaten out with a staff, because the heavy drag would have crushed the seeds. The "fitches" of Ezek. 4:9 was spelt.

Flood. One of the most remarkable events in the history of our world. The biblical narrative is given in Gen. 6-8. The scripture account of it says, "And I, behold, I do bring a flood of waters upon the earth, to destroy all flesh, wherein is the breath of life, from under heaven; every thing that is in the earth shall die." Gen. 6:17; comp. 7:4, 21, 23. "And all the high mountains that were under the whole heaven were covered. Fifteen cubits upward did the waters prevail; and the mountains were covered. ... And every living thing was destroyed which was upon the face of the ground, both man, and cattle, and creeping things, and fowl of the heaven; and they were destroyed from the earth; and Noah only was left, and they that were with him in the ark." Gen. 7:19-23, R. V. There is no fact in history better attested, independent of the word of God, than the flood; and none more universally acknowledged by all nations, accounts of it being in their legends. Many evidences of some such great catastrophe exist at the present day. The highest mountains in every part of the earth furnish proofs that the sea has spread over them, shells, skeletons of fish and sea monsters being found on them. The universality of a flood is shown by the fact that the remains of animals are found buried far from their native regions. Elephants and skeletons of whales have been found buried in England; mammoths near the north pole; crocodiles in Germany, etc. It is well to bear in mind that God has said, "I will establish my covenant with you; neither shall all flesh be cut off any more by the waters of the flood; neither shall there any more be a flood to destroy the earth." Gen. 9:11, 15. And also has said, "The world that then was, being overflowed with water, perished: but the heavens that now are, and the earth, by the same word have been stored up for fire, being reserved against the day of judgment, . . . in the which the heavens shall pass away with a great noise, and the elements shall be dissolved with fervent heat, and the earth and the works that are therein shall be burned up." 2 Pet. 3:5–10. There is an abundance of material stored up in the earth and in the atmosphere to produce such a combustion at any moment.

Food. The diet of the ancients may be learned from that of oriental people now. Vegetable food is more used than animal. Bread was the principal food; preparations of corn were, however, common. The Hebrews used a great variety of articles, John 21:5, to give a relish to bread. Milk holds a conspicuous place in eastern diet; generally in the form of the modern *leben, i. e.*, sour milk, and "butter;" Gen. 18:8; Judg. 5:25; 2 Sam. 17:29. Fruit was another source of diet; figs were generally dried and pressed into cakes. Grapes were eaten in a dried state as raisins. Of vegetables we have most frequent notice of lentils, beans, leeks, onions and garlic, which were and still are of a superior quality in Egypt. Num. 11:5. Honey is extensively used, as is also olive oil. The orientals are sparing in the use of animal food; not only does the excessive heat of the climate render it both unwholesome to eat much meat and expensive from the necessity of immediately consuming a whole animal, but the regulations of the Mosaic law in ancient, as of the Koran in modern, times have tended to diminish its use. The prohibition against consuming the blood of any animal, Gen. 9:4, was more fully developed in the Levitical law, and enforced by the penalty of death. Lev. 3:17; 7:26; 19:26; Deut. 12:16. Certain portions of the fat of sacrifices were also forbidden, Lev. 3:9, 10, as being set apart for the altar. Lev. 3:16; 7:25. Christians were forbidden to eat the flesh of animals portions of which had been offered to idols. All beasts and birds classed as unclean, Lev. 11:1 ff.; Deut. 14:4 ff., were also prohibited. Under these restrictions the Hebrews were permitted the use of animal food; they availed themselves of it in the exercise of hospitality or at festivals of a religious, public or private character. The animals killed for meat were: calves, lambs, oxen, harts, roebucks and fallow deer, and other clean animals; birds of various kinds; fish, with the exception of such as were without scales and fins. Locusts, of which certain species only were esteemed clean, were occasionally eaten, Matt. 3:4, but were regarded as poor fare.

Fool. This term, in Scripture, implies moral pravity. The fool is not merely an unreasonable, he is a sinful person. 2 Sam. 13:13; Ps. 14:1; Prov. 19:1, 29; 20:3; 26:4, 5; Matt. 23:17; Rom. 1:21, 22. Hence the censure of one who unjustifiably cast so great a reproach upon a brother. Matt. 5:22.

Foreknowledge. The foreknowledge of God is repeatedly spoken of in Scripture. Acts 2:23; Rom. 8:29; 11:2; 1 Pet. 1:2. There are curious and intricate questions in reference to his foreknowledge, which it would be quite foreign to the character of this work to attempt to discuss. It must be sufficient to say that the Scripture attributes the most perfect prescience to the Deity. It is one of those high attributes which place him immeasurably above all pretended gods. Isa. 41:22, 23; 42:9; 44:6–8. God does not gather knowledge as we do: before his eye all things past, present, or to come, are spread with equal clearness: he sees all possibilities, those events which may happen as well as those which will happen. 1 Sam. 23:9–13; Jer. 38:17–23; 42:9–22; Matt. 11:21, 23; Acts 27:24, 31. Yet this divine foreknowledge does not compel men; it fetters not their free action; it does not deliver them from the responsibility of their own deeds. Gen. 50:20; Isa. 10:6, 7. And, if we are unable exactly to comprehend this, we may well remember that God's judgments are unsearchable, Rom. 11:33, his ways higher than our ways, his thoughts than our thoughts. Isa. 50:9.

Forerunner. A person sent before an army or a noted person. Thus John the Baptist was a messenger who went beforehand to prepare the way of the Lord. Mark 1:2, 3. And Christ is said to be "the forerunner for us," Heb. 6:20, representing and introducing us. For, when as a priest he entered into the holy place, he went thither not for himself merely, but as the head and guide of his people, to open the way and conduct the whole church into his glory.

Forgiveness. The remission of a fault. In the gospel of Christ, free forgiveness of sins is set forth. Acts 5:31; 13:38, 39; 1 John 1:6–9; 2:12. And the full remission, which transgressors have at God's hand for Christ's sake, is made the ground and the pattern of that forgiving spirit which is to be manifested by Christ's true followers. Matt. 6:12, 14, 15; 18:21–35; Mark 11:25, 26 A. V., but verse 26 is omitted in the R. V.; Eph. 4:32, and elsewhere. See **Justification**.

Fox. The jackal is probably meant in several passages where "fox" now occurs in Scripture. Both animals are cunning, voracious, and mischievous, Ezek. 13:4; Luke 13:32, are fond of grapes. Song of Sol. 2:15. Both burrow in the ground or among ruins. Luke 9:58. The jackal hunts its prey in large packs. It follows after caravans and armies, and devours the bodies of the dead, and even digs them up from their graves. Ps. 63:10; Lam. 5:18. See 2 Sam. 18:17. Samson used foxes or jackals, Judg. 15:4, 5, to destroy the grain of the Philistines by binding torches to the tails of the animals, and they ran round setting fire to fields of corn.

Frankincense. A vegetable resin, brittle, glittering, and of a bitter taste, used in Hebrew offerings and sacrifices. Ex. 30:31–36. It burns for a long time with a steady flame. It is obtained by successive incisions in the bark of a tree called *Arbor thuris*. The first incision yields the purest and whitest resin, while the product of the after incisions is spotted with yellow, and loses its whiteness altogether as it becomes old. The Hebrews imported their frankincense from Arabia. Isa. 60:6; Jer. 6:20.

Fringes. The Israelites were commanded to put fringes upon their garments, Num. 15:38, 39; Deut. 22:12, a kind of edging which would prevent the ends of the cloth from unravelling; also in the corners possibly of the outer garment, which was quadrangular, there was to be a narrow blue ribbon. These fringes or borders were in process of time enlarged; and it was one part of the superstition of the Pharisee so to enlarge them as to attract special notice. Matt. 23:5. Hence there was a kind of sacredness attributed to the hem of the garment; and this seems to have been the reason why diseased persons specially desired to touch the hem of Christ's garment. Matt. 9:20; 14:36; Luke 8:44.

Frog. The original Hebrew word signifies a marsh-leaper. We find frogs mentioned only in connection with the plague inflicted upon the Egyptians. Ex. 8:2–14; Ps. 78:45; 105:30, and for illustration. Rev. 16:13. Naturalists disagree as to the species of frogs at present found in Egypt.

Frontlets. See **Phylacteries.**

Fullers' Field. A spot close to the walls of Jerusalem. 2 Kings 18:17, 26; Isa. 36:2; 7:3.

Furnace. Furnaces are noticed in the Bible, such as a smelting or calcining furnace, Gen. 19:28; Ex. 9:8, 10; 19:18; especially a lime-kiln, Isa. 33:12; Amos 2:1; a refining furnace, Prov. 17:3; Nebuchadnezzar's furnace, a large furnace built like a brick-kiln, Dan. 3:22, 23, with two openings, one at the top for putting in the materials, and another below for removing them. The potter's furnace and the blacksmith's furnace are noticed in the Apocryphal books. Eccles. 27:5; 38:28. The Persians were in the habit of using the furnace as a means of inflicting punishment. Dan. 3:22, 23; Jer. 29:22.

G

Gaal (*gā'al*), *loathing*, the son of Ebed, led a revolt against Abimelech, king of the Shechemites. Judg. 9:26–46. He was defeated and his partisans were scattered.

Gaash (*gā'ash*), *earthquake*. The hill where Joshua was buried. Josh. 24:30; Judg. 2:9. South of Tibneh, which is identified as Timnath-serah, is a hill, upon the north side of which are tombs; hence it is supposed to be "the hill Gaash."

Gabbatha (*gab'ba-thah*), *platform*. The place of Pilate's judgment-seat; called also "the pavement." John 19:13. The judgment-hall was the Prætorium, on the western hill of Jerusalem, and the pavement, or Gabbatha, was a tesselated pavement outside the hall.

Gabriel (*gā'-bri-el*), *man of God*. An angel specially charged with the message to Zacharias respecting the birth of John, and to Mary respecting the birth of Christ. Luke 1:19-26. At an earlier period he was sent to Daniel to unfold a vision. Dan. 8:16; 9:21. See **Angels.**

Gad (*găd*), *good fortune*(?) 1. The seventh son of Jacob, and the first-born of Zilpah, Leah's handmaid. Gen. 30:11. 2. A prophet and particular friend of David, the history of whose reign he wrote. 1 Chron. 29:29. He came to David when the latter was in the cave of Adullam. 1 Sam. 22:5. He then began his career of counsellor, under divine direction, which eventually won him the title of "the king's seer," 2 Sam. 24:11, 13; 1 Chron. 21:9. In Hezekiah's day he was remembered. 2 Chron. 29:25.

Gad, the Tribe of. The territory given to the tribe of Gad lay east of the Jordan, north of that allotted to Reuben, and south of that given to Manasseh on that side of the river. It extended from the Jordan eastward to Aroer, Josh. 13:24, 25, including half of Mount Gilead and half of Ammon. Deut. 3:12; Josh. 13:24, 25. For physical features and history see **Gilead.** Its chief cities were Ramoth-gilead, Mahanaim, Heshbon, and Aroer. This tribe, in the wilderness, was placed with Simeon and Reuben on the south of the tabernacle; with Reuben and the half of Manasseh, it occupied the pasture grounds on the east of the Jordan. It was warlike, as is graphically stated. 1 Chron. 12:8. Two famous men came from Gad—Barzillai, 2 Sam. 17:27, and Elijah, 1 Kings 17:1. The territory was the battle field for wars between Syria and Israel. 2 Kings 10:33.

Gadarenes (*gād'a-renez*), **country of.** Possibly the same as that of the Gergesenes, R. V. "Gerasenes;" Matt. 8:28 R. V., but Gergesenes in A. V. Mark 5:1; Gadarenes, A. V., and so in Luke 8:26, but Gerasenes in R. V. in both passages. A region about Gadara, an important city about 6 miles south-east of the Sea of Galilee, and 16 miles from Tiberias; now called *Um Keis*. The town is about 1215 feet above the sea-level, on the western crest of a mountain. The tomb-caverns are very numerous, and some of them are still inhabited by the Arabs, illustrating Matt. 8:28. The place of the miracle of Matt. 8:28–33 has been in doubt, but it cannot be Gadara, which is too far from the lake for the herd of swine to rush into it precipitantly in one short run. Recent explorations fix it, with some certainty, about midway of the Lake of Galilee, on its eastern side and near Gerasa, or modern Kersa. Between two wadys, Semakh and Fik, which are 3 miles apart, the hills come within 40 feet of the lake, and present a steep slope, so that a herd of swine running swiftly down it would be carried on into the water. There are various readings of the name in the original text of the Gospels. The reading of Matt. 8:28 was probably "Gadarenes" (as in the R. V.), which Origen changed to "Gergesenes." In Mark 5:1 the readings are "Gerasenes" or "Gadarenes;" in Luke 8:26, "Gerasenes," "Gergesenes," or "Gadarenes." The explanation is, Gadara, a chief city, is named, as better known than Gerasa or Khersa.

Gaius (*gā'yus*). 1. A Macedonian, Acts 19:29, Paul's host at Corinth when the Epistle to the Romans was written, Rom. 16:23, and baptized with his household by Paul. 1 Cor. 1:14. He accompanied Paul to Ephesus, and was seized by the mob, Acts 19:29. The association of his name with that of Aristarchus seems to identify him with the Gaius of Derbe. Acts 20:4. Opinions differ on this point. 2. To one of this name is addressed the third Epistle of John. 3 John 1.

Galatia (*ga-lā'shĭ-ah*). A central province of Asia Minor, subject to the Roman rule, bounded by Bithynia and Paphlagonia on the north, Pontus on the east, Cappadocia and Lycaonia on the south, and Phrygia on the west. The country is chiefly high tableland between the two rivers Halys and Sangarius. The Galatians were originally Gauls or Celts who 300 years before Christ moved from the regions of the Rhine back toward the east, and there mingled with Greeks and Jews. Galatia was a part of Paul's missionary field. He visited it once with Silas and Timothy, Acts 16:6; again, on his third tour, he "went over *all* the country of Galatia," Acts 18:23, and received a collection for the saints from its churches. 1 Cor. 16:1. Crescens also appears to have been sent there near the close of Paul's life. 2 Tim. 4:10.

Galbanum. One of the ingredients of the sacred perfume (Ex. 30:34). It is a resinous gum of a brownish-yellow color, generally occurring in masses, and of a strong, disagreeable odor. When mixed with other fragrant substances, it made the perfume more lasting.

Galilee (*găl'ĭ-lee*), *circle, circuit*. A name in the Old Testament for a small district in the northern mountains of Naphtali, around Kedesh-naphtali, and including 20 towns given by Solomon to Hiram, king of Tyre, Josh. 20:7; 21:32; 1 Kings 9:11; 2 Kings 15:29, and called "Galilee of the nations" in Isa. 9:1. Devastated during the wars of the Captivity, it was repeopled by strangers. In the time of the Maccabees they probably outnumbered the Jewish population, and gave their new name to a much wider district. In the time of our Lord, Palestine was divided into three provinces, of which Galilee was the most northern. It included the whole region from the plain of Jezreel to the Litany (Leontes) river, being about 50 miles long by 20 to 25 miles wide. The northern part was known as Upper and the southern part as Lower Galilee. These included the territories given to Asher, Naphtali, Zebulun, and Issachar. The country was famed for its fertility, rich pastures, and fine forests. The portion west of the lake was the most beautiful. In the Roman period the population was dense, Josephus estimating it at 2,000,000 or 3,000,000, though that is probably an exaggeration. It had a mixed population of heathens, foreigners, and Jews. The latter, having a strong, if not dominant, influence, were less strict and less acquainted with the Law than their southern Judæan neighbors, by whom they were little esteemed. The noted mountains of Galilee were Carmel, Gilboa, and Tabor; the towns were Nazareth, Cana, Tiberias, Chorazin, Bethsaida, and Capernaum. Jesus spent the greater portion of his life and ministry in Galilee. Many of his most remarkable miracles, teachings, and labors were within this province of Galilee. His disciples were chiefly from this region. Acts 1:11. After the fall of Jerusalem, Galilee became the residence of celebrated rabbis and the centre of Jewish schools of learning.

Galilee, Sea of. Named from the province of Galilee, which bordered on its western side, Matt. 4:18. It was also called the "Sea of Tiberias," from the city of that name, John 6:1, and "Sea of Chinneroth" in the Old Testament. At its northwestern angle was a beautiful and fertile plain called "Gennesaret," and from that it derived the name of "Lake of Gennesaret." Luke 5:1; Num. 34:11; Josh. 12:3, and Galilee, Josh. 19:35. Its modern name is Bahr Tubariyeh. Most of our Lord's public life was spent in the environs of this sea. The Sea of Galilee is of an oval shape, about 12 miles long and 6 broad. It is 60 miles northeast of Jerusalem and 27 east of the Mediterranean sea. The river Jordan enters it at its northern end and passes out at its southern end. Its most remarkable feature is its deep depression, being no less than 700 feet below the level of the ocean. The scenery is bleak and monotonous, being surrounded by a high and almost unbroken wall of hills, on account of which it is exposed to frequent sudden and violent storms. The great depression makes the climate of the shores almost tropical. In summer the heat is intense, and even in early spring the air has something of an Egyptian balminess. The water of the lake is sweet, cool, and transparent; and as the beach is everywhere pebbly it has a beautiful sparkling look. It abounds in fish now as in ancient times. There were large fisheries on the lake, and much commerce was carried on upon it. There are only a few small boats now to be found on the lake.

Gall. A word which in the A. V. represents two or more Hebrew words. 1. The Hebrew word *rôsh*, rendered "hemlock" in Hos. 10:4; Amos 6:12, R. V., "gall," is generally rendered "gall," Deut. 29:18; Ps. 69:21, meaning most probably the poppy; and thus Jer. 8:14, "water of gall," would be poppy-juice. It stands sometimes for poison generally. Deut. 32:32. 2. Another word, *merêrah*, or *merorah*, means the gall of the human body, Job 16:13; 20:25, and that of asps, Job 20:14, the poison being supposed to lie in the gall. The Greek *cholē* means a bitter humor of man or beast, taking sometimes a more general signification. Matt. 27:34. It is used metaphorically in Acts 8:23. The draught offered to our Lord at his crucifixion is said by Matthew to be mingled with gall, by Mark with myrrh. Matt. 27:34; Mark 15:23. If the two refer to the same act, Mark specifies the ingredient, while Matthew shows that the effect

93

was to render the mixture bitter; as we say, "bitter as gall."

Gallio (*găl'li-o*). Marcus Annæus Novatus, brother of the eminent philosopher, Lucius Annæus Seneca, was adopted into the family of the rhetorician, Lucius Junius Gallio, and was thenceforth designated Junius Annæus Gallio. To him his brother Seneca dedicated one of his works, De Ira. He was proconsul of Achaia under the Emperor Claudius, about 53 and 54 A. D.; when Paul was accused before him. Acts 18:12-16.

Gamaliel (*ga-mā'li-el*), *recompense of God*. 1. Son of Pedahzur; prince or captain of the tribe of Manasseh at the census at Sinai, Num. 1:10; 2:20; 7:54, 59, and at starting on the march through the wilderness. Num. 10:23. (B. C. 1490.) 2. A Pharisee and celebrated doctor of the law, who gave prudent worldly advice in the Sanhedrin respecting the treatment of the followers of Jesus of Nazareth. Acts 5:34 ff. (A. D. 29.) He was Paul's teacher. Acts 22:3. He is generally identified with Gamaliel, the grandson of Hillel, who is referred to as authority in the Jewish Mishna.

Garden. Gardens in the East were surrounded by hedges of thorn, Isa. 5:5, or walls of stone. Prov. 24:31. For further protection lodges, Isa. 1:8; Lam. 2:6, or watchtowers, Mark 12:1, were built in them, in which sat the keeper, Isa. 5:2; 21:5, to drive away the wild beasts and robbers. The gardens of the Hebrews were planted with flowers and aromatic shrubs, Song of Sol. 6:2; 4:16, besides olives, fig trees, nuts or walnuts, Song of Sol. 6:11, pomegranates, and others for domestic use. Ex. 23:11; Jer. 29:5; Amos 9:14. Gardens of herbs, or kitchen gardens, are mentioned in Deut. 11:10 and 1 Kings 21:2. The retirement of gardens rendered them favorite places for devotion.

Garments. Notice: 1. Materials; 2. Color and decoration; 3. Name and mode of wearing the various articles; 4. Usages relating thereto.

1. *Materials.*—The first human dress was an "apron" of fig leaves, Gen. 3:7; then the skins of animals, Gen. 3:21; as later the "mantle" worn by Elijah. Sheepskin is still a common material of dress in the East. The art of weaving hair and wool was known to the Hebrews at an early period. Ex. 25:4; 26:7; Gen. 38:12. Linen and perhaps cotton fabrics were known, 1 Chron. 4:21; and silk was introduced much later. Rev. 18:12. The use of mixed material, such as wool and flax, was forbidden. Lev. 19:19; Deut. 22:11.

2. *Color and decoration.*—The prevailing color of the Hebrew dress was the natural white of the materials employed. Mark 9:3. The use of colors was known; notice the scarlet thread. Gen. 38:28. Also, the art of weaving with threads previously dyed, Ex. 35:25; of the introduction of gold thread or wire. Ex. 27:6 ff. Robes decorated with gold, Ps. 45:13, and with silver thread, cf. Acts 12:21, were worn by royal personages: other kinds of embroidered robes were worn by the wealthy, Judg. 5:30; Ps. 45:14; Ezek. 16:13; as well as purple, Prov. 31:22; Luke 16:19; and scarlet. 2 Sam. 1:24.

3. *The names and modes of wearing garments.*—Oriental dress has preserved a remarkable uniformity in all ages: the modern Arab dresses much as the ancient Hebrew did. The costume of the men and women was very similar; there was sufficient difference, however, to mark the sex, and it was strictly forbidden to a woman to wear the staff, signet-ring, and other ornaments of a man; as well as to a man to wear the outer robe of a woman. Deut. 22:5. The robes common to the two sexes were: (1) *The inner garment*, closely fitting, resembling in form and use our shirt, though unfortunately translated "coat" in the Authorized Version. It was made of either wool, cotton, or linen, was without sleeves, and reached only to the knee. Another kind reached to the wrists and ankles. It was kept close to the body by a girdle, and the fold formed by the overlapping of the robe served as an inner pocket. A person wearing the inner garment alone was described as *naked*. (2) *Upper* or *second* tunic, longer than the first. (3) The *linen cloth* appears to have been a wrapper of fine linen, which might be used in various ways, but especially as a night-shirt. Mark 14:51. (4) *The outer garment* consisted of a square piece of woolen cloth. The size and texture would vary with the means of the wearer. It might be worn in various ways, either wrapped round the body or thrown over the shoulders like a shawl, with the ends or "skirts" hanging down in front; or it might be thrown over the head, so as to conceal the face. 2 Sam. 15:30; Esther 6:12. The ends were skirted with a fringe and bound with a dark purple ribbon, Num. 15:38; it was confined at the waist by a girdle. The outer garment was the poor man's bed-clothing. Ex. 22:26, 27. The dress of the women differed from that of men in the outer garment; an inner garment being worn alike by both sexes. Song of Sol. 5:3. Among their distinctive robes was a kind of shawl, Ruth 3:15; Isa. 3:22; light summer dresses and gay holiday dresses. Isa. 3:24. The garments of females had an ample border of fringe (*skirts*, A. V.), which concealed the feet. Isa. 47:2; Jer. 13:22. The travelling *cloak* referred to by Paul, 2 Tim. 4:13, is sometimes explained as a travelling case for carrying clothes or books. The *coat of many colors* worn by Joseph, Gen. 37:3, 23, was a tunic furnished with sleeves and reaching down to the ankles.

4. *Usages in dress.*—The length of the dress rendered it inconvenient for active exercise; hence the outer garments were either left in the house by a person working close by, Matt. 24:18; or were thrown off, Mark 10:50; or were girded up. 1 Kings 18:46; 1 Pet. 1:13. On entering a house the upper garment was probably laid aside, and resumed on going out. Acts 12:8. The presentation of a robe was often an installation or investiture, Gen. 41:42; Esther 8:15; Isa. 22:21; taking it away a

dismissal from office. 2 Macc. 4:38. The best robe was a mark of honor. Luke 15:22. The number of robes kept in store for presents was very large, Job 22:6; Matt. 6:19; Jas. 5:2, and implied the possession of wealth and power. Isa. 3:6, 7. On wedding occasions the entertainer sometimes provided robes for his guests. Matt. 22:12; Luke 15:22. The business of making clothes devolved upon women in a family. Prov. 31:22; Acts 9:39.

Gate. Eastern cities anciently were walled and had gates. They are thus sometimes taken as representing the city itself. Gen. 22:17; 24:60; Deut. 12:12; Judg. 5:8; Ruth 4:10; Ps. 87:2; 122:2. Gateways were used: (1) As places of public resort. Gen. 19:1; 23:10; 34:20, 24; 1 Sam. 4:18, etc. (2) For public deliberation, holding courts of justice, or for meeting kings and rulers or ambassadors. Deut. 16:18; 21:19; 25:7; Josh. 20:4; Judg. 9:35, etc. (3) Public markets. 2 Kings 7:1. In heathen towns the open spaces near the gates appear to have been sometimes used as places for sacrifice. Acts 14:13; comp. 2 Kings 23:8. The gates of cities were carefully guarded, and closed at nightfall. Deut. 3:5; Josh. 2:5, 7; Judg. 9:40, 44. They contained chambers over the gateway. 2 Sam. 18:24. The doors of the larger gates mentioned in Scripture were two-leaved, plated with metal, closed with locks and barred with metal bars. Deut. 3:5; Ps. 107:16; Isa. 45:1, 2. Gates not covered by iron were liable to be set on fire by an enemy. Judg. 9:52. The gateways of royal palaces and even of private houses were often richly ornamented. Sentences from the law were inscribed on and above the gates. Deut. 6:9; Rev. 21:21. The gates of Solomon's temple were very massive and costly, being overlaid with gold and carvings. 1 Kings 6:34, 35; 2 Kings 18:16. Those of the holy place were of olive wood, two-leaved and overlaid with gold; those of the temple of fir. 1 Kings 6:31, 32, 34; Ezek. 41:23, 24.

Gath (găth), wine-press. One of the five cities of the Philistines, 1 Sam. 5:8; 6:17; Amos 6:2; Mic. 1:10; a stronghold of the Anakim, Josh. 11:22; home of Goliath, 1 Sam. 17:4; place whither the ark was carried, 1 Sam. 5:8; where David sought refuge, 1 Sam. 21:10-15; was strengthened by Rehoboam, 2 Chron. 11:8; taken by Hazael of Syria, 2 Kings 12:17; probably recovered by Jehoash, 2 Kings 13:25; broken down by Uzziah, 2 Chron. 26:6; was probably destroyed before the time of the later prophecies, as it is omitted from the list of royal cities. See Zeph. 2:4; Zech. 9:5, 6. Probably Tel es-Safi, 15 miles south of Ramleh and 12 miles southeast of Ashdod.

Gaza (gā'zah), Hebrew Azzah, strong. The chief of the five cities of the Philistines, 50 miles southwest of Jerusalem, 3 miles from the Mediterranean, now called Ghŭzzeh. Gaza was peopled by the descendants of Ham, Gen. 10:19; by the Anakim, Josh. 11:22; given to Judah, Josh. 15:47; the scene of Samson's exploits, Judg. 16; under Solomon's rule and called Azzah, 1 Kings 4:24; smitten by Egypt, Jer. 47:1, 5; prophesied against, Amos 1:6, 7; Zeph. 2:4; Zech. 9:5; noticed in New Testament only in Acts 8:26; a chief stronghold of paganism and the worship of the god Dagon. The town is now without walls or gates, but is in the midst of olive-orchards and has about 20,000 inhabitants.

Geba (gē'-bah), hill. A Levitical city of Benjamin, Josh. 21:17; 1 Chron. 6:60; also called Gaba. Josh. 18:24. It was held by the Philistines, but taken by Jonathan, 1 Sam. 13:3; was a northern landmark of Judah, 2 Kings 23:8; was rebuilt by Asa, 1 Kings 15:22; held by the Assyrians, Isa. 10:29; peopled by Benjamites after the captivity, Ezra 2:26. Geba and Gibeah appear to be sometimes confounded in the English Version (see 1 Sam. 14:5), though they were separate towns. Geba was near Michmash and on the south side of the ravine. It has been identified with Jeba, a deserted village 6 miles north of Jerusalem.

Gebal (gē'bal), mountain. 1. A place near Tyre. Ezra 27:9. 2. Some identify the Gebal of Ps. 83:7 with northern Edom, called el-Jebal, but others regard it as Geba No. 1.

Gedaliah (gĕd'a-lī'ah), whom Jehovah hath made powerful. The governor of Judæa, appointed by Nebuchadnezzar after its subjection. 2 Kings 25:22; Jer. 40:5. He was a friend of Jeremiah, Jer. 40:6; a party headed by Ishmael slew him. Jer. 41:2.

Gehazi (ge-hā'zī), valley of vision. The servant of Elisha. He was the prophet's messenger to the good Shunammite, 2 Kings 4 (B. C. 889-887); accepted money and garments from Naaman; was smitten with leprosy, and was dismissed from the prophet's service, 2 Kings 5. Later he related to king Joram all the things which Elisha had done. 2 Kings 8:4, 5.

Gemariah (gĕm'a-rī'ah), whom Jehovah has perfected. 1. The son of Hilkiah, sent on an embassy from Zedekiah to Nebuchadnezzar. Jer. 29:3. 2. The son of Shaphan, from whose chamber Baruch read to the people the roll of Jeremiah's prophecies. Jer. 36:10, 11, 12, 25.

Genealogy. Genealogical lists are found all through the historical books of the Old Testament. One great object in the preservation of these genealogical lists was to note Christ's descent. The first biblical genealogy is that of Cain's descendants, Gen. 4:16-24; then that of Seth. The tenth and eleventh chapters of Genesis are regarded by ethnologists as invaluable, since they contain a history of the dispersion of the nations in prehistoric times. The first eight chapters of 1 Chronicles are devoted to genealogical accounts, beginning with Adam, because, as it is stated, "all Israel were reckoned by genealogies." 1 Chron. 9:1.

GENEALOGY OF JESUS CHRIST.—Matt. 1:1-17; Luke 3:23-38. This is the only genealogy given us in the New Testament. We have two lists of the human ancestors of Christ: Matthew, writing for Jewish Christians, begins with Abraham; Luke, writing for Gentile Christians, goes back to

Adam, the father of all men. John, 1:1-18, begins his gospel by setting forth Christ's divine genealogy. The explanation of the differences in these two lists is, 1. One, or perhaps two, levirate marriages in the family of Joseph—*i. e.*, a marriage of a man to the childless widow of his elder brother, the children of the second marriage being reckoned as the legal descendants of the first husband. 2. That Matthew gives the *legal* or *royal* genealogy of Joseph, Luke the private line of Joseph. 3. That Matthew gives the genealogy of Joseph, Luke the genealogy of Mary. The Davidic descent of Jesus is a mark of the Messiah, and is clearly taught in the prophecy, and also in Rom. 1:3; 2 Tim. 2:8; Heb. 7:14; John 7:42; Acts 13:23.

Generation, or Generations, "has three secondary meanings in the A. V.: 1. A genealogical register, as Gen. 5:1. 2. A family history, Gen. 6:9; 25:1 ff., since early history among the orientals is drawn so much from genealogical registers. 3. A history of the origin of things as well as persons—*e. g.*, of the earth."—*Smith.*

Genesis (*jĕn'e-sĭs*). The first book of the Bible. The term signifies "beginning" or "origin." Genesis gives us a history of the origin of the world, of the human family, of sin, of the promise of redemption, and of the Jewish people. The first eleven chapters describe the creation of things, the history of Adam, the deluge, and the confusion of tongues at Babel. With the twelfth chapter begins the history of the patriarchs and Israel. There are no good grounds for doubting that Moses was the author. With the use of older documents and traditions, he compiled, under divine direction, the history as we have it. The order of created things in Genesis is substantially the order of geology and biology. Both begin with the formation of the earth and proceed from the vegetable to animal life; both stop with man. The word translated "day" probably means an indefinite period. The "seventh day," which has no evening, Chron. 2:2, cannot refer to a day of 24 hours, but to the long redemptive period in which we are living. Few if any existing documents have a more venerable age than has Genesis. Covering nearly 2500 years, it gives us the account of the preparation of this planet as an abode for man and the first annals of the race. Its value cannot be overestimated as a fragment of literature or as a work of history, and it has been well observed that in the first page of Genesis a child may learn more in an hour than all the philosophers in the world learned without it in a thousand years.—*Schaff.*

Gennesaret (*gĕn-nĕs'a-rĕt*), **the Land of.** A small strip of country on the northwest side of the Sea of Galilee. It is named only twice in Scripture. Matt. 14:34; Mark 6:53; comp. Luke 5:1. It lies along the lake for three or four miles, and extends back about a mile or more, where it is shut in by the hills. The plain was formerly very rich and fruitful, according to Josephus, and is supposed to be the scene of the parable of the sower, Matt. 13:1-8, but it is now fruitful in thorns. The banks of the lake and of the brook running from the fountain '*Ain Tŭbighah* are fringed with oleanders.

Gentile (*jĕn'tĭle*). This was the name by which the Jews designated all men but themselves—*i. e.*, all pagan nations who were ignorant of the true God, and idolaters. Luke 2:32; Acts 26:17, 20; Rom. 2:9, where the R. V. reads "Greek;" 9:24, etc. In opposition to the Gentiles, the Hebrews regarded themselves, and were in fact, the "chosen people of God." Sometimes the "Greeks," as the most cultivated among the heathen, stand for them. Rom. 1:16; Acts 16:1, 3, etc. Paul is called the "apostle to the Gentiles" on account of his special mission and work among them.

COURT OF THE GENTILES. See **Temple**.

ISLES OF THE GENTILES, R. V., "Isles of the nations." Gen. 10:5. The Hebrew word signifies any land bordering on the sea. It refers to land on the Mediterranean, Black, and Caspian seas.

Gerar (*gē'rär*), *residence*, or *water-pots*. A city and district in the south of Palestine, and near Gaza, Gen. 10:19; visited by Abraham, Gen. 20:1; by Isaac, Gen. 26:1; Asa pursued the defeated Ethiopians to it. 2 Chron. 14:13.

Gerizim (*gĕr'a-zĭm*), Mount. A mountain near Shechem, from which the blessings were pronounced, as the curses were from Mount Ebal, Deut. 11:29; 27:1-13; Josh. 8:30-33. Gerizim is 2849 feet above the level of the sea, and about 800 feet above *Nâblus* (Shechem). It is separated from Ebal by a narrow valley. Six tribes were placed on Gerizim, and six on Ebal, Deut. 27:12, 13; the ark was probably in the valley between them, and Joshua read the blessings and cursings successively. Josh. 8:33, 34; Deut. 27:14, 15. Gerizim was the scene of the first recorded parable—that of the trees and brambles. Judg. 9:7-21. It was the site of the Samaritan temple, and referred to by the woman at the well. John 4:20. See **Ebal**.

Geshur (*gĕ'shur*), *bridge*. A small district of Syria, east of the Jordan and northeast of Bashan; allotted to Manasseh, Deut. 3:14; 2 Sam. 15:8; 1 Chron. 2:23; Josh. 13:13; David married a daughter of its king, 2 Sam. 3:3; Absalom fled thither after the murder of Amnon, 2 Sam. 13:37. Now known as "the Lejah," and still the refuge of criminals and outlaws.

Gethsemane (*gĕth-sĕm'a-ne*), *oil press*. A place across the Kidron and at the foot of Olivet, noted as the scene of our Lord's agony. John 18:1; Mark 14:26; Luke 22:39. A garden or orchard was attached to it, and it was a place to which Jesus frequently resorted. Matt. 26:36; Mark 14:32; John 18:2. Tradition, since the fourth century, has placed it on the lower slope of Olivet, about 100 yards east of the bridge over the Kedron.

Gezer (*gē'zer*), *steep place*, called also Gazer, Gazara, Gazera, and Gad, a royal city of Canaan, and one of the oldest cities of the land. Josh. 10:33; 12:12. Gezer was in Ephraim; given to Kohath, Josh. 21:

21; 1 Chron. 6:67; noticed in the wars of David, 1 Sam. 27:8; 2 Sam. 5:25; 1 Chron. 20:4; burned by Pharaoh in Solomon's days, 1 Kings 9:15-17; given to Solomon's Egyptian wife, and rebuilt by him; was an important city in the time of the Maccabees.

Giant. Gen. 6:4. R. V., "Nephilim." The sons of Anak are usually looked upon as giants. Num. 13:33. The king of Bashan, Deut. 3:11, and Goliath, 1 Sam. 17:4, were warlike and dreaded giants.

Gibbethon (gĭb'be-thŏn), *height*. A town of Dan; given to the Kohathites, Josh. 19:44; 21:23; held by the Philistines in the reigns of Jeroboam, Nadab, Baasha, Elah, Zimri, and Omri. 1 Kings 15:27; 16:17. The siege lasted 27 years.

Gibeah (gĭb'e-ah), *a hill*. The name of several towns. 1. Gibeah in the hill-country of Judah, Josh. 15:57; now probably Jebah, ten miles north of Hebron. 2. Gibeah of Benjamin, 1 Sam. 13:2; first mentioned in Judg. 19; a shameful crime by some of its people nearly destroyed the tribe of Benjamin. Judg. 20, 21. 3. Gibeah of Saul, probably the same as Gibeah of Benjamin. For notices of Gibeah of Saul, see 1 Sam. 10:26; 11:4; 15:34; 22:6; 23:19; Isa. 10:29, etc. 4. Gibeah in Kirjath-jearim was no doubt a hill in that city, 2 Sam. 6:3, 4, on which the house of Abinadab stood, where the ark was left. 5. Gibeah in the field, Judg. 20:31; probably the same as Geba. 6. Gibeah-ha-araloth, Josh. 5:3, margin. See **Gilgal.**

Gibeon (gĭb'e-on), *of a hill*. A city of the Hivites, Josh. 9:3-21, about six miles north of Jerusalem. Near it Joshua commanded the sun to stand still, Josh. 10:12, 13; Isa. 28:21; the city was given to Benjamin and to the Levites, Josh. 18:25; 21:17; it was the scene of a notable battle, 2 Sam. 2:12-24; 20:8-10; of the hanging of seven of Saul's sons, 2 Sam. 21:1-6; the tabernacle was set up at Gibeon, 1 Chron. 16:39; and Solomon offered great sacrifices there, 1 Kings 3:4, 5; 9:2; 2 Chron. 1:3, 13; Jehoram recovered captives at Gibeon, Jer. 41:12-16; its people helped to rebuild the walls of Jerusalem after the captivity, Neh. 3:7; 7:25; Ezra 2:20, margin. It is now called el-Jib.

Gideon (gĭd'e-on), *he that cuts down*. Youngest son of Joash, whose family lived at Ophrah, Judg. 6:15, in the territory of Manasseh, near Shechem. He was the fifth and greatest recorded judge of Israel. He had sons, Judg. 6:11; 8:22; and was called by an angel to be a deliverer of Israel. Judg. 6. Clothed by the Spirit of God, Judg. 6:34; comp. 1 Chron. 12:18, he blew a trumpet and was joined by Zebulun, Naphtali and even the reluctant Asher. Strengthened by a double sign from God, he reduced his army by the usual proclamation, Deut. 20:1, 8. By a second test at "the spring of trembling" he further reduced the number of his followers to 300. Judg. 7:5, ff. The midnight attack upon the Midianites, their panic, and the rout and slaughter that followed, are told in Judg. 7. The memory of this splendid deliverance took deep root in the national traditions. 1 Sam. 12:11; Ps. 83:11; Isa. 9:4; 10:26; Heb. 11:32. After this there was a peace of forty years, Judg. 8:29-31. He refused the crown. Judg. 8:23.

Gihon (gī'hŏn), *fountain*, or *stream*. 1. The name of a river of Eden, Gen. 2:13. 2. A place near Jerusalem where Solomon was proclaimed king. 1 Kings 1:33-45. Hezekiah stopped the upper water-course of Gihon, and Manasseh built a wall on the west side of Gihon. 2 Chron. 32:30; 33:14.

Gilboa (gĭl-bō'ah or gĭl'bo-ah), *bubbling fountain*. A mountain east of the plain of Jezreel, and where Saul and Jonathan were slain in battle, and from whence Saul went to consult the witch of Endor. 1 Sam. 28:4; 31:1, 6; 1 Chron. 10:1; 2 Sam. 1:21.

Gilead (gĭl'e-ad), *hard*. 1. The grandson of Manasseh. Num. 26:29, 30, etc. 2. The father of Jephthah. Judg. 11:1, 2. 3. A Gadite. 1 Chron. 5:14.

Gilead, *rocky region*. Called also Mount Gilead and Land of Gilead, Gen. 31:25; Num. 32:1; and known in New Testament times as Peræa, or, "beyond Jordan." Matt. 4:15; John 1:28. 1. Gilead was a region of country bounded on the north by Bashan, east by the Arabian desert, south by Moab and Ammon, and west by the Jordan. Gen. 31:21; Deut. 3:12-17; 1 Sam. 13:7; 2 Kings 10:33. It was about 60 miles long, and 20 miles in its average breadth. Its mountains named in Scripture are Abarim, Pisgah, Nebo, and Peor, and are about 2000 to 3000 feet above the valley of the Jordan. Num. 32:1; Gen. 37:25. The balm of Gilead was held in high favor, Jer. 8:22; 46:11; it is said that only a spoonful could be collected in a day, and that was sold for twice its weight in silver. Jacob fled toward Gilead, Gen. 31:21; it was conquered by Israel, Num. 21:24; Judg. 10:18; Josh. 12:2; Deut. 2:36; was given to Reuben, Gad, and Manasseh, Josh. 17:6; under Jephthah it defeated the Ammonites, Judg. 10:18; was a refuge for Saul's son and for David, 2 Sam. 2:9; 17:22, 24; the home of Elijah, 1 Kings 17:1; taken in part by Syria, 2 Kings 10:33; by Assyria, 2 Kings 15:25-29; referred to in the minor prophets, Hos. 6:8; 12:11; Amos 1:3, 13; Ob. 19; Micah. 7:14; Zech. 10:10. 2. Mount Gilead of Judg. 7:3 was probably near Mount Gilboa.

Gilgal (gĭl'gal), *rolling*. 1. The name of the first station of the Israelites after crossing the Jordan, Josh. 4:19, 20, where the twelve stones were set up, and the tabernacle remained until removed to Shiloh. Josh. 18:1. Samuel judged, and Saul was made king there; 1 Sam. 7:16; 10:8; 11:14, 15; at Gilgal the people gathered for war; there Agag was hewn in pieces. 1 Sam. 13:4-7; 15:33. Gilgal is not named in the New Testament. Josephus places this Gilgal 10 furlongs from Jericho and 50 from the Jordan: Jerome had it pointed out 2 miles from Jericho. 2. The Gilgal in Elijah's time was above Bethel, since the prophet "went down" from that Gilgal to Bethel. 2 Kings 2:2. As Bethel is 3300 feet above the Jordan plain, it must have been a Gilgal not in that plain. It has identified with Jiljilia, 8 miles north of Bethel, where the school of the prophets was probably established. 3. Gilgal of Josh. 12:23 is supposed to be at a Jiljûlieh, near Antipatris, in the plain of Sharon.

Gittith (*gĭt'tĭth*), *a musical instrument.* A word found in the titles of Ps. 8; 81; 84. The derivation of the word is uncertain.

Glass was discovered by the Phœnicians, or perhaps earlier. Representations of the process of glass-blowing are found on Egyptian monuments, and glass beads and fragments of glass vases have been discovered of very ancient age. The only mention of glass in the Old Testament is in Job 28:17, R. V. It is translated "crystal" in the A. V. The mirrors referred to by the word "glass" in 1 Cor. 13:12; 2 Cor. 3:18; Jas. 1:23, were not made of glass. The word is translated "mirror" in these places in the R. V.

Glede. Some unclean bird of prey. Deut. 14:13. It is not certain what particular bird is meant, but most probably one of the buzzards, of which three species inhabit Palestine. The original Hebrew word is rendered "vulture" in Lev. 11:14, R. V., "kite."

Goad. Judg. 3:31. A rod or pole about eight feet long, armed at the larger end with a piece of iron, with which the plowshare was freed from clods and earth, and at the smaller with a sharp spike, by which the oxen were urged on in their labor. In the hands of Shamgar, Judg. 3:31, it was a powerful weapon.

Goat. There are many varieties of the goat; four were most likely known to the Hebrews: 1. The domestic Syrian long-eared breed, with horns rather small and variously bent; the ears longer than the head, and pendulous; hair long, often black. 2. The Angora, or rather Anadolia breed of Asia Minor, with long hair, more or less fine. 3. The Egyptian goat, with small spiral horns, long brown hair, and very long ears. 4. A goat of Upper Egypt without horns, having the nasal bones singularly elevated, the nose contracted, with the lower jaw protruding the incisors. Gen. 15:9. Several words are used in Hebrew for this animal. Goats constituted a large part of Hebrew flocks; for the milk and the flesh were articles of food. Gen. 27:9; 1 Sam. 25:2; Prov. 27:27. As clean animals they were used in sacrifice, Ex. 12:5; Heb. 9:13; and their hair was manufactured into a thick cloth. Of this, one of the coverings of the tabernacle was made, Ex. 25:4; 26:7; and it was on this material that in all probability Paul was employed. Acts 18:3. There is a Hebrew word also which occurs four times, rendered thrice "wild goats." 1 Sam. 24:2; Job 39:1; Ps. 104:18. and once "roe," R. V. "doe," Prov. 5:19. This, there can be little doubt, is the ibex, which is specially formed for climbing, its forelegs being shorter than the hinder. The word translated "devils," R. V. "he-goats," in Lev. 17:7; 2 Chron. 11:15, is one of the ordinary terms for a goat, signifying hairy. This animal is sometimes introduced in Scripture symbolically, as in Dan. 8:5, 21; comp. Matt. 25:32, 33.

God. The name of the Creator and the supreme Governor of the universe. He is a "Spirit, infinite, eternal, and unchangeable in his being, wisdom, power, holiness, justice, goodness, and truth." He is revealed to us in his works and providential government, Rom. 1:20; but more fully in the Holy Scriptures and in the person and work of his only begotten Son, our Lord. 1. *Names.* There are three principal designations of God in the Old Testament—Elohim, Jehovah (Javeh), and Adonai. The first is used exclusively in the first chapter of Genesis; chiefly in the second book of Psalms, Ps. 42–72, called the Elohim Psalms, and occurs alternately with the other names in the other parts of the Old Testament. It expresses his character as the almighty Maker and his relation to the whole world, the Gentiles as well as the Jews. The second is especially used of him in his relation to Israel as the God of the covenant, the God of revelation and redemption. "Adonai," *i. e.*, my Lord, is used where God is reverently addressed, and is always substituted by the Jews for "Jehovah," which they never pronounce. The sacred name Jehovah, or Yahveh, is indiscriminately translated, in the Common Version, God, Lord, and Jehovah. 2. *The Nature of God.* God is revealed to us as a trinity consisting of three Persons who are of one essence, Matt. 28:19; 2 Cor. 13:14; John 1:1–3—God the Father, God the Son, and God the Holy Ghost. To the Father is ascribed the work of creation, to the Son the redemption, to the Holy Spirit the sanctification; but all three Persons take part in all the divine works. To each of these Persons of the Trinity are ascribed the essential attributes of the Supreme God. Thus, the Son is represented as the Mediator of the creation. John 1:3; Col. 1:16; Heb. 1:4. 3. The *unity* of the Godhead is emphasized in the Old Testament, while the trinity is only shadowed forth, or at best faintly brought out. The reason for the emphasis of the unity of the Godhead was to show the fallacy of polytheism and to discourage idolatry, which the heathen practiced. God is denominated "one Lord." Deut. 6:4. Over against the false deities of the heathen, he is designated the "living" God. This belief in God as one was a chief mark of the Jewish religion.—*Condensed from Schaff.*

Gog and Magog (*gŏg* and *mā'gŏg*). Ezek. 38:2. Magog was the name of one of Japheth's sons. Gen. 10:2. It was also a general name of a country north of the Caucacus or Mount Taurus, or for the people of that district. Gog was the king of the country. This people seems to have sustained relations of hostility to Israel, and is associated with Antichrist. Rev. 20:8.

Golan (*gō'lan*), *circle.* One of the six cities of refuge. It was in Bashan, and the most northerly of the three cities of refuge east of the Jordan. Deut. 4:43; Josh. 20:8; 21:27; 1 Chron. 6:71.

Gold. Gen. 2:11. Several places are mentioned by the sacred writers as abounding in gold; such as Ophir, Job 28:16; Parvaim, 2 Chron. 3:6; Sheba and Raamah, Ezek. 27:22. Until long after the time of David gold was not coined, but was sold by weight as a precious article of commerce.

Goliath (go-lī'ath), *splendor.* A giant of Gath, who for forty days defied the armies of Israel. 1 Sam. 17. His height was "six cubits and a span," which, taking the cubit at 18 inches, would make him 9½ feet high. In 2 Sam. 21:19 we find that another Goliath of Gath was slain by Elhanan, also a Bethlehemite.

Gomer (go'mer), *perfect.* 1. The eldest son of Japheth, Gen. 10:2, 3, the father of the early Cimmerians, of the later Cimbri and the other branches of the Celtic family. 2. The wife of Hosea. Hos. 1:3.

Gomorrah (go-môr'rah), *submersion.* One of the five cities in the vale of Siddim, Gen. 14:1-11; destroyed for its wickedness, Gen. 18:20; 19:24, 28; made a warning by Moses, Deut. 29:23; 32:32; referred to by Isaiah, 1:9, 10; by Jeremiah, 23:14; 49: 18; 50:40; by Amos, 4:11; by Zephaniah, 2:9; by our Saviour, Matt. 10:15; Mark 6: 11, A. V.; by Paul, quoting Isaiah, Rom. 9: 29; by Peter and Jude, 2 Pet. 2:6. Its site is disputed. Some place it at the southern, others at the northern, end of the Dead Sea.

Gopher-wood. The ark was made of this material. Gen. 6:14. It was some resinous wood, such as cedar, pine, fir, or cypress, which was considered by the ancients as the most durable wood. It abounded in Syria, was used very commonly for shipbuilding, and was almost the only wood which could furnish suitable timber for so large a vessel as the ark.

Goshen (gō'shen). 1. The portion of Egypt assigned to Israel. Gen. 45:5, 10; 46:28; 47:27; 50:8. It probably bordered on the Tanitic branch of the Nile, hence called Zoan or Tanis, Ps. 78:12, and reached from the Mediterranean to the Red sea. It was suited to shepherds, and abounded in vegetables. It contained the treasure-cities Rameses and Pithom. Goshen was near the royal capital, Gen. 47:27 compared with 48:1, 2; Ex. 5:20; appears to have been the starting-place of the Israelites in their journey to the land of promise. Ex. 12:37, 38. 2. A district in Palestine, perhaps between Gibeon and Gaza. Josh. 10:41; 11:16. 3. A city in the hill-country of Judah. Josh. 15:51.

Gospel. From the Anglo-Saxon *Godspell,* "good tidings," is the English translation of the Greek *euaggelion,* which signifies "good" or "glad tidings." Luke 2: 10; Acts 13:32. The same word in the original is rendered in Rom. 10:15 by the two equivalents "gospel" and "glad tidings." The term refers to the good news of the new dispensation of redemption ushered in by the life, death, and resurrection of Jesus Christ. The "good news" is denominated either simply the "gospel," Matt. 26:13, or else "the gospel of the kingdom," Matt. 9:35; of "Jesus Christ," Mark 1:1; "of peace," Rom. 10:15 A. V., but omitted in R. V.; Eph. 6:15; of "salvation," Eph. 1:13; of "God," 1 Thess. 2:9; and of grace. Acts 20:24. The four Gospels were issued probably during the latter half of the first century—those of Matthew and Mark and Luke before the destruction of Jerusalem; and that of John towards the close of the century. Before the end of the second century, there is abundant evidence that the four Gospels, as one collection, were generally used and accepted. In the fourth Gospel the narrative coincides with that of the other three in a few passages only. The common explanation is that John, writing last, at the close of the first century, had seen the other Gospels, and purposely abstained from writing anew what they had sufficiently recorded. In the other three Gospels there is a great amount of agreement. If we suppose the history that they contain to be divided into 89 sections, in 42 of these all the three narratives coincide, 12 more are given by Matthew and Mark only, 5 by Mark and Luke only, and 14 by Matthew and Luke. To these must be added 5 peculiar to Matthew, 2 to Mark and 9 to Luke, and the enumeration is complete. But this applies only to general coincidence as to the facts narrated —the amount of verbal coincidence, that is, the passages either verbally the same or coinciding in the use of many of the same words, is much smaller. The *First Gospel* was prepared by Matthew for the Jew. He gives us the Gospel of Jesus, the Messiah of the Jews, the Messianic royalty of Jesus. Mark wrote the *Second Gospel* from the preaching of Peter. Luke wrote the *Third Gospel* for the Greek. It is the gospel of the future, of progressive Christianity, of reason and culture seeking the perfection of manhood. John, "the beloved disciple," wrote the *Fourth Gospel* for the Christian, to cherish and train those who have entered the new kingdom of Christ, into the highest spiritual life. See **Matthew, Mark, Luke, and John.** Paul says: "I am not ashamed of the gospel of Christ; for it is the power of God unto salvation to every one that believeth." Rom. 1:16. To the Corinthians he writes: "I came not to you with excellency of speech or of wisdom, declaring unto you the testimony of God. For I determined not to know anything among you, save Jesus Christ, and him crucified." 1 Cor. 2:1, 2.

Gourd. 1. Jonah 4:6-10. The plant intended is the *Ricinus communis,* or castor-oil plant, which, a native of Asia, is now naturalized in America, Africa, and the south of Europe. 2. The wild gourd of 2 Kings 4:39, gathered by one of "the sons of the prophets," is a poisonous gourd, supposed to be the colocynth, which bears a fruit of the color and size of an orange. Orientals can easily understand the cause of the mistake.

Governor. Various Hebrew terms are thus translated: thus it is used to designate certain provincial officers of the Assyrian, Babylonian, Median and Persian empires. The original word is *pechah,* probably akin to the modern pacha. Several of these governors presided over districts on the western side of the Euphrates, Neh. 2:7, 9; and they were inferior to the satraps, or king's lieutenants. Ezra 8:36. In the New Testament the Roman procurator of Judea is called the "governor," e. g., Matt. 27:2, 11, 14; a kindred word being used to describe the authority of Tiberius, Luke 3:1, where our version has "reign." The "governor" of a marriage-feast was the bridegroom's friend, who took charge of the entertainment, John 2:8, 9. The "governor" of Damascus would seem to have been the ethnarch who held the place as the king's lieutenant or vassal. 2 Cor. 11:32. The "governors" of a minor were the trustees of his property, R. V. "stewards." Gal. 4:2. The "governor" of a ship was the steersman. See R. V., Jas. 3:4.

Gozan (*gō'zan*), *quarry* (?). A district to which the Israelites were carried captive. 2 Kings 17:6; 18:11; 19:12; 1 Chron. 5:26; Isa. 37:12. Gozan must not be considered as a river; rather the river mentioned in 1 Chron. 5:26 ran through it; it was probably the region called Gauzanitis by Ptolemy, and Mygdonia by other writers.

Grapes. See Vine.

Grass. There are several Hebrew words which are translated "grass" in our version; but the translation is not uniform. Once, Num. 11:5, the word ordinarily translated "grass" is rendered "leeks." That which grows upon the flattened terraces of eastern house-tops is very soon withered by the scorching rays of the sun. 2 Kings 19:26; Ps. 90:5, 6; 129:6; Isa. 40:6-8; 1 Pet. 1:24.

Grasshopper. See Locust.

Great Sea. Num. 34:6. The Mediterranean sea; called also "utmost sea" and the "hinder sea;" R. V., "eastern sea" and "western sea." Joel 2:20; Zech. 14:8. See Sea.

Greece (*greece*), or **Hellas** (*hel'las*). The well-known country in the southeast of Europe. It is named four times in the Old Testament as Greece or Grecia, Zech. 9:13; Dan. 8:21; 10:20; 11:2, and once in the New Testament, Acts 20:2. It or its people are referred to in Hebrew history as Javan, Isa. 66:19; Ezek. 27:13, 19, and in apostolic history as Achaia. Its cities noticed in Scripture are Athens, Corinth, and Cenchrea.

Greeks, Grecians. The "Greeks" were those Greeks by race, Acts 16:1, 3; 18:17 A. V., but the R. V. omits "the Greeks" and reads "they all;" or else Gentiles as opposed to Jews, Rom. 2:9, 10, "Gentile" A. V., but the margin of the A. V. and the text of the R. V. read "Greek." But Grecians were foreign Jews as distinct from those in Palestine, who were called "Hebrews." Acts 11:20. The Greeks and Hebrews first met when the Tyrians sold the Jews to the Greeks, Joel 3:6. "Prophetical notice of Greece occurs in Dan. 8:21, etc., where the history of Alexander and his successors is rapidly sketched. Zech. 9:13 foretells the triumphs of the Maccabees over the Græco-Syrian empire, while Isaiah looks forward to the conversion of the Greeks, amongst other Gentiles, through the instrumentality of Jewish missionaries. Isa. 66:19."

Greyhound. Prov. 30:31. The Hebrew word means "one well girt or knit in the loins;" see margin of the R. V.; hence it may refer to the war-horse, or to a wrestler. Comp. Job 39:19-25.

Grove. The translation, except in Gen. 21:33 A. V. (the R. V. reads "tamarisk tree)," of the Hebrew word *asherah*; but since *asherah* is an idol or an idolatrous pillar—an image of Astarte, and not a "grove," the A. V. is misleading, as in 1 Kings 18:19; 2 Kings 13:6, and other places, where the R. V. transfers the Hebrew word and reads "Asherah."

H

Habakkuk (*hab-băk'kuk* or *hăb'ak-kŭk*), *embrace*. One of the twelve minor prophets. He lived in the reign of Jehoiakim or of Josiah. His prophecy relates chiefly to the invasion of Judæa by the Chaldæans, chap. 1, and the subsequent punishment of the Chaldæans themselves, chap. 2. The passage, 2:4, "the just shall live by his faith," furnished to Paul the text for his Epistle to the Romans. Rom. 1:17; comp. Gal. 3:11. The third chapter is an eloquent and sublime psalm upon the majesty of God. Bishop Lowth says, "This anthem is unequalled in majesty and splendor of language and imagery."

Habor (*hā'bôr*). Perhaps *rich in vegetation*. A river of Gozan, 2 Kings 17:6; 1 Chron. 5:26; probably identical with the modern *Khabour*, the *Aborrhas* and *Chaboras* of ancient writers, and a branch of the Euphrates.

Hachilah, Hill of (*hăk'al-ah*), *the darksome hill*. A place in Judah near Ziph, and where David with his 600 followers hid. 1 Sam. 23:19; compare 14, 15, 18; 26:3.

Hadad (*hā'dăd*), *clamor*, a Syrian deity, *the sun*. 1. One of the kings who reigned in Edom; his capital city was Avith. He defeated the Midianites in the field of Moab. Gen. 36:35; 1 Chron. 1:46. 2. Another later king of Edom, the last enumerated in the early genealogies. 1 Chron. 1:50, 51. In Gen. 36:39 he is called Hadar. In 1 Chron. 1:51, a later record, his death is noted. 3. An Edomite of the royal family. 1 Kings 11:14-25.

Hadadezer (*hăd-ad-ē'zer*), or **Hadarezer** (*hăd-ar-ē'zer*), *Hadad's help*. A king of Zobah. He was twice defeated by king David's armies. 2 Sam. 8:3; 10:16. On the first occasion 22,000 of the enemy were slain and 1000 chariots were taken. Among the spoils were shields of gold. 1 Chron. 18:4-7, which David took to Jerusalem. Some years afterward they became tributary to David. 1 Chron. 19:16-19.

Hadad-rimmon (*hā'dad-rĭm'mon*). A place probably named from two Syrian idols, Hadad, the sun-god, and Rimmon. It was in the valley of Megiddo, Zech. 12:

11, and the scene of a great lamentation over the death of Josiah. 2 Kings 23 : 29 ; 2 Chron. 35 : 20-25.

Hades. The unseen world, the spirit world. Occurs eleven times in the Greek Testament, Matt. 11 : 23 ; 16 : 18 ; Acts 2 : 31 ; Rev. 1 : 18, etc., and is retained in the R. V. to distinguish it from Gehenna ("hell"). The word is used in Homer as a proper noun for Pluto, the god of the unseen or lower world. In later writers it signifies the unseen spirit world, the abode of the dead. 1. The Greek view of *Hades* and the Roman view of *Orcus* is that of a place for all the dead in the depths of the earth. 2. The Hebrew *Sheol* is the equivalent for the Greek *Hades*, and is so translated in the Septuagint. It is likewise the subterranean abode of all the dead, but only their temporary abode until the advent of the Messiah or the final judgment, and is divided into two departments, called *Paradise* or *Abraham's bosom* for the good, and *Gehenna* or *hell* for the bad. 3. The New Testament *Hades* does not differ essentially from the Hebrew *Sheol*, but Christ has broken the power of death, dispelled the darkness of Hades, and revealed to believers the idea of heaven as the state and abode of bliss in immediate prospect after a holy life. The A. V. translates *Hades* and *Gehenna* by the same word, "hell," except in 1 Cor. 15 : 55, "grave," R. V. reads "death," and thus obliterates the important distinction between the realm of the dead or spirit world and the place of torment. Hades is a temporary abode—heaven and hell are permanent and final. Since Christ's descent into Hades, or the unseen, the spirit world, believers need not fear to enter this realm through death. Christ declares, "I am alive for evermore, Amen ; and have the keys of death and of Hades." Rev. 1 : 18, R. V.

Hagar (*hā'gar*), *flight*. An Egyptian woman, the bond-servant of Sarah, whom the latter gave as a concubine to Abraham, and Hagar despised her mistress. Gen. 16 : 1-4. Hagar fled. On her return she gave birth to Ishmael, and Abraham was then 86 years old. When Ishmael was about 16 years old, he was caught by Sarah making sport of her young son Isaac, and Sarah demanded the expulsion of Hagar and her son. Hagar again fled toward Egypt, and when in despair at the want of water, an angel again appeared to her, pointed out a fountain close by, and renewed the former promises to her. Gen. 21 : 9-21. Paul, Gal. 4 : 25, refers to her as the type of the old covenant.

Hagarenes, Hagarites (*hā'gar-ēnes', hā'gar-ītes*), (named from Hagar). A people dwelling to the east of Palestine, with whom the tribes of Reuben made war in the time of Saul. 1 Chron. 5 : 10, 18-20. The same people are mentioned in Ps. 83 : 6.

Haggai (*hăg'ga-ī* or *hăg'gāī*), *festive*. A prophet after the captivity, in the second year of Darius Hystaspes, or B. C. 520, Hag. 1 : 1. Nothing is known of his life.

THE PROPHECY OF, which is prose in form, concerns the repair of the temple, 1 : 1-12 ; 2 : 10-20, the glory of the second temple, 2 : 1-9, and the triumph of Zerubbabel over his enemies. 2 : 20-23.

Hair. The Hebrews allowed the hair to grow thick and somewhat long. Ezek. 8 : 3. Baldness was disliked, as sometimes symptomatic of leprosy, Lev. 13 : 40-44 : hence the reproach uttered against Elisha, 2 Kings 2 : 23. Cuttings of the hair, such as were usual in idolatrous worship, were forbidden. Lev. 19 : 27 ; Deut. 14 : 1. Still this seems to have been a Hebrew custom in mourning, Jer. 7 : 29 ; while, on the contrary, the Egyptians let their hair grow when in distress, and shaved or cut it on returning prosperity. Gen. 41 : 14 : comp. Herodotus, lib. ii. 36, iii. 12. The way in which Absalom let his hair grow was no doubt the vanity of a young and handsome man. 2 Sam. 14 : 26. Thus, to uncover the ear is a common phrase for communicating a secret, 1 Sam. 9 : 15, marg., 20 : 2, marg., as if it were necessary to put aside the locks in order to whisper in the ear. There was, however, a clear distinction made between the sexes in this respect, 1 Cor. 11 : 14, 15 ; so that the women wore their hair very long. Luke 7 : 38 ; John 12 : 3. Hence, perhaps, the long hair of the Nazirites was to indicate humility and subjection. Num. 6 : 5. The color of the hair was generally black, Song of Sol. 5 : 11 : but the gray hairs of age were regarded as especially venerable, Prov. 16 : 31 ; on this account, perhaps, the hairs of the Ancient of Days are likened to "pure wool." Dan. 7 : 9. Samson had seven plaits in his hair, Judg. 16 : 13,19 ; and these must have been fastened with a fillet. Ezek. 24 : 17. Of course greater pains were taken by females in thus adorning themselves ; so that we read in many passages of both scripture and the apocrypha of tiring the head and braiding the hair. 2 Kings 9 : 30 ; 1 Tim. 2 : 9 ; 1 Pet. 3 : 3 ; Judith 10 : 3. It was also worn in curls : the "well-set hair," Isa. 3 : 24, probably implied the artistical arrangement of these. There are several references to the curls in the descriptions of Solomon's Song. Thus "the chain of the neck," Song of Sol. 4 : 9, might be a long lock or curl falling down upon the neck ; and the "galleries," R. V., "tresses," 7 : 5, were the curls in orderly array. The hair was commonly anointed with fragrant oil or perfume. Ps. 23 : 5 ; 133 : 2 ; Matt. 6 : 17 ; Luke 7 : 46.

Ham, *hot*, or *multitude*. The son of Noah, known for his irreverence to his father, Gen. 9 : 22, and as the parent of Cush, Mizraim, Phut, and Canaan, Gen. 10 : 6, who became the founders of large nations. Cush seems to have been the father of the peoples dwelling in Babylonia, southern Arabia, and Ethiopia ; Nimrod was his son. Gen. 10 : 8. Mizraim, the Hebrew word for Egypt, was the ancestor of the Egyptians. Phut was also the ancestor of an African people, as appears from the association of his name with the descendants of Cush and the Lydians, Jer. 46 : 9 ; see margin. Canaan was the ancestor of the Phœnicians and other tribes inhabiting Palestine. Egypt is called "the land of Ham." Ps. 78 : 51 ; 105 : 23-27 ; 106 : 22.

Haman (hā'man), *celebrated*. Prime minister of Ahasuerus, the Persian monarch. Esth. 3:1. His pride was hurt because Mordecai, the Jew, refused to bow and do him reverence. Esth. 3:2. He was executed on the very gallows he had prepared for Mordecai. Esth. 7:10. The Jews, on the mention of his name on the day of Purim, hiss.

Hamath (hā'math), *fortress, citadel*. A city of Syria. It was founded by a son of Canaan, Gen. 10:18; Num. 34:8, and was situated in the valley of the Orontes. It was 165 miles in a straight line north of Jerusalem; was visited by the spies, Num. 13:21, and it is frequently noticed as the northern boundary of Palestine. Num. 34:8; Josh. 13:5. Its king, Toi, blessed David for his victory over Zobah, 2 Sam. 8:9-12; Solomon extended his kingdom to Hamath, 1 Kings 8:65; 2 Chron. 8:4, and built store-cities in that region; afterward the city and country became independent, but were again subdued by Jeroboam II. 2 Kings 14:25, 28. It was taken by the Assyrians, 2 Kings 18:34; Isa. 10:9; Amos calls it "Hamath the great," and speaks of its desolation. Amos 6:2. Its modern name is Hamah, and it is now a place of 30,000 inhabitants.

Hananiah (hăn'a-nī'ah), *whom God hath given*. 1. A false prophet and contemporary with Jeremiah. Jer. 28:3. He died that year. Jer. 28:17. There are 15 persons of this name mentioned in the Old Testament.

Handicraft. Acts 18:3; 19:25; Rev. 18:22. Says Rabbi Jehuda, "He who does not teach his son a trade is much the same as if he taught him to be a thief." *Metal-workers*. The preparation of iron for use either in war, in agriculture, together with iron, working in brass, or rather copper alloyed with tin (bronze), is mentioned as practiced in antediluvian times. Gen. 4:22. After the establishment of the Jews in Canaan, the occupation of a smith became a distinct employment. 1 Sam. 13:19. The smith's work and its results are often mentioned in Scripture. 2 Sam. 12:31; 1 Kings 6:7; 2 Chron. 26:14; Isa. 44:12; 54:16. The worker also in gold and silver must have found employment among the Hebrews in very early times. Gen. 24:22, 53; 35:4; 38:18. Various processes of the goldsmith's work are illustrated by Egyptian monuments. After the conquest frequent notices are found of both moulded and wrought metal, including soldering. *Carpenters* are often mentioned in Scripture. Gen. 6:14; Ex. 37; Isa. 44:13. In the palace built by David for himself the workmen employed were chiefly foreigners. 2 Sam. 5:11. That the Jewish carpenters must have been able to carve with some skill is evident from Isa. 41:7; 44:13. In the New Testament the occupation of a carpenter is mentioned in connection with Joseph the husband of Mary, and our Lord himself was a carpenter. Matt. 13:55; Mark 6:3. *Masons* and *stone-cutters* were employed by David and Solomon, many of whom were Phœnicians. 1 Kings 5:18. The large stones used in Solomon's temple are said by Josephus to have been fitted together exactly without either mortar or clamps, but the foundation stones to have been fastened with lead. For ordinary building mortar was used; sometimes bitumen, as at Babylon. Gen. 11:3; Ezek. 13:10. The use of whitewash on tombs is noticed by our Lord. Matt. 23:27. *Shipboat-building* was common to some extent, for there were the fishing-vessels on the Lake of Gennesaret. Matt. 8:23; 9:1; John 21:3, 8. Solomon built ships for his foreign trade. 1 Kings 9:26, 27; 22:48; 2 Chron. 20:36, 37. Apothecaries or perfumers appear to have formed a guild or association. Ex. 30:25, 35; 2 Chron. 16:14; Neh. 3:8; Eccles. 7:1; 10:1. The arts of *spinning* and *wearing* both wool and linen were carried on in early times by women. Ex. 35:25, 26; Lev. 19:19; Deut. 22:11; 2 Kings 23:7; Ezek. 16:16; Prov. 31:13, 24. The loom with its beam, 1 Sam. 17:7, pin, Judg. 16:14, and shuttle, Job 7:6, was perhaps introduced later, but as early as David's time. 1 Sam. 17:7. *Dyeing* and *dressing* cloth were practiced in Palestine, as were also tanning and dressing leather. Josh. 2:15-18; 2 Kings 1:8; Matt. 3:4; Acts 9:43. *Barbers*. Num. 6:5, 19; Ezek. 5:1. *Tent-makers* are noticed in Acts 18:3. *Potters* are frequently alluded to. Jer. 18:2-6. *Bakers* are noticed in Scripture, Jer. 37:21; Hos. 7:4; and the well-known valley Tyropœon probably derived its name from the occupation of the cheese-makers, its inhabitants. Dealers in meat, not Jewish, are spoken of in 1 Cor. 10:25.

Hannah (hăn'nah), *grace*. One of the wives of Elkanah, and the mother of Samuel. Her song of praise on this occasion, 1 Sam. 2:1-10, is a magnificent hymn to the holiness and justice of Jehovah, and has been compared with the song of Mary. Luke 1:46-55.

Hanun (hā'nun), *favored*. 1. The son of Nahash, king of the Ammonites. He disgraced David's ambassadors, and thus caused the ruin of his people. 2 Sam. 10; 1 Chron. 19. 2. One who, with the inhabitants of Zanoah, helped to repair the wall of Jerusalem. Neh. 3:13. 3. Another person, apparently, who also helped in repairing the wall. Neh. 3:30.

Haran (hā'ran), *a mountaineer*. 1. The brother of Abraham, and the father of Lot. Gen. 11:26. 2. A Levite. 1 Chron. 23:9.

Haran (hā'ran), *parched, dry;* called also **Charran** (kăr'ran). Acts 7:2, 4. The place to which Terah removed from Ur of the Chaldees. Terah died there, Gen. 11:31, 32; Abram and Lot moved to Canaan, Gen. 12:4, while Nahor remained at Haran, which was called the city of Nahor. Gen. 24:10. It was the early home of Rebekah, and Jacob afterward resided there with Laban. Gen. 27:43. The city was in Mesopotamia, and more definitely in Padan-aram, Gen. 24:10; 25:20, and also in western Assyria. It is generally identified with the modern Haran, the Roman Carræ, situated on the river Belik—the ancient Bilichus—about 50 miles above its entrance into the Euphrates.

Hare. Deut. 14:7. Of the hare, which resembles the rabbit, five species or varieties are found in Palestine. This animal was declared unclean by the Jewish law, Lev. 11:6, "because he cheweth the cud, but divideth not the hoof." For popular guidance this description was better than a more scientific one, and is explained under **Coney.**

Harod (ha'rod), *trembling, terror.* A spring by which Gideon encamped, and where probably the trial of the army by their mode of drinking was made, Judg. 7; perhaps the same with the fountain of Jezreel. 1 Sam. 29:1. It is likely that the modern 'Ain Jalûd is the spring of Harod.

Harosheth (ha-rō'shĕth), *working in wood, etc.,* **of the Gentiles.** So called from the mixed people who dwelt there. A place in the north of Palestine, the home of Sisera, Judg. 4:2, 13, 16, and the place of assembling of Jabin's army.

Harp. The national musical instrument of the Hebrews. Its invention is credited to Jubal before the flood, Gen. 4:21. Josephus records that the harp had ten strings and that it was played on with the plectrum. Sometimes it was smaller, having only eight strings, and was usually played with the fingers.

Harrow. It is very questionable whether the Hebrews used a harrow in our sense of the term. In Job 39:10; Isa. 28:24; Hos. 10:12, breaking the clods is alluded to; but this was before sowing the seed, just to level the ground. The word translated "harrow" in 2 Sam. 12:31; 1 Chron. 20:3, means a sharp threshing-sledge.

Hart, Hind. Ps. 42:1. The former is the male stag, one of the most graceful and beautiful of all animals. It was clean by the Levitical law, Deut. 12:15; 14:5, and the grace and agility of its motions are alluded to in Song of Sol. 2:9; Isa. 35:6. The stag lolls or pants like the dog, and is soon exhausted by hunger. Jer. 14:5; Lam. 1:6. The hind is the female stag. She is smaller and weaker than her mate, the hart, and has no horns. She is sure and swift of foot, and leaps fearlessly among the rocks and precipices. 2 Sam. 22:34; Ps. 18:33; Hab. 3:19. The instinctive affection of the hart and hind is alluded to, Prov. 5:18, 19, and Song of Sol. 2:7; 3:5. The figurative prediction of Jacob respecting Naphtali, Gen. 49:21, would be more appropriately rendered, "Naphtali is a deer roaming at large; he shooteth forth noble antlers." The antlers or horns indicate the strength and health of the stag, and the whole metaphor expresses the increase of the tribe and the fertility of their portion in Judæa.

Harvest in Palestine was in March and April, and the term is frequently employed to designate this season of the year. Josh. 3:15; Prov. 6:8. The harvests of the different grains happened in regular succession, and are known as the "wheat-harvest," 1 Sam. 12:17, and the "barley-harvest," Ruth 1:22. The grain was reaped with sickles, Jer. 50:16, gathered in handfuls, Ruth 2:16, and done up into sheaves, Ps. 129:7. It was then conveyed to the barns or threshing-floors, sometimes in carts, Amos 2:13, where it was threshed or winnowed. One mode of threshing was by the treading of oxen, which it was forbidden to muzzle. Deut. 25:4. Harvest was a season of great joy and merriment. Isa. 9:3. Our Lord refers to the end of the world under the term of harvest, Matt. 13:39, whose reapers will be the angels. The angel is represented figuratively as at that time thrusting in his sickle, "for the harvest of the earth is ripe." Rev. 14:15.

Hauran (haw'ran), *caves, caverns.* A country east of the Jordan; the northeastern boundary of Palestine, Ezek. 47:16, 18, and the Auranitis of the Greeks, and now known as the Hauran. When the Israelites conquered the land, the whole of this region appears to have been subject to Og, the king of Bashan, Num. 21:33-35; Deut. 3:1-5, and a large portion of it was allotted to Manasseh. The ruins scattered over the region are very extensive and remarkable; those built in the caverns are regarded by Wetzstein as the most ancient, and possibly reaching back to the times of the Rephaim. Gen. 14:5; 15:20, and Deut. 3:11.

Havilah (hăv'i-lah or ha-vī'lah), *circle, district.* A country abounding in gold, bdellium, and onyx stone. Gen. 2:11. Havilah is mentioned as a boundary of the children of Ishmael. Gen. 25:18. Kalisch supposes that it was a country between the Persian and the Arabian gulfs; others hold that the "country of Havilah" in 1 Sam. 15:7 refers to the region about Mount Seir, and that it was not probably identical with the Havilah of Gen. 2:11.

Havoth-Jair (hă'voth-jā'ir), *villages of Jair.* A title applied to certain villages east of the Jordan which Jair captured and held. Num. 32:41; Judg. 10:4. The towns of Jair are included with the 60 cities given to Manasseh, Josh. 13:30; 1 Chron. 2:23; but the word rendered "villages" usually means a small collection of hovels in a country place. These towns were a part of one of the revenue districts of Solomon. 1 Kings 4:13.

Hazael (hăz'a-el or hā'za-el), whom *God beholds, i. e., cares for.* A king of Syria. 1 Kings 19:15, 17. Jehu was to extirpate the authors of idolatry, Hazael to chastise the whole nation of Israel, and Elisha to slay with the quick and powerful sword of the divine word. Comp. Jer. 1:10. When Elisha visited Damascus, and Ben-hadad, who was sick, had sent Hazael, a trusted servant, to inquire whether he should recover, Elisha intimated his approaching sovereignty. Hazael was astonished. The next day, however, Ben-hadad died, apparently by Hazael's hand, though some question this; and Hazael succeeded as king; and his reign, with the exception of the time when he was called on to defend himself against the Assyrian power, was occupied with continual wars upon Israel and even against Judah. 2 Kings 8:7-15, 28, 29; 9:14, 15; 10:32, 33; 12:17, 18; 13:3; 2 Chron. 22:5, 6. Hazael is supposed to have reigned about 46 years, 886-840 B.C. He was succeeded by his son, Ben-hadad II. 2 Kings 13:22–25; Amos 1:4.

Hazor (hā'zŏr), *enclosure.* 1. The city of King Jabin; destroyed by Joshua, Josh. 11:1, 10, 11; given to Naphtali, Josh. 19:36; again possessed by the Canaanites, Judg. 4:2, who had for its king Jabin—a generic title, probably, like Pharaoh in Egypt—who reigned in Hazor and whose general was Sisera. It was fortified by Solomon, 1 Kings 9:15; its people were carried into captivity by Tiglath-pileser. 2 Kings 15:29. The city appears to have been situated on a hill in the midst of a plain, and was a stronghold. Josh. 11:4; Judg. 4:3. 2. A city in the south of Judah; probably should be written Hazor-ithman. Josh. 15:23. 3. Another town of Judah; called Hazor-hadattah, or New Hazor. Josh. 15:25. 4. Hezron, which is Hazor, Josh. 15:25; rendered by Canon Cook "Kerioth Hezron, which is Hazor." It is supposed to have been the home of Judas Iscariot, the man of Kerioth, Matt. 10:4; Conder suggested Kheshram, north of Beer-sheba, as the site of this Hazor.

Heart. Acts 16:14. The seat of the affections, desires, hopes, and motives. John 14:1; Esth. 1:10. The term is also used by the Bible writers to designate the understanding, 1 Cor. 2:9, and intellectual perceptions. It is further a general term for the spiritual nature of man. Isa. 1:5; 2 Cor. 4:6. In the latter passage the apostle speaks of the light shining in our hearts, teaching us of Christ as the one who reveals God. The heart is declared to be corrupt and full of evil, Eccl. 9:3, and deceit, Jer. 17:9, the seat of sin and crime, Matt. 15:19, as also of faith. Rom. 10:10. The Lord "looketh on the heart," 1 Sam. 16:7, in contrast to the outward appearance, and we are commanded to cultivate it, as the most important part of our nature, rather than external appearances. Prov. 4:4; Joel 2:13. The expression, "to speak in the heart," 1 Sam. 1:13, is synonymous with "to think."

Heaven. There are four Hebrew words thus rendered in the Old Testament. 1. *Rākî'a,* A. V. firmament. 2. *Shâmayim;* used in the expression, "the heaven and the earth," or "the upper and lower regions." Gen. 1:1. 3. *Mārôm,* used for heaven in Ps. 18:16; Isa. 24:18; Jer. 25:30. Properly speaking, it means a mountain, as in Ps. 102:19; Ezek. 17:23. 4. *Shechâkim,* "expanses," with reference to the *extent* of heaven. Deut. 33:26; Job 35:5. Paul's expression, "third heaven," 2 Cor. 12:2, has led to much conjecture. Grotius said that the Jews divided the heaven into three parts, viz., 1. The air or atmosphere, where clouds gather. 2. The firmament, in which the sun, moon, and stars are fixed. 3. The upper heaven, the abode of God and his angels.

Heber (hē'ber), *alliance.* Heber the Kenite, the husband of Jael, who slew Sisera. Judg. 4:21, 22. See Jael, Sisera. Heber appears to have led a life apart from the rest of his tribe. He must have been a person of consequence, from the fact that it is stated that there was peace between him and the powerful king Jabin. Judg. 4:17. There are seven persons of this name mentioned in the Scriptures.

Hebrew (hē'brew), a name given to Abram by the Canaanites, Gen. 14:13, because he had crossed the Euphrates. The name some derive from *'Eber,* "beyond, on the other side," Abraham and his posterity being called Hebrews in order to express a distinction between the races east and west of the Euphrates. It may also be derived from *Eber,* or *Heber,* one of the ancestors of Abraham. Gen. 10:24. See Jews.

Hebrews, Epistle to the. The aim of this epistle is to prove from the Old Testament the divinity, humanity, atonement and intercession of Christ, and his preeminence over Moses and the angels of God; to demonstrate the superiority of the gospel to the law, and the real object and design of the Mosaic institution. The name of the writer of this epistle is nowhere mentioned. Its authorship is disputed, many ascribing it to the apostle Paul, others to Apollos, Luke, or Barnabas. It is believed to have been written in Italy about A. D. 63.

Hebron (hē'bron), *friendship.* An ancient town of Palestine, about 20 miles south of Jerusalem, first called Kirjath-arba, or city of Arba. Josh. 21:11; 15:13, 14; Judg. 1:10. It lies about 3000 feet above the level of the sea, and is one of the oldest towns in the world and mentioned before Damascus, Gen. 13:18; 14:13; and was built 7 years before Zoan, or Tanis, in Egypt, Num. 13:22. Hebron is named about forty times in the Old Testament, but nowhere in the New. Abraham pitched his tent under the oaks of Mamre, near Hebron, Gen. 13:18, and he bought the cave of Machpelah, as a burial-place. Gen. 23:17–20. Hebron was taken by Joshua, Josh. 10:36, 37; 12:10, and the region given to Caleb, Josh. 14:13; was rebuilt and made a Levitical city and a city of refuge, Josh. 20:7; 21:11; was the royal residence of David, 2 Sam. 2:1–14; 1 Kings 2:11; became the headquarters of the rebellious Absalom, 2 Sam. 15:10; was fortified by Rehoboam and repeopled after the captivity. 2 Chron. 11:10; Neh. 11:25. A pool is still shown over which tradition says that David hung the murderers of Ishbosheth, and the tomb of Abner and Ishbosheth is also pointed out within an Arab house, and the mosque is known to conceal the noted cave of Machpelah, the burial-place of Abraham, Isaac, and Jacob and their wives except Rachel. The mosque is closed against visitors and guarded with the strictest care by the Moslems.

Helbon (hĕl'bŏn), *fertile.* A Syrian city celebrated for its wine, Ezek. 27:18, and formerly identified with Aleppo, but later with Helbôn, in a wild glen high up in the Anti-Lebanon. This valley is celebrated for its fine grapes and vineyards. Robinson says "the wine of Helbon" is the best and most famous wine in the country.

Hell. The English word hell is used to designate the place of the dead, the grave, and also the place of punishment after death and the abode of evil spirits.

It represents four different words in the original of Scripture—*Sheōl, Hades, Gehenna,* and *Tartarus.* 1. *In the Old Testament* it is used 31 times to render the Hebrew word *Sheōl.* Sheōl at first seems to have denoted the common subterranean abode of all human spirits, good and bad (Gen. 37:35, R. V., death; Num. 16:30), but afterward is represented as having in it two distinct regions, one for the righteous, Ps. 16:11; 17:15, the other for the wicked. Ps. 9:17; 49:14. All the dead are alike in *Sheōl,* but in widely different circumstances. *Sheōl* is variously translated in our English Bible by the terms "hell," "pit," and "grave." In many places it is rightly translated "grave." 1 Sam. 2:6; Job 14:13, etc. *Sheōl* is represented as in the depths of the earth, Job 11:8; Prov. 9:18; Isa. 38:10, all-devouring, Prov. 1:12, destitute of God's presence, Ps. 88:10-12, a state of forgetfulness, Ps. 6:5, insatiable, Isa. 5:14, remorseless, Song of Sol. 8:6, and a place of silence, Eccl. 9:10.

2. *The New Testament.*—The two words translated "hell" are Hades and Gehenna. Hades occurs eleven times, and is once rendered "grave," R.V., "death," 1 Cor. 15:55; in all other places "hell." Hades does not always refer to the ultimate abode of the impenitent and the final state of exclusion from God. Matt. 16:27. After the crucifixion, our Lord descended into hades, Acts 2:27, and this is an article of the Apostles' Creed, where, however, we use wrongly the word "hell." It was in this realm that our Lord "preached to the spirits in prison." 1 Pet. 3:19.

The Greek word *Gehenna* occurs twelve times in Scripture. It early designated a place in the valley of Hinnom, which had been the seat of the worship of Moloch, Jer. 7:31; 2 Chron. 33:6; 2 Kings 23:10, and for the deposit of the filth and dead animals of the city. Hence it was used to denote the final state and abode of lost souls. Matt. 5:29; 10:28; 23:15; Jas. 3:6, etc. It is here that "their worm dieth not" and the "fire is not quenched." Mark 9:48. Into this realm the rebellious angels were cast, 2 Pet. 2:4 (where the word is a derivative from the Greek word "Tartarus"). At the great day of judgment the cursed shall go away into this abode and receive everlasting punishment. Matt. 25:46. It is referred to by our Lord in solemn and awful tones. Matt. 5:22, 29, 30; 10:28; Mark 9:43-48; Luke 12:5, and with such accompaniments as indicate everlasting and remediless ruin. Retribution will have degrees, Matt. 10:15, in character, but none in duration.

Heresy. Acts 24:14, A. V. This term, as generally used by the sacred writers, signifies a party or division, R. V. "a sect." It is derived from a word meaning "to choose." The Pharisees, Acts 15:5; 26:5, and the Sadducees, Acts 5:17, as well as the Nazarenes, Acts 24:5, 12, 14, were denominated heresies. In these passages the word is translated "sects." In Acts 24:14, where Paul speaks of the Christian religion as "the way which they call heresy," he undoubtedly means to imply that the Christian organization was not a separation from the Old Testament Church, but the true Church itself. In 1 Cor. 11:19; Gal. 5:20, and 2 Pet. 2:1 heresies are referred to in connection with the apostolic Church, and in the last two cases the implication is that they are departures from the fundamental truth of the gospel, and to be condemned. Early in the history of the Christian Church the word acquired the signification it now has, of a departure from the fundamentals of gospel truth.

Hermon (her'mon), *a peak, summit.* The highest mountain in Palestine, Deut. 3:8; Josh. 12:1; Josh. 11:17; 1 Chron. 5:23. It towers high above the ancient border city of Dan and the fountains of the Jordan, and is the most conspicuous and beautiful mountain in Palestine or Syria. Hermon has three summits, situated like the angles of a triangle, and about a quarter of a mile from each other. In two passages of Scripture this mountain is called Baal-hermon, Judg. 3:3; 1 Chron. 5:23, possibly because Baal was there worshipped. Hermon was probably the scene of the transfiguration, as it stands near Cæsarea Philippi, where we know Christ was just before that event. The height of Hermon is reckoned at 10,000 feet.

Herod (hĕr'od), *hero-like.* A family of Idumean origin. Not less than six Herods exclusive of Archelaus are noted in Scripture.

1. *Herod the Great* was the second son of Antipater and appointed procurator of Judæa by Julius Cæsar, B. C. 47. In B. C. 41 he was appointed by Antony tetrarch of Judæa. Forced to abandon Judæa the following year, he fled to Rome, and received the appointment of king of Judæa. It was some time before his fatal illness that he must have caused the slaughter of the infants at Bethlehem. Matt. 2:16-18. He adorned Jerusalem with many splendid monuments of his taste and magnificence. The temple, which he built with scrupulous care, was the greatest of these works. The restoration was begun B. C. 20, and the temple itself was completed in a year and a half. But fresh additions were constantly made in succeeding years, so that it was said that the temple was building forty and six years, John 2:20, the work continuing long after Herod's death. Herod died at Jericho, B. C. 4.

2. *Herod Antipas,* the son of Herod the Great, first married a daughter of Aretas, "king of Arabia Petræa," but afterward Herodias, the wife of his half brother, Herod Philip. Aretas, indignant at the insult to his daughter, invaded the territory of Herod, and defeated him with great loss. This defeat, according to the famous passage in Josephus, was attributed by many to the murder of John the Baptist, which had been committed by Antipas shortly before, under the influence of Herodias. Matt. 14:4; Mark 6:17 ff.; Luke 3:19. At a later time Herodias urged him to go to Rome to gain the title of king, cf.

105

Mark 6:14; but he was opposed at the court of Caligula by the emissaries of Agrippa, and condemned to perpetual banishment at Lugdunum, A. D. 39. Herodias voluntarily shared his punishment, and he died in exile. Pilate took occasion from our Lord's residence in Galilee to send Jesus to Herod Antipas, Luke 23:6 ff. The city of Tiberias, which Antipas founded and named in honor of the emperor, was the most conspicuous monument of his long reign.

3. *Herod Philip I.*, Philip, Mark 6:17, was the son of Herod the Great and Mariamne. He married Herodias, the sister of Agrippa I., by whom he had a daughter, Salome. He was excluded from all share in his father's possessions in consequence of his mother's treachery, and lived afterward in a private station.

4. *Herod Philip II.* was the son of Herod the Great and Cleopatra. He received as his own government Batanea, Trachonitis, Auranitis (Gaulanitis), and some parts about Jamnia, with the title of tetrarch, Luke 3:1. He built a new city on the site of Paneas, near the sources of the Jordan, which he called Cæsarea Philippi, Matt. 16:13; Mark 8:27, and raised Bethsaida to the rank of a city under the title of Julias, and died there A. D. 34. He married Salome, the daughter of Herod Philip I. and Herodias.

5. *Herod Agrippa I.* was the son of Aristobulus and Bernice, and grandson of Herod the Great. Caligula made him king, first of the tetrarchy of Philip and Lysanias; afterward the dominions of Antipas were added, and finally Judea and Samaria. Agrippa was a strict observer of the law, and he sought with success the favor of the Jews. It is probable that it was with this view he put to death James the son of Zebedee, and further imprisoned Peter. Acts 12:1 ff. But his sudden death interrupted his ambitious projects. Acts 12:21, 23.

6. *Herod Agrippa II.* was the son of Herod Agrippa I. In A. D. 52 the emperor gave him the tetrarchies formerly held by Philip and Lysanias, with the title of king. Acts 25:13. The relation in which he stood to his sister Bernice, Acts 25:13, was the cause of grave suspicion. It was before him that Paul was tried. Acts 26:28.

Herodians (he-rō'di-anz), (from Herod). Matt. 22:15 ff.; Mark 12:13 ff. Canon Cook describes these persons as "that party among the Jews who were supporters of the Herodian family as the last hope of retaining for the Jews a fragment of national government, as distinguished from absolute dependence upon Rome as a province of the empire. Supporters of the family of Herod, who held their dominions by the grant of the Roman emperor, would be in favor of paying tribute to the supreme power." Matt. 22:16.

Herodias (he-rō'di-as). Daughter of Aristobulus, one of the sons of Mariamne and Herod the Great, and consequently sister of Agrippa I. She first married Herod Philip I.; then she eloped from him to marry Herod Antipas, her step-uncle. The head of John the Baptist was granted at the request of Herodias. Matt. 14:8-11; Mark 6:24-28, A. D. 29.

Heshbon (hĕsh'bŏn), *reason, device*. A city of the Moabites, taken by Sihon, king of the Amorites, and made his capital; captured and occupied by the Israelites, Num. 21:25, 26; situated on the boundary between Reuben and Gad; rebuilt by Reuben and made a Levitical city, then being territorially a Gadite city. Num. 32:3, 37; Deut. 1:4; 2:24-30; 3:2, 6; 4:46; 29:7; Josh. 9:10; 12:2, 5; 13:10-27; 21:39; Judg. 11:19, 26; 1 Chron. 6:81. In later times the Moabites regained possession of Heshbon, so that it is mentioned as a Moabitish town in the prophetic denunciations against that people. Isa. 15:4; 16:8, 9; Jer. 48:2, 34, 45; 49:3. The ruins of the city still exist some 15 miles east of the northern end of the Dead sea, on the great table land of Moab. A small hill rises 200 feet above the general level, and upon this is Heshbon, now called Hesbân. East of the city are the remains of water-courses and an enormous cistern, or "fish-pond," which illustrates Song of Sol. 7:4.

Hezekiah (hĕz'e-kī'ah), *whom God strengthens*. A good king of Judah, who succeeded his father Ahaz about 726 B. C., and died about 698 B. C. For his history see 2 Kings 18-20; 2 Chron. 29-32. Compare Isa. 36-38. He tried to restore the worship of Jehovah, removing "high places," and destroying the brazen serpent; consult 2 Chron. 28:22-25; for the final deportation of the Ten Tribes see 2 Kings 17; 18:9-12; and for his revolt against the Assyrians compare 2 Kings 18; 2 Chron. 32. Hezekiah's payment of tribute is noted in 2 Kings 18:13-16. Assyrian annals of Sennacherib discovered at Nineveh agree with this account. A second invasion seems to have followed when Sennacherib, Isa. 30:1-7, returned, Isa. 33:1. Then came Sennacherib's letters from Lachish and Libnah, the destruction of a great part of his army, and the retreat of the rest to Assyria, in answer to Hezekiah's prayer. Compare Isa. 31:8, 9; 37:33-37. Hezekiah's sickness, humiliation, and prolongation of life 15 years in peace, and the prediction that Babylon, then feeble and friendly, would one day carry his descendants into captivity are noticed in Old Testament history, Isa. 39; Micah 4:10. Hezekiah collated the Proverbs of Solomon. Prov. 25:1. The prophecies of Hosea and Micah were delivered partly in his reign; compare Jer. 26:17-19; and Nahum was perhaps his contemporary.

Hiddekel (hĭd'de-kĕl), *rapid*. One of the rivers of Eden, the river which "goeth eastward to Assyria," Gen. 2:14, and which Daniel calls "the great river," Dan. 10:4, rightly identified with the Tigris. The name now in use among the inhabitants of Mesopotamia is Dijleh.

Hierapolis (hī'e-răp'o-lĭs), *sacred city*. A city in Proconsular Asia, Col. 4:13, near the river Lycus, and in sight of Laodicea, which was about 5 miles to the south. It stood on a high bluff, with a high mountain behind it. In the city was the famous temple of Pluto, remains of which are still to be seen. The ruins of the city are extensive, as temples, churches, a triumphal arch, a theatre, gymnasium, baths, and highly ornamented sarcophagi.

Higgaion (*hig-gā'yon*). A term occurring three times, Ps. 9:16; 19:14 (translated "meditation"), and Ps. 92:3 (translated "solemn sound"). It probably was originally a musical term which acquired the additional signification of solemn thought or meditation.

High Places. The Hebrew word *bamah* is a general term, comprehending mountains and hills; but in Ezek. 20:29, it is given as the proper name of a place; while in other passages it is usually and correctly translated "high place." The Hebrews, like most other ancient nations, frequently offered sacrifices upon "high places," notwithstanding the prohibition in Deut. 12, both to Jehovah and to idols, 1 Sam. 9:12-14; 1 Kings 3:2, 4; 2 Kings 12:3; 1 Chron. 16:39; and erected chapels thereon, and had ministers of the sacred rites. 1 Kings 12:32; 13:32; 2 Kings 17:29, 32. Even Solomon, after the erection of the temple, and other kings, till the time of Josiah, frequently sacrificed on hills and mountains. 1 Kings 11:7; 2 Kings 14:4; 15:4, 35; 2 Chron. 20:33; Ezek. 6:3; Lev. 26:30. Probably the massive circular ruins on the summits of Hermon are the remains of such places of ancient idolatrous worship. 2 Kings 23:7; Ezek. 16:16; Amos 5:8.

High Priest. The head of the Jewish priesthood. Lev. 21:10. Aaron was the first to hold the office, Ex. 28:1, and his descendants filled it after him. Eleazar was his immediate successor, Num. 3:32; 20:28; Deut. 10:6, and the priesthood remained in his family till Eli, 1 Chron. 24:3, 6, who was of the house of Ithamar. The office of the high priest was originally held for life. This rule was disregarded by Solomon, who appointed Zadok and deposed Abiathar, 1 Kings 2:35, because he had espoused the cause of Adonijah, 1 Kings 1:7, 25. In the years succeeding the close of the canon the office became a tool in the hands of the rulers of the land. Herod particularly and his successors disregarded the tradition of the Jews on this point. This people, who held the office so sacred, now often begged their rulers to remove the incumbents, who were parasites of the throne. Herod appointed no less than five high priests himself, and one of them, Simon, as the price of his daughter in marriage. We consequently read in the New Testament of several high priests living at the same time, and Annas and Caiaphas are particularly mentioned. Luke 3:2. The services of consecration were prolonged, lasting seven days, Ex. 29:35, and elaborate. They consisted of sacrifices, Ex. 29; of anointing with oil, Ex. 29:7; 30:22-33; Lev. 21:10, and of putting on of garments. Ex. 29:5, 6, 8, 9. The dress of the high priest was much more costly and magnificent than that of the inferior order of priests. It is described Ex. 39:1-9. The high priest's most solemn, peculiar, and exclusive duty was to officiate in the most holy place on the great day of atonement. Heb. 9:7, 25. See **Atonement, Day of**. In Lev. 16 we have a full account of this most interesting service and the imposing ceremonies which preceded it. The high priest might at any time perform the duties assigned to the ordinary priests. He was in general the overseer of the temple, 2 Kings 12:10, and at the time of our Lord presided over the Sanhedrin. Acts 5:17; John 18:13, 14, etc. Jesus is the great High Priest who once for all sprinkled with his own blood the threshold of the holy of holies (heaven), where he ever liveth to make intercession for us. Heb. 4:14; 7:25:9:12, etc.

Hinnom (*hĭn'nom*), perhaps *lamentation*. The valley of the son or sons of Hinnom, or, more concisely, the valley of Hinnom, the boundary between Judah and Benjamin. Josh. 15:8; 18:16. It was the place where children were made "to pass through the fire to Molech," and was defiled by Josiah, in order to extinguish forever such detestable rites. 2 Kings 23:10; 2 Chron. 28:3; 33:6; Jer. 7:31, 32; 19:2, 6; 32:35. It is mentioned after the captivity again as the frontier of Judah and Benjamin. Neh. 11:30. From the fires of Moloch and from the defilement of the valley, comp. Isa. 30:33; 66:24, if not from the supposed everburning funeral fires, the later Jews applied the name of the valley (in the Septuagint *Geënna*), to the place of eternal suffering for lost angels and men; and in this sense it is used in the New Testament. Matt. 5:22, 29, 30; 10:28; Mark 9:43, 45, 47; Luke 12:5; Jas. 3:6.

Hiram (*hī'ram*), *noble*. 1. A distinguished king of Tyre. He was contemporary with David and Solomon, and on terms of political and personal friendship with them. Under his reign the city of Tyre became celebrated for its wealth and magnificence, and the vast supplies he furnished to the kings of Israel show the greatness of his resources. He aided David with materials for a palace, 2 Sam. 5:11; 1 Chron. 14:1, and Solomon in the construction of the temple, 1 Kings 5:1-12; 9:11-14, furnishing workmen as well as materials. He also allowed Solomon to send ships with the Tyrian ships under Tyrian management. 1 Kings 9:26-28; 10:11-28. 2. An eminent artificer of Tyre who was employed by Solomon on some of the most difficult of the fixtures and furniture of the temple. 1 Kings 7:13.

Hittites (*hĭt'tītes*). The tribe or nation descended from Heth, the son of Canaan. Gen. 10:15; 1 Chron. 1:13. They were inhabitants of Canaan in the time of Abraham. Gen. 15:20. They then occupied the southern part of the land, as Hebron, Gen. 23:3-18, extending towards Beersheba; since Esau married Hittite wives, and Isaac and Rebekah feared that Jacob might follow his example. Gen. 26:34; 27:46; 28:9. Hittites evidently, therefore, were in the neighborhood; they were subsequently in the mountainous region near the Amorites and Jebusites, Num. 13:29; Josh. 11:3: and were perhaps some of the original inhabitants of Jerusalem, Ezek. 16:3, 45, as well as in the neighborhood of Bethel. Judg. 1:22-26. Indeed, they had spread so extensively, that Canaan, or at least the northern part of it, was called the "land of the Hittites." Josh. 1:4. Some suppose them to have been a commercial people. Gen. 23:16. In subsequent times we find two of David's warriors Hittites, Ahimelech, 1 Sam. 26:6, and Uriah, 2 Sam. 11:3. Solomon rendered those that yet remained in Palestine tributary, 1 Kings 9:20; and they are mentioned after the captivity. Ezra 9:1. But there are some remarkable notices of Hittites, Judg. 1:26; 1 Kings 10:29; 2 Kings 7:6; 2 Chron. 1:17, which point to a people, a branch of the great family, or the descendants of those expelled from Palestine, who were settled independently beyond Lebanon, and it may be on the southeastern frontier towards Arabia. And Egyptian annals speak of a war with Hittites; and Egyptian pictures are believed to represent Hittites. These representations may be taken not unfairly to figure the old Hittites of Canaan. We are learning much of the Hittites from recent explorations, but their inscriptions lately discovered have not been certainly deciphered nor their records indisputably determined.

Hivites, Land of the (*hi'vites*). A region in Canaan, along the coast of the Mediterranean, peopled by some of the descendants of Canaan, the son of Ham. Gen. 10:17; 1 Chron. 1:15. On Jacob's return to Canaan, Shechem was in possession of the Hivites, Hamor the Hivite being the "prince of the land." Gen. 34:2. They voluntarily surrendered their country to Joshua. Josh. 9:7; 11:19. The main body of the Hivites were then living on the northern confines of western Palestine—"under Hermon in the land of Mizpeh," Josh. 11:3; "in Mount Lebanon, from Mount Baal-hermon unto the entering in of Hamath." Judg. 3:3. They paid tribute to Solomon. 1 Kings 9:20; 2 Chron. 8:7. Their country appears to have been afterward absorbed by the surrounding nations.

Holy Spirit or **Holy Ghost.** The Holy Spirit or Holy Ghost is the third Person of the Holy Trinity, of one essence or nature with the Father and the Son, yet distinct from them. He applies the work of redemption to us, and makes us partakers of all the benefits of Christ, of his righteousness, life, and death. He is an Advocate, who pleads our cause, who strengthens and comforts us and prepares us for glory in heaven. Matt. 1:18, 20; 28:19; John 1:33; 14:26; 16:7, 8; 20:22; Acts 2:4; Rom. 5:5; 2 Cor. 13:14; 1 Thess. 4:8. Our A. V. uses, in most passages, the term Holy *Ghost;* but in four passages, Holy *Spirit*, which is better; see the R. V. See **God.**

Honey. Canaan is described as a land "flowing with milk and honey." Ex. 3:8, 17; 13:5; Ps. 19:10; 81:16. And travellers now speak of the immense swarms of bees found in some rocky parts of the country, Deut. 32:13. With this "wild honey" John Baptist was fed. Matt. 3:4. There was a kind of honey-syrup obtained from dates. 2 Chron. 31:5. Honey was forbidden as an offering, Lev. 2:11. It is often joined with milk, both being natural products; and "honey and milk" are sometimes figuratively put for pleasant discourse. Song of Sol. 4:11. Honey was sometimes made from the juice of grapes boiled down to the half or third part. This, called *dibs*, is still prepared in many parts of Syria and Palestine, especially in the neighborhood of Hebron, and is in great quantities exported into Egypt.

Hor (*hôr*), *mountain*, Mount. 1. The mountain on which Aaron died. Num. 20:25-27; 33:37. It was on the "boundary line," or "at the edge" of the land of Edom. It was the halting-place of the people next after Kadesh, Num. 20:22; 33:37, and they quitted it for Zalmonah, Num. 33:41, in the road to the Red sea. Num. 21:4. It was during the encampment at Kadesh that Aaron died. Mount Hor is on the eastern side of the great valley of the Arabah, the highest and most conspicuous of the whole range of the sandstone mountains of Edom, having close beneath it on its eastern side the strange city of Petra. It is now called Jebel Nebi-Harûn, "the mountain of the prophet Aaron." Its height is 4800 feet above the Mediterranean; or about 1700 feet above the town of Petra, and more than 6000 above the Dead sea. The mountain is marked far and near by its double top, which rises like a huge castellated building from a lower base and is now surmounted by a circular dome of the tomb of Aaron, a distinct white spot on the dark red surface of the mountain. The chief interest of Mount Hor consists in the prospect from its summit, the last view of Aaron—that view which was to him what Pisgah was to Moses. 2. A mountain, distinct from the preceding, named in Num. 34:7, 8, only, as one of the marks of the northern boundary of the land which the children of Israel were to conquer. This Mount Hor is the great chain of Lebanon itself.

Horeb (*hō'reb*), *dry, desert*. A mountain or range frequently mentioned in Scripture. The special application of Horeb and Sinai in the Old Testament has been much discussed. Robinson and Hengstenberg think that Horeb is the name for the whole range —Sinai for a particular peak; Gesenius and others hold precisely the opposite view. Stanley suggests that there is more a distinction of usage than of place. 1. In Leviticus and Numbers Sinai is exclusively used of the scene of the giving of the Law. 2. In Deuteronomy Horeb is substituted for Sinai. 3. In the Psalms the two are used indifferently. See *Sinai and Palestine*, p. 31. The mountain of Sinai and its wilderness are distinguished as the theatre of events that took place in the district of Horeb, and the whole of Horeb is called "the mountain of God." Ex. 3:1, 12; 4: 27; 17:6; 18:5; 33:6. Hence, sometimes "Sinai" alone is spoken of. Ex. 19:11, 20, 23; 24:16; 31:18; 34:29, 32; Lev. 7:38; 25:1; 26:46; 27:34; Num. 1:1; 3:1, 14; 33:15. But frequently "Horeb" alone is named, and the same events are spoken of as occurring on Horeb which are described as taking place on Sinai. Deut. 1:2, 6, 19; 4:10, 15; 5:2; 9:8; 18:16; 29:1. Later sacred writers employ both names: *e. g.*, "Horeb," 1 Kings 8:9; 19:8; 2 Chron. 5: 10; Ps. 106:19; Mal. 4:4; "Sinai," Judg. 5:5; Ps. 68:8, 17.

Horn. The word "horn" is often used to signify power and honor. Of *strength*, the horn of the unicorn, R. V. "wild ox," was the most frequent representative. Deut. 33:17, etc., but not always; comp. 1 Kings 22:11, where probably horns of iron, worn defiantly and symbolically on the head, are intended. Among the Druses upon Mount Lebanon the married women wear silver horns on their heads. In the sense of *honor*, as "my horn," Job 16:15; "all the horn of Israel," Lam. 2:3—and hence for the supreme authority. It also stands for honor or power, whence it comes to mean king, kingdom. Dan. 8:3, etc.; Zech. 1:18. It was also a symbol of victory. 1 Kings 22:11; Rev. 5:6.

Hornet. The hornet resembles the common wasp, only it is larger. It is exceedingly fierce and voracious, especially in hot climates, and its sting is frequently dangerous. In Scripture the hornet is referred to only as the means which Jehovah employed for the extirpation of the Canaanites. Ex. 23:28; Deut. 7:20; Josh. 24:12.

Horse. This most valuable animal was first domesticated in the East, and was probably brought by those who emigrated westward from Asia into Arabia and Egypt. No mention is made of horses as forming any part of the possessions of the patriarchs; nor are any noticed among the presents Abraham received from the kings of Egypt and Gerar. Gen. 12:16; 20:14. The horse was probably not in those early times used except for military purposes; indeed we find scarcely an allusion in Scripture to its employment for the farm or any ordinary domestic service. Once the horse is said to tread out some species of corn, Isa. 28:28; but it is a war-horse, strong and fierce, that is poetically described in Job 39:19–25.

Horse-leech, *the adherer*. A well-known kind of worm very common in all the stagnant waters of Palestine. Prov. 30:15. It fastens itself within the nostrils or mouths of animals as they drink, and will suffer itself to be nearly torn in two before relaxing its hold. Its thirst for blood —never satisfied till its body is completely filled—may illustrate the insatiable cravings of lust, avarice, and cruelty.

Hosanna, *save, we beseech!* The exclamation with which Christ was greeted at his last entry into Jerusalem. Matt. 21:9. It is a Hebrew phrase, known in earlier times and taken from Ps. 118:25, which was recited as a part of the Great Hallel, Ps. 113– 118, at the feast of tabernacles, and which was therefore familiar to the Jews.

Hosea (*ho-zē′ah*), *salvation*. Son of Beeri, and one of the minor prophets. His prophetic career extended from B. C. 784 to 725, a period of 59 years. The prophecies of Hosea were delivered in the kingdom of Israel. Jeroboam II. was ruler, and Israel was at the height of its splendor. Nothing is known of the prophet's life excepting what may be gained from his book.

Hosea, Book of. Consists of 14 chapters. It is easy to recognize two great divisions in the book: 1, chap. 1 to 3; 2, chap. 4 to end. The prophecies were probably collected by Hosea himself toward the end of his career. Of his style Eichhorn says: "His discourse is like a garland woven of a multiplicity of flowers; images are woven upon images, metaphor strung upon metaphor. Like a bee, he flies from one flowerbed to another, that he may suck his honey from the most varied pieces. . . . Often he is prone to approach to allegory; often he sinks down in obscurity." His prophecies are frequently referred to in the New Testament. Matt. 9:13; 12:7; Luke 23:30, etc.

Hoshea (*ho-shē′ah*), *salvation*. 1. The 19th, last and best king of Israel. He succeeded Pekah, whom he slew in a successful conspiracy, thereby fulfilling a prophecy of Isaiah. Isa. 7:16. In the third year of his reign (B. C. 726) Shalmaneser cruelly stormed the strong caves of Beth-arbel, Hos. 10:14, and made Israel tributary, 2 Kings 17:3, for three years. At the end of this period Hoshea entered into a secret alliance with So, king of Egypt, to throw off the Assyrian yoke. The alliance did him no good: it was revealed to the court of Nineveh by the Assyrian party in Ephraim, and Hoshea was immediately seized as a rebellious vassal, shut up in prison, and apparently treated with the utmost indignity. Micah 5:1. Nothing is known of Hoshea after this event. 2. The son of Nun, *i. e.*, Joshua, Deut. 32:44; and also in Num. 13:8, R. V., though there the A.V. has Oshea. 3. Son of Azaziah, 1 Chron. 27:20; like his great namesake, a man of Ephraim, ruler of his tribe in the time of king David. (B. C. 1019.) 4. One of the heads of the people who sealed the covenant with Nehemiah. Neh. 10:23. (B. C. 410.)

Hour. The twenty-fourth part of the day. Such a mode of dividing time was not originally employed among the Hebrews. And, when the word "hour" first occurs, it is used loosely and indefinitely, Dan. 3:6, 15; 4:33; 5:5; as it is frequently in the New Testament, Mark 13:32; John 2:4; and as very commonly among ourselves. At a very early period the Egyptians divided the day into twelve hours; and the same reckoning prevailed among the Babylonians, from whom the Greeks took it. It is likely that the Jews learned and adopted it at the period of the captivity. In our Lord's time, the day, that is, the space between sunrise and sunset, was commonly distributed into twelve hours, John 11:9; these, therefore, varied in length according to the season of the year. Generally, however, we may say that the third hour corresponded with our 9 A. M., the sixth with our noon, the ninth with our 3 P. M., etc. In Acts 23 : 23 the hours of the night were reckoned from sunset; consequently the time named would nearly correspond with our 9 P. M.

House. See **Dwelling.**

Hushai (hū'shāi or hū'sha-ī), *rapid*. An Archite, and a particular and faithful friend of David. 2 Sam. 16 : 16. He gained such influence over Absalom as to prevail with his advice over Ahithophel, 2 Sam. 17 : 14. During this time he remained David's friend.

Husks. This word in Luke 15 : 16 describes really the fruit of the carob. It belongs to the locust family. This tree is common in Syria and Egypt; it produces pods, shaped like a horn, varying in length from six to ten inches, and about a finger's breadth, or rather more; it is dark brown, glossy, filled with seeds, and has a sweetish taste. It is used much for food by the poor, and for the feeding of swine.

Hyssop. Ex. 12 : 22. A plant often used in the ceremonies of purification. Lev. 14 : 4, 6, 51 ; Ps. 51 : 7. One of its characteristics is referred to in 1 Kings 4 : 33. It is associated with our Saviour's last hours. John 19 : 29. More than twenty different plants have been urged as the species intended. Tristram and other recent authorities favor the caper-bush. Dr. Post, of Syria, argues very conclusively in favor of a species of marjoram.

I

Iconium (ī-cō'-ni-ŭm). *place of images* (?). A large and rich city of Asia Minor, in the province of Lycaonia. It was on the great Roman highway from Ephesus to Tarsus, Antioch, and the Euphrates, and at the foot of Mount Taurus, in a beautiful and fertile country, about 300 miles southeast of Constantinople and about 120 miles inland from the Mediterranean. Paul visited it on his first and second missionary journeys. Acts 13 : 51 ; 14 : 1, 19, 21 ; 16 : 2 ; 2 Tim. 3 : 11. It is now called Konieh, and has a population of about 30,000.

Idolatry. The worship of other objects or beings than the one true God. Probably the heavenly bodies were among the earliest objects of idolatrous reverence. Thus the sun and moon, the Baal and Astarte of Phœnician worship, were regarded as embodying these active and passive principles respectively. And the idol deities of other nations bore similar characters. It is easy to see how such worship would be tainted by licentiousness of thought, and that the rites of it would be immoral and obscene. Unnatural lusts would be indulged, till the frightful picture drawn by the apostle Paul of heathenism was abundantly realized among even the most refined nations of antiquity. Rom. 1 : 18-32. It was in order to guard the Israelites against such abominable things that many of the enactments of the Mosaic law were directed. Deut. 22 : 5. The ancient Hebrews had no fixed form of idolatry; but they frequently imitated the superstitions of other nations. Gen. 31 : 30 ; Josh. 24 : 23 ; Judg. 2 : 11, 12 ; 8 : 27 ; 17 : 5 ; 18 : 30, 31. Solomon, seduced by his strange wives, caused temples to be erected in honor of their gods, and himself impiously offered incense to them. 1 Kings 11 : 5-7. Under the reign of Ahab, idolatry reached its greatest height; and the impious Jezebel endeavored to destroy the worship of Jehovah. Even the sacrifice of children, forbidden as it was under the most severe and summary penalties, became common. Lev. 20 : 2 ; Jer. 7 : 31 ; Ezek. 16 : 21. The severe chastisement of the captivity in a great measure uprooted Hebrew idolatry. Perhaps those who went into Egypt were the worst class of the Jews. Jer. 44 : 15-30. Yet even there idolatry did not last among them. And, though after the return there was much lukewarmness shown, and alliances were made afresh with ungodly nations, and false prophets appeared, Ezra 9 : 1, 2 ; Neh. 6 : 14, yet so far as we can judge by the national covenant, Neh. 10, and the general tone of the post-exilian prophets, Haggai, Zechariah, and Malachi, idolatry ceased to flourish. In the New Testament the Christians, who were continually brought into contact with idolaters through the extent of the Roman empire, were cautioned as to their behavior. Not only were they to abhor idol-worship itself, but they were also to abstain from meats which had been offered to idols. Acts 15 : 29. It was true that the meat itself was not thereby defiled, for an idol was nothing; and therefore Christians need not be too particular in inquiring into the history of what was set before them But, if any one apprised them that it had been so presented, they were not to eat, lest an occasion of offence should be given to a weak brother or to a censorious heathen. 1 Cor. 8 : 4-13 ; 10 : 25-32.

Idumæans, or Edomites (ĭd'u-mē'anz, or ē'dom-ītes). The inhabitants of Idumæa or Edom, descendants of Esau, Gen. 36 : 1, 8, and dwellers in the clefts of the rocks in the Sinaitic peninsula. Jer. 49 : 16. Petra, called "Selah" or "Joktheel," their stronghold in Amaziah's day, 2 Kings 14 : 7, and chief city, was literally cut in the rocks, and the southern part of the country abounds in cave-dwellings. They had kings long before the Hebrews. Gen. 36 : 31. Though they were of the same primitive parentage as the Hebrews, they were by no means friendly to them. They perpetuated the enmity between Esau and Jacob. They opposed their passage through their country when Israel came from the wilderness. Num. 20 : 20, 21. But finally they allowed a passage through their eastern border, accepting also Israel's offer to pay for provisions. Deut. 2 : 28, 29. The Edomites were conquered by Saul in the early part of his reign, 1 Sam. 14 : 47, and by David likewise, 2 Sam. 8 : 14 ; but at the instigation of Hadad they revolted against Solomon. 1 Kings 11 : 14. Edom was for a long time a vassal of the kingdom of Judah, but again revolted, and after a struggle got its independence in the reign of Jehoram. 2 Kings 8 : 20-22. The later kings attacked and were attacked by the Edomites. The prophets foretold the desolation of the descendants of Esau and their country. Jer. 49 : 17, 18 ; Obadiah 8. Thirty ruined towns within three days' journey from the Red sea attest their former greatness and their present desolation.

Illyricum (*il-lĭr'i-kŭm*). A Roman province of southeastern Europe, lying along the eastern coast of the Adriatic, from the boundary of Italy on the north to Epirus on the south, and contiguous to Mœsia and Macedonia on the east. On account of the insurrection of the Dalmatians, B. C. 11, the province was divided, and the northern portion called Dalmatia : the southern portion remained one of the Senate's provinces. Paul preached round about unto Illyricum. Rom. 15 : 19.

Immanuel (*im-măn'u-el*), *God with us.* The name given to the child whose birth the prophet Isaiah was authorized to announce to Ahaz when the confederacy was formed by Israel and Syria against Judah. Isa. 7 : 1-16. This passage has been cited by Matthew, and specially applied to the birth of Christ, Matt. 1 : 22, 23, who is rightly regarded as "God with us" and as ever present in his church and with his people through the ages of the world. Matt. 28 : 20.

Incense. The sacred perfume offered to God by burning on the incense altar. The gums which composed it are mentioned in Ex. 30 : 34-38, including salt, for v. 35 reads, "seasoned with salt" in the R. V. Incense was to be burnt on the altar made for the purpose twice a day, in the morning when the lamps were dressed, and also when they were lighted in the evening. It might seem as if this work were restricted to the high priest, Ex. 30 : 7, 8; but certainly the ordinary priests are found burning incense, Lev. 10 : 1; and, in later times at least, those who so officiated were chosen by lot, Luke 1 : 8, 9; the people being of course without, v. 10, and probably praying in silence : comp. Rev. 8 : 1, 3. There was another solemn burning of incense—and this was the high priest's peculiar office—on the great day of atonement. Lev. 16 : 13. Jewish writers have said that the incense was to counteract the unpleasant smell which might arise from the carcases of victims. But it had a higher purpose. The psalmist, Ps. 141 : 2, indicates this; his words implying that prayer was in reality what incense was in symbol.

Ink, Inkhorn. Jer. 36 : 18 ; Ezek. 9 : 2. It is supposed that the common ink of early ages was made of water and pulverized charcoal, or the black of burnt ivory, with the addition of some kind of gum. Other substances were doubtless used both for writing and coloring matter. The Romans used a dark purple liquid, which was obtained from a species of fish, for this purpose. The ink in common use at this day has been known for several centuries in Europe, and is usually made of nutgalls, vitriol, and gum. Ancient ink was more caustic, and less liable to fade or decay. Chinese ink is of the same quality. The professed writers or scribes carried with them, as they do at the present day in eastern countries, writing instruments, and among them was an inkhorn, thrust into the girdle at the side.

Inn. In the Bible the "inn" was not a hotel in our sense. The word so translated means either a "lodging-place for the night"—not necessarily a covered place, but a mere station of caravans, where water could be obtained ; such was the "iun," R. V. "lodging-place," at which Joseph's brethren stopped, Gen. 42 : 27 ; Ex. 4 : 24—or else a khan or caravanserai, which was, and is, a large square building enclosing an open court, in whose centre is a fountain ; the building contains a number of rooms. There is no provision for meals or feed for the animals ; the travellers carry such necessaries with them. These caravanserais are often built by benevolent persons. Jer. 9 : 2. Another kind of "inn" is that mentioned in the parable of the Good Samaritan. Luke 10 : 34. This had a host, who was probably paid to attend to the wants of travellers. And it was in one of the stables of a mere caravanserai provided for the horses of travellers that our Lord was born. In modern Syria, in villages where there is no khan, there is a house for the entertainment of travellers, with a man appointed to look after it : for its accommodations, meagre as they are, payment is exacted, and the keeper likewise gets a fee.

Inspiration. The influence of the Spirit of God on the mind, such as to guard against error in communicating God's will. The prophets and apostles spake "as they were moved by the Holy Ghost." 2 Pet. 1 : 21. The divine Spirit acted upon each author according to his individuality, and used him, not as a machine, but as a free and responsible agent. Hence the differences of style and mode of treatment. The Bible is both human and divine, like the person of Christ, whom it reflects. There are various theories of inspiration, as to its modes and degrees ; but all Christians agree that in the Bible, and in the Bible alone, we have a full and perfectly trustworthy revelation of God, and that it is the infallible rule of our faith and practice.

Iron is mentioned with brass as the earliest of known metals. Gen. 4 : 22. The natural wealth in iron of the soil of Canaan is indicated by describing it as "a land whose stones are iron." Deut. 8 : 9. The book of Job contains passages which indicate that iron was a metal well known. Sheet-iron was used for cooking utensils. Ezek. 4 : 3 ; cf. Lev. 7 : 9. That it was plentiful in the time of David appears from 1 Chron. 22 : 3. The market of Tyre was supplied with bright or polished iron by the merchants of Dan and Javan. Ezek. 27 : 19. Iron ore is now abundant in northern Palestine.

Isaac (i'zak), *laughter, sporting.* The heir of promise, son of Abraham by his wife Sarah, born when his father was 100 years old. His name, given before his birth, Gen. 17:19, was significant. Abraham had smiled incredulously when the promise was renewed to him and Sarah designated as the mother of the promised seed, and Sarah laughed derisively afterwards when she heard the reiterated word. Gen. 17: 17; 18:12. The son by his name, therefore, was to warn the parents against unbelief, and expressed the joy with which they received at last the fulfilment of the promise. Gen. 21:6. Isaac's life was far less stirring than that of his father Abraham, or that of his son Jacob. He was a man of mild contemplative character, suffering more than acting, easily persuaded, yet upon occasion firm. Isaac stands forth the model of that loving submission which those who become sons and heirs of God ought to pay to their heavenly parent, as inheritors of his father Abraham's faith. We best love to contemplate Isaac as bearing the wood with his father up the slopes of Moriah. Gentle, pious, conciliating as he was through the rest of his days, he never rose higher in after life; he hardly fulfilled this promise of his youth. Yet Isaac was a man of faith and prayer; and God was not ashamed to be called his God. Heb. 11:16. His history conveys many instructive lessons.

Isaiah (i-zā'yah or ī-zā'yah), *salvation of Jehovah.* One of the great Hebrew prophets. Of his personal history very little is known. He was the son of Amoz, Isa. 1:1, whom rabbinical tradition represents as the brother of king Amaziah. He was married, his wife being called "the prophetess," Isa. 8:3, not because she exercised the prophetic gift herself, but simply because she was married to a prophet. He had at least two sons, with symbolical names, Shear-jashub and Maher-shalal-hash-baz. Isa. 7:3; 8:1-3. It is presumed that he ordinarily wore a hair-cloth garment, Isa. 20:2; but there is no reason for believing that he was an ascetic. He probably resided at Jerusalem, where he exercised his prophetic ministry during a long course of years. Isaiah prophesied under Uzziah, receiving the divine call in the last year of that monarch's reign, Isa. 6; and under the succeeding kings, Jotham, Ahaz, and Hezekiah. Isa. 1:1. Whether he lived on into Manasseh's reign is uncertain. Jewish tradition asserts that he did, and that he was martyred by being sawn asunder; and this has been supposed to be alluded to in Heb. 11:37. Isaiah is the evangelist among the Old Testament prophets. He is more frequently quoted in the New Testament than any other. In him the Messianic prophecies reach their highest perfection. He draws the picture of the suffering and triumphing Saviour of Israel and the world, until at last he stands before us in unmistakable clearness and fulness. Isaiah is also one of the greatest of poets. "Everything conspired to raise him to an elevation to which no prophet, either before or after, could as writer attain. Among the other prophets each of the more important ones is distinguished by some one particular excellence and some one peculiar talent; in Isaiah all kinds of talent and all beauties of prophetic discourse meet together, so as mutually to temper and qualify each other; it is not so much any single feature that distinguishes him as the symmetry and perfection as a whole. . . . In the sentiment he expresses, in the topics of his discourses and in the manner, Isaiah uniformly reveals himself as the king prophet."—*Ewald.*

Isaiah, Book of. Isaiah is divided into two parts. The first, comprising the first 39 chapters, is composed of a variety of individual prophecies against nations and denunciations of sin. Social vices, chap. 3, and idolatry, chap. 8, are rebuked without mercy. Assyria, Babylon, 13:19 *sq.*, Moab, 15; Ethiopia, 18; Egypt, 19; and Tyre, 23, pass successively before the prophet's mind, and their doom is predicted. The prophecies of Babylon's desolation and of Tyre's ruin are among the most poetic and the sublimest passages in all literature. Chaps. 36-39 are concerned with Sennacherib's invasion and episodes in the life of Hezekiah. The second part of Isaiah begins abruptly with the fortieth chapter: "Comfort ye, comfort ye my people." It takes its position at the close of the Babylonian captivity, and prophesies its close and the glories of the Messianic period of Israel's history. Of all the prophetic writings, none are more evidently inspired and truly evangelical than these last 27 chapters. Isaiah prophesies of the Messiah with distinctness and in a way that his predecessors had not done. We find prophecies of his birth, 7:14; 9:6, of his Davidic descent, 11:1, 2, etc. But the fullest as well as the most distinct of the predictions is contained in the fifty-third chapter. It may be called the gospel of the Old Testament, on account of the graphic and faithful picture it gives of the Messiah, as the "Man of sorrows," suffering in the stead of mankind. This chapter of itself will stand always as an evidence of prime importance for the divine mission of Christ. "The authenticity of the second part of Isaiah, from chaps. 40-66," says Schaff, "has been assailed by modern critics, who regard it as a later production of some 'great unknown prophet' at the end of the Babylonian exile. But it is characteristic of prophetic vision to look into the far future as if it were present; and it makes not much difference for the divine character of the prophecy whether it was uttered 500 or 700 years before its fulfilment. The description of the servant of God who suffers and dies for the sins of the people in chap. 53 applies to no other person in history, with any degree of propriety, but to Jesus Christ."

Ish-bosheth (ĭsh'bō'sheth or ĭsh'bo-sheth), *man of shame.* Son and successor of Saul, who was persuaded by Abner to go up to Mahanaim and assume the government while David reigned at Hebron, 2 Sam. 2:8, 11; and all Israel except Judah acknowledged him as king. A severe battle soon after occurred at Gibeon, between the army of Joab, under David, and the army of Ish-bosheth, under Abner, in which the latter was utterly defeated. Abner was killed afterward by Joab. Ish-bosheth, thus deprived of his strongest supporter, was assassinated at noonday upon his bed, after a brief reign of two years. 2 Sam. 4:5-7.

Ishi (ish'ī or ī'shī), Hos. 2:16, signifying *my husband*, and **Baali** (bā'al-ī), in the same passage, signifying *my Lord*, are figuratively used to denote that Israel once played the whore in serving idols, but would now serve the living God. The latter having been used in idol-worship, would become obsolete in this sense. Hos. 2:17.

Ishmael (ish'ma-el), whom *God heareth*. 1. The son of Abraham by Hagar, and the ancestor of Arabian tribes, generally called "Ishmaelites." Gen. 25:12-18; 1 Chron. 2:17; 18:3. Previous to his birth Hagar was informed by an angel what would be the character of her son, and that his posterity would be innumerable. Gen. 16:11. When Hagar was banished to the wilderness, God directed her to a fountain, and renewed his promise to make him a great nation. Ishmael married an Egyptian woman, and dwelt in the wilderness, Gen. 16:12; he was distinguished for lawless predatory habits, as his descendants have always been. Gen. 21:20, 21. So rapidly did Ishmael's family multiply, that in a few years afterwards they are spoken of as a trading nation. Gen. 37:25; 39:1. Isaac and Ishmael amicably met at the burial of their father. Gen. 25:9. Ishmael died, perhaps in battle, at the age of 137 years. He was the father of twelve sons, who gave their names to as many tribes, who dwelt in the wilderness, from Havilah unto Shur. Gen. 17:20. The prophecies concerning him, Gen. 16:12; 17:20; 21:13, 18, confirm the Bible; being literally carried out for nearly 4000 years to the present day. Ishmael no doubt became a wild man of the desert, the progenitor of the roaming Bedouin tribes of the East, so well known as robbers to this day that travellers through their territory must be well armed and hire a band of robbers to protect them against their fellow-robbers. Ishmael is also the spiritual father of the Mohammedans, who are nothing but bastard Jews. They apply to themselves the promise of a large posterity given to Ishmael. Gen. 21:13, 18. 2. A prince of the royal family of Judah, who murdered the governor Gedaliah, with several of the Hebrews and Chaldeans who were attached to him. He fled to the Ammonites. Jer. 40:7-16; 41:1-18. There are six persons of this name mentioned in the Scriptures.

Israel (iz'ra-el), *the prince that prevails with God*. 1. The name given to Jacob after his wrestling with the angel at Peniel. Gen. 32:28; Hos. 12:4. It became the national name of the twelve tribes collectively. They are so called in Ex. 3:16 and afterward. It is used in a narrower sense, excluding Judah, in 1 Sam. 11:8; 2 Sam. 20: 1; 1 Kings 12:16. Thenceforth it was assumed and accepted as the name of the northern kingdom. After the Babylonian captivity, the returned exiles resumed the name Israel as the designation of their nation. The name Israel is also used to denote laymen, as distinguished from priests, Levites, and other ministers. Ezra 6:16; 9:1; 10:25; Neh. 11:3, etc. See **Jews**.

Israel, Kingdom of. A term not infrequently applied to the united kingdom before the revolt of the ten tribes, 1 Sam. 13: 1, 4; 15:28; 16:1; 2 Sam. 5:12; 7:16; 1 Kings 2:46; 4:1; but the term was also used to designate the country of the ten tribes only during the dissensions which followed the death of Saul. After the death of Solomon and the revolt under Rehoboam, 1 Kings 12:20, 28, 32, it was generally, but not uniformly, applied to the independent kingdom formed by the ten tribes in the north of Palestine, so that thenceforth the kings of the ten tribes were called "kings of Israel," and the descendants of David, who ruled over Judah and Benjamin, were called "kings of Judah." In the prophets "Judah" and "Israel" are often mentioned. Hos. 4:15; 5:3, 5; 6:10; 7: 1; 8:2, 3, 6, 8; 9:1, 7; Amos 1:1; 2:6; 3: 14; Micah 1:5; Isa. 5:7. The two kingdoms are sometimes called "the two houses of Israel." Isa. 8:14. The area of the kingdom of Israel is estimated at about 9000 square miles, or about the same as that of the State of New Hampshire. The kingdom lasted 254 years, B. C. 975-721. The capitals were Shechem, 1 Kings 12:25, Tirzah, 1 Kings 14:17, and Samaria, 1 Kings 16:24. Jezreel was also a summer residence of some of its kings. Of the nineteen kings, not counting Tibni, not one was a godly man. The idolatry introduced by Jeroboam was continued, notwithstanding the partial reformations of Elijah, Elisha, and other faithful prophets. The following admirable summary of the history of the kingdom in four periods is condensed from Smith's *Dictionary*:

"1. *B. C. 975-929.*—Jeroboam had not sufficient force of character in himself to make a lasting impression on his people. A king, but not a founder of a dynasty, he aimed at nothing beyond securing his present elevation. The army soon learned its power to dictate to the isolated monarch and disunited people. Baasha, in the midst of the army at Gibbethon, slew the son and successor of Jeroboam; Zimri, a captain of chariots, slew the son and successor of Baasha; Omri, the captain of the host, was chosen to punish Zimri; and after a civil war of four years he prevailed over Tibni, the choice of half the people.

"2. *B. C. 929-884.*—For forty-five years Israel was governed by the house of Omri. That sagacious king pitched on the strong hill of Samaria as the site of his capital. The princes of his house cultivated an alliance with the kings of Judah, which was cemented by the marriage of Jehoram and Athaliah. The adoption of Baal-worship led to a reaction in the nation, and to the moral triumph of the prophets in the per-

113

son of Elijah, and to the extinction of the house of Ahab, in obedience to the bidding of Elisha.

"3. B. C. 884-772.—Unparalleled triumphs, but deeper humiliation, awaited the kingdom of Israel under the dynasty of Jehu. Hazael, the ablest king of Damascus, reduced Jehoahaz to the condition of a vassal, and triumphed for a time over both the disunited Hebrew kingdoms. Almost the first sign of the restoration of their strength was a war between them, and Jehoahaz, the grandson of Jehu, entered Jerusalem as the conqueror of Amaziah. Jehoash also turned the tide of war against the Syrians, and Jeroboam II., the most powerful of all the kings of Israel, captured Damascus and recovered the whole ancient frontier from Hamath to the Dead sea. This short-lived greatness expired with the last king of Jehu's line.

"4. B. C. 772-721.—Military violence, it would seem, broke off the hereditary succession after the obscure and probably convulsed reign of Zachariah. An unsuccessful usurper, Shallum, is followed by the cruel Menahem, who, being unable to make head against the first attack of Assyria, under Pul, became the agent of that monarch for the oppressive taxation of his subjects. Yet his power at home was sufficient to insure for his son and successor, Pekahiah, a ten years' reign, cut short by a bold usurper, Pekah. Abandoning the northern and trans-Jordanic regions to the encroaching power of Assyria under Tiglath-pileser, he was very near subjugating Judah, with the help of Damascus, now the coequal ally of Israel. But Assyria, interposing, summarily put an end to the independence of Damascus, and perhaps was the indirect cause of the assassination of the baffled Pekah. The irresolute Hoshea, the next and last usurper, became tributary to his invader, Shalmaneser, betrayed the Assyrian to the rival monarchy of Egypt, and was punished by the loss of his liberty and by the capture, after a three-years' siege, of his strong capital Samaria. Some gleanings of the ten tribes yet remained in the land after so many years of religious decline, moral debasement, national degradation, anarchy, bloodshed, and deportation. Even these were gathered up by the conqueror and carried to Assyria, never again, as a distinct people, to occupy their portion of that goodly and pleasant land which their forefathers won under Joshua from the heathen."

After the destruction of the kingdom of Israel, B. C. 721, the name "Israel" began again to be applied to the whole surviving people. "Israel" is sometimes put for the *true* Israelites, the faithful worthy of the name. Ps. 73:1; Isa. 45:17; 49:3; John 1:47; Rom. 9:6; 11:26. See **Judah and Jews.**

Issachar (*Is'sa-kar*), *God hath given me my hire*. The fifth son of Jacob and Leah. Gen. 30:18. The prophetical description of him uttered by his father, Gen. 49:14, 15, was fulfilled in the fact that the posterity of Issachar were a laborious people and followed rural employments, and were subject to the tributes of marauding tribes.

Issachar (*Is'sa-kar*), **The Territory of,** included the great plain of Esdraelon, or Jezreel, and lay above that of Manasseh; its boundaries are given in Josh. 19:17-23. It extended from Mt. Carmel to the Jordan, and from Mt. Tabor to En-gannim. Zebulun was on the north, Manasseh on the south, and Gilead on the east, across the Jordan. It contained sixteen noted cities and their villages. Among them were Megiddo, Jezreel, Shunem, Beth-shan, Endor, Aphek, Taanach; and Jezreel stood almost exactly in the centre of the territory. This region was one of the richest and most fertile in Palestine. Many historical events of great interest took place within the territory. It furnished two kings to Israel—Baasha and Elah. 1 Kings 15:27; 16:6. Their portion of Palestine is still among the most fertile of the whole land. See **Jezreel, Plain of, and Palestine.**

Ituræa (*It-u-rē'ah*), *an enclosed region*. A small province on the northwestern border of Palestine. It derived its name from "Jetur," a son of Ishmael. Gen. 25:15; 1 Chron. 1:31; 5:19. This district is now called Jedur, and is about 17 miles from north to south by 20 from east to west. Philip was tetrarch of Ituræa and of the region of Trachonitis. Luke 3:1.

J

Jabbok (*jăb'bok*), *emptying*. A stream rising about 25 miles east of the north end of the Dead sea, and flowing east, then northward and westward, and finally into the Jordan about midway between the Sea of Galilee and the Dead sea. It is now called the Zerka or "blue" river. Across this stream Jacob sent his family, and here his wrestling for a blessing occurred. Gen. 32:22-24. The Israelites conquered the kingdoms of Og and Sihon, but not the Ammonite country nor the upper Jabbok, which explains Deut. 2:37. Compare Num. 21:24; Deut. 3:16; Josh. 12:2; Judg. 11:13, 22. The Jabbok, before it enters the Jordan valley, flows through a deep, narrow ravine, the hills being from 1500 to 2000 feet in height. The stream abounds in small fish of excellent flavor.

Jabesh and Jabesh-Gilead (*jā'besh-gĭl'e-ad*), *dry Gilead*. A city east of the Jordan; destroyed by the Israelites, Judg. 21:8-14; delivered from Nahash by Saul, 1 Sam. 11:1-11, and in gratitude therefor, its people brought the bodies of Saul and his sons, which the Philistines hung upon the walls of Beth-shan, to Jabesh, and caused them to be buried in a wood near by. 1 Sam. 31:11-13. David blessed them, 2 Sam. 2:4-6, but afterward removed the bones to Saul's ancestral burying-place. 2 Sam. 2:4-6; 21:12-14. Robinson identifies it with ed-Deir, 23 miles southeast of the Sea of Galilee on the south side of Wady Yabis. Merrill, however, would identify Jabesh with the ruins of a town found about 7 miles from Pella and about 2300 feet above the Jordan valley. This seems to conform to the Biblical statements concerning the place.

Jabin (jā'bĭn), *whom he—i. e., God—observes.* 1. King of Hazor, a northern district of Canaan. Josh. 11 : 1. He and his allies were utterly defeated in a battle with Joshua at Merom, the city of Hazor was taken, and Jabin put to death. 2. Another king of the same name and place, who had great wealth and power, and oppressed the children of Israel for 20 years. Judg. 4 : 2. His army was defeated by Deborah and Barak, and Sisera, his principal general, put to death.

Jabneel (jăb'ne-el or jăb'neel), *Jehovah causes to be built.* A town of Judah; called also Jabneh. Josh. 15 : 11 ; 2 Chron. 26 : 6. Uzziah captured it from the Philistines. It was called by Josephus, Jamnia, and after the destruction of Jerusalem was for some time the seat of a famous Jewish school of learning. It is identified with Yebnah, a village about three miles from the Mediterranean and 12 miles south of Joppa.

Jacinth or **Hyacinth,** "amber" margin R. V. Ex. 28 : 19. Probably the same as the ligure, a gem of a yellowish-red or a dark purple color, Rev. 9 : 17 ; called "sapphire" in margin of R. V. Rev. 21 : 20. In the former passage there is reference merely to its color.

Jacob (jā'kŏb), *supplanter.* The second son of Isaac and Rebekah. He was born with Esau probably at the well of Lahai-roi, about B. C. 1837. His history is related in the latter half of the Book of Genesis. He bought the birthright from his brother Esau, and afterward acquired the blessing intended for Esau by practicing a well-known deceit on Isaac. Gen. 25 : 21-34 ; 27 : 1-40. Jacob, in mature years, was sent from the family home to avoid his brother, and to seek a wife among his kindred in Padan-aram. As he passed through Bethel, God appeared to him. After the lapse of 21 years he returned from Padan-aram with two wives, two concubines, eleven sons and a daughter, and large property. He escaped from the angry pursuit of Laban, from a meeting with Esau, and from the vengeance of the Canaanites provoked by the murder of Shechem ; and in each of these three emergencies he was aided and strengthened by the interposition of God, and in sign of the grace won by a night of wrestling with God his name was changed at Jabbok into Israel. Deborah and Rachel died before he reached Hebron ; Joseph, the favorite son of Jacob, was sold into Egypt eleven years before the death of Isaac; and Jacob had probably reached his 130th year when he went thither. He was presented to Pharaoh and dwelt for 17 years in Rameses and Goshen, and died in his 147th year. His body was embalmed, carried with great care and pomp into the land of Canaan, and deposited with his fathers, and his wife Leah, in the cave of Machpelah. Gen. chs. 27 to 50. The example of Jacob is quoted by the first and the last of the minor prophets. Besides the frequent mention of his name in conjunction with the names of the other two patriarchs, there are distinct references to the events in the life of Jacob in four books of the New Testament—John 1 : 51 ; 4 : 5, 12 ; Acts 7 : 12-15 ; Rom. 9 : 11-13 ; Heb. 11 : 21 ; 12 : 16.

Jacob's Well. See **Sychar.**

Jaddua (jăd-dū'a or jăd'du-ah), *known.* 1. Son and successor in the high priesthood of Jonathan or Johanan, and last of the high priests mentioned in the Old Testament. R. V. Joiada. Neh. 12 : 11, 22. B. C. 406–332. 2. One of the chief of the people who sealed the covenant with Nehemiah. Neh. 10 : 21.

Jael (jā'el), *a wild goat.* Wife of Heber, the Kenite who slew Sisera, general of the Canaanitish army. While Sisera was sleeping in her tent Jael drove a large nail or tent-pin through his temples. Judg. 4 : 17-23.

Jah (jäh). Ps. 68 : 4. A form of the Hebrew word "Jehovah." It is part of the compound words "Adonijah" ("God is my Lord") and "hallelujah" ("Praise the Lord"). See **Jehovah.**

Jahaz (jā'hăz), *place trodden down.* A Moabitish city situated near the desert ; afterward reckoned to the tribe of Reuben and assigned to the priests. Num. 21 : 23; Deut. 2 : 32 ; Isa. 15 : 4 ; Jer. 48 : 34. It is also called Jahaza, Josh. 13 : 18, A. V. Jahazah, Josh. 21 : 36 ; Jer. 48 : 21, A. V., and Jahzah. 1 Chron. 6 : 78 A. V., and Jer. 48 : 21 R. V. At this place the Israelites gained a victory over Sihon and conquered the territory between the Arnon and the Jabbok ; but in later times Jahaz seems to have been occupied by the Moabites.

Jair (jā'ir), *whom Jehovah enlightens.* 1. A chief warrior under Moses, descended from the most powerful family of Judah and Manasseh. He took all the country of Argob (the modern Lejah) on the east side of Jordan, and, besides, some villages in Gilead, which he called Havoth-jair, "villages of Jair." 1 Chron. 2 : 21-23 ; Num. 32 : 41 ; Deut. 3 : 14 ; comp. Josh. 13 : 30. 2. Jair the Gileadite, who judged Israel 22 years. "He had thirty sons who rode on thirty ass-colts, and they had thirty cities, which are called Havoth-jair, which are in Gilead." Judg. 10 : 3-5. 3. A Benjamite, father of Mordecai. Esth. 2 : 5. 4. In 1 Chron. 20 : 5, in the A. V., Jair occurs, but it is a totally different name in Hebrew, meaning "whom God awakens." This Jair was the father of Elhanan, who killed Lachmi, the brother of Goliath. He is called Jaare-oregim in 2 Sam. 21 : 19.

Jairus (ja-ī'rus), *whom God enlightens.* 1. A ruler of a synagogue in some town near the western shore of the Sea of Galilee. Matt. 9 : 18 ; Mark 5 : 22 ; Luke 8 : 41. (A. D. 28.) 2. Same as Jair. 3. Esth. 11 : 2.

James (jāmez), *same name as Jacob.* 1. James the son of Zebedee, one of the twelve apostles, and elder brother of John. His mother's name was Salome. He was a fisherman, Mark 1 : 19, when at the call of the Master he left all, and became a disciple. Matt. 10 : 2 ; Mark 3 : 7 ; Luke 6 : 14 ; Acts 1 : 13. The name of Boanerges was given to him and his brother. The "sons of thunder" had a burning and impetuous spirit, which twice exhibits itself. Mark 10:37; Luke 9:54. He was one of the three who witnessed the raising of Jairus' daughter, the transfiguration, and the agony of Jesus in Gethsemane. On the day of the ascension he is mentioned as persevering, with the rest of the apostles and disciples, in prayer. Acts 1:13. Shortly before the passover, in the year 44, he was put to death by Herod Agrippa I. Acts 12:1, 2. 2. James the son of Alphæus, one of the twelve apostles. Matt. 10:3. Called also James the Less. Mark 15:40; 16:1; Matt. 27:56; Acts 1: 13. Tradition says he labored in Palestine and Egypt. By some he is regarded as a cousin of Jesus. 3. James the " brother of the Lord." Gal. 1:19. At some time in the 40 days that intervened between the resurrection and the ascension, the Lord appeared to him. 1 Cor. 15:7. Ten years after we find James mentioned with Peter, and with him deciding on the admission of Paul into fellowship with the church at Jerusalem, Acts 15:13; and from henceforth we always find him equal to, and sometimes presiding over, the very chiefest apostles, Peter, John, and Paul. Acts 9:27. This pre-eminence is evident throughout the after-history of the apostles, whether we read it in the Acts, in the epistles, or in ecclesiastical writers. Acts 12:17; 15:13, 19; 21:18; Gal. 2:9. According to tradition, James was thrown down from the temple by the scribes and Pharisees; he was then stoned and his brains dashed out with a fuller's club while praying for his murderers. Josephus places his death in 62 A.D., but Hegesippus in 69 A.D.

James, the General Epistle of. The author of this epistle was in all probability James the "brother of the Lord." It was written from Jerusalem, probably before A. D. 62. Its object is to comfort the dispersed Jews, commending to them patience in suffering, joy in sorrow, and prayer in trouble. There is a close resemblance between the pastoral letter in Acts 15:23 and this epistle. Both commence with "greeting." Jas. 1:1.

Japheth (jā'pheth), *enlargement*. One of the three sons of Noah. The descendants of Japheth occupied the "isles of the Gentiles," R. V. "isles of the nations," Gen. 10:5—*i. e.*, the coast lands of the Mediterranean sea in Europe and Asia Minor— whence they spread northward over the whole continent of Europe and a considerable portion of Asia.

Jason (jā'son), *one who will heal*. A Thessalonian, and probably a relative of Paul, whom he entertained, and in consequence received rough treatment at the hands of the unbelieving Jews. Acts 17; with Rom. 16:21.

Jasper. The last stone in the breastplate of the high priest, and the first in the foundations of the new Jerusalem. Ex. 28:20; Rev. 21:19. Jasper is an opaque species of quartz, of different colors, often banded or spotted, and susceptible of a high polish. The dark-green kind is supposed to be the variety of the Bible.

Javan (jā'van), *clay*. 1. A son of Japheth. Gen. 10:2, 4; Isa. 66:19; Ezek. 27: 13. Javan was regarded as the representative of the Greek race. The name was probably introduced into Asia by the Phœnicians, to whom the Ionians were naturally better known than any other of the Hellenic races, on account of their commercial activity and the high prosperity of their towns on the western coast of Asia Minor. 2. A town in the southern part of Arabia (Yemen), whither the Phœnicians traded. Ezek. 27:19.

Jazer, Josh. 21:39, or **Jaazer** (jā'zer, jā'a-zer or ja-ā'zer). Num. 21:32, A. V., a city of the Ammonites, near the river Jabbok. Its ruins are at Sar, about 15 miles from Hesbân.

SEA OF. Jer. 48:32. May be a lake existing in ancient times near the city of Jazer. But scholars are not agreed what the Sea of Jazer refers to.

Jebus (jē'bus), *place trodden down, threshing-floor*. The ancient name of Jerusalem among the Canaanites, Judg. 19:10, 11; 1 Chron. 11:4, 5; probably derived from a descendant of Canaan the son of Ham. Gen. 10:16. The tribe of Jebusites were partially subdued by Joshua, Josh. 10:23, 40; 12:10; 15:63; and they were permitted to remain after the conquest of Jebus, by David. Num. 13:29; 2 Sam. 5:6-9; 24:16-25; 1 Chron. 11:4-8; Ezra 9:1, 2. "Jebusi" or "Jebusite" is sometimes put for the city Jebus. Josh. 15:8; 18:16; Zech. 9:7.

Jeduthun (je-dū'thun or jĕd'u-thŭn), *praising*. A Levite of the family of Merari, probably the same as Ethan. Compare 1 Chron. 15:17, 19, with 1 Chron. 16:41, 42; 25:1, 3, 6; 2 Chron. 35:15. His office was generally to preside over the music of the temple service. Jeduthun's name stands at the head of the 39th, 62d, and 77th Psalms.

Jehoahaz (je-hō'a-hăz), *whom Jehovah holds*. 1. Son and successor of Jehu, king of Israel for 17 years, B. C. 856-840. See 2 Kings 13:1-9. His reign was disastrous to the kingdom. The kings of Syria, Hazael and Benhadad, oppressed and spoiled the country. When his troubles multiplied he sought the Lord, whom he had forsaken, and God ultimately raised up a deliverer in the person of Jehoash, his son. 2 Kings 5: 25. 2. Son and successor of Josiah, king of Judah, 2 Kings 23:30; called Shallum, 1 Chron. 3:15; Jer. 22:11. Though he was the fourth son, yet the *people* chose him king. He was an evil-doer, 2 Kings 23:32, and referred to as a young lion by Ezek. 19:3. He reigned only three months. B. C. 610. Pharaoh-necho sent him a prisoner loaded with chains into Egypt, and there he died, Jer. 22:11, 12, and his brother Jehoiakim became king in his stead. 2 Kings 23:30, 35. 3. The same with Ahaziah and Azariah. Compare 2 Chron. 21:17; 22:1, 6, 8, 9.

Jehoash (je-hō'ash), *whom Jehovah bestowed*. Full form of the name commonly written Joash, and applied to two kings. See **Joash**, 3 and 4.

Jehoiachin (je-hoi'a-kĭn), *whom Jehovah*

has appointed. Jeconiah, 1 Chron. 3:17; Coniah, Jer. 22:24; Jeconias, R. V. "Jechoniah." Matt. 1:12. Son and successor of Jehoiakim, king of Judah, B.C. 598. 2 Kings 24:8. In his brief reign Nebuchadnezzar besieged Jerusalem and carried the king and royal family, the chief men of the nation, and great treasures, unto Babylon. 2 Kings 24:6-16. Jehoiachin merited this punishment. Jer. 22:24-30. For 37 years he was a captive, but Evil-merodach liberated him and made him share the royal bounty and be head of all the captive kings in Babylon.

Jehoiada (*je-hoi'a-dah*), *whom Jehovah knows*. 1. The father of Benaiah, which see. 2 Sam. 8:18; 1 Kings 1:32 ff.; 1 Chron. 18:17. This Jehoiada was the chief priest, 1 Chron. 27:5, and therefore he was the leader of the priests who came to David at Hebron. 1 Chron. 12:27. By a copyist's error, Benaiah is said to have been the father of Jehoiada instead of the son. 1 Chron. 27:34. 2. A high priest of the Jews, and husband of Jehosheba. 2 Kings 11:4. See **Athaliah** and **Joash**. His administration was so auspicious to the civil and religious interests of the nation, 2 Kings 12:2; 2 Chron. 23:16, that when he died, at an advanced age, he was buried in the royal sepulchres at Jerusalem. 2 Chron. 24:16. Many do not accept the age of 132 years assigned to him, for the reason that if he lived so long, then, when he married the daughter of Jehoram, he must have been 80, while Jehoram was only 32. It has been proposed to read "83" instead. 3. The second priest in the reign of Zedekiah. Jer. 29:25-29. 4. One who helped repair the wall. Neh. 3:6. R. V. "Joiada."

Jehoiakim (*je-hoi-a-kim*), *whom Jehovah sets up*. Called Eliakim, son of Josiah and king of Judah. After deposing Jehoahaz, Pharaoh-necho set Eliakim, his elder brother, upon the throne, and changed his name to Jehoiakim. For four years Jehoiakim was subject to Egypt, when Nebuchadnezzar, after a short siege, entered Jerusalem, took the king prisoner, and bound him in fetters to carry him to Babylon. Jehoiakim became tributary to Nebuchadnezzar, but after three years broke his oath of allegiance and rebelled against him. 2 Kings 24:1. Nebuchadnezzar sent against him numerous bands of Chaldeans, with Syrians, Moabites, and Ammonites, 2 Kings 24:2, and who cruelly harassed the whole country. Either in an engagement with some of these forces, or else by the hand of his own oppressed subjects, Jehoiakim came to a violent end in the eleventh year of his reign. His body was cast out ignominiously on the ground, and then was dragged away and buried "with the burial of an ass," without pomp or lamentation, "beyond the gates of Jerusalem." Jer. 22:18, 19; 36:30. All the accounts we have of Jehoiakim concur in ascribing to him a vicious and irreligious character. 2 Kings 23:37; 24:9; 2 Chron. 36:5. The reign of Jehoiakim extends from B. C. 609 to B. C. 598, or, as some reckon, 599.

Jehonadab (*je-hŏn'a-dăb*), or **Jonadab**, *whom Jehovah incites*. The son of Rechab, the founder of the Rechabites, which see. He joined Jehu in the slaughter of the Baalites. 2 Kings 10:15-23.

Jehoram (*je-hō'ram*), *whom Jehovah has exalted*. 1. The son and successor of Jehoshaphat, king of Judah. He reigned eight years, three of which he was associated with his father, though some suppose that he reigned eight years alone. He married Athaliah, the daughter of Ahab and Jezebel; and, through her influence, all the brothers of the king were murdered, and the gross idolatries of the Phœnicians were introduced into the kingdom of Judah. The Edomites revolted, and made themselves independent. The Philistines on one side, and the Arabians on the other, ravaged the country, and even Jerusalem and the royal palace. Jehoram was at length smitten with a malignant dysentery. He died miserably, and was denied the honors of a royal burial. He is also called Joram. 2 Kings 8:16, 21, 24; 2 Chron. 21. 2. One of the priests. 2 Chron. 17:8. 3. See **Joram**.

Jehoshaphat (*je-hŏsh'a-făt*), *whom Jehovah judges*. 1. King of Judah, son of Asa, succeeded to the throne B. C. 914, when he was 35 years old, and reigned 25 years. His history is in 1 Kings 15:24; 2 Kings 8:16, or in a continuous narrative in 2 Chron. 17:1 to 21:3. He was contemporary with Ahab, Ahaziah, and Jehoram. He was one of the pious and prosperous kings of Judah. At first he strengthened himself against Israel, but soon afterward formed an alliance with Israel. Jehoshaphat tried to put down the high places and groves in which the people of Judah burned incense, and sent the wisest Levites through the cities and towns to instruct the people in religion. He received tribute from the Philistines and Arabians, and kept up a large standing army in Jerusalem. He became Ahab's ally in the great battle of Ramoth-gilead, for which he was severely reproved by Jehu. 2 Chron. 19:2. He built at Eziongeber, with the help of Ahaziah, a navy designed to go to Tarshish; but it was wrecked. He was miraculously delivered from a threatened attack of the people of Ammon, Moab, and Seir. He also had war against the rebellious king of Moab. 2 Kings 3. In his declining years the administration of affairs was placed, probably B. C. 891, in the hand of his son Jehoram. There are five persons of this name mentioned in the Scriptures.

Jehoshaphat, Valley of, *valley of the judgment of Jehovah*. A place named only in Joel 3:2, 12. Three leading explanations have been given. 1. That the valley referred to is the same as the "valley of Berachah," where the forces allied against Israel were defeated by Jehoshaphat. 2 Chron. 20:16-26. This event took place 100 years before Joel, and may have given rise to this expression of the prophet. 2. That the valley is that of the Kedron, east of Jerusalem. This identification of Jehoshaphat with the Kedron is now generally regarded as based upon a misinterpretation of Joel. 3. That the name does not refer to any special place (see margin of R. V., which reads, "The Lord judgeth"), but to either (*a*) the scene of great victories, as those of the Maccabees; or (*b*) the general judgment at the end of the world; or (*c*) the truth that God's persecuted people he will defend and vindicate.

Jehovah (*je-ho'vah*), *he will be.* A title of the supreme Being, indicative of eternal and immutable self-existence. Ex. 6:3. It is similar to the title "I AM." Ex. 3:14. In the English Bible it is usually translated "Lord" and printed in small capitals. It occurs first in the second chapter of Genesis. As distinct from Elohim, it signifies the God of revelation and redemption, the God of the Jews, while Elohim is the God of nature, the Creator and Preserver of all men. See **Jah, God**.

Jehu (*jē'hu*), *Jehovah is He.* 1. The son of Jehoshaphat, king over Israel. 1 Kings 19:16, 17. Having been proclaimed king in the presence of the whole army, he proceeded towards Jezreel, and executed the predicted judgments upon the house of Ahab. He slew Joram, the reigning king, and mortally wounded Ahaziah, king of Judah, who was with him. 2 Kings 9:24. Jehu then entered Jezreel, and had Jezebel thrown out of the window of the palace, and her body was trodden under foot, fulfilling another prophecy. Jehu then secured possession of Samaria, and slew all that remained unto Ahab, till he had extirpated him, according to the word of the Lord. 2 Kings 10:1-17. He then, at a great festival, exterminated all the idolatrous priests and prophets of Baal, as traitors to King Jehovah, and turned the temple of Baal into a draughthouse. 2 Kings 10:18-28. For his services he received a divine promise, that his descendants, for four generations, should possess the throne. Jehu, himself, was a decisive, terrible, and ambitious man. He erred in allowing the golden calves at Dan and Bethel to remain. He reigned 28 years. 2 Kings 10:29-36. The name of Jehu occurs on the black obelisk, in the British Museum: "Yaua, the son of Khumri," *i. e.*, Jehu, the successor of Omri, the founder of Samaria. 1 Kings 16:23, 24. 2. A descendant of Judah. 1 Chron. 2:38. 3. A descendant of Simeon. 1 Chron. 4:35. 4. One of David's distinguished officers. 1 Chron. 12:3. 5. The son of Hanani, a prophet of Samaria. 1 Kings 16:1-12; 2 Chron. 19:1-3. He wrote the annals of Jehoshaphat. 2 Chron. 20:34.

Jephthah (*jeph'thah*), *whom God sets free.* A judge about B. C. 1143-1137. His history is contained in Judg. 11:1 to 12:8. He was a Gileadite, the son of Gilead and a concubine. Driven by the other sons from his father's inheritance, he went to Tob and became the head of a marauding party in a debatable land, probably belonging to Ammon. 2 Sam. 10:6. When a war broke out between the children of Israel and the Ammonites, he signalized himself for courage and enterprise. This led the Israelites to seek his aid as their commander-in-chief; and though he objected at first on the ground of their ill-usage of him, yet, upon their solemn covenant to regard him as their leader, in case they succeeded against the Ammonites, he took command of their army. After some preliminary negotiations with the Ammonites, in which the question of the right to the country is discussed with great force and ingenuity, and finding every attempt to conciliate them vain, the two armies met; the Ammonites were defeated with great loss of life, and their country scoured by the Israelites. On the eve of the battle Jephthah made a vow, that if he obtained the victory, he would devote to God whatever should come forth from his house to meet him on his return home. His daughter, an only child, welcomed his return with music and dancing. Jephthah was greatly afflicted by this occurrence; but his daughter cheerfully consented to the performance of his vow, which took place at the expiration of two months; and the commemoration of the event by the daughters of Israel was required by a public ordinance. Whether Jephthah actually offered up his daughter as a burnt-offering is a question that continues to be much disputed. Those who maintain the negative allege, that by translating the Hebrew prefix *or*, rendered *and* in our version, all difficulty will be removed. His vow will then read, "shall surely be the Lord's, *or*, I will offer a burnt-offering:" and not unfrequently the sense requires that the Hebrew should be thus rendered. Moreover, when Jephthah made this vow, he could not have intended to insult the Lord by promising a sacrifice of which he had expressed the utmost abhorrence, Lev. 20:2-5; Deut. 12:31; especially as it is recorded that the Spirit of the Lord was upon him when he uttered his vow. Suppose a dog had come out of the house of Jephthah, can any one suppose that he would have offered this unclean animal as a burnt-offering to the Lord? And why, then, should we suppose that he would offer a human sacrifice, which would have been so much more abominable? It is, moreover, argued that no mention is made of any bloody sacrifice of the young woman. But merely that *he did with her according to his vow which he had vowed;* and *she knew no man;* or, "she had not known man." R. V. These last words seem to convey, not obscurely, the idea that Jephthah devoted his daughter to the Lord, by consecrating her to a life of celibacy. And it should not be forgotten, that in the Epistle to the Hebrews (ch. 11), Jephthah is placed among the worthies who were distinguished for their faith. Now can we suppose that such a man would be guilty of the crime of sacrificing his own daughter? Compare Heb. 11:32 with 2 Sam. 12:9; 1 Kings 11:5, 7. Hence, against the view that he offered his daughter as a burnt-offering, the sums of the argument are: 1. Jephthah must have known that human sacrifices were contrary to God's law. 2. That, being under the influence of the Spirit, Judg. 11:29, he would be prevented from slaying his child, as Abraham was. 3. The law allowed him to redeem his daughter for 30 shekels. Lev. 27:4. 4. No account of the bloody sacrifice is given, but another disposition of her case is intimated. 5. Jephthah is in the list of worthies named in Heb. 11 for their faith. Those who urge the strict literal interpretation think these arguments inconclusive; and urge that Jephthah was a wild character in a rude period, and that there is not a particle of evidence that God approved his rash vow, or this part of his conduct. In the early period there are instances of persons guilty of some great sins, yet who were generally eminent for their piety. Josephus says: "Such an oblation was neither conformable to the law, nor acceptable to God." His next act was one of severity in dealing with the Ephraimites, who were not invited to war against the Ammonites, hence had a battle with the Gileadites, and were defeated; and the latter, seizing the fords of the Jordan, slew every Ephraimite who attempted to escape by crossing the river; and the method employed to ascertain whether they belonged to Ephraim was, to cause them to pronounce the word "shibboleth," which they sounded "sibboleth;" for, it seems that, by this time, a difference in the manner of pronouncing at least one Hebrew letter had arisen between the inhabitants on the different sides of the Jordan. On this occasion 42,000 men of Ephraim were slain; which was a punishment for commencing a war with so small a provocation. Judg. 11 and 12. Jephthah died after judging six years, and was buried among his people, the Gileadites, in one of their cities. Judg. 12:7.

Jeremiah (jĕr-e-mī'ah), whom *Jehovah setteth up* or *appointeth*. 1. The distinguished prophet, son of Hilkiah, a priest of Anathoth. Jer. 1:1-6. He was called to assume the prophetic office when a youth, and on that account declined it: but God promised him grace and strength sufficient for his work. He prophesied under Josiah, Jehoiakim, Jehoiachin, and Zedekiah; and for some time during the exile. During the course of his predictions, Jerusalem was in a distracted and deplorable condition, and the prophet was calumniated, imprisoned, and often in danger of death. Jeremiah expressly foretold that the captivity would endure for 70 years; he also predicted the return of the people to their own country. He appears to have stood high in the estimation of Nebuchadnezzar. Jer. 39:11-14. Towards the close of his life he was carried into Egypt against his will, by the Jews who remained in Judea after the murder of Gedaliah, where he probably died. Jeremiah is called "Jeremy," Matt. 2:17 A. V., and "Jeremias," Matt. 16:14 A. V. The name Jeremy, in Matt. 27:9, 10, is probably an error of the transcribers for Zechariah. The R. V. reads Jeremiah in all these places. Canon Cook says of Jeremiah: "His character is most interesting. We find him sensitive to a most painful degree, timid, shy, hopeless, desponding, constantly complaining, and dissatisfied with the course of events, but never flinching from duty. . . . Timid in resolve, he was unflinching in execution; as fearless when he had to face the whole world as he was dispirited and prone to murmuring when alone with God. Judged by his own estimate of himself, he was feeble, and his mission a failure; really, in the hour of action and when duty called him, he was in very truth 'a defenced city and an iron pillar, and brazen walls against the whole land.' Jer. 1:18. He was a noble example of the triumph of the moral over the physical nature." There are eight persons of this name mentioned in the Scriptures.

Jeremiah, Book of. This prophecy embraces a period of upwards of 40 years, between B. C. 628 and B. C. 586. It relates to the judgments that were to come upon the people for their gross idolatry and corruption; to the restoration which awaited them, whenever they would repent of and forsake their sins; and to the glory which would arise on the church in future times. Melancholy, tender sensibility, and a tone of grief, are the distinguishing characteristics of Jeremiah's style. The several prophecies may be arranged thus: I. The introduction, chap. 1. II. Reproofs of the sins of the Jews, consisting of seven sections—*a.* chap. 2, *b.* 3-6, *c.* 7-10, *d.* 11-13, *e.* 14-17:18, *f.* 17:19, 20, *g.* 21-24. III. A general review of the heathen nations, and also of the people of Israel, consisting of two sections—*a.* 46-49, which may have been transposed, *b.* 25, and an historical appendix in three sections—*a.* 26, *b.* 27, *c.* 28, 29. IV. Two sections picturing the hopes of brighter times—*a.* 30, 31, *b.* 32, 33, to which is added an historical appendix in three sections—*a.* 34:1-7, *b.* 34:8-22, *c.* 35. V. The conclusion, in two sections—*a.* 36, *b.* 45. Added some time afterwards—*a.* 37-39, *b.* 40-43, *c.* 46:13-26. The fifty-second chapter of Jeremiah is nearly the same with 2 Kings 24:18-25:30. Both were mainly drawn from the same sources. The order of the prophecies of Jeremiah, from chap. 21:15 to the end of the book, is different in the Septuagint version from that of the Hebrew text; for those prophecies which, in the Hebrew, occupy the last place—46-51—are found in the Greek translation after chap. 25:14, and in a different order. In some editions of the Septuagint the chapters are as in the Hebrew.

Jericho (jĕr'i-kō), *city of the moon*, or *place of fragrance*. A city of Benjamin, situated in the valley of the Jordan, on the west side of that river, and north of its entrance into the Dead sea. Josh. 2:1-3; 1 Kings 16:34. It was also called the City of Palm-trees. Deut. 34:3; Judg. 1:16. As Jericho was the first city that was taken, on the west of the Jordan, the ban was laid on all the property in it. Joshua burned the city with fire, and pronounced a solemn curse upon the person who, at any succeeding period, should build its walls or set up its gates, Josh. 4:13; which was executed upon Hiel, 533 years afterward. 1 Kings 16:33, 34. Previous to this, however, the city had been rebuilt, but not upon its ancient foundations. Judg. 3:13;

2 Sam. 10:5; 2 Kings 2:4, 5. The more ancient city was probably in the neighborhood of the beautiful fountain, which is apparently the same whose waters Elisha healed. 2 Kings 2:18-22. The later Jericho appears to have occupied the site of the miserable and filthy village, Er-Riha, nearly two miles from the fountain. Ezra 2:34; Neh. 3:2; Matt. 19:1; 20:29-34; Mark 10:1, 46, 52; Luke 18:35-43; 19:1-10. Riha lies almost desert; and even that "one solitary palm tree" which Dr. Robinson saw is gone. The inhabitants are a feeble and licentious race. The road between Jerusalem and Jericho still retains its ancient character for scenes of assault and robbery. Luke 10:30.

Jeroboam (*jĕr'o-bō'am*), *whose people are many*. There were two kings of this name: 1. The first king of the divided kingdom of Israel, B. C. 975-954, was the son of Nebat. He was made by Solomon the superintendent of the taxes exacted from the tribe of Ephraim. 1 Kings 11:28. He made the most of his position, and at last was perceived by Solomon to be aiming at the monarchy. He was leaving Jerusalem, when he was met by Ahijah the prophet, who gave him the assurance that, on condition of obedience to his laws, God would establish for him a kingdom and dynasty equal to that of David. 1 Kings 11:29-40. Solomon attempting to arrest Jeroboam, caused his flight into Egypt. There he remained until Solomon's death. Jeroboam married Ano, the elder sister of the Egyptian queen Tahpenes, and returned to Shechem, where took place the conference with Rehoboam, and the final revolt which ended in the elevation of Jeroboam to the throne of the northern kingdom. Fearing that the yearly pilgrimages to Jerusalem would undo all the work which he effected, he boldly decided to rend the religious unity of the nation, which was as yet unimpaired. He caused two golden calves to be made and set up at the two extremities of his kingdom, one at Dan and the other at Bethel. It was while dedicating the altar at Bethel that a prophet from Judah suddenly appeared, who denounced the altar, and foretold its desecration by Josiah. The king, stretching out his hand to arrest the prophet, felt it withered and paralyzed, and only at the prophet's prayer saw it restored. Jeroboam was at constant war with the house of Judah, and in a battle with Abijah was defeated, and soon after died in the 22d year of his reign, 2 Chron. 13:20, and was buried in his ancestral sepulchre. 1 Kings 14:20. 2. Jeroboam II., the son of Joash, the fourth king of the dynasty of Jehu, B. C. 825-784. He was one of the most prosperous of the kings of Israel. He repelled the Syrian invaders, took their capital city Damascus, 2 Kings 14:28, and recovered the whole of the ancient dominion from Hamath to the Dead sea. 2 Kings 14:25. Ammon and Moab were reconquered, and the trans-Jordanic tribes were restored to their territory, 2 Kings 13:5; 1 Chron. 5:17-22; but it was merely an outward restoration.

Jerusalem (*je-ru'sa-lĕm*). The religious and political capital of Israel; called also "the Holy City," Neh. 11:1; "City of the Great King," Ps. 48:2; "City of David" and "Zion," 1 Kings 8:1; 2 Kings 14:20. Jewish writers held that it was the same as Salem. Gen. 14:18; Ps. 76:2. The first notice of it as Jerusalem is in Josh. 10:1. It was a boundary mark between Benjamin and Judah. Josh. 15:8; 18:16, 28, where it is called Ha-jebusi, that is, the Jebusite—in A. V. Jebusi—and in Judg. 19:10, 11, "Jebus, which is Jerusalem," because it was then a city inhabited by Jebusites. Jerusalem is in latitude 31° 47′ north, and in longitude 35° 18′ east from Greenwich, or about the latitude of Savannah, Ga. It is 35 miles east from the Mediterranean sea, and 18 miles west of the north end of the Dead sea. It stands on four peaks of the mountain ridge of Western Palestine, at a general elevation of about 2600 feet above the sea, the English survey placing the height of Moriah at 2440 feet, Mount Zion 2550 feet, Mount of Olives 2665 feet. The hill on which the temple stood is 2440 feet high, "dropping abruptly," says Selah Merrill, "at the northeast corner 100 feet, at the southeast corner 250 feet, at the southwest corner 140 feet, and on the west side about 100 feet, while toward the north, beyond what afterward became the temple area, the ridge rose gradually about 100 feet, its highest point being at the spot now known as Jeremiah's Grotto. Excluding the extension of the ridge to Jeremiah's Grotto, the horizontal area thus bounded is the same as the present Haram Area. Zion was 100 feet higher than the temple mount, and the distance across from summit to summit was less than one-third of a mile; but the descent to the bottom of the ravine separating the two was 100 feet on the side of the temple mount, and 200 feet on the side of Zion. Olivet is 90 feet higher than the highest point of Jerusalem, 143 feet higher than Mount Zion, and 243 feet higher than the temple mount. But the distance from the highest point of Jerusalem to the top of Olivet is scarcely more than a mile. Thus Olivet overlooks Jerusalem, and from its summit the best view of the city is obtained." "In several respects," says Dean Stanley, "its situation is singular among the cities of Palestine. Its elevation is remarkable; occasioned, not from its being on the summit of one of the numerous hills of Judæa, like most of the towns and villages, but because it is on the edge of one of the highest table-lands of the country. Hebron, indeed, is higher still by some hundred feet, and from the south, accordingly (even from Bethlehem), the approach to Jerusalem is by a slight descent. But from any other side the ascent is perpetual; and to the traveller approaching the city from the east or west it must always have presented the appearance, beyond any other capital of the then known world—we may say beyond any important city that has ever existed on the earth—of a mountain city; breathing, as compared with the sultry plains of Jordan, a mountain air; enthroned, as compared with Jericho or Damascus, Gaza, or Tyre, on a mountain fastness." *Sinai and Palestine*, 170, 1. The elevation of Jerusalem is a subject of constant reference and exultation by the Jewish writers. Their fervid poetry abounds with allusions to its height, to the ascent thither of the tribes from all parts of the country. It was the habitation of Jehovah, from which "He looked upon all the inhabitants of the world," Ps. 33: 14; its kings were "higher than the kings of the earth," Ps. 89:27. Jerusalem, if not actually in the centre of Palestine, was yet virtually so. This central position as expressed in the words of Ezekiel 5:5, "I have set Jerusalem in the midst of the nations and countries round about her," led in later ages to a definite belief that the city was actually in the centre of the earth.

Roads.—There were 3 main approaches to the city: 1. From the Jordan valley by Jericho and the Mount of Olives. This was the route commonly taken from the north and east of the country—as from Galilee by our Lord, Luke 17:11; 18:35; 19: 1, 29, 37, etc., from Damascus by Pompey, to Mahanaim by David, 2 Sam. 15 and 16. It was also the route from places in the central districts of the country, as Samaria. 2 Chron. 28:15. The latter part of the approach, over the Mount of Olives, as generally followed at the present day, is identical with what it was, at least in one memorable instance, in the time of Christ. 2. From the great maritime plain of Philistia and Sharon. This road led by the two Bethhorons up to the high ground at Gibeon, whence it turned south, and came to Jerusalem by Ramah and Gibeah, and over the ridge north of the city. 3. There was also the route from Hebron, Bethlehem, and Solomon's pools on the south.

To the four hills, Zion, Ophel, Acra, and Moriah, in the ancient city may be added the hill of Goath, and Bezetha, the new town. The precise topography of the city has long been in dispute, and while recent explorations have added much to our knowledge of the city, many points are yet unsettled. The western hill was called *Mount Zion*, and it is also clear that Zion and the city of David were identical. "David took the castle of Zion, which is the city of David." "And David dwelt in the castle, therefore they called it the city of David. And he built the city round about, even from Millo round about, and Joab repaired the rest of the city." 2 Sam. 5:7-9; 1 Chron. 11:5-8. *Mount Moriah* was the eastern hill, 2 Chron. 3:1, and the site of the temple. It was situated in the southwest angle of the area, now known as the Haram area, and was, Josephus tells us, an exact square of a stadium, or 600 Greek feet, on each side. At the northwest angle of the temple was the Antonia, a tower or fortress. North of the side of the temple is the building now known to Christians as the Mosque of Omar, but by Moslems it is called the Dome of the Rock. *Ophel* was the southern continuation of the eastern hill, which gradually came to a point at the junction of the valleys Tyropœon and Jehoshaphat. *Bezetha*, "the New City," noticed by Josephus, was separated from Moriah by an artificial ditch, and overlooked the valley of Kidron on the east; this hill was enclosed within the walls of Herod Agrippa. Lastly, *Acra* lay westward of Moriah and northward of Zion, and formed the "Lower City" in the time of Josephus.

Gates.—The following list of gates, named in the Bible and Josephus, are given by Smith: 1. Gate of Ephraim. 2 Chron. 25: 23; Neh. 8:16; 12:39. This is probably the same as the 2. Gate of Benjamin. Jer. 20: 2; 37:13; Zech. 14:10. If so, it was 400 cubits distant from the 3. Corner gate. 2 Chron. 25:23; 26:9; Jer. 31:38; Zech. 14:10. 4. Gate of Joshua, governor of the city. 2 Kings 23:8. 5. Gate between the two walls. 2 Kings 25:4; Jer. 39:4. 6. Horse gate. Neh. 3:28; 2 Chron. 23:15; Jer. 31:40. 7. Ravine gate, R. V., valley gate, *i. e.*, opening on ravine of Hinnom. 2 Chron. 26:9; Neh. 2: 13, 15; 3:13. 8. Fish gate. 2 Chron. 33:14; Neh. 12:39. 9. Dung gate. Neh. 2:13; 3: 13. 10. Sheep gate. Neh. 3:1, 32; 12:39. 11. East gate. Neh. 3:29. 12. Miphkad. R. V., "Hammiplikod." Neh. 3:31. 13. Fountain gate (Siloam?). Neh. 12:37. 14. Water gate. Neh. 12:37. 15. Old gate. Neh. 12: 39. 16. Prison gate. Neh. 12:39. 17. Gate Harsith (perhaps the Sun), A. V., East gate. Jer. 19:2. 18. First gate, Zech. 14:10. 19. Gate Gennath (gardens). Joseph. *B. J.* v. 4, ᶟ 4. 20. Essenes' gate. Joseph. *B. J.* 4, ᶟ 2. To these should be added the following gates of the temple: Gate Sur. 2 Kings 11: 6. Called also Gate of foundation. 2 Chron. 23:5. Gate of the guard, or behind the guard. 2 Kings 11:6, 19 ; called the High gate, R. V., "Upper gate." 2 Chron. 23:20; 27:3 ; 2 Kings 15:35. Gate Shallecheth. 1 Chron. 26:16. It is impossible to say which or how many of these names designate *different* gates. The *chief* gates of Jerusalem now are four: the Damascus gate on the north, the Jaffa gate on the west, David or Zion gate on the south, and St. Stephen's gate on the east. The Mohammedans have other names for these gates. Only during the past six centuries have traditions connected the martyr Stephen with the present St. Stephen's gate; before that they were located to the north about the Damascus gate. The small door in the gate, to admit persons to enter after the gate was locked at night, is in the Jaffa gate, but it was built only 30 years ago. There is no evidence that there was such a door in our Lord's time, and to use it, as illustrating "the needle's eye," Luke 8:25, is without warrant from ancient history.

Walls.—According to Josephus, the first or old wall began on the north at the tower called Hippicus, the ruins now called Kasr Jalud at the northwest angle of the present city, and, extending to the Xystus, joined the council house, and ended at the west cloister of the temple. The second wall began at the gate Gennath, in the old wall, probably near the Hippicus, and passed round the northern quarter of the city, enclosing the great valley of the Tyropœon, which leads up to the Damascus gate; and then, proceeding southward, joined the fortress Antonia. The points described by Josephus in the course of this wall have not been identified, and have given rise to sharp disputes, as the course of this wall goes far towards deciding the true site of Calvary. John 19 : 20 ; Luke 23 : 33. The third wall was built by King Herod Agrippa; and was intended to enclose the suburbs on the northern sides of the city, which before this had been left exposed.

Extent.—After describing the walls, Josephus adds that the whole circumference of the city was 33 stadia, or nearly four English miles, which is as near as may be the extent indicated by the localities. He then adds that the number of towers in the old wall was 60, the middle wall 40, and the new wall 99. Jerusalem of to-day as walled in would require about an hour to walk around it. The walls, measuring straight from point to point, are about 12,000 feet in length; the north wall being 3930 feet, the east wall 2754 feet, the south wall 3245 feet, and the west wall 2086 feet. The area in the present city is about 210 acres. The ancient city included the southern slopes of Zion and Ophel, which in modern times have been under cultivation, thus fulfilling the prediction, "Zion shall be ploughed like a field." Jer. 26 : 18.

The Pools of Gihon, Siloam, Hezekiah, Bethesda, En-rogel, etc., will be noticed under their proper titles.

The king's garden, Neh. 3 : 15, was probably outside the city at the south, as Gethsemane, Matt. 26 : 36, was eastward at the foot of the Mount of Olives. Of the various so-called streets, as the "east street," R V., "the broad place on the east," 2 Chron. 29 : 4; the "street of the city," *i. e.*, the city of David, R. V., "broad place at the gate of the city," 2 Chron. 32 : 6; the "street," R. V., "broad place facing the water gate," Neh. 8 : 1, 3, or, according to the parallel account in 1 Esdr. 9 : 38, the "broad place of the temple towards the east;" the "street of the house of God," Ezra 10 : 9, R. V., "broad place;" the "street," R. V., "broad place of the gate of Ephraim," Neh 8 : 16 ; and the "open place of the first gate toward the east" could not have been "streets," in our sense of the word, but rather open spaces found in eastern towns near the inside of the gates. Streets, properly so called, there were, however, Jer. 5 : 1 ; 11 : 13, etc.; but the name of only one, "the bakers' street," Jer. 37 : 21, is preserved to us.

History.—Only a brief notice of its history can be given. We catch our earliest glimpse of Jerusalem in Josh. 10 : 1, and in Judg. 1, which describes how the "children of Judah smote it with the edge of the sword, and set the city on fire;" and almost the latest mention of it in the New Testament is contained in the solemn warnings in which Christ foretold how Jerusalem should be "compassed with armies," Luke 21 : 20, and the "abomination of desolation" be seen standing in the Holy Place, Matt. 24 : 15. In the 15 centuries which elapsed between those two periods, the city was besieged no fewer than 17 times; twice it was razed to the ground; and on two other occasions its walls were levelled. In this respect it stands without a parallel in any city, ancient or modern. David captured the city, B. C. 1046, and made it his capital, fortified and enlarged it. 2 Sam. 5 : 7 ; 6 : 2-16 ; 1 Kings 11 : 36. Solomon adorned the city with beautiful buildings, including the temple, but made no additions to its walls. 1 Kings 7 : 2-7; 8; 10 : 7 ; 2 Chron. 9 : 1-12. The city was taken by the Philistines and Arabians in the reign of Jehoram, B. C. 886, and by the Israelites in the reign of Amaziah, B. C. 826. The books of Kings and of Chronicles give the history of Jerusalem under the monarchy. It was thrice taken by Nebuchadnezzar, in the years B. C. 607, 597, and 586, in the last of which it was utterly destroyed. Its restoration commenced under Cyrus, B. C. 536, and was completed under Artaxerxes I., who issued commissions for this purpose to Ezra, B. C. 457, and Nehemiah, B. C. 445. Neh. 4 : 7-22; 6 : 1-16. In B. C. 332 it was captured by Alexander the Great, and again under Antiochus Epiphanes, B. C. 170. Under the Maccabees Jerusalem became independent and retained its position until its capture by the Romans under Pompey, B. C. 63. The temple was subsequently plundered by Crassus, B. C. 54, and the city by the Parthians, B. C. 40. Herod took up his residence there, and restored the temple with great magnificence. It was taken and destroyed by the Romans under Titus, when it had held out nearly five months, A. D. 70, fulfilling Christ's prophecy, Matt. 24. Hadrian restored it as a Roman colony, A. D. 135. The emperor Constantine erected a church on the supposed site of the holy sepulchre, A. D. 336, and Justinian added several churches and hospitals, about A. D. 532. It was taken by the Persians under Chosroes II. in A. D. 614. In A. D. 637 the patriarch Sophronius surrendered to the khalif Omar, and the Holy City passed into the hands of the Fatimite dynasty. About 1084 it was bestowed upon Ortok, whose severity to the Christians became the proximate cause of the Crusades. It was taken by the Crusaders in 1099, and for 88 years Jerusalem remained in the hands of the Christians. In 1187 it was retaken by Saladin after a siege of several weeks. In 1277 Jerusalem was nominally annexed to the kingdom of Sicily. In 1517 it passed under the sway of the Ottoman sultan Selim I., whose successor, Suliman, built the present walls of the city in 1542. Mohammed Ali, the pasha of Egypt, took possession of it in 1832; and in 1840, after the bombardment of Acre, it was again restored to the sultan and has since remained in the hands of the Turks. A steam railway was opened from Jaffa (Joppa) to Jerusalem in October, 1892.

Population.—It is estimated that modern Jerusalem has from 50,000 to 75,000 inhabitants, of whom 12,000 are Mohammedans, 8000 Christians, and 25,000 to 30,000 (Conder says 40,000) Jews, nearly 30,000 depending largely for their living upon benevolent gifts from religious brethren elsewhere. The population of Jerusalem in ancient times probably did not exceed 75,000 at any period of Bible history.

Recent Explorations.—Besieged 17 times, twice destroyed, ancient Jerusalem is now buried under 80 feet of earth and rubbish. Of the explorations and present condition of the city, Selah Merrill, United States consul at Jerusalem (in Jackson's concise *Dictionary*), says: "One would suppose that in a place like Jerusalem, which has always been a centre of special interest, there would be many remains of antiquity and a large number of historical sites whose genuineness no person would question. The truth is just the contrary of this. Very many things are doubtless buried which will, from time to time, be brought to light, as has been the case during the past 25 years. Thanks to recent excavations, certain points and objects have been recovered which may be accepted as authentic beyond dispute. Thus we have the actual site of the Herodian temple, together with portions of the wall which supported its area, also the remains of a bridge of the same period which led from the temple to Mount Zion. We have the point of the native rock over which the altar was built, and from this are able to determine the site of the Holy of Holies. We can point to the spot where the castle of Antonia stood, and thus fix the eastern terminus of the 'second wall.'" Near the Jaffa gate Dr. Merrill "discovered, in 1885, a section of this wall, whose position has been so long in dispute. One hundred and twenty feet of it were exposed, consisting of one, two, and in a single place of three layers of massive stones, and from this the position of the Gennath Gate can be determined within a few yards. The lower portion of the so-called 'Castle of David' belongs to the time of Herod, if not to an earlier period. In the northwest corner of the city the foundations of one of the great towers of ancient Jerusalem have been uncovered, and massive work of the same age is found at the Damascus Gate. Under the mosque El Aksa are the columns of the Double Gate and the Porch belonging to it, through which our Lord must have often entered the temple. There is no question about the valleys Hinnom, Jehoshaphat, and the Tyropœan, or the pool of Siloam. The rock-cut conduit, leading for 1700 feet under Ophel, connecting the Pool of Siloam with the Virgin's Fountain, in which the Siloam inscription was discovered in 1880, dates from the time of the Hebrew kings. North of the city we have the tomb of Helena, the mother of Izates, built in the last century before Christ; and there are a few other objects, as the Tomb of Absalom and that of Jehoshaphat, which certainly belong to ancient times, but whose exact date cannot be determined." The old Pool of Bethesda was lately discovered by Conrad Schick, under the Church of St. Anne. Beyond these, our knowledge of the various places in ancient Jerusalem, noticed in the Bible and Josephus, is indefinite if not chaotic. Jerusalem is not a centre of trade, and it has few manufactures or business by which wealth can be acquired. Money-changers are numerous because people from many other countries are found there, most of whom bring with them coin that is not current in the city. Shopkeepers are seldom able to make change themselves, and it is understood that the purchaser must come prepared to pay the exact amount of his purchase. Upward of 40 different languages and dialects are spoken in Jerusalem. Society is of a low order. The people are slow to adapt themselves to new conditions. There is, however, reason to hope for improvement under better religious and educational influences, and under a wise and helpful government.

In Scripture and Prophecy. Jerusalem is named 799 times in the Bible, and many times alluded to in sacred history and prophecy. Its strength and beauty are noticed, Ps. 48:2, 11-13; 122:2-5; its peace is prayed for, Ps. 51:18; 122:6-8; its glory noticed, Ps. 87:1-6. The siege and desolation of the city for sins were predicted, Isa. 29:1-3; 27:10; Jer. 4:11; 19:8; 21:10; 22:28, 31; especially its destruction by the Chaldeans, Jer. 13:9, 18; 34:22; Ezek. 24:2; Amos 2:5. These predictions were literally fulfilled. See 1 Kings 14:25, 26; Jer. 51:50, 51; Lam. 2:13; 5:11-22. Its preservation and restoration at times promised and performed, 2 Kings 19:10; 2 Chron. 32:9-20; Isa. 37:17, 20, 33-35; Ps. 69:35, where it is called Zion: compare Isa. 11:9, 10; Jer. 31:1, 4, 38-40; Zech. 8:3-5. Again its destruction by the Romans was predicted, Zech. 14:2; Luke 19:41-44; and 21:9, 10, 20, 24; and Josephus' description of the siege and destruction of the city under Titus (*Wars, Bk.* vi.) shows how terrible was the fulfillment of this prophecy of Christ. It is still the "Sacred City," however, to the Jew, the Christian, and the Moslem, hallowed by the footsteps and sufferings of the Son of God.

Jeshurun (*jĕsh'u-rŭn* or *je-shū'run*), *happy*, and once in A. V. **Jesurun**, Isa. 44:2, a symbolical name for Israel in Deut. 32:15; 33:5, 26; Isa. 44:2. It is most probably derived from a root signifying "to be blessed."

Jesse (*jĕs'se*), *wealthy*. The father of David, the son of Obed, and grandson of Boaz and the Moabitess Ruth. He was also a descendant of Rahab the Canaanite, of Jericho. Matt. 1:5. Jesse's genealogy is twice given in full in the Old Testament, viz., Ruth 4:18-22 and 1 Chron. 2:5-12. He is commonly designated as "Jesse, the Bethlehemite," 1 Sam. 16:1, 18; 17:58; but his full title is "the Ephrathite of Bethlehem Judah." 1 Sam. 17:12. He was an "old man" when noticed in 1 Sam. 17:12, with eight sons, 1 Sam. 16:10; 17:12, residing at Bethlehem. 1 Sam. 16:4, 5. Jesse's wealth seems to have consisted of sheep and goats, which were under the care of David. 1 Sam. 16:11; 17:34, 35. After David was compelled to leave the court of Saul, he took his father and his mother into the country of Moab, and there they disappear from the records of Scripture, B. C. 1068–61.

Jesus Christ. The name of the Saviour, signifying his work and authority; Jesus (the Greek form of the Hebrew Joshua) means *Jehovah saves*, or Saviour. Matt. 1 : 21. Christ (the Greek translation of the Hebrew Messiah) means anointed. Jesus was his common name during his life on earth, generally used in the gospels. Christ is his official name, frequently used alone or with Jesus in the epistles. Jesus occurs in the Bible 711 times; Christ 304 times; Jesus Christ, Lord Jesus Christ, and Christ Jesus (anointed Saviour), 244 times, and Messiah 4 times. He has many other titles and names in Scripture, as "Immanuel," Matt. 1 : 23; "Son of God," John 1 : 34; "Son of man," John 8 : 28; "Son of David," etc., Mark 10 : 47, 48; in all, upwards of 100 titles, indicating his character, life, and work.

The predictions concerning Christ were many—about 150 or more—and were made at various periods of Old Testament history. He was to be born in Bethlehem, a small village, Micah 5 : 2; he was to be a king with a universal and perpetual empire. Ps. 2 : 6; 45 : 2-7; 72; Isa. 9 : 6, 7; yet would be despised and rejected. Isa. 53. He was to open the eyes of the blind and the ears of the deaf, Isa. 35 : 5, 6, and yet to be betrayed, sold and slain and his grave appointed with the wicked. Yet his sufferings should make many righteous. Isa. 11 : 1-9; 60 : 1-11. He was to do the work of a prophet, Isa. 42 : 1-7; of a priest, Ps. 110 : 4: Zech. 6 : 13; and of a king. Dan. 7 : 14. These predictions, and many others of like nature, were all fulfilled in Jesus the Son of Mary.

He is the centre of all Jewish and Christian history; the "Holy of Holies" in the history of the world. There is space here for the briefest outline only of his human life, his mysterious person, and his work.

HIS LIFE.—While Augustus was emperor of Rome, and Herod the Great king in Jerusalem, Jesus was born four years before 1 A. D., the Christian era having been fixed by Dionysius Exiguus of the sixth century, four years too late. Mary, a virgin, betrothed to Joseph of Nazareth, gave birth to Jesus at Bethlehem according to Micah's prophecy. Micah 5 : 2. Angels celebrated it with songs, and wise men from the East brought precious gifts to the new-born babe. To escape Herod's threats, the child Jesus was taken to Egypt, but later settled with his parents at Nazareth. Only one event of his childhood is known—a visit when 12 years old to Jerusalem, when he astonished the doctors by his words and questions. He was trained as other Jewish lads of his station. At three the boy was weaned, and wore for the first time the fringed or tasselled garment prescribed by Num. 15 : 38–41 and Deut. 22 : 12. His education began at first under the mother's care. At five he was to learn the law, at first by extracts written on scrolls of the more important passages, the *Shema* or creed of Deut. 2 : 4; the *Hallel* or festival psalms, Ps. 114, 118, 136, and by catechetical teaching in school. At 12 he became more directly responsible for his obedience to the law; and on the day when he attained the age of 13, put on for the first time the phylacteries which were worn at the recital of his daily prayer. In addition to this, Jesus learned the carpenter's trade of Joseph.

Ministry.—His public ministry is usually regarded as lasting upwards of three years. John records more of the Judæan ministry, Luke more of his Peræan ministry, while Matthew and Mark give his Galilean ministry, as does Luke also. John the Baptist, in the fifteenth year of Tiberius, Luke 3 : 1, produced a deep impression by preaching repentance. Jesus sought baptism at his hands, and was tempted of the devil. He then went to Cana of Galilee, where he worked his first miracle at a wedding. With some disciples, he set out for Jerusalem to keep the passover. His first work was the cleansing of the temple from traffickers and money-changers—which he repeated near the close of his ministry. Matt. 21 : 12. He received a visit by night from Nicodemus. Presently the Baptist was thrown into prison and the Saviour withdrew to Galilee. On his way through Samaria he conversed with a woman at Jacob's well. At Nazareth he was rejected by the people, and went to Capernaum, which henceforth became "his own city." Here he called Peter and Andrew and James and John, and made his first tour through Galilee, performing many miracles. Early in the second year of his ministry Jesus went up to Jerusalem to a feast of the Jews, John 5 : 1, and healed a lame man at the pool of Bethesda, explained the right use of the Sabbath, a subject which he resumed when his disciples were plucking ears of corn on his return to Galilee. When he reached the Sea of Galilee multitudes followed him. He appointed the twelve apostles and delivered the Sermon on the Mount, and commenced a second tour in Galilee, during which he delivered the series of parables in Matt. 13, stilled the storm on Galilee, healed the demoniacs of Gadara, raised the daughter of Jairus, and after other miracles came again to Nazareth, where he was again rejected. He then made a third tour in Galilee, and sent forth the apostles, giving the instructions recorded in Matt. 10 : 11. After an interval of some months the twelve returned, and with them he retired to the Sea of Galilee, fed the 5000, walked on the water, and delivered his sermon on the bread of life, John 6, in the synagogue at Capernaum. Early in the third year of his ministry, Jesus disputed with the Pharisees about eating with unwashed hands, and went toward the northwest, healed the daughter of the Syrophœnician woman, and then passed around to Decapolis, where he wrought many miracles and fed 4000. Near Cæsarea Philippi Peter made his confession of faith, and then Jesus foretold his own death and resurrection and the trials of his followers. The transfiguration followed, and the next morning the healing of an epileptic child. On the way back to Capernaum he again foretold his sufferings, and exhorted the disciples to humility, forbearance, and brotherly love. About this time he instructed and sent out the 70 on their mission. Then he left Galilee, and having cleansed ten lepers came to Jerusalem at the Feast of Tabernacles. John 7:2. Here he taught in public, and answered a lawyer's question with the parable of the Good Samaritan. The healing of the man born blind led to a long discourse, which aroused the rulers, and Jesus retired beyond Jordan. In Peræa, on his way to Jerusalem, he uttered the parables of the lost sheep, the unjust steward, the rich man and Lazarus, and the pharisee and the publican: gave precepts concerning divorce: blessed little children: taught the rich young ruler. He raised Lazarus at Bethany. A third time he foretold his death and resurrection, and approaching Jericho healed blind men, called Zacchæus, and gave the parable of the pounds. He arrived at Bethany six days before the passover. At supper, in Simon's house, he is anointed. At the beginning of the last week before the crucifixion Jesus made a public entry into the city, spoke parables and warnings, lamented over Jerusalem, praised the widow's mite, met certain Greeks and predicted his second coming with solemn warnings confirmed by the parables of the ten virgins, the five talents, and the sheep and the goats. At the last or fourth passover with the twelve, Jesus instituted the Lord's Supper, delivered his farewell discourses, and withdrew to Gethsemane. After the agony in the garden he was arrested and in the night brought before Annas, and then Caiaphas and the Sanhedrin, and in the morning before Pilate and Herod. Pilate yielded to the Jews, delivered Jesus to be mocked and crucified. He was buried and a watch set upon the tomb. On the morning of the third day the tomb was found empty, and soon he appeared to the women, then to the disciples, who could hardly believe the fact. During 40 days he taught them, and then, near Bethany, ascended to heaven in their sight.

Mysterious Person.—The great peculiarity of the Scripture doctrine of the *person* of Christ is that he is God and man united, two natures forming one personality. "He is not divine alone, nor human alone, but divine-human." He is the Eternal Word, John 1, the Son of God, and he is also the Son of man. Mark 11:13. This may be difficult for us to comprehend; but if a finite mind could comprehend the whole of Christ's nature, Christ could not be the infinite God he is declared to be. John 1:4.

Work and Offices of Christ.—These are usually presented as threefold. The Bible and Evangelical creeds describe the Mediator as a prophet, priest, and king. As prophet he perfectly reveals the will of the Father to man; as priest he is the perfect offering for sin, procuring redemption for all who will accept of it; as king, he is and will become rightful ruler and judge of this world, and be exalted above every name that is named, putting all things under him,

receiving the praises of all created intelligences.

Jethro (*jē'thro* or *jĕth'ro*), *his excellence.* A priest or prince of Midian, and father-in-law of Moses. Ex. 3:1. He is called Raguel (R. V. "Reuel"), Num. 10:29, and Reuel, Ex. 2:18, and was probably known by either name, while Jethro was his official title. It is highly probable, too, that he was a descendant of Abraham by Keturah, the mother of Midian, Gen. 25:2; but what was the nature of his office as priest—or prince, as some say it should be rendered—we know not.

Jew. 2 Kings 16:6. A name applied first to men of Judah. The most common title for Jews in the Old Testament is "Israel" or "Israelites," but in the New Testament "Jews" is most frequently used. The terms "Israel" and "Israelites" occur in Scriptures about 2460 times; "Jew" and "Jews" about 275 times, and "Hebrew" or "Hebrews" about 50 times. "Jew" is a broader title than Hebrews, as it may include Hellenists, Greek proselytes who became Jews, Acts 6:1; 24:18, and less specific than Israelites. See John 1:47; 2 Cor. 11:22.

Hebrew is probably from *Eber*, a Hebrew word meaning "to pass over," and the name of an ancestor of Abram, Gen. 10:24; 11:13. Abram is first called "the Hebrew" in Gen. 14:13. The Egyptians, Gen. 39:14; 41:12, and the Philistines, 1 Sam. 4:6, knew the people by this title. But they sometimes use it of themselves, but only when foreigners are thought of. Gen. 40:15; Ex. 2:7. The favorite name was "Israelites," and after the captivity the title "Jews" came into vogue, but the title "Hebrews" was still used for the more strict Jews, who preferred the Hebrew language, in distinction from the Hellenists or Grecian Jews. The Hebrew people were descended directly from Abram, Gen. 12:1, through Isaac and Jacob, and are frequently called the "seed of Abraham," Ps. 105:6; John 8:37, or "children of Abraham," Gal. 3:7, or "children of Israel," Ex. 1:13. God, to carry out his purpose and preserve his church, called Abraham to leave his father's house and his country, and separated him and his household from the rest of mankind; gave him special promises, made covenants with him, and constituted him the "Father of the Faithful" to the world. From that time, for two thousand years, the visible church of God was confined to the family of this man; and for fifteen centuries the history of this family is the only sacred history of the world. During fifty generations of the children of Adam the family of this man, or rather the descendants of a part of it, "elected according to the purpose of God," Rom. 9:11, enjoyed exclusive privileges; to the Israelites alone "*pertaineth* the adoption, and the glory, and the covenants, and the giving of the law, and the service of God, and the promises, whose *are* the fathers, and of whom as concerning the flesh Christ *came*, who is over all, God blessed forever. Amen." Rom. 9:45. They were separated from the world by most stringent laws; and it was necessary during all that time for the rest of mankind, through the Jews, to learn the way to be saved. The darkness of death overshadowed all other lands. Thanks be to God! when the fullness of time was come, when salvation was completed by the life, death, and resurrection of the Lord Jesus Christ, and the reservoir of truth was thus filled, the gates were opened; and the command was given to the church to go forth and to proclaim the glad tidings of salvation to all nations and to preach the gospel to every creature. "The gospel preached unto Abraham," before the giving of the law: "In thee shall all nations be blessed" was the first proclamation "that God would justify the heathen through faith." Gal. 3:8. Nothing can more conclusively show the hand of God in directing the history of the world, and in controlling the affairs of nations, than the prophecies and the facts connected with the history of Abraham and of his descendants. Two thousand years after the promise was made to him; in thy seed shall all the families and all the nations of the earth be blessed. Gen. 12:3; 18:18; 22:18. It was fulfilled in the advent of the Son of God, born of the seed of Abraham. The fearful prophecies of God concerning the descendants of Abraham, uttered before they entered the promised land, have been continually in progress of fulfillment to the letter. The Jews have not only undergone the horrors of the siege and the loss of their country, so graphically foretold and described in the 28th chapter of Deuteronomy; but they are, at this day, living witnesses to the truth of God's word. More than three thousand years ago, while on a conquering march, with visions of glory before them, they were warned of their future apostacy, and were told of the judgments that would fall upon them and upon their land. It was said to them, "Thou shalt become an astonishment, a proverb and a by-word among all nations, whither the Lord shall lead thee." Deut. 28:37. "These curses shall be upon thee for a sign and for a wonder, and upon thy seed." Deut. 28: 45, 46. "The Lord shall scatter thee among all people, from the one end of the earth even unto the other; . . . and among these nations shalt thou find no ease, neither shall the sole of thy foot have rest." Deut. 28:64, 65. This has been literally the sad lot of this wonderful people for the last eighteen hundred years. Besides these foretold judgments upon the Jews there are also in the word of God promises of blessings yet to be enjoyed by them. In some of these the world has an interest. While telling the Israelites of the woes that should come upon them, God added: "And yet, for all that, when they be in the land of their enemies, I will not cast them away, neither will I abhor them, to destroy them utterly, and to break my covenant with them: for I am the Lord their God." Lev. 26:44. We are told "Blindness in part is happened to Israel, until the fulness of the Gentiles be come in. And so all Israel shall be saved: as it is written, There shall come out of Sion the Deliverer, and shall turn away ungodliness from Jacob." Rom. 11:25. Paul tells us, "Through their fall salvation *is come* unto the Gentiles." Rom. 11:11. And he informs us that the world is again to be indebted to the Jews; he says: "Now if the fall of them be the riches of the world and the diminishing of them the riches of the Gentiles; how much more their fulness?" Rom. 11:11, 12. The restoration and conversion of the Jews is thus connected with the great ingathering of all nations into the Church of Christ; and the time of this is at hand. The Jews by their talents and industry exert great influence among Christian nations. They have long been the great bankers of the world. The Rothschild family with its immense wealth has controlled the money market. The Jews have furnished great scholars and statesmen. Neander, the church historian, and Stahl, the jurist, were converted Jews; the great musician, Mendelssohn, Bartholdi, Lord Beaconsfield, Gambetta, Castelar, were of Jewish extraction. They have distinguished themselves in all the occupations except agriculture and manufactures. They are divided into orthodox and liberal or reform Jews, who differ from each other as the Pharisees and Sadducees of old. The former prevail in Russia, Poland and the East; the latter in Germany and America. Many of the Jews to-day are deists, or rationalists. The number of Jews in the world is estimated at 9,000,000, of whom 50,000 live in New York city, where they accumulate great wealth. The last word of Christ and the apostles concerning this wonderful people—which, like the burning bush, are never consumed—is a word of promise and hope that their blindness will be removed, and that after the fulness of the Gentiles has come in "all Israel shall be saved." Rom. 11:26. We are indebted to the Jews for our knowledge of God, and of the way of salvation. All of the Scriptures were written by Jews. Moses, the prophets, and the apostles were all Jews. Jesus Christ, our Lord, "was made of the seed of David according to the flesh;" and he says: "Salvation is of the Jews." John 4:22.

Jewry (*jew'ry*), a word elsewhere rendered "Judah" and "Judæa." It occurs once in the Old Testament, Dan. 5:13, where it is rendered "Judah" in the R. V., and several times in the Apocryphal and New Testament books. See **Judah** and **Judæa**.

Jezebel (*jĕz'e-bĕl*), *chaste. Isabella.* 1. The daughter of Ethbaal, king of Tyre, and wife of Ahab, king of Israel, infamous for her idolatry, wickedness and cruel persecution of the prophets of Jehovah. She established the worship of Baal and other idols in the kingdom of Israel. 1 Kings 18: 3-19. When Elijah caused 450 prophets of Baal to be put to death this wicked woman threatened to slay Elijah, but he escaped. Jezebel planned and executed the murder of Naboth, using the authority and name of the king, and showing her remarkable influence over the wicked Ahab and over the leading men in the kingdom. 1 Kings 21:1-13. Indeed, her character throughout exhibits her as a remarkably able and decisive but impious woman. For even after Ahab's death she maintained the ascendency over her son Joram. The doom of this impious queen was predicted by the prophet Elijah, and was in due time visited upon her to the very letter. See 1 Kings 21:23, and 2 Kings 9:36, 37. See Ahab. 2. A symbolical name of a woman in the church at Thyatira, who corrupted the people; so called in allusion to Ahab's idolatrous wife. Rev. 2:20-24.

Jezreel (jĕz're-el). *God hath planted.* 1. A city in the plain of the same name between Gilboa and Little Hermon. It was a boundary of Issachar. Josh. 19:18. Ahab chose it for his chief residence. The selection shows the ability of this wicked king. Near by were a temple and grove of Astarte, with an establishment of 400 priests supported by Jezebel. 1 Kings 18:19; 2 Kings 10:11. The palace of Ahab, 1 Kings 21:1, probably containing his "ivory house," 1 Kings 22:39, was on the eastern side of the city. Compare 1 Kings 21:1; 2 Kings 9:25, 30, 33. Jezebel lived by the city wall, and had a high window facing eastward. 2 Kings 9:30. It had a watch-tower, on which a sentinel stood. 2 Kings 9:17. The gateway of the city on the east was also the gateway of the palace. 2 Kings 9:34. The vineyard of Naboth was probably on the vineclad hill outside the city to the eastward. A spring near is now called '*Ain-Jalûd*, or the "Spring of Goliath," and is the "fountain" or "spring" in "Jezreel." 1 Sam. 29:1. After the fall of the house of Ahab, Jezreel also fell into a decline. It is now a miserable village of a dozen houses, and known as Zerin. 2. A town in Judah, in the neighborhood of the southern Carmel. Josh. 15:56. Here David in his wanderings took Ahinoam the Jezreelitess for his second wife. 1 Sam. 27:3; 30:5.

Jezreel, Valley of. A triangular plain extending from the Mediterranean to the Jordan, and from the ridge of Carmel to the mountains in Galilee. It is about 25 miles long from east to west, and 12 miles wide from north to south. There Barak and Gideon triumphed; Deborah sung her war song; Saul and Jonathan fell near by, on the mountains of Gilboa; here king Josiah was mortally wounded by the Egyptians. From the base of this triangular plain three branches stretch out eastward, divided by two bleak gray ridges, one called Mount Gilboa, the other Little Hermon. The central branch is the richest as well as the most celebrated. It is the valley of Jezreel proper; the battle-field where Gideon triumphed and Saul and Jonathan were overthrown. Judg. 7:1, ff.; 1 Sam. 29 and 31. The plain is noted for its wonderful richness.

Joab (jō'ab), *whose father is Jehovah.* 1. The son of Zeruiah, and nephew of David, and commander-in-chief of his army. He was an accomplished warrior, but a most unscrupulous man. 1 Chron. 2:16; 11:6. He treacherously assassinated Abner. 2 Sam. 2:23; 3:27. When Absalom rebelled Joab adhered to David; and contrary to express orders he put Absalom to death. 2 Sam. 18:14. David then made Amasa general of his army, but Joab was so offended that he also assassinated Amasa, as he had done Abner. 2 Sam. 20:10. Joab combined in the plot to set Adonijah on the throne, in defiance of the will of David, who had, by divine direction, resolved to make Solomon king. 1 Kings 2:28. After the death of David, Joab was slain at the altar, whither he had fled for protection; and was buried in his own domain in the wilderness. 2 Kings 2:5-34. 2. A descendant of Judah. 1 Chron. 4:14. 3. One whose posterity returned from exile. Ezra 2:6; 8:9; Neh. 7:11.

Joash (jō'ăsh), *Jehovah gives.* 1. The son and successor of Ahaziah, king of Judah, called also Jehoash. On the murder of his brethren by Athaliah, he was saved by his aunt Jehosheba, the wife of Jehoiada the high priest, who hid him for six years in one of the rooms of the temple. When Joash was 7 years of age, Jehoiada planned with Azariah and others, to place young Joash upon the throne, and to dethrone his grandmother, the wicked Athaliah; and the young king was crowned in the court of the temple with great solemnity. 2 Kings 11. Joash behaved himself well while Jehoiada lived and was his guide; but no sooner was this good man dead than he began to listen to the counsels of his wicked courtiers. Zechariah the priest, son of Jehoiada, warned him of his sin and danger; but as a reward of his fidelity, he was, by order of Joash, stoned to death between the porch and the altar, prophesying that God would avenge his death. 2 Chron. 24:20-22. After suffering a variety of injuries from the Syrians, and after being loaded with ignominy, Joash was murdered by his own servants, after a reign of 41 years. His remains were refused a place in the royal sepulchre. See also 2 Kings 12; 13:1; 2 Chron. 22:10-12; 23; 24. 2. The son and successor of Jehoahaz, king of Israel. He reigned two or three years with his father and alone 14 years. He departed not from the sins of Jeroboam, the son of Nebat; nevertheless he was successful in three campaigns against the Syrians; and in one against Amaziah, king of Judah. Joash seems to have been possessed of more talents than virtues. He is also called "Jehoash." 2 Kings 13:10-25; 14:1-16. 3. The father of Gideon. Judg. 6:11. 4. A son of Ahab, king of Israel. 1 Kings 22:26; 2 Chron. 18:25. 5. One of David's distinguished warriors. 1 Chron. 12:3, 21. 6. A descendant of Judah. 1 Chron. 4:22.

Job (jŏb). 1. The patriarch, from whom one of the poetical books of the Old Testament is named. He lived in the land of Uz and belonged to the Aramean race, which had settled in the lower part of Mesopotamia (probably to the south or southeast of Palestine, in Idumean Arabia), adjacent to the Sabeans and Chaldeans. The opinions of Job and his friends are thus interesting as showing a phase of patriarchal religion outside of the family of Abraham, and not controlled by the legislation of Moses. The form of worship is similar to the early patriarchal type; with little of ceremonial ritual, without a separate priesthood. Job is represented as a chieftain of immense wealth and high rank, blameless in all the relations of life, subjected to special trials, which he endured with humility, and finally was rewarded by marked blessings and great prosperity. 2. Son of Issachar, called Jashub. Gen. 46:13; 1 Chron. 7:1.

Job, Book of. This is an historical poem, as is shown by the narrative prologue and epilogue in prose. Some ascribe its authorship to Moses in Midian, others bring it down to the age of Solomon. It is written in pure Hebrew, and shows intimate acquaintance with both Egyptian and Arabian scenery and usages. Its theme is the problem of evil, why the righteous suffer and the wicked prosper in this world. After the outbreak of Job's despair, chap. 3, there are three series of controversies, in which each of Job's friends makes an address, to which Job replies—save that in the 3zd series Zophar is silent. Chaps 4–26. Then Job makes a closing address to all three, 27, 28, followed by a striking soliloquy, 29–31. Elihu utters four discourses, 32–37, after which Jehovah speaks out of the whirlwind, 38–41, and Job is humbled and yet vindicated. The best critics of every age count this poetical book as one of the immortal master-pieces of genius. Carlyle said that "there is nothing written of equal literary merit." But it is no less estimable for its religious and ethical worth, setting forth as it does the being and perfections of Jehovah, the apostasy and guilt of evil spirits and of mankind, the sovereignty of divine providence, the mercy of God on the basis of sacrifice and penitence, the disciplinary nature of his people's sorrows, the wisdom of submission to his will, and the assurance, in view of his infinite power and wisdom, that all shall be well with his followers in the end. The Book of Job may be better understood by reading it in the Revised English Version.

Jochebed (jŏk'e-bĕd), *whose glory is Jehovah.* The wife and at the same time the aunt of Amram and the mother of Moses and Aaron. Ex. 2:1; 6:20; Num. 26:59.

Joel (jō'el). One of the minor prophets and son of Pethuel. Nothing is recorded of his personal history, but he belongs most likely to the reign of Uzziah, and resided in Judah. There are 14 persons of this name mentioned in the Bible.

Joel, Book of. It may be divided into two parts: I. 1–2:17 describes a sore judgment which is to come upon the land, and is used as a call to repentance. II. 2:18–3:21 contains the blessings which Jehovah will confer upon the chosen people, and announces when the Messiah has come, the outpouring of the Spirit and the complete conquest of Judah over her foes, resulting in absolute and unbreakable peace. The second chapter contains a prophecy of a terrible plague of locusts, but a symbolical use is made of the incursion to foretell the attack of Judah's foes. Joel's style is classical; "it is elegant and perspicuous, and at the same time nervous, animated, and sublime."—*Ayre.* The fulfillment of his Messianic prophecies is noticed in the New Testament. Acts 2:16–21; Rom. 10:13.

John the Apostle. The son of Zebedee and Salome, of Bethsaida. His father was able to have "hired servants" and his mother was one of the women who aided in Jesus' support, Luke 8:3, and took spices to embalm his body. Mark 16:1. He is regarded as the youngest of the twelve apostles, but had been a disciple of John the Baptist, who pointed out Jesus as the Lamb of God to him. John 1:35–37. John is noted as "the disciple whom Jesus loved," and as one of the three chosen to witness the restoration of Jairus' daughter, the transfiguration, and the agony in the garden. At the last supper he reclined on Jesus' bosom, and to his care Jesus on the cross committed his mother. He with Peter on the resurrection morn ran to the empty tomb of Jesus, and "he saw and believed." When with some others he was fishing on the Sea of Galilee, he was the first to recognize the Lord standing on the shore. After the ascension, he and James and Peter were the leading apostles, Gal. 2:9, of the infant church, and guided its counsels. He was banished for a time to the isle of Patmos. Tradition represents him as closing his career at Ephesus. He was naturally bold and severe. Our Lord called him a "son of thunder," but he became amiable though firm and fearless.

John, Gospel of. The fourth Gospel is ascribed to John, and was probably composed, or at least put in its present shape, at Ephesus, between A. D. 70 and 95. The particular design of it is expressed by the author to be that we might believe that Jesus is the Christ, the Son of God, and that, believing, we might have life through his name. John 20:31. Hence the subjects and discourses of this book have special relation to our Lord's character and offices, and are evidently intended to prove his nature, authority, and doctrines as divine. The gospel contains: A. The prologue, 1:1–18; B. The history, 1:19 to chap. 21. 1. The preparation for Jesus' public ministry, (a) by John, 1:19–36; (b) by the choice of disciples. 1:37–51. 2 The public labors of Jesus in doctrine and miracle, chaps. 2–12. 3. Jesus in the private circle of his disciples. Chaps. 13–17. 4. The history of the passion and resurrection or public glorification of the Lord. Chaps. 18–21. "The Gospel of John is," says Schaff, "the gospel of gospels. It is the most remarkable as well as most important literary production ever composed. . . . It is a marvel even in the marvellous Book of books. It is the most spiritual and ideal of gospels. It brings us, as it were, into the immediate presence of Jesus. It gives us the clearest view of his incarnate divinity and his perfect humanity."

John, the Epistles of, are three in number. They were written in Ephesus, between A. D. 80 and 95, or possibly later. The first has always been attributed to John, though his name is neither prefixed nor subscribed. It is a kind of practical application of the gospel. It is addressed to Christians. The second epistle is addressed to the "elect lady and her children." The elect lady is supposed to have been some honorable woman distinguished for piety, and well known in the churches as a disciple of Christ. Some, however, have thought some particular church and its members might be denoted. Those who adopt the latter opinion apply the term to the church at Jerusalem, and the term "elect sister," 2 John 13, to the church at Ephesus. The third epistle, which is addressed to Gaius, or Caius, a private individual, and is commendatory of his piety, was written about the same time with the others.

John (jŏn) **the Baptist,** *whom God loves.* The forerunner of our Saviour. He was the son of Zacharias and Elisabeth, both belonging to priestly families. Luke 1:5. His birth, name, and work were foretold by the angel Gabriel. He grew up a Nazirite, and when about 30 years old began to preach in the wilderness of Judæa. His dress, food, and manner of life were like Elijah. He was fearless and faithful, and met with success among the people; yet he was humble and gave great honor to Jesus, who came to his baptism. At the request of Jesus, John, however, baptized him. John continued his labors with growing popularity for a year and a half, when he was cast into prison by Herod, whom he reproved for marrying his brother Philip's wife. In prison his faith seemed to waver, for he sent to Jesus to know if he were really the Messiah, and received a satisfactory answer. Matt. 11:4-6. But the malice of Herodias, whose connection with Herod whom John had rebuked, wrought his death. Matt. 14:6-12. John was beheaded in prison on Herod's birthday, at the request of the wicked Herodias. His disciples buried his body and went and told Jesus.

John (Mark). The Hebrew name of the evangelist Mark. Acts 12:12, 25; 13:5, 13; 15:37. See **Mark.**

John, Revelation of. See **Revelation.**

Jonadab (jŏn'a-dăb), *whom Jehovah impels.* 1. The son of Shimeah, and nephew of David. "He seems to have been one of those characters who, in the midst of great or royal families, pride themselves and are renowned for being acquainted with the secrets of the whole circle in which they move."—*Stanley.* He advised the outrage of Tamar. 2 Sam. 13:3-5. 2. The form, oft-repeated, in Jer. 35 for **Jehonadab,** which see.

Jonah (jō'nah), *dove.* The fifth of the minor prophets; was the son of Amittai, and a native of Gath-hepher. 2 Kings 14:25. He flourished in or before the reign of Jeroboam II., about B. C. 820. His story is related in the book that bears his name. Christ tells of "the sign of the prophet Jonah." Luke 11:29, 30. But the resurrection of Christ itself was also shadowed forth in the history of the prophet. Matt. 12:39, 41; 16:4. The mission of Jonah was highly symbolical. The old tradition made the burial place of Jonah to be Gath-hepher; the modern tradition places it at *Nebi-Yunus,* opposite Mosul.

Jonathan (jŏn'a-thăn), *the gift of Jehovah.* 1. A son of Gershom and a Levite, who impiously served as a priest, first to Micah, and then to the Danites in Laish or Dan. Judg. 17:18. 2. A son of Saul, 1 Chron. 8:33, distinguished for his lovely character. His brilliant exploit in Michmash, 1 Sam. 13 and 14, illustrates his pious faith, his bravery, see also 1 Sam. 13:3, when he was about 30 years old, and his favor with the people, who would not suffer him to be put to death for violating Saul's foolish vow. This valiant and generous prince, "strong like a lion and swift like an eagle," 2 Sam. 1:23, loved David as his own soul. 1 Sam. 18:1-4; 19:2; 20. When he knew that David was chosen of God for the throne, he nobly yielded his own claims, and while holding to his father he had a pure and disinterested friendship for David. 1 Sam. 23:16-18. He was slain with his father, in battle with the Philistines at Mount Gilboa. The beauty and pathos of the elegy in which David laments his friend are unsurpassed in literature. 2 Sam. 1. David found and cared for the only son Mephibosheth. 2 Sam. 9. There are 14 persons of this name mentioned in the Bible.

Joppa (jŏp'pah), or **Japho** (jā'pho), *beauty,* now *Jaffa.* A town on the southwest coast of Palestine, in the territory of Dan. Josh. 19:46. The harbor, though always as now a dangerous one, became the port of Jerusalem in the days of Solomon, and has been ever since. Here Jonah took ship to flee from the presence of his Maker. Here, on the housetop of Simon, the tanner, "by the seaside," Peter had his vision that led him to preach the gospel to Gentiles. Acts 11:5. In population Joppa has greatly increased within 25 years. A Turkish calendar enumerates 865 Moslem, 135 Greek, 70 Greek Catholic, 50 Latin, 6 Maronite, and 5 Armenian families. The city contains from 15,000 to 20,000 inhabitants. There are flourishing colonies settled in the vicinity, which foster various industries.

Jordan (jŏr'dan), *the descender,* called "the river," Gen. 31:21; Josh. 1:11, has a course of little more than 200 miles, from the foot of Anti-Lebanon to the head of the Dead sea—136 miles in a straight line. It is the river of the great depressed valley of Palestine—the "descender," if not "the river of God" in the book of Psalms. There were fords opposite Jericho, to which the men of Jericho pursued the spies. Josh. 2:7; compare

Judg. 3:28. Higher up were the fords or passages of Bethbarah, where Gideon lay in wait for the Midianites, Judg. 7:24, and where the men of Gilead slew the Ephraimites. Judg. 12:6. At one of these fords was made the first recorded passage of the Jordan in the Old Testament. Gen. 32:10. Jordan was next crossed, over against Jericho, by Joshua. Josh. 4:12, 13. From their nearness to Jerusalem the lower fords were much used. David, it is probable, passed over them in one instance to fight the Syrians. 2 Sam. 10:17; 17:22. Thus there were two or more places at which the Jordan was usually forded; and it must have been at one of these, if not at both, that baptism was afterwards administered by John the Baptist, and by the disciples of our Lord. Our Lord was baptized probably at the ford near Bethabara or Bethany. The rains and the melting of the snows on Lebanon caused it to rise and flood the valley. "The Jordan overflowed all his banks all the time of harvest." Josh. 3:15. The channel or bed of the river became brimful, so that the level of the water and of the banks was then the same. The bridges over the river did not exist in early times, although there are evidences of one near the lake of Galilee in the Roman period, and perhaps in the time of Christ. See *Galilee*, by S. Merrill. In the scriptural accounts of the Jordan it is frequently mentioned as a boundary; "over Jordan," "this" and "the other side," or "beyond Jordan," were expressions familiar to the Israelites. In one sense, indeed, that is, in so far as it was the eastern boundary of the land of Canaan, it was the eastern boundary of the promised land. Num. 34:12. The Jordan rises from several sources near Panium (*Bânids*), and passes through the lakes of Merom (*Hûleh*) and Gennesaret. The two principal features in its course are its descent and its windings. From its fountain heads to the Dead sea it rushes down one continuous inclined plane, only broken by a series of rapids or precipitous falls. Between the Lake of Gennesaret and the Dead sea there are 27 rapids. The depression of the Lake of Gennesaret below the level of the Mediterranean is 653 feet, and that of the Dead sea 1316 feet. The whole descent from its source to the Dead Sea is 3000 feet. Its width varies from 45 to 180 feet, and it is from 3 to 12 feet deep.—*Schaff*. The only tributaries to the Jordan below Gennesaret are the *Yarmûk* (Hieromax) and the *Zerka* (Jabbok).

Joseph (*jō'zef*), *increase*. 1. The elder of Jacob's two sons by Rachel, Gen. 37:3, and beloved by his father. The gift of the new robe, or coat of many colors, was perhaps intended to give him the rights of primogeniture, as the son of his first wife, in place of Reuben who had forfeited them. Gen. 35:22; 1 Chron. 5:1. He was born in Mesopotamia, Gen. 30:22-24. By a wonderful providence of God he was raised from a prison to be the chief ruler of Egypt under Pharaoh. "The story of his father's fondness, of his protest against sin among his brothers, of their jealous hostility and his prophetic dreams, of his sale by his brethren to Midianites and by them to Potiphar in Egypt, of the divine favor on his pure and prudent life, his imprisonment for three to twelve years for virtue's sake, his wonderful exaltation to power and his wise use of it for the good of the nation, of his tender and reverent care of his father, his magnanimity to his brethren, and his faith in the future of God's chosen people, is one of the most pleasing and instructive in the Bible, and is related in language inimitably natural, simple, and touching. It is too beautiful for abridgment, and too familiar to need full rehearsal."—*Rand*. The history of Joseph is strikingly confirmed by the Egyptian monuments. Joseph married the princess Asenath, daughter of Potipherah, priest of On; and his two sons, Manasseh and Ephraim, Gen. 41:50, whom Jacob adopted, Gen. 48:5, became the heads of two of the twelve tribes of Israel. 2. The son of Heli and reputed father of Jesus Christ. He was a just man, and of the house and lineage of David. He lived at Nazareth in Galilee. He espoused Mary, the daughter and heir of his uncle Jacob, and before he took her home his wife received the angelic communication recorded in Matt. 1:20. When Jesus was twelve years old, Joseph took his mother and Jesus to keep the passover at Jerusalem, and when they returned to Nazareth he continued to act as a father to the child Jesus, and was reputed to be so indeed. But here our knowledge of Joseph ends. That he died before our Lord's crucifixion is indeed tolerably certain, by what is related, John 19:27; and, perhaps, Mark 6:3, may imply that he was then dead. But where, when, or how he died, we know not. 3. Joseph of Arimathæa, a rich and pious Israelite, probably a member of the Great Council or Sanhedrin. He is further characterized as "a good man and a just." Luke 23:50. We are told that he did not "consent to the counsel and deed" of his colleagues in the death of Jesus. On the evening of the crucifixion Joseph "went in boldly unto Pilate and craved the body of Jesus." Pilate consented. Joseph and Nicodemus then, having enfolded the sacred body in the linen shroud which Joseph had bought, placed it in a tomb hewn in a rock, in a garden belonging to Joseph, and close to the place of crucifixion. There is a tradition that he was one of the seventy disciples. 4. Joseph, called Barsabas, and surnamed Justus: one of the two persons chosen by the assembled church, Acts 1:23, as worthy to fill the place in the apostolic company from which Judas had fallen.

Joshua (*jŏsh'u-ah*), *Saviour*, or *whose help is Jehovah*. Written also **Hoshea, Oshea, Jehoshua, Jeshua,** and **Jesus.** 1. The son of Nun, of the tribe of Ephraim. 1 Chron. 7:27, and minister of Moses. Ex. 24:13. He is mentioned first in connection with the fight against Amalek at Rephidim, when he was chosen by Moses to lead the Israelites. Ex. 17:9. He was one of the twelve spies who were sent, Num. 13:17, to explore the land of Canaan, and one of the two, Num. 14:6, who gave an encouraging report of their journey. Moses, shortly before his death, was directed, Num. 27:18, to appoint Joshua leader over the people. God himself gave Joshua a charge through the lawgiver. Deut. 31:14, 23. Under God's direction, Josh. 1:1, Joshua assumed the command of the people at Shittim, sent spies into Jericho, crossed the Jordan, fortified a camp at Gilgal, circumcised the people, kept the passover, and was visited by the Captain of the Lord's Host. The miraculous fall of Jericho terrified the Canaanites. In the great battle of Beth-horon the Amorites were signally routed, and the south country was open to the Israelites. Joshua returned to the camp at Gilgal, having conquered half of Palestine. He defeated the Canaanites under Jabin king of Hazor. In six years six tribes, with 31 petty chiefs, were conquered. Joshua, now stricken in years, proceeded to make the division of the conquered land. Timnath-serah in Mount Ephraim was assigned as Joshua's peculiar inheritance. After an interval of rest, Joshua convoked an assembly from all Israel. He delivered two solemn addresses, recorded in Josh. chaps. 23, 24. He died at the age of 110 years, and was buried in his own city, Timnath-serah. Joshua's character is a very noble one; and few blemishes are found in it. The favored disciple of Moses, he learned to be faithful to the Lord God. Once, indeed, he was too jealous for what he conceived to be Moses' honor. Num. 11:28, 29. He was generally bold and fearless, though an unexpected check at one time dispirited him. But, with these small exceptions, an able commander, a wise ruler, a faithful servant of the Lord, Joshua shines as a bright star among the noble worthies of Old Testament history. 2. An inhabitant of Beth-shemesh, in whose land was the stone at which the milch-kine stopped when they drew the ark of God with the offerings of the Philistines from Ekron to Beth-shemesh. 1 Sam. 6:14, 18, B.C. 1124. 3. A governor of the city who gave his name to a gate of Jerusalem, 2 Kings 23:8, in the reign of Josiah, B.C. 628. 4. Jeshua the son of Jozadak. Hag. 1:14; 2:2; Zech. 3:1, etc.

Josiah (jo-si'ah), whom *Jehovah heals.* One of the pious kings of Judah. He reigned 31 years, B.C. 640-610. He ascended the throne at the early age of eight years, and before his eighteenth year he had cut off and destroyed all the idols of the land, with their temples, groves, and monuments; and had ransacked the sepulchres of the idolatrous priests, and burned their bones upon the altars, in accordance with the prophecy of the man of God, announced in the presence of Jeroboam 326 years before Josiah was born. 1 Kings 13:2; 2 Kings 22:1, 2; 2 Chron. 34:1, 2. In the prosecution of the thorough repair and purification of the temple, Hilkiah "found the book of the Law of the Lord by Moses." Josiah immediately convoked the whole realm, and in person read the book of the Law to them, and exacted from them a promise to obey it. 2 Kings 22:8-20; 2 Chron. 31:14-33. The Scythians are supposed to have invaded Palestine between the thirteenth and the eighteenth year of his reign. Josiah was mortally wounded at Megiddo, and died at Jerusalem. Jeremiah the prophet was greatly affected by it, and composed an elegy on the occasion, 2 Chron. 35:25, and all those accustomed to celebrate in song the worth and achievements of men of great eminence, both men and women, mourned for Josiah for ages after his death. Indeed, the mourning was such as to become proverbial. Zech. 12:11. He was only 39 years of age when he died.

Jot, the English form of the Greek *iota, i. e.*, the smallest letter of the Greek alphabet. The Hebrew *yod,* or *y* formed somewhat like a comma ('). It is used metaphorically to express the minutest thing.

Jotham (jō'tham), *Jehovah is upright.* 1. The youngest son of Gideon, Judg. 9:5, who escaped from the massacre of his brethren. His parable of the reign of the bramble is the earliest example of the kind. Judg. 9:7-21. 2. The son of king Uzziah or Azariah and Jerushah. After ruling the kingdom for some years during his father's leprosy, he succeeded to the throne B.C. 758, when he was 25 years old, and reigned 16 years in Jerusalem. He was contemporary with Pekah and with the prophet Isaiah. His history is contained in 2 Kings 15 and 2 Chron. 27.

Journeyings of Israel. Num. 9:17-23. See **Exodus, Sinai,** and **Wilderness of the Wanderings,** and Table in Appendix.

Jubilee. Lev. 25. A festal year prescribed by the Hebrew law. It recurred every fiftieth year, *after* seven Sabbaths of years—not being, as some have supposed, the seventh sabbatical year—marking off a great cycle of time, so that at each half century the Israelitish polity began, as it were, afresh; a new morning of holy gratulation and recovered strength dawning on the land. All Hebrew servants were set free, pledges of lands, personal property rights alienated for any reason, were restored, there being only one exception—that of houses built in walled towns. Lev. 25:29-31. All were to be put back, as far as possible, into the position in which they began the 50 years. The account of this institution, which had its type in the weekly Sabbath, is carefully given in the law. Lev. 25:8-16, 23-55. The jubilee commenced on the tenth day of the seventh month, and was proclaimed through the whole country. It was to be a year when, as in the sabbatical year, the land lay untilled: nor was there any formal gathering of its spontaneous produce, which was to be absolutely free to all comers. It has been disputed whether the law of the jubilee ever came into full operation. Little is directly recorded: but there are several allusions to it. Num. 36:4; Isa. 61:1, 2; Ezek. 7:12, 13; 46:16-18. No doubt, like other commandments of the law, it was neglected in days of declension and apostasy. It must have pointed forward also to that future state of glorious spiritual freedom, where the inheritance of each redeemed one is his forever, no forfeiture of his high privileges to be dreaded in God's eternal kingdom.

Judæa (*ju-dē'ah*), or **Judea, Province of.** A name applied to that part of Canaan occupied by those who returned after the Assyrian and Babylonian captivities. The word first occurs, Dan. 5:13 (A. V. "Jewry"), and the first mention of the "province of Judæa" (R. V. "Judah") is in Ezra 5:8; it is alluded to in Neh. 11:3 (A. V. "Judah"); in the Apocrypha the word "province" is dropped, and throughout it and in the New Testament the expressions are the "land of Judæa" and "Judæa." In a wider and more improper sense "Judæa" was sometimes applied to the whole country of the Canaanites, its ancient inhabitants, and even in the gospels we read of the coasts of Judæa "beyond Jordan." Matt. 19:1; Mark 10:1. Judæa was strictly the southern district, west of the Jordan, and south of Samaria. It was made a portion of the Roman province of Syria after Archelaus was deposed, A. D. 6, and was governed by a procurator, who was subject to the governor of Syria. See **Canaan, Palestine,** and **Judah.**

Judæa, the Hill Country of. The central ridge of mountains stretching from north to south, and forming as it were the backbone of the land of Palestine. Luke 1:65.

Judæa, Wilderness of. A wild and desolate region extending from the hill-country near Jerusalem southeast to the Dead Sea, and averaging about 15 miles in breadth. Matt. 3:1. It is a limestone country, rough and barren, with only patches of grass. It seems never to have had many inhabitants, and no cities. The traditional scene of the temptation of Christ is in this district, on a high mountain behind Jericho, very desolate, and now infested with beasts and reptiles. See Matt. 4:1; Mark 1:13.

Judah (*jū'dah*), *praise*. 1. The fourth son of Jacob and Leah, was born in Mesopotamia. Gen. 29:35. The name was given as an expression of the mother's gratitude. We know more of him than of the other patriarchs except Joseph, whose life he saved, advising the sale. Gen. 37:26-28. His marriage, an incident in his son's life, and his intrigue with Tamar are recorded in Gen. 38. Judah became the surety for the safety of Benjamin on the second journey to Egypt. Gen. 43:3-10. His conduct is worthy of all praise, and his plea for Benjamin's liberty is one of the most touching speeches in the Bible. Gen. 44:14-34. He went down into Egypt with three sons. Gen. 46:12 The tribe of Judah was always large and prominent, vying with Ephraim for the supremacy. The prophetic blessing which his father pronounced on Judah, Gen. 49:8-12, is very remarkable. It describes the warlike character and gradually increasing strength of the tribe, comp. Num. 2:3; Josh. 14:11; 15:1; Judg. 1:1, 2; 1 Chron. 14:17; Ps. 18:40; Isa. 29:1 (where its capital is called Ariel, "lion of God"); Rev. 5:5; the duration of its power —viz., until the coming of Christ, when Judæa became a province of Rome, comp. Luke 2:1-7; John 18:31; Acts 5:37; and the destruction of their city, A. D. 70, when the Christian dispensation had become established, compare Matt. 24:14; Acts 2:8; Rom. 10:18, in the glory and triumph of the Messiah.

Judah, the Kingdom of. The kingdom of Judah embraced not only the territory of the tribe of Judah (see below), but also included the larger part of Benjamin on the northeast, Dan on the northwest, and Simeon on the south. The area thus under the dominion of Judah is estimated at 3435 square miles. Besides this, Edom, subdued by David, continued faithful to Judah for a time, and the Red Sea ports furnished an outlet for commerce.

The family of David furnished all the 19 kings of Judah, but the eldest son did not always succeed. Judah outlasted Israel 135 years. After the division of the kingdom, B. C. 975, Judah maintained its separate existence for 389 years, until B. C. 586. During this period there were 19 rulers, all of the lineage of David, except Athaliah. During the first three reigns Israel and Judah were in an attitude of hostility. Israel under Jeroboam was signally defeated. 2 Chron. 13. Later, an alliance was formed by the marriage of Jehoshaphat's son with Ahab's daughter, Athaliah, 1 Kings 22; 2 Chron. 18, who usurped the crown. The two kingdoms combined against Syria. The two great foes of Judah were Egypt on the south and Assyria on the east. From Egypt came Shishak, who humbled Judah, 2 Chron. 12:2-12; Zerah, whose million of men were routed by king Asa 2 Chron. 14:9-12; and Josiah was slain at Megiddo. 2 Chron. 35:23. The children of Ammon, Moab, and Mount Seir also invaded Judah during Jehoshaphat's reign, but they only destroyed one another. 2 Chron. 20:22-25. The armies of Assyria met with varied fortune. Tiglath-pileser distressed Judah during the reign of Ahaz, 2 Chron. 28:20; Sennacherib's host of 185,000 men was destroyed by the angel of the Lord in Hezekiah's reign, 2 Chron. 32:21; 2 Kings 19:35; Manasseh was carried away captive into Babylon, 2 Chron. 33:11; Jeholachin was also made captive; Zedekiah rebelled against Nebuchadnezzar, and was defeated, his sons slain before his eyes, and he made captive; Jerusalem was taken in B. C. 586, and the history of the kingdom of Judah was ended.

Judah, Territory of. *Extent.*—The district assigned to the tribe of Judah in the Promised Land, with its cities, is described in Josh. 15. It extended across the whole of Western Palestine, from the Dead Sea on the east to the Mediterranean on the west. The average extent of this district was 50 miles from east to west and 45 miles from north to south, and its area about half that of the State of Connecticut. A portion of this territory was subsequently cut off for Simeon, which thus became the frontier tribe on the south. Josh. 19:1-9. A portion of the northwestern part was also given to Dan. Comp. vs. 40-48.

The territory of Judah comprised four regions quite distinct in physical features: 1. The south country, or Negeb, where the fertile land shaded off into the wilderness. 2. The valley, plain, or Shefelah, lying between the Mediterranean and the central hill-country. Josh. 15:33-47. This was an exceedingly fertile country, occupied by the Philistines, who constantly disputed possession. 3. The hill-country, occupying the central range of mountains. Josh. 15: 48-60. This region was favorable for the olive and vine. 4. The wilderness, sloping from the central hills to the Dead Sea, at which it terminates in precipitous cliffs. Josh. 15:61, 62. This barren tract has evidently been uncultivated and uninhabited from the remotest times, for here alone, of all Palestine, are found no traces of the ruins of former cities. An exception must be made of the fringe of the Dead Sea, where were six cities. Josh. 15:21-62.

Judas (jū'das). 1. The son of Jacob, "Judah" in R. V. Matt. 1:2,3. 2. The faithless apostle who betrayed his master. Matt. 10:4; Mark 3:19; Luke 6:16. He was Simon's son, John 6:71, and is called Iscariot, probably from his birthplace, perhaps from Kerioth in Judah, Josh. 15:25, or from Kartan, or Kartah, in Galilee. Josh. 21:32, 34. Of this man's earlier life we know nothing, nor for what reason he was induced to follow Jesus. Why our Lord appointed Judas an apostle, the sacred narrative does not tell us. Jesus knew and expressed his knowledge of Iscariot's character. John 6:64, 70, 71. In calling him our Lord acted only in accordance with the general administration of his kingdom. This is illustrated by one of his parables, Matt. 13:24-30; and it is no more than we continually see,—ungodly men in place and power, both in the world and in the church, with gifts which they abuse and responsibilities which increase their condemnation. It has often been a puzzle to those who did not understand the moral government of God, comp. Ps. 73; but he will eventually vindicate his wisdom and his justice. Meanwhile valuable lessons of warning and circumspection are taught by the fate of such as have perverted their privileges to their own ruin. Judas maintained a fair character among his fellow-apostles, and was entrusted with the custody of their money, John 12:6; 13:29; nor do they seem to have suspected him even when our Lord was distinctly warning them that one of their number would betray him. Matt. 26:21-24; John 13:22. This was Judas' question to the priests: "What will ye give me?" Matt. 26:15. Satan espied his opportunity and took it. Luke 22:3. Probably Judas began to see that he was suspected, and, when the Lord in answer to his hypocritical question, had distinctly told him of his treason, full of additional passion, he went recklessly about his work. Matt. 26:25; John 13:26-30. He was fulfilling prophecy, but was unconscious of it. His own evil heart it was that prompted him; and therefore the guilt of his deed was upon himself. When confronted with the results of his base treachery, he was seized with remorse, returned the bribe, and hanged himself. 3. One described as one of the Lord's brethren, Matt. 13:55, called also Juda. Mark 6:3 A. V. An interesting story is related of his family by Eusebius. The emperor Domitian was alarmed by what he had heard of Messiah's kingdom, and ordered some of the descendants of the house of David to be sought out and brought to him. Those so presented to the emperor were the grandsons of Judas; but the hardness of their hands, proving that they were but ordinary peasants, and their description of the spiritual nature of the new sovereignty, removed all apprehensions. They were let go, and lived on, honored as the Lord's relatives, into the reign of Trajan. 4. A brother of James, and one of the apostles; called also Thaddæus and Lebbæus. Matt. 10:3; Mark 3:18; Luke 6:16; John 14:22; Acts 1: 13; Matt. 13:55. 5. Judas of Galilee, a leader of an insurrection "in the days of taxing"—i. e., the census—A. D. 6, and who, according to Gamaliel, was very successful for a time, but was ultimately completely defeated. Acts 5:37. We find in Josephus an allusion to a man, who is there said to have been born in the city of Gamala in Gaulanitis, and to have been the founder of a new sect, which did not differ from that of the Pharisees save in a fanatical love of liberty and refusal to support the Roman state. 6. The one whose house in Straight street, Damascus, sheltered Paul during his blindness. Acts 9:11, 17. This Judas may have kept an inn; it is unlikely that he was a disciple. 7. Judas, surnamed Barsabas, a "chief man among the brethren," a "prophet," who was chosen along with Paul and Barnabas and Silas to carry the decisions of the council of Jerusalem, A. D. 50, to Antioch. Acts 15:22-33.

Jude (jūde), **Epistle of.** It is referred to by Clement of Alexandria, Tertullian, and Origen. It was probably written in Palestine, about A. D. 65. This epistle seems to have been intended to guard the faithful against prevalent errors, and to urge them to constancy in the faith. It is not improbable that Peter had read Jude's epistle, when he wrote his Second epistle; and that the thoughts, under the influence of the Holy Spirit, had made a strong impression upon his mind.

Judges. The judges were rulers sent of God to deliver the Israelites from their oppressors. Their power extended over portions of the country only, and some of them were contemporaneous. Their chief work was that of deliverers and captains in war. While Samuel as a judge gave something like a settled government to the south, there was scope for the irregular exploits of Samson on the borders of the Philistines. Samuel at last established his authority as judge and prophet, but still as the servant of Jehovah, only to see it so abused by his sons as to exhaust the patience of the people, who at length demanded a *king*, after the pattern of the surrounding nations. The following is a partial list of the judges, and the approximate length of their rule: First oppression, by Mesopotamia—8 years. First judge: Othniel—40 years. Second oppression, by Moab—18 years. Second judge: Ehud—50 years; third judge: Shamgar—unknown. Third oppression, by Jabin and Sisera—20 years. Fourth judge: Deborah and Barak—40 years. Fourth oppression, by Midian—7 years. Fifth judge: Gideon—40 years; sixth judge: Abimelech—3 years; seventh judge: Tola—23 years; eighth judge: Jair—22 years. Fifth oppression, by Ammon—18 years. Ninth judge: Jephthah—6 years; tenth judge: Ibzan—7 years; eleventh judge: Elon—10 years; twelfth judge: Abdon—8 years. Sixth oppression, by the Philistines—40 years. Thirteenth judge: Samson—20 years; fourteenth judge: Eli—40 years; fifteenth judge: Samuel.

Judges, Book of, derives its title from the fact that it gives us the history of the Israelites under the administration of 15 Judges, viz., from 18 or 20 years after the death of Joshua to the time of Saul. The chronology is uncertain. This book has been well styled a commentary upon the text: "Righteousness exalteth a nation; but sin *is* a reproach to any people." Prov. 14:34. It may be divided into two parts: 1. Chaps. 3-16, an account of God's successive deliverances; 2. Chaps. 17-21, an account, detached from the preceding and out of chronological order, of the invasion of Laish by the Danites, in connection with the story of Micah and his priest, Jonathan, chaps. 17-18; and an account of the revenge of the insult to the Levite, chaps. 19-21, the whole prefaced with an introduction, chaps. 1-3. The book is quite evidently a compilation from existent and trustworthy materials. Its date is uncertain.

Judgment, the Day of. God is called "the Judge of all the earth," Gen. 18:25, and it is reasonable to suppose that he will righteously administer his dominions. In the world, however, the ungodly are often seen to prosper, and the righteous to be oppressed. And this has sometimes grievously perplexed God's servants, who have not known how to reconcile the fact with his holy justice. Ps. 73. Scripture, therefore, points onward to a time when all these apparent anomalies will be explained, when a great assize will sit, and a just recompense of reward will be meted out to men. Eccl. 11:9; 12:14; Acts 24:25. This judgment, we are told, shall be exercised by Christ, Acts 10:42; 17:31; Rom. 14:10. Men might be judged either individually, each on his departure from the world, or collectively. Scripture gives us reason to believe that the latter will be the course of God's procedure, Matt. 25:31-46; Rev. 20:12, 13; and a day is spoken of, sometimes called the "last day," John 11:24, sometimes the "great day," Jude 6, when this shall be. The space of time to be so occupied it is impossible for us to calculate; about the nearness or distance of that day it is useless to speculate, Matt. 24:36; it will be a strict and searching judgment, Matt. 12:36, so that the practical lesson we have to learn is, to be prepared, to judge ourselves, that we be not judged and condemned of the Lord. 1 John 2:28; 4:17.

Judgment Hall. The word *prætorium* is so translated five times in the A. V. of the New Testament, and in those five passages it denotes two different places. 1. In John 18:28, 33; 19:9, it is the residence, R. V., "palace," which Pilate occupied when he visited Jerusalem. The site of Pilate's prætorium in Jerusalem has given rise to much dispute, some supposing it to be the palace of king Herod, others the tower of Antonia; but it was probably the latter, which was then and long afterward the citadel of Jerusalem. 2. In Acts 23:35 Herod's judgment hall (R. V. reads palace) or prætorium in Cæsarea was doubtless a part of that magnificent range of buildings the erection of which by king Herod is described in Josephus. The word "palace," or "Cæsar's court," in the A. V., Phil. 1:13, R. V., "prætorian," is a translation of the same word prætorium. It may here have denoted the quarter of that detachment of the prætorian guards which was in immediate attendance upon the emperor, and had barracks in Mount Palatine at Rome.

Julius (*jū'li-ŭs* or *jūl'yus*). A centurion of **Augustan Band** (which see), under whose charge Paul was conveyed to Rome. Acts chaps. 27, 28. He was courteous to the apostle, and may be the same with Julius Priscus, subsequently prefect of the prætorian guards.

Juniper. Unquestionably, the original intends the *rĕtem* (*Rĕtama rætam*), a shrub of the broom family, attaining a height of about 12 feet. Under its shade travellers are glad to creep on a sultry day for a noontime nap, and thus Elijah lay and slept after his long journey. 1 Kings 19:4, 5.

Jupiter (*jū'pi-ter*). The heathen god worshipped by the Greeks under the name of Zeus. He was supposed to exercise supreme power; but the actions attributed to him were frequently in the highest degree sensual and abominable. Antiochus Epiphanes dedicated the temple at Jerusalem to this deity as Zeus Olympius, that on Gerizim to him as Zeus Xenius, the "defender of strangers." 2 Macc. 6:2. He is two or three times mentioned in the New Testament. Acts 14:12, 13; 19:35.

Justification. A term used to imply the declaring or accounting of a person just or righteous before God. If any one were free from sin, if he perfectly obeyed God's commandments, he would really be just, not exposed to the penalty of transgression. Rom. 2:13. But mankind, as sinful, are not just in this sense, and cannot be so treated. Ps. 143:2; Rom. 3:19, 20, 23; 1 John 1:8. If, then, they are to be freed from the condemnation of sin, if they are to be dealt with as those not amenable to God's law, it must be not by the establishment of their innocence, but by the remission of their guilt. And it was for this that the Lord Jesus Christ came into the world, and offered himself a sacrifice for sin, that men might be delivered from the condemnation into which their sins had cast them. Rom. 3:24, 25; 2 Cor. 5:21; 1 John 1:7; 2:2. The Scripture therefore teaches that we are justified by faith in Christ. Rom. 3:28; Gal. 2:16. This doctrine is thus expressed in the eleventh article of the Anglican church: "We are accounted righteous before God only for the merit of our Lord and Saviour Jesus Christ by faith, and not for our own works or deservings. Wherefore that we are justified by faith only is a most wholesome doctrine, and very full of comfort." The originating cause of justification is God's free grace and loving pity for a fallen world. John 3:16; Rom. 5:8; Eph. 2:4-8. The meritorious cause is the sinless life and sacrificial death of Christ, Rom. 4:25, for the virtue of which God could without moral fault, or detriment to justice, remit sin. The instrumental cause is faith, whereby we receive the atonement, accepting God's mercy on the terms on which he offers it. Rom. 3:30; 5:11. Those who are so justified are at peace with God, and have all the advantages of such a state of reconciliation. Rom. 5:1, 2. Justified men desire and endeavor to walk in holiness of life. Rom. 8:1. Gratitude for the mercy received will incline them to do that which is well pleasing in God's sight. They feel that they have been purchased to be his, and must glorify him in their body and their spirit. 1 Cor. 6:20. This will be their mark, the token, the proof that they are no longer enemies, but friends; not sentenced culprits, but beloved children. Should any not so walk and act, they cannot be God's children. Such a faith as theirs, a faith which worketh not by love, is empty and useless. Jas. 2:17, 26. Abraham's obedience was the proof that he possessed that faith which was counted to him for righteousness. Of justification, then, it may be briefly said that—1, its source is the grace of God; 2, its ground the mediatorial work of Christ; 3, faith is the way by which we receive it; and, 4, the holy life of a believer the evidence of its possession; or, yet more briefly, it is originally by grace, meritoriously by Christ, instrumentally by faith, evidentially by good works.

K

Kab or Cab. See **Measures**.
Kabzeel ($kăb'ze$-el), *gathered by God*. Called **Jekabzeel** when rebuilt after the captivity, Neh. 11:25, a city of the tribe of Judah, situated farthest to the south, Josh. 15:21; was the birthplace of Benaiah, the son of Jehoiada. 2 Sam. 23:20; 1 Chron. 11:22.
Kadesh, *sacred*, or **Kadesh-barnea** ($kā'desh$-$bär'ne$-ah). A place on the southern frontier of Canaan. It was "eleven days," or about 165 miles, distant from Horeb, Deut. 1:2: on the border of Edom, Num. 20:16; not far from Gerar, Gen. 20:1; to the east of Bered, Gen. 16:14; in the desert of Zin, Num. 20:1; 27:14; 33:36; Deut. 32:51; and the point to which Chedorlaomer returned, having driven the Horites over the Arabah into the Et Tih region, and then going northward. Gen. 14:7. In Scripture it is sometimes called Kadesh alone, and sometimes Kadesh-barnea, and is identical with Meribah-kadesh, Ezek. 47:19; Josh. 15:3, 23; with En-Mishpat — the fountain of judgment, Gen. 14:7; and with Rithmah — the broom, Num. 33:18, thus called from a shrub growing in the desert. Spies were sent into the land of Canaan. The people rebelled, and were condemned to 40 years sojourn in the wilderness, Num. 13:14, during which time Kadesh seems to have been their chief centre. At the end of 40 years they encamped again at Kadesh for a march to Canaan. Num. 20:1. Here Miriam died and was buried, and the rock was smitten for water. Num. 20:1-21. It was 40 to 50 miles directly south of Beersheba.
Kanah ($kā'nah$), *place of reeds*. 1. A town in the district of Asher, Josh. 19:28; now a village, 'Ain Kana, six miles southeast of Tyre. 2. A river forming the boundary between Ephraim and Manasseh. Josh. 16:8; 17:9.
Kedar ($kē'dar$), *dark-skinned*. Second son of Ishmael. Gen. 25:13. From him descended the leading tribes of Arabia and of the land east of Palestine. They and the country bear the name of Kedar. Isa. 21:16; Jer. 49:28. They were nomads, living in black hair-tents, Song of Sol. 1:5, as the modern Bedouins do, or in villages, Isa. 42:11, and were rich in flocks and herds, and noted as archers and mighty men.
Kedesh ($kē'desh$), *sanctuary*. 1. A town on the southern boundary of Judah, Josh. 15:23; perhaps identical with Kadesh or Kadesh-barnea. 2. A city of Issachar; assigned to the Gershonite Levites. 1 Chron. 6:72. In the parallel list, Josh. 21:28, its name is Kishon. 3. A fortified city belonging to the tribe of Naphtali; allotted to the Gershonite Levites, Josh. 20:7; 21:32; 1 Chron. 6:76, and made a city of refuge. It was the residence of Barak, Judg. 4:6, and here Deborah assembled the tribes of Zebulon and Naphtali. Judg. 4:11. It was taken by Tiglath-pileser in the reign of Pekah, 2 Kings 15:29, and here the battle took place between Jonathan Maccabæus and Demetrius. 1 Macc. 11:63. Now it is a small village, Kades, ten miles north of Safed and four miles northwest of Merom, beautifully situated on a high ridge jutting out in the depressed basin through which the Jordan flows to the Sea of Merom. It is surrounded with ruins; numerous sarcophagi have been found here.
Keilah ($keī'lah$ or $keī'lah$), *fortress*. A city in the lowland of Judah, near the Philistine frontier. Josh. 15:44. When

captured and plundered by a Philistine invasion David came to its rescue, but the inhabitants treacherously plotted with Saul for his betrayal. 1 Sam. 23 : 1-13. After the captivity its rulers aided in restoring the walls of Jerusalem, Neh. 3 : 17, 18; now Kila, seven miles east of Beit Jibrin.

Kenath (kē'nath), *possession.* A city of Gilead, in the tribe of Manasseh; captured by Nobah, Num. 32 : 42; a place of splendor and importance under Rome; a Christian bishop's see; 20 miles from Bostra; now called Kunawat.

Kenite (kē'nite or kĕn'īte), *smith.* A tribe of Midian, between Palestine and Sinai, and east of the Gulf of Akabah. Their land was promised to Abraham. Gen. 15 : 19. Jethro, Moses' father-in-law, was a Kenite. Judg. 1 : 16. They were mentioned in Balaam's prophecy. Num. 24 : 21. Part of the tribe joined Israel and lived south of Judah. Judg. 1 : 16. One family migrated to the far north. There Heber dwelt. Judg. 4 : 11. The Kenites were friendly with the Canaanites, Amalekites, and Israelites. Saul and David spared them in their raids on Amalek on account of their former kindness. 1 Sam. 15 : 6 ; 27 : 10 ; 30 : 29. A family of Kenites came of Hemath, father of the house of Rechab. 1 Chron. 2 : 55.

Kidron or **Cedron**, John 18 : 1, A. V., (kĭd'ron or kē'dron), or **Kedron**, 2 Sam. 15 : 23; 1 Kings 15 : 13: *black brook.* From a Hebrew root signifying "black," not from cedars, cedar-brook. It is a small stream, dry in summer, but growing into a torrent in the rainy season; rises 1½ miles northwest of Jerusalem; runs in a southeastern direction until it reaches the northwestern shore of the Dead Sea. Here Athaliah was executed, 2 Kings 11 : 16; here Maachah's idols were burnt, 1 Kings 15 : 13 ; 2 Chron. 15 : 16 ; and hither the impurities and abominations of idol-worship were regularly carried and destroyed. 2 Chron. 29 : 16 ; 30 : 14 ; 2 Kings 23 : 4, 6, 12. In the time of Josiah it became the common burial-place of the city, 2 Kings 23 : 16, and so it is to-day. The two events, however, connected with it, and which give it its greatest interest, are David's crossing it on his flight from Jerusalem when Absalom rebelled, 2 Sam. 15 : 23, 30; and Christ's crossing it on his way to Gethsemane. John 18 : 1; Mark 14 : 26; Luke 22 : 39. As Cæsar crossed the Rubicon for the military conquest of the world, so Christ crossed the Kedron for the salvation of the world.

Kingdom of God, of Christ, of Heaven. These terms describe: 1, a life of righteous allegiance to Christ, entered by faith, lived by love, and crowned with glory, Matt. 6 : 33, etc.; 2, the condition of things Christ came to explain, Luke 1 : 33; Acts 1 : 3, and to bring on earth, Matt. 4 : 17; 3, Christ's rule over Israel, Matt. 21 : 13 ; 4, the rule that God offered or committed to Israel, Matt. 21 : 43; 1 Chron. 17 : 14 ; 5, the state of things in the history of the church during the conflict on earth of the so-called kingdom of grace, preparatory to the kingdom of glory, Matt. 13 ; 6, Christ's rule in spiritual and eternal righteousness over the redeemed earth, Rev. 12 : 10, in contrast with the world-powers, Dan. 7 : 18 ; then the kingdom will destroy and take the place of the four monarchies, Dan. 7, and have its glorious manifestation ; 7, the visible glory of Christ, Matt. 16 : 28 ; 8, the rule of God the Father over earth and heaven, Matt. 6 : 10 ; 9, the heavenly state. Matt. 8 : 11. The kingdom of God is perfectly established in the heavens. Matt. 6 : 10. The power and glory of the divine kingdom are shown in a measure in creation and providence. From the moral kingdom the earth has revolted. God reestablished it in Israel, taking the kingship himself. Ex. 19 : 6 ; Hos. 13 : 10. He made the kingship visible in David, 1 Sam. 16, and permanent in his family. Ps. 89 : 20, 28, 36. The kingdom ceased as a visible power, with the loss of its inner spirit, when the nation lapsed and persisted in idolatry. The prophets foretold its restoration, Dan. 12 : 7-13 ; Ps. 2 ; Isa. 2 ; Mic. 4 ; Jer. 23 : 5 ; Ezek. 34 : 23 ; John the Baptist came to announce it. Matt. 3 : 2. Jesus Christ preached it, Matt. 4 : 17; explained its character and demands, as, for instance, that its citizens must be holy, meek, Christ-like, etc., that when established it will be a condition of peace, purity, and glory, Matt. 25 : 34; Mark 9 : 47; Acts 14 : 22 ; Christ came as the King to Jerusalem, Luke 19 : 38; comp. Luke 1 : 32, but was rejected, and took the kingdom from Israel. Matt. 21 : 43. He taught its mysteries to the disciples, especially after his resurrection, Acts 1 : 3 ; and sent them forth to preach it. He declared that the time of its manifestation was known only to the Father. Acts 1 : 7. He laid the foundations of it on the day of Pentecost by the outpouring of the Holy Spirit, and rules it from his throne in heaven. The disciples went everywhere preaching the word of grace, 1 Thess. 2 : 12, and persuading men to enter the kingdom by faith and holiness. Acts 8 : 12 ; 20 : 25 ; 28 ; 23. The kingdom is to be fully manifested at the coming of Christ, the Son of man. 2 Tim. 4 : 1 ; Dan. 7 : 13; Matt. 13 : 43; Luke 22 : 29. At "the end" Christ is to deliver up to the Father the mediatorial kingdom that he received at his ascension, Eph. 1 : 20, after having reigned and put down all rule, authority, and power, and all enemies under his feet, 1 Cor. 15 : 24 ; and the kingdom of God, without distinction of persons, shall be complete and forever. Heb. 1 : 8. The members of the "invisible church" are citizens of the kingdom of heaven.

Kings, the Books of. In the Hebrew canon they formed one book, as did the books of Samuel, which were also called books of the Kings. The two books of Kings deal especially with the theocratic promise of 2 Sam. 7 : 12; see 1 Kings 14 : 7-11 ; 15 : 29 ; 16 : 1-7 ; and treat the history from the kingly side, and show the evil of schism and the worship of idols set up for political reasons, as by Solomon, 1 Kings 11, and Jeroboam, 1 Kings 12 : 26. The reign of Solomon is described, with a minute account of the glorious temple and the royal houses. The story of the revolt of the larger part of the land to form the kingdom of Israel follows, and of the frequent changes of dynasty, no less than seven, which furnished 19 kings, every one evil, during the 253 years of its existence. Captivity of the best of the land closed the history of this kingdom. The same books also show that David's royal house continued unbroken through a series of 19 kings, reigning in Jerusalem about 130 years longer, till Judah was punished for its idolatry. See list of kings and prophets in Appendix.

The author cannot be identified. Ancient tradition in the Talmud names Jeremiah; some have supposed them compiled by Ezra or Baruch. The books, originally one, have a very marked unity of design, plan, and style, and were first divided in the Septuagint. They are in large measure a compilation from existent documents. They have always had a place in the Jewish canon. The concise narrative is illustrated, enlarged, and confirmed by the books of Isaiah and Jeremiah. This history is referred to in the New Testament, Luke 4 : 25 ; Acts 7 : 47 ; Rom. 11 : 2 ; Jas. 5 : 17, and modern research is continually bringing new evidence to the truth of the history.

Kir (*kir*), *wall*, or *place surrounded with walls*. The city from which the Syrians emigrated when they came to settle in the region north of Palestine, and to which Tiglath-pileser sent the captive Syrians after the conquest of Damascus. 2 Kings 16 : 9 ; Amos 1 : 5 ; 9 : 7. About the location of this city scholars disagree, some placing it in Armenia, on the river Kar; others identifying it with Carena, or Carna, in Media.

Kir-haraseth (*kir′hăr′a-sĕth*), *brick fortress*, 2 Kings 3 : 25 A.V. ; or **Kir-hareseth**, Isa. 16 : 7; or **Kir-haresh** (*kir-hā′resh*), Isa. 16 : 11 A. V. ; or **Kir-heres** (*kir-hē′res*), Jer. 48 : 31, 36 ; or simply **Kir of Moab**, Isa. 15 : 1. A strong fortress in Moab, situated near the southeastern shore of the Dead Sea. It is now called Kerak.

Kirjath-arba (*kir′jath-är′bah*), R. V., *Kiriath-arba*. The city of Arba, Arba being its founder, or the city of Four—Abraham, Isaac, Jacob, and Adam having been buried there—is mentioned Gen. 23 : 2; 35 : 27 ; Josh. 14 : 15 ; 15 : 13, 54 ; 20 : 7 ; 21 : 11 ; Judg. 1 : 10 ; Neh. 11 : 25. See **H e b r o n** and **Mamre**.

Kirjath-jearim (*kir′jath-jē′a-rĭm*), R. V., *kiriath-jearim, the city of woods*. One of the four cities of the Gibeonites, Josh. 9 : 17, situated on the border of Judah and Benjamin, Josh. 15 : 9 ; 18 : 14, 15, but belonging to Judah, Josh. 15 : 60 ; Judg. 18 : 12 ; was also called Baalah, Josh. 15 : 9, 10, or Baale of Judah, 2 Sam. 6 : 2, or Kirjath-baal. Hither the ark was brought from Beth-shemesh, 1 Sam. 6 : 21 ; 7 : 1, 2, and here it remained until it was removed by David. 1 Chron. 13 : 5 ; 2 Chron. 1 : 4. The prophet Urijah, who was put to death by Jehoiakim, Jer. 26 : 20, was born here, and after the captivity the people of the city returned in numbers to it. Neh. 7 : 29.

Kishon (*kī′shon*), *bending, curved*, or in one place, Ps. 83 : 9, **Kison** (*kī′son*), the present Nahr Mukutta, a river which drains the plain of Esdraelon, passes through the plain of Acre, and falls into the Mediterranean. Only the lower part of it is perennial, fed by some springs at the foot of Mount Carmel. The upper part, rising on Tabor and Little Hermon, is dry in the summer, but becomes a torrent in the winter, rushing along with great impetuosity and transforming parts of the plains it traverses into swamps. The total defeat of Sisera, Judg. 4 : 7 ; 5 : 21, and the executions of the idol-priests by Elijah, 1 Kings 18 : 40, took place on the shores of this river.

Kiss. Kissing the lips in salutation was customary among near relatives of both sexes. Gen. 29 : 11 ; Song of Sol. 8 : 1. Between individuals of the same sex, and in a limited degree between those of different sexes, the kiss on the cheek as a mark of respect or an act of salutation has at all times been customary in the East. In the Christian Church the kiss of charity was practiced not only as a friendly salutation, but as an act symbolical of love and Christian brotherhood. Rom. 16 : 16 ; 1 Cor. 16 : 20 ; 2 Cor. 13 : 12 ; 1 Thess. 5 : 26 ; 1 Pet. 5 : 14. Among the Arabs the women and children kiss the beards of their husbands or fathers. The superior returns the salute by a kiss on the forehead. In Egypt an inferior kisses the hand of a superior, generally on the back, but sometimes, as a special favor, on the palm also. Kissing is spoken of in Scripture as a mark of respect or adoration to idols. 1 Kings 19 : 18 ; Hos. 13 : 2.

Knop. An ornament of the golden candlestick, Ex. 25 : 31 ; 37 : 17, and elsewhere, probably formed like a pomegranate. Also a carved ornament of the cedar-work of the temple, and the molten sea, 1 Kings 6 : 18 ; 7 : 24, perhaps like wild gourds or cucumbers.

Kohath (*kō′hath*), *assembly*. One of the three sons of Levi, from whom the three principal divisions of the Levites derived their origin and their name. Gen. 46 : 11 ; Ex. 6 : 16. In the journeyings of the tabernacle the sons of Kohath (Kohathites) had charge of the most holy portions of the vessels. Num. 4. Of the personal history of Kohath we know nothing, except that he came down to Egypt with Levi and Jacob, Gen. 46 : 11 ; that his sister was Jochebed, Ex. 6 : 20, and that he lived to the age of 133 years. Ex. 6 : 18.

Korah (*kō′rah*), *ice* or *baldness*. 1. Second son of Esau and Aholibamah, a prince of Edom. Gen. 36 : 5, 14, 18. 2. A son of Hebron, tribe of Judah. 1 Chron. 2 : 43. 3. A Levite who rebelled against Moses and Aaron. He was a cousin of Moses, for their fathers Izhar and Amram were brothers. Ex. 6 : 16-21. Korah and the 250 Levites whom he had enticed to join him were destroyed by fire from the Lord ; while Dathan and Abiram were swallowed by the miraculous opening of the earth. Num. 16; Ps. 106:17, 18; Jude 11. But Korah's children escaped, Num. 26:11; and the Korahites, or "sons of Korah," were a celebrated family of doorkeepers, singers, and poets in the time of David. 1 Chron. 9:17-19; 26:1; 2 Chron. 20:19. To them are inscribed several psalms. Ps. 42, 44–49, 84, 85, 87, 88.

L

Laban (lā'ban), *white.* 1. Son of Bethuel, brother of Rebekah and father of Leah and Rachel. The elder branch of Abram's family remained at Haran, in Mesopotamia, when Abraham removed to the land of Canaan. There Laban was, and took the leading part in the betrothal of his sister Rebekah to Isaac. Gen. 24:10, 29-60; 27:43; 29:5. Laban again appears as the host of his nephew Jacob at Haran. Gen. 29:13, 14. Jacob married Rachel and Leah, daughters of Laban, and remained with him 20 years. But Laban's conduct toward his nephew shows from what source Jacob inherited his tendency to sharp dealing. Nothing is said of Laban after Jacob parted from him.

Lachish (lā'kish), *invincible.* A city of the Amorites, lying south of Jerusalem, and toward the border of Simeon. Josh. 10:3. It was one of the Canaanitish cities which was subdued by Joshua and included in Judah; fortified by Jeroboam. 2 Chron. 11:9. King Amaziah was killed there. 2 Kings 14:19. Lachish was besieged by Sennacherib and perhaps taken. 2 Kings 18:13, 14; Isa. 36:1, 2. The siege is considered by some to be depicted on the slabs found in one of the chambers of the palace at Kouyunjik. Lachish has lately (1892) been identified with Tel-el-Hissy on the Mediterranean Sea, where remarkable tablets, records, and letters of the king of Lachish have been found, written before the exodus.

Lamb. Ex. 12:3. The young of the sheep, though the original word means also the kid or young of the goat; and by the Jewish law it is expressly provided that the sacrifice at the passover might be a lamb, either of the sheep or goat. Ex. 12:5. Sundry peculiar enactments are contained in the same law, respecting the qualities of the animal. Ex. 22:30; 23:19; Lev. 22:27. The prophet represents Christ as a lamb led to the slaughter, Isa. 53:7, and the same figure is employed by John the Baptist. John 1:29, 36. It expresses the meekness and gentleness of Christ, and designates him as the great sacrifice for sin. Throughout the Scriptures, from the beginning to the end, the lamb and the sacrifice of a lamb are used as a type of the Lord Jesus Christ and of his blood shed for our sins. In the Revelation he is expressly called "The Lamb" 27 times. He is represented as now standing in the midst of the throne of God, as a "Lamb as it had been slain, having seven horns, and seven eyes, which are the seven spirits of God." "And they sung a new song saying, Thou art worthy to take the book, and to open the seals thereof: for thou wast slain, and hast redeemed us to God by thy blood out of every kindred, and tongue, and people, and nation, and hast made us unto our God kings and priests." "And every creature which is in heaven, and on the earth, and under the earth, and such as are in the sea, and all that are in them, heard I saying, Blessing, and honor, and glory, and power, *be* unto him that sitteth upon the throne, and unto the Lamb, for ever and ever." Rev. 5:6, 8, 9, 12, 13; 6:1, 16; 7:9, 10, 14, 17; 12:11; 13:8; 17:14; 21:9, 22, 23, 27, etc. See **Sheep.**

Lamech (lā'mek), *strong.* 1. The fifth descendant from Cain, the first polygamist, father of Jabal, Jubal, the inventor of musical instruments, and Tubal-cain, the worker of metals. He was the author of the earliest poetry extant, in which he addresses his wives on account of having slain a man. Gen. 4:18-24. 2. Son of Methusaleh and father of Noah. Gen. 5:25, 31; 1 Chron. 1:3; Luke 3:36.

Lamentations of Jeremiah. *Contents.*—The lamentations are an elegiac poem on the destruction of Jerusalem and Judah by Nebuchadnezzar. The book consists of five separate poems, each complete in itself. The poetical form of this composition is a very elaborate alphabetical structure. The first four chapters are acrostics, like Ps. 25, 34, 37, 119, etc.—that is, every verse begins with a letter of the Hebrew alphabet in regular order. Chaps. 1, 2, and 4 contain 22 verses each, according to the number of Hebrew letters. The third chapter has three successive verses beginning with the same letter, making 66 verses in all. It soothed the weary years of the Babylonian exile, and afterward kept up a lively remembrance of the days of the deepest humiliation. On the ninth day of the month of Ab (July) it was read, year by year, with fasting and weeping, to commemorate the national misery and the final deliverance. The author is not named anywhere in the Bible, and the book is not quoted in the New Testament; but general tradition assigns the composition to Jeremiah, and this is the prevailing opinion.

Lamp. The lights of the East are of various kinds; not only oil, but pitch, naphtha, and wax are used to maintain the flame. The wicks were generally made of cotton or of flax. According to rabbinical tradition, the wicks of the sacred lamps were made of the old linen garments of the priests. The form of Oriental lamps was fanciful, and often elegant, of which we have numerous specimens found in the ruined cities of the East. The materials of which lamps were made were baked clay, terra cotta, bronze, etc. The lamps of the Hebrews, it is probable, were suffered to burn all night, and this occasioned no great expense in a country so rich in oil. The putting out of the light denoted the ruin and extinction of the family and the desertion of the house. This gives force to the words in Job 18:5, 6; 21:17; 29:3;

"The light of the wicked shall be put out; ... light shall be dark in his tabernacle, and his candle shall be put out with him." Jer. 25:10, 11; Prov. 20:20. Also in Prov. 13:9; "The light of the righteous rejoiceth, but the lamp of the wicked shall be put out;" and of the prudent wife, "Her candle goeth not out by night." Prov. 31:18.

Land-mark. The removing of a land-mark was specially prohibited by the Mosaic law. Deut. 19:14; 27:17; Prov. 22:28; 23:10. See also Job 24:2. As this was so flagrant an offence, the expression seems to have become proverbial to designate unprincipled conduct. See Hos. 5:10.

Laodicea (la-ŏd-i-sē'ah), the old city (Greek Diospolis), stood on the banks of the Lycus, a branch of the Meander, a few miles distant from Colosse and Hierapolis, in the Roman province of Asia, in Asia Minor. Seleucus II. enlarged it, and named it after his wife Laodicea. A Christian church was early established here, probably from Ephesus, and to this church Paul sent a salutation when writing to the Colossians, Col. 4:15; it is also mentioned in Rev. 1:11; 3:14. From Col. 4:16 it appears that Paul wrote a letter to the Laodiceans, which some think is the same as the Epistle to the Ephesians.

Lappeth. Judg. 7:5. Orientals are accustomed to take up water in the hollow of the hand to drink with surprising agility. When Gideon's army came to the water side, some drank of it with the hand quickly, to be ready without delay to follow Gideon; while the thousands of fainthearted, that were sent away, stooped down to drink with so much tardiness and ceremony as to show that their hearts were not with Gideon in his contemplated enterprise. The three hundred showed themselves men of alacrity and promptness, and therefore fit for the work.

* Lapwing. Occurs only in A. V. of Lev. 11:19, R. V. Hoopoe, and in the parallel passage of Deut. 14:18, amongst the list of those birds which were forbidden by the law of Moses to be eaten by the Israelites. Probably the hoopoe is intended, a bird about the size of a pigeon.

Latchet. Mark 1:7. The fastening of a sandal or shoe. See Garments, Clothing.

Lattice. 2 Kings 1:2. See Dwelling.

Laver. 1. A circular vessel of brass, in the tabernacle containing water for the priests to wash their hands and feet, before offering sacrifice. It stood in the court between the altar and the door of the tabernacle. Ex. 30:18-21. It rested on a basis, i. e., a foot, which, as well as the laver itself, was made from the mirrors of the women who assembled at the door of the tabernacle court. Ex. 38:8. Like the other vessels belonging to the tabernacle, it was, together with its "foot," consecrated with oil. Lev. 8:10, 11. 2. In Solomon's temple, besides the great molten sea, there were ten lavers of brass, raised on bases, 1 Kings 7:27, 39, five on the north and five on the south side of the court of the priests. They were used for washing the animals to be offered in burnt offerings. 2 Chron. 4:6.

Law, The. This term is applied in the New Testament to the old covenant and revelation, in distinction from the new; the dispensation under the law in distinction from the dispensation under the gospel; that by Moses and the prophets in distinction from the dispensation by Christ. John 1:17; Acts 25:8; Heb. 10:1-18. It was the title applied by the Jews to the first five books of the Bible. The law, the prophets, and the psalms, Luke 24:27, 44; Acts 13:15, thus designate the entire Old Testament. The term often refers more specially to the Mosaic legislation, including the moral, Matt. 5:17, the ceremonial, Eph. 2:15, and the political, but particularly the first. Sometimes Paul uses the word "law" (without the article) in a wider sense—of principle, rule of moral conduct—and speaks of the heathen as having such a law written on their conscience or being a law to themselves. Rom. 2:14, 15.

Lawyers, Luke 7:30, called also "doctors of the law," Luke 5:17, among the Hebrews, were not pleaders before a court, but expounders of the Mosaic and priestly law, and copied it, so that it is not certain what was the difference between a lawyer and a scribe. Matt. 22:35; Luke 10:25; comp. Mark 12:28.

Lazarus (lăz'a-rŭs), an abbreviation of Eleazar, whom God helps. 1. A person of Bethany residing with his two sisters, in whose household Christ was a frequent guest. He was raised from the tomb by Christ in the presence of the family and a number of Jews, after he had been dead four days. So incensed were the Jews at this that they sought to kill not only Christ, but even Lazarus. John 11; 12:1-11. 2. In the parable by which our Saviour illustrates the retributions of the future world one of the parties is named Lazarus. Luke 16:19-31.

Lead. A metal known to the ancients from a very early period, and alluded to in Ex. 15:10 on account of its weight. It is mentioned several times in Scripture as entering into the process of purifying more precious metals, Jer. 6:29; Ezek. 22:18, 20; for which purpose quicksilver is now used. The words of Job 19:24, "that they were graven with an iron pen and lead in the rock forever," refer to the custom of pouring molten lead into letters carved in the rock in order to make them more striking to the eye.

Leah (lē'ah), wearied. The elder daughter of Laban. Her eyes were delicate and weak. Gen. 29:16, 17. By her father Laban's deceit she was married to Jacob; she bore him six sons and a daughter; but seems to have been ever painfully sensible that her husband's affections were given mainly to her sister Rachel. Gen. 29:21-25, 31-35; 30:1-21. She willingly accompanied Jacob into Canaan, Gen. 31; and there she died, when, is not stated, but it was before the family of Israel went down into Egypt, and she was buried in the cave of Machpelah. Gen. 49:31.

Leasing. Ps. 4:2, A. V., "falsehood," R. V. An old English word for falsehood, lying.

Leaven. Any substance that promotes fermentation. Sour dough is generally used in the East for this purpose; lees of wine are also employed. The fermentation produced is a kind of putrefaction; indeed it is distributed into three kinds, the vinous, the acetous, the putrefactive. All leaven was prohibited in meat-offerings, Lev. 2:11; 7:12; 8:2; Num. 6:15, and specially in the paschal feast of the Hebrews, Ex. 12:3, 19, 20; whence this was often called "the feast of unleavened bread." Matt. 26:17. The nature of leaven, affecting the whole lump of the substance to which it is added, furnishes some striking illustrations in Scripture, Matt. 13:33; 16:6; 1 Cor. 5:6; as also does the corruption it had undergone; thus we have warnings in Luke 12:1; 1 Cor. 5:7, 8, where the word is symbolically used for corruptness of life, or doctrine.

Lebanon (*leb'a-non*), *exceeding white*. A double mountain range to the north of Palestine, consisting of a western chain, Lebanon proper, and an eastern. "Lebanon toward the sun-rising," Josh. 13:5, called by classic writers Anti-Libanus, and enclosing a valley from five to eight miles broad—"the valley of Lebanon," Josh. 11:17; called by classic writers Cœlo-Syria. The western range, the Lebanon proper, begins on the north near the banks of the Eleutherus, which passes through the plain of Emesa, the "entrance of Hamath," Num. 34:8, to the Mediterranean, and runs for a distance of 90 geographical miles, in the direction from northeast to southwest, parallel with the Mediterranean, to the banks of the Litany, the ancient Leontes, which, draining Cœlo-Syria and breaking through the Lebanon by a wild gorge, enters the Mediterranean a few miles north of Tyre. The average height of this range is from 6000 to 8000 feet. "The smell of thy garments *is* like the smell of Lebanon." Song of Sol. 4:11. The eastern chain, the Anti-Lebanon, runs nearly parallel with the western. Its highest point is Mount Hermon. Its western descent toward Cœlo-Syria is abrupt and steep; to the east it gradually sinks into the plains of the desert. Its general aspect is bleak and barren, the abode of wild beasts and birds of prey. From both ranges numerous rivers descend—the Eleutherus, Leontes, Jordan, Abana, and Pharpar (which see); and the cold-flowing waters of the springs and streams of Lebanon were and are still proverbial.

Leek. A vegetable similar to the onion, after which the Israelites longed in the wilderness. Num. 11:5. The same word is elsewhere rendered "grass," 1 Kings 18:5; 2 Kings 19:26; Job 40:15; Ps. 37:2; "herb," Job 8:12; "hay," Prov. 27:25, Isa. 15:6. The specific translation "leek" is questionable.

Lees. The settlings of a liquor; its sediment or dregs. "Wine on the lees" means a generous, full-bodied liquor. Isa. 25:6. Before the wine was consumed, it was necessary to strain off the lees; such wine was then termed "well refined." Isa. 25:6. To drink the lees, or "dregs," was an expression for the endurance of extreme punishment. Ps. 75:8.

Legion. A division of the Roman army. The number of men in it differed at various times. Originally a legion consisted of about 3000; but in the time of Augustus it contained about 6000: there were also cavalry attached, to the amount of one-tenth of the infantry. Each legion was divided into ten cohorts, each cohort into three maniples, and each maniple into two centuries, which, according to the name, should comprise 100 men. The word legion came in the course of time to express indefinitely a large number; so it is used in Matt. 26:53; Mark 5:9, 15; Luke 8:30; and so we frequently now use it.

Lentiles. A leguminous plant, producing a kind of pulse resembling small beans. They are chiefly used for pottage, which is of a red or chocolate color. Such was that for which Esau sold his birthright. Gen. 25:29–34. An illustration of this is furnished in the tomb-paintings of Egypt, where there is a representation of a man cooking lentiles for soup or porridge. Sometimes lentiles, in seasons of scarcity, and by the poor, were employed for making bread. Ezek. 4:9. Mixed with barley they are said to be frequently so used in the southern parts of Egypt.

Leopard. Isa. 11:6. An animal of the cat tribe, which is often mentioned by the sacred writers. The Hebrew name is nimrah. Num. 32:3. Beth-nimrah, Num. 32:36, means the house of the leopards; and in Song of Sol. 4:8, are mentioned the mountains of the leopards. Allusions are made in the Bible to its manner of watching for its prey, Jer. 5:6; Hos. 13:7; its fleetness, Hab. 1:8; its fierceness and cruelty, Isa. 11:6, and in Dan. 7:6 it is made the emblem of power.

Leper. Leprosy is the name of a loathsome disease taking various forms; some curable, some not. In the worst form the bones and the marrow are pervaded with the disease, so that the joints of the hands and feet lose their power, the limbs of the body fall together, and the whole system assumes a most deformed and loathsome appearance. The progress and effect of the disease are described in Job 2:7, 8, 12; 6:2; 7:3–5; 19:14–21. There are two forms of the disease—the tuberculated, incrusting the whole person with ulcerous tubercles, and the anæsthetic, making the skin mummylike—but under both forms "Death lives," and the diseased is a walking tomb, a parable of death. There was also a milder form of the disease, the so-called white leprosy, often attacking only one limb and generally curable, as when "Moses' hand *was* leprous as snow." Ex. 4:6. Notice also the cases of Miriam, Num. 12:10; Gehazi, 2 Kings 5:27; and Uzziah, 2 Chron. 26:16–23. Although the laws respecting this dis-

LET   OF THE BIBLE.   LEVITES

ease which we find in the Mosaic code are exceedingly rigid, it is by no means clear that the leprosy was considered contagious. The horror and disgust which was felt toward a disease so foul and loathsome might be a sufficient reason for such severe enactments, and strict seclusion was at all events an effective means of arresting the progress of the disease by preventing intermarriage between "lepers" and the healthy. The leper was excluded from the tabernacle and the camp, and when he was healed his restoration to social intercourse with his fellow-men was twofold; performed both in the camp and in the tabernacle. Lev. 14 : 3–32. A house for lepers was built outside Jerusalem on the hill of Jareb—*i. e.*, "the hill of scraping," Jer. 31 : 40; Job 2 : 8—and the leper was compelled to wear mourning. Lev. 13 : 45. Of leprosy in garments and houses, Lev. 13 : 47–59; 14 : 33–53, little can be said. It might be propagated by animalculæ or germs; and the regulations concerning it must have been of a sanitary as well as moral character. It is well known that the disease is now frequently conveyed by clothes.

Let. Ex. 5 : 4, R. V., "loose;" Isa. 43 : 13; Rom. 1 : 13, R. V., "hindered;" 2 Thess. 2 : 7, R. V., "restraineth." This word is used in old English for "to hinder," "to stop."

Letter. The letters mentioned, 2 Sam. 11 : 14; 2 Kings 10 : 1; Ezra 4 : 11, were in the form of rolls, not unlike those used in the East at the present day. Thus the Arabs roll up their letters, and then flatten them to the breadth of an inch and paste up the end instead of sealing them; and the Persians make up their letters in the form of rolls, about six inches long, and paste a bit of paper around them with gum and seal them with an impression of ink. When sent to inferiors they were often sent open, Neh. 6 : 5; but when sent to equals or superiors they were enclosed in a purse or bag.

Levi (*lē'vī*), *a joining*. 1. The third son of Jacob by Leah, who gave him his name as trusting that her husband would, now that she had borne him three sons, be joined in affection with her. Gen. 29 : 34. Levi, with his brother Simeon, took the lead in the dreadful vengeance inflicted upon the Shechemites for the defilement of their sister Dinah. Gen. 34 : 25–31. Jacob viewed their conduct with abhorrence, and, before his death, while prophetically describing the future fortunes of his sons and their posterity, uttered a solemn denunciation upon Simeon and Levi. Gen. 49 : 5–7. This appears to have come upon Simeon; but the holy zeal of the Levites on occasion of the golden calf procured them a remarkable blessing and distinction. Ex. 32 : 26–29. Levi had three sons, Gershon, Kohath, and Merari, the heads of the families of the tribe. He died in Egypt at the age of 137. Ex. 6 : 16. See **Levites.** 2. The same as Matthew. Mark 2 : 14; Luke 5 : 27. See **Matthew.** 3, 4. Two of our Lord's ancestors. Luke 3 : 24, 29.

Leviathan (*jointed monster*). This word occurs five times in the A. V., and once in the margin, Job 3 : 8, where the text has "mourning." In Hebrew the word *livyathan* is found only in Job 3 : 8; 41 : 1; Ps. 74 : 14; 104 : 26; Isa. 27 : 1. In the margin of Job 3 : 8 and text of Job 41 : 1 the crocodile is no doubt the animal meant, and also in Ps. 74 : 14. In Ps. 104 : 26 the name represents some animal of the whale tribe in the Mediterranean; but it is uncertain what animal is intended in Isa. 27 : 1. The term may denote some species of snakes which are common in south and west Africa.

Levites (*lē'vītes*). A term applied sometimes to all the descendants of Levi. Num. 35 : 2; Josh. 21 : 3, 41; Ex. 6 : 25; Lev. 25 : 32, etc. But the "sons of Aaron" were separated from the rest of the descendants of Levi and consecrated priests: hence, after this the Levites comprised only those descendants of Levi who were not "sons of Aaron" —that is, priests. 1 Kings 8 : 4; Ezra 2 : 70; John 1 : 19, etc. Sometimes, also, the term was used to show from what tribe the priests came—"the priests the Levites." Josh. 3 : 3; Deut. 17 : 18. The Levites numbered 22,000 in the wilderness, and took the place of the first-born, part of whom were redeemed at five shekels each, Num. 3 : 45–51, the fixed ransom for a victim vowed in sacrifice. Num. 18 : 16; Lev. 27 : 6. Thus the Levites came to occupy in the Hebrew theocracy a position midway between the priests and the people. They consisted of three great families, the Kohathites, the Gershonites, and the Merarites, of which the first carried the sacred vessels, the second the hangings and curtains of the tabernacle, and the third the boards and pillars. They also kept the book of the Law, Deut. 17 : 8–12, and served as judges, etc. Forty-eight cities, with 1000 cubits of the country surrounding, were appropriated for the residence and maintenance of the Levites. Besides these cities, with adjacent districts, the Levites received a tithe of all produce, animal and vegetable, but of this they paid a tithe to the priests. Num. 18 : 20–32. Another tithe they received every third year, and special provision was made for them during the term they administered in the sanctuary. In the time of David their number had increased to 38,000, of which 24,000 were set apart for the ordinary services, 6000 for the teaching of the Law and the administration of justice, 4000 as porters, and 4000 as musicians. They were divided into courses, and came up from their cities to the sanctuary in regular rotation. 1 Chron. 23 ; 24 : 20–31 ; 25 ; 26. When the separation took place between the kingdom of Israel and the kingdom of Judah, all the Levites gathered to Judah, 2 Chron. 11 : 13–15, and they continued to play a conspicuous part in the destinies of this kingdom. After the captivity, however, only a small number of them returned, Ezra 2 : 36–42; 3 : 10; 6 : 18; but in the new organization they assumed their old positions. They settled in the villages near Jerusalem, received their old tithes, etc. Neh. 10:37-39; 12:29. In the New Testament they occur as representatives of a formal worship destitute of love. Luke 10:32. The distinction of Levite is still maintained among the Jews.

Leviticus (*le-vit'i-kŭs*), *relating to the Levites*. The name of the third book of the Pentateuch. Only the chapters 8-10 are history; the rest treats of the Levitical services—namely, chaps. 1-7, the laws of offerings; 8-10, the consecration of Aaron and his family; 11-15, the laws concerning that which is clean and that which is unclean; 16, the atonement as the sum-total of all means of grace; 17-20, the separation of Israel from heathendom in food, marriage, etc.; 21, 22, the holiness of priests and offerings; 23, 24, the holiness of convocations, Sabbaths; 25, on redemption; 26, on repentance; 27, on vows.

Libertines (*lib'er-tines*). The descendants of Jewish freedmen at Rome, who had been expelled, 19 A. D., by Tiberius. Acts 6:9. They might very well have a synagogue of their own at Jerusalem, as they were numerous, and as there are said to have been not fewer than 460 or 480 synagogues in that city.

Libnah (*lib'nah*), *whiteness*. 1. The fifth station at which Israel encamped on their journey from Sinai; situated between Rimmon-parez and Rissah, Num. 33:20, 21, but not yet identified. 2. A city of Canaan, in the lowland of Judah, was taken by Joshua. Josh. 10:29-32, 39; 12:15, and assigned to the priests, Josh. 15:42; 21:13; 1 Chron. 6:57; revolted against Joram, 2 Kings 8:22; 2 Chron. 21:10; was besieged by Sennacherib, 2 Kings 19:8; Isa. 37:8.

Libya (*lib'y-ah*), occurring only in Ezek. 30:5 A. V. (R. V. "Put,"), and Acts 2:10, and Lybia is the classic name of northern Africa, west of Egypt. It was inhabited by a Hamitic race, spoken of in the Old Testament under the name of Lehabim or Lubim.

Lice. Ex. 8:16. These parasitic insects are still a pest in the Nile valley. Herodotus tells us that the ancient Egyptians peculiarly abhorred such vermin, and were taught by their priests that contact with lice rendered them ceremonially unclean. Some authorities have held that gnats were here intended, but more probably *ticks* are meant. These ticks are much larger than lice. The body is ordinarily about the size of a small pea; the legs are long, and the creature runs rapidly.

Ligure, Heb. *leshem*. A precious stone mentioned in Ex. 28:19; 39:12, R. V. "Jacinth," as the first in the third row of the high priest's breastplate. Perhaps tourmaline, or more definitely the red variety known as rubellite, is the stone meant. Rubellite is a hard stone, and used as a gem, and is sometimes sold for red sapphire.

Lily. A flower repeatedly mentioned in Scripture in both the Old and the New Testaments. It was of gorgeous beauty, Matt. 6:28, 29, growing near the place where the Sermon on the Mount was delivered, luxuriant and probably rapid in its growth, Hos. 14:5; it was found in the valleys among thorns and on pasture land, Song of Sol. 2:1, 2, 16; 4:5; 6:3; still, whether it was scarlet, or emitted a fragrant odor, we cannot gather with certainty from Song of SoL, 5:13, as critics differ in their interpretation of this verse. If the former idea be preferred, the flower may be supposed to be the *Lilium Chalcedonicum*, or scarlet martagon, which is found plentifully in Galilee in spring-time. If the lily was fragrant, it was probably the *Lilium candidum*, or common white lily, which also grows in Palestine; or it may designate some species of anemone.

Linen. A cloth made from flax. Lev. 13:47. Several Hebrew words are rendered linen. Egypt was the great centre of the linen trade. Prov. 7:16; 1 Kings 10:28, A. V., but the R. V. reads differently. Some linen made from the Egyptian byssus, a flax that grew on the banks of the Nile, was soft like silk and of dazzling whiteness. This linen has been sold for twice its weight in gold. Sir J. G. Wilkinson says of it: "The quality of the fine linen fully justifies all the praises of antiquity, and excites equal admiration at the present day, being to the touch comparable to silk, and not inferior in texture to our finest cambric."

Lion. Lions do not now exist in Palestine; but they must in ancient times have been numerous there. The names Lebaoth, Josh. 15:32; 19:6; Laish, Judg. 18:7; 1 Sam. 25:44, indicate the presence of the lion in those regions. The lion of Palestine was in all probability the Asiatic variety, described by Aristotle and Pliny as distinguished by its short curly mane, and by being shorter and rounder in shape, like the sculptured lion found at Arban. When driven by hunger it not only ventured to attack the flocks in the desert in presence of the shepherd, 1 Sam. 17:34; Isa. 31:4, but laid waste towns and villages, 2 Kings 17:25, 26; Prov. 22:13; 26:13, and devoured men. 1 Kings 13:24; 20:36. Among the Hebrews, and throughout the Old Testament, the lion was the symbol of the princely tribe of Judah, while in the closing book of the Bible it received a deeper significance as the emblem of him who "prevailed to open the book, and to loose the seven seals thereof." Rev. 5:5. On the other hand its fierceness and cruelty rendered it an appropriate metaphor for a fierce and malignant enemy, Ps. 7:2; 22:21; 57:4; 2 Tim. 4:17, and hence for the archfiend himself, 1 Pet. 5:8.

Locust. A well-known insect which commits terrible ravages on vegetation in the countries which it visits. The common brown locust is about three inches in length, and the general form is that of a grasshopper. Locusts occur in great numbers, and sometimes obscure the sun. Ex. 10:15; Judg. 6:5; Jer. 46:23. Their voracity is alluded to in Ex. 10:12, 15; Joel 1:4, 7. They make a fearful noise in their flight, Joel 2:5; Rev. 9:9. Their irresistible progress is referred to in Joel 2:8, 9. They enter dwellings, and devour even the woodwork of houses. Ex. 10:6; Joel 2:9, 10. They do not fly in the night. Nah.

3:17. The sea destroys the greater number. Ex. 10 : 19; Joel 2 : 20. The flight of locusts is thus described: "It is difficult to express the effect produced on us by the sight of the whole atmosphere filled on all sides and to a great height by an innumerable quantity of these insects, whose flight was slow and uniform, and whose noise resembled that of rain; the sky was darkened, and the light of the sun considerably weakened. In a moment the terraces of the houses, the streets, and all the fields were covered by these insects, and in two days they had nearly devoured all the leaves of the plants." Locusts have been used as food from the earliest times. Lev. 11 : 21, 22; Matt. 3 : 4; Mark 1 : 6. Herodotus speaks of a Libyan nation who dried their locusts in the sun and ate them with milk. The more common method was to pull off the legs and wings and roast the bodies in an iron dish. Then they were thrown into a bag, and eaten like parched corn, each one taking a handful when he chose. Sometimes locusts are ground and pounded, and then mixed with flour and water and made into cakes, or they are salted and then eaten; sometimes smoked; sometimes boiled or roasted; or stewed or fried in butter.

Lod (lŏd). 1 Chron. 8 : 12. See **Lydda**.

Lodebar (lō-dē'bar or lō'de-bär), *without pasture*. A place in the tribe of Gad, not far from Mahanaim, north of the Jabbok, east of the Jordan. 2 Sam. 9 : 4; 17 : 27. Here dwelt Machir the Ammonite, who assisted David in his flight from Absalom, and there lived Mephibosheth, Jonathan's lame son. Some suppose it to be the same as Debir, Josh. 13 : 26, but by modern travellers it has not yet been identified.

Log. See **Measures**.

Looking-glass. This word occurs in Ex. 38 : 8; Job 37 : 18; also in Isa. 3 : 23, where it is simply "glasses." The R. V. reads mirrors in these three places. The articles intended were mirrors, tablets, or plates of polished metal, mostly of a round form, and furnished with handles. Those carried by the Hebrew women at the time of the construction of the vessels of the tabernacle were used for making "the laver of brass and the foot of it of brass." Many mirrors have been discovered in Egypt, and are to be seen in museums. They are of mixed metal, chiefly copper, very carefully wrought, and highly polished.

Lord. The rendering of the two Hebrew words "Jehovah" and "Adonai." When it represents the former it is printed with capitals. Gen. 15 : 4. When it represents the latter it is printed with a capital initial. Ps. 97 : 5.

Lord's Day. Rev. 1 : 10. From the times of the apostles, the first day of the week has been kept sacred by Christians in commemoration of the resurrection of Christ, and it is invariably designated as the Lord's day by the fathers of the primitive church up to the time of the edict of Constantine, when the name Sunday became common. "On the first day of the week when the disciples came together to break bread, Paul preached unto them." Acts 20 : 7. His charge "concerning the collection for the saints" to the church in Corinth is, "Upon the first day of the week let every one of you lay by him in store, as God hath prospered him." 1 Cor. 16 : 1, 2. John commences the Revelation saying: "I was in the Spirit on the Lord's day." Rev. 1 : 10. The Lord's day, as the Sabbath, reminds us of the finished work of creation and redemption. See **Sabbath**.

Lord's Prayer. The name given to the prayer which our Lord taught his disciples, after their request, "Lord, teach us to pray," recorded in Matt. 6 : 9-13; Luke 11 : 2-4. Our Lord warns them against praying to be seen of men, and against using " vain repetitions, as the heathen do," and adds: "After this manner pray ye: Our Father which art in heaven," etc. This prayer is a model prayer, divinely authorized: simple, short; complete, so far as adoration, confession, supplication, and intercession go. As it is, a Jew, a Mohammedan, or a heathen, may use it with propriety; but it would not be a complete Christian prayer without it is offered in accordance with our Lord's additional teachings concerning prayer to his disciples. We must come to God through him. "No man cometh unto the Father, but by me." John 14 : 6. We must offer our prayers in his name. "Verily, verily, I say unto you, Whatsoever ye shall ask the Father in my name, he will give it you. Hitherto have ye asked nothing in my name: ask, and ye shall receive, that your joy may be full." "Whatsoever ye shall ask in my name, that will I do, that the Father may be glorified in the Son. If ye shall ask anything in my name, I will do it," John 16 : 23, 24, 26; 14 : 13, 14; 15 : 16. In the use of the Lord's Prayer, so called, we should remember our Lord's injunction when teaching it, "Use not vain repetitions, as the heathen do." Matt. 6 : 7.

Lord's Supper. The passover was instituted in the Jewish church as a perpetual reminder of their deliverance from Egypt until, as a type, it was fulfilled by the death of the Lord Jesus Christ for his people. Just before his death he instituted what is called "The Lord's Supper," to be observed by his followers as a perpetual reminder until he comes again. As the passover was not a new deliverance, but simply a reminder and commemoration to be observed with joy and thanksgiving, so is the Lord's Supper to be observed. There is no new sacrifice of Christ. The adoration of the bread or wafer is the grossest perversion and idolatry. "Christ was once offered to bear the sins of many." "We are sanctified through the offering of the body of Jesus Christ once for all." "But this man, after he had offered one sacrifice for sins for ever, sat down on the right hand of God." "For by one offering he hath perfected for ever them that are sanctified." Heb. 9 : 25-28; 10 : 10, 12, 14. The connection of the passover feast with the Lord's Supper is shown by such passages as the following. At the institution of the latter,

Christ said, "With desire I have desired to eat this passover with you before I suffer. For I say unto you, I will not any more eat thereof, until it be fulfilled in the kingdom of God," Luke 22 : 15, 16; and, "For even Christ our passover is sacrificed for us." 1 Cor. 5 : 7. The Lord's Supper was instituted before Christ's body was broken or his blood shed. The accounts of it given, Matt. 26 : 26; Mark 14 : 22; Luke 22: 14-20, are exceedingly touching, and the injunction very plain : "This do in remembrance of me." Luke 22 : 19; 1 Cor. 11: 24, 25. It is also a continual reminder of the second coming of our Lord ; "For as often as ye eat this bread, and drink this cup, ye do shew the Lord's death till he come." 1 Cor. 11 : 26. The Scripture account of it is simple. The Lord Jesus, after eating the paschal supper with his disciples, took bread and blessed *it*, and brake *it*, and gave *it* to the disciples and said, Take, eat, this is my body, which is broken for you : this do in remembrance of me. After the same manner also *he took* the cup, and gave thanks and gave *it* to them, saying, Drink ye all of it ; for this is the new covenant in my blood, which is shed for many unto remission of sins; this do ye as oft as ye drink-it in remembrance of *me*. Matt. 26 : 19-30; Mark 14 : 16-26; Luke 22 : 13-20; 1 Cor. 11 : 23-26. R. V. Nothing can surpass the touching simplicity and appropriateness of this memorial service.

Lot (*lŏt*), *veil* or *covering*. The son of Haran and nephew of Abraham. Gen. 11: 27, 31. His sisters were Milcah the wife of Nahor, and Iscah, by some identified with Sarah. Haran died before the emigration of Terah and his family from Ur of the Chaldees, ver. 28, and Lot was therefore born there. He removed with the rest of his kindred to Haran, and again subsequently with Abraham and Sarai to Canaan. Gen. 12 : 4, 5. With them he took refuge in Egypt from a famine, and with them returned first to the "South," Gen. 13 : 1, and then to their original settlement between Bethel and Ai. vs. 3, 4. Later, they separated, Lot choosing the fertile plain of the Jordan, near Sodom. Gen. 13 : 10-14. Lot was captured by the four kings of the East, and rescued by Abram. Gen. 14. He was still living in Sodom, Gen. 19, from which he was rescued by angels on the day of its final overthrow. He fled first to Zoar, in which he found a temporary refuge during the destruction of the other cities of the plain. The end of Lot's wife is commonly treated as one of the difficulties of the Bible ; but it surely need not be so. The value and the significance of the story to us are contained in the allusion of Christ. Luke 17 : 32. It is folly to think of identifying the "pillar" with some one of the fleeting forms which the perishable rock of the south end of the Dead Sea is constantly assuming. From the incestuous intercourse between Lot and his two daughters sprang the nations of Moab and Ammon.

Lot. Casting lots or a pebble is an ancient custom of deciding doubtful questions. Prov. 16 : 33. Among the Jews lots were used with the expectation that God would so control them as to give a right direction to them, as in the choice of the apostle Matthias, Acts 1 : 26, and in the cases of Saul and Jonathan, and Jonah and his companions to determine who had offended God. 1 Sam. 14 : 41, 42; Jonah 1 : 7. In the division of the Promised Land among the tribes of Israel the use of the lot was expressly commanded by God himself, it being understood that the extent of territory should be proportioned to the population of each tribe. Num. 26 : 55. So the selection of the scapegoat on the day of atonement was to be determined by lot. Lev. 16 : 8. Property was divided in a similar way. Ps. 22 : 18 ; Matt. 27 : 35. The orders of the priests and their daily services were also assigned by lot. 1 Chron. chaps. 24, 25. The manner of casting lots is supposed to have been by stones or marks which were thrown together into the lap or fold of a garment, or into an urn or vase, and the person holding them shook them violently, and they were then drawn. The passage, Prov. 16 : 33, is paraphrased thus : "In a lot-vase the lots are shaken in all directions; nevertheless, from the Lord is the whole decision or judgment."

Love Feasts, *Agapē*. Jude 12; 2 Pet. 2 : 13. A meeting accompanying the Lord's Supper in which the poorer members of the church were provided for by the contributions of Christians, but whether before or after the celebration is uncertain. Chrysostom says that after the early community of goods had ceased, the richer members brought to the church contributions of food and drink, of which, after the conclusion of the services and the celebration of the Lord's Supper, all partook together, by this means helping to promote the principle of love among Christians. The love feasts were forbidden to be held in churches by the Council of Laodicea, A. D. 320; but in some form or other they have been continued in some churches.

Lucifer (*lū'sĭ-fẽr*), *light-bringer*. The original word signifies brilliant star, *i. e.*, the morning star. The title is applied to the king of Babylon in Isa. 14 : 12, R. V., day star; he had outshone other kings, as the bright star of the morning surpasses other stars. Falling from heaven denotes a sudden political overthrow or catastrophe. In popular language Lucifer is regarded as an appellation of Satan.

Lucius (*lū'shĭ-ŭs*). A Cyrenian, a Christian teacher at Antioch. Acts 13 : 1. It is probably the same person whom Paul calls his kinsman, *i. e.*, of his own tribe, and whose salutation he conveys to the Roman church. Rom. 16 : 2.

Luke (*lūke*), Col. 4 : 14; called also Lucas, Philemon 24, A. V. A physician and distinguished companion of Paul, and writer of the third Gospel and the book of the Acts. The diction of these books in the New Testament, the gospel and the Acts, is such as to persuade some that he must have been a Jew. But Paul, writing to the Colossians, after mentioning all "of the circumcision" who had been a comfort unto him, adds the salutation of "Luke, the beloved physician." Col. 4 : 10-14. The inference is that Luke was not a Jew. Luke is traditionally said to be a native of Antioch; this, however, has no better foundation than the confounding of him with that Lucius who is reckoned among the teachers at Antioch, Acts 13 : 1 ; from whom he must certainly be distinguished.

Luke, the Gospel of. This is the third in order of the gospels, attributed commonly to the evangelist whose name it bears. It is addressed to Theophilus, and begins by stating the object of writing, namely, to put on record an authentic orderly account of our Lord's history from his birth to his ascension. 1 : 1-4. Then follows a narrative of Christ's birth with attendant circumstances, and particulars of his infancy and youth. 1 : 5-2 : 52. Afterwards we have a notice of John's ministry, to his imprisonment. 3 : 1-20. And then commences the history of Christ's public ministration, headed with a mention of his baptism, vs. 21, 22; his genealogy, vs. 23-38; his temptation, 4 : 1-13 ; his discourses, miracles, and transactions in Galilee. 4 : 14-9 : 50. The gospel closes with Christ's Peræan ministry, his last journey to Jerusalem, his passion, death, resurrection, and ascension. 9 : 51-24 : 53. Luke wrote his gospel in Greek. His writings prove him to have been a man of education and attainment. His style is pure, copious, and flowing, more classical than that of the other evangelists : the preface, indeed, is pure classical Greek. Still, there are many Hebraisms, and certain peculiarities of diction apparent. The writer, moreover, evinces a thorough acquaintance with Jewish customs. This is not surprising in so clear-sighted an observer, especially as he certainly visited and perhaps more than once resided in Palestine. He had, too, the close intimacy of the apostle Paul. A singular propriety has been observed in the way in which he names and describes the various diseases he has occasion to mention. The thoughtful comments, too, which he frequently makes upon the circumstances he records, with the notice of the causes which led to particular events, admirably correspond with what we might expect from a well-informed medical man.

Lunatics. Latin *luna*, the moon. Insane persons were supposed to be affected by the changes of the moon. This word is used twice in the New Testament—Matt. 4 : 24 ; 17 : 15; but rendered epileptic in the R. V. The word refers to some disease affecting both the body and the mind, which might or might not be a sign of possession. By the description of Mark 9 : 17-26 it is inferred that this disease was epilepsy.

Luz (*lŭz*), *almond tree*. 1. The Canaanite name for the place in which Jacob rested and had a prophetic vision, and afterward the city of Bethel; now Beitin. Gen. 28 : 19 ; 35 : 6 ; 48 : 3; Josh. 16 : 2 ; 18 : 13 ; Judg. 1 : 23. 2. A city in the land of the Hittites, built by an inhabitant of the original Luz, who was spared when the city was sacked, Judg. 1 : 23; now Luweiziyeh, four miles northwest of Banias.

Lycaonia (*ly-ka-ō'ni-ah*). A province of Asia Minor which the apostle Paul twice visited. Acts 14 : 1-23 ; 16 : 1-6. It was separated from Phrygia, and bounded north by Galatia, east by Cappadocia, south by Cilicia, and west by Pisidia and Phrygia. Its chief towns were Iconium, Derbe, and Lystra. The speech of this province, Acts 14 : 11, is supposed to have been either a Syrian or a corrupted Greek dialect.

Lycia (*lĭsh'i-ah*), a region of Asia Minor, on the Mediterranean, between Caria and Pamphylia. It acquired some political importance, as shown by 1 Macc. 15 : 23. In the reign of Claudius it became a Roman province. Paul visited it, and preached the gospel in its two largest cities, Patara, Acts 21 : 1, and Myra, Acts 27 : 5.

Lydda (*lyd'dah*). Ezra 2 : 33. The Greek name for the Hebrew *Lud*, the present *Lydd*, now a village, but in ancient times a large town situated in the plain of Sharon, a few miles east of Joppa, on the road to Jerusalem. It was burnt several times by the Romans, but again rebuilt. Here Peter healed the paralytic Æneas. Acts 9 : 32.

Lydia (*lyd'i-ah*). 1. A Jewish proselyte from the city of Thyatira, in Lydia, engaged in the purple trade, possessed of wealth, and temporarily residing at Philippi, where she heard Paul preach. Acts 16 : 14. She accepted the gospel, was baptized together with her household, and Paul stayed at her house. 2. Ezek. 30 : 5, R. V. "Lud," where it probably refers to a people or place in Africa. It was also a coast region of Asia Minor, and formed in olden times the centre of a great empire under Crœsus ; afterward it belonged successively to Syria, Pergamus, and the Romans. Its principal cities were Sardis, Thyatira, and Philadelphia. It is mentioned in 1 Macc. 8 : 8 among the provinces which the Romans transferred from Syria to Pergamus.

Lystra (*lys'trah*). A city of Lycaonia, probably at the present Bin bir-Kilisseh. Paul visited this place twice, the first time in company with Barnabas, Acts 14, when he was saluted as the god Mercury, but afterward stoned ; the second time in company with Silas. Acts 16. Timothy was probably born here. 2 Tim. 3 : 11.

M

Maacah (*mā'a-kah*), *oppression*, 2 Sam. 3 : 3 : or **Maachah**, 1 Chron. 3 : 2. 1. A daughter of Talmai, king of Geshur, was taken in battle by David, according to Hebrew tradition, and made one of his wives and bore him Absalom. 2. A small district or kingdom on the northeastern frontier of Palestine, in Syria, near Ammon and toward Mesopotamia, 2 Sam. 10 : 6 ; or **Maachah**, 1 Chron. 19 : 6, 7.

Maachah (*mā'a-kah*). 1. The daughter of Nahor, Abraham's brother. Gen. 22 : 24. 2. The father of Achish, who was king of Gath in Solomon's reign, 1 Kings 2 : 39; is also called Moach, 1 Sam. 27 : 2. 3. The daughter or more probably the granddaughter of Absalom, and the third wife of Rehoboam, mother to Abijah and grandmother to Asa, 1 Kings 15:2; 2 Chron. 11: 20-22; but the R. V. reads "Maacah." In 2 Chron. 13:2 she is called "Michaiah, the daughter of Uriel of Gibeah," "Michaiah" being a variation of "Maachah," and Uriel being the husband of Absalom's daughter Tamar. In the beginning of Asa's reign she held the dignity of queen-mother, 1 Kings 15:2, 10, 13; 2 Chron. 11: 20-22; but when Asa came of age she lost the dignity as a punishment because she had introduced idolatry. 2 Chron. 15:16. There are eight persons of this name mentioned in the Bible.

Macedonia (*măs-e-dō'nĭ-ah*), *extended land*. Macedonia is situated in a great basin north of Greece, nearly surrounded by the mountains and the sea. The third great world-kingdom, the Macedonian empire, received its name from this comparatively little spot. Comp. Dan. 8:5-8, 21. The Romans conquered the territory from Perseus. It was at first divided into four districts, afterward consolidated into one with its capital at Thessalonica, where the proconsul resided. In New Testament history Macedonia holds an important place because of the labors of the apostles. Paul was called there by the vision of the "man of Macedonia," and made a most successful missionary tour. Acts 16:10; 17:1-12. He visited it again, Acts 20:1-6, and probably for a third time. Comp. 1 Tim. 1:3; Phil. 2:24. His Epistles to the Thessalonians and Philippians show that the Macedonian Christians exhibited many excellent traits. The details of his work can be studied in connection with the cities of Macedonia visited by him. See **Neapolis, Philippi, Apollonia, Thessalonica, Berœa.**

Machpelah (*mak-pē'lah*), *double cave*. A field in Hebron containing the cave which Abraham bought of Ephron the Hittite as a burial-place for his family. A full account of the negotiations, carried on after the oriental forms still prevalent, is given in Gen. 23. That cave became the burial-place of Abraham and Sarah, Isaac and Rebekah, Jacob and Leah. Gen. 23: 19:25:9; 49:29-32; 50:12, 13. The name does not occur except in the book of Genesis. The cave Machpelah is one of the Bible sites which are positively known. It was situated on the western slope of a hill in Hebron, the town lying for the most part to the south and west. Within an enclosure is a mosque, which was probably erected in the time of Justinian as a Christian church. Visitors are rigidly excluded, but by a special firman of the sultan the Prince of Wales was admitted in 1862, and others have since entered it. Of the cave itself there is no trustworthy account. Captain Warren was told that it had not been entered for 600 years. The Moslems have a superstition that whoever attempts to enter it will be struck dead, and their fanaticism causes them to prohibit any one from making the attempt. It is thought to be possible that the embalmed body of Jacob may still be preserved in the cave, as Egyptian mummies have been found of as early a date.

Magdala (*măg'da-lah*), *tower*. In the chief manuscripts and versions the name is given as "Magadan." Magdala is found only in Matt. 15:39. The parallel passage, Mark 8:10, has the "parts of Dalmanutha," on the western edge of the lake. The two regions or districts were probably near each other. The Magdala from which Mary Magdalene was named is perhaps identical with Migdal-el, Josh. 19:38, and may be the modern el-Mejdel.

Magi, *great, powerful*. Wise men, "rabmag," Jer. 39:3, which is used as a proper name, and properly signifies the prince Magus, or chief of the Magi. In Babylon the magi were known by the name of "wise men" and "Chaldeans." Isa. 44: 25; Jer. 50:35; Dan. 2:12-27; 4:6, 18; 5:7, 8, 11, 12, 15. To their number, doubtless, belonged the "astrologers" and "stargazers," Isa. 47:13; also the "soothsayers" and the "dream interpreters." Dan. 1:20; 2:2, 27; 4:7; 5:7, 11. Daniel describes them as men of wisdom, Dan. 1:20; he intercedes for them with Nebuchadnezzar, Dan. 2:24; and accepts a position as their chief or master. Dan. 5:11. The same impression of dignity, truthfulness, and aspiration after the true religion is conveyed by the narrative in Matt. 2:1-14. Whence these Magi came we do not certainly know, but probably from the lands of the Jewish captivity on the Euphrates.

Magic was the art of influencing future events and changing their course by dark and secret means. Of the religion of the Egyptians, Chaldæans, Persians, etc., magic formed an essential element, and of the Egyptian magicians, in their conflict with Moses and Aaron, Exodus gives a vivid account. 7:11, 12, 22; 8:7. Of the religion of the Jews magic did not only not form a part, but the law forbade the consulting of magicians, under penalty of death. Lev. 19:31; 20:6. Nevertheless, from their neighbors magic crept in among the Israelites. The most remarkable instance is that of Saul and the sorceress of Endor. 1 Sam. 28:3-20. Also in the New Testament we find it mentioned. Acts 8:9.

Mahanaim (*mā'ha-nā'ĭm*), *two camps*. A town east of the Jordan, named by Jacob. Gen. 32:1, 2. It was assigned to the Levites. Josh. 13:26, 30; 21:38; 1 Chron. 6: 80, and lay within the territory of Gad, north of the torrent Jabbok. Mahanaim became in the time of the monarchy a place of mark. 2 Sam. 2:8, 12; 2 Sam. 19: 32. Abner fixed Ishbosheth's residence there, and David took refuge in it when driven out of the western part of his kingdom by Absalom. 2 Sam. 17:24; 1 Kings 2:8. Mahanaim was the seat of one of Solomon's commissariat officers, 1 Kings 4: 14, and it is alluded to in his Song, 6:13. Dr. Merrill locates Mahanaim in the Jordan valley, six miles north of the Jabbok, at a ruin called Suleikhat.

Makkedah (*mak-kē'dah*), *place of shep-*

herds. A royal city of the Canaanites in the plains of Judah, where Joshua executed the five confederate kings. Josh. 10:10; 12:16; 15:41. Warren would identify it with el-Mŭghâr.

Malachi (măl'a-ki), *messenger of Jehovah*. The last of the prophets of the Old Testament, and called "the seal" because his prophecies form the closing book of the canon of the Old Testament. Of his personal life nothing is known but what can be gleaned from his book. He flourished after the captivity, later than Haggai and Zechariah, at a time when the temple was completed, and was probably a contemporary of Nehemiah, B. C. 433. His prophecies are at once denunciatory of prevailing vices, and close with a prophecy of the coming of Messiah, and foretells that Elijah will return as a forerunner of Messiah—a prediction which found its striking fulfilment by the mission of John the Baptist. Mal. 4:5; Luke 1:17; Matt. 11:14; 17:12.

Mallows. The Hebrew word *malluahh*, rendered "mallows," R. V. "salt-wort," Job 30:4, is derived from *melahh* — "salt;" and seems to designate a saline plant—perhaps a species of salt-wort; or perhaps the garden mallow, reared in Egypt, and boiled with meat, is intended.

Mammon (măm'mon), *wealth*. A Chaldee or Syriac word used by our Lord in uttering two severe admonitions. In the one, Matt. 6:24, he would intend a carnal worldly possession-loving spirit, which unfits a man for the high service of God. In the second place, Luke 16:9, 11, mammon is more explicitly wealth, called "mammon of unrighteousness" because it is the substance of a system, an avaricious system, which never could have existed had original righteousness not been lost.

Manasseh (ma-năs'sch), *forgetting*. 1. The first-born of Joseph. When he and his brother Ephraim were boys, and Jacob, their grandfather, was about to die, Joseph took them into the patriarch's presence to receive his blessing. Gen. 48:5-20. Nothing further is known of the personal history of Manasseh. The eastern part of the tribe of Manasseh prospered much and spread to Mount Hermon, but they finally mixed with the Canaanites, adopted their idolatry, became scattered as Bedouins in the desert, and were the first to be carried away into captivity by the kings of Assyria. 1 Chron. 5:25. The western Manasseh, of which only a few glimpses are visible in the later history of Israel, always showed itself on the right side; as, for instance, in the cases of Asa, 2 Chron. 15:9; Hezekiah, 2 Chron. 30:1, 11, 18, and Josiah, 2 Chron. 34:6, 9. 2. Son and successor of Hezekiah, king of Judah, ascended the throne at the age of twelve years, B. C. 696. The earlier part of his reign was distinguished for acts of impiety and cruelty, 2 Kings 21, and he succeeded in drawing his subjects away from the Lord to such an extent that the only kind of worship which was not allowed in Judah was that of Jehovah. 2 Kings 21:2-9. Having supported the Babylonian viceroy in his revolt against Assyria, he was at last taken captive by the Assyrian king and ignominiously transported to Babylon. Upon his repentance, however, he was liberated, and returned to his capital, where he died B. C. 641, after having done much to repair the evils of his former life. 2 Chron. 33:1-20.

3. The territory of Manasseh occupied by a tribe descended from Joseph, and divided into two portions—one east of the Jordan, and the other west of it. 1. *East of the Jordan*.—The country of Manasseh east of the Jordan included half of Gilead, the Hauran, Bashan, and Argob. 1 Chron. 5:18-23. The extensive pastures of Gilead and Bashan gave the best scope for the half-nomad and herdsman's life led by this portion of the tribe. Ps. 68:15. The people were powerful and brave, taking a leading part in the wars of Gideon, of Jephthah, and of David. See also **Gilead and Bashan**. 2. *West of the Jordan*.—The portion of the half-tribe of Manasseh on the west of the Jordan extended from the Mediterranean to the Jordan, and lay between Asher and Issachar on the north and Ephraim on the south. Josh. 17:7-10. They also gained some towns in Carmel within the bounds of Issachar, probably by capturing them from the ancient Canaanites. Josh. 17:11-18. The dominant position of Ephraim seems to have obscured the power of Manasseh, and this portion of their country is frequently joined with Ephraim in the biblical allusions.

Mandrakes (Heb. *love plants*). Modern Bible scholars apply this name to a member of the potato family (*Mandragora officinalis*). This is a stemless plant with a disk of leaves almost as long, but not nearly as broad, as those of the garden rhubarb, which it somewhat resembles, except in its blossoms. The odor of the plant seems to be enjoyed by Orientals, Song of Sol. 7:13, and by *some* Occidentals. Many strange superstitions are connected with this plant, and the idea of Rachel's time still prevails that conception is ensured by eating the fruit of this plant. Gen. 30:14-16.

Manna (*what is this?* Heb. *măn*). The chief food of the Israelites in the wilderness. Ex. 16:14-36; Num. 11:7-9; Deut. 8:3, 16; Josh. 5:12; Ps. 78:24, 25. The most remarkable things about the manna of the Israelites were: 1. That double the quantity was supplied on the day preceding the Sabbath or seventh day; 2. That on the Sabbath or seventh day none was furnished; 3. That what they kept from the sixth day to the seventh was sweet and good, while what they kept from any other day to the next day bred worms and became offensive. These miracles were wrought in attestation of the sanctity of the Sabbath. The manna of the Jews is described as "a small round thing," as small as "the hoarfrost on the ground," "like coriander seed" (in shape doubtless, perhaps in size and density), "of the color of bdellium," "and the taste of it like wafers made with honey." For forty years this miraculous supply of food was furnished daily to between 3,000,000 and 4,000,000 of people. Deut. 29:5, 6. It ceased while they were encamped at Gilgal, immediately after they had celebrated the passover for the first time in the Land of Promise. To commemorate this wonderful miracle a golden pot was provided, Ex. 16:33; Heb. 9:4, and an omer (or one man's portion) of the manna put up for preservation and placed in or near the ark, that succeeding generations might see with their own eyes the very substance on which their fathers were miraculously fed in their long and perilous journeyings from Egypt to Canaan. The manna which is now used in medicine as a mild laxative is the juice of the flowering ash, a native of Sicily, Calabria, and other parts of the south of Europe. It is either naturally concreted, or exsiccated, and purified by art. The best manna is in oblong pieces or flakes of a pale yellow color; light, friable, and somewhat transparent. It has no characteristics in common with the manna miraculously supplied to the Israelites while journeying through the wilderness. Wherever the manna is referred to in Scripture, it is invariably regarded as a miraculous food sent directly from God. The Lord Jesus accepted the manna as a type of himself—the living bread which came down from heaven. "For the bread of God is he which cometh down from heaven and giveth life unto the world." John 6:33, 48, 50. The phrase "hidden manna," Rev. 2:17, figuratively describes the spiritual food which Christ supplies to those who believe in him and live by faith in him.

Maon (mā'on). 1. Founder of Beth-zur, 1 Chron. 2:45. 2. One of the cities of Judah, in the mountains, Josh. 15:55, and a district where David hid from Saul, and near which Nabal had possessions. 1 Sam. 23:24, 25. The name of Maon still exists in Main, a lofty conical hill 100 feet high, about eight miles south from Hebron.

Marah (mā'rah), *bitterness*. A place in the wilderness of Shur or Etham, three days' journey, Num. 33:8, 9, from the place at which the Israelites crossed the Red Sea. There was at Marah a spring of bitter water, sweetened subsequently by the casting in of a tree which "the Lord showed" to Moses. Ex. 15:23, 24; Num. 33:8, 9. Probably 'Ain Hawarah, 47 miles from Ayun Mousa, where is a spring.

Maranatha (măr'a-năth'ah). An Aramaic expression signifying "Our Lord will come." 1 Cor. 16:22.

Mareshah (ma-rē'shah), *top of a hill*. A city of Judah in the low country. Josh. 15:44. It was fortified and garrisoned by Rehoboam after the rupture with the northern kingdom. 2 Chron. 11:8. Near it the great battle between Zerah and Asa was fought. 2 Chron. 14:9-12. It is mentioned once or twice in the history of the Maccabean struggles. 1 Macc. 5; 2 Macc. 12:35.

Mark (märk). John whose surname was Mark, Acts 12:12, was the son of Mary, a woman of piety who lived at Jerusalem. The disciples occasionally assembled at her house for prayer, and she was sister to Barnabas. Col. 4:10. He is also called Marcus. Peter styles Mark his son, 1 Pet. 5:13; meaning his spiritual son—that he was converted by that apostle. Mark left Jerusalem for Antioch with Paul and Barnabas, Acts 12:25, and accompanied them on their first missionary journey. He left them at Perga and returned to Jerusalem. This afterward led to a serious dispute between Paul and Barnabas. Acts 13:5, 13; 15:39. They therefore separated, Mark sailing with his uncle Barnabas to Cyprus. Acts 15:36-39. At a later period he was again with Paul during his first imprisonment at Rome, Col. 4:10, and he regained Paul's confidence. 2 Tim. 4:11. We find him also with Peter, 1 Pet. 5:13, with whom he is said to have travelled, and to have been his amanuensis. Nothing further of him is recorded in the Scripture; but we may identify him with the author of the second Gospel, and may readily believe ecclesiastical history which tells us that he was bishop of the church in Alexandria. Whether he died a natural death or by martyrdom is uncertain.

Mark, the Gospel of. The universal consent of the ancient church ascribed the second gospel to John Mark. It has also been said that he wrote under the superintendence of Peter. The arrangement of this gospel appears to be: 1. A short introduction noticing the mission of John Baptist. 1:1-8. 2. The public ministry of Christ, his discourses and actions in Galilee, prefaced by an account of his baptism. 1:9-9:50. 3. Our Lord's last journeyings toward Jerusalem, with the narrative of his passion, death, resurrection, and ascension. 10 to 16:20. It exhibits Christ as the spiritual conqueror and wonder-worker, the lion of the tribe of Judah, filling the people with amazement and fear. Mark introduces several Latin terms; he even substitutes Roman money for Greek, 12:42, which Luke does not, and notices that Simon of Cyrene was the father of Alexander and Rufus, 15:21, who probably were Christians in Rome. Rom. 16:13. It is, therefore, most likely that the Gospel was written in that city.

Market, or Market Place. In the Old Testament this word occurs only once. Ezek. 27:13, A. V.; in the New Testament oftener, Matt. 23:7; Mark 12:38; Luke 11:43; 20:46; Acts 16:19, etc., and we learn from Matt. 20:3 that not only were all kinds of produce offered for sale here, but hither resorted also the laborers to find employment. It was frequented by business men and by crowds of idlers and loungers. In a strictly Oriental city, such as Jerusalem, the market had not, like the forum, this character of being the centre of all public life. Still it was always a lively place, generally situated just within the gate, and the principal scene of trade and traffic.

Marriage. The institution of marriage dates from the time of man's original creation. Gen. 2:18-25. The marriage bond is not to be dissolved except on the strongest grounds. Comp. Matt. 19:9. On the relation of the wife to the husband, see 1 Cor. 11 : 8, 9; 1 Tim. 2 : 13. In the patriarchal age polygamy prevailed. Gen. 16 : 4; 25 : 1, 6; 28 : 9; 29 : 23, 28; 1 Chron. 7 : 14. Divorce also prevailed in the patriarchal age, though but one instance of it is recorded. Gen. 21 : 14. The Mosaic law discouraged polygamy, restricted divorce, and aimed to enforce purity of life. It was the best civil law possible at the time, and sought to bring the people up to the pure standard of the moral law. Our Lord and his apostles re-established the integrity and sanctity of marriage, Matt. 19 : 4, 5; 5 : 32; 19 : 9; Rom. 7 : 3; 1 Cor. 7 : 10, 11, and enforced moral purity, Heb. 13 : 4, etc., especially by the formal condemnation of fornication. Acts 15 : 20. In the Hebrew commonwealth an Israelite and a non-Israelite were not allowed to marry, except in a few special cases, and Israelites closely related could not marry. See Lev. 18 : 6-18, and for exceptions, Deut. 25 : 5-9. The law which regulates this exception has been named the "levirate" law, from the Latin *levir*, "brother-in-law." The choice of the bride devolved not on the bridegroom himself, but on his relations or on a friend deputed for this purpose. The consent of the maiden was sometimes asked, Gen. 24 : 58; but this appears to have been subordinate to the previous consent of the father and the adult brothers. Gen. 24 : 51; 34 : 11. The act of betrothal was celebrated by a feast, and among the more modern Jews it is the custom in some parts for the bridegroom to place a ring on the bride's finger. The ring was regarded among the Hebrews as a token of fidelity, Gen. 41 : 42, and of adoption into a family. Luke 15 : 22. During the interval between betrothal and marriage, the bride lived with her friends; her communications with her future husband were carried on through a friend deputed for the purpose, termed the "friend of the bridegroom." John 3 : 29. She was regarded as the wife of her future husband; hence faithlessness on her part was punishable with death, Deut. 22 : 23, 24, the husband having, however, the option of "putting her away." Deut. 24 : 1; Matt. 1 : 19. At the marriage ceremony the bride removed from her father's house to that of the bridegroom or his father. The bridegroom prepared himself for the occasion by putting on a festival dress, and especially by placing on his head a handsome nuptial turban. Ps. 45 : 8; Song of Sol. 4 : 10, 11. The bride was veiled. Her robes were white, Rev. 19 : 8, and sometimes embroidered with gold thread, Ps. 45 : 13, 14, and covered with perfumes, Ps. 45 : 8; she was further decked out with jewels. Isa. 49 : 18; 61 : 10; Rev. 21 : 2. When the fixed hour arrived, which was generally late in the evening, the bridegroom set forth from his house attended by his groomsmen (A. V. "companions," Judg. 14 : 11; "children of the bride-chamber," Matt. 9 : 15), preceded by a band of musicians or singers, Gen. 31 : 27; Jer. 7 : 34; 16 : 9, and accompanied by persons bearing flambeaux, Jer. 25 : 10; 2 Esdr. 10 : 2; Matt. 25 : 7; Rev. 18 : 23, and took the bride with the friends to his own house. At the house a feast was prepared, to which all the friends and neighbors were invited, Gen. 29 : 22; Matt. 22 : 1-10; Luke 14 : 8; John 2 : 2, and the festivities were protracted for seven or even fourteen days. Judg. 14 : 12; Tob. 8 : 19. The guests were sometimes furnished with fitting robes, Matt. 22 : 11, and the feast was enlivened with riddles, Judg. 14 : 12, and other amusements. The last act in the ceremonial was the conducting of the bride to the bridal chamber, Judg. 15 : 1; Joel 2 : 16, where a canopy was prepared. Ps. 19 : 5; Joel 2 : 16. The bride was still completely veiled, so that the deception practiced on Jacob, Gen. 29 : 23, was not difficult. A newly married man was exempt from military service, or from any public business which might draw him away from his home, for the space of a year, Deut. 24 : 5; a similar privilege was granted to him who was betrothed. Deut. 20 : 7.

The conditions of married life.—The wife appears to have taken her part in family affairs, and even to have enjoyed a considerable amount of independence. Judg. 4 : 18; 1 Sam. 25 : 14; 2 Kings 4 : 8, etc. In the New Testament the mutual relations of husband and wife are a subject of frequent exhortation. Eph. 5 : 22, 33; Col. 3 : 18, 19; Titus 2 : 4, 5; 1 Pet. 3 : 1-7. The duties of the wife in the Hebrew household were multifarious, Gen. 18 : 6; 2 Sam. 13 : 8, the distribution of food, Prov. 31 : 15, the manufacture of the clothing, Prov. 31 : 13, 21, 22; and the legal rights of the wife are noticed in Ex. 21 : 10, under the three heads of food, raiment, and duty of marriage or conjugal right. Marriage is used to illustrate the spiritual relationship between God and his people. Isa. 54 : 5; Jer. 3 : 14; Hos. 2 : 19. In the New Testament the image of the bridegroom is transferred from Jehovah to Christ, Matt. 9 : 15; John 3 : 29, and that of the bride to the church. 2 Cor. 11 : 2; Rev. 19 : 7; 21 : 2, 9. For full account, see Bissell's *Biblical Antiquities.*

Mars' Hill (*märz hĭll*), or **Areopagus** (*är'e-ŏp'a-gŭs* or *ā're-ŏp'a-gŭs*). Acts 17 : 19, 34. This was a rocky height in Athens, opposite the western end of the Acropolis. From this spot Paul delivered his address to the men of Athens. Acts 17 : 22-31. He also "disputed" in the "market," or *agora*, "daily," 17 : 17, which was south of the Areopagus, in the valley lying between this hill and those of the Acropolis, the Pnyx, and the Museum.

Martha (*mär'thah*), *bitterness.* One of the family at Bethany whom Jesus loved. Martha has been supposed the elder sister, as the house is called hers, and she undertook the special charge of entertaining the Lord. Luke 10 : 38-42. Some have imagined that she was the wife or widow of Simon the leper; which would account for the place where Mary anointed Christ being termed his house. Matt. 26 : 6, 7; Mark 14 : 3; John 12 : 1-3. Martha made a noble confession when she met the Saviour on his way to raise her brother Lazarus; though even her expectation reached not to the mighty work he was about to do. John 11:1-46. Nothing certain is known of her later history.

Mary (*mā'ry*). The name of several women in the New Testament. 1. The mother of our Lord. She was, like Joseph, of the tribe of Judah and of the lineage of David. Ps. 132:11; Luke 1:32; Rom. 1:3. She was connected by marriage, Luke 1:36, with Elisabeth, who was of the tribe of Levi and of the lineage of Aaron. She was betrothed to Joseph of Nazareth; but before her marriage she became with child by the Holy Ghost, and became the mother of Jesus Christ, the Saviour of the world. She was at Jerusalem with Joseph, at Cana and at Capernaum. John 2:12; Matt. 4:13; 13:54, 55; Mark 6:1-4. Lastly she was at the cross, and was there commended to the care of the disciple whom Jesus loved: "Woman, behold thy son." And from that hour John assures us that he took her to his own abode. In the days succeeding the ascension of Christ Mary met with the disciples in the upper room, Acts 1:14, waiting for the coming of the Holy Spirit with power. Such is all the authentic history we have of the "blessed among women," taught, as no other woman was, the hard lessons which were to guide her to her Son's eternal kingdom. Some of them were joyful; and some were very grievous; but she learned them thoroughly, till she loved the Lord Jesus as her Saviour far more than as her Son. 2. The wife of Cleophas, was present at the crucifixion and burial of our Lord, Matt. 27:56, 61, was among those who went to embalm him, Mark 16:1-10, was among the earliest to whom the news of his resurrection was announced, Luke 24:6, 10, and on her way to the disciples with the intelligence she met her risen Lord and worshipped him. Matt. 28:1, 9. 3. The mother of John Mark, Acts 12:12, and aunt to Barnabas, Col. 4:10, a godly woman residing at Jerusalem at whose house the disciples were convened the night Peter was miraculously delivered from prison. 4. The sister of Lazarus and Martha, and a devoted friend and disciple of our Saviour, from whom she received the testimony that she had chosen the good part which should not be taken from her. Luke 10:41, 42. Compared with her sister she appears of a more contemplative turn of mind and more occupied with the "one thing" needful. John 11:1; 12:2. 5. Mary Magdalene, or Mary of Magdala. Luke 8:2. The general impression that she was an unchaste woman is entirely without foundation. Having been cured of a demoniacal possession by our Saviour, she became his follower, Luke 8:2, 3, and showed her attachment to him to the last. She was at his crucifixion, John 19:25, and burial, Mark 15:47, and was among those who had prepared the materials to embalm him, Mark 16:1, and who first went to the sepulchre after the resurrection: and she was the first to whom the risen Redeemer appeared, Mark 16:9, and his conversation with her has an interest and pathos unsurpassed in history. John 20:11-18. 6. A Christian woman in Rome to whom Paul sends his salutation. Rom. 16:6.

Matthew (*măth'thu*). Derived from the same word as Matthias, Acts 1:23, 26 (*gift of God*), apostle, and author of the first gospel. His original name was Levi, Mark 2:14; Luke 5:27, 29, which, like that of Simon and of Saul, was changed on his being called to the apostleship. He first appears in the gospels as a publican or tax-gatherer near the Sea of Galilee, and the last mention of him is in the list of those who met in the upper room at Jerusalem after the ascension of our Lord. Acts 1:13. The tradition of his martyrdom in Ethiopia is not very trustworthy.

THE GOSPEL ACCORDING TO MATTHEW was probably written in Palestine, and for Jewish Christians. It was probably first composed in Hebrew—*i. e.*, Syro-Chaldaic, or Western Aramaic, the dialect spoken in Palestine by the Jewish Christians, and then later in Greek, as we now possess it. The date of its composition was clearly before the destruction of Jerusalem, Matt. 24, and yet some time after the crucifixion of Christ. Matt. 27:7, 8; 28:15. Some of the ancients give the eighth year after the ascension as the date, others the fifteenth. We would place it between 60 and 66 A. D.—a period during which both Mark and Luke probably wrote their gospels.

Matthias (*măth-thī'as* or *măt-thī'as*). A disciple of Christ, and witness of his ministry from the commencement, who was appointed by lot to supply the vacancy in the company of the twelve apostles occasioned by the apostacy of Judas. Acts 1:21-26. Of his after life and ministry nothing is known with certainty.

Mazzaroth (*măz'za-rŏth*), *the twelve signs*. The margin of the A. V. of Job 38:32 gives Mazzaroth as the name of the twelve signs of the zodiac.

Meals. The Hebrews took a light meal in the forenoon, consisting of bread, milk, cheese, etc. 1 Kings 20:16; Ruth 2:14; Luke 14:12. The dinner was at mid-day among the ancient Egyptians. Gen. 43:16. Supper, after the labors of the day were over, appears to have been the principal meal among the Hebrews, as it was among the Greeks and Romans. Mark 6:21; Luke 14:16, 24; John 12:2. In eating, knives and forks were not used, but each morsel of food was conveyed from the dish to the mouth by the hand. This mode of eating made it necessary to wash the hands before and after meals. Ruth 2:14; Prov. 26:15; John 13:26; Matt. 15:2, 20; Luke 11:38. In ancient times, at formal entertainments, every one seems to have had his separate portion of meat placed before him, Gen. 43:34; 1 Sam. 1:4, 5; 9:23, 24; in later times every one helped himself from the dish nearest to him. Matt. 26:23. The Orientals do not drink during meals, but afterwards water or wine is handed round. Matt. 26:27. The Hebrews seem to have had two modes of sitting: seldom used seats or chairs, like the ancient

Egyptians, but they sat on the floor, and the meal was laid on a cloth spread on the floor, or on a table raised only a few inches. During the captivity the Jews acquired the Persian practice of reclining at meals upon couches, or upon mats or cushions, around the tables, in such a way that the head of every person approached the bosom of the one who reclined next above him. John 13 : 23 ; Luke 7 : 38. In the time of Christ it was common before every meal to give thanks. Matt. 14 : 19 ; 15 : 36.

Measures and Weights. The following is condensed from *Schaff's Dictionary:* The Jewish law contains two precepts respecting weights and measures. The first, Lev. 19 : 35, 36, refers to the standards kept in the sanctuary, and the second, Deut. 25 : 13-15, to copies of them kept by every family for its own use. The standards of the weights and measures preserved in the temple were destroyed with the sacred edifice, and afterward the measures and weights of the people among whom the Jews dwelt were adopted; which, of course, adds to the perplexities of the subject.

I. *Measures of Length.* — The Hebrews, like all other ancient nations, took the standard of their measures of length from the human body. They made use, however, only of the finger, the hand, and the arm, not of the foot or the pace. The handbreadth or palm, 1 Kings 7 : 26, was four digits, or the breadth of the four fingers—from three to three and a half inches. A span, Lam. 2 : 20 A. V., but the R. V. reads, "the children that are dandled in the hands," which expresses the distance across the hand from the extremity of the thumb to the extremity of the little finger, when they are stretched as far apart as possible, say nine to ten inches. A cubit, the distance from the elbow to the extremity of the middle finger, or about eighteen inches. The different expressions used in the Old Testament about this measure—such as "after the cubit of a man," Deut. 3 : 11; "after the first measure," 2 Chron. 3 : 3 ; "a great cubit," Ezek. 41 : 8—show that it varied. A fathom, Acts 27 : 28, was from six to six and a half feet. The measuring-reed, Ezek. 42 : 16, comprised six cubits, or from ten to eleven feet, and the measuring-line, Zech. 2 : 1, a hundred and forty-six feet. The furlong, Luke 24 : 13, was a Greek measure, and nearly the same as at present—viz., one-eighth of a mile, or forty rods. The mile, mentioned only once, Matt. 5 : 41, belonged to the Roman system of measurement, as stadium to the Greek. The Roman mile was 1612 yards. The Jewish mile was longer or shorter, in accordance with the longer or shorter pace in use in the various parts of the country. The Sabbath day's journey, Acts 1 : 12, was about seven-eighths of a mile, and the term denoted the distance which Jewish tradition said one might travel without a violation of the law. Ex. 16 : 29. The term, a day's journey, Num. 11 : 31 ; Luke 2 : 44, probably indicated no certain distance, but was taken to be the ordinary distance which a person in the East travels on foot, or on horseback or camel, in the prosecution of a journey—about 20 miles.

II. *Measures of Capacity.*—1. Dry. A cab or kab (hollow), 2 Kings 6 : 25, one-third of an omer, or two pints. An omer (heap, sheaf), Ex. 16 : 36, one-tenth of an ephah, or six pints. The seah (measure), Gen. 18 : 6 ; Matt. 13 : 33; Luke 13 : 21, one-third of an ephah, or 20 pints, was the ordinary measure for household purposes. The ephah—a word of Egyptian origin, but often occurring in the Old Testament, Ex. 16 : 36; Lev. 5 : 11; Num. 5 : 15; Judg. 6 : 19, etc.—ten omers, or three seahs, or 60 pints. The homer (heap), Isa. 5 : 10, when used for dry measure, 100 omers, or 600 pints. The Greek word translated "bushel," Matt. 5 : 15, is supposed by some to answer to the Hebrew word seah. The Roman bushel was very nearly the same with the English peck. 2. Liquid. The log (basin), Lev. 14 : 10, six egg-shells full, one-tenth of a hin, or nearly one pint. The hin—a word of Egyptian origin, but often used in the Old Testament, Ex. 29 : 40 ; 30 : 24; Num. 15 : 4, etc.—one-sixth of a bath or ten pints. The bath (measured), the largest of the liquid measures, contained one-tenth of a homer, seven and a half gallons, or 60 pints. 1 Kings 7 : 26 ; 2 Chron. 2 : 10; Isa. 5 : 10. The firkin, John 2 : 6, was a Greek measure, containing seven and a half gallons.

III. *Weights.*—In the time of Moses the common weight was a shekel, which signifies a "weight." There were also the parts of a shekel, as the fourth, third, and half. The shekel, the maneh, and the talent, were all originally names of weights. When the phrase "shekel of the sanctuary" is used, Ex. 30 : 13, it means, not that this was different from the common shekel, but that it was a true standard weight, according to the authorized standard preserved in the sanctuary, or, as we should say, a sealed weight or measure, to denote that its accuracy is certified by authority. To weigh substances the Jews had : the shekel, Amos 8 : 5, half an ounce avoirdupois. The minch or "manch," A. V., Ezek. 45 : 12, 100 shekels or 50 ounces, equal to three pounds two ounces avoirdupois. The talent, 2 Sam. 12 : 30, 3000 shekels, 30 maneh, 1500 ounces, equal to 93 pounds 12 ounces avoirdupois. See **Money.**

Meat, Meats. This word as it occurs in our version is frequently used for food in general, Lev. 22 : 11, 13, R. V., "bread;" 1 Sam. 20 : 5, 34 ; 2 Sam. 3 : 35, R. V., "bread," and elsewhere, or for what is allowed to be eaten, proper for sustenance, Gen. 1 : 29, 30, and 9 : 3, where the R. V. reads "food." More specially, though perhaps sometimes indicating, as in our ordinary employment of the term, flesh-meat, Gen. 27 : 4, 7, 31, it is almost exclusively applied to vegetables or vegetable products. Thus a meat-offering, R. V. "meal-offering," was a kind of cake made of flour and oil. Lev. 2.

Meat-offering. R. V. "meal-offering." Lev. 2 and 6 : 14-23. David gives its meaning. 1 Chron. 29 : 10-21. It was a meal-offering. This involves neither of the main ideas of sacrifice—the atonement for sin and self-dedication to God. It takes them for granted, and is based on them. Rather it expresses gratitude and love to God as the giver of all. Accordingly the meal-offering, properly so called, was introduced by the sin-offering, which represented the idea atonement, and to have formed an appendage to the burnt-offering, which represented the sacrifice. The unbloody offerings offered alone did not properly belong to the regular meal-offering; they were usually substitutes for other offerings. Comp. Lev. 5:11; Num. 5:15.

Medeba (*mĕd'e-bah*), *waters of quiet*. A city of Moab, first mentioned with Heshbon and Dibon. Num. 21:30. It was afterward taken by the Israelites and allotted to the tribe of Reuben, Josh. 13:16; held by the Ammonites during the reign of David, 1 Chron. 19:7-15, it later again reverted to Moab. Isa. 15:2. After the return from the captivity it was alternately in the possession of the Jews and of the Gentiles.

Medes and **Media** (*mē'di-ah*), *name*. The same as Madai, "middle land," one of Japheth's sons. Gen. 10:2. The Hebrew word thus translated "Madai" is also rendered "Medes," 2 Kings 17:6, etc., and "Media," Esth. 1:3, etc., and also "Mede." Dan. 11:1. In the period of which Herodotus writes the people of Media were called Aryans. Its greatest length from north to south was 550 miles, its average breadth 250 to 300 miles, and its area 150,000 square miles. Media was divided originally into six provinces, which in Greek and Roman times were reduced to two. The early history of the Medes is very obscure. Their origin is given in Gen. 10:2, and they were connected with the captivity of Israel. 2 Kings 17:6; 18:11. Isaiah, in his prophecy against Babylon, reveals the agency and character of the Medes. Isa. 13:17, 18; 21:2. But Media was not incorporated with Assyria, although Sargon, and afterward Sennacherib, subdued its people and exacted tribute. In B.C. 633 an independent kingdom was set up by Cyaxares, who in B.C. 625 took a leading part in the destruction of Nineveh. Media then became a great and powerful monarchy, comprising, besides Media proper, Persia, Assyria, Armenia, and other adjoining countries. The empire was 1500 miles long, 450 miles wide, and had an area of 600,000 square miles. Under Cyrus the two kingdoms of Babylonia and Media were united, B.C. 538. There are references in Scripture to this kingdom under the title of the "Medes and Persians." Dan. 5:28; 6:8, 12, 15; comp. Esth 1:19. The only city in Media alluded to in Scriptures is Achmetha, or Ecbatana. Ezra 6:2. This region was absorbed in the Macedonian empire of Alexander the Great. Later an independent Median kingdom held sway until the Christian era, after which it became a part of the Parthian empire. Medes are mentioned in connection with Parthians, etc., in the New Testament. Acts 2:9.

Mediator. One who interposes between two parties in order to bring them to agreement, or to a common purpose. Gal. 3:20. Moses so interposed between God and Israel. Exod. 20:19; Deut. 5:5; Gal. 3:19. But the Lord Jesus Christ is the only mediator in the highest sense between God and man; so that we find this special designation given him. 1 Tim. 2:5; Heb. 8:6; 9:15; 12:24. See **Jesus Christ.**

Megiddo (*me-gĭd'do*), *place of crowds*. Josh. 12:21. A city of one of the kings whom Joshua defeated on the west of the Jordan, in the great plain of Esdraelon. The song of Deborah notes the place as the scene of the great conflict between Sisera and Barak. Judg. 4:6-17. When Pharaoh-necho came from Egypt against the king of Assyria, Josiah joined the latter, and was slain at Megiddo. 2 Kings 23:29; 2 Chron. 35:22-24. Megiddo is the modern *el-Lejjûn*, which is probably the Legio of Eusebius and Jerome. A stream flows down the gorge, and joins the Kishon. Here are probably the "waters of Megiddo" of Judges 5:19.

Melchizedek, or **Melchisedec** (*mel-kĭz'-e-dĕk*), the Greek form in the New Testament (*king of righteousness*), is mentioned in Gen. 14:18-20 as king of Salem and priest of the Most High God, meeting Abram in the valley of Shaveh, bringing out bread and wine to him, blessing him, and receiving tithes from him; in Ps. 110:4, where Messiah is described as a priest "after the order of Melchizedek;" and finally, in Heb. 5:6, 7, where the typical relations between Melchizedek and Christ are defined, both being priests without belonging to the Levitical tribe, superior to Abram, of unknown beginning and end, and kings of righteousness and peace. The short but impressive account of Melchizedek in Genesis, and the striking though mystical applications made in the Psalms and the Epistle to the Hebrews, have given rise to various interpretations. One Jewish tradition considers him to be a survivor of the Deluge, the patriarch Shem, and thus entitled by his very age to bless the father of the faithful, and by his position as ruler of Canaan to confer his rights to Abram. Another tradition, equally old, but not so widely accepted, considers him to be an angel, the Son of God in human form, the Messiah. Modern scholars, arguing back from the expositions given in the Epistle to the Hebrews, consider him to be a descendant of Ham, a priest among the heathen, constituted by God himself, and given a title above that of the ordinary patriarchal priesthood, even above that of Abram.

Melita (*mĕl'i-tah*), *honey*, modern *Malta*. A small island in the Mediterranean Sea, 60 miles south of Sicily. It is 17 miles long by 9 or 10 broad. This island is noted in Scripture as the scene of the shipwreck of Paul. Acts 27. The wreck probably happened at the place known as St. Paul's Bay, an inlet with a creek two miles deep and one broad. Its chief officer (under the Roman governor of Sicily) appears from inscriptions to have had the precise title which Luke uses. Acts 28:7.

Melons. Num. 11:5. Melons of all kinds have ever been largely cultivated in Egypt, and in summer often form the chief food and drink of the lower classes.

Memphis (*Měm'phis*), in Hebrew *Noph, place of Phtah*. An ancient royal city of lower Egypt. From the ancient hieroglyphic name *Ma-m-Phtah* came the Hebrew "Moph," Hos. 9:6, and "Noph," and the Greek form "Memphis." Isa. 19:13; Jer. 2:16; 44:1; Ezek. 30:13,16. Memphis is said to have been about 19 miles in circumference. Its overthrow was distinctly predicted by the Hebrew prophets; Isa. 19:13; Jer. 46:19; and it never recovered from the blow inflicted upon it by Cambyses, 525 B.C. After the founding of Alexandria, Memphis rapidly fell into decay. It is now marked by mounds of rubbish, a colossal statue sunk deep in the ground, and a few fragments of granite.

Menahem (*měn'a-hěm*), *consoler*. A king of Samaria. His reign, which lasted ten years, B.C. 771-760, was distinguished for cruelty and oppression. 2 Kings 15:14-20.

Mene (*me'ne*), **Tekel, Upharsin.** This sentence, which appeared on the wall of Belshazzar's banqueting-hall to warn him of the impending destruction of Babylon, is in the Chaldee language. Translated literally, *Mene*, "he is numbered;" *Mene*, "he is numbered;" *Tekel*, "he is weighed;" *Upharsin*, "they are divided." "Peres," in the original language, is the same word with "Upharsin," but in a different case or number. It means "he was divided." Dan. 5:25.

Mephibosheth (*me-phĭb'o-shĕth*), *end of shame* or *abasement*. 1. The son of Jonathan and grandson of Saul, 2 Sam. 4:4; also called "Meribbaal"—*contender against Baal*. 1 Chron. 8:34; 9:40. He was only about five years of age when his father was slain, and on the news of this catastrophe the nurse who had charge of him, apprehending that the whole house of Saul would be exterminated, fled away with him; but in her flight stumbled with the child, and lamed him for life. David made provision for Mephibosheth and his family. 2 Sam. 9:9-13; 16:1-4; 19:24-30. 2. A son of Saul by his concubine Rizpah. 2 Sam. 21:8.

Merab (*mē'răb*), *increase*. The eldest daughter of Saul, 1 Sam. 14:49, promised to David, but given to Adriel in marriage. 1 Sam. 18:17, 19.

Mercurius (*mer-kū'ri-ŭs*), identical with the Greek Hermes (*the speaker*). One of the heathen deities fabled to be the son of Jupiter and Maia. He was supposed to preside over eloquence and merchandise, and to be the messenger of the gods. Barnabas and Paul were taken by the people at Lystra for Jupiter and Mercury. Acts 14:11-13. Ovid has a story of these two deities wandering in the adjacent country of Phrygia.

Mercy-seat was the name of the lid or cover of the ark of the covenant. It was made of gold, two and a half cubits long and one and a half cubits broad, and two cherubs, also of gold, were placed one at each end, stretching their wings toward each other, and forming a kind of throne, upon which God was believed to be present in a peculiar manner to hear and answer prayer, and to make known his holy will. Ex. 25:17-22; 30:6; 31:7; 37:6-9; 1 Chron. 28:11; 2 Chron. 5:7, 8; Ps. 80:1; 99:1. Before and upon the mercy-seat the high priest sprinkled the blood of the sin-offerings on the day of atonement as a propitiation, Lev. 16:11-16, which, under the new dispensation, received its fulfillment. Heb. 9:5; Rom. 3:25.

Meribah (*mer'i-bah*), *quarrel, strife*. 1. The fountain near Rephidim which Moses smote by the divine command; also called "Massah" ("temptation, trial"). Ex. 17:1-7; Deut. 6:16; 9:22. 2. Another fountain, produced in the same manner and under similar circumstances as the preceding, near Kadesh, in the desert of Zin; also called waters of Meribah and Meribah Kadesh. Deut. 33:8; Ps. 95:8; 106:32. This miracle occurred near the close of the wanderings of the Hebrews in the desert. Num. 20:1-24; 27:14; Deut. 32:51; Ps. 81:7; Ezek. 47:19. Some erroneously regard the two as identical, but this view is inconsistent with the scriptural narrative. See **Kadesh**.

Merodach (*me-rō'dak*, or *měr'o-dak*), *death*, Jer. 50:2, identical with the Babylonian Bel or Belus, the term being probably at first a mere epithet of the god.

Merodach-baladan (*me-rō'dak-băl'a-dăn*), *worshipper of Baal*. King of Babylon. 2 Kings 20:12; Isa. 39:1. In the former passage he is called Berodach-baladan. The name Merodach-baladan has been found in the Assyrian inscriptions. It appears there were two reigns of this king, the first from B.C. 721 to B.C. 709, when he was deposed; and the second after his recovery of the throne in B.C. 702, which lasted only half a year. He sent ambassadors to Hezekiah, 2 Chron. 32:31, about B.C. 713.

Merom, Waters of (*mē'rom*), *waters of the high place*. A lake in northern Palestine, where Joshua won a victory. Josh. 11:5, 7. It is usually identified with the modern el-Huleh of the Arabs. Lake Huleh is eleven miles north of the Sea of Galilee.

Meroz (*mē'rŏz*), *refuge*. A place in the northern part of Palestine, the inhabitants of which were accursed for not having taken the field with Barak against Sisera. Judg. 5:23.

Mesech (*mē'sĕck*), Ps. 120:5, or **Meshech** (*mē'shek*), Ezek. 32:26, a son of Japheth, whose descendants are supposed to have settled in Armenia. They had considerable commerce with Tyre. Ezek. 27:13. Some suppose the Muscovites were of this race.

Mesha (*mē'shah*), *deliverance*. 1. A king of Moab who refused to pay tribute to Jehoram, king of Israel. Jehoram determined to punish him; but Mesha made the horrible sacrifice of his eldest son to some idol god, openly upon the wall, in sight of the Israelites, who fearing that they might incur the anger of God by having given occasion to a human sacrifice, retreated to their own country. 2 Kings 3:4-27. A most wonderful corroboration of the Scripture history is found in the famous Moabite stone. See **Dibon**. 2. A son of Caleb, and brother of Mareshah. 1 Chron. 2:42. 3. A Benjamite, son of Shaharaim. 1 Chron. 8:9.

Mesopotamia (*mĕs-o-po-tā'mi-ah*), *the region between the rivers*. The name given by the Greeks and Romans to that tract of fertile country lying between the rivers Euphrates and Tigris. Acts 2:9; 7:2. It was called by the Hebrews Aram-naharaim, or "Aram (or Syria) of the two rivers;" Gen. 24:10; Deut. 23:4; Judg. 3:8,10; 1 Chron. 19:6; and Padan-aram or "Plain of Syria," Gen. 25:20; 28:2-7; 46:15; also Aram or "Syria," Num. 23:7; Gen. 31:20, 24. The great plains of Mesopotamia possess a nearly uniform, level, good soil, but barren from want of irrigation. Mesopotamia was the country of Nahor, R. V., "city of Nahor." Gen. 24:10. Here lived Bethuel and Laban, and hither Abraham sent his servant to fetch Isaac a wife. Gen. 5:38. A century later Jacob came on the same errand, and hence he returned with his two wives after an absence of 21 years. Mesopotamia again occurs at the close of the wanderings in the wilderness. Deut. 23:4. About a half century later, Mesopotamia appears as the seat of a powerful monarchy. Judg. 3. The children of Ammon, having provoked a war with David, "sent a thousand talents of silver to hire them chariots and horsemen out of Mesopotamia, and out of Syria-maachah, and out of Zobah." 1 Chron. 19:6. Assyrian inscriptions and the Scripture record show that Mesopotamia was inhabited in the early times of the empire, B. C. 1200-1100, by a vast number of petty tribes, each under its own prince, and all quite independent of each other, Judg. 3:8-10; 2 Kings 19:12, 13; Isa. 37:12, until subjugated by the kings of Assyria. Mesopotamia became an Assyrian province. The conquests of Cyrus brought it wholly under the Persian yoke, and thus it continued to the time of Alexander. The whole region is studded with mounds and ruins of Assyrian and Babylonian greatness. See **Assyria**.

Messiah (*mes-sī'ah*). This is a Hebrew word signifying "anointed," and corresponding exactly to the Greek *Christos*. As in ancient times not only the king, but also the priest and the prophet, was consecrated to his calling by being anointed, the word "Messiah" often occurs in the Old Testament in its literal sense, signifying one who has been anointed, 1 Sam. 24:6; Lam. 4:20; Ezek. 28:14; Ps. 105:15; but generally it has a more specific application, signifying the One who was anointed, the supreme Deliverer who was promised from the beginning, Gen. 3:15, and about whom a long series of prophecies runs through the whole history of Israel from Abram, Gen. 12:3; 22:18; Jacob, Gen. 49:10; Balaam. Num. 24:17; Moses, Deut. 18:15, 18; and Nathan. 2 Sam. 7:16; through the psalmists and prophets, Ps. 2:16; 22:40; 45:110; Isa. 7:10-16; 9:1-7; 11; 13; 53; 61; Jer. 23:5,6; Micah 5: 2; Mal. 3:1-4, to his immediate precursor, John the Baptist. The character of these prophecies is very definite. The lineage from which Messiah should descend was foretold, Gen. 49:10; Isa. 11:1, the place in which he should be born, Micah 5:2, the time of his appearance, Dan. 9:20, 25; Hag. 2:7; Mal. 3:1, etc. Nevertheless, in the vanity of their hearts, the Jews mistook the true meaning of these prophecies. They expected a triumphant worldly king, according to Ps. 2; Jer. 23:5,6; Zech. 9:9, and that his triumph was to be accomplished by sufferings and death they did not understand. See **Jesus Christ**.

Methuselah (*me-thū'se-lah*), *man of dart*, or *he dies and it is sent*—namely, the flood. The son of Enoch, and, according to Hebrew chronology, 969 years old when he died, in the first year of the flood. The longest-lived man was the son of the saintliest of his time. Gen. 5:27; 1 Chron. 1:3. He lived 243 years with Adam and 600 years with Noah. The history of the fall and of the world before the flood was carried thus through only one person to Noah.

Micah (*mī'kah*), *who is like Jehovah?* 1. An idolater in Mount Ephraim. Judg. 17:18. 2. The sixth of the minor prophets, is called the Morashite, from his birthplace Moresheh, in the territory of Guth, westward from Jerusalem. He prophesied during the reigns of Jotham, Ahaz, and Hezekiah, kings of Judah, B. C. 750-698, and was a contemporary of Isaiah, whom he often resembles in style and expressions. Compare, for instance, Isa. 2:2 with Micah 4:1, or Isa. 41:15 with Micah 4:13.

THE BOOK OF MICAH contains prophecies concerning Samaria and Jerusalem. In his prophecies concerning Messiah he is very precise. The prediction that Christ should be born in Bethlehem belongs to him. 5:2. His style is poetic throughout, pure, rich in images and plays upon words, bold and lofty, but sometimes abrupt and obscure. There are seven persons of this name mentioned in the Bible.

Micaiah (*mī-kā'yah*). The son of Imlah. A faithful prophet who predicted in vain to Ahab the fatal termination of his expedition against Ramoth-gilead. 1 Kings 22:8-28; 2 Chron. 18:7-27. He delivered his warning in the form of a remarkable vision, in which the weighty lesson is conveyed that God blinds judicially those who have shut their eyes and ears to his monitions, letting them be deceived by lying spirits.

Michael (*mī'ka-el* or *mī'kel*), *who as God?* 1. A chief angel, who is represented as the patron of the Hebrews before God. Dan. 12:1. In Jude 9 Michael is represented "as contending with Satan about the body of Moses." So again in Rev. 12:5, 7, 9, the symbolic scenery which represents the malignity of Satan towards the "man-child"—Christianity—the child of Judaism, caught up to the throne of God, i. e., placed under the divine protection, and invested with sovereign power—Michael and his angels are represented as waging war with Satan and his angels in the upper regions; from

MICHAL OF THE BIBLE. MILLO

which the latter are cast down upon the earth. There are ten persons of this name mentioned in the Bible.

Michal (*mi'kal*). The second daughter of Saul, 1 Sam. 14:49, and the wife of David. During David's exile she was married to another, Phalti, or Palti, 1 Sam. 25:44; 2 Sam. 3:15, with whom she lived for ten years. After the accession of David to the throne she was restored to him, 2 Sam. 3:13, 14; but an estrangement soon took place between them, and on the occasion of one of the greatest triumphs of David's life—the bringing up of the ark to Jerusalem—it came to an open rupture between them, after which her name does not again occur. 2 Sam. 6:23.

Michmas (*mik'mas*), or **Michmash** (*mik'mash*), *something hidden*. A town of Benjamin noted in the Philistine war of Saul and Jonathan. 1 Sam. 13:11. Isaiah refers to it in connection with the invasion of Sennacherib in the reign of Hezekiah. Isa. 10:28. After the captivity it was repeopled. Ezra 2:27; Neh. 7:31. Later it became the residence of Jonathan Maccabæus and the seat of his government. 1 Macc. 9:73. Michmash is identified with the modern village of Mukmas, about five miles north of Jerusalem, where are considerable ruins of columns, cisterns, etc. In plain view, about a mile away, is the ancient Geba or Gibeah, where Saul was encamped. 1 Sam. 13:16.

Midian (*mid'i-an*), *strife*. The territory of Midian extended, according to some scholars, from the Elanitic Gulf to Moab and Mount Sinai; or, according to others, from the Sinaitic peninsula to the desert and the banks of the Euphrates. The people traded with Palestine, Lebanon, and Egypt. Gen. 37:28. Joseph was probably bought by them, perhaps in company with Ishmaelites. See Gen. 37:25, 27, 28, 36, and Gen. 25:2, 4, 12, 16. Moses dwelt in Midian. Ex. 2:15-21; Num. 10:29. Midian joined Moab against Israel and enticed that nation into sin, for which it was destroyed. Num. chaps. 22, 24, 25. Later, Midian recovered, became a powerful nation, and oppressed the Hebrews, but were miraculously defeated by Gideon. Judg. 6; 7; 8:1-28; Ps. 83:9, 11; Isa. 9:4; Hab. 3:7. The Midianites henceforward became gradually incorporated with the neighboring Moabites and Arabians. In the region east of Edom and Moab are many ancient ruins, and portions of the territory are of great fertility, producing bountiful crops for the modern Arabs—the tribe of Beni Sakk'r, which bears considerable resemblance in race, character, and habits to what is known of the ancient Midianites. "Curtains of Midian," Hab. 3:7, is a figurative expression denoting the borders or inhabitants of Midian.

Migdol (*mig'dol*), *tower*. 1. A place near the head of the Red Sea. Ex. 14:2; Num. 33:7,8. 2. A fortified city in the northern limits of Egypt toward Palestine. Jer. 44:1; 46:14. This name is rendered "tower" in the phrase "from the tower of Syene," R.V. reads "Seveneh," Ezek. 29:10; 30:6; but the margin correctly has "from Migdol to Syene"—*i. e.*, Syene the most southern border of Egypt, and Migdol the most northern.

Migron (*mig'ron*), *precipice*. A place near Gibeah. 1 Sam. 14:2. Migron is also mentioned in Sennacherib's approach to Jerusalem. Isa. 10:28. It was near Michmash.

Mile, the Roman, equal to 1618 English yards—4854 feet, or about nine-tenths of an English mile. It is only once noticed in the Bible. Matt. 5:41.

Miletus (*mi-lē'tus*), Acts 20:15, 17, less correctly called Miletum in 2 Tim. 4:20, A.V. It was on the coast, 36 miles to the south of Ephesus. Acts 20:15. The site of Miletus has now receded ten miles from the coast, and even in the apostles' time it must have lost its strictly maritime position. Miletus was far more famous 500 years before Paul's day than it ever became afterward. Now the small Turkish village *Melas* is near the site of the ancient city.

Mill. Matt. 24:41. The Jewish handmill consisted of two circular stones, each about 18 inches or two feet in diameter, the lower of which is fixed, and has its upper surface slightly convex, fitting into a corresponding concavity in the upper stone. In the latter is a hole through which the grain passes, immediately above a pivot or shaft which rises from the centre of the lower stone, and about which the upper stone is turned by means of an upright handle fixed near the edge. It is worked by women, sometimes singly and sometimes two together, who are usually seated on the bare ground, Isa. 47:1, 2, facing each other; both have hold of the handle by which the upper is turned round on the "nether" millstone. The one whose right hand is disengaged throws in the grain as occasion requires through the hole in the upper stone. It is not correct to say that one pushes it half round and then the other seizes the handle. This would be slow work, and would give a spasmodic motion to the stone. Both retain their hold; and pull *to* or push *from*, as men do with the whip or cross-cut saw. The proverb of our Saviour, Matt. 24:41, is true to life, for *women* only grind. So essential were millstones for daily domestic use that they were forbidden to be taken in pledge. Deut. 24:6. There were also larger mills driven by cattle or asses. Matt. 18:6. With the movable upper millstone of the hand-mill the woman of Thebez broke Abimelech's skull. Judg. 9:53.

Millet, the grain of the cultivated panicgrass (*Panicum miliaceum*), or of du-rah (variously spelled, but thus pronounced). Ezek. 4:9. Durah or Egyptian corn (*Sorghum vulgare*) resembles maize in size and general appearance, and is largely cultivated upon the Nile.

Millo (*mil'lo*), *a mound, rampart*. "Millo" is used for a part of the citadel of Jerusalem, probably the rampart, or entrenchment. 2 Sam. 5:9; 1 Kings 9:15-24; 11:27; 1 Chron. 11:8. The same, or part of it, was probably the "house of Millo;" margin

"Beth Millo." 2 Kings 12:20; 2 Chron. 32:5. Some think it means the "stronghold of Zion."

Mint. Matt. 23:23; Luke 11:42. A well-known herb, much used in domestic economy. The Jews are said to have scattered it, on account of its pleasant smell, on the floors of their houses and synagogues. The species most common in Syria is the *Mentha sylvestris*, horse-mint.

Miracle, in the A. V., represents three Greek words: 1. *Semeion*, sign, by which a divine power is made known and a divine messenger attested. Matt. 12:38, 39; 16:1, 6; Mark 8:11; Luke 11:16; 23:8; John 2:11, 18, 23, etc.; Acts 6:8; 1 Cor. 1:22. 2. *Teras*, wonder or portent, with regard to their astounding character. John 4:48; Acts 2:22, 43; 7:36; Rom. 15:19; usually in connection with "signs." 3. *Dunamis*, power or powers, mighty deeds, with reference to their effect. Matt. 7:22; 11:20, 21, 23; Luke 10:13; Rom. 15:19. A miracle is not, philosophically speaking, a violation of the ordinary laws of nature, nor does it necessarily require a suspension of those laws, as some have imagined; but is either a manifestation of divine power, superior to natural causes, or an increase of the action of some existing law, accomplishing a new result. Such were the miracles which God wrought by the prophets; and those wrought by Christ and by the apostles and disciples in his name. Though miracles are supernatural facts, in one sense they are also natural facts. They belong to a superior order of things, to a superior world; and they are perfectly conformed with the supreme law which governs them. They belong to the vast plan of Jehovah, which contains at once both the natural course of events and these supernatural manifestations. And when, on remarkable occasions, his plans and purposes have required preternatural interposition of his power, it has always been exerted; but, with the unusual occasion, the unusual agency has ceased, and the extraordinary result has no longer occurred. Such interferences are not required in the established course and usual sequences of nature. The miracles of Christ as reported in the gospels present many noticeable features. They were numerous; a multitude more having been performed than are described in detail. John 20:30; 21:25. They exhibit great variety: they were wrought almost always instantaneously, by a word of power, without the use of auxiliary means, sometimes taking their effect at a distance from the place in which Christ personally was. They were permanent in their results, were subjected at the time to keen investigation, and convinced a hostile people of the truth of them, to such an extent that, though there were persons who concealed or resisted their convictions, very many in consequence attached themselves, to the great detriment of their worldly interests, in several cases with the sacrifice of their lives, to the person and doctrine of this extraordinary Teacher. They were miracles, too, of mercy, intended to relieve human suffering, and to promote the well-being of those on whom or for whom they were wrought. And the power of working miracles was conveyed by our Lord to his followers, was repeatedly exercised by them, and was continued for a while in the church. Acts 19:11; 1 Cor. 12:10, 28, 29. For list of miracles in the Bible, see Appendix.

Miriam (*mir'i-am*), *rebellion*. 1. The daughter of Amram and the sister of Moses and Aaron, 1 Chron. 6:3, appointed to watch the ark of bulrushes in which her infant brother was laid among the flags of the river. She was there when Pharaoh's daughter came down and discovered it, and proposed to go for a nurse. She immediately called her mother as the nurse, and the infant was placed under her care. Ex. 2:4-10. After the passage of the Red Sea, she led the choir of the women of Israel in the sublime song of deliverance, Ex. 15:20, but afterward, having joined Aaron in murmuring against Moses, she was smitten with leprosy, and restored only in answer to the prayers of Moses. Num. 12:1-15. She died and was buried at Kadesh. Num. 20:1. 2. A descendant of Judah. 1 Chron. 4:17.

Mite. A coin of Palestine in the time of our Lord. Mark 12:41-44; Luke 21:1-4. It was the smallest piece of money and worth about one-fifth of a cent—two mites making a farthing. See Farthing.

Mitre. The head-dress of the Jewish priest. It was of fine flax or linen, made with many folds, making in length eight yards, and wreathed round the head in the shape of an Eastern turban. It bore upon its front a gold plate, on which was inscribed: "Holiness to the Lord." Ex. 28:4, 37, 39; 29:6; 39:28, 30; Lev. 8:9; 16:4.

Mitylene (*mit-y-lē'ne*), *hornless*. The chief town and capital of the isle of Lesbos. Acts 20:14, 15. In Paul's day it had the privileges of a free city.

Mizpah (*miz'pah*) and **Mizpeh** (*miz'peh*), *watch-tower*. The name of several places in Palestine. 1. On Mount Gilead, also called Mizpeh of Gilead, Judg. 11:29, and elsewhere, probably Ramoth-mizpeh, Josh. 13:26, and Ramoth-gilead, 1 Kings 4:13, and elsewhere, the place where Laban and Jacob set up a heap of stones as a witness and landmark between them. Gen. 31:23, 25, 48, 52. Here, also, the Israelites assembled to fight against the Ammonites, Judg. 10:17; and here Jephthah was met by his daughter. Judg. 11:29. Some suppose that this was the place also where the tribes assembled to avenge the great sin committed in Benjamin, Judg. 20:1, 3; 21:1, 5, 8; but this is more usually applied to the Mizpah in Benjamin. See No. 6. This Mizpah has been identified, with great probability, with Kulat er Rubad on the Wady 'Ajlûn, about ten miles east of the Jordan. The summit commands a wide view, and is in harmony with the name Mizpeh, or "watch-tower." 2. Mizpeh of Moab, where the king of that nation was living when David committed his parents to his care, 1 Sam. 22:3; possibly now Kerak. 3. The land of Mizpeh, in the north of Palestine, the residence of the Hivites, Josh. 11:3; possibly identical with—4. The valley of Mizpeh, Josh. 11:3, 8, whither the confederate hosts were pursued by Joshua; perhaps the modern Buka'a, the great country of Cœle-Syria, between Lebanon and Anti-Lebanon. 5. A city in Judah, Josh. 15:38; possibly identical with the modern Tell es-Sâfiyeh. This others have identified with Misrephothmaim. Josh. 11:8. 6. A city in Benjamin, Josh. 18:26, where Israel assembled. 1 Sam. 7:5-7, 11, 12, 16. Here Saul was elected king. 1 Sam. 10:17-21. Asa fortified Mizpah, 1 Kings 15:22; 2 Chron. 16:6; it was where Gedaliah was assassinated, 2 Kings 25:23, 25; Jer. 40:6-15; 41:1-16; the men of Mizpah joined in rebuilding a par of the wall of Jerusalem. Neh. 3:7, 15, 19. Probably identical with Neby Samwil, standing on a peak about four miles northwest of Jerusalem. Whether the Mizpah of Hosea, 5:1, was in Benjamin or in Gilead is uncertain.

Mizraim (miz'rā-im or miz-rā'im), *limits, borders*. The name by which the Hebrews generally designated Egypt, apparently from Mizraim, the son of Ham. Gen. 10:6, 13. Called in English versions Egypt. Gen. 45:20; 46:34; 47:6, 13. Sometimes it seems to be employed to designate *lower* Egypt, to the exclusion of Pathros or *upper* Egypt. Isa. 11:11; Jer. 44:15. See Egypt.

Moab (mō'ab), *from the father*. The son of Lot and his eldest daughter, and founder of the Moabite people. Gen. 19:30-38. Moab is also used for the Moabites; and also for their territory. Num. 22:3-14; Judg. 3:30; 2 Sam. 8:2; 2 Kings 1:1; Jer. 48:4.

The territory of the Moabites, originally inhabited by the Emims, Deut. 2:10, lay on the east of the Dead Sea and the Jordan, strictly on the highlands south of the Arnon; Num. 21:13; Ruth 1:1, 2; 2:6; but in a wider sense it included also the region anciently occupied by the Amorites over against Jericho, usually called the "Plains of Moab." Num. 21:13; 22:1; 26:3; 33:48; Deut. 34:1. When the Hebrews advanced to Canaan, they did not enter the territory of Moab proper, Deut. 2:9; Judg. 11:18; but there was always a great antipathy between the two peoples, which arose from Balaam having seduced the Hebrews to sin by the daughters of Moab. Num. 25:1, 2; Deut. 23:3-6. After the death of Joshua the Moabites oppressed the Hebrews, but they were delivered by Ehud. Judg. 3:21. David subdued Moab and Ammon, and made them tributary. 2 Sam. 8:2-12; 23:20. Soon after the death of Ahab they began to revolt, 2 Kings 3:4, 5; Isa. 16:1, 2, and were subsequently engaged in wars with the Hebrews. 2 Chron. 20:1, 10; 27:5. Under Nebuchadnezzar the Moabites acted as the auxiliaries of the Chaldeans, 2 Kings 24:2; Ezek. 25:8-11; and during the exile they took possession once more of their ancient territory, vacated by the tribes of Reuben and Gad; as did the Ammonites also. Jer. 49:1-5. Some time after the exile their name was lost under that of the Arabians, as was also the case with the Ammonites and Edomites. The famous Moabite Stone, bearing an inscription of Mesha, a king of Moab, about 900 B. C., was found at Dibon, in Moab, within the gateway by, Rev. F. A. Klein—a German missionary at Jerusalem—in 1868. The stone is of black basalt, 3 feet 8½ inches high, 2 feet 3½ inches wide, and 1 foot 1.78 inches thick. It has 34 lines of Hebrew-Phœnician writing, and contains a most remarkable corroboration of the Scripture history in 2 Kings 3. The long-predicted doom of Moab is now fulfilled, and the 48th chapter of Jeremiah is verified on the spot by the traveller. There are 27 references to Moab in this chapter, and 121 in the Scriptures.

Mole. In Lev. 11:30 A. V. the Hebrew word is believed to denote the chameleon. The R. V. reads: "And the gecko, and the land-crocodile, and the lizard, and the sand lizard, and the chameleon." Another word rendered "mole," in Isa. 2:20, means "the burrower." As no true moles have been found in Palestine, this term may comprehend the various rats and weasels that burrow about ruins.

Molech (mō'lek), *the ruler*, Lev. 18:21, or **Milcom** (mil'kom), 1 Kings 11:5, or **Moloch**, Acts 7:43. The name of an idol-god worshipped by the Ammonites with human sacrifices, especially of children. The rabbins tell us that it was made of brass and placed on a brazen throne, and that the head was that of a calf with a crown upon it. The throne and image were made hollow, and a furious fire was kindled within it. The flames penetrated into the body and limbs of the idol; and when the arms were red-hot, the victim was thrown into them, and was almost immediately burned to death, while its cries were drowned by drums. Though warned against this idolatry, common to all the Canaanite tribes, though probably not of Canaanite origin, the Jews were repeatedly allured to adopt it. 2 Kings 23:10; Ezek. 20:26. In the Valley of Hinnom they set up a tabernacle to Molech, and there they sacrificed their children to the idol.

Money. Gen. 17:12. This word occurs about 130 times in the A. V., and represents three Hebrew words: *keseph* or *k'saph* occurring most frequently (about 110 times) in historical books, only a few times in the poetical books, as Ps. 15:5; Prov. 7:20; Lam. 5:4. Two other Hebrew words, *qesitah* and *qinyon*, also appear early in the Old Testament, Gen. 33:19; Lev. 22:11. Money also represents six Greek words in the New Testament: *argurion*, meaning "silver," Matt. 25:18; *kerma*, a small coin. John 2:15; *nomisma*, meaning possibly "legal coin," Matt. 22:19; *chalkos*, a copper coin, Mark 6:8; *chrema*, Acts 8:18, and *stater*, rendered "shekel" in the R. V., equal to 24 *drachmas*. Matt. 17:27. Coined money, as now in use among civilized nations, was unknown in the world until about six hundred years before Christ. The Assyrians, Babylonians, and Egyptians had no coins until about B. C.

300. David and Solomon never saw any coined money. The Jews had none until the time of the Maccabees, about B. C. 139. Before the periods named, gold and silver were used as money by weight; and are now so used in some eastern countries. The first mention of money is in the touching story of Abraham's buying a burial place for his wife. It is said, "Abraham weighed the silver, four hundred shekels, current with the merchant." Gen. 23:4-16. It appears to have been then in general use. The study of ancient coined money is interesting, showing the rise of the arts and their fall during the dark ages of priestcraft, from the fourth to the fifteenth centuries; the coins of 400 years before Christ being superb, while those a thousand years after Christ are hardly discernible. The early coins show, not only the likenesses of kings and emperors, but also many of the most important events of their reigns. For the coins mentioned in the Bible, see **Shekel, Penny, Farthing.**

Money-changers. Matt. 21:12; Mark 11:15; John 2:15. According to Ex. 30: 13-15, every Israelite who had reached the age of twenty must pay into the treasury, whenever the nation was numbered, a half-shekel as an offering to Jehovah. The money-changers whom Christ, for their impiety, avarice, and fraudulent dealing, expelled from the temple were the dealers who supplied half-shekels, for such a premium as they might be able to exact, to the Jews from all parts of the world who assembled at Jerusalem during the great festivals, and were required to pay their tribute or ransom money in the Hebrew coin.

Month. Gen. 8:4. The ancient Hebrews called the months by their numbers; as first month, second month, third month, etc., and also had a name for each month. They likewise had a civil and a sacred year. The sacred year was used in computing their festivals, and chiefly by sacred writers. The civil year was used in reckoning their jubilee, the reign of kings, and birth of children. The length of the month depended on the changes of the moon. The names of the Hebrew months follow:

Civil.	Sacred.		Beginning with the new moon.	Feasts.
VII	I.	Nisan, or Abib	March, April......Neh. 2:1....	Passover, Unleavened Bread.
VIII	II.	Zif, or Ziv	April, May............1 Kings 6:1...	Pentecost.
IX	III.	Sivan	May, June...............Esther 8:9.....	
X	IV.	Thammuz	June, July..............	
XI	V.	Ab	July, August...........	
XII	VI.	Elul	August, September..Neh. 6:15......	
I	VII.	Tishri, or Ethanim	Septem'r, October ..1 Kings 8:2	Feast of Trumpets. Atonement. Feast of Tabernacles.
II	VIII.	Bul	October, Novem'r...1 Kings 6:38.	
III	IX.	Kisleu, or Chislen. R. V. Chislev	November, Dec'r....Neh. 1:1........	Dedication.
IV	X.	Tebeth	December, Jan'y.....Esther 2:16...	
V	XI.	Shebat	January, February..Zech. 1:7......	
VI	XII.	Adar	February, March....Esther 3:7.....	Purim.

Twelve lunar months, making 354 days and six hours, made the Jewish year short of the Roman by twelve days. To compensate for this difference, the Jews about every three years, or seven times in 19 years, intercalated a *thirteenth* month, which they called *Vedar*, the second *Adar*. By this means their lunar year equalled the solar.

Mordecai (*môr'de-kâi*), *little man*. A Jew in the Persian court who caused the deliverance of the Jews from the destruction plotted by Haman. This led to the institution of the feast of Purim. See Esther.

Moreh (*mō'reh*). 1. The halting place of Abram after his entrance into the land of Canaan. Gen. 12:6. It was near Shechem, Gen. 12:6, and the mountains Ebal and Gerizim. Deut. 11:30. 2. The hill of Moreh, where the Midianites and Amalekites were encamped before Gideon's attack upon them. Judg. 7:1. It lay in the valley of Jezreel, on the north side.

Moriah (*mo-rī'ah*), *chosen of Jehovah?* 1. The place where Abraham was directed to offer Isaac as a sacrifice. Gen. 22:2. 2. A mount on which Solomon built the temple in Jerusalem. 2 Chron. 3:1. It was in the eastern part of the city, overlooking the valley of the Kedron, and where was the threshing-floor of Araunah. 2 Sam. 24:24; 1 Chron. 21:24. See **Jerusalem.**

Moses (*mō'zez*), *from the water*, i. e., *drawn from the water*. The prophet and legislator of the Hebrews and the son of Amram and Jochebed, and of the tribe of Levi, the son of Jacob. Ex. 2:1, 10; 6:16-20; Josh. 1:1, 2, 15; 1 Kings 8:53, 56; 2 Chron. 1:3; Dan. 9:11; Deut. 34:5; Ps. 90: title; Ezra 3:2. He was born in Egypt, about B. C. 1571. In his infancy, because of the cruel edict of Pharaoh, he was hid in a boat-cradle in the Nile; but was found and adopted by the daughter of Pharaoh. He was educated at the Egyptian court, and "was learned in all the wisdom of the Egyptians, and was mighty in words and in deeds." **Ex.** 2:1-10; Acts 7: 20-22. When Moses had grown up, he resolved to deliver his people. Having slain an Egyptian, however, he fled into the land of Midian, where he was a shepherd chief. Among the Midians, the Minni, who we now know were a cultured and literary people, God further prepared him to be the deliverer of his chosen people. By a succession of miracles, which God wrought by his hand, Moses brought the Hebrews out of Egypt, and through the wilderness, unto the borders of Canaan. See Sinai. He was only allowed to behold, not to enter the Promised Land. Having accomplished his mission and attained to the age of 120 years, with the faculties of mind and body unimpaired, the legislator transferred his authority to Joshua; and, ascending the summit of Pisgah, he gazed on the magnificent prospect of the "goodly Land." There he died, and "the Lord buried him in a valley in the land of Moab, over against Beth-peor; but no man knoweth of his sepulchre unto this day." Deut. 34:1-7. God buried Moses. It was fitting, therefore, that he too should write his epitaph. "And there arose not a prophet since in Israel like unto Moses, whom the Lord knew face to face, in all the signs and the wonders which the Lord sent him to do in the land of Egypt, to Pharaoh, and to all his servants, and to all his land, and in all that mighty land, and in all the great terror which Moses showed in the sight of all Israel." Deut. 34:10-12.

Moth. The clothes-moth, which, in its caterpillar state, is very destructive to woven fabrics. In Job 4:19 man is said to be "crushed before the moth"—that is, more easily than the moth.

Mourning. Oriental mourning is public and careful of prescribed ceremonies. Gen. 23:2; Job 1:20; 2:12. Among the forms observed the following may be mentioned: Rending the clothes, Gen. 37:29, 34; 44:13, etc.; dressing in sackcloth, Gen. 37:34; 2 Sam. 3:31; 21:10, etc.; ashes, dust or earth sprinkled on the person, 2 Sam. 13:19; 15:32, etc.; black or sad-colored garments, 2 Sam. 14:2; Jer. 8:21, etc.; removal of ornaments or neglect of person, Deut. 21:12, 13, etc.; shaving the head, plucking out the hair of the head or beard, Lev. 10:6; 2 Sam. 19:24, etc.; laying bare some part of the body, Isa. 20:2; 47:2, etc.; fasting or abstinence in meat and drink, 2 Sam. 1:12; 3:35; 12:16, 22, etc. In later times for the employment of persons hired for the purpose of mourning, Eccl. 12:5; Jer. 9:17; Amos 5:16; Matt. 9:23, friends or passersby to join in the lamentations of bereaved or afflicted persons, Gen. 50:3; Judg. 11:40; Job 2:11; 30:25, etc.; and in ancient times the sitting or lying posture in silence indicative of grief, Gen. 23:3; Judg. 20:26, etc. The period of mourning varied. In the case of Jacob it was seventy days, Gen. 50:3; of Aaron, Num. 20:29, and Moses, Deut. 34:8, thirty. A further period of seven days in Jacob's case, Gen. 50:10. Seven days for Saul, which may have been an abridged period in the time of national danger. 1 Sam. 31:13.

Mouse. Tristram found 23 species of mice in Palestine. In Lev. 11:29, and Isa. 66:17 this word is doubtless used generically, including as unclean even the larger rat, jerboa, dormouse, and sand-rat. They made great havoc in the fields of the Philistines after that people had taken the ark of the Lord. 1 Sam. 6:4, 5.

Mulberry Trees. Some of the best recent authorities advocate the aspen or poplar, a few species of which grow in Palestine. The "going" in the tree-tops, which was to be the sign that God went out before the host, 2 Sam. 5:23, 24, may have been the rustle of these leaves, which are proverbial for their readiness to tremble before the slightest breeze.

Murrain. Ex. 9:3. See **Plagues of Egypt.**

Music. 1 Sam. 18:6; Isa. 30:29. The practice of music was not restricted to any one class of persons. 1 Chron. 13:8; 15:16. The sons of Asaph, Heman, and Jeduthun were set apart by David for the musical service. They were divided, like the priests, into 24 courses, which are enumerated. 1 Chron. 25. Of the 38,000 Levites, "four thousand praised the Lord with the instruments." 1 Chron. 23:5. Each of the courses or classes had 154 musicians and three leaders, and all were under the general direction of Asaph and his brethren. Each course served for a week, but upon the festivals all were required to be present, or four thousand musicians. Heman, with one of his leaders, directed the central choir, Asaph the right, and Jeduthun the left wing. These several choirs answered one another, as is generally supposed, in that kind of alternate singing which is called "antiphonal," or responsive. The priests, in the meantime, performed upon the silver trumpets. 2 Chron. 5:11-14; Num. 10:2.

Musical Instruments. Eccl. 2:8, A. V. They were invented by Jubal, the son of Lamech, Gen. 4:21, and had appropriate names. Gen. 31:27. They may be divided into three classes—stringed instruments, wind instruments, and such as gave their sounds on being struck. Of stringed instruments were the harp, the instrument of ten strings, the sackbut, and the psaltery. They are described under their proper names. The instruments of music mentioned in 1 Sam. 18:6, as used by women, are supposed to have been metallic triangles, as the name indicates.

Mustard. Matt. 13:31, 32; 17:20; Luke 17:6. This plant is the black mustard (*Sinapis nigra*). In the fertile and warm soil of Palestine, especially when cultivated, this herb must have reached considerable size. Dr. Thomson has seen it there as tall as the horse and his rider, and the ground near the Sea of Galilee is often "*gilded* over with its yellow flowers."

Myra (*my'rah*), *flowing, weeping*. An ancient port in Lycia, on the southwest coast of Asia Minor. Acts 27:5. It was on the river Andriacus, about 2½ miles from its mouth. The magnificent ruins of the city stand upon a hill not far from the sea.

Myrrh. A gum resin, celebrated for its aromatic properties. It derives its name from the Hebrew word *mór*, which implies "flowing" or "distilling," Greek *murrha*. The *Balsamodendron myrrha*, of the natural order *Terebinthaccæ*, is the tree found in Arabia and Africa, from which myrrh is chiefly procured. It exudes from the bark, and is at first soft, oily, and yellowish-white; it afterwards acquires the consistency of butter, and becomes still harder by exposure to the air, changing to a reddish hue. In commerce it is of two kinds, "myrrh in tears" and "myrrh in sorts." Myrrh is frequently mentioned in Scripture. It was an ingredient in the holy anointing oil, Ex. 30:23; it was used in perfumes, Ps. 45:8; Prov. 7:17; Song of Sol. 1:13; 3:6; in unguents, Esth. 2 : 12; Song of Sol. 5 : 5; for strengthening wine, Mark 15:23; also in embalming, John 19:30. Myrrh was among the offerings made by the eastern sages. Matt. 2:11. The best was that which flowed spontaneously from the tree.

Myrtle. This plant, *Myrtus communis*, grows in the east into a tree of twenty feet in height. The myrtle was an emblem of peace and quietude; hence allusions to it are frequently introduced by the sacred writers. Isa. 41:19; 55:13; Zech. 1:8-11. Branches of it were used for constructing booths and arbors at the feast of tabernacles. Neh. 8:15.

Mysia (*mĭsh'ĭ-ah*), or *mĭzh-ĭ-ah, beech region?* A province in the northwestern angle of Asia Minor, celebrated for its fertility. Acts 16:7, 8; 20:5.

Mystery. Eph. 1:8, 9. This word does not mean something absolutely hidden and unintelligible. It is rather a design hidden in God's counsels until revealed to mankind in and by Christ. Hence we find it continually employed in the New Testament to indicate those gracious purposes and plans, which were by degrees elaborated and illustrated, and on which the teaching of our Lord and his apostles threw the clearest light, but which remained hidden to those who would not understand, and who had their minds blinded against the truth. Thus the gospel is called "the mystery of the faith," "the mystery of godliness," 1 Tim. 3:9, 16, which mystery is immediately after explained to be the revelation and glorious work of the Lord Jesus Christ. So the calling of the Gentiles and their union into one body, God's church, with the Jews, is called a mystery, long hidden, but at last made known. Eph. 1:9, 10; 3:8-10; Col. 1:25-27. In the same way it is elsewhere used for a truth or doctrine, which required elucidation, and which received it. Matt. 13:11; Rom. 11:25; 1 Cor. 13:2; 15:51, 52. The word is also employed symbolically. Thus Paul treating of the primary institution of marriage introduces the term, because the marriage tie was a figurative representation of that yet closer union into which Christ brings his church, wherein the two are "one spirit." Eph. 5:31, 32; comp. 6:17. In prophetical language there is a similar use of the word mystery. Thus the "seven stars" symbolized "the angels of the seven churches," and the "seven candlesticks" the "seven churches." Rev. 1:20; comp. 17:5, 7.

N

Naaman (*nā'a-măn*), *pleasantness*. 1. "Naaman the Syrian," to whose cure our Lord referred. Luke 4:27. Naaman was commander-in-chief of the army of Syria, and was nearest to the person of the king, Ben-hadad II., whom he accompanied officially when he went to worship in the temple of Rimmon, 2 Kings 5:18, at Damascus, the capital. Naaman was afflicted with a leprosy of the white kind, which had hitherto defied cure. A little Israelitish captive maiden tells him of the fame and skill of Elisha, and he is cured by him by following his simple directions to bathe in the Jordan seven times. See 2 Kings 5:14. After his cure he gratefully acknowledged the power of the God of Israel, and promised " henceforth to offer neither burnt offering nor sacrifice unto other gods, but unto the Lord." How long Naaman lived to continue a worshipper of Jehovah while assisting officially at the worship of Rimmon we are not told; "but his memory is perpetuated by a leper hospital which occupies the traditional site of his house in Damascus, on the banks of the Abana." 2. One of the family of Benjamin who came down to Egypt with Jacob, as read in Gen. 46:21. He was the son of Bela, and head of the family of the Naamites. Num. 26:40; 1 Chron. 8:3, 4.

Nabal (*nā'băl*), *foolish, impious*. A man of the house of Caleb, who had large possessions in Carmel. He treated David very churlishly, and was saved from the disastrous consequence by his wife Abigail, whom David married after Nabal's death. 1 Sam. 25; 27:3; 30:5; 2 Sam. 2:2; 3:3.

Naboth (*nā'bŏth*), *fruits*. An Israelite of Jezreel who owned a vineyard adjoining the palace of king Ahab. 1 Kings 21:1. Anxious to secure this spot to use it for a garden, the king proposed to buy it; but Naboth declined to sell. So Jezebel, the wife of Ahab, made a wicked plan to have Naboth condemned to death on a false charge of blasphemy, and thus allow the king to seize upon the vineyard. The murder was avenged by the doom immediately passed upon Ahab and Jezebel, the royal murderers. 1 Kings 21:19.

Nadab (*nā'dăb*), *spontaneous, liberal*. 1. The eldest son of Aaron. Ex. 6:23; 24:1, 9; 28:1; Lev. 10:1; Num. 3:2, 4; 26:60, 61; 1 Chron. 6:3; 24:1, 2. 2. The son and successor of Jeroboam I., king of Israel, whose sinful conduct he imitated. He reigned two years, 954-953 B. C., and while engaged at the siege of Gibbethon he and all his house were slain by Baasha. 1 Kings 14:20; 15:25-31. 3. One of Judah's posterity. 1 Chron. 2:28, 30. 4. A Benjamite, one of the family from which Saul descended. 1 Chron. 8:30; 9:36.

Nahash (*nā'hăsh*), *serpent*. 1. An Ammonite king. He offered to Jabesh-gilead a treaty on condition that the citizens should submit to the loss of their right eyes. This cruelty aroused the indignation of Saul, who defeated their enemies. At a subsequent period he was on friendly relations with David. 2 Sam. 10 : 2. 2. Mentioned as father of Abigail. 2 Sam. 17 : 25. Some identify him with Jesse, and others with Nahash, king of the Ammonites.

Nahor (nā'hôr), *snorting*. 1. One of the patriarchs, father of Terah and grandfather of Abraham. Gen. 11 : 22-25 ; 1 Chron. 1 : 26. He is called Nachor in Luke 3 : 34, A.V. 2. A son of Terah. It would seem that he must have accompanied his father to Haran; for it is sometimes styled the city of Nahor. Gen. 11 ; 26, 27, 29 ; 22 : 20-24 ; 24 : 10, 15, 24, 47 ; 29 : 5 ; 31 : 53. He is called Nachor in Josh. 24 : 2, A. V.

Nahum (Nā'hum), *consolation*. One of the twelve minor prophets. In Nah. 1 : 1 he is called an Elkoshite. Some refer this name to a place in Galilee, others to a village on the Tigris. The intimate acquaintance the book shows with Syrian affairs makes it probable that Nahum lived an exile in Assyria, and perhaps at the village on the Tigris. Nahum prophesied before the destruction of Nineveh, which he predicts, and probably in the reign of Hezekiah.

BOOK OF. It is a poem of great sublimity, and admirable for the elegance of its imagery. It describes with much beauty and poetic force the siege and destruction of Nineveh as a punishment for her wickedness. Nah. chaps. 2 and 3.

Nain (nā'in), *beauty*. A town in Galilee where Christ raised the widow's dead son to life. Luke 7 ; 11. It is now called Nein, and is on the northwestern edge of Little Hermon, six miles southeast of Nazareth, and 25 miles southwest of Tell Hum (Capernaum ?).

Naioth (nā'yoth), *habitations*. A place near Ramah where Samuel dwelt. 1 Sam. 19 : 18-23 ; 20 : 1. Some interpret the word to mean a school of prophets over which Samuel presided.

Name. Gen. 2 : 19. This sometimes has a peculiar signification, as in Prov. 18 : 10, where the term denotes God himself. See, also, Ps. 20 : 1, 5, 7. In the New Testament it usually means the character, faith, or doctrine of Christ. Acts 5 : 41 ; 8 : 12 ; 9 : 15, and 26 : 9. The names of God are expressive of some element of his character—are the symbol of some revealed attribute of his nature. We name him only because we know him, and we know him only because he has made himself known. Names among the Jews usually had a meaning and a relation of some peculiar circumstances in the character, birth, or destiny of the person. Ex. 2 : 10 and 18 : 3, 4 ; Matt. 1 : 21. The same person often had two names. Names were changed, and are still, in Eastern countries, for slight reasons. A change of office or station often occasioned a change of name. "And upon his thigh a name written." Rev. 19 : 16. This alludes to an ancient custom among Eastern nations of adorning the images of their gods and the persons of princes and heroes with inscriptions expressive of their character, titles, etc. They were made on the garment, or on one of the thighs, and several ancient statues have been discovered, with inscriptions of one or two lines, written sometimes horizontally and sometimes perpendicularly, both on the inside and outside of the thigh, and sometimes upon both thighs. Men surname themselves by the name of Israel, when, having been before Gentiles and sinners, they join themselves to Jesus and his church. Isa. 44 : 5.

Naomi (na-o'mi or nā'o-mi), *my delight*. The wife of Elimelech, and the mother-in-law of Ruth, and who moved with their two sons from Judæa to Moab in the time of a famine. Ruth 1 : 2. Elimelech died, and also his two sons, each leaving a widow ; Naomi, thus bereaved, started back to her native country. Orpah remained behind, but Ruth accompanied her. Once back in Bethlehem, she wished to be known by the name Mara—"bitterness." She thenceforth acted the part of a faithful mother to Ruth.

Naphtali (năph'ta-li), *my wrestling*. The sixth son of Jacob, by Bilhah, Rachel's handmaid. Gen. 30 : 7, 8. He had four sons. Gen. 46 : 24 ; Ex. 1 : 4 ; 1 Chron. 7 : 13. Jacob said, "Naphtali is a hind let loose, he giveth goodly words," graceful and eloquent. Gen. 49 : 21.

TERRITORY OF NAPHTALI, peopled by his descendants, called Nephthalim, Matt. 4 : 15, A. V., was called "the west and the south," A.V., literally "the sea and the circuit." Deut. 33 : 23 ; Josh. 19 : 32-39. It lay in a rich and fertile portion of Northern Palestine, partly along the Lebanon range, called "the mount of Naphtali." Josh. 19 : 32-39 ; 20 : 7, R. V., "Hill country of Naphtali." They attended in force at the coronation of David, 1 Chron. 12 : 34, and are mentioned with honor in the wars of the Judges, Judg. 1 : 33 ; 5 : 18 ; 6 : 35 ; 7 : 23, as much reduced by the Syrians, 1 Kings 15 : 20, and as among the first captives to Assyria, 2 Kings 15 : 29 ; Isa. 9 : 1. Barak was their most notable leader. Judg. 4 : 6-16. Our Saviour spent much time in the southern part of this region ; Matt. 4 : 13-15 ; Mark 2 : 1-12, partially fulfilling Isa. 9 : 1, 2.

Nathan (nā'than), *given*. 1. A distinguished prophet of Judæa, in the reigns of David and Solomon. 2 Sam. 7 : 2. Nathan was to tell David that he could not build the temple, and to point out David's sin against Uriah, which he conveyed under the striking allegory of the rich man and the ewe-lamb. Nathan was one of David's biographers, 1 Chron. 29 : 29, and also Solomon's. 2 Chron. 9 : 29. 2. One of the sons of David by Bathsheba. 1 Chron. 3 : 5. 3. Father of one of David's warriors. 2 Sam. 23 : 36. 4. One of the chief men who returned to Jerusalem with Ezra. Ezra 8 : 16. 5. A descendant of Caleb. 1 Chron. 2 : 36.

Nathanael (Na-thăn'a-el), *gift of God*. A native of Cana of Galilee, John 21 : 2, whom our Lord called an Israelite without guile. John 1 : 47. He was led by Philip to Jesus. He went doubting, with the words on his lips, "Can there any good thing come out of Nazareth ?" Jesus, however, at once convinces him that he is the Messiah by the exhibition of his knowledge, declaring that he had seen Nathanael under the fig tree before ever Philip had called him. Nathanael confesses him to be the Son of God and the King of Israel. The name Nathanael occurs only in John. For this reason, combined with the fact that John never mentions the name of Bartholomew, it is generally supposed that the two are identical.

Nazarene (*năz'a-rēne*). When our Lord was taken as a child to Nazareth, which thus became for many years his dwelling-place, the evangelist records this as a fulfilment of prophecy, Matt. 2:23, citing no particular place, but referring generally to "the prophets," who predicted Messiah's humble and despised condition. See Isa. chaps. 52, 53. The words, "He shall be called a Nazarene," do not occur in the writings of the Old Testament; but the thing or meaning conveyed by them is sufficiently obvious. Jesus, living at Nazareth, was from that very circumstance contemned; and we find in the course of his public career his connection with that town repeatedly used against him. John 1:46; 7:41, 52. Matthew notes that event which branded him with an ill-omened name, "Jesus of Nazareth," and his followers as Nazarenes, comp. Acts 24:5, as an exact fulfilment of what ancient seers had foretold. It is an error to connect Matt. 2:23 with Isa. 11, from a fancied relation of the original Hebrew word there translated "branch" with the name Nazareth.

Nazareth (*năz'a-rĕth*), *separated?* Matt. 2:23. A city of Galilee, famous as the home of Jesus during his childhood and youth until he began his public ministry. It was about 14 miles from the Sea of Galilee, and 66 miles north of Jerusalem in a straight line. It is one of the most beautiful sites in the Holy Land. Nazareth is not mentioned in the Old Testament, nor by any classical author, nor by any writer before the time of Christ. It was for some unknown reason held in disrepute among the Jews of Judæa. John 1:46. It was situated in a mountain, Luke 4:29, within the province of Galilee, Mark 1:9, and near Cana, as John 2:1, 2, 11 seems to imply. There was a precipice near the town, down which the people proposed to cast Jesus. Luke 4:29. It is mentioned 29 times in the New Testament. At Nazareth the angel appeared to Mary: the home of Joseph, Luke 1:26; 2:39, and to that place Joseph and Mary returned after their flight into Egypt. Matt. 2:23. The hills and places about the town possess a deep and hallowed interest to the Christian as the home of Jesus during his childhood and youth, until he entered upon his ministry, and had preached in the synagogue, and was rejected by his own townspeople. Even after Capernaum became "his own city" he was known as "Jesus of Nazareth," Matt. 13:54-58; Mark 6:1-6; Acts 2:22; 3:6; 4:10; 6:14, and his disciples were called "Nazarenes." The town is now called En-Nâsirah, or Nasrah, and has from 5000 to 6000 population, though the Turkish officials estimate it at 10,000. The brow of the hill over which the enraged Nazarenes threatened to cast Jesus is probably near the Maronite church, though tradition places it at the "Mount of Precipitation," two or three miles south of the town.

Nazarites (*năz'a-rītes*), properly *Nazirites*, Num. 6:2, from a Hebrew word signifying "to separate." A Nazirite, under the ancient law, was one, either male or female, under a vow to abstain from wine and all intoxicating liquors and the fruit of the vine. The hair should be allowed to grow without being shorn, and all contamination with dead bodies should be avoided. The Nazirite was not even to approach the corpse of father or mother, Num. 6:7, and if by accident this should occur, he was required to shave his head, make offerings, and renew the vow. When the time of the vow expired, the person brought an offering to the temple; the priest then cut off his hair and burnt it; after which the Nazirite was free from his vow and might again drink wine. The term of the vow is left indefinite. "The days of the vow" is the expression in Num. 6. We know, however, that there were perpetual Nazirites. Samson and probably Samuel and John the Baptist were perpetual Nazirites. Hannah promised the Lord that no razor should touch the head of her child if the Lord would give her one, 1 Sam. 1:11, and the angel predicted to Zacharias that John would abstain entirely from wine and strong drink. Luke 1:15.

Neapolis (*ne-ăp'o-lĭs*), *new city.* A place in Northern Greece where Paul first landed in Europe, and where he probably landed on his second visit, Acts 16:11; comp. 20:1, and whence he embarked on his last journey to Jerusalem. Acts 20:6. It is now a Turco-Grecian town of 5000 or 6000 population, and called Kavalla; it has numerous ruins.

Nebaioth (*ne-bā'yoth*). Isa. 60:7, or **Nebajoth** = *heights*, R.V., "Nebaioth," Gen. 25:13, the first-born, 1 Chron. 1:29, son of Ishmael, whose descendants are supposed to have settled in Arabia, and to have been the Nabathæans of Greek and Roman history. They were a pastoral people, Isa. 60:7, whence the beautiful figure of the prophet above cited respecting the gathering of the Gentile nations to the sceptre of the Messiah. Petra was their chief city.

Nebo (*nē'bo*), *proclaimer.* 1. One of the Assyrian deities, who is represented, with Bel, as being unable to resist the destruction to which Cyrus subjected their idols. Isa. 46:1. This god was called "he who possesses intelligence," and statues of him are still preserved. 2. A mountain of Moab "over against Jericho." Deut. 32:49. "And Moses went up from the plains of Moab unto the mountain of Nebo, to the top of Pisgah, ... and the Lord showed him all the land of Gilead unto Dan." Deut. 34:1. Nebo was a mountain in the range of mountains called Abarim. While the discussions respecting Pisgah have been sharp, the majority of explorers and scholars agree in identifying Nebo with the northern end of the Abarim range. See Pisgah. 3. A city east of the Jordan; rebuilt by the Gadites, Num. 32:3, 38; 33:47; captured by the Moabites. Isa. 15:2; Jer. 48:1, 22. It was eight miles south of Heshbon; perhaps el Hâbis. 4. A town in Benjamin, Neh. 7:33; possibly Nûba, 7 miles northwest of Hebron.

Nebuchadnezzar (*něb'u-kad-něz'zar*), *may Nebo protect the crown!* or, more correctly, **Nebuchadrezzar**, the son and successor of Nabopolassar, the founder of the Babylonish monarchy, was the most illustrious of these kings. 2 Kings 24:1; Dan. chaps. 1–4. We know of him through the book of Daniel. In the Berlin Museum there is a black cameo with his head upon it, cut by his order, with the inscription: "In honor of Merodach, his lord, Nebuchadnezzar, king of Babylon, in his lifetime had this made." Nebuchadnezzar was intrusted by his father with repelling Pharaoh-necho, and succeeded in defeating him at Carchemish, on the Euphrates, B. C. 605, Jer. 46:2, taking Jerusalem and carrying off a portion of the inhabitants as prisoners, including Daniel and his companions. Dan. 1:1–4. Having learned that his father had died, Nebuchadnezzar hastened back to Babylon. Thus the remark, "In his days Nebuchadnezzar, king of Babylon, came up, and Jehoiakim became his servant three years," 2 Kings 24:1, is easily explained. The title is given by anticipation, and the "three years" are to be reckoned from 605 to 603 inclusive. The rebellion of Jehoiakim, entered upon, probably, because Nebuchadnezzar was carrying on wars in other parts of Asia, took place B. C. 602, and was punished by the irruption of Chaldæans, Syrians, Moabites, and Ammonites, incited, perhaps, by Nebuchadnezzar, who, as soon as possible, sent his troops against Jerusalem, and had him taken prisoner, but ultimately released him. 2 Kings 24:2. After his death his son Jehoiachin reigned, and against him Nebuchadnezzar, for the third time, invaded Palestine and besieged Jerusalem, and all the principal inhabitants were carried to Babylon. 2 Kings 24:12–16. Mattaniah, whose name was changed to Zedekiah, after a reign of nearly ten years, rebelled, and was punished by Nebuchadnezzar, who went up against Jerusalem and reduced the city to the horrors of famine before taking it. Zedekiah's two sons were killed before his eyes, and then his eyes put out, and he, as a captive, was carried to Babylon, B. C. 588. 2 Kings 25:7. On Nebuchadnezzar's order, Jeremiah was kindly treated. Jer. 39:11–14. The words, "The king spake and said, Is not this great Babylon, that I have built for the house of my kingdom, by the might of my power, and for the honor of my majesty?" Dan. 4:30, are proved to be characteristic by those on an inscription: "I say it, I have built the great house which is the centre of Babylon for the seat of my rule in Babylon." Of the king's madness there is, of course, no direct mention. There is an inscription which is read by Sir H. Rawlinson in a manner which finds its readiest explanation in the fact stated in Dan. 4:33: "For four years the residence of my kingdom did not delight my heart: in no one of my possessions did I erect any important building by my might. I did not put up buildings in Babylon for myself and for the honor of my name. In the worship of Merodach, my god, I did not sing his praise, nor did I provide his altar with sacrifices, nor clean the canals." Nebuchadnezzar is denominated "king of kings" by Daniel, 2:37, and ruler of a "kingdom with power and strength and glory." He built the hanging-gardens of Babylon on a large and artificial mound, terraced up to look like a hill. This great work was called by the ancients one of the seven wonders of the world. An idea of the extent of this monarch's building enterprises may be drawn from the fact that nine-tenths of the bricks found amongst the ruins of the ancient capital are inscribed with his name. He is said to have worshipped the "King of heaven," Dan. 4:37, but it may be questioned whether he did not conceive of the Jehovah of the Hebrews to be only one of many gods. He died about B. C. 561, after a reign of 44 years.

Nebuzaradan (*něb'u-zăr-ā'dan* or *něb'u-zăr'a-dăn*), *prince favored by Nebo.* Nebuchadnezzar's general, who effected the ruin of Jerusalem. 2 Kings 25:8; Jer. 39:9–13; 40:1; 52:12, 15, 16, 26.

Necho (*nē'ko*) or **Pharaoh-necho**. King of Egypt. 2 Chron. 35:20, R. V., "Neco." Son of Psammetichus. Josiah, king of Judah, being tributary to the king of Babylon, opposed Necho on his first expedition against Nebuchadnezzar, and gave him battle at Megiddo, where he received the wound of which he died. On Necho's return from the Euphrates, where he had taken and garrisoned the city of Carchemish, B.C. 610, he halted in Riblah in Syria, and sending for Jehoahaz, king of the Jews, he deposed him, loaded him with chains, and sent him into Egypt. 2 Chron. 36:4. Then coming to Jerusalem, he set up Eliakim, or Jehoiakim, Josiah's first-born, in his place. Carchemish was retaken by the army of the king of Babylon, in the fourth year of Jehoiakim, king of Judah, Jer. 46:2: so that Necho did not retain his conquests in Syria more than four years. 2 Kings 23:29 to 24:7. "Pharaoh-necoh" in the R. V. 2 Chron. 35:20 to 36:6.

Necromancer. Deut. 18:11. One who professed to reveal future events by pretended converse with the dead.

Nehemiah (*ně'he-mī'ah*), *comforted of Jehovah.* 1. A Jew of piety and zeal, born during the exile; but his family and tribe are not known. Raised to the office of cup-bearer to the Persian monarch, Nehemiah did not forget his desolated country, and was commissioned, at his own request, to visit Jerusalem and rebuild the city; which he accomplished under the most perplexing difficulties. The twentieth year of Artaxerxes, when Nehemiah went to Jerusalem, is usually fixed in B. C. 444; others, with some degree of probability, fix it in B.C. 454. Neh. 1:1:7:2. Nehemiah was made *tirshatha* — " governor " of Judea, under Artaxerxes Longimanus. Neh. 8: 9; 10:1; 12:26. He is also called the *pechah*, whence the modern *pasha*, a governor of a province. Neh. 12 : 26. Nehemiah was governor of Jerusalem twelve years, Neh. 5:14-19; and then returned to the Persian court, where he remained "certain days." Neh. 13 : 6. After nine or ten months he returned to Jerusalem, as governor, the second time; and corrected the abuses which had crept in during his absence. Neh. 13:7-31; Mal. 2:9-17; 3:6-12. He remained in power till the restoration of affairs in Jerusalem, probably about ten years; and died at an advanced age, probably in that city.

NEHEMIAH, BOOK OF, is the 16th in the order of the books of the Old Testament. It supplements the book of Ezra. It relates Nehemiah's great work of rebuilding Jerusalem and the reclamation of the customs and laws of Moses, which had fallen into disuse. The account of the walls and gates in chap. 8 is among the most valuable documents for the settlement of the topography of ancient Jerusalem. The registers and lists of names are also of value. Nehemiah is the author of the first seven chapters, and part of the twelfth and thirteenth. The change from the use of the first person to that of the third in the remaining chapters, and the fact that some names in the lists were not extant till after Nehemiah's death, point to some other hand as their author. 2. One who returned in the first expedition from Babylon under Zerubbabel. Ezra 2:2; Neh. 7: 7. 3. The son of Azbuk, who helped to repair the gates of Jerusalem. Neh. 3:16.

Nehiloth (*ne'hi-loth*), Ps. 5, title, meaning "perforated," as flutes, "wind instruments," R. V.

Nehushtan (*ne-hŭsh'tan*), *the brazen thing*. The serpent of brass—or copper—which Moses made by God's command in the wilderness, Num. 21:8, 9, was preserved for many ages. Hezekiah, perceiving that the people had been in the habit of paying a superstitious reverence to it, broke it up. 2 Kings 18:4. Probably Nehushtan was the name by which it had been ordinarily known; though some believe it a term of contempt then first applied.

Nergal (*ner'gal*), *man-devourer*, *great hero*. An idol of the Cuthites. 2 Kings 17: 30. The Jewish rabbins fancied that this idol was figured by a cock. It is now very commonly supposed to be the planet Mars. The word is used in titles, as Nergal-sharezer, the name of two princes of Babylon. Jer. 39:3, 13.

Nero (*nē'ro*). L. Domitius Nero succeeded Claudius as emperor of Rome, 54 A.D., and killed himself to avoid a public execution, 68. In his reign that war commenced between the Jews and Romans which terminated later in the destruction of Jerusalem by Titus and the overthrow of the Jewish polity. It was under Nero, too, that a fierce persecution of the Christians began, about 64 A.D., which lasted till his death. Paul suffered martyrdom in it at Rome. So great were this monarch's cruelties that his name has ever since served specially to distinguish a tyrant. He is frequently indicated as Cæsar in the New Testament, Acts 25:8, 10-12. 21; 26:32; 28:19; Phil. 4: 22, and as Augustus, Acts 25:21, 25; but his name Nero does not occur. See Cæsar.

Nethinim (*nĕth'ĭ-nim*), *given*, *dedicated*. The name of the Hebrew temple servants, under the Levites. The whole of the Nethinim do not appear to have been, in their origin, Gibeonites, as it is not improbable that other foreigners were occasionally added to the staff. Josh. 9:3-27; Ezra 8: 20. The employment of the Nethinim, though the lowest in the service of the sanctuary, was not regarded as degrading, but rather as a sort of honorable servitude. 1 Chron. 9:2; Ezra 2:43-58, 70; Neh. 3: 31; 7:46-60, 73; 11:3, 21.

Nettle. A well-known plant covered with minute sharp hairs, containing a poison that produces a painful, stinging sensation. It grows on neglected ground. A different Hebrew word in Job 30 : 7; Prov. 24:31; Zeph. 2:9, seems to indicate a different species.

Nibhaz (*nĭb'hăz*), *barker*. An idol-god of the Avites. 2 Kings 17:31. The name being derived from a word meaning "to bark," it is supposed that the god was represented by the figure of a dog. It would, therefore, be allied to Anubis of the Egyptians.

Nicodemus (*nĭk-o-dē'mus*), *conqueror of the people*. A Pharisee, a ruler of the Jews, and a teacher of Israel, John 3:1, 10, whose secret visit to our Lord was the occasion of the discourse recorded only by John. Nicodemus was a member of the Sanhedrin, and finally became a follower of Christ, and came with Joseph of Arimathæa to take down and embalm the body of Jesus. John 7:50; 19:39.

Nicolaitans (*nĭk-o-lā'ĭ-tanz*). Heretical persons or teachers. mentioned in Rev. 2: 6, 15. Compare 2 Pet. 2:12, 19; Jude 4, 7, 8, 11, 12. Some suppose them to have been followers of Nicolas the deacon, but there is no good evidence that he ever became a heretic.

Nicolas (*nĭk'o-las*), *conqueror of the people*. A Jewish proselyte of Antioch, who afterwards embraced Christianity, and was among the most zealous of the first Christians, so that he was chosen one of the seven to minister in the church at Jerusalem. Acts 6 : 5.

Nicopolis (*nĭ-cŏp'o-lĭs*), *city of victory*. There were many ancient cities which bore this name: three in particular have been supposed by different critics the one meant. Tit. 3:12. One of these was in the northeastern corner of Cilicia; another on the Nessus in the interior of Thrace; the third in Epirus (though Pliny assigns it to Acarnania). This last, most probably the Nicopolis intended by Paul, was built by Augustus in commemoration of his victory at Actium.

Nile, *blue*, *dark*. The great river of Egypt and of Africa, its entire length being about

4000 miles. The word "Nile" does not occur in the A. V., but the river is frequently referred to as Sihor or Shihor, which means a "black" or "turbid" stream, Josh. 13:3; Isa. 23:3; where the R. V. reads "Nile;" Jer. 2:18; 46:7, 8, R. V. "Nile;" 1 Chron. 13:5. It is also designated simply the "river," R. V. margin, "Nile," Gen. 41:1; Ex. 1:22; 2:3, 5, and the "flood of Egypt," R. V., "River of Egypt," Amos 8:8; 9:5. In the plural form this word *yeor*, rendered "river," frequently refers to the branches and canals of the Nile. This famous river is connected with the earliest history of the Egyptian and the Israelitish nations. Ex. 2:3; 7:20, 21; Num. 11:5; Ps. 105:29; Jer. 46:7, 8. The Nile is not named in the New Testament. As rain seldom falls in Egypt proper, the fertility of the country is entirely dependent upon the annual rise of the Nile. This usually begins in June and continues until near the end of September, the river remaining stationary for two or more weeks, and then attaining its highest level in October, when it begins to subside. The successive years of famine in the days of Joseph were doubtless due to a deficient overflow of the Nile for those years. Formerly this annual inundation turned Egypt into a vast lake, but in later times the water has been distributed by a great network of canals, from which the huge basins of cultivated land into which the canals divide the country, are supplied with water of the depth required to leave a deposit of mud to fertilize the land. The native uses his feet to regulate the flow of water into each of the squares or basins of land, and by a dexterous movement of his toes forms or removes a tiny embankment, as may be required to admit the proper flow of water. Another common mode is to use the "shadoof," a bucket attached to a long pole hung on a pivot, balanced by a stone or a lump of clay at one end, and having the bucket on the other end. To this day the Nile is lined for hundreds of miles with these shadoofs, worked by men, women, and children, who lift the water out of the river to irrigate their fields. Both these methods are believed to be very ancient, and may be alluded to by Moses in contrasting the fountains and rainfalls in Palestine with the absence of this supply in Egypt: "For the land, whither thou goest in to possess it, *is* not as the land of Egypt, from whence ye came out, where thou sowedst thy seed, and wateredst *it* with thy foot as a garden of herbs." Deut. 11:10, 11. The ancient Egyptians worshipped the river Nile as a god. Two of the ten plagues sent upon Pharaoh and Egypt before the departure of the Israelites were turning the water of the Nile into blood and bringing forth frogs from the river. Ex. 7:15-25; 8:3-7. The papyrus reeds—whence paper is designated —the flags, the lotus, and the various colored flowers formerly beautifying the banks of the river have nearly all disappeared, thus fulfilling prophecy. Isa. 19:6, 7.

Nimrim (*Nim'rim*) pure, plural of Nimrah, a brook in Moab. Isa. 15:6; Jer. 48:34.

Nimrod (*nim'rŏd*), *rebellion;* or *the valiant.* A son of Cush and grandson of Ham. Gen. 10:8 ff. He established an empire in Shinar, the classical Babylonia, the chief towns being Babel, Erech, Accad, and Calneh: and extended this empire northward along the course of the Tigris over Assyria, where he founded a second group of capitals, Nineveh, Rehoboth, Calah, and Resen.

Nineveh (*nin'e-veh*), perhaps *dwelling of Nin,* the capital and greatest city of Assyria. It was founded by Nimrod, Gen. 10:11, and was on the eastern bank of the river Tigris, about 250 miles in a direct line north of the rival city of Babylon, and not far from 550 miles northwest of the Persian Gulf. Assyrian scholars are not agreed in respect to the size of this ancient city. Some, as Layard, regard it as covering a large parallelogram, whose sides were each from 18 to 20 miles long, and the ends 12 to 14 miles wide. This view would include the ruins now known as Konyunjik, Nimrud, Khorsabad, and Keremles. Diodorus Siculus makes the circumference of the city 55 miles, including pastures and pleasure grounds. This view of the great extent of the city is, on the other hand, sharply disputed by Rawlinson, who thinks it highly improbable that this ancient city should have had an area about ten times that of London. He would reject it on two grounds, the one historical and the other topographical. He maintains that the ruins of Khorsabad, Keremles, Nimrud, and Konyunjik bear on their bricks distinct local titles, and that these titles are found attaching to distant cities in the historical inscriptions. According to his view, Nimrud would be identified with Calah, and Khorsabad with Dur-sargina, or "the city of Sargon." He further claims that Assyrian writers do not consider these places to be parts of Nineveh, but distinct and separate cities; that Calah was for a long time the capital, while Nineveh was a provincial town; that Dur-sargina was built by Sargon—not at Nineveh, but near Nineveh; and that Scripture similarly distinguishes Calah as a place separate from Nineveh, and so far from it that there was room for a great city between them. See Gen. 10:12. He also suggests that a smaller city in extent would answer the requirements of the description in the book of Jonah, which makes it a city of "three days' journey." Jonah 3:3. As already stated, Nineveh was founded by Asshur, or, as the marginal reading of Gen. 10:11 states, Nimrod. When Nineveh became the capital of Assyria is not definitely known, but it is generally believed it was during the reign of Sennacherib. The prophecies of the books of Jonah and Nahum are chiefly directed against this city. The latter prophet indicates the mode of its capture. Nah. 1:1-8; 2:6, 8; 3:18. Nineveh was the capital of Assyria during the height of the grandeur of that empire, and in the time of Sennacherib, Esar-haddon, and Assur-bani-pal. It was besieged for two years by the combined forces of the Medes and Babylonians, was captured, and finally destroyed B.C. 606.

Excavations have been made by M. Botta, Layard, Hormuzd Rassam, Loftus, and George Smith. They have brought to light, among others, the following noted buildings: 1. Three ruined temples, built and restored by many kings in different ages. 2. The palace of Shalmaneser, as improved by subsequent rulers. 3. A palace of another ruler, restored by Sennacherib and Esar-haddon. 4. A palace of Tiglath-pileser II. 5. A temple of Nebo. 6. The southwest palace of Sennacherib. 7. The northwest palace of the same ruler. 8. The city walls built by the latter king and restored by Assur-bani-pal. See Assyria. The prophecies respecting the destruction of Nineveh are very specific; the prophet seemed to see her in her desolation and exclaims: "Nineveh hath been from of old like a pool of water. . . Nineveh is laid waste; who will bemoan her? . . . Thy worthies are at rest; thy people are scattered upon the mountains, and there is none to gather them." Nah. 2:8; 3:7, 18, R. V. "The Lord . . . will make Nineveh a desolation, and dry like the wilderness. And herds shall lie down in the midst of her, all the beasts of the nations; both the pelican and the porcupine shall lodge in the chapiters thereof; *their* voice shall ring in the windows; desolation shall be in the thresholds . . . how is she become a desolation, a place for beasts to lie down in!" Zeph. 2: 11, 13, 14, 15. These prophecies have been literally fulfilled. The city was destroyed; its very site was lost and unknown for centuries; it has now been found, its ruins opened, but are uninhabited except by wild beasts.

Nisroch (*nĭs'rŏch*), *great eagle?* An Assyrian deity in whose temple at Nineveh Sennacherib was murdered by his sons, Adrammelech and Sharezer. 2 Kings 19: 37; Isa. 37:38.

Nitre. Prov. 25:20. This is, no doubt, the natron found abundantly in certain Egyptian lakes, 50 miles west of Cairo. The Egyptians use it in bread and for soap; also, it is said, mixed with vinegar as a cure for toothache. The contrariety between these two ingredients illustrates the place referred to.

Noah (*nō'ah*), *rest*. Gen. 6:8. The son of Lamech and grandson of Methuselah. Noah begat three sons, Shem, Ham, and Japheth. In consequence of the hopeless wickedness of the world at this time, God resolved to destroy it. During this age of almost universal apostasy we are told that Noah was a righteous man and perfect in his generations—*i. e.*, among his contemporaries—and that he, like Enoch, walked with God. Gen. 6:9. Peter calls him "a preacher of righteousness." 2 Pet. 2:5. He had three sons, each of whom married a wife; he built the ark in accordance with divine direction; and was 600 years old when the flood came. Gen. 6:7. On coming from the ark he built an altar, made an offering, and received a promise that the world should never again be destroyed by a flood. Gen. 8:20. The closing history in his eventful life of 950 years is given in Gen. 9. Noah was to be the father of a new race. From his small family the earth was to be repeopled. And 350 years did he live among his posterity, a monument of God's justice and God's faithfulness. One more incident is related of him. Gen. 9: 20-27. He planted a vine and drank, knowingly or not we cannot say, too freely of the fruit of it. A shameful scene ensued. But the patriarch recovered, and in the spirit of prophecy predicted happiness to his faithful sons, judgment to the ungodly. "Let him that thinketh he standeth take heed lest he fall." The days of Noah were 950 years when he died.

No-amon (*nō-ā'mon*), *portion*, or, *temple of Amon?* A large and most important city of Egypt. Nah. 3:8-10. This city was as mighty as Nineveh; yet judgment and ultimate desolation were threatened against it. There can be no doubt that the city intended was that called Thebes, in upper Egypt, seated on both banks of the Nile, renowned for its hundred gates and vast population, and as being the principal seat of the worship of the god Amon. Some of the mightiest Egyptian dynasties reigned at Thebes, and embellished it with crowds of unrivalled palaces and temples. But the voice of prophecy proclaimed that it should be "rent asunder." This doom began to be fulfilled first by the Assyrians. See Isa. 20. It is evident from the words of Nahum that Thebes fell earlier than Nineveh. Nah. 1:1. According to Sir H. Rawlinson, Esar-haddon and his son Assur-bani-pal both conquered Egypt, and the latter took Thebes twice. Cambyses, king of Persia, ruthlessly destroyed it and burnt and mutilated its remaining monuments; and its ruin was completed by Ptolemy Lathyrus, about 81 B. C. The remains of this vast city, which appears to have been quadrangular, four miles by two, still astonish those who visit them. They lie 260 miles south of Cairo, including Karnak and Luxor. Fragments of colossal obelisks, pillars, and statues are scattered over the wide space. The grand hall of the temple at Karnak is described as "170 feet by 329, supported by a central avenue of twelve massive columns, 66 feet high—without the pedestal and abacus—and 12 in diameter, besides 122 of smaller or rather less gigantic dimensions, 41 feet 9 inches in height, and 27 feet 6 inches in circumference, distributed in seven lines on either side of the former." Pictured records and hieroglyphic inscriptions abound in the temples and the tombs; and when these shall be fully deciphered we may hope for much additional information in regard to Egyptian history and customs, illustrating and corroborating the sacred books.

Nob (*nŏb*), *height, hill*. A city in Benjamin, on the great road from the north to Jerusalem, in the immediate neighborhood of which it must have been; perhaps on the ridge of Olivet. The tabernacle seems to have been here in the time of Saul, who, for the alleged favor shown by the high priest Ahimelech to David, destroyed the city, which was, however, afterwards rebuilt. 1 Sam. 21:1; 22:9-19; Neh. 11:32; Isa. 10:32.

Nod (nŏd), *flight*. The region eastward of Eden, to which Cain fled from the presence of Jehovah. Gen. 4:14-16. The Chaldee interpreters apply the term to Cain, and not to a land: "He dwelt a fugitive in the land."

Noph. See Memphis.

Numbers, Book of. The fourth book of Moses, and so called on account of the two censuses to which it refers. It gives some detached legal enactments and many valuable historical facts. In the first division, chaps. 1-10:10, an account is given of the preparations for the departure from Sinai. In chap. 6 we have the description of the *Nazirite's* vow. The second division, chap. 10:11 to chap. 14, contains an account of the journey from Sinai to the borders of Canaan. In chaps. 13, 14, the spies are mentioned by name, and a most interesting description is given of their discoveries in Canaan, their return to the camp, and the treatment they received. The third division, chaps. 15-19, gives various legal enactments and a few historical facts. The last division, chaps. 20-36, contains an account of the events of the last year before crossing the Jordan. In chap. 20 we have the description of Moses smiting the rock, and the notices of Miriam's and Aaron's deaths. In chap. 21 we have a picture of the discontentment and rebellion of the Israelites, their punishment through fiery serpents, and the simple remedy of a brazen serpent erected on a pole. Comp. John 3:14, 15. Chaps. 22-24 are concerned with Balaam. In chap. 32 the land east of the Jordan is assigned to Reuben and Gad, and in chap. 33 a list is given of the various stations in the wilderness.

Nuts. Those mentioned in Gen. 43:11 are doubtless pistachio-nuts, which were produced in Syria, but not in Egypt. Another word translated "nuts" in Song of Sol. 6:11 denotes what are known in our markets as "English walnuts," produced by a noble tree—*Juglans regia*—which is everywhere cultivated in the East.

O

Oak, *strong*. Gen. 35:4. No less than six Hebrew words are represented by oak in the A. V. Sometimes, evidently, the terebinth, elm, or teil tree is intended; at others, the oak. There are a number of varieties of oak in Palestine. Hos. 4:13; Judg. 6:11; Isa. 1:30; Amos 2:9.

Oath. The forms of solemn affirmation mentioned in Scripture are: 1. Lifting up the hand. Witnesses laid their hands on the head of the accused. Gen. 14:22; Lev. 24:14; Deut. 17:7; Isa. 3:7, A. V., but the R. V. reads "he shall lift up *his voice*." 2. Putting the hand under the thigh of the person to whom the promise was made. Gen. 24:2; 47:29. 3. Oaths were sometimes taken before the altar, or by an appeal to Jehovah; "as the Lord liveth." 2 Kings 2:2. Comp. 1 Kings 8:31; 2 Chron. 6:22. 4. Dividing a victim and passing between or distributing the pieces. Gen. 15:10, 17; Jer. 34:18. As the sanctity of oaths was carefully inculcated by the law, so the crime of perjury was strongly condemned; and to a false witness the same punishment was assigned which was due for the crime to which he testified. Ex. 20:7; Lev. 19:12. The New Testament has prohibitions against swearing. Matt. 5:34-37; Jas. 5:12. It cannot be supposed that it was intended by these to censure every kind of oath. For our Lord himself made solemn asseverations equivalent to an oath; and Paul repeatedly, in his inspired epistles, calls God to witness the truth of what he was saying. The intention was, as Alford well notes upon Matt. 5:34-37, to show "that the *proper* state of Christians is to require no oaths; that, when evil is expelled from among them, every yea and nay will be as decisive as an oath, every promise as binding as a vow."

Obadiah (ō′ba-dī′ah or ŏb′a-dī′ah), *servant of Jehovah*. The name of 13 persons in Scripture. The most noted of these were: 1. The officer of Ahab's court who hid 150 prophets from Jezebel. 2. The prophet whose prophecy is placed fourth among the minor prophecies. Absolutely nothing is known of his life. His prophecy was possibly uttered subsequently to B.C. 588, as we draw from verse 11. The captivity of this verse is in all probability that by Nebuchadnezzar in B.C. 588.

PROPHECY OF, contains a general accusation of Edom, and an account of the prosperity of Zion when Jacob should return from his captivity and Esau be discomfited. There is a striking resemblance between the first nine verses of this prophecy and Jer. 49:7-16. One prophet must have read the other's prophecy.

Obed-edom (ō′bed-ē′dom) *servant of Edom*. 1. A Gittite who lived in David's time, 1 Chron. 13:13, and at whose house the ark was left, after the dreadful death of Uzzah. 2 Sam. 6:6-10. The blessing which came on the house of Obed-edom for the ark's sake encouraged David to remove it to Jerusalem. 2 Sam. 6:10-12. 2. The temple-treasurer in the reign of Amaziah. 2 Chron. 25:24.

Oded (ō′ded), *erecting*. 1. The father of the prophet Azariah, who flourished in Asa's reign. 2 Chron. 15:1-8. In v. 8 Oded is called "prophet," where probably "the son" is meant. 2. A prophet at the time of Pekah's invasion of Judah who prevailed upon the victorious army to let the captives free. 2 Chron. 28:9-11.

Offering, Gen. 4:3, **Oblation,** Lev. 2:7. The offerings in Jewish worship were either bloody or bloodless, or animal and vegetable. Of animals only tame ones were used, as oxen, goats, and sheep, and the dove. Lev. 5:11, etc. From the vegetable kingdom, wine, flour, etc., were set apart. Human sacrifices or offerings were especially forbidden. Lev. 18:21; 20:2. The first offerings of which record is made are those of Cain and Abel. Gen. 4:3-8. The second offering is that of Noah, Gen. 8:20, after the flood. The various offerings were the burnt-offerings, meat-offerings, peace-offerings, and the sin and trespass-offerings. The burnt-offering was to be a male without blemish, of the herd and of the flock, offered voluntarily at the door of the tabernacle, the hand of the offerer being upon the head of the victim. Lev. 1:2–4. The design of the burnt-offering was an atonement for sin. Lev. 1:4; comp. Heb. 10:1-3, 11. It was presented every day, Ex. 29:38-42, on the Sabbath, Num. 28:9, 10, and on the great day of atonement, Lev. 16:3, and the three great festivals. Num. 28:11-31; 29. The meat-offering, R. V., "meal-offering," consisted of flour, or cakes, prepared with oil and frankincense. Lev. 2:1; 6: 14–23. It was to be free from leaven and honey, but was to have salt. Lev. 2:11, 13. With this was connected the drink-offering, which was never used separately, but was an appendage of wine to some sacrifices. Ex. 29:41. A meal-offering was presented every day with the burnt-offering. Ex. 29: 40, 41. The first-fruits, offered at Pentecost, Lev. 23:17-20, and at the Passover, Lev. 23: 10-14, were called wave-offerings; those offered in harvest-time, Num. 15:20, 21, heave-offerings. Peace-offerings were eucharistic in their nature, and were offered in thanksgiving or at a special dedication of something to the Lord. Lev. 3; 7:11-21. The animal as well as the vegetable kingdom contributed to this class of offerings. The sin and trespass-offerings were expiatory. They included an offering for the sins of ignorance. Lev. 4:2. There are sins that are "debts" to God, more numerous, it may be, than our transgressions. The prayer the Lord taught regards sins as "debts." Matt. 6:12. Our thanksgivings now are to be offered through Christ, and the Hebrews were required to present sacrifices with their thanksgivings. Lev. 7:15. Sin-offerings were presented by the high priest for personal offences, for national sins, and on the great day of atonement, when he confessed the sins of the whole nation with his hand on the scapegoat's head, and the goat was driven off into the wilderness. Lev. 16, etc. These offerings all had a typical significance, and prefigured the atonement of Jesus Christ, on whom was laid the iniquity of us all, and "his own self bare our sins in his own body on the tree." 1 Pet. 2:24.

Og (ōg) long-necked? A king of Bashan, of gigantic stature. Deut. 3:11, who opposed the passage of the Israelites through his territories. Deut. 3:1. He was defeated in a pitched battle in Edrei, and, together with his sons, was slain. Deut. 1:4; Num. 21:33, 34. His sixty fenced and walled cities were given with Bashan and all his kingdom to the half-tribe of Manasseh. Deut. 3:3, 4; Num. 32:33. He was a giant. Josh. 13:12, and his long iron bedstead was regarded as a curiosity, and was preserved as a memorial of his huge stature. Deut. 3:11.

Oil. The Hebrews used olive oil as butter and as animal fat is used with us. Deut. 32:13; Job. 24:11; Ezek. 16:13. In some of the Hebrew thank-offerings oil was taken with the meat-offering. Lev. 5:11; 7:12; Num. 5:15; 6:15; Ex. 29:40. Oil was used for anointing the head and the body; and in the preparation of ointments. Ex. 30:24; 2 Sam. 14:2; Ps. 23:5; 92:10; 104: 15; Prov. 21:17; Luke 7:46. The application of oil for medicinal purposes prevailed in the earliest periods. Isa. 1:6; Hos. 12:1; Mark 6:13; James 5:14, 15. Olive oil was extensively used for the lamps in the tabernacle. Ex. 27:20. The use of oil is significant of gladness, Ps. 141:5; Isa. 61:3, and the omission of it betokened sorrow. 2 Sam. 14:2; Matt. 6:17. Oil was also the symbol of abundance and festivity. Deut. 28:40; Ezek. 27:17. The anointing with oil was symbolical of the unction of the Holy Spirit. Ps. 45:7; Zech. 4:14; Isa. 61: 1; 1 John 2:20.

Old Testament. See Scriptures.

Olive, Olive-Tree. 1 Kings 6:23. The olive, *olea Europaea*. It grows plentifully almost everywhere near the shores of the Mediterranean, and is abundant in Palestine. Deut. 6:11; 8:8. Olive yards are therefore commonly mentioned as a considerable part of a man's property. 1 Sam. 8: 14; 1 Chron. 27:28. This tree flourishes in Syria, in warm and sunny situations, on a rocky soil, at a height not greater than about 3000 feet above the level of the sea. It increases slowly to a moderate altitude of twenty or thirty feet, with a knotty trunk, and numerous extended branches. The leaves grow in pairs, of a pale dusty color, and are not deciduous. The white flowers appear in June; and the fruit is an oblong berry, first green, and, when fully ripe, a blackish-purple. The wood is something like box, but softer, with dark gray veins. The olive tree lives to a great age. With an olive leaf in her mouth the dove returned to Noah when the waters of the flood were abated. Gen. 8:11. The high estimation in which the olive tree was held is seen by its being placed first in Jotham's parable. Judg. 9:8, 9. And it is often mentioned as indicating plenty, prosperity, and strength: the allusion taking its force from the products, from the evergreen character, and the protracted existence of the tree, *e. g.*, Ps. 52:8. an olive being often planted in the court of a building, Ps. 128: 3, young shoots springing, from an old trunk: Jer. 11:16; Hos. 14:6. And various applications of the berries are referred to, Deut. 24:20, the oil, Lev. 24:2, which was an article of commerce, 1 Kings 5:11, and the wood, 6:31-33.

Olives, the Mount of, Olivet, Mount. A mountain ridge to the east of Jerusalem, from which it is separated by the valley of Jehoshaphat. It has three or four summits or peaks. The mount of Olives, called also Olivet, and by the Arabs at present Jebel et-Tur, a name they give to elevated summits generally, was so styled from the olive trees which clothed its sides. Some of these still remain; and on part of the hill are corn-fields; and in a few half-cultivated gardens are fig and pomegranate trees.

Olivet is mentioned several times in the Old Testament. Up its slopes David, fleeing from Jerusalem for fear of Absalom, went wearied and weeping. Here he met Hushai and Ziba. 2 Sam. 15:30; 16:4. It is also referred to by Zechariah. Zech. 14:4. From Olivet our Lord looked down upon Jerusalem and wept bitter tears over its perverseness. Over Olivet he passed to and fro visiting Bethany. On the side of Olivet was Gethsemane. On Olivet, the last charge was given to the disciples who were thenceforth to build up the Christian church, and from its top Christ ascended to reign till every enemy shall be subdued beneath his feet. Matt. 24:3; 26:30; Mark 11: 1-20; 13:3; 14:26; Luke 19:29-44; 21:37; 22:39; John 8:1; Acts 1:9-12. Christ did not ascend from the spot where now stands the church of the Ascension: it was rather from some point over the summit, near to Bethany. Luke 24:50, 51. The views from this mount in different directions are extensive; Jerusalem on one side, on another there are the dreary hills over which the road passes to Jericho, with the northern end of the Dead Sea visible, and the mountains of Moab beyond. The highest point of Olivet is 2682 feet above the sealevel.

Omega (*o-mē'gah*, or *ō'me-gah*). The last letter in the Greek alphabet. See **Alpha**.

Omri (*ŏm'rī*), *pupil of Jehovah*. 1. 1 Kings 16:16. A general of the Israelitish army, who was made king during the siege of Gibbethon. The army had heard that Zimri had assassinated Elah the king, and had usurped the throne; instantly the siege was raised, they forthwith marched to Tirzah, where Zimri resided, and captured it. The Israelites were then divided into two parties, one of which had made Tibni king; but after a struggle of about six years, Omri prevailed, and took the throne, which he disgraced, from 928-917 B.C. Omri, who is called on an Assyrian monument Khumri, founded Samaria, which thenceforth became the capital of the ten tribes. 1 Kings 16:16-30; Micah 6:16. 2. A descendant of Benjamin. 1 Chron. 7:8. 3. A descendant of Judah. 1 Chron. 9:4. 4. A descendant of Issachar. 1 Chron. 27:18.

On (*ŏn*), *sun, light*. A noted city of Lower Egypt, Gen. 41:45, 50; called Beth-shemesh, or "house of the sun," Jer. 43:13, and known to the Greeks as Heliopolis, or "city of the sun." Ezek. 30:17, A. V., margin. Some suppose it to be referred to as the "city of destruction" in Isa. 19:18, 19. On was situated upon the Pelusiac branch of the Nile, about 20 miles northeast of ancient Memphis, and 6 miles north from Cairo. The origin and founder of On are unknown, but it has an obelisk which has been standing about 4000 years. It has been considered the Rome and the Athens of ancient Egypt, the centre of its religion and learning. In it stood the great temple of Ra, with one exception the most famous ancient shrine in Egypt. Its companies of priests and attendants are reputed to have numbered over 12,000. The legend of the wonder-bird Phœnix, early used to illustrate the doctrine of the resurrection, arose here; to this city Joseph, delivered from prison, came with royal honors to marry the daughter of Potipherah, "dedicated to Ra." Josephus reports that On was the home of Jacob on his arrival in Egypt. In its grandeur it was the resort of men of learning from all countries. In its schools and universities Moses, according to Manetho, was instructed in all the learning of the Egyptians, and hither came Plato, Eudoxus, and the wisest of the Greeks to be initiated into the mystic lore of its priests. From the teachers of its ancient schools Herodotus gained his knowledge of the country and its history. The site of this once famous city is now marked with a few ruins of massive walls, fragments of sphinxes, a noted obelisk of red granite of Syene (one of the two which stood before the temple of the Sun). The obelisk, bearing the name of Usurtesen I., and rising amid the desolation, is 66 feet high. 2. Name of a person. Num. 16:1.

Onesimus (*o-nĕs'ĭ-mŭs*), *useful*. A slave of Philemon, in whose behalf Paul wrote the Epistle to Philemon. Col. 4:9.

Onesiphorus (*ŏn'e-sĭf'o-rŭs*), *profit-bringing*. A primitive Christian who ministered to the wants of Paul at Ephesus, and afterward sought him out at Rome and openly sympathized with him. 2 Tim. 1:16-18; 4:19.

Ono (*ō'no*), *strong*. A town in Benjamin and reoccupied after the captivity. 1 Chron. 8:12; Ezra 2:33; Neh. 7:37. A plain and a valley—the two perhaps identical—were connected with it. Neh. 6:2; 11:35; 1 Chron. 8:12. It is named with Lod, and may be a few miles north of Lydda (Lod).

Onyx. Gen. 2:12; Ex. 28:9, 20; 35:9, 27; 1 Chron. 29:2; Job 28:16; Ezek. 28: 13. Opinions differ as to the gem intended by this word; some prefer translating it "beryl." The onyx has its particles arranged in parallel layers; white alternating with blue, gray, or brown. It was much used by the ancients for cameos.

Ophel (*ō'fel*), *hill, swelling*. A hill of ancient Jerusalem and fortified by a wall. 2 Chron. 27:3; 33:14; Neh. 3:26 27; 11: 21, but it is now outside the walls of the city. See **Jerusalem**.

Ophir (*ō'fĭr*), *abundance*. 1. One of the sons of Joktan. Gen. 10:29; 1 Chron. 1: 23. 2. A seaport or region from which the Hebrews in the time of Solomon obtained gold. The gold was proverbial for its fineness, so that "gold of Ophir" is several times used as an expression for fine gold, 1 Chron. 29:4; Job 28:16; Ps. 45:9; Isa. 13: 12; and in one passage, Job 22:24, the word Ophir by itself is used for gold of Ophir, and for gold generally. In addition to gold the vessels brought from Ophir almug wood and precious stones. The precise situation of Ophir has long been a subject of discussion. It is safe to conclude that Ophir was in southern Arabia, upon the border of the Indian Ocean; for even if all the things brought over in Solomon's ships are not now found in Arabia, but are found in India, yet there is evidence that they once were known in Arabia.

Ophrah (ŏf'rah), *female fawn*. 1. A town in Benjamin toward which an invading company of Philistines went. Josh. 18:23; 1 Sam. 13:17. Some suppose it is identical with Ephrain or Ephron, 2 Chron. 13:19, and with the city of Ephraim, to which our Lord retired after raising Lazarus, John 11:54. Eusebius and Jerome located it about five Roman miles east of Bethel. 2. Ophrah of the Abi-ezerite. Judg. 6:11, 24. This was the place where Gideon saw the angel, erected an altar, and where he was buried. Judg. 8:27, 32. Here Abimelech slew 70 of his kindred, and the town appears to have been near Shechem, in the territory of Manasseh. Judg. 9:1, 5, 6, 15. The Palestine Memoirs suggest as its site the village of Ferata, near Shechem.

Oreb (ō'reb), *raven*. The "rock of Oreb" was named after Oreb, one of the princes of Midian, whom the men of Ephraim slew. Judg. 7:25; Isa. 10:26. Reland and others would locate Oreb east of the Jordan and in the neighborhood of Bethshean, at a place called Orbo.

Organ. Gen. 4:21, A. V., "pipe," R. V., meaning a wind instrument of music, like a flute or clarionet.

Orion (o-rī'on). A constellation of about 80 stars, south of Taurus, and, partly, of the equator. Job 9:9. The constellation is also mentioned in Job 38:31 and Amos 5:8.

Ossifrage (os'si-frage), *bone-breaker*. Lev. 11:13; the "gier-eagle," R. V.

Ostrich. Job 30:29; Isa. 13:21; 34:13; Jer. 50:39; Micah 1:8; Lam. 4:3. The largest of the feathered tribe, exceedingly swift, employing its wings which are useless for flight to aid it in running. It is voracious, and will swallow any hard substance, as stones or metal; but these are to assist the action of the gizzard. Sometimes, however, it is said that its indiscriminating appetite proves fatal to it. Several female ostriches lay their eggs in a single nest, a mere shallow hole in the sand, and then carefully cover them. In very hot climates the sun's heat on them is sufficient in the daytime without incubation by the parent birds; but in less sultry regions both male and female are said to sit upon the eggs. There are also other eggs scattered near which are apparently neglected, but are really designed for the food of the young birds when hatched. These habits are the result of the instinct with which the Deity has endowed the ostrich; but some of them are so strange as to have given rise to an Arabian proverb, "As foolish as an ostrich." And this is sufficient to justify the statement in the book of Job. Scripture must, of course, be composed in popular language; and the meaning here is evidently not that the bird is through stupidity unfaithful to its instinct, but that that instinct is of a kind which seems to imply want of forethought and natural care.

Othniel (ŏth'ni-el), *lion of God*. The successor of Joshua. He was the son of Kenaz, the younger brother of Caleb, of the tribe of Judah; and for his valor in seizing the city of Debir, he was rewarded by the gift of Achsah, the daughter of Caleb, in marriage. He delivered the Hebrews from the bondage in which they had been held for eight years by the Mesopotamians, and during the 40 years of his administration the Hebrews remained faithful to Jehovah. Josh. 15:16-19; Judg. 1:11-15; 3:8-11; 1 Chron. 4:13.

Ouches. The Hebrew word *mishbetzoth*, rendered ouches, signifies settings, bezels, in which gems are set, hence the sockets for fastening the precious stones in the shoulder-pieces of the high priest's ephod. Ex. 28:11, 14, 25; 39:13-16.

Oven. The Eastern oven is of two kinds—fixed and portable. The former is found only in towns, where regular bakers are employed. Hos. 7:4. The latter is adapted to the nomad state. It consists of a large jar made of clay, about three feet high and widening toward the bottom, with a hole for the extraction of the ashes. Each household possessed such an article, Ex. 8:3; and it was only in times of extreme dearth that the same oven sufficed for several families. Lev. 26:26. It was heated with dry twigs and grass, Matt. 6:30, and the loaves were placed both inside and outside of it.

P

Padan-aram (pā'dan-ā'ram), *the low highland*, where Abraham got a wife for his son Isaac, Gen. 25:20; 28:2, 5, 7, and Jacob found his wives, and where Laban lived. Gen. 31:18; 33:18; 35:9, 26; 46:15. It is the region between the two great rivers Euphrates and Tigris.

Palestine (păl'es-tīne), *land of sojourners*. Joel 3:4; comp. Ex. 15:14; Isa. 14:29, 31. A small country east of the Mediterranean Sea, sacred alike to Jew, Mohammedan, and Christian. In length it is about 140 miles, in average breadth not more than 40 between the Mediterranean westward, and the deep Jordan valley to the east, while to the north it is closed in by Lebanon and Anti-libanus, and bordered on the south by the desert. It lay on the direct route between the great ancient empires of Asia and northern Africa, and exposed to peril from both. The physical structure of Palestine is peculiar. It is mountainous, but among these mountains are plains and valleys and torrent-beds. The mountain mass which occupies the central part is bordered on each side east and west by a lowland belt. On the west the plains of Philistia and Sharon lie between the Mediterranean and the hills, interrupted by a ridge which, shooting out from the main highlands, terminates in the bold promontory of Carmel. To the north of this ridge the low plain widens and extends in one part its undulating surface quite across the country to the Jordan. And still farther to the north is Phœnicia with headlands down to the sea. The eastern depression is most remarkable. It is a deep cleft in which lie a chain of lakes connected by the Jordan. And the bottom of this cleft is, in its lower part, far below (1300 feet) the level of the Mediterranean Sea. Owing to this extraordinary depression, the slopes on the eastern side of the central elevated land are much more abrupt and rugged than on the west. The southern hill country is dry and bare. There is little wood; it is near upon the desert, and possesses few springs of water. The hill tops are rounded and monotonous—the eastern part of the tract being but an arid wilderness. And a noteworthy feature in these hills is the abundance of caverns, partly natural, partly, perhaps, artificial. Northward the country improves. There are more fertile plains winding among the hills, more vegetation and more wood, till in the north the swelling hills are clothed with beautiful trees, and the scenery is pleasing, oftentimes romantic. In central and north Palestine, too, there are gushing fountains of water, imparting fertility to the valleys through which they pour their streams. The Philistine plain is one vast grainfield, yielding the most abundant increase. And dry and barren as are many of the hills at present, there is evidence enough that in earlier happier days they were terraced, wooded, and productive: "a good land, a land of brooks of water, of fountains and depths that spring out of valleys and hills; a land of wheat, and barley, and vines, and fig trees, and pomegranates; a land of oil olive and honey . . . a land whose stones *are* iron, and out of whose hills thou mayest dig brass." Deut. 8:7-9. Palestine was early inhabited by seven tribes—as, Hittites, Gergashites, Amorites, Canaanites, Perizzites, Hivites, and Jebusites, Deut. 7:1; and other tribes are also noted as occupying adjacent regions. Gen. 10:15-19; 15:18-21; Num. 13:28, 29. It became afterwards the land of Israel; but, when judgment fell upon the Hebrews for their sins, they were removed, and there was at different times a large influx of foreign population, eastern nations, 2 Kings 17:24; Ezra 4:9, 10, Greeks, etc.; so that even in our Lord's time the inhabitants of Palestine were of a mixed character; and in later ages additional foreign elements were introduced. See Judæa, Galilee.

Palm, Palm Tree. Ex. 15:27; Lev. 23:40; Deut. 34:3. There are several hundred species of palm; but the *Phœnix dactylifera*, or date-palm, is that which, growing in Palestine, is often referred to in Scripture. Its fruit furnishes a considerable part of subsistence to the inhabitants of Egypt, Persia, and Arabia. A conserve is also made of it with sugar; while the stones are ground in the handmills for the food of camels. Baskets, bags, mats, etc., are manufactured of the leaves; the trunk is split up, and is serviceable in various ways; the weblike integuments at the bases of the leaves are twisted into ropes; the sap is collected, and is at first a sweetish mild beverage, but afterwards ferments, and a kind of arrack is produced from it by distillation. Every part, therefore, of the tree has its use. The names of many places show that palms were abundant: Elim, Elath, Hazezon-tamar—"felling of palm tree" —Gen. 14:6; Bethany, "house of dates." John 11:1; 12:13.

Palmer-worm. Heb. *gâzâm*. Joel 1:4; 2:25; Amos 4:9. Probably some species of locust or caterpillar is intended.

Palsy. Matt. 4:24; 8:6; Luke 6:6. The loss of sensation or power of motion in any part of the body. A hand thus affected was called "a withered hand." Matt. 12:10-13. Several palsied or paralytic persons were cured by Jesus. Matt. 4:24; 8:13; John 5:5-7.

Pamphylia (*pam-fil'i-ah*), *of every tribe.* A Roman province in the south of Asia Minor. It was in Pamphylia that Paul first entered Asia Minor, after preaching the gospel in Cyprus. Acts 13:13; 14:24; 27:5.

Pannag. Ezek. 27:17. Some kind of spice or millet, or "perhaps a kind of confection," R. V. margin.

Paphos (*pā'fos*), *boiling,* or *hot.* Acts 13:6. A town at the west end of the island of Cyprus. It was founded B. C. 1184. Paul and Barnabas travelled, on their first missionary tour, "through the isle," from Paphos to Salamis. Acts 13:6. Paphos was given to the worship of Aphrodite or Venus, who was fabled to have here risen from the sea.

Parable (from a Greek word signifying comparison) is used in the Bible in both the wide and a narrow sense. In the first case it comprises all forms of teaching by analogy, and all forms of figurative speech, and is applied to metaphors, whether expanded into narratives, Ezek. 12:22, or not, Matt. 24:32; to proverbs and other short sayings, 1 Sam. 10:12; 24:13; 2 Chron. 7:20; Luke 4:23; to dark utterances or signs of prophetic or symbolical meaning. Num. 23:17, 18; 24:3; Ezek. 20:49; Heb. 9:9, etc. In the second case it means a short narrative of some every-day event, by which some great spiritual truth is conveyed to the hearer. For list of parables of Christ see Appendix.

Paran, El-paran (*pā'ran*), *place of caverns.* A desert or wilderness south of Palestine, and near the wilderness of Etham, which separated it from the Gulf of Suez and Egypt. Paran is named in connection with the invasion of the confederate kings, Gen. 14:6, and in the story of Hagar, Gen. 21:21. In the detailed itinerary of the children of Israel, Num. 33, many stations in Paran are recorded, Num. 33:17-49, and probably all the eighteen stations there mentioned between Hazeroth and Kadesh were in Paran. Through this very wide wilderness, from pasture to pasture, as do modern Arab tribes, the Israelites wandered in irregular lines of march.

Parthians (*pär'thi-anz*). Acts 2:9. The inhabitants of Parthia. It lay east of Media. Parthia was raised into a distinct kingdom by Arsaces, B. C. 256. It soon extended itself over a great part of the ancient Persian empire. The Parthians were esteemed the most expert horsemen and archers in the world; and their skill in discharging arrows while in full flight is frequently celebrated by Roman poets.

Pas-dammim (*pās'dăm'mĭm*), *boundary of blood*. The scene of fierce contests between the Israelites and the Philistines. 1 Chron. 11:13. It is called Ephes-dammim in 1 Sam. 17:1; perhaps Damum, about 11 miles southwest of Jerusalem.

Passover, the principal annual feast of the Jews. Comp. 1 Cor. 5:7, 8. It was appointed to commemorate the "passing over" of the families of the Israelites when the destroying angel smote the first-born of Egypt, and also their departure from the land of bondage. Ex. 12. At even of the 14th day of the first month (Nisan) the Passover was to be celebrated, and on the 15th day commenced the seven days' feast of unleavened bread. The term "Passover" is strictly applicable only to the meal of the paschal lamb, and the feast of unleavened bread was celebrated on the 15th onward for seven days to the 21st inclusive. This order is recognized in Josh. 5:10, 11. But in the sacred history the term "Passover" is used also to denote the whole period—the 14th day, and the festival of the seven days following. Luke 2:41; John 2:13, 23; 6:4; 11:55. As to the time of the celebration of the Passover, it is expressly appointed "between the two evenings," Ex. 12:6; Lev. 23:5; Num. 9:3, 5, or, as it is elsewhere expressed, "at even, at the going down of the sun." Deut. 16:6. This is supposed to denote the commencement of the 15th day of Nisan, or at the moment when the 14th day closed and the 15th began. The twenty-four hours, reckoned from this point of time to the same period of the next day, or 15th, was the day of the Passover. At sunset of the 14th day the 15th began, and with it the feast of unleavened bread. The lamb was to be selected on the 10th day, and kept till the 14th day, in the evening of which day it was to be killed. Ex. 12:3-6. The feast began by the handing around of a cup of wine mixed with water; over which the head of the family or the chief of the association pronounced the benediction. The lamb, roasted whole, and the other dishes were then placed on the table, and after a second cup of wine the meal was eaten. Everybody present partook of the lamb, the bitter herbs, and the unleavened bread, and care was taken that no bone was broken. What was left of the flesh was immediately burnt. After the meal followed the third cup of wine, then the singing of psalms and hymns, and finally a fourth, and perhaps a fifth, cup of wine. Then followed the feast of unleavened bread, occupying seven days, the first and last of which were peculiarly holy, like the Sabbath. Ex. 12:15, 16. That the Passover was a type of the sacrifice of Christ is clearly shown by Christ himself, where he says, "With desire I have desired to eat this passover with you before I suffer: For I say unto you, I will not any more eat thereof, until it be fulfilled in the kingdom of God." Luke 22:15, 16. He at that time instituted what is called the Lord's Supper to commemorate his death and which since then has taken the place of the Passover in his church.

Pastors (*shepherds*). This word occurs but once in the New Testament, Eph. 4:11. In all other places where the Greek word occurs it is translated shepherd, and shepherds. It is often applied to Christ as the Shepherd and Bishop of our souls. John 10:11; 1 Pet. 2:25. It refers to the elders of the church, who are to "feed (shepherd) the flock of God which is among you, taking the oversight *thereof*." 1 Pet. 5:1, 2; Acts 20:28.

Patara (*păt'a-rah*), a seaport town on the southwest shore of Lycia, near the left bank of Xanthus, and opposite Rhodes. Acts 21:1, 2. It was about seven miles east of the mouth of the river, had a convenient harbor, and was visited by ships of all nations. The gospel was early preached there. The city was given up to the worship of Apollo, its founder, Patarus, being reputed to be a son of that god. Patara is now in ruins, but retains its ancient name.

Pathros (*păth'ros*), *region of the south*. A district of Egypt near Thebes. The country is mentioned in the Prophets, and nearly always in connection with Egypt. Isa. 11:11; Jer. 44:1-15; Ezek. 29:14. Its inhabitants were known as the Pathrusim, the descendants of Ham through Mizraim. Gen. 10:14; 1 Chron. 1:12.

Patmos (*păt'mos*). Rev. 1:9. A little rugged island in the Ægean Sea, 24 miles west of Asia Minor. It is from 15 to 25 miles in circumference, and is very rocky and barren. The barrenness of the island made it a suitable spot for the banishment of Roman criminals. To it the apostle John was banished by the emperor Domitian, A. D. 95. Its rocky solitude well suited the sublime nature of the Revelation.

Paul (*pawl*), *small*. Originally named Saul, he is first called Paul in Acts. He was a Jew of pure Hebrew descent, of the tribe of Benjamin, circumcised according to the law when eight days old, born at Tarsus in Cilicia, and by birth a free Roman citizen. Acts 22:28. He was taught, according to Jewish custom, a trade, that of tentmaker—*i. e.*, the manufacturing of goats' hair cloth, commonly used for tents. But he was early sent to Jerusalem, where he was trained under the famous Gamaliel. Acts 21:39; 22:3, 27, 28; Phil. 3:5. Of his family we know nothing, save that he had a nephew, who detected a conspiracy against his life. Acts 23:16-22. He was a fierce defender of Judaism and a bitter enemy of Christianity. Acts 8:3; 26:9-11. Of his miraculous conversion, we have three accounts—Acts, chaps. 9, 22, 26. Christ revealed himself to him near and at Damascus. Acts 26:15; 1 Cor. 15:8. His advocacy of Jesus as the Jewish Messiah exposed him everywhere to the hatred and malice of his countrymen. He made four missionary tours, preaching Christ and planting churches in Asia Minor, Macedonia, and Greece, and making several visits to Jerusalem, narrated in the Acts. He was accused by the rulers of the Jews, arrested at Jerusalem by the Roman officers, and after being detained for two years or more at Cæsarea, he was sent to Rome for trial, having himself appealed to Cæsar. It is quite probable, as Christians believed in the earlier centuries, that the apostle was acquitted and discharged from his first imprisonment in Rome at the end of two years, and that he afterwards returned to Rome, where he was again imprisoned and put to death by Nero. The following is a summary of the chief events in the life of Paul, taken from Schaff's *Dictionary of the Bible*:

	A. D.
Paul's conversion	37
Sojourn in Arabia	37–40
First journey to Jerusalem after his conversion, Gal. 1:18; sojourn at Tarsus, and afterward at Antioch. Acts 11:26	40
Second journey to Jerusalem, in company with Barnabas, to relieve the famine	44
Paul's first great missionary journey, with Barnabas and Mark: Cyprus, Antioch in Pisidia, Iconium, Lystra, Derbe; return to Antioch in Syria	45–49
Apostolic Council at Jerusalem; conflict between Jewish and Gentile Christianity; Paul's third journey to Jerusalem, with Barnabas and Titus; settlement of the difficulty; agreement between the Jewish and Gentile apostles; Paul's return to Antioch; his difference with Peter and Barnabas at Antioch, and temporary separation from the latter	50
Paul's second missionary journey from Antioch to Asia Minor, Cilicia, Lycaonia, Galatia, Troas, and Greece (Philippi, Thessalonica, Berœa, Athens, and Corinth). From this tour dates the Christianization of Europe	51
Paul at Corinth (a year and a half). First and Second Epistles to the Thessalonians	52–53
Paul's fourth journey to Jerusalem (spring); short stay at Antioch. His third missionary tour (autumn)	54
Paul at Ephesus (three years); Epistle to the Galatians (56 or 57). Excursion to Macedonia, Corinth, and Crete (not mentioned in the Acts); First Epistle to Timothy (?). Return to Ephesus. First Epistle to the Corinthians (spring, 57)	54–57
Paul's departure from Ephesus (summer) to Macedonia. Second Epistle to the Corinthians	57
Paul's third sojourn at Corinth (three months). Epistle to the Romans	57, 58
Paul's fifth and last journey to Jerusalem (spring), where he is arrested and sent to Cæsarea	58
Paul's captivity at Cæsarea. Testimony before Felix, Festus, and Agrippa (the Gospel of Luke and the Acts commenced at Cæsarea, and concluded at Rome)	58–60
Paul's voyage to Rome (autumn); shipwreck at Malta; arrival at Rome (spring, 61)	60, 61
Paul's first captivity at Rome. Epistles to the Colossians, Ephesians, Philippians, Philemon	61–63
Conflagration at Rome (July); Neronian persecution of the Christians; martyrdom of Paul (?)	64
Hypothesis of a second Roman captivity and preceding missionary journeys to the East, and possibly to Spain. First Epistle to Timothy; Titus (Hebrews?), Second Timothy	63–67

The epistles of Paul are 13, or, if we count the Hebrews, 14 in number. They are inspired tracts for the times, and for all times. They may be arranged:

1. *Chronologically:*

1 and 2 Thessalonians, written A. D. 52, 53, from Corinth.
Galatians, written A. D. 56–57, from Ephesus.
1 Corinthians, written A. D. 57, from Ephesus.
2 Corinthians, written A. D. 57, from Macedonia.
Romans, written A. D. 58, from Corinth.
Colossians, Ephesians, Philippians, and Philemon, written A. D. 61–63, from Rome.
Hebrews, written A. D. 64 (?), from Italy.
1 Timothy and Titus, written A. D. 65 or 57 (?) *, from Macedonia.
2 Timothy, written A. D. 67 or 64 (?) *, from Rome.

*The time of the composition of the Pastoral Epistles depends upon the question of the second Roman captivity. The Second Epistle to Timothy was at all events the last, whether written in the first or second captivity.

2. *Topically:*

Romans and Galatians: doctrines of sin and grace.
1 and 2 Corinthians: moral and practical questions.
Colossians and Philippians: person of Christ.
Ephesians: the Church of Christ.
1 and 2 Thessalonians: the second advent.
1 and 2 Timothy and Titus: church government and pastoral care.
Philemon: slavery.
Hebrews: the eternal priesthood and sacrifice of Christ.

Pekah (*pē'kah*), *open-eyed.* 2 Kings 15: 25. The son of Remaliah, a captain in Pekahiah's army who conspired against his master, slew him, and reigned over Samaria in his stead for 20 years (758–738 B. C.). His conduct was evil; he maintained the sinful worship set up by Jeroboam I. He was slain by conspirators headed by Hoshea, who afterwards obtained the crown. 2 Kings 15:25–38; 16:1–9; 2 Chron. 28:6; Isa. 7:1–16; 8:6.

Pekahiah. *Jehovah has opened his eyes.* The son of Menahem, king of Israel. He succeeded his father and reigned wickedly two years (760–758 B. C.). He was murdered in his palace by Pekah, one of his officers, 2 Kings 15:22–26.

Pelican. Heb. *the vomiter*. A voracious water-bird, unclean by the Levitical law, Lev. 11:18, of singular construction and habits, resembling the goose, though nearly twice as large. Its bill is 15 inches long. The female has a large pouch or bag capable of containing two or three gallons of water, and food enough for six common men. Out of this pouch she feeds herself and her young, and from this habit and the red nail at the end of her bill came the notion that she fed her offspring on her own blood. The pelican was formerly more abundant than now in the East. Having gorged itself with fish, this bird flies miles into the wilderness, where it sits in some lonely place "for hours, or even days, with its bill resting on its breast, a picture of melancholy." Ps. 102:6. The R. V. and the margin of the A. V. read "pelican" for "cormorant" in Isa. 34:11; Zeph. 2:14.

Peniel (*pe-ni'el*), *face of God*. The name which Jacob gave to the place in which he had wrestled with God: "He called the name of the place Peniel; (face of God), for..I have seen God face to face." Gen. 32:30. Called also Penuel. Gen. 32:31; Judg. 8:17; 1 Kings 12:25. Peniel lay somewhere on the Jabbok, now Zerka, a few miles north of the glen where the Jabbok falls into the Jordan.

Penny. Matt. 20:2; 22:19; Luke 20:24. This word in the English version is misleading at the present time. When the translation was first made the English penny was a silver coin. The Greek word is *dēnarion*, the Roman *denarius*, which was a silver coin worth about 16 cents. The penny shown to Christ was a Roman *denarius*, bearing the likeness and name of Tiberius Cæsar, who was emperor of Rome at that time. Agreeing "to pay the laborer a *denarius* a day" shows that 16 cents was then about the value of a day's labor in Judea.

Pentecost. Acts 2:1. From a Greek word signifying fiftieth. The name in the New Testament for the second great festival of the Jews, called by them "the feast of weeks," or "the day of first-fruits." It was celebrated on the fiftieth day—hence the name—after the passover, reckoning from the second day of the passover—the 16th of Nisan—Lev. 23:11, 15, to the morrow after the end of the seventh week. Lev. 23:15, 16; Deut. 16:9. It was originally a simple thanksgiving for the harvest, which in Palestine fell in the weeks between the passover and the pentecost. The festival was kept only for one day, and the principal rite consisted in the offering of two loaves made of the finest flour of the last crop's wheat. In some branches of the Christian Church pentecost is celebrated seven weeks after Easter, in commemoration of the outpouring of the Holy Spirit on the disciples, as the birthday of the Christian Church. See Acts 2:1-14.

Pergamos (*per'ga-mŏs*, Rev. 1:11, A. V., but in R. V. *Pergamum*), *height, elevation*. A city of Mysia, about three miles to the north of the river Caicus, and 20 miles from its present mouth. The city was noted for its vast library, containing 200,000 volumes. Here were splendid temples of Zeus or Jupiter, Athene, Apollo, and Æsculapius. One of "the seven churches of Asia" was in Pergamos. Rev. 1:11; 2:12-17. It is called "Satan's seat" by John, which some suppose to refer to the worship of Æsculapius, from the serpent being his characteristic emblem. The modern name of the city is Bergama.

Peor. Num. 23:28. See **Pisgah.**

Perizzites (*pĕr'iz-zītes*), *villagers*. The Perizzites lived apparently in villages in the open country in the south part of Palestine, and were expelled during the conquest. Gen. 13:7; 34:30; Josh. 17:15; Judg. 3:5; 1 Kings 9:20; 2 Chron. 8:7; Ezra 9:1.

Persia (*pĕr'shĭah*, or *shah*), Heb. *Pharas, pure,* or *tigers?* Ezek. 38:5. A country in Central Asia. The term is generally applied in Scripture to the Persian empire, but in Ezek. 38:5 it designates Persia proper. The Persian empire extended from the Indus on the east to Thrace on the west, and from the Black and Caspian Seas on the north to the Indian Ocean, the Persian Gulf, and the Red Sea on the south. It, at times, included Western Asia and portions of Europe and Africa. Persia proper was an unproductive country south of Media. The interior was a great plateau, having an average elevation of 4000 feet above the sea, broken by mountains and valleys and interspersed with fruitful plains. The founder of the Persian dynasty was Achæmes, and it was tributary to the Medes until a revolt under Cyrus about B. C. 558, when it rapidly extended its sway over Asia Minor, and in B. C. 538 over Babylon, where the Persians came into contact with the captive Jews. Cyrus issued a decree permitting the Jewish captives to return to their own land. 2 Chron. 36:20-23; Ezra 1:8. A later king, called Artaxerxes in Scripture, forbade the rebuilding of the temple, but Darius Hystaspes authorized the work to go on. Ezra 4:5-24; 6:7-12. Xerxes, who was probably the Ahasuerus of the book of Esther, succeeded him, and was defeated by the Greeks, assassinated, and succeeded by his son Artaxerxes Longimanus, who was friendly to the Jews. Ezra 7:11-28; Neh. 2:1-9. Only one of his successors is noticed in Scripture, Darius the Persian. Neh. 12:22. After lasting about 200 years the Persian empire was overthrown by Alexander the Great, B. C. 330, and followed by the Macedonian, the third great world-empire. Dan. 8:3-7, 20.

Peter (*pē'ter*), *stone,* or *rock;* Syriac *Cephas;* Greek *Petros*. One of the twelve apostles, one of the three favorite disciples, with John and James. His original name was "Simon" or "Simeon." He was a son of Jonas (John, so read the best manuscripts), a brother of Andrew, probably a native of Bethsaida in Galilee. He was a fisherman and lived at Capernaum with his wife and mother-in-law, whom Christ healed of a fever. See John 1:42; 21:15; Matt. 16:18; Luke 5:3-10; Matt. 8:14, 15; Mark 1:29-31; Luke 4:38. Peter forsook all to follow Christ. His new name "Peter" ("rock-man") was given him when he was called to the apostleship. John 1:42. He made a remarkable confession of the divinity of our Lord. Matt. 16:18. The name "Peter" or "Cephas" was a prophecy of the prominent position which he, as the confessor of Christ, would occupy in the primitive age of the church. The church was built (not on Petros, but Petra—a rock), on his confession of the foundation, "Thou art the Christ, the Son of the living God." Matt. 16:16, 18. The keys of the kingdom of heaven, to bind, and to loose, on earth and in heaven, were given to the church. Matt. 18:17, 18; 1 Cor. 5:11, 13; 2 Cor. 2:7, 10. Peter was not infallible, for Paul "withstood him to the face because he was to be blamed." Gal. 2:11. He laid the foundation of the church among the Jews on the day of Pentecost, Acts 2, and, after a special vision and revelation, among the Gentiles also, in the conversion of Cornelius. Acts 10. He appears throughout in the Gospels and the first part of the Acts as the head of the twelve. He was the first to confess and the first to deny his Lord and Saviour, yet he repented bitterly, and had no rest and peace till the Lord forgave him. He had a great deal of genuine human nature, but divine grace did its full work, and overruled even his faults for his advancement in humility and meekness. The labors of Peter are recorded in the Acts, chaps. 1 to 12 and chap. 15. He was the leading apostle from the day of Pentecost to the Council of Jerusalem, in A. D. 50. After that time his labors are involved in obscurity. According to the testimony of Christian antiquity, Peter suffered martyrdom in Rome under Nero, but his residence in Rome is disputed, and the year of his martyrdom is uncertain. When Paul arrived at Rome, A. D. 61, and during his imprisonment, A. D. 61-63, no mention is made of Peter. He is said to have been crucified, and thus he followed his Lord literally in the mode of his death. Comp. John 21:18, 19. Origen adds, however, that Peter, deeming himself unworthy to suffer death in the same manner as his Master, was at his own request crucified with his head downward.

EPISTLES OF PETER. The genuineness of 1 Peter has never been seriously questioned. It was addressed to Christian churches in Asia Minor, and written probably at Babylon on the Euphrates. 1 Pet. 5:13. Some, however, interpret this of Rome, and others of a town in Egypt called Babylon, near Old Cairo. 2 Peter was less confidently ascribed to Peter by the early church than the first epistle. There is no sufficient ground, however, for doubting its canonical authority, or that Peter was its author. 2 Pet. 1:1, 18; 3:1. Compare also 1 Pet. 3:20; 2 Pet. 2:5. In many passages it resembles the Epistle of Jude. Both epistles attest the harmony between the doctrines of Peter and Paul. "The faith expounded by Paul kindles into fervent hope in the words of Peter, and expands into sublime love in those of John."

Pharaoh (*fā'ro*, or *fā'ra-o*). Gen. 12:15. The common title of the king of Egypt—also called Pharaoh-necho and Pharaoh-hophra. 2 Kings 23:29; Jer. 44:30; 46:2. Ten Pharaohs are mentioned in the Old Testament. 1. The Pharaoh of the time of Abraham. Gen. 12:15. The date of Abraham's visit to Egypt is most probably fixed at about B. C. 2080. 2. The Pharaoh of Joseph, Gen. 41, was the last, or the last but one, of the fifteenth dynasty; probably identical with Apophis, who reigned at least 26 years, B. C. 1876-1850. 3. The Pharaoh of the Oppression—"the new king over Egypt who knew not Joseph," Ex. 1:8, and under whose reign Moses was born—probably Rameses II., the Sesostris of the Greeks, the masterbuilder of Egypt, whose statues and temples in ruins are found all over the Nile valley from Zoan (Tanis) to Karnak. His mummied body was taken from the tomb in 1881 and unwrapped in the Bulak museum. 4. The Pharaoh of the Exodus, Ex. 5:1, before whom Moses wrought his miracles, was Menephtha, son of Rameses II. On a monument of Tanis mention is made of the fact that he lost a son, and Dr. Brugsch connects this with the death of the first-born, the last of the plagues. 5. The Pharaoh whose daughter, Bithiah, was given in marriage to Mered, a descendant of Judah. 1 Chron. 4:18. 6. The Pharaoh who gave the sister of his queen in marriage to Hadad, an Edomite of royal blood, who escaped the massacre of Joab and fled to Egypt. 1 Kings 11:18-20. 7. The Pharaoh whose daughter Solomon married and brought "into the city of David until he had made an end of building his own house, and the house of the Lord," 1 Kings 3:1, consequently before the eleventh year of his reign, in which year the temple was finished. 1 Kings 6:37, 38. This Pharaoh afterward made an expedition into Palestine, took Gezer, and gave it to his daughter, Solomon's wife. 1 Kings 9:16. 8. The Pharaoh to whom king Hezekiah was allied in his war with Sennacherib. 2 Kings 18:21. 9. Pharaoh-nechoh, also called simply Necho, reigned from B. C. 610 to 594. He made an expedition against Assyria, but was encountered by Josiah, king of Judah, at Megiddo. 2 Chron. 35:20-24; 2 Kings 23:29, 30. Necho's army was afterward defeated at Carchemish by Nebuchadnezzar, and he lost all his Asiatic possessions. 2 Kings 24:7. 10. Pharaoh-hophra, the Apries of secular history, was the second successor of Necho, and entered Palestine, probably in B. C. 590, in order to relieve Jerusalem, which was besieged by Nebuchadnezzar. Jer. 37:5-8; Ezek. 17:11-13; comp. 2 Kings 25:1-4. The campaign was of no avail. Jerusalem fell, and Nebuchadnezzar made a successful invasion into Egypt. Pharaoh-hophra was afterward deposed by his own subjects, and finally strangled. In their prophecies Jeremiah and Ezekiel (see above) give a very striking picture of this king, his arrogance and conceit, which corresponds closely with that given by Herodotus.

Pharisees (*far'i-sees*), a religious sect

among the Jews at the time of Christ. Matt. 15:1–8. Their name is from the Hebrew word *perŭshim*, " separated." The chief sects among the Jews during Christ's ministry were the *Pharisees*, the *Sadducees*, and the *Essenes*. Christ denounced the Pharisees in the strongest language; see Matt. 15:1–8; 23:13–25; Mark 7:5, 6; Luke 11:42–44. To understand the Pharisees is an aid toward understanding the spirit of pure Christianity. The principle of the Pharisees, common to them with all orthodox modern Jews, is that by the side of the written law there was an oral law to complete and to explain the written law, given to Moses on Mount Sinai and transmitted by him by word of mouth. They were particular to avoid anything which the law declared unclean, but they forgot to acquire that cleanness which is the most important of all, and which consists in the purity of the heart. Matt. 15:11. It would be a great mistake to suppose that the Pharisees were wealthy and luxurious, or that they had degenerated into the vices which were imputed to some of the Roman popes and cardinals during the 200 years preceding the Reformation. Josephus compared the Pharisees to the sect of the Stoics. He says that they lived frugally, in no respect given to luxury. We are not to suppose that there were not many individuals among them who were upright and pure, for there were such men as Nicodemus, Gamaliel, Joseph of Arimathæa, and Paul. See Sadducees.

Pharpar (*fär'par*), *swift*. A river of Damascus—Abana and Pharpar—alluded to by Naaman. 2 Kings 5:12. See Abana.

Phenice (*fĕ-nī'se* or *fē'nice*). 1. Another and more accurate form for Phœnicia. Acts 11:19; 15:3, A. V. See Phœnicia. 2. A town and harbor, more properly Phœnix (from the Greek word for the palm tree which was indigenous to Crete). Acts 27:12. The town was on the southwest coast of the island of Crete.

Philadelphia (*fĭl'a-dĕl'fĭ-a*), *brotherly love*. Rev. 3:7. A city on the borders of Lydia and Phrygia, about 25 miles southeast of Sardis. It was built by Attalus Philadelphus, king of Pergamos, who died B. C. 138. Philadelphia is mentioned in the New Testament as the seat of one of the seven churches. Rev. 1:11; 3:7–13. The church at this place was highly commended, and it is noticeable that the city has survived all the vicissitudes of earthquakes and wars until the present day.

Philemon (*fĭ-lē'mon*), **Epistle to**. Written by Paul from Rome, probably near the close of A. D. 62. It is cited by Tertullian, Origen, and Eusebius. Onesimus, a servant of Philemon, had fled to Rome, was there converted, serving Paul for a season, but was sent back to his former master by Paul, who wrote this epistle, chiefly to conciliate the feelings of Philemon toward his penitent servant, and now fellow-disciple. Philem. 1.

Philip (*fĭl'ip*), *lover of a horse*. 1. One of the apostles, a native of Bethsaida; he had been a disciple of John the Baptist. John 1:43–48; 6:5–7; 12:21, 22; 14:8, 9; Matt. 10:3; Mark 3:18; Luke 6:14. He was with the rest of the apostles and disciples who had assembled for prayer in the upper room in Jerusalem, after the ascension of our Lord. Acts 1:13, 14. 2. One of the seven deacons of the church at Jerusalem; also called " the Evangelist." Acts 6:5; 21:8. He preached the gospel in Samaria with great success. Acts 8:5–13. He was directed of the Spirit to proceed toward Gaza, where he preached Christ to the treasurer of Candace, queen of Ethiopia. After a short stay at Azotus, Philip preached the gospel from town to town till he came to Cæsarea, where he probably settled. Acts 8:26–40. He had four daughters who were endued with the gifts of prophecy. Acts 21:8, 9. 3. A tetrarch of Trachonitis, and Ituræa. Luke 3:1. He was the son of Herod the Great, by his wife Cleopatra; and at his death his tetrarchy was annexed to Syria. Matt. 16:13; Mark 8:27. 4. A son of Herod the Great by Mariamne the daughter of Simon the high priest. He was the first husband of Herodias, who was taken from him by his brother Herod Antipas. Matt. 14:3; Mark 6:17; Luke 3:19.

Philippi (*fĭ-lĭp'pī*). A city of Macedonia. It was on the borders of Thrace, 33 Roman miles northeast of Amphipolis, and about ten miles from Neapolis its port, where Paul landed. It was built on the site of a village, called Krenides (also Datos), by Philip king of Macedon, and made a strong military station. From the New Testament history Philippi appears to have been the first city in Europe which heard the gospel. The account of Paul's visit and of his founding of a church there is given in Acts 16.

Philippians (*fĭ-lĭp'pĭ-anz*), **Epistle to the**. This epistle, written by Paul while a prisoner at Rome, A. D. 62 or 63, is remarkable for its Christian joy and for the love the apostle shows for the Philippian converts. Phil. 4:1. The Philippian Christians are reminded, as believers in Christ, of their dignity and privileges, see Acts 16:12–40, and are exhorted to live worthily of their heavenly citizenship. Phil. 3:20; 1:27, R. V.

Philistia (*fĭ-lĭs'tĭ-ah* or *-lĭst'yah*), *land of sojourners*. In Ps. 60:8; 87:4; 108:9, the only places where the word "Philistia" occurs, is the same Hebrew word elsewhere translated "Palestine." Palestine originally meant only the district inhabited by Philistines. In Ps. 83:7 A. V. the word is rendered "Philistines." Josephus calls these people "Palestines." Philistia, or the "land of the Philistines," included the coast plain on the southwest of Palestine, from Joppa on the north to the valley of Gerar on the south, a distance of about 40 miles. Its breadth at the northern end was ten miles, and at the southern about 20. It appears to have extended as far inland as Beersheba. Gen. 21:33, 34; 26:1, 14–18; Ex. 23:31; Josh. 13:2, 3. At the Exodus the Philistines seem to have been such a mighty and warlike people, that the Israelites deemed it prudent to avoid their land, lest "the people repent when they see war, and they return to Egypt." Ex. 13:17. Thenceforward, during the whole period of Old Testament history, the Israelites and the Philistines were frequently brought in contact. The Philistines are mentioned 310 times in the Old Testament, from Genesis to Zechariah. They were a commercial as well as a warlike people. Their chief god was Dagon, Judg. 16:23; 1 Sam. 5:1–5, who, as well as the goddess Derketo, had the form of a fish.

Phinehas (*fĭn'e-has*), *brazen mouth.* 1. A son of Eleazar and grandson of Aaron, Ex. 6:25; 1 Chron. 6:4, 50, was high priest of the Jews for nearly 20 years. His zeal and promptitude in punishing the sin of Zimri was rewarded by the promise to his family of perpetual succession in the Jewish priesthood. Num. 25:6–15. This promise was fulfilled; for except the interval from Eli to Zadok, the priesthood continued in the family of Phinehas until the destruction of the temple and the Babylonian captivity. 2. A son of Eli, and noted for his wickedness. 1 Sam. 1:3; 2:34; 4:4, 11, 17, 19; 14:3. 3. A Levite in the time of Ezra. Ezra 8:33.

Phœnicia (*fe-nĭsh'ĭ-ah*). A country north of Palestine, and on the Mediterranean Sea. Its extreme length was about 120 miles, and its width about 20 miles. Its chief cities were Tyre and Sidon. Phœnicia was included in the land of promise, but it was not occupied by the Israelites. Josh. 13:4–6; Judg. 1:31, 32. David and Solomon traded with its king, receiving timber from its territory, and employing its sailors, laborers, and skilled workmen. 2 Sam. 5:11; 1 Kings 5:9, 17, 18. Ahab married a princess of this country, and there Elijah found a refuge. 1 Kings 16:31; 17:9; Luke 4:26. Jesus also visited this country —the only time he passed the borders of Palestine. Matt. 15:21; Mark 7:26. Paul visited Tyre, Sidon, and Ptolemais. Acts 21:2, 3, 7; 27:3. The name "Phœnicia" does not occur in the Old Testament; in the New Testament it appears once as Phœnicia and twice as Phenice. Acts 21:2; 11:19; 15:3, A. V. The R. V. reads Phœnicia in all these places. There are numerous prophecies in the Old Testament, however, concerning the overthrow of cities in this country, which have been signally fulfilled. See **Tyre** and **Sidon**.

Phrygia (*frȳj'ĭ-ah*), *dry, barren*. A district of Asia Minor whose limits varied at different times. Within its limits were the cities of Laodicæa, Hierapolis, Colossæ, and Antioch of Pisidia. People from Phrygia were present at Pentecost, Acts 2:10; and the apostle Paul twice traversed the country. Acts 16:6; 18:23. Some converts were made, and we find Paul "strengthening all the disciples." Acts 18:23. At the Council of Nice, A. D. 325, the Phrygian churches were represented by eight bishops, and still more attended the Council of Constantinople, A. D. 381.

Phut (*phŭt*), *afflicted*, or *a bow?* Gen. 10:6. More properly Put, as in R. V., and 1 Chron. 1:8, A. V. Phut was a son of Ham, and progenitor of an African people of the same name, though sometimes the name is rendered "Libya" or "Libyans." Jer. 46:9; Ezek. 27:10; 30:5; 38:5; Nah. 3:9, A. V. But the R. V. reads "Put" in all cases. These people probably occupied Libya, in north Africa, near the Mediterranean coast. This is the land of the Moors in modern times.

Phylactery. Matt. 23:5. A strip of parchment on which some verses of Scripture were written, *e. g.*, Ex. 13:2–10, 11–16; Deut. 6:4–9; 11:13–21. Such strips were enclosed in small leathern boxes, and during the time of prayer worn by men on the forehead between the eyebrows, or on the left arm near the region of the heart, being attached by leathern straps. They were supposed to be preservatives against the power of demons; hence the name phylacteries, *i. e.*, safeguards. The practice was founded upon a literal interpretation of Ex. 13:9, 16; Deut. 6:8; 11:18, and is continued to the present day.

Pilate (*pī'late*), Pontius Pilatus, the sixth Roman procurator of Judea, succeeding Valerius Gratus. Under his rule John the Baptist commenced his ministry, Luke 3:1, and our Lord was put to death. Luke 23:6, 13; John 19:6, 19. Pilate entered on his office at the end of 25 or beginning of 26 A. D., in the reign of Tiberius. He held it about ten years, till a short time before that emperor's death. He was unscrupulous in the exercise of his authority. See Luke 13:1. Malicious, artful, yet not free from superstition, he was not destitute of some sense of justice, as his weak efforts to secure the acquittal of Jesus show. Vitellius, president or prefect of Syria, ordered Pilate to Rome to answer for his conduct before the emperor. His deposition must have occurred in 36 A. D., most probably prior to the passover. Before he arrived in Rome, however, Tiberius was dead, March 16, 37 A. D. Pilate is said to have been banished by Caligula to Vienne in Gaul. According to Eusebius, he put an end to his own life.

Pisgah (*pĭz'gah*), *hill*, or *the height*. The summit from which Moses, before his death, gained his view of the promised land. Peor was a peak near it. It was in Moab, one of the mountains of Abarim, and the top of Nebo. It was in the territory afterward assigned to Reuben, and thus was north of the Arnon. Num. 21:20; Deut. 3:27; 4:49; 34:1; Josh. 13:20. Pisgah had cultivated land. Balak brought Balaam "into the *field* of Zophim, to the top of Pisgah," and there "built seven altars." Num. 23:14.

Pisidia (*pĭ-sĭd'ĭ-ah*), *pitchy*. A district of Asia Minor. The ranges of the Taurus mountains extended through it. Notorious robbers were in this region, and here Paul may have been "*in* perils of waters, *in* perils of robbers." 2 Cor. 11:26. Paul twice visited Pisidia, passing directly north from Perga to Antioch, Acts 13:14, and again returning through Pisidia to Pamphylia. Acts 14:21–24.

Pit. This term is used to render several Hebrew words. It denotes a cistern or reservoir. It was into such a dry cistern that

Joseph was cast. In old decayed cisterns the water leaks out or becomes slimy, and such a pit becomes the image of dreariness and misery. Jer. 2:13; Ps. 40:2; Zech. 9:11.

Pithom (*pi'thom*), *house* or *temple, of Tum*, who was the sun-god of Heliopolis, a "treasure city," or *dépôt* of provisions, built by the Israelites in Goshen. Ex. 1:11. M. Naville has identified Pithom with Pa-Tum, "setting sun," and with *Tel el-Mashûta*, where he found remarkable ruins, brick grain-chambers, and similar evidences of a "store city."

Plagues of Egypt. The ten plagues narrated in Ex. 7-12 stand in close connection with the natural phenomena of Egypt, still they maintain their character as miracles. They are introduced and performed by Moses; they cease at his request. Ex. 8:5, etc. These ten plagues were doubtless spread over a long time, and probably they followed, as much as possible, the order of the seasons; for some of them were not only distinctively Egyptian, but really only an aggravation of yearly maladies. Canon Cook, in the *Bible Commentary*, distributes them thus: The first was toward the end of June, when the Nile begins to overflow. The second came three months later, at the time of the greatest inundation, in September, and was an attack on a native worship. The third was early in October, and the fourth after the subsidence of the inundation. The fifth was in December or January; the sixth, shortly after; the seventh, at the time when hailstorms occur now in Egypt, from the middle of February to early March. The eighth was when the leaves are green, toward the middle of March. The ninth was peculiarly Egyptian, and was the immediate precursor of the tenth. During this time the Israelites had frequent opportunities to gather, and thus were prepared for their exodus.

Plough. The plough of the east was very light and simple, perhaps merely a forked stick, having a wooden share, shod with one of those triangular or heart-shaped points of iron which the inhabitants of the Palestine towns still use. 1 Sam. 13:20. A single upright held by one hand, Luke 9:62, while the goad was carried in the other, guided this primitive instrument, which turned the earth equally on both sides. The slight scratching which constitutes eastern ploughing never requires more than one pair of cattle, and often a single cow or ass or camel was doubtless used, as now.

Poetry, Hebrew. Poetry was the delight of orientals. About one-third of the Old Testament is poetry, the oldest, the purest, and the most sublime in the world. Strictly there is neither epic nor dramatic poetry in Hebrew. The reason is obvious. Epic poetry springs from an effort to glorify human greatness—the heroic in man; the Hebrew was taught to glorify God. Hebrew poetry is almost wholly lyric and didactic, and some add also gnomic. There are no lyrics in the world comparable with the Psalms of David, no gnomic poetry equal to the Proverbs, and no didactic poem so perfect in form, so profound and majestic in thought or so exalted and spiritual in conception as the book of Job. Rhyme and metre, common in modern poetry, are seldom found in Hebrew. Hebrew poetry consists chiefly of parallelisms and a certain swing and balance in the sentences which give an indescribable charm to their poetic compositions. The parallelisms in Hebrew have been roughly divided into three kinds: 1, Synonymous, that is, where each line of the distich or tristich has the same thought, but in varied expression; 2, Antithetic, where the thought of the second member of the parallelism is in contrast with that of the first; and 3, Synthetic, where the thought is cumulative upon the same topic. There are five so-called poetical books in the Old Testament: Job, Psalms, Proverbs, Ecclesiastes, and Song of Solomon. But beside these, large portions of other books are in poetic language. The prophetical books except Daniel are largely in poetry. See Rice: "Our Sixty-six Sacred Books."

Pomegranate (*pum-gran'nate*). The pomegranate has been cultivated from early times in Syria, Num. 13:23; Deut. 8:8, and the warmer regions of the east. It rarely exceeds ten feet in height, and has small lance-shaped, glossy leaves, of a reddish-green when young, but becoming pea-green and remaining alive through the winter. The flowers are of a brilliant scarlet or orange, and in August or September the fruit ripens. This is of the size of an orange, flattened at the ends like an apple, is of a beautiful brown-red color, Song of Sol. 4:3; 6:7, has a hard rind and is filled with pulp of a highly grateful flavor. The abundant juice was made into wine, Song of Sol. 8:2, and used for a cooling drink. Some cultivated trees bear sweet and some sour fruit, while the wild pomegranates yield only a small and worthless apple.

Pontus (*pŏn'tus*). A Roman province in the north of Asia Minor, along the coast of the Euxine Sea (Pontus), from which circumstance the name was derived. It is three times mentioned in the New Testament, Acts 2:9; 18:2; 1 Pet. 1:1. There were many Jewish residents in the district.

Potiphar (*pŏt'i-far*). Potiphar, with whom the history of Joseph is connected, is described as "an officer of Pharaoh, chief of the executioners, an Egyptian." Gen. 39:1; comp. 37:36. He appears to have been a wealthy man. Gen. 39:4-6. The view we have of Potiphar's household is exactly in accordance with the representations on the monuments. When Joseph was accused, his master contented himself with casting him into prison. Gen. 39:19, 20. After this we hear no more of Potiphar.

Pottage. Gen. 25:29. See **Lentiles.**

Potter, Jer. 18:2; Lam. 4:2, and pottery are frequently alluded to in Scripture, showing that the art was known at an early period.

Prayer. All the noted saints of Scripture were mighty in prayer; but there is no mention of special prayer before the flood.

See Gen. 20:17; 32:26; Num. 11:2. For list of special prayers see "Index to the Bible."

Prevent, and Prevented. Job 3:12; 41:11; Ps. 59:10; 79:8; 88:13; 119:148; Matt. 17:25. These words in the A. V. never mean, as at present, "to hinder," but "to go before," "to anticipate." 1 Thess. 4:15.

Priest. In the sacred Scriptures priest denotes one who offers sacrifice. In patriarchal times the fathers were the priests of their own families, though perhaps a more general priestly office existed, such as that exercised by Melchizedek. The patriarchs—Noah, Abraham, and others—officiated as priests of their households. Gen. 8:20; 12:8. The male descendants of Aaron were priests by birthright, and the first-born, in regular succession, was entitled to the office of high priest. Certain blemishes, however, specified in Lev. 21:16-24, disqualified a man, not for the order, but for performing the functions of the office. The number of priests was at first very small, Josh. 3:6; 6:4; but in the time of David it had greatly increased; 3700 priests joined him at Hebron. 1 Chron. 12:27. He divided them into 24 courses—16 of the family of Eleazar, and eight of the family of Ithamar; and, as these courses officiated in regular succession, changing every Sabbath, 2 Chron. 23:8, each course would be in attendance at the sanctuary at least twice a year. During the period of the captivity this division into courses seems to have fallen into some confusion. Among the 4289 priests who accompanied Zerubbabel, only four courses were represented, Ezra 2:36-39; Neh. 7:39-42, and courses are afterward mentioned which cannot be identified with any of the original ones. The duty of the priests was to prepare and offer the daily, weekly, and monthly sacrifices. In war they sounded the holy trumpets and carried the ark of the covenant. In peace they ministered as judges and expounded the law to the people. It appears, however, from 2 Chron. 17:7-10; 19:8-10; Ezek. 44:24, etc., that the priests often neglected the judicial and teaching functions of their office. The consecration of a priest took place with great solemnity. The ceremonies, which were minutely prescribed by Moses, Ex. 29:1-37; Lev. chaps. 8, 9, lasted for seven days, and consisted in sacrifices, washings, the putting on of the holy garments, the sprinkling of blood, and anointing with oil. The consecration of the high priest was distinguished by pouring the sacred oil upon his head, Ex. 29:7; 30:22-33; Lev. 8:12; 21:10, 12; Ps. 133:2, in addition to the washing and the sprinkling with oil, etc., which he shared with all priests, Ex. 29:4, 20, 21; Lev. 8:6, 23, 24, 30. So Christ, our great High Priest, was anointed with the Holy Spirit. Dan. 9:24; Acts 10:38; John 3:34. Peculiar garments were put upon the high priest, Ex. 29:5, 6, 29, 30; Lev. 8:7-9, and sacrifices were offered seven days. Ex. 29:1-37; Lev. 8:14-36. The high priest's sacred garments, besides the drawers, linen tunic, and girdle of other priests, were four, Ex. 28:4, 39-43; Lev. 8:7-9: the robe of the ephod, Ex. 28:31-35; the ephod, with its "curious girdle," Ex. 28:6-12; the breast-plate, with the Urim and Thummim, vs. 15-30; and the mitre, vs. 36, 39. See the respective titles. These garments were worn only when the high priest was ministering in the sanctuary. Ezek. 42:14; 41:17-19; Acts 23:5. On the day of atonement his dress was of plain white linen. Lev. 16:4, 23, 24. The high priest was to enter the Holy of Holies once a year on the day of atonement, to make expiation for the sins of the nation. Lev. 16. The high priest was president of the Sanhedrin in our Lord's time. Matt. 26:62. The office of the priesthood was abolished when Christ died. There were to be no more offerings for sin. "Christ was once offered to bear the sins of many." Heb. 9:28. "We are sanctified through the offering of.. Jesus Christ once." Heb. 10:10. "By one offering he hath perfected forever them that are sanctified." Heb. 10:14. The words priest and priesthood do not occur in the New Testament in connection with any order in the church. The only mention of them is, Christ, as our Priest, and all believers, as priests, and a priesthood. 1 Pet. 2:5, 9; Rev. 1:6; 5:10; 20:6.

Prophecy. Prophecy is not only the predicting of future events: it included the larger office of receiving and communicating the will and purposes of God. So that we find in Scripture prophecy instructions, warnings, rebukes, as largely as predictions of things to come. And men are termed prophets, Abraham for example, Gen. 20:7, of whom it is nowhere recorded that they uttered a single prophecy in the sense of foretelling future events. Christ, moreover, in whom the promise of Deut. 18:15-19 was to have its ultimate and complete fulfilment, and who was to be the great prophet of the church, performed that office, not so much by many predictions as by teaching all that it was needful the world should know. The way, too, in which prophecy is spoken of in the apostolic writings goes to establish the same view. It is described as touching the heart and conscience, convicting, instructing, edifying, comforting. 1 Cor. 14:1, 3, 24, 25. The heathen had little conception of prophecy in this its largest and most excellent sense: they deemed it but an inexplicable knowledge of futurity. What, then, are the characteristics of the 16 prophets thus called and commissioned and intrusted with the messages of God to his people? 1. They were the national poets of Judea. 2. They were annalists and historians. A great portion of the prophecies of Isaiah, of Jeremiah, of Daniel, of Jonah, of Haggai, is direct or indirect history. 3. They were preachers of morals and of spiritual religion. The system of morals put forward by the prophets, though not higher or purer than that of the law, is more plainly declared, and with greater, because now more needed, vehemence of diction. 4. But the prophets were something more than national poets and annalists, preachers of patriot-

179

ism, moral teachers, exponents of the law, pastors, and politicians. Their most essential characteristic is that they were instruments of revealing God's will to man, as in other ways, so specially by predicting future events, and, in particular, by foretelling the incarnation of the Lord Jesus Christ and the redemption effected by him. We have a series of prophecies which are so applicable to the person and earthly life of Jesus Christ as to be thereby shown to have been designed to apply to him. And if they were designed to apply to him, prophetical prediction is proved. The weight of prophecy as an evidence of the truth of the religion of the Bible can hardly be overestimated. It stands alone. No other claim to supernatural foreknowledge can be put in comparison with it. And no petty objection to this or that detail, no fancied discovery that here or there fulfilment has not answered to prediction, can be admitted to shake such evidence of such a comprehensive character. The supposed chronological arrangement of the prophecies is as follows:

	B. C.
Jonah	856-784
Amos	810-785
Hosea	810-725
Isaiah	810-698
Joel	810-660
Micah	758-699
Nahum	720-698
Zephaniah	640-609
Jeremiah	628-586
Habakkuk	612-598
Daniel	606-534
Obadiah	588-583
Ezekiel	595-536
Haggai	520-518
Zechariah	520-518
Malachi	436-420

Propitiation. A reconciliation. Thus, Christ is the "propitiation for our sins." Rom. 3:25; 1 John 2:2; 4:10. He reconciles us to God, not God to us. The same Greek word is used by the Septuagint to denote "sin-offering," Ezek. 44:27 and 45:19; "atonement," Num. 5:8; the "mercyseat," Heb. 9:5; and the covering of the ark of the covenant. Lev. 16:14.

Proselyte, *a stranger, sojourner.* In the later Jewish sense this term designates a convert from Paganism to Judaism. Matt. 23:15; Acts 2:11; 6:5; 13:43. The Rabbins distinguish two kinds of proselytes. 1. Perfect proselytes, who, submitting to circumcision, embraced the Jewish religion in its full extent, and enjoyed all the rights and privileges of Jewish citizenship. Ex. 12:48; 20:10; Josephus *Ant.* xx. 2 4. 2. Proselytes of the gate, *i. e.,* foreigners, dwelling among the Jews, who, without being circumcised, conformed to certain Jewish laws and customs. Proselytes were found in great numbers, not only in Judea, but in all the principal cities of the empire. Acts 13:43; 16:14; 17:4, 17; 18:7.

Proverbs, Book of. This is a collection of wise maxims woven into a didactic poem, and making up a popular system of ethics. They are a guide of practical wisdom, the moral philosophy of the Hebrews. We may divide the book of Proverbs into four parts. 1. Prov. 1-9, a discourse extolling true wisdom, and specially urging the young to secure so excellent a possession. To this we find prefixed a title and introduction, 1:1-6, intended possibly to apply to the whole book. 2. A collection of maxims generally unconnected, inculcating moral precepts which respect both man's duty towards God and his behavior to his fellow-creatures. 10:1-22:16. 3. A more connected address, with various admonitions, and a charge to listen to the words of the wise. 22:17-24:34. 4. An appendix, chaps. 25-31, comprising (1) a collection of Solomon's proverbs which Hezekiah's servants copied out, chaps. 25-29; many of those which are comprised in the second part are here repeated; and (2) chaps. 30, 31, the words of Agur, etc. The book of Proverbs is frequently cited or alluded to in the New Testament. It is, indeed, a treasure-house of ethical wisdom, filled with choice sententious aphorisms, far excelling those of all secular and uninspired sages, and inculcating all moral duties.

Psalms, the Book of. The "praise" or hymn-book of Jew and Christian for thousands of years. The following description of the book is given in Rice's *Our Sixty-six Sacred Books:* The book of Psalms in the Hebrew Bible was the first of the third division called K'thubim, or "Writings." The Psalms, Proverbs, and Job were regarded as pre-eminently poetical books, and the Massoretes distinguished them by a peculiar accentuation. The Psalms were called "Sepher T'hellim," or "Book of Praises." The Greeks called it "Psalmos," from which the English "Psalms" is derived. The Psalms counted one book in the A. V., in the Hebrew Bible are divided into five collections, rather inaptly termed "books" in the Revised English Version. The end of each of the first four "books" is indicated by a doxology. The books are: 1. Ps. 1-41; 2. Ps. 42-72; 3. Ps. 73-89; 4. Ps. 90-106; 5. Ps. 107-150. The topics of the Psalms have been compared to an oratorio in five parts: 1. Decline of man; 2. Revival; 3. Plaintive complaint; 4. Response to the complaint; 5. Final thanksgiving and triumph. This fivefold division of the Psalms is very ancient, but when or by whom it was made is uncertain. Some ascribe it to Nehemiah or his time; it certainly is two or three centuries older than the Christian era. The division appears in the Septuagint. Why it was made is not clear. Some conjecture that it was in accord with the supposed chronological order of the Psalms, or was an arrangement according to authors, topics, or for liturgical use. The collection could not have been completed before the time of Ezra. About fifty Psalms are quoted in the New Testament. The titles or inscriptions of the Psalms are not by the original authors, but belong to an early age. They are attached to 101 Psalms. The 49 not having titles, the Talmud calls "Orphan Psalms." According to these titles, 73 Psalms are ascribed to David, 12 to Asaph, one of David's singers, 12 to the sons of Korah, a priestly family of singers of David's time, 2 (72d and 127th) to Solomon, 1 (90th) to Moses, and 1 (89th) to Ethan. The other 49 are anonymous. But the Septuagint assigns 85 Psalms to David, the 127th to Jeremiah, the 146th to Haggai, and the 147th to Zechariah. The New Testament also cites Psalms 2 and 95 as if David were the author. It is worthy of note that the great Hallel songs, Ps. 115–118, and the famous alphabetic hymn, the 119th, are among the anonymous songs. The most ancient classification, aside from the division into five collections, is found in the titles. The meaning of these is obscure. Some are termed *Shir*, a solo for the voice; *Mizmor*, song of praise accompanied with an instrument; *Maschil*, ode or didactic song; *Michtam*, a catch-word poem (Delitzsch); *Shiggaion*, an excited ode; *Tephillah*, a prayer-song; *Shir jediduth*, a song of loves; *Shir hamma'aloth*, a song of ascent or pilgrim songs; *Kinah*, dirge or elegy. Modern groups are based upon the contents, as seven (some say eight) penitential (6th, 25th, 32d [38th], 51st, 102d, 130th, 143d), seven imprecatory psalms (35th, 52d, 58th, 59th, 69th, 109th, 137th), pilgrim songs, psalms of thanksgiving, of adoration, of faith and hope, Messianic psalms, and historic psalms. Some psalms have parallelisms or longer stanzas, each beginning with an initial letter corresponding to the twenty-two letters of the Hebrew alphabet. There are seven of these alphabetic psalms and five other alphabetic poems in the Old Testament. Some psalms are choral, as 24th, 115th, 135th; some gradational, as 121st, 124th. Of the psalms ascribed to David, several have Aramaic forms, but according to the latest linguistic researches these forms may betray an earlier rather than a later author. The psalms have suggested many of the noblest Christian hymns.

Publican, a collector of Roman tribute. Matt. 18:17. The principal farmers of this revenue were men of great credit and influence, but the under-farmers, or common publicans, were remarkable for their rapacity and extortion, and were accounted as oppressive thieves and pickpockets. Hence the Jews classed them with sinners, and would not allow them to enter the temple or the synagogues, to partake of the public prayers or offices of judicature, or to give testimony in a court of justice.

Pul (*pŭl*), *lord!* The first king of Assyria who invaded Canaan, and by a present of 1000 talents of silver, equivalent to nearly $2,000,000 in our day, was prevailed on by Menahem to withdraw his troops and recognize the title of that wicked usurper. 2 Kings 15:19.

Pulse, *seed*. Our English word means peas, beans, lentiles, and the produce of similar podded plants, but in Dan. 1:12, 16 the Hebrew word probably denotes vegetable food in general, and in 2 Sam. 17:28 parched peas, which are still a favorite food in the east.

Purple. Ex. 25:4. The purple dye so famous among the orientals of ancient days was produced from a species of shellfish peculiar to the Mediterranean Sea. As each fish yielded but a few drops of coloring matter, the choicest purple bore a very high price. Purple robes were worn by the kings and first magistrates of ancient nations. Esth. 8:15. Comp. Luke 16:19.

Purse. A fold in the girdle, such as is often found at the present day in eastern countries. But Hebrews also had a bag which was used to hold money. The first fold in a girdle had an opening, closed with a leathern strap, where the money was carried. Matt. 10:9; Mark 6:8.

Puteoli (*pu-tē'o-lī*). The principal port of southern Italy, in the most sheltered part of the bay of Naples. It was the great emporium for the Alexandrian wheat-ships. Seneca gives an interesting account of the arrival of a fleet of these. All other vessels when they entered the bay were obliged to strike their topsails. These, therefore, could be distinguished in a crowd of ships as soon as they hove in sight. Paul was permitted to tarry seven days at Puteoli on his way from Malta to Rome. Acts 28:13, 14.

Pygarg. Deut. 14:5, A. V. Probably the antelope known as the addax.

Q

Quails. Ex. 16:13; Num. 11:31, 32; Ps. 105:40. The great quantity of quails taken by the Israelites has its parallel in modern times. Pliny states that they sometimes alight on vessels in the Mediterranean and sink them. Colonel Sykes states that 160,000 quails have been netted in one season on the island of Capri. The Israelites would have had little difficulty in capturing large quantities of these birds, as they are known to arrive at places sometimes so completely exhausted by their flight as to be readily taken, not in nets only, but by the hand. Yet the feeding of the Israelites for a month was a miracle.

Quaternion. A body of four. Acts 12:4–10. Four soldiers were appointed to keep guard during each of the four watches of the night. There were therefore sixteen in all. Of each quaternion probably two were in the prison, Peter being chained to them, and the other two were sentinels before the gate—the first and second guard.

Queen. This title in the A. V. represents three Hebrew words. It is applied to a ruling queen, as the queen of Sheba, 1 Kings 10:1; and to Athaliah, 2 Kings 11; to the wives of the king, Esth. 1:9; 7:1; and to the queen-mother, as Bathsheba, Maachah, 1 Kings 2:19; 15:13; and to Jezebel, 2 Kings 10:13.

Queen of heaven, Jer. 7:18; 44:17, 18, 19, 25, is the moon, worshipped as Ashtaroth or Astarte, to whom the Hebrew women offered cakes in the streets of Jerusalem.

Quicksands, The. More properly the Syrtis, as in the R. V., Acts 27:17, the broad and sandy gulf on the north African coast between Carthage and Cyrene. There were properly two Syrtes—the eastern or larger, now called the Gulf of Sidra, and the western or smaller, now the Gulf of Cabes. The former is mentioned in the Acts.

Quiver. Gen. 27:3. A case for arrows. See Armor.

R

Raamah (rā'a-mah), *trembling.* A commercial country which traded with Tyre. Ezek. 27:22. It furnished spices, gems, and gold, and was probably named after a son of Cush, whose descendants are believed to have settled upon the southwestern shore of the Persian Gulf.

Raamses (ra-ăm'sĕz). Ex. 1:11. See Rameses.

Rabbah (răb'bah), *greatness.* The chief city and capital of the Ammonites. Josh. 13:25. Its full name is "Rabbath of the children of Ammon." Deut. 3:11 A. V. It is also called "Rabbath of the Ammonites." Ezek. 21:20 A. V. Greek and Roman writers call it "Philadelphia," a name given by Ptolemy Philadelphus, by whom it was rebuilt. Its modern name is Amman. Rabbath was situated on the upper Jabbok, about 22 miles east of the Jordan.

Rabbi (răb'bī), literally *my master.* A title given by the Jews to teachers of the law, and frequently applied to our Lord by the disciples and the people. Matt. 23:7, 8; 26:25, 49; Mark 9:5; 11:21; 14:45; John 1:38, 49; 3:2, 26, etc. The usual Greek word in the gospels as the title of Christ means "teacher." Matt. 8:19; 9:11.

Rabshakeh (răb'sha-kēh or rab-shā'keh). An officer—the chief butler or cupbearer—who was sent with Rab-saris, the chief of the eunuchs, and Tartan, messengers of the king of Assyria, to Hezekiah, summoning him, in the most indecent and blasphemous manner, to surrender his capital. 2 Kings 18:17-37.

Rachel (rā'chel), *an ewe.* The daughter of Laban and wife of Jacob. Her history is given in Genesis, chaps. 29-35. She died after giving birth to Benjamin, and was buried near the road from Bethlehem to Jerusalem. Gen. 35:19.

Rahab (rā'hăb), *large.* 1. A woman of Jericho, who received and concealed two Hebrew spies. In the siege of the city Rahab and her family were spared by the Hebrews from the general massacre of the inhabitants. Josh. 2; 6:17-27. She is called "a harlot;" but the proof of her reformation is found in the eminence of her faith. Heb. 11:31; Jas. 2:25. She subsequently married Salmon, a prince of Judah, and became an ancestress of David, and appears in the genealogy of Christ. Ruth 4:20; Matt. 1:5. 2. Rahab, *pride.* An appellation for Egypt, designating the insolence and violence of its princes and inhabitants. Ps. 87:4; 89:10; Isa. 51:9.

Rain. "Early rain" signifies the rain of the autumn, Deut. 11:14, and "latter rain" the rain of spring. Prov. 16:15. For six months in the year, from May to October, no rain falls, the whole land becomes dry, parched, and brown. The early rains commence about the latter part of October, continuing through November and December. Rain continues to fall more or less during the month of March; it is very rare in April. Robinson observes that there are not, at the present day, "any particular periods of rain or succession of showers which might be regarded as distinct rainy seasons. The whole period from October to March now constitutes only one continued season of rain, without any regularly intervening term of prolonged fine weather. Unless, therefore, there has been some change in the climate the early and the latter rains, for which the husbandman waited with longing, seem rather to have implied the first showers of autumn—which revived the parched and thirsty soil and prepared it for the seed—and the later showers of spring, which continued to refresh and forward both the ripening crops and the vernal products of the fields. Jas. 5:7; Prov. 16:15. The rainbow was appointed as a sign that God would not again destroy the earth by a flood. Gen. 9:12-17.

Ramah (rā'mah), *a hill.* 1. One of the cities of Benjamin. Josh. 18:25. Its site is at er-Râm, about five miles from Jerusalem, and near to Gibeah. Judg. 4:5; 19:13; 1 Sam. 22:6. Its people returned after the captivity. Ezra 2:26; Neh. 7:30. 2. The home of Elkanah, Samuel's father, 1 Sam. 1:19; 2:11, the birthplace of Samuel himself, his home and official residence, the site of his altar, 1 Sam. 7:17; 8:4; 15:34; 16:13; 19:18, and finally his burial-place. 1 Sam. 25:1; 28:3. It is said that its situation was in Mount Ephraim, 1 Sam. 1:1, a district without defined boundaries. The position of Ramah is a much disputed question. The latest map of the Palestine fund places it a short distance east of Bethlehem. 3. A name applied to four other places.

Rameses (răm'e-sĕz or ra-mē'sez), *son of the sun*). A province and city in Egypt; called also **Raamses.** Gen. 47:11; Ex. 12:37; Num. 33:3, 5. The district was, without doubt, identical with Goshen.

Ramoth (rā'moth), *heights,* and **Ramoth Gilead.** 1. A city in Gilead, within the limits of the tribe of Gad, Josh. 21:38; called also Ramah and Ramoth-Gilead. 2 Kings 8:28, 29; 1 Kings 4:13; 22:1-37; 2 Chron. 18; 22:5, 6. It was one of the cities of refuge. Deut. 4:43; Josh. 20:8; 1 Chron. 6:80. During the reigns of the later kings of Israel, Ramoth was the occasion of several wars between them and the kings of Syria. 1 Kings 22:3; 2 Kings 8:28; 9:1. It may be identical with es-Salt, but more probably with Gerash.

Rebekah (re-bĕk'ah), *a cord with a noose, enchaining.* The daughter of Bethuel and sister of Laban. She was a woman of personal attractions and became the wife of Isaac, to whom late in life she bore Esau and Jacob. Gen. 22:23; 24:15-67; 25:20-28. Of her sons, Jacob was Rebekah's favorite; and she persuaded him to obtain his father's blessing by fraud. Gen. 26:7, 8, 35; 27. In consequence Jacob had to flee from his brother's wrath; and it is probable that Rebekah saw her best-loved son no more. Gen. 28:5; 29:12; 35:8; 49:31. She died before Isaac.

Rechabites (rĕ'kab-ītes or rĕk'ab-ītes). A Kenite tribe descended from Rechab. Jonadab, one of their chiefs, laid an injunction on his posterity to drink no wine, to build no houses, but to dwell in tents. This injunction they obeyed fully for 300 years; but upon the Chaldean invasion they were forced to quit the open country and live in Jerusalem. Jer. 35. Afterwards they probably withdrew into the desert. For their obedience a promise was given them that their family should never be extinct. And accordingly, at the present day, there is an Arabian tribe who claim a descent from Rechab, and profess a modified Judaism.

Red Sea. The Greeks meant by the Erythræan or Red Sea not only the Arabian Gulf but also the ocean between the Indian and Arabian peninsulas. Some suppose it was so named from the red color of the mountains on the western shores, some from the red coral, or the red appearance of the water occasioned by certain zoophytes; others think that, as the Edomitish territory reached down to this gulf, it might be the Sea of Edom, Edom meaning red. The Red Sea, from the straits of Bab el-Mandeb to its most northerly point at Suez, is about 1400 miles in length, its greatest width being about 200 miles; it is divided by the Sinaitic peninsula into two large arms or gulfs, the eastern extending northeast or northerly about 100 miles, with an average width of 15 miles, while the western extends northwest near 180 miles, with an average width of 20 miles. The great event associated with the Red Sea is the passage of the Israelites and the overthrow of the Egyptians. Ex. chaps. 14, 15. This miraculous event is frequently referred to in the Scriptures. Num. 33:8; Deut. 11:4; Josh. 2:10; Judg. 11:16; 2 Sam. 22:16; Neh. 9:9-11; Ps. 66:6; Isa. 10:26; Acts 7:36; 1 Cor. 10:1, 2; Heb. 11:29, etc. The place of the crossing has been a matter of much controversy. The head of the gulf is probably at least 50 miles farther south than it was at the time of the Exodus. If the Red Sea then included the Bitter Lakes of Suez, the crossing may have been farther north than would now appear possible. Thus the predictions of Isaiah, 11:15; 19:5, "The Lord shall utterly destroy the tongue of the Egyptian Sea," "The waters shall fail from the sea," are fulfilled. After crossing, the Israelites marched down and encamped on the east side of the Red Sea (Gulf of Suez). Num. 33:10. From the way of the Red Sea came locusts, Ex. 10:12-19, and the quails which supplied them with food came from the same source. Num. 11:31. They journeyed by the way of the Red Sea (the eastern arm or Gulf of Akabah) to compass Edom. Num. 21:4. In the prosperous reign of Solomon he "made a navy of ships" at Ezion-geber and Elath, which were ports at the head of the Gulf of Akabah. 1 Kings 9:26; 10:22; 2 Chron. 8:17, 18.

Rehoboam (rē-ho-bō'am), *enlarges the people*. The son and successor of Solomon. He reigned 17 years, B. C. 975-958. His insolent conduct hastened the political crisis which resulted in the division of the Hebrew kingdom into the two kingdoms of Judah and Israel. 1 Kings 12:21-24; 14:21, 31; 2 Chron. 10:1-14. Within five years of Rehoboam's accession to the throne, the kingdom of Judah was invaded by Shishak, king of Egypt, who desolated the country, and made it tributary to Egypt, and Shishak's victory is noted in the great temple at Karnak.

Rehoboth (re-hō'both), *wide places*. 1. A city of Assyria, near Nineveh, founded by Asshur or Nimrod. Gen. 10:11. 12. 2. A city on the Euphrates, Gen. 36:37, supposed to be represented by the modern Rahabah. 3. A well belonging to Isaac. Gen. 26:22.

Remphan (rĕm'fan). Acts 7:43, and quoted from Amos 5:26, where the word in Hebrew is "Chiun." It is probable, therefore, that they are names for a god worshipped secretly by the Israelites in Egypt and in the wilderness, answering, probably, to Saturn or Moloch, the star-god.

Rephaim (rĕph'a-ĭm or re-phā'im), **Valley of.** Josh. 15:8; 18:16; and translated "the valley of the giants" in the A. V., but vale of "Rephaim" in the R. V. It was one of the landmarks of the land of Judah, named after the Rephaim, or "giants," who at an early period were found on both sides of the Jordan. Comp. Gen. 14:5; Deut. 3:11-13; Josh. 13:12; 17:15. David twice defeated the Philistines in this valley. 2 Sam. 5:17-25; 23:13; 1 Chron. 11:15, 16; 14:9-16. The valley was noted for its fertility. Isa. 17:5. Its position as a boundary of Judah would indicate it to have been south of the valley of Hinnom.

Rephidim (rĕf'i-dĭm), *resting-place*. A station of the Hebrews before reaching Sinai. Num. 33:14, 15. Near it was the fountain which flowed from the rock in Horeb, called "Meribah," and "Massah," whence they were miraculously supplied with water. Ex. 17; 19:2. It may have been in Wady Feiran or in some part of Wady esh-Sheikh. See *Journeys of Israel.*

Reuben (reu'ben), *behold a son!* The eldest son of Jacob and Leah. Gen. 29:32; Deut. 33:6. He was deprived of the privileges of his birthright, in consequence of his improper intercourse with Bilhah, his father's concubine. Gen. 35:22; 49:3, 4. The portion of the Promised Land assigned to the tribe of Reuben lay on the east of the Jordan, in the district now called the Belka, and is still famous for its fine pasture lands, as in ancient times. Num. 32:1-38; 34:14; Josh. 1:12-18; Deut. 3:12-16.

Revelation, Book of. This book, frequently called by its Greek name, the *Apocalypse*, was written by John the apostle and the evangelist, about A. D. 95. "This is the last and the most mysterious book of the Bible. It is the divine seal of the whole. It is for the New Testament what Daniel is for the Old Testament. It gathers up all the former prophecies and extends them to the remotest future. It represents the church in conflict with the great secular powers. It unrolls a sublime panorama of Christ's victorious march through the world's history till the appearance of the new heaven and the new earth, when the aim of creation and redemption shall be fully realized. The theme is the divine promise, 'I come quickly,' with the corresponding human prayer, 'Even so, come, Lord Jesus.' It gives us the assurance that the Lord is coming in every great event, and overrules all things for his glory and the ultimate triumph of his kingdom."—*Schaff.*

Rezin (rē'zin), *stable, firm.* 1. King of Damascus; allied himself with Pekah and defeated Ahaz, but was himself defeated by Tiglath-pileser II., his capital destroyed and his people carried away into captivity. 2 Kings 15 : 37; 16 : 5–9; Isa. 7 : 1–8; 8 : 6; 9 : 11. 2. One whose descendants returned with Zerubbabel. Ezra 2 : 48; Neh. 7 : 50.

Rezon (rē'zon), *prince.* Son of Eliadah, a Syrian, who when David defeated Hadadezer king of Zobah, put himself at the head of a band of adventurers and set up a petty kingdom at Damascus. 1 Kings 11 : 23. He harassed the kingdom of Solomon during his whole reign.

Rhegium (rē'ji-ŭm), *breach.* A city on the coast near the southwestern end of Italy. Paul was detained at this place for a day when on his voyage to Rome. Acts 28 : 13. It is now called Rheggio, the capital of Calabria, having about 10,000 inhabitants.

Rhodes (rōdz), *a rose.* A noted island in the Mediterranean, 13 miles from the coast of Asia Minor. Paul visited it on his return from his third missionary journey. Acts 21 : 1. He might have there seen fragments of the greatest of the Seven Wonders of the world—the famous Colossus of Rhodes. This was made of brass, and was 105 feet high. It stood at the right of the port as vessels entered, and not astride the channel, as so generally represented in pictures. It was erected B. C. 290, and overthrown by an earthquake B. C. 224. The modern city is a place of considerable trade.

Riblah (rĭb'lah), *fertility.* An ancient city in the northeastern frontier of Canaan. Num. 34 : 10, 11. The ancient town was upon the great road from Palestine to Babylon, and was a convenient military headquarters for the Babylonian kings and others invading the country. Here the Egyptian king Pharaoh-nechoh put Jehoahaz in chains and made Eliakim king, and here Nebuchadnezzar brought Zedekiah, murdered his sons before his eyes, and then put out his eyes and bound him in chains to be carried to Babylon. 2 Kings 23 : 29–35; 25 : 1–7; Jer. 39 : 5–7. Riblah is now a mean and poor village.

Rimmon (rĭm'mon), *pomegranate.* 1. The name of an idol worshipped in Damascus. 2 Kings 5 : 18. See Naaman. 2. A Benjamite, father of the two men who slew Ish-bosheth. 2 Sam. 4 : 2, 5, 9. 3. A town in Judah, afterward given to Simeon. Josh. 15 : 21, 32; 19 : 7; 1 Chron. 4 : 32; Neh. 11 : 29; Zech. 14 : 10. 4. A Levitical city in Zebulun. 1 Chron. 6 : 77, R. V., Rimmono. It is also called Remmon-methoar. Josh. 19 : 13 A. V. It is identified with the present village Rummaneh, about six miles north of Nazareth. 5. A rock whither the 600 surviving Benjamites retreated after the slaughter of their tribe. Judg. 20 : 45, 47; 21 : 13.

Rizpah (rĭz'pah), *a coal, a hot stone for baking.* A concubine of Saul whom Abner was accused for appropriating, as if thereby aiming at the crown. 2 Sam. 3 : 7. This caused a breach between him and Ishbosheth. Her two sons were delivered to the Gibeonites to be hanged: and the story of her affection as she watched her dead is peculiarly touching. 2 Sam. 21 : 8–11.

Roman Empire. The empire of Rome succeeded the Macedonian empire founded by Philip and Alexander. It controlled the greater part of the then known world. The references to the Roman dominion in the Bible chiefly allude to the empire in its earlier history, including the reigns of Augustus, Tiberius, Claudius, and Nero. The extent and power of the empire during this period were greater than at any earlier and possibly than at any later time. It reached to the Atlantic on the west, the Euphrates on the east, the African desert, the Nile cataracts, and the Arabian deserts on the south, the Rhine, the Danube, and the Black Sea on the north. It also conquered Great Britain. Augustus divided the provinces into two classes—1. Imperial. 2. Senatorial. These divisions are recognized in the New Testament. The ruler of a senatorial province is "proconsul," and of an imperial province a "governor." Thus Cyrenius was governor of Syria. Luke 2 : 2. Pilate, Felix, and Festus are spoken of as "governors," that is, procurators, of Judæa. Matt. 27 : 2; Acts 23 : 24; 24 : 27.

Romans (rō'manz), **Epistle to.** It was written at Corinth, A. D. 58, as Paul was leaving that city for Jerusalem. Rom. 15 : 25; comp. Acts 20 : 2, 3, 16; Rom. 16 : 1, 23; 1 Cor. 1 : 14; 2 Tim. 4 : 20. It is the fullest exposition of the great truth that the gospel is the power of salvation unto all who believe. This epistle is designed to correct certain misapprehensions, and to show that the system of Jewish rites and ceremonies is done away by the gospel dispensation, and that the way of salvation through Christ is opened alike to Jews and Gentiles, and that whosoever will may come directly and hopefully to Jesus Christ for salvation and pardon from sin.

Rome (rōme). In the New Testament times Rome was the capital of the empire in its greatest prosperity. Among its inhabitants were many Jews. Acts 28 : 17. They had received the liberty of worship and other privileges from Cæsar, and lived in the district across the Tiber. We know that as early as A. D. 64, eight or ten years after a church was established there and addressed by Paul, Rom. 1 : 8; 16 : 19, the emperor Nero commenced a furious persecution against its members, which the emperor Domitian renewed A. D. 81, and the emperor Trajan carried out with implacable malice, A. D. 97–117. Seasons of suffering and repose succeeded each other alternately until the reign of Constantine, A. D. 325, when Christianity was established as the religion of the empire. Within the gardens of Nero in the Neronian persecution, A. D. 64, after the great conflagration, Christians, wrapped in skins of beasts, were torn by dogs, or, clothed in inflammable stuffs, were burnt as torches during the midnight games; others were crucified. In the colosseum, a vast theatre, games of various sorts and gladiatorial shows were held, and within its arena many Christians, during the ages of persecution, fought with wild beasts, and many were slain for their faith. The catacombs are vast subterranean galleries (whether originally sand-pits or excavations is uncertain). Their usual height is from eight to ten feet, and their width from four to six feet, and they extend for miles, especially in the region of the Appian and Nomentane Ways. The catacombs were early used by the Christians as places of refuge, worship, and burial. More than four thousand inscriptions have been found in these subterranean passages, which are considered as belonging to the period between the reign of Tiberius and that of the emperor Constantine. Among the oldest of the inscriptions in the catacombs is one dated A. D. 71. Rome, as a persecuting power, is referred to by the "seven heads" and "seven mountains" in Rev. 17:9, and is probably described under the name of "Babylon" elsewhere in the same book. Rev. 14:8; 16:19; 17:5; 18:2, 21.

Ruth (*ruth*), *a friend*, or, according to others, *beauty*. Ruth 1:4. A Moabitish woman who married a son of Naomi and left her own country to follow her mother-in-law into Judæa. Her kindness was abundantly rewarded, as she soon after married Boaz, and became the ancestor of the royal family of David, and appears in the genealogy of Christ. Matt. 1:5.

Ruth, Book of. This beautiful narrative belongs to the period of the Judges. Ruth 1:1. The object of the writer was to trace the genealogy of David, and his descent from a Moabitish mother, who had been reduced to extreme poverty. The simplicity, integrity, and kind feelings of the principal persons exhibited are altogether remarkable; and the narrative shows that David had at least some ancestors who were nature's noblemen. 1 Chron. 2:11, 12. The writer of the book is not known, but the Hebrews ascribed it to Samuel.

Rye. The word, so rendered in Exod. 9:32; Isa. 28:25, A. V., is translated "fitches" in Ezek. 4:9, "spelt" in the margin. There is little doubt that the plant intended by the Hebrew word is not rye, but spelt, as it is translated in the R. V.

S

Sabachthani (*sa-băk'tha-nī*, or *sä'bak-thä'nī*), *thou hast forsaken me*. One of the words uttered by Christ on the cross. Matt. 27:46; Mark 15:34. It is part of the phrase which is in Syro-Chaldee.

Sabaoth (*săb'a-ŏth* or *sa-bā'oth*), *hosts*. The phrase "Lord of Sabaoth" occurs twice in the New Testament, in Rom. 9:29 and James 5:4. It should not be mistaken as referring to the Sabbath. But it is the Greek transliteration of the Hebrew *Tsebaoth*, "hosts" or "armies," so often recurring in the Old Testament, "the Lord of *hosts*," Isa. 1:9, "the Lord God of *hosts*," *i. e.*, the heavenly bodies, the angels, or the people of God.

Sabbath (*rest*). Ex. 16:23. The institution of a day of rest is founded in man's nature, and dates back to Paradise. Gen. 2:2, 3. The term is used of days or times, generally every seventh day, or a seventh portion of time, separated and sanctified for God's service, Lev. 19:3, 30; 25:4, and in the original text of the New Testament for a whole week. Matt. 28:1; Mark 16:2; Luke 24:1; John 20:1; Acts 20:7; 1 Cor. 16:2. In a spiritual sense it designates the eternal rest in heaven. Heb. 4:9 margin, and Greek. The fourth commandment, Ex. 20:8–11; Deut. 5:12–15, enjoins no specific religious service, except in the general direction to keep it holy. Subsequent legislation made it a day of holy convocation. The sacrifices of the temple were doubled; the shew-bread was changed; the inner court of the temple was opened for solemn services: the prophets and the Levites took the occasion for imparting religious instruction to the people. It was a day of holy joy. Indeed, the fear was that the day would be "wasted by idleness and degraded by sensuality and drunkenness," because it was so joyous. Neh. 8:9–12; Hos. 2:11. Christ kept the Sabbath in the highest sense of the term. He observed every jot and tittle of the Mosaic Law in the freedom of the spirit. From him we learn that acts of necessity and mercy are to be performed on that day, but that worldly occupations are to be put as far as possible out of our thoughts. It is true we transfer the observance of the Sabbath to the first day of the week, but we do not thereby violate the spirit of the divine law: for what God asked for was the seventh of our entire time. We have a warrant for this change. Upon the first day of the week Christ arose from the dead. We find the disciples, before the Ascension, assembled on that day, and Jesus appeared to them. John 20:26. According to tradition, which is confirmed by every probability, the outpouring of the Holy Ghost on the day of Pentecost was on Sunday. Paul preached at Troas on the first day of the week—evidently, among those Christians, the day of religious service. Acts 20:7. Paul tells the Corinthians that every one is to lay by him in store upon the first day of the week as he is prospered. 1 Cor. 16:2. It was upon the Lord's day—and by this name he calls it—that John on Patmos saw through the opened door into heaven. Rev. 1:10. Around the Lord's day we do well to throw safeguards. It is, in a sense, the palladium of Christian liberty. The various states and cities have good laws for the protection of the *civil* Sabbath and against its open desecration. The American churches are unanimously in favor of a quiet Sabbath, in opposition to the evils of the so-called "continental Sunday," and earnest efforts have been made to protect us against them. See **Lord's Day.**

Sabeans (sa-bē'anz). 1. Descendants of Seba. Isa. 45:14. It should be simply "people of Seba," son of Cush. 2. In Joel 3:8 the descendants of Sheba, son of Joktan, are meant. Possibly a third tribe is spoken of in Job 1:15. The translation "Sabeans" in Ezek. 23:42 is incorrect; read "drunkards," as in the margin and in the R. V.

Sackbut. A musical instrument. The word thus (probably erroneously) translated, *sabbecā*, occurs only in Daniel. Dan. 3:5, 7, 10, 15. It seems really to have been a triangular instrument with four or more strings, played on with the fingers, and emitting a sharp, clear sound.

Sackcloth. A coarse black cloth commonly made of hair, Rev. 6:12, such as that of goats or camels. It was used for straining liquids, for sacks, and for mourning garments. Sometimes it was worn under the ordinary clothes, bound upon the loins, or instead of any other kind of dress; occasionally it was spread on the ground to be lain upon. Gen. 37:34; 1 Kings 21:27; 2 Kings 6:30; Isa. 58:5; Joel 1:8; Jonah 3:5, 6, 8. Deep sorrow was hence denoted by sackcloth and ashes. Matt. 11:21. Such garments were sometimes the dress of prophets and ascetics. Isa. 20:2; Zech. 13:4.

Sacrifice. Gen. 31:54. Sacrifices were in use from the earliest periods of the world, and among all nations. The universality of sacrificial rites is a powerful argument on behalf of their naturalness; they meet the demand of the sinner for some way of appeasing the offended divinity. But Christians have no need of them, simply because of the one perfect Sacrifice once offered on the cross. See **Offerings, Altar,** and **Lamb.**

Sadducees (săd'du-seez). One of the Jewish sects of which we read in the New Testament. They were in sharp opposition to the Pharisees, but ready to work with them against the person and teaching of Jesus. Their origin is involved in some obscurity; probably sprung from Zadok. See Bissell's *Biblical Antiquities.* The tenets of the Sadducees may be gathered from the notices we have of them in the New Testament, illustrated by the account given by Josephus, *Antiq.* lib. xiii. 5, § 9, 10, § 6, lib. xviii. 1, § 4. They disregarded the traditions and unwritten laws which the Pharisees prized so highly, and professed to take the Scriptures as the sole authoritative guide of religion. They denied the existence of angels and spirits, and maintained that there was no resurrection, Matt. 22:23; Acts 23:8, the soul according to them dying with the body; hence they denied a future state of reward or punishment. It was their maxim therefore that actions to be virtuous must not be done in hope of recompense. Another principle of their belief was the absolute freedom of man's will, so that he had full power of himself to do good or evil as he chose; and then only could his actions have a moral value. But this view was pushed so far as almost entirely to exclude the divine interposition in the government of the world. The Sadducees were not so numerous as the Pharisees; nor were their tenets so acceptable to the people. Yet many of their body were men of wealth and influence. They were found in the supreme council; and in the time of Christ and the apostles a Sadducee filled the office of high priest. Acts 4:1; 5:17; 23:6. Their party had, moreover, a political complexion; they were austere, it may be added, in their habits, and severe in the administration of justice. After the first century of the Christian era they disappear from history.

Salamis (săl'a-mis), *peaceful,* or *beaten.* A sea-port town with a good harbor, on the eastern coast of Cyprus. It was visited by Paul and Barnabas on their first missionary journey. Acts 13:5. The city was once the capital of Cyprus, and stood on the north side of the river Pediæus. Its site is now traced by broken cisterns and columns and the foundations of ancient buildings. The ruins are known as Old Famagusta.

Salem (sā'lem), *peace.* The city of Melchizedek. Gen. 14:18; Heb. 7:1, 2. Jewish commentators affirm that Salem is Jerusalem, on the ground that Jerusalem is so called in Ps. 76:2. Nearly all Jewish commentators hold this opinion. Jerome, however, states that the Salem of Melchizedek was not Jerusalem, but a town eight Roman miles south of Scythopolis, and identifies it with Salim, where John baptized. See **Salim.**

Salim (sā'lim), *peace* or *fountains?* A place named to mark the locality of Ænon, where John baptized. John 3:23. Some identify it with Salem. Eusebius and Jerome mention Salim as near the Jordan, eight Roman miles south of Scythopolis. Robinson suggested that it was identical with the village of Salim, three miles east of Nablûs.

Salmon (săl'mon), *shady.* Ps. 68:14, A. V., or **Zalmon.** Judg. 9:48. This was one of the high hills which environed the ancient Shechem and afforded pasturage for Jacob's flocks.

Salome (sa-lōme'; Greek and Latin, Salō'me. 1. The wife of Zebedee, and the mother of James the elder and John the Evangelist, and was one of the followers of Christ, Matt. 27:56; Mark 15:40; 16:1. though she seems, like many others, to have at first mistaken the true nature of his kingdom. Matt. 20:21. 2. The name of the daughter of Herodias, who danced before Herod. Matt. 14:6; Mark 6:22. She is not named in the New Testament, but is by Josephus.

Salt. See Lev. 2:13; Matt. 5:13.

Salt Sea or **Dead Sea.** *Names.* This sea is called in the Scriptures the "sea of the plain," R. V. "of the Arabah," Deut. 4:49; 2 Kings 14:25; the "salt sea," Deut. 3:17; Josh 3:16; 12:3; the "east sea," Joel 2:20; Ezek. 47:18; Zech. 14:8; and "the sea," Ezek. 47:8. It also appears as the "vale of Siddim." Gen. 14:3. The title "Dead Sea" is not found in Jewish writers, but was introduced at an early period by the Greek authors. This remarkable sheet of water is of an elongated oval shape; but the regularity of the figure is broken by a large peninsula projecting from the eastern shore near to the southern end, dividing the whole into two reaches which communicate by a somewhat narrow channel. The extreme length is about 46 miles, the greatest breadth above ten miles. The superficial area has been estimated at about 300 square miles; but, as it would seem that the water does not constantly stand at the same level, that carried off by evaporation not always balancing that brought in by streams, the dimensions of the lake are subject to not inconsiderable variation. A line of drift-wood encircles the lake, branches and limbs of trees, brought down by the Jordan and other torrents, and marking the highest level of the water. There is a salt and stony plain at the northeast corner, but the eastern side has been less explored. The Jordan, also, and various streams east and west empty themselves into it. And, as there is no outlet, the waters are intensely salt. Its specific gravity is therefore higher than that of the ocean, so that persons unable to swim elsewhere cannot sink in this lake. It was once imagined that life could not subsist above it. The waters were said to be almost motionless, and their steam pernicious. Birds and wild fowl are found on it, but no fish in it. The most extraordinary fact in regard to the Dead Sea is that it lies in so deep a cleft among its mountains that its surface is about 1293, or according to Lynch 1316, feet below the level of the Mediterranean. The Jordan flows through a sunken valley, the fall along its course being rapid and considerable, till it reaches its lowest point in this lake. Moreover, the depth of the water of the lake is very great, 1310 feet at its deepest point towards the northern end; the southern end is shallow. The cities of the plain, which were destroyed by "brimstone and fire from the Lord out of heaven," were near the Dead Sea. Gen. 19:24. The supposition formerly most common was that these cities were submerged by the waters of the sea at the time of the great catastrophe—a theory which appears to be inconsistent with the geological and physical character of the region. See **Sodom**.

Salt, Valley of. Apparently the Ghor or valley at the southwestern extremity of the Dead Sea, adjacent to the mountain of salt; where the Hebrews gained two decisive victories over the Edomites. The "Syrians" is read in 2 Sam. 8:13, by a copyist's error. 1 Chron. 18:12; 2 Kings 14:7; 2 Chron. 25:11. In this neighborhood lay also the City of Salt. Josh. 15:61, 62.

Salute, Matt. 10:12; **Salutation,** Luke 1:41. The salutations of the Jews were usually of a religious character—at least, in form—and were attended with much ceremony, as they are to this day among the orientals. Sometimes there was nothing but the simple exclamation, "The Lord be with you!" or "Peace be with you!" To this last and most common form striking allusion is made by our Saviour. John 14:27; 20:19, 26. It passed into the epistolary salutation. Rom. 1:7, etc. The time occupied in the ceremonies of salutation, repeatedly bowing, kissing the beard, etc., was often very considerable, Gen. 33:3, 4, and hence the caution in 2 Kings 4:29; Luke 10:4, against saluting.

Samaria (*sa-mā'ri-ah*; Lat. *săm'a-ri'ah*), *watch-post.* A city and district of Palestine. The city was founded by Omri. 1 Kings 16:23, 24. The palace at Tirzah, where the preceding monarch had resided, was burnt by Zimri. A hill admirably adapted for the site of a great city and capital belonged to Shemer. Omri purchased it for two talents of silver; and the city that he built thereon he called "Samaria," after the name of the former owner. 1 Kings 16:18, 23, 24. Thenceforth it was the metropolis of the northern kingdom, the rival of Jerusalem, and generally the residence of the Israelitish monarchs, 1 Kings 16:29; 20:43; 2 Kings 1:2, though they had also a palace at Jezreel. 1 Kings 21:1; 2 Kings 8:29. The worship of Baal was set up in Samaria by Ahab, who built there an altar and a temple to the idol-god, 1 Kings 16:32, which were destroyed by Jehu. 2 Kings 10:18-28. Samaria was unsuccessfully besieged by the Syrians in the reigns of Ahab and Joram. 1 Kings 20:1-21; 2 Kings 6:24-33; 7. It was ultimately taken by the Assyrians after a siege of three years in the reign of Hoshea. 2 Kings 17:5, 6; 18:9, 10. The inhabitants were carried into captivity and colonists put in their place. 2 Kings 17:24; Ezra 4:9, 10. The city was taken by Alexander the Great, who placed a body of Syro-Macedonians in it. Subsequently Samaria was utterly destroyed by John Hyrcanus. It must, however, have been rebuilt; for in the time of Alexander Jannæus it was reckoned one of the cities possessed by the Jews. Pompey assigned it to the province of Syria. Augustus gave it to Herod the Great, who adorned it, settled a colony of veterans there, and strengthened its defences. He also gave it the name of Sebaste in honor of the emperor—Sebastos being the Greek equivalent of Augustus. But it began to decay, overshadowed by its neighbor Nablous, and it is now but a mass of ruins, adjacent to the modern village of Sebustieh. Samaria was gloriously beautiful, "a crown of pride," Isa. 28:1, upon its fruitful hill. "The site of this celebrated capital," says Dr. Thomson, "is delightful, by universal consent." The name Samaria is often applied to the northern kingdom. Thus the sovereigns are called kings of Samaria as well as of Israel, 1 Kings 21:1; 2 Kings 1, 3; and we also read of "the cities of Samaria." 2 Kings 17:24. In New Testament times Samaria was one of the Roman divisions of Palestine lying between Galilee and Judæa; so that any one who would pass straight from one of these provinces to the other "must needs go through Samaria." John 4:4. It occupied the ancient territories of the tribes of Ephraim and western Manasseh.

Samaritans (sa-măr'i-tans). 2 Kings 17:29; comp. vs. 9-12. In the New Testament the word denotes the mixed race which sprang from the remnant of Israel and the colonists brought from various parts of Assyria at the captivity. 2 Kings 17:23, 24. The colonists lived at first in heathenism; but they afterwards sought to propitiate "the god of the land" by bringing back an Israelitish priest to Bethel, and mingling with their own idolatries a corrupt worship of Jehovah. 2 Kings 17:25-33, 41. The Jews, on their return from captivity, B. C. 536, declined the Samaritans' request to be permitted to help build the temple. Ezra 4. In consequence of this refusal the Samaritans hindered the erection of the temple and afterwards the rebuilding of the walls of Jerusalem, B. C. 445. Neh. 4:6. The enmity was increased by the erection of a rival temple on Mount Gerizim, where the Samaritans offered sacrifices according to the Mosaic law, referring to Deut. 27:11-13, as proof that this was the proper site for the temple. The bitter animosity between the two races must be understood in order to understand many facts in New Testament history.

Samos (sā'mos), *a height.* An island in the Ægean Sea, a few miles from the main land, and 42 miles southwest of Smyrna. The island is 27 miles long, ten miles wide, and has an area of 165 square miles. It was the seat of Juno-worship, the birthplace of Pythagoras, and noted for its valuable pottery. Paul visited the island on his third missionary journey. Acts 20:15. Samos was then the capital of the island.

Samson (săm'son), *sunlike.* The son of Manoah, and noted as the strongest man. He was judge of a portion of Israel for 20 years, during the latter part of "the 40 years" period, and partly contemporary with Eli and Samuel. Judg. chaps. 13-16. His birth was miraculously foretold; he was a Nazirite from infancy; celebrated for his fearless and wonderful exploits, for his moral infirmities, and for his tragical end. He was not a giant in size; his exploits were wrought by special divine aid; "the Spirit of God came mightily upon him." Judg. 13:25; 14:6, 19; 15:14; 16:20, 28. The providence of God was signally displayed in overruling for good the hasty passions of Samson, the cowardice of his friends, and the malice of his enemies. Samson is ranked with the heroes of the faithful. Heb. 11:32, 33. But we must, of course, not judge him from the standpoint of the New Testament. He lived in the wild anarchial period of the judges, when might was right, and he was just the man for that time.

Samuel (săm'u-el), *heard of God.* A great prophet, the last judge of Israel before the monarchy, which he introduced by anointing Saul. He appears also as the head of a school of prophets. 1 Sam. chaps. 1-5. He was the son of Elkanah a Levite, descended from that Korah who perished in the wilderness. Num. 16; 26:11. Little is recorded in detail of his administration. For a number of years he judged Israel—this is the sum of what is told—though whether his authority was recognized by all the tribes may admit of question. The places to which he is said to have gone on circuit were all in the south of Palestine, 1 Sam. 7; and when he appointed his sons to office it was in Beer-sheba, the extreme south.

Samuel, First and Second Books of. We cite this from Rice's *Our Sixty-six Sacred Books:* The two books of Samuel were originally one in the Hebrew Bible. Even the Massoretic note at the end of the second book, giving the number of verses, treats them as one book. The Septuagint regarded the books of Samuel and of Kings as a complete history of the Hebrew kingdom, and divided them into four books, calling them "Books of the Kingdoms." This division is followed in the Latin and Douay versions, where they are named the first, second, third, and fourth books of Kings. The modern division was introduced into Hebrew printed Bibles in 1518. The author of the two now called 1 and 2 Samuel is unknown. The name of the books probably arises from the fact that Samuel is the hero of the first part. Samuel could have written only 24 chapters of the first book, since the 25th chapter records his death. The contents indicate that official records may have been consulted by the writer, and national hymns were incorporated in the work, as the song of Hannah, 1 Sam. 2:1-10; David's song over Abner, 2 Sam. 3:33, 34; his thanksgiving song, and his farewell song, 2 Sam. 22; 23:1-7. The date of composition was not later than Solomon's time, as the language proves. "It is pure Hebrew, free from Aramaisms and late forms. Constructions such as are found in Kings are not found in Samuel." The difficulties are chiefly the adjustment of the chronology, the variations between the Hebrew and Greek texts, and the apparent discrepancies, as 1 Sam. 23:19; 24:22, and chap. 26. The first book covers a period of about 80 years —1171 to 1056 B. C.—and the second book from 1056 to 1015 B. C.—the important era of the reign of David

Sanballat (san-băl'lat), *heroes.* A satrap of the king of Persia, in Samaria. He was a native of Horonaim, a town of Moab. He endeavored by every means to hinder Nehemiah in the work of rebuilding Jerusalem. Neh. 2:10; 4:1; 6:1-14; 13:28.

Sarah (sā'rah), *princess.* 1. The wife and half-sister, Gen. 20:12, of Abraham, and mother of Isaac. Her name is written Sarai in Gen. 11:29. The change of her name from Sarai, *my princess* (*i. e.* Abraham's), to Sarah, *princess,* was made when Abram's name was changed to Abraham.

She died at Hebron at the age of 127 years, 28 years before her husband, and was buried by him in the cave of Machpelah. She is referred to in the New Testament as a type of conjugal obedience in 1 Pet. 3:6, and as one of the types of faith in Heb. 11:11.

Sardine, Rev. 4:3, A. V., or **Sardius**, Ex. 28:17. A gem of a blood-red or flesh color, susceptible of a high polish, and also called "sard" or "carnelian." Its former name it obtains from Sardis, in Asia Minor, where it was first found. This stone has long been a favorite for the engraver's art.

Sardis (*sär'dis*). A city in Asia Minor, and the capital of Lydia. Sardis was situated at the foot of Mount Tmolus, about 50 miles northeast of Smyrna and on the river Pactolus, celebrated for its "golden sands." It was the residence of the famous Crœsus, whose name is the synonym for riches. When Cyrus conquered him, B. C. 548, he is said to have taken treasure of the value of $600,000,000. Sardis was the seat of one of the seven churches of Asia, and the Christians seem to have been so corrupted by the prevailing worldliness that they received a severe rebuke. Rev. 3:1–5.

Sargon (*sar'gon*), *firm king*. An Assyrian king, successor of Shalmaneser and father of Sennacherib. For centuries nothing was known of him only one fact, Isa. 20:1, that Ashdod was taken by his command. The exhumed ruins of the Khorsabad palace show him to have been a great warrior with able generals, the chief of whom was Tartan. He reigned from 722 to 705 B. C., and was murdered in the magnificent palace he had built.

Satan (*sā'tan*), *adversary*. 1 Chron. 21:1. The adversary of God and man, the foe to goodness, and the tempter to evil. The proper name appears five times in the Old Testament, 1 Chron. 21:1; Job 1:6,12; 2:1; Zech. 3:1; in the New Testament 25 times; the word "devil" occurs 25 times; "the prince of this world," three times; "the wicked one," six times; "the tempter," twice. In one remarkable verse several epithets are combined—the old serpent, the devil, and Satan, who deceiveth the whole world. Rev. 12:9. The most striking mention of Satan is in Job, where he appears among "the sons of God." This is in itself sufficient to prove the subordination of the powers of evil unto God and the permissive nature of sin, and that Satan has no authority to vex save as God grants it. The existence of Satan is a perpetual menace to godliness. See **Devil**.

Satyr (*sat'ir*). A fabled creature of Greek mythology, part man and part goat, and supposed to be the deity of forests and rural places. The expression "satyrs shall dance there," Isa. 13:21 (the R. V. margin reads "he goats," comp. also Isa. 34:14), denotes that the place shall become a rude, wild, uncultivated waste.

Saul (*sawl*), *asked for, desired*. 1. The first king of Israel. He was the son of Kish, of the tribe of Benjamin. 1 Sam. 9:1, 2; 10:1, 21, 23, 24. In personal appearance he was tall, remarkably fine and noble. After his signal defeat of the Ammonites, Saul was confirmed on the throne by the army at Gilgal, 1 Sam. 11, though the continuance of the theocracy was earnestly insisted on by Samuel. 1 Sam. 12. He carried on successful wars against the Ammonites, the Philistines, the Moabites, and the Amalekites. 1 Sam. 13:1-21; 14:46-52. Saul, however, in two instances, forgot that he was subject to Jehovah, the invisible King. 1 Sam. 13:11-14; 15. Hence Jehovah commanded Samuel to anoint David privately, as Saul's successor to the kingdom. 1 Sam. 16:1-13. From this time Saul is exhibited as the slave of jealousy, duplicity, and malice; he fell at last into a deep melancholy. David was introduced to the court to soothe Saul, and there he became acquainted with the manners of the court, and the business of government. 1 Sam. 16:14-23. See **David**. The Philistines mustered an army so formidable, that Saul, finding himself abandoned of God, applied in his emergency to a witch at Endor. Disheartened by the ambiguous answer of the wily sorceress, Saul advanced against the Philistines. The Hebrews were routed, and Saul, finding himself wounded, fell upon his own sword, B. C. 1056, after a reign of forty years. 1 Sam. 28:1-25; 31. There is no character in history more pitiable than this wretched king, swayed by evil impulse, tormented by his own conscience, powerless as it seemed for everything but mischief. His better thoughts, if temporarily awakened, were stings and scourges to him. 1 Sam. 24:17; 26:21.

Saviour. See **Jesus Christ**.

Scapegoat. Lev. 16:8, 10, R. V. Azazel. See **Goat and Atonement**.

Scarlet. Gen. 38:28. The Hebrew word *tolah* signifies *a worm*, *i. e.*, the *coccus worm*, from which the color was made.

School, Acts 19:9; **Scholar**, 1 Chron. 25:8; **School-master**, R. V. "tutor," Gal. 3:24. Schools were established under the prophets to train young men to become expounders of Jewish law, and to fit them for the priestly and prophetical offices. 1 Sam. 19:18-24; 2 Kings 2:3, 5, 7, 15. The office nearly answered to that of a governor or tutor, Gal. 4:2, 3, who constantly attends his pupil, teaches him, and forms his manners. Maimonides thus describes a Jewish school: "The teacher sat at the head, and the pupils surrounded him as the crown the head, so that every one could see the teacher and hear his words. The teacher did not sit in a chair while the pupils sat on the ground, but all either sat on chairs or on the ground." The children read aloud to acquire fluency. The number of school-hours was limited, and during the heat of the summer was only four hours. The punishment employed was beating with a strap, never with a rod. The chief studies were their own language and literature; the chief school-book the Holy Scriptures.

Scorpion. 1. A venomous creature allied to the spider, but resembling the lobster. Its usual length is one or two inches, but in tropical climates it is sometimes found six or eight inches in length, and its sting is attended with excruciating pain, Rev. 9:

3-6, terminating often in violent convulsions and death. Scorpions are abundant in Palestine, and are especially common about Mount Sinai. Deut. 8:15. They remain dormant during the cold season, but through the rest of the year swarm under stones and in all the crannies and crevices of walls and houses. The sting is a curved claw at the end of the tail, and this latter the animal, in running, carries over its back in a threatening attitude. Luke 11:12 seems to mean merely the bestowal of a dangerous and unwelcome gift rather than a good one, and may refer to the Greek proverb: "A scorpion instead of a perch." 2. An instrument resembling a whip, with knots, bits of lead, or small stones at the end. 1 Kings 12:11. See **Scourge.**

Scourge. Deut. 25:1-3. An instrument of punishment in Egypt and Rome. The number of stripes was limited by Moses to forty; which the Jews, in later times, were so careful not to exceed, that they inflicted only thirty-nine. Deut. 25:3; 2 Cor. 11:24. There were two ways of scourging; one with thongs or whips; the other with rods or twigs. Sometimes sharp iron points or sharp-cornered pieces of metal were fastened to the end of the thongs, to render the suffering still more extreme. The punishment was inflicted on the offender lying on the ground. Ex. 21:20; Lev. 19:20; Deut. 22:18; Prov. 10:13; 13:24; 20:30; 23:13, 14; Ps. 89:32. In later times the offender was tied by his arms to a pillar, and his back laid bare to the *virgæ* or rods of the lictor. To this degrading punishment no Roman citizen could be subjected. Matt. 10:17; 27:26; John 2:15; Acts 16:23; 22:25; 26:11; Heb. 11:35.

Scribe. There are two Hebrew words which mean "a writer," but one is usually translated in the A. V. by "officer," the other is rendered "scribe." The art of writing among the Hebrews may not have been in early times generally learned, and therefore a class of men would arise who earned their living by carrying on correspondence or conducting accounts. Sheva was the scribe of David. 2 Sam. 20:25. The king's scribe recorded the edicts, and sometimes acted as treasurer. 2 Kings 12:10. Scribes also officiated in the army. Jer. 52:25. Scribes in the New Testament were the copyists of the law, and were popularly regarded as the teachers or expounders of the law. Ezra was their leader and pattern. Ezra 7:6. But these learned expounders of the law took greater liberties with the text and made it void through their traditions. Mark 7:13. Some were members of the Sanhedrin. Matt. 26:3 (A. V. but omitted in R. V.); 21:15. Jesus reproved them repeatedly and in the most unmeasured terms. Matt. 23; 1-33. They were his determined and wily foes. Luke 5:30; 6:7; 11:53. That there were exceptions is manifest, for Jesus speaks of scribes being sent of God, Matt. 23:34, and one of his parables relates to a scribe "instructed unto the kingdom of heaven." Matt. 13:52. The scribes and lawyers were one class.

Scripture, *writing,* and **Scriptures,** *writings.* The name given in the Bible to portions of the recorded will of God; called also "Holy Scriptures," Rom. 1:2; 2 Tim. 3:15, and once "the Scripture of truth." Dan. 10:21. The more common title in the Bible is "Law," and "Law of Moses." Christ refers frequently to passages in the Old Testament in this way, and once designates the entire collection by the three divisions known to the Jews, "the Law of Moses, and the Prophets, and the Psalms." Luke 24:44. The term Scripture occurs 52 times in the A. V., only once in the Old Testament: but compare 2 Kings 22:13; Ps. 40:7, and Ps. 119. "Law," "Law of Moses," occur 426 times, and "Gospel" in the New Testament only 101 times. The prophets frequently used the phrase, "the word of the Lord." Isa. 1:10; Jer. 2:4; Ezek. 12:17; Dan. 9:2; Hos. 1:1; Joel 1:1. Scripture is called in the New Testament "the word of God," "oracles of God," and "God's words." Acts 4:31; 6:7; 12:24; Rom. 3:2; and John 8:47. In the New Testament Paul's epistles are classed with the Old Testament as "Scripture." 2 Pet. 3:16. The term Bible comes from the Latin *Biblia,* and Greek *Biblos* or *Biblion,* meaning book. It was used by Josephus—70-100 A. D., and Philo, to designate single books of the Old Testament; and later by Chrysostom—350-407 A. D.—for the whole collection. "The Jews have the books—*biblia*—" . . . "Provide yourselves with books, . . . at least procure the new, the Apostolos, the Acts, the Gospels." *Hom.* 2 and 9. He also called them "the divine books." It was applied to the Holy Scriptures by Chaucer—1400, and Wyckliffe—1384, and used as a title by Coverdale—1535. Since then the "Holy Bible" has become the common English title for the collection of 66 sacred books, accepted by all Christians as the authoritative word of God. The Bible is divided into the Old and the New Testaments, a name based upon 2 Cor. 3:14; testament referring there to the old covenant. Thus we read of the "book of the Covenant," Ex. 24:7; 2 Kings 23:2, a phrase which was transferred in time to the entire Hebrew Sacred Scriptures, and the New Testament or Covenant to the Christian. There are 39 separate books in the Old Testament, and 27 in the New Testament, making 66 books in the Bible. They are called "holy" or "sacred" because they are the written revelations of God. "For the prophecy came not in old time by the will of men; but holy men of God spake as they were moved by the Holy Ghost." 2 Pet. 1:21 A. V., or in R. V., "for no prophecy ever came by the will of man; but men spake from God, being moved by the Holy Ghost." Comp. 2 Tim. 3:16, and 2 Pet. 3:16. The Jews, besides dividing the Old Testament into the Law, the Prophets, and the Psalms, or the writings, as before noted, made other divisions in the text of separate books for convenience in reading in public worship. For example, they divided the "Law," the five books of Moses, into 54 portions, and these were subdivided into smaller sections. From these grew the modern division of the Old Testament into chapters and verses. The New Testament was divided into chapters and verses by Stephens in 1551, and likewise first appeared in the Genevan English Bible in 1557-1560. The chronological dates were first inserted by Lloyd in 1701, and are from Ussher. The marginal references to facilitate finding texts on the same or similar topics, were greatly improved by Drs. Paris and Blayney, 1762, 1769. The *italics* in the English versions do not indicate emphatic words, but are inserted by the translators to complete the sense and to show that there are no words in the original Hebrew or Greek to correspond with these English words in italics. The original text of the Old Testament is Hebrew (except a small portion in Chaldaic); the New Testament was written in Greek. The text of the Hebrew Bible has been carefully preserved by the labors of men who regarded it with great reverence. The Massoretic text of to-day is the work of a body of scholars living at Tiberias, in Galilee, and at Sora in the Euphrates valley, who added the vowel points. The oldest extant Hebrew Old Testament manuscripts date from the tenth century. The entire Hebrew Bible was first printed in 1488. Besides the Jewish Massoretes, able Hebrew scholars have carefully and conscientiously compared various Hebrew copies with the old Greek translations, to give us a more accurate Hebrew text than could be gained from a single ancient manuscript. The New Testament Greek text has received greater critical study than even the Old Testament text. Copies of the gospels and epistles were early multiplied in great numbers. These manuscripts are of two classes —uncials, written in capitals and with no division of words or sentences and very few marks of punctuation, and cursives, written in running hand. The former are the older, dating from the fourth to the tenth century. The material used, the style of writing, and other peculiarities, enable experts to tell very nearly to what century any given manuscript belongs. The first printed New Testament text that was published was that of Erasmus in 1516. What is called the Received Text (Greek) is that of the Elzevir Edition, 1633. The toils of a long succession of scholars have sufficed to furnish a text that satisfactorily represents the original. Chief among these scholars were Beza, Mill, Bengel, and Bentley in the centuries that followed the Reformation. They were followed by Griesbach — 1754-1812, Lachmann — 1793-1851, Tischendorf — 1815-1874, Tregelles — 1813-1875, Westcott, and Hort, and through their labors we have a satisfactory and pure text of the Greek Testament.

Order of the Books.—The order of the various books differs in Hebrew manuscripts, according as they are Talmudic or Massoretic. The Talmudic order is: the Law, or five books of Moses; the Prophets, viz., Joshua, Judges, 1 and 2 Samuel, 1 and 2 Kings, Jeremiah, Ezekiel, Isaiah, the twelve minor Prophets; the Writings, viz., Ruth, Psalms, Job, Proverbs, Ecclesiastes, Song of Solomon, Lamentations, Daniel, Esther, Ezra with Nehemiah, 1 and 2 Chronicles. The Massoretes order is: the Law, the earlier Prophets, then Isaiah, Jeremiah, and Ezekiel; and the *k'thubim* or Writings are thus arranged: Psalms, Proverbs, Job, the five *megilloth*, viz., Song of Solomon, Ruth, Lamentations, Ecclesiastes, Esther, then Daniel, Ezra with Nehemiah. 1 and 2 Chronicles. The order in the Septuagint varies considerably from that of the Hebrew. The books of the New Testament may be classed as historical, doctrinal, and prophetical. The historical, viz., the four Gospels, and the Acts of the Apostles, always stand first. Of the doctrinal class, some leading manuscripts — including the Alexandrine and Vatican — make the catholic epistles precede those of Paul; the Hebrews following 2 Thessalonians. The Western church has generally placed the Pauline epistles first, namely, those to churches, then those to individuals, with the Hebrews last, the author being, according to many, uncertain. The prophetical book, Revelation, always closes the sacred volume. See Rice's *Our Sixty-six Sacred Books* for further account of the text, versions, etc.

Ancient Translations.—1. The oldest translation of the Old Testament is the Greek, made about two centuries before Christ. It is called the Septuagint—*i. e.*, seventy, a round number for the more exact seventy-two—from a tradition that the work was executed by 72 Jewish scholars. It was in universal use among the Jews in Christ's day, and is continually quoted by the New Testament writers. This translation instead of the Hebrew was translated into Latin by the early Christian fathers, and is the authority in the Greek Church to-day. The Jews, however, abandoned it, and returned to the study and use of the original Hebrew. 2. A translation into Syriac was made by Christians, direct from the Hebrew, called the Peshitâ (*simple*), because it was literal, and not paraphrastic, was in common use in the fourth century. 3. Of Latin translations are the Itala, made from the Septuagint, and the translation by Jerome, the most learned Christian of his day, directly from the Hebrew, A. D. 385-405, which is called the Vulgate. All Roman Catholic versions must be conformed to it.

Modern Translations.—Only a few leading modern versions can be noticed: 1. German, by Luther, New Testament, in 1522, and Bible, 1534; revised version, 1892. 2. French, by Le Fevre, at Antwerp, 1530; Olivetan, 1535, and Segonds, 1880. 3. Dutch, synod of Dort, 1637, Staats Bibel. 4. Italian, Diodati, 1607. 5. Spanish, by Valero, and by San Miguel, 1602, 1794. 6. Arabic, by E. Smith and Van Dyck, 1866. Many translations have been made by missionaries.

English Translations.—Translations of portions of the Bible were made into Anglo-Saxon in the eighth century and into early English in the thirteenth century. The chief translations are: Wyckliffe's New Testament, from the Latin in 1380, and his followers also translated the Old Testament; these were written. Tyndale's, from the Greek, first English New Testament, printed 1526. Coverdale's Bible, 1535, chiefly from the Latin. This was the first entire Bible printed in English, and probably at Zurich. Matthews' Bible, a fusion of the translations by Tyndale and Coverdale, and made by John Rogers, the martyr, under the name of Matthews, 1537. It was published with the English king's license, and hence was the first authorized version in English. Taverner's Bible was a revision of Matthews' issued in 1539. Cranmer's, or the Great Bible, was simply a new edition of Matthews', issued under the sanction of and with a preface by, Cranmer, also in 1539. The Genevan New Testament, 1557, and Genevan Bible, 1560, were made by English refugees at Geneva, during the persecution under the English queen, Mary, who was a Roman Catholic. It was the first complete English translation from the original Hebrew and Greek texts, and the first English Bible divided into modern chapters and verses. The Bishops' Bible, 1568-1572, a revision of the Great Bible, made by 15 scholars, eight of whom were bishops. The Rheims, New Testament, 1609, and Douai Bible, 1610, made by Roman Catholic scholars at Douai. The King James', or so-called Authorized Version, made from the Hebrew and Greek by 47 scholars, under sanction of James II., king of England, 1611. The Anglo-American revised Bible, New Testament, 1881, Old Testament, 1885. This is a revision of the so-called A. V. made by a company of 67 British and 34 American scholars appointed by a Committee of the Church of England, through the Convocation of Canterbury, in 1870.

Evidences of Scripture.—Concerning the evidences, external and internal, of the truth of Scripture, it may briefly be said that no books have been subjected to such severe critical examination into every statement, and clause, and particular, as the Bible, and never have the arguments for its integrity and authority been as strong as they are to-day. The fulfillment of prophecy, the minute accuracy of descriptions, formerly supposed to be inaccurate, but which later and more thorough researches have found to be true, sustain the historic verity of the Scriptures. For instance, a searching examination of Paul's shipwreck has proved it to be minutely accurate. The explorations made of late years in Nineveh and Babylon, Egypt and Palestine, have tended to confirm the credibility of Scripture in many hitherto disputed points. It is true that we must receive the evidence so produced with care. Inscriptions and monumental records are more likely to exaggerate the successes than to chronicle the disasters of the people by whom they were made. We could not reasonably expect to find in Egyptian monuments any detail of the judgments which forced the release of Israel. Neither was it likely that Sennacherib would record the fatal overthrow of his vast army at Jerusalem. But much information has been obtained by incidental notices. Thus it had been questioned whether such a king as Nebuchadnezzar ever reigned. His name, it was said, did not appear in Herodotus: and objectors, if they did not deny the existence of the conqueror, at least insinuated that a petty satrap had been magnified into a great king. But now bricks in abundance have been found inscribed with Nebuchadnezzar's name, proving that he had built and adorned a magnificent capital. Dan. 4:30. Yet more serious doubt was expressed in regard to Belshazzar; and consequently the narrative of his feast and the awful sign which interrupted it was pronounced a fable. But it is now distinctly proved by the discovery of unquestionable records that a sovereign of that name was associated in power with his father during the last days of Babylon's independence. These instances could be multiplied many times, from the discoveries at Tanis, Lachish, Nineveh, Memphis, and from the recovery of inscriptions and letters, and from the mummies of the Pharaohs, of priests, and princes, almost without number. The results of Christianity, its effects on individuals, families, nations; its wonderful missions, are an unanswerable proof of the verity of this one Book, the Bible. The Scriptures are the only written revelation of God, and the only authoritative record of his plan of salvation. The Old Testament was given specially at first to the Jews, and the New Testament to the disciples of Christ. The Old Testament is fulfilled in the New. There are not less than 265 direct quotations from the Old Testament in the New, and 350 further allusions in the New Testament to the Old Testament, which imply that the latter was the word of God. Again and again Christ and his apostles cited and approved of the Old Testament as the truth of God, and the New Testament expressly declares: "All Scripture *is* given by inspiration of God, and *is* profitable for doctrine, for reproof, for correction, for instruction in righteousness: that the man of God may be perfect, thoroughly furnished unto all good works." 2 Tim. 3:16, 17, A. V. (The R. V. modifies, but on the whole rather strengthens this, as a proof text on the subject.) God's word is not to be diminished, or added to, see Deut. 4:2; 12:32; Rev. 22:19; nor is God's plan of salvation to be modified: "If any *man* preach any other gospel unto you . . . let him be accursed." Gal. 1:9. The Scriptures from the beginning to their end point to and reveal the living "Word made flesh," even the Lord Jesus Christ, and the eternal life in him. John 1:1-14; Col. 1:12-20; Heb. 1:1-3. From the Mosaic book of Deuteronomy in the Old Testament Jesus quoted texts to withstand the awful conflict in the temptations of the devil. Matt. 4:4. It was from the Old Testament books that Jesus talked on the way to Emmaus with two disciples, "beginning at Moses and all the prophets, he expounded unto them in all the Scriptures the things concerning himself." Luke 24:27. These scriptures are sufficient to guide and persuade any who will be reasonably persuaded to salvation. When the rich man in torment plead with Abraham for his five brethren, saying: "If one went unto them from the dead, they will repent," the answer was, "If they hear not Moses and the prophets, neither will they be persuaded, though one rose from the dead." Luke 16:30, 31. They make a fatal mistake who do not so study the Bible as to find Christ in it from beginning to end, a personal Saviour through whom comes eternal, spiritual life.

Circulation of the Bible. — The following statements are from Rice's *Our Sixty-six Sacred Books:* The Bible and portions of the Scriptures are printed in 367 versions and 287 dialects, according to the American Bible Society reports (founded 1816). The reports of the British and Foreign Bible Society (founded 1804) show that over 60 new versions of the Bible were added to its list in eleven years, and that the Scriptures are now published in 510 versions in upwards of 300 languages. A conservative estimate is that the Bible, or portions, are now issued in 390 languages and dialects by the Bible and mission societies and private publishers of the world. It is computed that 60,000 copies of the gospels were circulated among Christians before the end of the second century after Christ. Over 100,000 copies of Luther's German version were sold within 40 years of its issue. Between 1524 and 1611 not less than 278 editions of English Bibles and Testaments were printed. In the first 15 years of this century private publishers in America issued 134 editions of the Bible and 65 of the New Testament. Not less than 1000 editions, some having a very large circulation, were issued in the first 65 years of this century in America alone. The total circulation of the Scriptures and portions, for the nineteenth century, is placed at 300,000,000 copies. Never was the annual circulation greater than now. Bible and mission societies of the world circulate yearly about 6,500,000 copies, and private publishers swell this number to more than 10,000,000 annually. The copies of the Scriptures circulated in heathen lands, in this century, are believed to exceed in number all that there were in the world from Moses to Martin Luther. "This word of God has held a thousand nations for thrice a thousand years spell-bound," says F. W. Robertson, " held them by an abiding power, even the universality of its truth." "Blessed are" they . . "who walk in the law of the Lord." Ps. 119:1.

Scythian (*sĭth'ĭ-an*). Wandering tribe or tribes north of the Black and Caspian Seas. Col. 3:11.

Sea. The Hebrew word *yam*, or "sea," is used in Scripture: 1. For the "gathering of waters," or the ocean. Gen. 1:2, 10; Deut. 30:13. 2. As referring to the Mediterranean Sea, under the title of the "binder," the "western," the "utmost," sea, or the "sea of the Philistines," the "great sea," or simply "the sea." Deut. 11:24; 34:2; Joel 2:20; Ex. 23:31; Num. 34:6, 7; Josh. 15:47; Gen. 49:13; Ps. 80:11; 107:23; 1 Kings 4:20. 3. As referring to the Red Sea. Ex. 15:4. 4. As referring to inland lakes, like the Salt or Dead Sea. 5. To any great collection of waters, as the Nile or the Euphrates in time of a flood or high water. Isa. 19:5; Amos 8:8, A. V., "flood;" Nah. 3:8; Ezek. 32:2; Jer. 51:36.

Sea of Chinnereth (*kĭn'ne-rĕth*). Num. 34:11. See Galilee, Sea of.

Sea of Jazer (*jā'zer*). Jer. 48:32. See Jazer.

Sea of Tiberias (*tī-bē'rĭ-as*). John 21:1. See Galilee, Sea of.

Sea, the Molten, or Brazen. The name of the large copper or bronze laver made by Solomon for the temple, and which stood upon twelve metal oxen in the southeast corner of the court of the priests. It is described in 1 Kings 7:23-26. It was 7½ feet high, 15 feet in diameter, and 45 feet in circumference, and contained 16,000 gallons—2 Chron. 4:5 says 24,000 gallons. Solomon made it of the copper captured from Tibbath and Chun, cities of Hadarezer, king of Zobah. 1 Chron. 18:8. Ahaz took down the sea from off the brazen oxen and put it upon a pavement of stones. 2 Kings 16:17. The Assyrians broke it in pieces. 2 Kings 25:13.

Sea, the Salt. Gen. 14:3. See Salt Sea.

Seal. Among seals used in Egypt at a very early period were engraved stones, pierced through their length and hung by a string or chain from the arm or neck, or set in rings for the finger. The most ancient form used for this purpose was the *scarabæus* (beetle), formed of precious or common stone, or even of blue pottery or porcelain, on the flat side of which some inscription or device was engraved. In many cases the seal consisted of a lump of clay, impressed with the seal and attached to the document by strings. In sealing a sepulchre the fastening was covered with clay or wax, and the seal was stamped upon it, so that it could not be broken open without discovery. The signet-ring was an ordinary part of a man's equipment. Gen. 38:18. The ring or the seal as an emblem of authority in Egypt, Persia, and elsewhere is mentioned in Gen. 41:42; 1 Kings 21:8; Esther 3:10, 12; 8:2; Dan. 6:17; and as an evidence of a covenant, in Jer. 32:10, 44; Neh. 9:38; 10:1; Hag. 2:23. Engraved signets were in use among the Hebrews in early times. Ex. 28:11, 36; 39:6.

Seba (*sē'bah*), *man!* A wealthy and commercial region of Ethiopia. Ps. 72:10; Isa. 43:3; 45:14. Seba appears to have corresponded to the northern portion of Abyssinia. Its inhabitants are mentioned with Sheba, Ps. 72:10, the trading people of the other side of the Red Sea. The inhabitants of both Sheba and Seba were called Sabæans by Greek and Latin writers, but the Hebrew words are distinct.

Seir (*sē'ir*). 1. Mount Seir, Gen. 14:6, or land of Seir, Gen. 32:3; 36:30, the mountainous region lying north of the eastern gulf of the Red Sea. Deut. 2:1-8. The rugged appearance of the tract as viewed from the mountain generally recognized as Mount Hor, the central and highest peak, 4800 feet high, justifies its name. See Idumæa. 2. Mount Seir, Josh. 15 : 10, was a landmark on the northern boundary of Judah, between Kirjath-jearim and Bethshemesh.

Sela or **Selah** (*sĕ'lah*), *the rock*, and named Joktheel. 2 Kings 14 : 7; Isa. 16 : 1. Rendered "rock" in Judges 1 : 36; 2 Chron. 25 : 12. Probably the city later known as Petra, the ruins of which are found about two days' journey north of the Gulf of Akabah. It was in the midst of Mount Seir, in the neighborhood of Mount Hor, and therefore Edomite territory. About 70 B. C. Petra appears as the residence of the Arab princes named Aretas. Trajan reduced it to subjection to the Roman empire. Petra lay, though at a high level, in a hollow three-quarters of a mile long and from 800 to 1500 feet wide, shut in by mountain cliffs, and approached only by a narrow ravine, through which the river winds. There are extensive ruins at Petra of Roman date.

Selah. This Hebrew musical term, which occurs 73 times in the Psalms, and elsewhere only in Hab. 3 : 3, 9, 13, is supposed to be connected with the use of the temple music.

Seleucia (*se-leū'shĭ-ah*; Lat. *sĭl'eu-si'a*). Acts 13 : 4; 14 : 26. The seaport of Antioch, and the place at which Paul and Barnabas embarked, and to which they returned on their first missionary journey. It was on the Mediterranean, about five miles north of the river Orontes, and was founded by Seleucus Nicator, died B. C. 280.

Sennacherib (*sen-nak'e-rĭb*, or *sĕn-na-kē'rĭb*), *sin, the moon, increases brothers*, was the son and successor of Sargon. In the third year of his reign, B. C. 700, Sennacherib turned his arms toward the west, attacked Sidon, and finally marched against Hezekiah, king of Judah. "Sennacherib came up against all the fenced cities of Judah, and took them." 2 Kings 18 : 13. There can be no doubt that the record which he has left of his campaign against "Hiskiah" in his third year is the war with Hezekiah so briefly touched in 2 Kings 18 : 13-16. In the following year, B. C. 699, Sennacherib made his second expedition into Palestine. Hezekiah had revolted, and claimed the protection of Egypt. Sennacherib therefore attacked Egypt, and from his camp at Lachish and Libnah he sent an insulting letter to Hezekiah at Jerusalem. 2 Kings 19 : 14. In answer to Hezekiah's prayer the Assyrians lost, in a single night, by some awful manifestation of divine power, 185,000 men! The camp immediately broke up: the king fled. 2 Kings 19 : 35-37. Sennacherib reached his capital in safety, engaged in other wars, though he seems to have carefully avoided Palestine, and was slain by two of his sons, 15 or 20 years after his flight from Jerusalem. Isa. 37 : 38. He reigned 22 years, and was succeeded by Esar-haddon, B. C. 680. Sennacherib was one of the most magnificent of the Assyrian kings. He seems to have been the first who fixed the seat of government permanently at Nineveh, which he carefully repaired and adorned with palaces and splendid buildings.

Seraphim, *princes*. The name given by Isaiah to the spirits waiting on the Lord, and which are apparently the most exalted of the angelic host. Isa. 6 : 2, 6.

Sergius Paulus (*ser'jĭ-ŭs pau'lus*), proconsul of Cyprus. Acts 13 : 7, etc. A. D. 44. He is described as an intelligent man, and yielded to the claims of the gospel.

Serpent. The serpent is a creature distinguished for its subtility, Gen. 3 : 1, and wisdom in avoiding danger, Matt. 10 : 16, as well as for the instinctive dread which it inspires in man and most animals. About one-sixth of all the species known are venomous. The devil is called "the serpent" and "the old serpent," Rev. 12 : 9, 14, 15, probably in allusion to his subtility and malice, and also to the fact that in tempting our first parents to disobey God he employed a serpent or assumed the form of one. 2 Cor. 11 : 3. We frequently find references in Scripture to serpent-charming. Ps. 58 : 4, 5; Eccles. 10 : 11; Jer. 8 : 17; James 3 : 7. This practice is still common in the east. Serpent-charmers carry enormous snakes, generally black, about them, allow them to crawl all over their persons and into their bosoms—always, however, with certain precautions, either necessary or pretended to be so. They repeatedly breathe strongly into the face of the serpent, and occasionally blow spittle or some medicated composition upon them. In Ps. 58 : 4, 5, 6, there is evidently an allusion to certain kinds of serpents which cannot be charmed. Such serpents there still are, which the charmer cannot subdue; and instances are related in which they have fallen victims to their daring attempts. When God punished the murmurs of the Israelites in the wilderness by sending among them serpents whose fiery bite was fatal, Moses, upon their repentance, was commanded to make a serpent of brass, whose polished surface shone like fire, and to set it up on the bannerpole in the midst of the people; and whoever was bitten by a serpent had but to look up at it and live. Num. 21 : 4-9. This brazen serpent was a type of Christ: "As Moses lifted up the serpent in the wilderness, even so must the Son of man be lifted up, that whosoever believeth in him should not perish, but have eternal life." John 3 : 14, 15. To present the serpent form, as deprived of its power to hurt, impaled as the trophy of a conqueror, was to assert that evil, physical and spiritual, had been overcome, and thus help to strengthen the weak faith of the Israelites in a victory over both. The "fiery flying serpent" of Isa. 30 : 6 has no relation to the "fiery" or "burning serpents" of Num. 21 : 6, 8. The latter were so called from the "fiery" or burning nature of their bite or sting.

Servant. This word is frequently used in our version of both Testaments, when "slave" would have been much more fitting. Joshua was Moses' attendant, Ex. 24:

13; 33:11—clerk or secretary we might in modern language say—it being understood that the designation in the last-named passage does not define Joshua's age. But the words '*ebed*, implying "laborer" in Hebrew, and *doulos* in Greek, are spoken of slaves. It does not at all follow, because the Mosaic law and the Christian dispensation found slavery existing in the world, and made regulations for it, that God approved the system of one man's holding another as his property. Laws have to deal with persons as they are, in order to make them what they ought to be. The kidnapping or unlawful stealing of men for slavery was branded as a capital crime. Ex. 21:16; Deut. 24:7; 1 Tim. 1:10. Slaves among the Hebrews were of two general classes: I. Hebrews; II. Non-Hebrews. I. Hebrews. There were three ways by which a Hebrew might become a slave: 1. Poverty. He might sell himself in default of payment of debt. Lev. 25:39. 2. Theft. When he could not pay the amount required. Ex. 22:1, 3. According to Josephus, he could only be sold to a Hebrew. 3. Parents could sell their daughters as maid-servants, but they were ultimately to be their masters' concubines. Ex. 21:7. There were three ways by which the servitude might end: 1. When the debt or other obligation was met. 2. When the year of Jubilee had come. Lev. 25:40. 3. At the conclusion of six years of service. Ex. 21:2; Deut. 15:12. Indeed no servitude could last longer than six years. The owner was expressly forbidden to "rule over him with rigor." Lev. 25:43. Nor was he suffered to go away empty, but must be furnished liberally out of the flock, out of the floor, and out of the wine-press. Deut. 15:14. A slave might even marry a daughter of his master. 1 Chron. 2:35. In the case of a female Hebrew slave, there was not the release at the end of six years: but if marriage with the owner or his son did not take place, she was not to be sold to a foreigner, but "he shall cause her to be redeemed," *i. e.*, he should return her to her father or find her another Hebrew master, or else free her absolutely. Ex. 21:7-11. When Hebrews became the slaves of non-Hebrews, they might be redeemed or redeem themselves, or else go free at the year of Jubilee. Jewish Hebrew slavery terminated at the captivity. II. Non-Hebrews. They were mostly captives made in war from the neighboring tribes, but besides were purchased of dealers. Lev. 25: 45; Gen. 14:14; Eccl. 2:7. This sort of slavery survived the captivity, but was opposed by the Pharisees. Thirty shekels seems to have been the average price of a slave. Ex. 21:32. Slaves were protected against violence; for if they lost an eye or a tooth from rough handling they got their liberty. Ex. 21:26, 27. To kill one was murder. Lev. 24:17, 22. They had full religious privileges, since they were circumcised. Gen. 17:12.

Seven. Among the Hebrews this was a kind of complete or sacred number. It was noted also among the Persians, ancient Indians, Greeks and Romans. The peculiarity of the Hebrew view consists in the special dignity of the *seventh*, and not simply in that of *seven*. The Sabbath being the seventh day suggested the adoption of seven as the coefficient, so to say, for the appointment of all sacred periods, and we thus find the seventh month ushered in by the Feast of Trumpets, and signalized by the celebration of the Feast of Tabernacles and the Great Day of Atonement; seven weeks as the interval between the Passover and the Pentecost: the seventh year as the sabbatical year; and the year succeeding 7×7 years as the Jubilee year. Seven days were appointed as the length of the feasts of Passover and Tabernacles; seven days for the ceremonies of the consecration of priests, and so on; seven victims to be offered on any special occasion, as in Baalam's sacrifice, Num. 23:1, and especially at the ratification of a treaty, the notion of seven being embodied in the very term signifying to swear, literally meaning to *do seven times*. Gen. 21:28. As to the reason of the fact, three is the signature of God, in the ever-blessed Trinity; four of the world—four elements, four seasons, four winds, etc., etc. There are reasons, then, amply sufficient, why seven, being thus, as it is, made up of three and four, should be itself the signature of the covenant. No mere accident or caprice dictated the selection of it. Seven is used for any round number, or for completeness, as we say a *dozen*, or as a speaker says he will say *two or three* words. Notice, the animals went into the ark by sevens; the years of plenty and famine were marked by sevens, Gen. 7:2: 41:2, 3; the golden candlestick had seven branches, and there were "seven stars" and seven churches. Rev. 1:20; 2:1. In the same book we read of seven spirits, seven seals, seven trumpets, seven thunders, seven vials, seven plagues, and seven angels. Rev. 8:1; 15:1.

Shadrach (shă'drak). See **Abednego.**

Shallum (shăl'lum), *retribution.* The murderer of Zachariah, king of Israel. He usurped the crown, but was slain by Menahem at the end of the first month of his reign, B. C. 771. 2 Kings 15:10-15.

Shalmaneser (shăl-ma-nē'zer), *Salman is gracious.* A king of Assyria, B. C. 727-722. Hoshea, king of Israel, had revolted, but was conquered by Shalmaneser. 2 Kings 17:3. Hoshea revolted a second time and allied himself with So, king of Egypt, and Shalmaneser returned, ravaged Samaria, besieged Hoshea, and after three years Samaria fell. But meantime a rebellion headed by Sargon had broken out in Assyria, and Shalmaneser was deposed. It is not stated in 2 Kings 17:6 that *Shalmaneser* took Samaria, but that the *king of Assyria* did, probably Sargon.

Sharon (shăr'on), *the plain.* 1. A district in Palestine lying upon the seacoast. It extended from Joppa to Cæsarea (whence it is frequently in Scripture coupled with Carmel), and from the central hills to the Mediterranean. It was a region well adapted for pasture, 1 Chron. 27:29; Isa.

65:10, very fertile, Isa. 33:9; 35:2, and celebrated for its roses. Song of Sol. 2:1. Its locality is further indicated as being in the neighborhood of Lydda, Acts 9:35, where it is called Saron, A. V., but Sharon in R. V.

Sheba (*shē'ba*), *seven* or *an oath*. 1. A wealthy region in Arabia bordering on the Red Sea. The queen of Sheba visited Solomon, coming "to Jerusalem with a very great train, with camels that bear spices, and very much gold, and precious stones." 1 Kings 10:1-13; 2 Chron. 9:1-12. Many ancient writers noted the abundance of spices in the Yemen or Sabæan country. Strabo asserts that the enormous profits of the spice trade made the Sabæans one of the wealthiest nations on the face of the earth. They used gold and silver most lavishly in their furniture, their utensils, and even on the doors and roofs of their houses. 2. A town in Simeon, mentioned between Beer-sheba and Moladah. Josh. 19:2. Shema is named next to Moladah in Josh. 15:26, and is probably identical with this Sheba.

Shechem (*shē'kem*), *shoulder*. Gen. 35:4. A town in the valley between Mounts Ebal and Gerizim; called also Sichem, Sychem, Sychar. Neapolis, and now Nablûs, were successively on or near the site of Shechem. It was 34 miles north of Jerusalem, about seven miles southeast of Samaria, and its site is unrivalled for beauty in Palestine. Two mountains parallel to each other, Ebal and Gerizim, almost meeting at their bases and only a mile and a half apart at their summits, enclose a beautiful little valley extending east and west, not more than a hundred yards wide at the narrowest part, and widening out in both directions. The city is mentioned 48 times in the Bible. Its history begins 4000 years ago, before Jerusalem was founded, and extends through Scripture from Abraham to Christ. Jesus visited the region, preached to a woman at Jacob's well, and many from Sychar believed on him. John 4:5, 39-42. Whether Sychar occupied precisely the same site as ancient Shechem has been a question in dispute among scholars. Dr. Thomson describes the situation thus: "Nothing in Palestine surpasses (the vale) in fertility and natural beauty; and this is mainly due to the fine mill-stream which flows through it. The whole country is thickly studded with villages, the plains clothed with grass or grain, and the rounded hills with orchards of olive, fig, pomegranate, and other trees. . . Nablûs is a queer old place. The streets are narrow and vaulted over; and in the wintertime it is difficult to pass along many of them on account of brooks, which rush over the pavement with deafening roar. In this respect I know no city with which to compare it except Brusa; and, like that city, it has mulberry, orange, pomegranate, and other trees mingled in with the houses, whose odoriferous flowers load the air with delicious perfume during the months of April and May. Here the bilbûl delights to sit and sing, and thousands of other birds unite to swell the chorus. See **Samaritans**.

Sheep, Shepherd. Gen. 4:2; 46:32. Sheep were used in the sacrificial offerings, both the adult animal, Ex. 20:24, and the lamb. Ex. 29:38; Lev. 9:3; 12:6. Sheep and lambs formed an important article of food. 1 Sam. 25:18. The wool was used as clothing. Lev. 13:47. "Rams' skins dyed red" were used as a covering for the tabernacle. Ex. 25:5. Sheep and lambs were sometimes paid as tribute. 2 Kings 3:4. Sheep-shearing is alluded to. Gen. 31:19. Sheep-dogs were employed in biblical times. Job 30:1. Shepherds in Palestine and the East generally go before their flocks, calling to them, and the sheep follow; comp. John 10:4; Ps. 77:20; 80:1, though they also drive them. Gen. 33:13. Rev. John Hartley gives an illustration of John 10:1-16: "Having had my attention directed to John 10:3, I asked a shepherd to call one of his sheep. He did so, and it instantly left its pasturage and its companions and ran up to the hands of the shepherd with signs of pleasure and with a prompt obedience which I had never before observed in any other animal. It is also true in this country that 'a stranger will they not follow, but will flee from him.'" The common sheep of Syria and Palestine are the broad-tailed, which, when fattened, have tails of an enormous size. "I have seen many in Lebanon so heavy," says Dr. Thomson, "that the owners could not carry them without difficulty. . . The cooks use this mass of fat instead of Arab butter. . . . This is the 'rump' so often mentioned in the Levitical sacrifices, which was to be taken off hard by the backbone. Ex. 29:22; Lev. 3:9; 7:3; 9:19. It is, in fact, not properly a tail, but a mass of marrow-like fat, which spreads over the whole rump of the sheep, and down the caudal extremity, till near the end." The shearing of the sheep was celebrated anciently, as often now, with much festivity. Gen. 31:19; 38:12, 13; 1 Sam. 25:4-8, 36; 2 Sam. 13, 23-28.

Shekel, Gen. 24:22; Ex. 30:13, means "weight," and was the name of a particular weight of uncoined gold or silver, and in later history of a silver coin worth about 65 cents. See **Money, Measures and Weights**.

Shem (*shĕm*), *name*. The eldest son of Noah. His conduct toward his father on one occasion is noted with praise. Gen. 9:20-27. The Jews are his descendants, and, besides, there are the Aramæans, Persians, Assyrians, and Arabians. The languages spoken by the descendants of Shem—the Hebrew, Chaldee, Assyrian, and Arabic—are called Semitic languages.

Shewbread. Ex. 25:30. Unleavened bread offered every Sabbath on the golden table in the holy place, made into twelve cakes, according to the twelve tribes of Israel, and placed in two piles or rows. The old cakes remained till replaced by the new, and hence the name "continual bread." Num. 4:7; Lev. 24:8. As a general rule the old could be eaten by the priests alone, and by them only in the court of the sanctuary. 1 Sam. 21 : 1-6; Matt. 12 : 3.

Shibboleth (shĭb'bo-lĕth), *stream*. A word which the Gileadites required the fugitive Ephraimites to speak, in order to detect by their pronunciation whether or no they were really of that tribe. Judg. 12 : 4-6. The variations of dialect in the spoken language of Palestine made it difficult for the Ephraimites to speak it.

Shiloh (shī'loh). 1. The word "Shiloh," as used in Gen. 49 : 10, has given rise to much discussion. Some consider it as referring to the town; others apply it to the Messiah. 2. A city of Ephraim, north of Bethel, and where the tabernacle was set up. Josh. 18 : 1. It was thus the sacred capital where solemn assemblies were held, Josh. 18 : 8-10; 19 : 51 ; 21 : 2; 22 : 12; not, however, to the entire exclusion of other places. Josh. 24 : 1, 25, 26. Through the period of the judges' administration the tabernacle seems to have remained at Shiloh. Judg. 18 : 31 ; 21 : 12, 19, 21. It was there in the priesthood of Eli. Samuel was there called to be a prophet. 1 Sam. 1 : 3, 9, 24 ; 2 : 14 ; 3 : 21 ; 4 : 3, 4, 12 ; 1 Kings 2 : 27. After the ark of God had been taken by the Philistines we do not find that it was ever restored to the tabernacle at Shiloh. It was sometimes with the army, 1 Sam. 14 : 18 ; but its resting-place was with Abinadab at Kirjath-jearim. 1 Sam. 7 : 1, 2. And then we hear little more of Shiloh ; the tabernacle itself was removed, 2 Chron. 1 : 3 ; and Jerusalem became ultimately the city which the Lord chose, to place his name there.

Shimei (shĭm'e-ī), *famous*. The name of 14 or more Hebrews, of whom the two following may be described. 1. A son of Gershon the son of Levi, Num. 3 : 18 ; 1 Chron. 6 : 17, 42 ; 23 : 7, 9, 10 ; called Shimi, Ex. 6 : 17, A. V. It is to his descendants, probably, that reference is made in Zech. 12 : 13 ; comp. Num. 3 : 21. 2. The son of Gera, a Benjamite and a kinsman of Saul, who insulted king David when fleeing before Absalom, and humbled himself on David's return. Shimei gave his parole never to leave Jerusalem, but broke it by pursuing his fugitive servants to Gath, and was put to death on returning. 2 Sam. 16 : 5-14 ; 19 : 16-23 ; 1 Kings 2 : 8, 9, 36-46.

Shinar (shī'nar), **the Land of,** *casting out? country of two rivers?* The region where the people, after the Flood, made bricks and used slime (bitumen) for mortar. Gen. 11 : 2, 3. It would seem originally to have denoted the northern part of Babylonia, as "Chaldæa" denoted the southern part ; but subsequently, like Chaldæa, it was sometimes used for the whole. Gen. 10 : 10 ; Isa. 11 : 11 ; Dan. 1 : 2 ; Zech. 5 : 11. In Josh. 7 : 21 it is rendered "Babylonish." Among its cities were Babel (Babylon), Erech or Orech (Orchoi), Calneh or Calno (probably Niffer), and Accad.

Shishak (shī-shăk). King of Egypt, known as Sheshonk I. The first year of Shishak would about correspond to the 26th of Solomon, B. C. 989, and the 20th of Shishak to the 5th of Rehoboam. Shishak at the beginning of his reign received the fugitive Jeroboam, 1 Kings 11 : 40 ; and it was probably at the instigation of Jeroboam that he attacked Rehoboam.

Shittim (shĭt'tim), *acacias*. The scene of the sin with the Midianites, and of its terrible punishment, Num. 25 ; 31 : 1-12 ; the sending forth of the spies to Jericho ; and the final preparation before crossing the Jordan. Josh. 2.

Shittim-wood, from the *shittah tree*, Isa. 41 : 19, A. V. ; the R. V. reads "acacia," was much used in constructing and furnishing the tabernacle. Ex. 25 : 5, 13, A. V. The only timber tree of any size now found in the Arabian desert is the *seyal* (*Acacia seyal*).

Shunem (shu'nem), *two resting-places*. A city in the territory of Issachar. Josh. 19 : 18. The Philistines encamped there before the great battle of Gilboa. 1 Sam. 28 : 4. David's nurse, Abishag, was of Shunem, 1 Kings 1 : 3, and it was the residence of the Shunammite woman who entertained Elisha. 2 Kings 4 : 8. It answers to the modern Sulem, on the southwestern slope of Little Hermon, about 53 miles north of Jerusalem.

Shushan (shu'shan), *a lily*. A celebrated city, called by the Greeks Susa, in the province of Elam. There are various accounts of its origin ; it must have existed at an early period. The site of Shushan has been identified with the modern Shush or Sus, between the river Choaspes (*Kherkhah*) and the Ulai (*Eulæus*). These are really two branches of the same river, which divides about 20 miles above Susa. Hence, Daniel might be standing on the "banks of the Ulai" and also "between Ulai." Dan. 8 : 2, 16. The site is nearly due east of Babylon and north of the Persian Gulf. The great central hall of the palace at Shushan was 343 feet long by 244 feet wide. The king's gate, where Mordecai sat, was probably a hall 100 feet square, 150 feet from the northern portico. Between these two was probably the inner court, where Esther appeared before the king.

Siddim (sĭd'dim), *a depression*. The vale in which were "slime pits," near the plain whereon stood the cities of Sodom and Gomorrah. Gen. 14 : 3, 10 ; 19 : 28. See Sodom.

Sidon. Gen. 10 : 15, A.V. See **Zidon.**

Sihon (sī'hon), *sweeping away*. A king of the Amorites at Heshbon, who was slain, and his kingdom taken by the Hebrews. Num. 21 : 21-31 ; Deut. 2 : 26 ; Ps. 135 : 11, 12 ; Jer. 48 : 45.

Silas (sī'las), Acts 15 : 40, contracted from **Silvanus** (sĭl-vā'nus), *woody*, 2 Cor. 1 : 19, is called one of the chief of the brethren, Acts 15 : 22, and a faithful brother. 1 Pet. 5 : 12. He is supposed to have been a native of Antioch, and a member of the Christian church there. Acts 15 : 37-41. He was the associate of Paul in several of his missionary tours, and his fellow-prisoner at Philippi. Acts 15 : 40 ; 16 : 25, 29 ; 17 : 4, 10, 15. He is called a prophet. Acts 15 : 32.

Siloah (sĭ-lō'ah or sĭl'o-ah), R. V., "Shelah," Neh. 3 : 15 ; or **Siloam,** John 9 : 7, 11 ; or **Shiloah.** Isa. 8 : 6. A rivulet on the southeast of Jerusalem, at the foot of Zion and Moriah; supposed by some to be the same with En-rogel and Gihon. There were two pools, the upper, Isa. 7:3, or king's pool, Neh. 2:14, and the lower pool. Isa. 22:9. There was also a tower at Siloam. Luke 13:4.

Simeon (sĭm'e-on), *a hearkening*. 1. The second son of Jacob, born of Leah. Gen. 29:33. He participated in the revenge of Levi against the Shechemites for the outrage upon Dinah. Gen. 34; 25, 30; 49:5-7. Before entering Canaan, the tribe of Simeon had become the lowest of the tribes in point of number. Num. 1:23; 26:14. To the Simeonites was assigned the territory in the southwest, with a number of towns, which had been allotted to Judah. Josh. 19:1-9. An emigration from this tribe took place, at an early period, towards Gedor, and afterwards to Mount Seir. 1 Chron. 4: 24-43; Ezek. 48:24; Rev. 7:7. 2. One of the ancestors of Mary, Luke 3:30, A. V., but R. V. reads "Symeon." 3. An aged godly Jew residing at Jerusalem, who had been favored with a divine intimation that he should live to see the Lord's Christ. And being led by the Spirit, at the time when Jesus was presented by his mother at the temple, he recognized the infant as the expected Messiah, and took him in his arms and blessed him, glorifying God. Luke 2: 25-35. 4. A Christian teacher at Antioch, surnamed Niger (black), evidently from his dark complexion. Acts 13:1, R. V. "Symeon."

Simon (sī'mon), *a hearing*, contracted from **Simeon**, a sorcerer, who professed to be a convert to the Christian faith, and was baptized by Philip at Samaria, but was severely rebuked by Peter as a hypocrite, because he desired to buy the gift of the Spirit. Acts 8:9. Hence the buying and selling of ecclesiastical rights, benefits, or privileges is called simony, a high offence against the purity and integrity of the Christian faith. 2. Simon Peter. Matt. 4:18. See **Peter**. 3. Simon the Canaanite, Matt. 10:4, or Simon Zelotes, or the zealous, one of the twelve apostles; was one of the party called Zealots, hence his name. The epithet "Canaanite" is properly "Kananite," the Chaldee for "zeal," and has no reference to locality. 4. The brother of our Lord, Matt. 13:55; Mark 6:3; not to be confounded with the preceding, nor with Symeon, who succeeded James as bishop of the church in Jerusalem. 5. A Pharisee. Luke 7:36, 40. 6. A leper. Matt. 26:6. 7. The father of Judas Iscariot. John 6:71. 8. The man of Cyrene who was compelled to bear our Saviour's cross. Matt. 27:32; Mark 15:21; Luke 23:26. 9. The tanner at Joppa with whom Peter lodged. Acts 9:43.

Sin, Wilderness of (sĭn). A region between Elim and Rephidim. Ex. 16:1; 17: 1; Num. 33:11, 12. Here the Israelites were first fed with manna and quails. The wilderness extends 25 miles along the east shore of the Red Sea, from Wâdy Taiyibeh to Wâdy Feiran; it is now called the plain of el-Markha. It is barren, but has a little vegetation.

Sinai (sī'nâi, or sī'naĭ, or sī'na-ī), *broken* or *cleft rocks?* The name of a district, a range of mountains and a mountain peak. The district is in the peninsula lying between the Gulf of Suez and the Gulf of Akaba, and the mountains in the district are celebrated as the place where the Mosaic law was given. Ex. 16:1; 19:2-25; 24:12, 18; 25:40; 34:2-35; Lev. 7:38; 25: 1; 26:46; 27:34; Deut. 33:2; Judg. 5:5; Heb. 8:5; 12:18-21. The "peak" where the law was given is now generally believed to be identical with Ras Sufsafeh, the northern portion of Jebel Musa.

Slave. See **Servant.**

Smyrna (smir'nah), *myrrh*. An ancient Ionian city on the western coast of Asia Minor. Rev. 1:11; 2:8. Smyrna has been repeatedly overthrown by earthquakes. Some few of the ruins of ancient Smyrna are still visible to the south of the modern city. The first cotton-seeds were conveyed to the United States from Smyrna, and planted in 1621.

Sodom (sŏd'om), *burning?* The principal city in a group of cities in the vale of Siddim, which were destroyed on account of the great wickedness of their inhabitants. Gen. 10:19; 13:3, 10-13; 19:1-29. The history of its great wickedness and its terrible punishment is given in Gen. 18:16-33; 19:1-29. Sodom is often held up as a warning to sinners to escape the terrible vengeance of God. Deut. 29:23; Isa. 1: 9, 10; 3:9; 13:19; Jer. 23:14; 49:18; Ezek. 16:49, 50; Amos 4:11; Zeph. 2:9; Matt. 10:15; 11:23, 24; 2 Pet. 2:6-8; Rev. 11:8. There are only two possible localities for these cities—the lower end of the lake, or the upper end of the same. Tradition, from the time of Josephus and Jerome, has pointed to the southern site. The northern site has been strongly advocated by Grove, Tristram, Thomson, and others, and it is probably the true one, though the question is one which is undecided.

Solomon (sŏl'o-mon), *pacific*. The son of David by Bathsheba, and the third king of Israel. 2 Sam. 12:24; 1 Chron. 22:9; Matt. 1:6; 1 Kings 2:12. He was also called the wisest of men, and Jedidiah — friend of Jehovah. 2 Sam. 12:24, 25; 1 Kings 4:29, 30; 7:51; 10:1; 11:41-43; 2 Chron. 9. David voluntarily resigned the government to Solomon, giving him at the same time a solemn charge respecting the administration of it. 1 Kings 2:1-11. Solomon was celebrated for his wealth, splendor, and wisdom. The great event of his reign, however, was the erection of the temple at Jerusalem. 1 Kings 5. Solomon also established a navy of ships at the port of Ezion-geber, on the Red Sea. 1 Kings 9:26-28. Jerusalem, the capital of his vast dominions, became renowned for wealth and splendor. Matt. 6:29; 12:42; Acts 7: 47. His arbitrary exercise of the royal power, however, his numerous harem, the introduction of cavalry, the expenditure of the royal house, and his toleration of idolatry in the land of Jehovah, led him into weak and sinful indulgences. 1 Kings 11:1-11; 12:1-4. The prosperity of his reign was interrupted by disquiets in Edom and Syria ; and he was foretold of the revolt of the ten tribes. Solomon died B.C. 975, after a reign of 40 years; and, notwithstanding his glory, was little lamented. 1 Kings 11:11-43; 2 Chron. 9:31. He is said to have written 3000 proverbs, 1005 Songs, and much on natural history. 1 Kings 4:32, 33. Some of his proverbs and songs probably exist in the Book of Proverbs, in Song of Solomon, and in the Psalms. The Acts of Solomon appears to have been a full history of his reign. 1 Kings 11 : 41 ; 2 Chron. 9 : 29.

Solomon, the Song of. This book, called also Canticles, and according to its Hebrew appellation "the Song of Songs," always had a place in the Jewish canon, and has consequently been received into that of the Christian church. This book, according to its spiritual meaning, is understood to delineate the mutual love of God and his people, in which there are vicissitudes and trials, and backslidings and repentance, and finally a perfect union betwixt the Redeemer and his ransomed church. The same similitude, not indeed wrought out with such particularity, is to be found in other parts of Scripture. God frequently condescends to take the marriage-tie as illustrative of the close fellowship of himself with his chosen. Departure from him is spiritual adultery. His kindness is pre-eminent in receiving back the polluted one. And the last glorious triumph is called the marriage-supper of the Lamb, where the bride is presented pure and undefiled, every stain obliterated, resplendent in glistening robes, the meet consort of a royal spouse. The idea is repeated in both the Old and New Testaments. See, for example, Ps. 45: Isa. 54: 4-6; 62:4, 5; Jer. 2:2; 3:1, 20; Ezek. 16; Hos. 2:16, 19, 20; Matt. 9:15; John 3:29; 2 Cor. 11 : 2 ; Eph. 5:23, 29, 30, 32; Rev. 19 : 7-9; 21 : 2. Such passages as these show how familiarly the idea was used, even in prose composition; we need not be surprised to find it expanded in impassioned poetry. Another view is that the book presents a picture of pure domestic love and happiness.

Son of God. This title is continually given to the Lord Jesus Christ, and as appropriated by him it is a full proof of his divinity. Luke 1:32; 22:70, 71; Rom. 1: 4. The title was applied to Adam, who had no human father. Luke 3 : 33. And there is a sense in which other men, as the creatures of God's hand, and still more as received into his reconciled family by adoption, may be called God's sons. Hos. 1:10; John 1:12; Acts 17: 28, 29; Rom. 8: 14; Gal. 3:26; 4:5-7; 1 John 3:1, 2. But it was evidently with a much higher meaning that our Lord is termed "The Son of God." For the Jews rightly judged that by the assumption of this title he laid claim to equality with God, and, regarding it as blasphemy, and a breach of the first commandment, they determined to put him to death. John 5 : 17, 18. In fact, it was on this charge that ultimately they condemned him. And that it was not in the lower and common sense that Christ claimed God as his Father is evident from the fact that he did not correct the Jews' opinion; which most unquestionably he would have done, had they been under a mistake in supposing him to have broken the great commandment of the law. See **Jesus Christ.**

Son of Man. Matt. 8:20. This title is given to our Saviour 80 times in the New Testament. See also Dan. 7 : 13. The Jews perfectly understood it to denote the Messiah. He calls himself not *a* son of man (among other children of men), but *the* Son of man (above all others)—the ideal, the universal, the perfect Man. So, on the other hand, he calls himself not *a*, but *the*, Son of God—the only-begotten and eternal Son of the Father. Comp. such passages as John 1:51; 3:13; 6:53; Matt. 9:6; 12: 8; Mark 2 : 10, 28. See **Jesus Christ.** The term *son of man* is applied to Ezekiel and Daniel, meaning merely "man," as it does in Num. 23 : 19 ; Job 25 : 6 ; Ps. 8 : 4, etc.

Sosthenes (sŏs'the-nēz), *saviour of his nation.* A Jew at Corinth who was seized and beaten in the presence of Gallio. Acts 18 : 12-17.

Spikenard (Heb. *nĕrd*). Song of Sol. 1 : 12; 4 : 13, 14. The ointment with which our Lord was anointed in Simon's house at Bethany was this *nĕrd*, and was very costly. See Mark 14 : 3-5; John 12 : 3, 5. The ointment was made from an aromatic herb of the valerian family, imported from an early age from Arabia, India, and the Far East.

Spirit. John 3:8. Both in Greek and Hebrew the word for this implies a "blowing" or "breathing;" its primary sense is "wind." In 2 Thess. 2:8 it is used for "breath;" in Eccles. 8:8 for the vital principle; while in other places it denotes the soul. Angels, both good and bad, souls without bodies, are thus designated. Matt. 14 : 26; Luke 24 : 39. The inclination is similarly expressed; hence we have a spirit of grace and of supplication, Zech. 12: 10, a spirit of infirmity, Luke 13: 11. See **Holy Spirit.**

Stephen (stē'vn), *a chaplet, crown.* One of the seven and the first martyr of the Christian church. Acts 6 : 5. After a noble defence, he was dragged without the city, where, while praying, he was stoned to death. Acts 6 : 11-15; 7; 8:2; 11:19; 22: 20.

Stoics (stō'ĭks). Acts 17 : 18. A sect of Grecian philosophers who derived their name from *stoa*, "a porch," because Zeno, their founder, in the fourth century before Christ, and succeeding leaders, used to teach in the painted porch or colonnade at Athens. In their physical doctrines they maintained two first principles, the active and the passive; the passive was matter; the active was God, who was one, though called by many names. Of him they pantheistically believed that all souls were emanations. They held the entire independence of man. The humbling doctrines of the cross, the preaching of Jesus, and the resurrection would, it is clear, be distasteful to such philosophers. Acts 17 : 18. Epictetus and the emperor Marcus Aurelius were stoics.

Stoning. The capital punishment generally inflicted on notorious criminals among the Hebrews and among the Egyptians. Ex. 8 : 26 ; 17 : 4 ; Lev. 20 : 2-27 ; 24 : 14-23 ; Num. 14 : 10 ; Josh. 7 : 25. The culprit was led out of the city to the place of execution ; and the witnesses against him were required to begin the work of death. He was stoned in one of two ways ; either stones were thrown upon him till he died ; or he was thrown headlong down a steep place, and large stones rolled upon his body. Acts 7 : 58, 59 ; 14 : 19 ; Matt. 21 : 44.

Stork, *the pious.* A bird of passage, much like the crane, but larger. It feeds on insects, snails, frogs, and offal, and was reckoned among unclean birds. The common stork (*Ciconia alba*) stands nearly four feet high, and is white except the extremities of the wings, which are black. Its long legs enable it to seek its food in the water as well as on the land, and its bill is so formed as to retain its slippery prey. In Palestine it builds its nest on trees. Ps. 104 : 17. "The beauty and power of the stork's wings are seized on as an illustration by Zechariah : 'The wind *was* in their wings, for they had wings like the wings of a stork.' Zech. 5 : 9. The black pinions of the stork, suddenly expanded from their white body, have a striking effect, having a spread of nearly seven feet, and the bird on the wing, showing its long, bright-red bill and steering itself by its long red legs, stretched out far behind its tail, is a noble sight. The stork has no organs of voice, and the only sound it emits is caused by the sharp and rapid snapping of its bill, like the rattle of castanets."—*Tristram.*

Succoth (*suk'koth*), *booths.* 1. An ancient town on the journey of Jacob from Padan-aram. Gen. 33 : 17. Succoth lay between Peniel, near the ford of the torrent Jabbok and Shechem. Comp. Gen. 32 : 30 and 33 : 18. In accordance with this is the mention of Succoth in the narrative of Gideon's pursuit of Zeba and Zalmunna. Judg. 8 : 5-17. It was allotted to the tribe of Gad. Josh. 13 : 27. Succoth is named once again after this—in 1 Kings 7 : 46 ; 2 Chron. 4 : 17—as marking the spot at which the brass founderies were placed for casting the metal work of the temple. 2. The first camping-place of the Israelites when they left Egypt. Ex. 12 : 37 ; 13 : 20 ; Num. 33 : 5, 6.

Swine. The flesh of the hog was strictly forbidden to the Hebrews. Lev. 11 : 7 ; Deut. 14 : 8. It seems to have been offered in idol-worship, and the worshipper no doubt feasted on the sacrifice. Isa. 65 : 4 ; 66 : 3, 17. Wild hogs are now common on the Syrian hills ; perhaps they were equally common in ancient times. Ps. 80 : 13. And certainly in our Lord's days the breeding of swine was common. Matt. 7 : 6 ; 8 : 30-32 ; Luke 15 : 15, 16 ; 2 Pet. 2 : 22.

Sycamine Tree. This must be carefully distinguished from the sycamore. It is mentioned but once, Luke 17 : 6 ; referring to the black mulberry tree.

Sycamore Tree. The tree so called in Scripture is not the sycamore of this country, which is a species of maple. It rather belongs to the genus *Ficus*, and may be identified with the *Ficus sycomoris*, or sycamore fig. It is common both in Egypt and Syria. It is a tender tree, flourishing in sandy plains and warm valleys, but is not hardy enough for the mountain, and would be killed by a sharp frost. Ps. 78 : 47. It is lofty and wide-spreading, often planted by the wayside, over which its arms extend, just adapted to the purpose for which Zaccheus selected it. Luke 19 : 4. The sycamore yields several crops of figs in the year, which grow on short stems along the trunk and large branches. These figs are often small and insipid. Amos 7 : 14.

Sychar (*sy'kar*), *drunken.* A small village near Jacob's well, John 4 : 5, formerly supposed to be another name for Shechem. But this is now known to be a mistake ; Sychar is represented by the modern Aksar.

Synagogue. The Greek word for synagogue properly denotes an assembly, a congregation. Synagogues were not in use till after the exile. In Ps. 74 : 8 we read that the invading Chaldean armies had "burned up all the synagogues of God in the land," but this can only refer to the temple, with all its courts, etc. Synagogues were probably instituted by Ezra and Nehemiah. See Acts 15 : 21 : "For Moses of old time hath in every city them that preach him, being read in the synagogues every sabbath day." In the later periods of Jewish history synagogues were not only found in all the chief cities and lesser towns in Syria, but in the principal cities of the Roman empire. Mark 1 : 21 ; Acts 6 : 9 ; 9 : 2-20 ; Luke 7 : 5. The establishment of these synagogues providentially prepared the way for the preaching of the gospel. As any one who happened to be present was at liberty to read and expound the sacred books, Acts 13 : 14, 15 ; 15 : 21, this privilege afforded our Lord and his disciples many opportunities for preaching the gospel of the kingdom in the various synagogues. Isa. 61 : 4 ; Luke 4 : 16, 28 ; Matt. 13 : 54 ; Mark 6 : 2 ; John 18 : 20 ; Acts 13 : 5-44 ; 14 : 1 ; 17 : 2, 17 ; 18 : 4, 26 ; 19 : 8. The "ruler of the synagogue" granted permission to read or speak. Luke 8 : 49 ; 13 : 14 ; Mark 5 : 35 ; Acts 18 : 8. The "minister," answering nearly to the modern sexton of the synagogue, was the attendant who handed the books to the reader, and opened and closed the synagogue. Luke 4 : 20. The "elders" of the synagogue preserved order in the assembly, Luke 7 : 3 ; Mark 5 : 22 ; Acts 13 : 15, and appear also to have constituted the lowest tribunal, which took cognizance mainly of religious matters, and sometimes inflicted the punishment. Matt. 10 : 17 ; 23 : 34 ; Mark 13 : 9 ; Luke 12 : 11 ; 21 : 12 ; John 16 : 2 ; Acts 22 : 19 ; 26 : 11. Ruins of synagogues, in several places in Palestine, have been found.

Syracuse (*syr'a-kūse*). The celebrated city on the eastern coast of Sicily. Paul arrived there in an Alexandrian ship from Melita, on his voyage to Rome. Acts 28 : 12. The site of Syracuse rendered it a convenient place for the African corn-ships to touch at, for the harbor was an excellent one, and the fountain Arethusa in the island furnished an unfailing supply of excellent water.

Syria (*syr'i-ah*); Hebrew, *Aram*. Syria proper was bounded by Amanus and Taurus on the north, by the Euphrates and the Arabian desert on the east, by Palestine on the south, by the Mediterranean near the mouth of the Orontes, and then by Phœnicia on the west. This tract is about 300 miles long from north to south, and from 50 to 150 miles broad, between the Libanus and the Anti-Libanus ranges. Of the various mountain ranges of Syria, Lebanon possesses the greatest interest. The principal rivers of Syria are the Litany and the Orontes. Among the principal cities are Damascus, Antioch, Hamath, Gebal, Beirut, Tadmor or Palmyra, Heliopolis or Baalbec, and Aleppo. Baalbec is one of the most wonderful ruins in Syria; Damascus is the oldest and largest city. Syria is now one of the divisions of Asiatic Turkey, and contains about 60,000 square miles. The population is estimated at about 2,000,000—Mohammedans, Jews, and Christians of various churches. The language usually spoken is the Arabic.

T

Taanach (*tā'a-năk*), *sandy soil*. A royal Canaanitish city in Issachar, but assigned to Manasseh, Josh. 12 : 21; 17 : 11; Judg. 1 : 27; 5 : 19; 1 Kings 4 : 12, also written "Tanach." Josh. 21 : 25, A. V. This city is perhaps the same as "Aner." 1 Chron. 6 : 70. It is now called Taanuk, with ruins about four miles southeast of Megiddo, on the western side of the plain of Esdraelon.

Tabering. Nah. 2 : 7. An old English word, meaning "to beat as a taber" or "tabret," a small drum beaten with one stick.

Tabernacle, Ex. 25 : 9, literally means "a tent." The sanctuary where in the earlier times the most sacred rites of the Hebrew religion were performed. The command to erect a tabernacle is recorded in Ex. 25 : 8; and in that place, and in Ex. 29 : 42, 43, 45, the special purpose is declared for which it was to be made. And so we find the various names of it, the "tent," Ex. 26 : 11, 12; the "tabernacle," dwelling or habitation, Ex. 26 : 13; the "tent of meeting," Ex. 29 : 43, for so the words should be rendered; the "tent of the testimony" or "tabernacle of witness," Num. 9 : 15; 17 : 7; 18 : 2; the "house of the Lord," Deut. 23 : 18; Josh. 9 : 23; Judg. 18 : 31; all these appelations pointing to the covenant-purpose of God. The command to make it began by inviting the people to contribute suitable materials. They were to be offered with a willing heart. These materials are described in Ex. 25 : 3–7. And the tabernacle was to be built according to the pattern given of God. It was as to its general plan like an ordinary tent, which is usually divided into two compartments, the inner lighted by a lamp and closed against strangers. Such tents are longer than they are broad. And so the tabernacle was an oblong square or rectangle, 30 cubits (45 feet or perhaps 50 feet) long, ten cubits in breadth and in height. The frame-work on these sides was perpendicular boards of shittim-wood, that is, acacia, overlaid with gold, kept together by means of transverse bars passing through golden rings, and each with two tenons, fitting into silver sockets, on which they stood. There were four coverings. The first was ten curtains of *byssus*, or fine linen, blue, purple, and scarlet, with cherubim embroidered on them, coupled together by loops and gold hooks. The second covering was of goats' hair in eleven curtains. The third covering was of rams' skins dyed red, like our morocco leather; and the fourth of "badgers' skins," more probably a kind of seal skin. These were to protect the tabernacle from the weather. The inner apartment or most holy place was a cube of ten cubits, the outer apartment 20 cubits in length and ten in breadth. They were separated by a veil of the same kind as the innermost covering, suspended on four gilded acacia pillars reared upon silver sockets. The east end or entrance of the tabernacle had also a large curtain suspended from five gilded acacia pillars set in sockets of brass or copper.

The Furniture.—In the most holy place, which the high priest alone entered, was the ark of the covenant: in the holy place, where the priests ministered—to the north the table of shew-bread, to the south the golden candlestick, in the centre the altar of incense. Round about the tabernacle was an open court into which the people were admitted, 100 cubits in length and 50 broad. It was formed by columns, 20 on each side, 10 at each end, raised on brazen or copper sockets. Hangings fastened to the pillars formed three sides and part of the fourth; on the east the breadth of four pillars was reserved for a central entrance, where was an embroidered curtain suspended from the four pillars. Immediately opposite the entrance was the great altar of burnt offering; and between that and the door of the tabernacle was the laver. Ex., chaps. 26, 27, 38, 40. There are some parts of the description of the pillars and hangings of the court which it is not easy to understand. The tabernacle was completed in about nine months: and as the people offered most liberally, Ex. 36 : 5, it was a costly structure; the value of the materials being estimated at $1,000,000. It was erected on the first day of the first month of the second year after leaving Egypt. It was carried by the Israelites into Canaan, and there set up, possibly first at Gilgal, then, when the land was subdued, at Shiloh, Josh. 18 : 1, and also at Bethel, perhaps afterwards at Nob, and then at Gibeon. 1 Chron. 16 : 39; 21 : 29. It was removed, when the temple was built, to Jerusalem, and possibly deposited in the temple. 1 Kings 8 : 4; 2 Chron. 5 : 5. For the regulations about its removal see Num. 4. David seems to have constructed a second tabernacle to receive the ark when it was brought to Jerusalem. 2 Sam. 6:17; 1 Chron. 15:1. Doubtless the first one had perished or worn out. See Bissell. *Bib. Antiq.*

Tabernacles, Feast of. Num. 29:12-40. One of the three great annual festivals which all the Hebrews were to keep. During the seven days of its celebration the people dwelt in booths made of the branches and leaves of trees, in commemoration of the 40 years' wandering in the wilderness. Lev. 23:34-44. As the season of thanksgiving for the fruits of the earth, it is also called the "Feast of Ingathering." Ex. 23:16; 34:22. It commenced on the fifteenth day of Tisri, October: the first day and the eighth day were distinguished as Sabbaths. Num. 29:12-40; Deut. 16:13-15; Zech. 14:16-19. In every seventh year during this festival, the law of Moses was read in the hearing of all the people. Deut. 31:10-13; Neh. 8:14-18. In later times, the priests went every morning during the festival, and drew water from the fountain of Siloam, and poured it out to the southwest of the altar, the Levites, in the meanwhile, playing on instruments of music, and singing the Psalms 113-118. This ceremony is said to have been founded on Isa. 12:3; and was probably a memorial of the abundant supply of water which God afforded to the Hebrews during their wanderings in the wilderness. John 7:2-39.

Tabitha (*tab'i-tha*), *gazelle*. Acts 9:36-40. A female disciple at Joppa, called also Dorcas, restored to life in answer to Peter's prayer.

Tabor (*tā'bôr*), *a mound*: or **Mount Tabor.** Judg. 4:6. A single limestone mountain in central Palestine. It rises abruptly from the northeastern arm of the plain of Esdraelon, and stands entirely isolated except on the west, where a narrow ridge connects it with the hills of Nazareth. It is six miles east of Nazareth, and about 50 miles north of Jerusalem. As seen from a distance, it presents the appearance of a beautiful flattened cone, being symmetrical in its proportions, and rounded off like a hemisphere or the segment of a circle. Tabor makes a prominent figure in the Old, but is not named in the New Testament. It was the boundary between Issachar and Zebulun. Josh. 19:12, 22. Barak, at the command of Deborah, assembled his forces on Tabor, and descended thence, with "ten thousand men after him," into the plain, and conquered Sisera on the banks of the Kishon. Judg. 4:6-15. The brothers of Gideon, each of whom "resembled the children of a king," were murdered here by Zebah and Zalmunna. Judg. 8:18, 19. There are the ruins of a fortress on the summit of Tabor.

Tadmor (*tăd'môr*). Heb. *Tamar, palms.* A city in the wilderness, built by Solomon. 1 Kings 9:18, R. V., "Tamar;" 2 Chron. 8:4. There is no other Scripture mention of this city. It has usually been identified with the famous city of Palmyra. Palmyra occupied the most favorable position on the great caravan route between the rich cities of the East and the ports of the Mediterranean. Palmyra was mentioned by Pliny, Josephus, Jerome. and other early writers. The ruins extend over a plain about three or four miles in circuit.

Tahpanhes (*tăh'pan-hēz*). A city on the Tanitic branch of the Nile, in lower Egypt, and called Tahapanes and Tehaphnehes, Ezek. 30:18; possibly the Hanes of Isa. 30:4; Jer. 2:16; 43:7, 8, 9; 44:1; 46:14. Jeremiah, after the murder of Gedaliah, was taken to this place, and Pharaoh had a palace built or restored there, made of bricks in a brick-kiln. The children of Noph (Memphis) and of Tahpanhes are used to represent the entire body of the Egyptians. Jer. 2:16. It is identical with the Daphne of the Greeks. The site of Tahpanhes was discovered by M. Naville, and the palace of Psammetichus I. found.

Talent. See **Measures and Weights.** Ex. 25:39; 37:24; 2 Sam. 12:30; Matt. 25:25. A Jewish talent in weight contained about 3000 shekels, and is estimated to equal 125 pounds Troy measure. Reckoning silver at about 80 cents an ounce, a talent of silver would then be equal to about $1200. A talent of gold by the Oxford tables is estimated equal to $28,280, and about $27,300 by Bagster's Bible tables. An Attic talent was equal to about $960. This may be alluded to in Matt. 18:24; 25:15. Talents of silver, by weight, are frequently mentioned in the Old Testament. Ex. 38:27; 1 Kings 20:39; 2 Kings 5:22; 15:19; 1 Chron. 29:7. Talents of gold are also noticed. Ex. 25:39; 2 Chron. 36:3; 1 Chron. 29:7. Also a talent of lead. Zech. 5:7. See **Money.**

Tappuah (*tăp'pu-ah* or *tap-pū'ah*), *apple region.* 1. A town in the plain country of Judah. Josh. 15:34. 2. A city on the border of Ephraim and Manasseh; the city belonged to Ephraim, the land or district named from it to Manasseh. Josh. 16:8; 17:8. This was no doubt identical with En-tappuah. It is not certain which of these two places is intended in Josh. 12:17.

Tares. Bearded darnel (*Lolium temulentum*), a grass sometimes found in our own grain-fields, but very common in Eastern countries. Matt. 13:25. Until the head appears its resemblance to wheat is very close. Travellers describe the process of pulling up this grass and separating it from the genuine grain. and their descriptions perfectly accord with the language of our Saviour in the parable.

Tarshish (*tär'shish*), *a breaking.* 1 Kings 10:22; 22:48. 1. An ancient commercial city whose situation is not certainly determined. Some place it not far from the Straits of Gibraltar. Gen. 10:4; Ps. 72:10. The region of Tarshish, also written Tharshish, 1 Kings 10:22; 22:48, is possibly the *Tartessus* of the Greeks and Romans. The Hebrews and the Phœnicians imported silver, iron, tin, lead, and other articles of merchandise from this place of trade. Isa. 23:1, 6, 10; 66:19; Jer. 10:9; Ezek. 27:12, 25; 38:13. "Ships of Tarshish" designated ships employed by the Tyrians in voyages to and from Tarshish. Isa. 60 : 9; Jonah 1 : 3 ; 4 : 2; possibly all large merchant ships. Isa. 2 : 16 ; Ps. 48 : 7.

Tarsus (*tär'sus*). A town of Cilicia, the birthplace of the apostle Paul. Acts 9 : 11 ; 21 : 39 ; 22 : 3. Augustus made it a "free city." It was renowned as a place of education under the early Roman emperors. Strabo compares it in this respect to Athens and Alexandria. Tarsus also was a place of much commerce. It was situated in a wild and fertile plain on the banks of the Cydnus. No ruins of any importance remain.

Taverns, the Three. A place where some of the "brethren" came to meet Paul on his journey to Rome, and by their coming the apostle took fresh courage. Acts 28 : 13-15. It was on the Appian Way, 33 miles southeast from Rome, and ten miles from Appii Forum.

Tax, Taxing, Taxation. Luke 2 : 1, 2, R. V. "enroll, enrollment." 1 Kings 10 : 28, 29. The Israelites were expected to pay, in their earlier history, sacred offerings which were connected with their religious services. From them the priests and Levites, and in a measure the poor, were to be maintained. To these must be added the capitation tax to be paid when a census of the people was taken. Ex. 30 : 11-16. This, however, was but occasional—yet see perhaps some traces of it in 2 Kings 12 : 4 ; 2 Chron. 24 : 6-9; but it formed the basis of the annual impost agreed to after the captivity, Neh. 10 : 32, 33, then the third of a shekel, but afterwards a half-shekel, Matt. 17 : 24, 27, levied on all Jews wheresoever they resided. On the establishment of kingly government additional burdens were necessarily laid upon the nation—as for Solomon's great works, 1 Kings 12 : 4, and when foreign enemies required large sums as fines or annual tribute. 2 Kings 15 : 19, 20 ; 17 : 4 ; 23 : 33-35. Under the Persian government, after the return from Babylon, there was a regular system of taxation, to which doubtless the provinces of the empire generally were subjected. Three branches are enumerated, from which, however, the priests and sacred classes were specially exempted, "toll, tribute, and custom," Ezra 4 : 13 ; 7 : 24, probably implying direct money payments, excise, and tolls by travellers at bridges, fords, etc. The Jews had also to defray the charges of the governor by supplying his table, and by a money payment. This Nehemiah when in office did not exact. Neh. 5 : 14, 15. The Egyptian and Syrian kings imposed yet more oppressive taxes. In later times it appears that, though relief was sometimes granted, direct tribute, duties on salt, crown taxes, and a certain proportion of the produce of fruit trees, and corn land, with a tax on cattle were ordinarily required. 1 Macc. 10 : 29-31 ; 11 : 34, 35 ; 13 : 39. When Judea was made a Roman province the taxes were systematically farmed, and publicans were stationed through the country. There were the duties to be paid at harbors, and the gates of cities, a poll-tax, and perhaps a kind of property tax. Mark 12 : 14, 15 ; Rom. 13 : 6, 7. These imposts were regarded with great jealousy, as paid to a foreign power. There was also a house tax in Jerusalem, remitted by Agrippa I. *Josephus' Ant.* 19 : 6, 3. For the taxing or registration in order to taxation, said to be conducted by Cyrenius, Luke 2 : 1, 2, see **Cyrenius**. There was another at a later period. Acts 5 : 37.

Tekoa (*te-kō'ah*), *a fixing* or *pitching of tents*. A fortified city, twelve miles south by east from Jerusalem, 1 Chron. 2 : 24 ; Jer. 6 : 1 ; Amos 1 : 1 ; also written "Tekoah." 2 Sam. 14 : 2, 4, 9, A. V. The inhabitants were called "Tekoites." Neh. 3 : 5. It had a desert lying east of it, toward the Dead Sea. 2 Chron. 20 : 20. Tekoa, now called Teku'a, is situated on a hill.

Tel-abib (*tĕl-ā'bib*), *corn hill*. A place in Babylonia where some of the Jewish captives were stationed. It was by the river of Chebar; but its precise site is doubtful. Ezek. 3 : 15.

Teman (*tē'man*), *south desert*. A country named from the oldest son of Eliphaz, the son of Esau. Gen. 36 : 11. These people were called Temani, or Temanites, and seem to have been noted for wisdom. Jer. 49 : 7 ; Obad. 9. They are especially mentioned in the prediction against Edom. Jer. 49 : 7 ; Ezek. 25 : 13 ; Amos 1 : 12 ; Obad. 9 ; Hab. 3 : 3. Their country seems to have been the southeastern part of Edom.

Temple. A place or building dedicated to religious worship. "God . . . dwelleth not in temples made with hands." Acts 17 : 24. The word temple occurs in the A. V. about 200 times, generally referring to the one at Jerusalem. But the temple at Babylon is alluded to, 2 Chron. 36 : 7 ; Ezra 5 : 14 ; the temple of Diana at Ephesus, Acts 19 : 27 ; the temple of God, 2 Cor. 6 : 16, meaning the saints, and the temple in the Holy City—the New Jerusalem. Rev. 21 : 22. The word specially designated the sanctuary of Jehovah at Jerusalem. There were three successive temples there : 1. Solomon's; 2. Zerubbabel's, known as the Second temple ; 3. Herod's temple.

1. *Solomon's Temple*, was built on Mount Moriah, in the eastern part of Jerusalem, by Solomon, the king, as conceived and planned by his father David. 1 Chron. 17 : 1. David gathered the materials and funds to build it—" an hundred thousand talents of gold, and a thousand thousand talents of silver; and of brass and iron without weight." 1 Chron. 22 : 14. The silver and gold would be equal to from $2,000,000 to $4,000,000. Besides gold and silver, David collected immense quantities of "brass" (bronze or copper), iron, stone, timber, etc., and he secured skilful mechanics and artificers for every branch of the work. 1 Chron. 22 ; 29 : 4, 7. He also furnished the design, plan, and location of the building; in all which he was divinely instructed. 1 Chron. 21 ; 22 ; 28 : 11-19. There were 183,600 Jews and strangers employed on it—of Jews 30,000, by rotation 10,000 a month ; of Canaanites, 153,600, of whom 70,000 were " bearers of burdens," 80,000 hewers of wood and stone, and 3600 overseers. The

parts were all prepared at a distance from the site of the building, and when they were brought together the whole structure was erected without the sound of hammer, axe, or any tool of iron. 1 Kings 6:7. It required seven and one-half years to complete it in all its splendor, the glory of Jerusalem, and the most magnificent edifice in the world, B.C. 1005. Like the tabernacle, it had its front toward the east. All the arrangements of the temple were identical with those of the tabernacle, and the dimensions of every part exactly double those of the previous structure. It was 70 cubits long and 20 wide, and had in front a porch more than 200 feet high. All around the main structure there were attached to the north and south sides and at the west end certain buildings called side chambers, 1 Kings 6:10, three stories in height, which were much more extensive than the temple itself. The material was white stone: the woodwork of cedar, overlaid with fine gold; the floor of cedar, with planks of fir. 1 Kings 6:15. The holy of holies was a small square chamber, absolutely dark except by the light received through the entrance. In it were two huge golden figures, standing upright on their feet, on each side of the ark, which rested upon a protuberance of rough rock. Above the ark the wings of these cherubim met. The walls of the chambers which ran round the rest of the building were not allowed to lean against the outer walls of this sanctuary. The quarries of Solomon have been discovered under the present city of Jerusalem, near the Damascus gate. They are very extensive. The temple of Solomon stood 424 years; at times was allowed to fall into decay; was plundered by Shishak, king of Egypt, during the reign of Rehoboam. 1 Kings 14:25, 26. After this it was frequently profaned and pillaged: was repaired by Joash, 2 Kings 12:5-14, and by Josiah, 2 Chron. 29:3-9. Its destruction was prophesied by Jeremiah, Jer. 7:2, 14, and it was at last broken down and destroyed by the king of Babylon, and the nation itself carried into captivity. 2 Kings 25:8, 9, 13-17; 2 Chron. 36:18, 19, B.C. 586.

2. *The Temple of Zerubbabel.*—In B.C. 536 Cyrus the Persian king of Babylon gave permission to the Jews to return. Zerubbabel, as Jewish governor, and Joshua, the high priest, superintended the people in rebuilding the temple. Cyrus permitted and encouraged them to do this work, Ezra 3:8. Owing to the opposition of their enemies, it was not, however, completed for 20 years, B.C. 515. The story of this long struggle and trouble is told in the book of Ezra. This second temple, though inferior in many respects to the first—having no ark, no mercy-seat, no visible revelation of the divine glory, no sacred fire, no Urim and Thummim, and no spirit of prophecy, Ezra 3:12, 13—still was in breadth and height, in almost every dimension, one-third larger than Solomon's.

3. *Temple of Herod.*—The temple of Zerubbabel after nearly 500 years had suffered much from wars, age, and decay, when Herod the Great, to secure the favor of the Jews, undertook to rebuild it. He began the work 20 years before the birth of Christ and completed the main building in one year and a half, and the adjoining buildings in eight years. But the work was not entirely ended till A.D. 64, under Herod Agrippa II. So the statement in John 2:20 is correct. The building stood upon Mount Moriah, in an area which was 500 cubits square. Along the ramparts of the temple hill ran double cloisters or arcades, and there the money changers sat. Matt. 21:12. There were several courts about the temple which were upon different levels. The outer court, or court of the Gentiles, came first; then the court of the women, the court of Israel, the court of the priests, and then the temple itself. Between the first two came the "soreg" ("interwoven"), or "middle wall of partition." Eph. 2:14. It had 13 openings; upon it, at intervals, were stones with Greek inscriptions, threatening death to the Gentile who entered. A stone thus inscribed was discovered lately by an explorer in Palestine. The charge that Paul had brought such a Greek into the enclosure aroused the Jerusalem mob. Acts 21:28. The court of Israel, 10 cubits by 135, was 15 steps higher up, and upon them the 15 Songs of Degrees—Ps. 120-134, inclusive—were sung. The musical instruments were kept there. It was merely a platform, and had no cloisters or columns. Only men especially purified could enter it. The court of the priests, or sanctuary, 135 by 176 cubits, was 2½ cubits higher than the court of Israel, the wall being 1 cubit high, with 3 steps above it. On the wall there was a platform from which the priests blessed the people. The entrance of the temple was 20 cubits wide and 40 high. Over it hung the golden vine, supported, probably, by nails. The temple was of two stories; in the lower there were 38 chambers in three tiers; in the upper, none. The holy house was entered from the porch by a gate 20 cubits high and 10 broad, with double doors, opening out and in; before it hung a veil of equal width with the doors. Before the entrance to the holy of holies hung two veils or two curtains, 1 cubit apart, and, inasmuch as the opening of the outer curtain was upon the north, while the inner was on the south, no glimpse of the holy of holies could be obtained by any one but the high priest. The purification of Mary, Luke 2:22, must have been near the gate Nicanor. The Child Jesus was found amid the doctors of the law in the temple courts. Luke 2:46. The Beautiful Gate, Acts 3:2, was one of the finest entrances to the temple. The castle of Antonia, from which, by a secret passageway, the Roman soldiery could be led down into the temple area to preserve order—as notably to rescue Paul, Acts 21:31, 32—was situated upon the north-western corner of the outer cloister, and had four towers with a large interior space. Jesus foretold the destruction of the third

temple: "There shall not be left here one stone upon another, that shall not be thrown down." Matt. 24:2; Mark 13:2; Luke 21:6. This prophecy was made about 30 A. D., and was fulfilled about 40 years afterward, by the Roman soldiers, who set the temple on fire and destroyed it in 70 A. D., although the Roman commander had given strict orders to have it preserved. About three centuries later, the emperor Julian attempted to rebuild it, but was prevented, for the terrific explosions that took place, as the workmen dug down for the foundations, caused them to throw away their implements, and the work was abandoned. See Milman's *Hist. Christianity*, iii. 27.

Up to quite recent times the Haram— as the enclosure containing the site of the temple is called, and where the mosques of Omar and el-Aksar now stand—was closed to all non-Mohammedans; but the pressure brought to bear after the Crimean war, 1856, was too great, and now travellers find little difficulty in gaining admittance.

The temple was a type of the Christian, for every Christian is a temple of the Holy Ghost. 1 Cor. 3:16, 17; 6:19; 2 Cor. 6:16; 1 Pet. 2:5. The temple seen by Ezekiel in vision is very fully described, and is supposed by some to be a figure of the actual temple. See Ezek. 40 to 47.

Ten Commandments, the. Deut. 4:13. Or, more exactly, the Ten Words. Ex. 34:28, margin; Deut. 10:4, margin. They were proclaimed from Sinai, amid mighty thunderings and lightnings, Ex. 20:1-22, and were graven on tablets of stone by the finger of God. Ex. 31:18; 32:15, 16; 34:1, 28. Ten was a significant number, the symbol of completeness; and in these ten words was comprised that moral law to which obedience forever was to be paid. On these, summed up as our Lord summed them up, hung all the law and the prophets. Matt. 22:36-40. There were two tables, the commandments of the one more especially respecting God, those of the other, man. These are usually divided into four and six. Perhaps they might better be distributed into five and five. The honor to parents enjoined by the fifth commandment is based on the service due to God, the Father of his people. Paul, enumerating those which respect our neighbor, includes but the last five. Rom. 13:9.

Terah (*te'rah*), *delay*. The father of Abraham, who left Ur to go to Canaan, but died at Haran, in Mesopotamia. Gen. 11:24-32; Josh. 24:2, 14; Acts 7:2-4. He is called "Tharah" in Luke 3:34.

Teraphim (*ter'a-phim*), *givers of prosperous life?* Images kept in the houses and honored with a certain kind of reverence. Laban had some of them; and Rachel took these when leaving Padan-aram. Gen. 31:19, 30, 32-35. So we find that they were employed for purposes of divination among the Babylonians. Ezek. 21:21. It is possible that Rachel imagined that some augury of the future might be obtained from them; and she must have considered them as having a tutelary power. These images were probably some of the strange gods of which Jacob subsequently cleansed his household. Gen. 35:2, 4. Micah had them in his house, and felt sure that Jehovah would bless him when he had a Levite to minister before them. Judg. 17:5, 13. These the Danites eagerly carried off. Judg. 18:14-21. It is still more perplexing to find them in David's house. 1 Sam. 19:13, 16. And it does not seem that they were altogether put away till the thorough reformation of Josiah's days. 2 Kings 23:24. Then, indeed, they were classed with abominable things. The word is used, 1 Sam. 15:23, rendered in our version "idolatry," in expressing the truth that obstinacy was sinful, "iniquity, and teraphim worship." We find them also censured in Zech. 10:2; and Hosea employed the term to signify the state of Israel with no kind of worship either of the true God or of false deities. Hos. 3:4. We may gather that they were made of various materials, as of silver, Judg. 17:4, and that they resembled a human figure sometimes of the natural size. 1 Sam. 19:13. Perhaps they were like the Roman Penates or household gods. Small figures of baked clay, some with a human head and a lion's body, and others with a human body and lynx head, have been found under the pavement of the porch of the Khorsabad palace.

Tertullus (*ter-tŭl'lus*). "A certain orator," Acts 24:1, who was retained to accuse the apostle Paul at Cæsarea before the Roman procurator Felix.

Tetrarch. This title strictly denotes one who governs the fourth part of a province or kingdom. Matt. 14:1. In Scripture, however, it is applied to any one who governed a province of the Roman empire, whatever portion of the territory might be within his jurisdiction. Matt. 14:9.

Thebez (*thē'bez*) *brightness*. The town where Abimelech was killed. Judg. 9:50; 2 Sam. 11:21. It is now Tubâs, a place 11 miles northeast of Shechem, Nablûs.

Theophilus (*the-ŏph'i-lŭs*), *lover of God*. A noted person to whom Luke addressed his gospel and his history of the Acts of the Apostles. Luke 1:3. The title "most excellent" probably denotes official dignity. Acts 23:26; 24:3; and 26:25.

Thessalonians (*thĕs'sa-lō'ni-anz*), **Epistles to the.** These epistles are ascribed to Paul by Irenæus, Clement of Alexandria, and Tertullian. The First Epistle was probably the first of all the Pauline letters, and written, not at Athens, but at Corinth, about A. D. 52. The design of the epistle was to establish the followers of Christ in those graces for which they were conspicuous, and to encourage them under severe persecutions. Acts 17:1-11; 1 Thess. 1:5, 6. The Second Epistle, also written at Corinth, near the close of A. D. 53 or early in 54, was designed to correct some misapprehensions respecting the First Epistle. Some misunderstood the apostle's words, and taught that the day of the Lord was very near at hand. 1 Thess. 5:2-4. Paul corrects this misapprehension and assures them that the "man of sin," or "son of perdition," must reach the highest pitch of arrogance before final ruin from the Lord be hurled upon the "mystery of iniquity," which was already working. 2 Thess. 2:3-12.

Thessalonica (*thĕs'sa-lo-nī'kah*). A city of Macedonia. It was in Paul's time a free city of the Romans, the capital and most populous city in Macedonia. Paul and Silas, in A. D. 58, came to Thessalonica from Philippi, which was 100 miles northeast. For at least three Sabbaths the apostles preached to their countrymen. A church was gathered, principally composed of Gentiles. At length the persecution became so violent as to drive the apostles away. Paul desired to revisit the church there, and sent Timothy to minister to them. Among his converts were Caius, Aristarchus, Secundus, and perhaps Jason. Acts 17:1-13; 20:4; 27:2; comp. Phil. 4:16; 2 Tim. 4:10. Paul wrote two epistles to the Thessalonian church from Corinth, 1 Thess. 1:1; 2 Thess. 1:1. The "rulers" of the city, Acts 17:6, 8, are called, in the original, "politarchs." This is a peculiar term, not elsewhere found in the New Testament, but this very word appears in the inscription on a triumphal arch believed to have been erected after the battle of Philippi. The names of seven politarchs are given. During several centuries Thessalonica was an important centre of Christianity in the oriental church, and from it the Bulgarians and Slavonians were reached. The population now is about 80,000, of whom 30,000 are Jews and 10,000 Greeks.

Theudas (*theū'das*), *God-given*. An insurrectionary chieftain mentioned by Gamaliel. Acts 5:36. This Theudas was an obscure individual who is not mentioned elsewhere. The name was a common one.

Thomas (*tŏm'as*), *twin*. Also called *Didymus*, a Greek term meaning *twin*. Matt. 10:3; Mark 3:18; Luke 6:15; Acts 1:13. There can be little doubt that this apostle was a native of Galilee. John 21:2. In the character of Thomas we observe a desire for a sufficient evidence of facts. John 14:5; 20:24,25. He was of a thoughtful mind; his affection for his Master was warm and disinterested, John 11:16; and his faith was not, as some have characterized it, inconsiderate, running easily from one extreme to the other. He had doubted the resurrection, and described the kind of proof be required; but, when the Lord appeared, and showed by his address to him that he knew his thoughts, then the apostle naturally desired nothing more. His reason was convinced: it was his Lord and his God. John 20:26-29. There is nothing in Thomas' behavior to surprise those accustomed to analyze the workings of the human mind. The Scripture is afterwards silent as to this apostle. According to earliest tradition, he preached in Parthia, and was buried at Edessa; later histories say that he went to India, and was martyred there; and the Syrian Christians in that country claim him as the founder of their church.

Thresh, Threshing. Different modes of threshing are used in the East. A level spot was selected for the threshing-floor, generally in an exposed situation where advantage might be taken of the wind for winnowing or separating the corn from the chaff when the threshing process was completed. Robinson observed several of these floors near together of a circular form hardened by beating down the earth, and about 50 feet in diameter, the sheaves being thickly spread on them. Near Jericho "were no less than five such floors, all trodden by oxen, cows, and younger cattle, arranged in each case five abreast, and driven round in a circle, or rather in all directions, over the floor. . . By this process the straw is broken up and becomes chaff. It is occasionally turned up with a large wooden fork having two prongs, and when sufficiently trodden is thrown up with the same fork against the wind in order to separate the grain, which is then gathered up and winnowed. The whole process is exceedingly wasteful."

Thyatira (*thȳ'a-tī'rah*). A city of Asia Minor, on the northern border of Lydia. Dyeing was an important branch of its business from Homer's time, and the first New Testament mention of Thyatira, Acts 16:14, connects it with the purple-seller, Lydia. Three votive inscriptions have been found among its ruins purporting to have come from the guild of "The Dyers." Thyatira was the seat of one of the seven churches of Asia. Rev. 2:18-29. Its population now is estimated at from 17,000 to 20,000.

Thyine-wood. A kind of cedar growing in Spain, and on the coast of Africa. It was the *Citrum* or citron-wood of the Romans, the *Thuja articulata* of Linnæus. It was frequently employed to give fragrance to sacrifices. Rev. 18:12, margin, *sweet*. The tree grows to the height of 30 feet, or even more, and resembles the cypress in its boughs, leaves, and fruit.

Tiberias (*ti-bē'ri-as*). A town in Galilee, on the western shore of the sea of Tiberias. John 6:1, 23. Our Lord never visited it. He was often in the immediate neighborhood; but we never read of his entering Tiberias. It was the seat for centuries of a famous academy, and to the present day it is one of the four holy cities. Near to Tiberias are the celebrated hot baths of Hammam. The present city contains about 2000 inhabitants.

Tiberius (*tī-bē'ri-ŭs*). Luke 3:1. Tiberius Claudius Nero, the second Roman emperor, from A. D. 14 until A. D. 37. He was the son of Tiberius Claudius Nero and Livia, and hence a stepson of Augustus. He was despotic in his government, cruel and vindictive in his disposition. He died A. D. 37, at the age of 78, after a reign of 23 years. Our Saviour was put to death in the reign of Tiberius. John 19:12, 15.

Tiglath-pileser (*tĭg'lath-pĭ-lē'zer*). The second Assyrian king mentioned in the Scriptures as having come into contact with the Israelites, and the second of the name. He invaded Samaria, 2 Kings 15 : 29, and after some years destroyed Damascus, taking many captives. 1 Chron. 5 : 26. The occasion of the first attack was probably the refusal of Pekah to pay tribute ; of the second, the call of Ahaz upon him for assistance against Pekah and Rezin, the king of Syria. Tiglath-pileser at Damascus met Ahaz, who became his vassal. 2 Kings 16 : 10. He reigned B. C. 747-730.

Timnath (tĭm′nath) and **Timnathah** (tĭm′na-thah), *portion assigned*. 1. A place to which Judah was going when he was met by his daughter-in-law Tamar, Gen. 38 : 12-14 ; R. V., "Timnah." 2. The home of Samson's wife, Judg. 14 : 1, 2, 5 ; R. V., "Timnah ;" probably also identical with Timnah, the modern Tibneh, west of Bethshemesh.

Timnath-serah (tĭm′nath-sē′rah), *portion of abundance*. A town in the mountains of Ephraim, which was assigned to Joshua ; and in which he was buried. Josh. 19 : 49, 50 ; 24 : 30. It is also written "Timnath-heres"—*portion of the sun*. Judg. 2 : 9.

Timothy (tĭm′o-thy), *honoring God*. Called also **Timotheus**, A. V. An evangelist and helper of Paul. His father was a Greek and a heathen ; his mother, Eunice, was a Jewess, and a woman of piety, as was also his grandmother, Lois, 2 Tim. 1 : 5, and by them he was early taught in the Scriptures of the Old Testament. 2 Tim. 3 : 15. Paul selected him as an assistant in his labors, and, to avoid the cavils of the Jews, had him circumcised. 1 Cor. 9 : 20. He was left in charge of the church at Ephesus. 1 Tim. 4 : 12. A post-apostolic tradition makes him bishop of Ephesus.

Epistles of Paul to. These, with that to Titus, are commonly called the Pastoral Epistles, because they give directions about church work. First Timothy is supposed to have been written about the year 65, and contains special instructions respecting the qualifications and the duties of officers and other persons in the church. The second epistle was written a year or two later and while Paul was in constant expectation of martyrdom. 2 Tim. 4 : 6-8.

Tin. Num. 31 : 22 ; Ezek. 27 : 12. Burton has recently found tin-ore in the land of Midian. In Isa. 1 : 25 the word "tin" doubtless means a sort of dross. The margin of the R. V. reads "alloy."

Tiphsah (tĭf′sah), *passage, ford*. A city on the western bank of the Euphrates, supposed to be the *Thapsacus* of the Grecks and Romans. It was the northeastern extremity of Solomon's dominions. 1 Kings 4 : 24.

Tirhakah (tir′ha-kah), *exalted?* King of Ethiopia and upper Egypt. 2 Kings 19 : 9 ; Isa. 37 : 9. In legends he was one of the greatest conquerors of antiquity. His triumphs westward are said to have reached the Pillars of Hercules. When Sennacherib heard of his coming he demanded the immediate surrender of Jerusalem. 2 Kings 19 : 9, 16. Tirhakah reigned, probably, 28 years. The dates are uncertain, but perhaps his rule extended from B. C. 695 to 667.

Tirzah (tir′zah), *delight*. One of the 31 cities of the Canaanites taken by Joshua, Josh. 12 : 24, and for 50 years the capital of the northern kingdom of Israel, until Omri built Samaria. 1 Kings 14 : 17 ; 15 : 21, 33 ; 16 : 6, 23. It is also mentioned in the reign of Menahem, B. C. 772, 2 Kings 15 : 14, 16, and its fame for beauty appears from Song of Sol. 6 : 4. Tirzah has been usually identified with Telluzah, five miles east of Samaria, and 30 miles north of Jerusalem. The village occupies a fine elevation in the midst of olive groves.

Tishbah (tĭsh′bah). The birthplace of Elijah, 1 Kings 17 : 1, who is therefore called the Tishbite, probably identical with el-Istib, or Listib, 22 miles in an air-line south of the Sea of Galilee, and ten miles east of the Jordan.

Tithes, or Tenths. A form of tax known long before the time of Moses, Gen. 14 : 20 ; 28 : 22, and practised under the civil and religious government of heathen nations. It required a fixed proportion of the produce of the earth and of herds, for the service of God. One-tenth of this produce went to the use of the Levites, who had no part in the soil, and of course were dependent on their brethren for the means of subsistence. One-tenth of their tenth they paid in their turn to the priests. Num. 18 : 21-32. The nine parts were tithed again, and of this second tithe a feast was made in the court of the sanctuary, or in some apartment connected with it. If, however, the Jew could not with convenience carry his tithe thither, he was permitted to sell it and to take the money, adding one-fifth of the amount— that is, if he sold the tithe for a dollar, he should bring, in money, a dollar and twenty cents—and to purchase therewith what was required at the feast after he came to the sanctuary. Lev. 27 : 31 ; Deut. 12 : 17, 18 ; 14 : 22-27. See for full account, Bissell's *Biblical Antiquities*.

Tittle, the very least point, Matt. 5 : 18 ; used of the fine stroke by which some letters were distinguished. To omit this stroke condemned the entire copy of the Law made by the scribe.

Titus (tī′tus). A Gentile by descent, and probably converted to Christianity under the preaching of Paul. Titus 1 : 4. He, however, refused to subject him to the rite of circumcision, though, as some have inferred, he was strongly urged so to do. Gal. 2 : 3-5. Titus was the companion of Paul in many of his trials and missionary tours, 2 Cor. 8 : 6, 16, 23, and was entrusted with several important commissions. 2 Cor. 12 : 18 ; 2 Tim. 4 : 10 ; Titus 1 : 5.

Epistle of Paul to, was designed to instruct Titus in the right discharge of his ministerial offices in Crete, a difficult field, owing to the character of the inhabitants, who were noted for lying, idleness, and gluttony. Titus 1 : 12. The Epistle was probably written from Asia Minor in the year 65, when Paul was on his way to Nicopolis.

Tob (tŏb), *good*. The place or district beyond the Jordan to which Jephthah fled,

Judg. 11:3, 5; also called Ish-tob. 2 Sam. 10:6, 8, A. V. It lay beyond Gilead, toward the eastern deserts.

Tobiah (*to-bi'ah*), *goodness of Jehovah*. 1. "The children of Tobiah" were a family who returned with Zerubbabel, but were unable to prove their connection with Israel. Ezra 2:60; Neh. 7:62. 2. Tobiah though a slave, Neh. 2:10, 19—unless this is a title of opprobrium—and an Ammonite, found means to ally himself with a priestly family, and his son Johanan married the daughter of Meshullam the son of Berechiah, Neh. 6:18. He himself was the son-in-law of Shechaniah the son of Arah, Neh. 6:17, and these family relations created for him a strong faction among the Jews.

Tongues, Gift of. Joel 2:28; Acts 2:16; Mark 16:17; comp. Matt. 10:19, 20; Mark 13:11. This gift was of two kinds. The first gift was the power to "declare the wonderful works of God" in languages ordinarily unknown to the speakers, for the instruction of foreign hearers. Acts 2:4-11. The other form of the gift of tongues is thought to have been an ecstatic form of worship, chiefly praise, but requiring interpretation. Acts 10:46; 1 Cor. 12:30.

Topaz. Ezek. 28:13; Rev. 21:20. The modern chrysolite, a rather soft and transparent or translucent gem, usually of a pale green. The true topaz is ordinarily pellucid and of a yellowish tint, but sometimes of a brown, blue, or green hue, or even colorless. A single gem of this kind has been sold (it is said) for upwards of $1,000,000. The finest specimens are found in the East Indies.

Topheth (*to'feth*), and once **Tophet** (*to'fet*), *place of burning*, first applied to a deep part of the "valley of the son of Hinnom," Jer. 7:31, "by the entry of the east gate," Jer. 19:2. It seems also to have been part of the king's gardens, and watered by Siloam. Tophet occurs only in the Old Testament. 2 Kings 23:10; Isa. 30:33; Jer. 7:31, 32; 19:6, 11-14. The New does not refer to it. Tophet has been variously translated. The most natural meaning seems that suggested by the occurrence of the word in two consecutive verses, in one of which it is a *tabret* and in the other *tophet*. Isa. 30:32, 33. Tophet was probably the king's "music-grove" or garden, denoting originally nothing evil or hateful. Certainly there is little evidence that it took its name from the drums beaten to drown the cries of the burning victims that passed through the fire to Molech. Afterward it was defiled by idols and polluted by the sacrifices of Baal and the fires of Molech. Then it became the place of abomination, the very gate or pit of hell. The pious kings defiled it, pouring into it all the filth of the city, till it became the "abhorrence" of Jerusalem. See **Hell.**

Trachonitis (*trăk'o-ni'tis*), *a rugged region*. One of the five Roman provinces into which the district northeast of the Jordan was divided in New Testament times. It lay to the east of Ituræa and Gaulonitis and to the south of Damascus, and included the remarkable region of the modern Lejah (see **Argob**) and part of the western slopes of Jebel Hauran. The emperor Augustus entrusted it to Herod the Great on the condition that he should clear it of robbers. Herod Philip succeeded to the tetrarchy. Luke 3:1. He died A. D. 33, and the emperor Caligula bestowed the province of Trachonitis upon Herod Agrippa I. Later it was part of the dominions of Herod Agrippa II., A. D. 53.

Tradition. Judg. 6:13. Tradition is usually considered to imply that which was taught by oral instruction, in distinction from that which was committed to writing. At the beginning of the gospel the Christian doctrine was taught orally. Paul refers to "traditions" which he commands to be held fast, being as binding as any commandments delivered in any other way. 2 Thess. 2:15; 3:6. The Jews had really contradicted God's law by their traditions, which they pretended were of equal or even superior authority. For this our Lord reproved them. Matt. 15:1-9. They attached more importance to their traditional exposition of the law than to the law itself, calling the latter water, the tradition the wine that must be mingled with it. Their traditions were subsequently collected into the Talmud.

Transfiguration, The. Matt. 17:1-13; Mark 9:2-13; Luke 9:28-36. Though tradition locates the transfiguration on Mount Tabor, there is little to confirm this view, and modern scholars favor some spur of Mount Hermon. Jesus frequently went to the mountains to spend the night in prayer. Matt. 14:23, 24; Luke 6:12; 21:37. The apostles are described as heavy with sleep, but as having kept themselves awake. Luke 9:32. Moses the law-giver and Elijah the chief of the prophets both appear talking with Christ the source of the gospel, to show that they are all one and agree in one. Luke 9:31 adds the subject of their communing: "They spake of his decease which he should accomplish at Jerusalem." Among the apostles the three favorite disciples, Peter, James, and John, were the sole witnesses of the scene. The cloud which overshadowed the witnesses was bright or light-like, luminous, of the same kind as the cloud at the ascension. It is significant that at the end of the scene the disciples saw no man save Jesus only. Moses and Elijah, the law and the promise, types and shadows, pass away; the gospel, the fulfilment, the substance, Christ remains—the only one who can relieve the misery of earth and glorify our nature, Christ all in all.

Tribes. Num. 13:2-15. The twelve sons of Jacob were heads of families, and each family a tribe. The two sons of Joseph were adopted by Jacob in place of Joseph. Gen. 48:5. So there were thirteen tribes. But in dividing Canaan there were only twelve, since the family of Levi was assigned to the Lord's service and had no separate lot or share in the division of the promised land. Josh. 13:7-14, 33. The tribes were continued under one head or nation until after the death of Solomon, when ten tribes revolted from Judah and

Benjamin, and set up the northern kingdom—Israel. They were carried into captivity in 721 B. C., and no account of their return is given. Judah was also carried into captivity, 606 to 588 B. C.; but a remnant returned under Zerubbabel, Ezra, and Nehemiah, 536 B. C. and later. Tribes are referred to as being in the Christian church. Christ tells the apostles: "Ye . . shall sit upon twelve thrones, judging the twelve tribes of Israel." Matt. 19:28; Luke 22:30. James addresses his epistle "To the twelve tribes which are scattered abroad." Jas. 1:1. In the Revelation "144,000 of all the tribes of the children of Israel" were sealed. Rev. 7:4. See Jews.

Trinity. This word does not occur in Scripture. As a fact the Scripture reveals the doctrine of the Trinity in two ways: first in passages in which the Father, Son, and Holy Spirit are mentioned together as God; and secondly, in passages which speak of each as divine. In the New Testament clear evidence is given. See Matt. 3:16, 17; 28:19; 1 Cor. 12:3-6; 2 Cor. 13:14; Eph. 4:4-6; Tit. 3:4-6; 1 Pet. 1:2; Jude 20, 21. These passages, carefully read, are sufficient to prove that "the Godhead of the Father, of the Son, and of the Holy Ghost is one, the glory equal, the majesty co-eternal; such as the Father is, such is the Son, and such is the Holy Ghost; the Father is God, the Son is God, and the Holy Ghost is God; and yet they are not three Gods, but one God."

Troas (trō'ăs). A city in the northwestern part of Asia Minor, on the sea-coast, six miles south of the entrance to the Hellespont, and four miles south of the Homeric Troy. Alexandria Troas, as its name implies, owed its origin to Alexander the Great. Its port was excellent, and made Troas for many centuries the key of the commerce between Asia and Europe. Paul visited Troas twice, and perhaps three times. The first visit was on his second missionary journey. It was from Troas that, after the visit of the "man of Macedonia," he sailed to carry the gospel into Europe. Acts 16:8-11. On his return journey he stopped at Troas for eight days and restored Eutychus to life. Acts 20:5-10. Upon one visit he left his cloak and some books there. 2 Tim. 4:13.

Trophimus (trŏf'ĭ-mŭs), *foster-child*. A native of Ephesus, Acts 21:29, and a convert to the gospel, probably under Paul's ministry. Acts 20:4. He became one of the apostle's companions and helpers in missionary travels and labors. 2 Tim. 4:20.

Trumpets, Feast of. This feast—described in Num. 29:1-6; Lev. 23:24—was the New Year's day of the civil year, coming on the first of Tisri (October), and was further called by the rabbins "the birthday of the world," because in Tisri the late fruits were gathered and seed was sown. It was one of the seven days of holy convocation. The feast differed from the other feasts of new moon, which also had their trumpet-blowings over the burnt-offerings, by its being a day of rest and service.

Tubal (tū'bal). Fifth son of Japheth, whose descendants probably peopled a country lying south of the Caucasus, between the Black Sea and the Araxes, whose inhabitants were the Tibareni of the Greeks. Gen. 10:2. The Circassians, who inhabit this region, were slave-dealers, and they of Tubal traded in the persons of men. Ezek. 27:13; 38:2; comp. Rev. 18:13.

Turtle-Dove. Ps. 74:19. By the Jewish law the poor who could not afford a more costly sacrifice were permitted to bring two turtle-doves or two young pigeons. Lev. 12:6-8. As the former are not domesticated and breed everywhere in prodigious numbers, this provision was a great boon to the needy. The outward circumstances of Christ's parents are thus indicated in Luke 2:24.

Tychicus (tyk'ĭ-kŭs). A companion of Paul, Acts 20:4, and evidently a devoted and faithful disciple. Eph. 6:21, 22; Col. 4:7, 8.

Tyrannus (ty-răn'nus), *tyrant*. The name of the Greek rhetorician of Ephesus in whose lecture-room Paul delivered discourses daily for two years. Acts 19:9.

Tyre (tyre) and **Tyrus** (ty'rus). Heb. *Tsor*, "rock;" Arabic *Sûr*. A celebrated city of Phœnicia, on the eastern coast of the Mediterranean Sea, 21 miles south of Sidon. Tyre was originally on an island, or perhaps two islands, about one mile long, and lying parallel to the shore at the distance of half a mile. There was also a city called "Palætyrus"—"Old Tyre"—upon the mainland. The first Scripture mention of Tyre is in the time of Joshua, B. C. 1444, and it was then "a strong city." Josh. 19:29. It was coupled with the Zidonians. Jer. 47:4; Isa. 23:2, 4, 12; Josh. 13:6; Ezek. 32:30. The two cities Tyre and Sidon, being only 21 miles apart, were intimately associated. Tyre, under king Hiram, held friendly relations with Israel, under David and Solomon. David's census extended thither to embrace the Jews. 2 Sam. 24:7. The Tyrians furnished the timber for the temple and great buildings of Jerusalem. The cedars of Lebanon were floated from Tyre to Joppa, some 85 miles, and thence taken to Jerusalem. Tyrian artists also were skilful in the fine work required. As a reward for his services, Hiram was presented with 20 cities in northern Galilee, but he was not well pleased with them and called them "Cabul"—"displeasing" or "despicable." 2 Sam. 5:11; 1 Kings 5:1; 7:13; 9:11, 12; 1 Chron. 14:1; 2 Chron. 2:2, 3, 11. Hiram and Solomon were also associated in commercial enterprises. 1 Kings 9:27; 10:11-22; 2 Chron. 8:17, 18; 9:21. From Tyre came the many fatal influences toward idolatry which corrupted the chosen people. At a later period the friendly relations were changed to hostility. Tyre rejoiced in the distress of Israel, and God's prophet predicted the terrible overthrow of the proud heathen city. Isa. 23:1, 5, 8, 15-17; Jer. 25:22; 27:3; 47:4; Ezek. 26:2-15; 27:2-8, 32; 29:18; Hos. 9:13; Joel 3:4; Amos 1:9, 10; Zech. 9:2, 3; comp. Ps. 45:12; 83:7; 87:4. The prophecies were notably fulfilled. Shalmaneser, king of Assyria, besieged Tyre in B. C. 721. The siege lasted for five years, but the city was not taken. Nebuchadnezzar besieged it for 13 years. But Tyre came under the Persian dominion and furnished that power with a large fleet. This excited the hostility of Alexander the Great, who determined to destroy the power of the city. Not being able to reach the walls with his engines, he collected together all the remains of the ancient city Palætyrus—stones, timber, rubbish—and threw them into the narrow channel. Thus was fulfilled in a most remarkable manner the prophecy of Ezekiel. 26:3, 4, 12, 21. After a siege of seven months the city was taken. Some 8000 men were slain in the massacre which followed; 2000 were crucified, and 30,000 men, women, and children were sold into slavery. The city was also set on fire by the victors. Zech. 9:4; Joel 3:7. Insular Tyre afterwards came under the Romans, and for ages continued a flourishing trading city. Matt. 11:21; 15:21; Mark 3:8; 7:24; Luke 6:17; 10:13; Acts 21:3. It fell finally in the hands of the Mohammedans, A. D. 1291; since then it has irrecoverably declined. The Hebrew prophets denounced fearful judgments against Tyre for her idolatry and wickedness. Isa. 23; Ezek. 26:7-21; 27; 28:1-19; 29:18. And how truthfully their predictions have been accomplished may be seen in the existing ruins scattered along the shore, and the number of splendid columns lying in heaps beneath the waves. This ancient city has indeed become like the top of a rock, "a place to spread nets upon!"

U

Ulai (*ū'lāi* or *ū'la-ī*), *strong water?* A river of Susiana, on whose banks Daniel saw his vision of the ram and he-goat. Dan. 8:2-16. Recent explorations have shown that the river Choaspes (Kerkhan) divides about 20 miles above Susa. The eastern branch, which received the Shapur and fell into the Kuran, was probably the Ulai. This bifurcation of the stream explains the otherwise difficult passage, "I heard a man's voice between the banks of Ulai," Dan. 8:16—that is, between the banks of the two streams of that divided river.

Unicorn, *reēm*, or *high*. Num. 23:22, A. V., but R. V. reads "wild ox." The word occurs seven times in the Old Testament. That fabulous creature the unicorn certainly is not meant by the Hebrew *reēm*. Critics are agreed that the passages mentioning it, correctly understood, require an animal with two horns. This animal was distinguished for his ferocity, Isa. 34:7, strength, Num. 23:22; 24:8, agility, Ps. 29:6, wildness, Job 39:9, as well as for being horned, and destroying with his horns. Deut. 33:17; Ps. 22:21. For various reasons this animal could not have been the rhinoceros. Probably it was the now extinct aurochs (*Bos primigenius*), a long-horned and powerful ox, which existed in the forests of Europe nearly, or quite, until the Middle Ages. An allied species of great size and strength is known to have existed in Palestine, as the bison (*Bison bonasus*), and some of these, now called aurochs, are still found in the forests of Lithuania.

Ur, *light*, land of *light?* Gen. 11:28, 31; 15:7; Neh. 9:7. Some have identified the city Ur with Edessa, the modern Orfah. Others suppose it to be Warka. But late explorations identify it with Mugheir, where considerable ruins exist. It is situated on the right bank of the Euphrates near the marshes, and in periods of inundation the ruins are surrounded by water. They are of an oval shape, and measure about half a mile from north to south. The temple ruins are in the form of a parallelogram 198 by 133 feet. The lower story is supported by thick buttresses; and the height of the whole is 70 feet. The exterior is faced with red kiln-baked bricks; and the interior is constructed of bricks burnt or sun-dried. The name of Urukh, an early king, 2230 B. C., has been found upon the bricks; and the place was probably the capital of this monarch. The temple was dedicated to the moon-god Hurki: hence perhaps the town derived its name.

Uriah (*u-rī'ah*), 2 Sam. 11:3, or **Urias** (*u-rī'as*), Matt. 1:6, A. V. A Hittite by descent, but probably converted to Judaism, commander of one of the bands of David's army, and the husband of Bathsheba. His death was purposely brought about by an understanding between Joab and David, in order that David's guilt in the case of Bathsheba might be concealed, and that he might obtain her for his wife.

Urim (*ū'rim*), and **Thummim** (*thŭm'mim*), *light* and *perfection*. Denote some part of the high priest's apparel. When Aaron was arrayed, Moses himself put the Urim and Thummim into the breastplate. Ex. 28:13-30; Lev. 8:8. Nowhere in Scripture are the Urim and Thummim described, and we do not know what they really were.

Usury, by modern usage, means exorbitant or unlawful interest, but in the Scriptures it means simply interest. The law of Moses prohibited the Jews from taking any interest of each other for the loan of money or of anything else, though they were allowed to take it of foreigners. The exchangers of money were in the habit of receiving it at low interest and loaning it at high interest, taking the difference for their gain. Ezek. 22:12. The practice of usury is severely denounced in the Scriptures. Neh. 5:7, 10; Ps. 15:5; Prov. 28:8.

Uz (*ŭz*), *light sandy soil?* 1. A region and tribe in the northeastern part of Arabia deserta, between the Euphrates, Palestine, and Idumea, probably including part of Bashan; called by Ptolemy Ausitis. Job was an inhabitant of "the land of Uz," which was probably an extensive district, and subject to the Edomites. Job 1:1; Jer. 25:20; Lam. 4:21. 2. A son of Aram. Gen. 10:23; 1 Chron. 1:17. 3. The son of Dishan, the Horite. Gen. 36:28; 1 Chron. 1:42.

Uzziah (uz-zī'ah), *might of Jehovah*. 1. The son and successor of Amaziah, king of Judah; called Azariah in 2 Kings 14 : 21 and elsewhere; began to reign at 16, and reigned 52 years, B. C. 808-756. His career was most prosperous. He walked in the ways of his father David, and as a consequence was blessed with victory over his enemies, and great fame and love. But he was puffed up by success so long continued, and presumed to burn incense on the altar like the priests. Azariah, the high priest, and 80 others opposed him; but God most effectually checked him by making him a leper, dwelling in a separate house until death. 2 Kings 15 : 1-7; 2 Chron. 26. A great earthquake occurred in his reign. Amos 1 : 1; Zech. 14 : 5. There are five persons of this name mentioned in the Bible.

V

Vale, Valley. Five Hebrew words are translated "vale" or "valley." 1. *Emek*, signifying a "deep" broad valley, as the valley of Achor, Aijalon, Elah, Jezreel, Succoth, etc. 2. *Gai* or *ge*, signifying a "bursting," and used to designate narrow ravines or glens, as of Hinnom or Salt. Deut. 34 : 6. 3. *Nachal*, meaning a "wâdy-bed," filled with water in winter, but dry in summer. Such beds or valleys were Chereth, Eshcol, Sorek, Zered, etc. 4. *Bik'ah*, properly a "cleft," but applied to a broader space than a cleft or valley, and meaning sometimes a "plain," as that between Lebanon and Anti-Lebanon and Megiddo. Josh. 11 : 17; 13 : 17; Zech. 12 : 11. 5. *Has-Shephelah*, wrongly rendered "vale" in A. V., but "lowland" in R. V., meant a broad tract of low hills between the mountains of Judah and the coast-plain. Deut. 1 : 7; Josh. 10 : 40.

Vashti (vâsh'ti), *beautiful*. The deposed "queen" of Ahasuerus. Esth. 1. B. C. 483.

Vine. The first mention of the vine occurs in Gen. 9 : 20, 21. It was cultivated in Egypt. Gen. 40 : 9-11; Ps. 78 : 47. The vines of Palestine were celebrated both for luxuriant growth and for the immense clusters of grapes which they produced, which were sometimes carried on a staff between two men, as in the case of the spies. Num. 13 : 23. Special mention is made in the Bible of the vines of Eshcol, Num. 13 : 24; 32 : 9, of Sibmah, Heshbon, and Elealeh, Isa. 16 : 8, 9, 10; Jer. 48 : 32, and of Engedi. Song of Sol. 1 : 14. To dwell under the vine and fig tree is an emblem of domestic happiness and peace, 1 Kings 4 : 25; Ps. 128 : 3; Micah 4 : 4; the rebellious people of Israel are compared to "wild grapes," "an empty vine," "the degenerate plant of a strange vine," etc. Isa. 5 : 2, 4; Jer. 2 : 21; Hos. 10 : 1. It is a vine which our Lord selects to show the spiritual union which subsists between himself and his members. John 15 : 1-6. The vine trailed on the ground or upon supports. This latter mode of cultivation appears to be alluded to by Ezekiel. Ezek. 19 : 11, 12. The vintage, which formerly was a season of general festivity, began in September. The towns were deserted; the people lived among the vineyards in the lodges and tents. Comp. Judg. 9 : 27; Isa. 16 : 10; Jer. 25 : 30. The grapes were gathered with shouts of joy by the "grape gatherers," Jer. 25 : 30, and put into baskets. See Jer. 6 : 9. They were then carried on the head and shoulders, or slung upon a yoke, to the "wine-press." The vineyard, which was generally on a hill, Isa. 5 : 1; Jer. 31 : 5; Amos 9 : 13, was surrounded by a wall or hedge in order to keep out the wild boars, Ps. 80 : 13, jackals and foxes. Num. 22 : 24; Neh. 4 : 3; Song of Sol. 2 : 15; Ezek. 13 : 4, 5; Matt. 21 : 33. Within the vineyard were one or more towers of stone in which the vine-dressers lived. Isa. 1 : 8; 5 : 2; Matt. 21 : 33. The vat, which was dug, Matt. 21 : 33, or hewn out of the rocky soil, and the press, were part of the vineyard furniture. Isa. 5 : 2.

Vine of Sodom. Only in Deut. 32 : 32. Josephus describes fruits growing near the Dead Sea, "which indeed resemble edible fruit in color, but on being plucked by the hand are dissolved into smoke and ashes." These are the apples of Sodom of which the poets sing, and which are supposed to be mentioned in the above passage. If we are to interpret Deuteronomy and Josephus literally, the colocynth seems best to answer the conditions.

Viper. This word in the Old Testament possibly designates some particular species of hissing and venomous serpent, but its exact application cannot be determined. In the New Testament the Greek word thus rendered was used for any poisonous snake. The viper which fastened on Paul's hand, Acts 28 : 1-6, was doubtless the snake of that name, *Vipera aspis*, still common in the Mediterranean islands. It has now disappeared from Malta with the woods to which it is partial. The viper is an emblem of whatever is deceitful and destructive. Matt. 3 : 7; 12 : 34; 23 : 33; Luke 3 : 7.

Vulture. In Lev. 11 : 14, Deut. 14 : 13. Isa. 34 : 15, in place of this word, we should probably read "black kite," *Milvus migrans*. This is a bird which, except in the winter months, collects in Palestine in great numbers and is very sociable in its habits, according to the reference in Isaiah. Another Hebrew word rendered "vulture," R. V. "falcon," in Job 28 : 7, is elsewhere correctly rendered kite. It is a striking instance of the accuracy of the Scripture writers that, while the peculiar faculty for discovering their food which carrion-devourers possess is popularly attributed to the sense of smell, the Bible rightly attributes it to sight. In the book of Job the characteristic of the eagle is that "her eyes behold afar off." Job 28 : 7 refers to the same peculiarity, "There is a path which the vulture's eye hath not seen," implying that its vision is most acute and penetrating. It is well proved that birds of prey discern their booty at vast distances, that the eager flight of one is observed and followed by another, and so on, till many are gathered together wheresoever the carcase is.

War. The ancient battles were truly murderous. Scarcely ever was any quarter given, except where the vanquished were retained as slaves. 2 Chron. 13: 17. Enemies were then, as now, surprised and overcome by unexpected divisions of the forces, by ambushes, and by false retreats. Gen. 14:15; Josh. 8: 12; Judg. 20:36-39; 2 Kings 7:12. In lack of artillery, unwieldy machines for casting heavy stones and other destructive missiles were invented. Uzziah "made in Jerusalem engines invented by cunning men, to be on the towers and upon the bulwarks, to shoot arrows and great stones withal." 2 Chron. 26:15. There was no part of the ancient military preparations more terrible than chariots. Ex. 14:7; Deut. 20:1; Josh. 17:16; Judg. 4:3. They were in common use wherever there was any cavalry. 2 Sam. 10:18; 1 Chron. 18: 4; 2 Chron. 12:3; 14:9. Walls and towers were used in fortifications, and the latter were guarded by soldiers, and are called "garrisons." 2 Sam. 8:6; Ezek. 26:11. Various passages lead to the opinion that divisions of the army were common, as in modern times. Gen. 14:15; Judg. 7:16; 1 Sam. 11:11. The most frequent division of the host was into tens, hundreds, and thousands, and each of these had its commander or captain. Judg. 20:10; 1 Sam. 8:12; 2 Kings 11:4. Among the Hebrews these divisions had some reference to the several families, and were under the heads of families as their officers. 2 Chron. 25: 5; 26:12. The captains of hundreds and of thousands were of high rank, or, so to speak, staff officers, who were admitted to share in the councils of war. 1 Chron. 13: 1. The whole army had its commander-in-chief or captain, who was over the host, and its scribe or keeper of the muster-roll. 1 Kings 4:4; 1 Chron. 18:15, 16; 27:32-34; 2 Chron. 17:14; 26:11. In Isa. 33:18 the words translated "he that counted the towers" probably indicate what we should call a chief engineer. Under David the army of 288,000 men was divided into twelve corps, each of which was consequently 24,000 strong and had its own general. 1 Chron. 27. Under Jehoshaphat this was altered, and there were five unequal corps, under as many commanders. 2 Chron. 17:14-19. The cohort had 500 or 600 men, and the legion embraced ten cohorts. The light troops were provided with arms which they used at some distance from the enemy, such as bows and arrows. They are designated in 2 Chron. 14:8; while the heavy-armed were those who bore shield and spear. 1 Chron. 12:24. The light troops of the army of Asa were taken principally from the tribe of Benjamin because of their extraordinary accuracy of aim. Judg. 20:16. See Arms, Armor. The troops were excited to ardor and bravery by addresses from their priests, who were commanded to appeal to them. Deut. 20:2. In later times kings themselves were accustomed to harangue their armies. 2 Chron. 13:4. Finally, perhaps, after the sacrifices had been offered, the summons was given by the holy trumpets. Num. 10:9, 10; 2 Chron. 13:12-14. It was the practice of the Greeks, when they were within half a mile of the enemy, to sing their war song. A similar custom probably prevailed among the Jews. 2 Chron. 20: 21. Next followed the shout, or war cry, which the Romans accompanied with the noise of shields and spears struck violently together. This war cry was common in the East, as it is to this day among the Turks. It was the "alarm" or "shout" so often mentioned in Scripture. 1 Sam. 17: 52; 2 Chron. 13:15; Job 39:25; Jer. 4:19.

Ward. A prison, or an apartment of it. Gen. 40:3; Acts 12:10. Also a garrison or military post, Neh. 12:25, or a class or detachment of persons for any particular service. 1 Chron. 9:23; 25:8; Neh. 13:30.

Washing of the Hands and Feet. This was rendered necessary by oriental costoms and climate. The hands should be clean, for all persons at table put their fingers into the same dish. The feet should be washed because the sandals afforded little protection against soil; and besides, the feet would be hot. The words of Christ against the handwashings of the Pharisees was directed against it as a religious observance. Mark 7:3; Matt. 15:2; Luke 11: 38. The washing by the host of the feet of the guest was a mark of respect, 1 Sam. 25: 41; Luke 7:38, 44; John 13:5-14; but usually water was provided and the guests washed their own feet, or had them washed by servants. Gen. 18:4; Judg. 19:21.

Watches of the Night. The original division of the night was into three watches —" the beginning of the watches," from sunset to 10 o'clock, Lam. 2:19; "the middle watch," from 10 to 2 o'clock, Judg. 7:19; and "the morning watch," from 2 o'clock to sunrise, Ex. 14:24; 1 Sam. 11:11—but after the captivity the Jews adopted the custom of Rome and Greece, which divided the twelve hours of the night into four watches, beginning with 6 in the afternoon —"even," from 6 to 9 o'clock; "midnight," from 9 to 12; "cock-crowing," from 12 to 3; and "morning," from 3 to 6. Matt. 14:25; Mark 13:35; Luke 12:38.

Weasel (*chôled*) occurs only in Lev. 11: 29, in the list of unclean animals; but the Hebrew word ought more probably to be translated "mole." Moles are common in Palestine.

Weaving. The art of weaving was practised with great skill by the Egyptians at a very early period. The "vestures of fine linen" such as Joseph wore, Gen. 41:42, were the product of Egyptian looms. The Israelites attained a proficiency which enabled them to execute the hangings of the tabernacle, Ex. 35:35; 1 Chron. 4:21, and other artistic textures. The textures produced by the Jewish weavers were very various. The coarser kinds, such as tent-cloth, sack-cloth, and the "hairy garments of the poor," were made of goat's or camel's hair. Ex. 26:7; Matt. 3:4. Wool was extensively used for ordinary clothing, Lev. 13 : 47; Prov. 27 : 26 ; 31 : 13; Ezek. 27 : 18; while for finer work flax was used, varying in quality, and producing the different textures described in the Bible as "linen" and "fine linen." The mixture of wool and flax in cloth intended for a garment was forbidden. Lev. 19 : 19; Deut. 22 : 11.

Wedding. Matt. 22 : 3, A. V. See **Marriage.**

Week. There can be no doubt about the great antiquity of measuring time by a period of seven days. Gen. 8 : 10 ; 29 : 27. The origin of this division of time has given birth to much speculation. The week and the Sabbath are as old as man himself. They who embrace this view support it by a reference to the six days' creation and the divine rest on the seventh. Whether the week gave its sacredness to the number seven, or whether the ascendency of that number helped to determine the dimensions of the week, it is impossible to say. The weekly division was adopted by the Semitic races, and, in the later period of their history at least, by the Egyptians. So far from the week being a division of time without ground in nature, there was much to recommend its adoption. It is clear that if not in Paul's time, yet very soon after, the Roman world had adopted the hebdomadal division.

Weeks, Feast of. Ex. 34 : 22. Pentecost.

Wells were necessary in a dry and hot country like Palestine. They were deep, John 4 : 11, and difficult both to dig and preserve, and hence were a valuable part of the husbandman's property. Num. 20 : 17-19. They were sometimes owned in common. Gen. 29 : 2, 3. To protect them from the sand and from being used by others, they were covered, usually with a stone, and surrounded with a low wall. Gen. 29 : 2, 8. To stop them up was, and still is, regarded as an act of hostility, Gen. 26 : 15, and to invade the right of property in them was often the cause of sharp contention. Gen. 21 : 25. The water was generally drawn by pitchers and a rope. The well naturally became the halting-place of the traveller, Gen. 24 : 11; the camping-place of armies, Judg. 7 : 1, etc.; and it furnished an appropriate emblem of rich blessings. Jer. 2 : 13; 17 : 13. See **Jacob's Well.**

Whale. The Greek word translated "whale" in Matt. 12 : 40, A. V., means a large fish, or a sea monster. So, also, in Gen. 1 : 21 the word is generic. The original word representing "whale" is often translated "dragon" or "leviathan," and according to the derivation of the Hebrew, the word denotes a creature of great *length*, without being restricted to marine animals. Neither the Old Testament nor the New Testament, when correctly rendered, affirms that it was a whale which swallowed Jonah, but "a great fish." Jonah 1 : 17; Matt. 12 : 40. The R. V. reads the same as the A. V., but in the margin reads, "Greek, sea monster." The creature referred to is very likely to have been the white shark, which is abundantly capable of such a feat. The whale is, however, occasionally found in the Mediterranean Sea. See **Jonah.**

Wheat. In Palestine this most important of all grains was sown after barley—late in the fall. It was not only scattered broadcast and then ploughed, harrowed, or trodden in, Isa. 32 : 20, but it seems, according to the Hebrew of Isa. 28 : 25, to have been planted in rows or drills, as it certainly often is at present in Syria. Wheat is still produced for export east of the Jordan. Ezek. 27 : 17; Deut. 8 : 8. In the days of Jacob this grain was already so much cultivated in Mesopotamia that "wheat harvest" denoted a well-known season. Gen. 30 : 14. The many-eared variety, or mummy wheat, is referred to in Pharaoh's dream. Gen. 41 : 22. In the A. V. and R. V. this grain is often mentioned under the general name of "corn."

Wilderness, The, in which the Israelites spent 40 years, between Egypt and Canaan, is called sometimes the "great and terrible wilderness" by way of eminence. Deut. 1 : 1 ; 8 : 2 ; Josh. 5 : 6 ; Neh. 9 : 19, 21 ; Ps. 78 : 40, 52; 107 : 4 ; Jer. 2 : 2. In general it may be identified with the peninsula of Sinai, the triangular region between the Gulf of Akabah, on the east, and the Gulf of Suez and Egypt on the west. See **Sinai.** In this region there are several smaller wildernesses, as Etham, Paran, Shur, Zin. What is known distinctively as the "wilderness of the Wandering" is the great central limestone plateau between the granite region of Sinai on the south, the sandy desert on the north, and the valley of the Arabah on the east. The explorations of travellers and the British Ordnance Survey have made this region quite well known. The route of the Israelites from Egypt to Kadesh can be traced with reasonable accuracy. Instead of entering the Promised Land immediately from Kadesh, they were driven back into the wilderness for their disobedience, and there wandered for 40 years. They probably lived a nomad life as do the Bedouin Arabs of the present day.

Wine. Gen. 9 : 20, 21. In the Bible, wine is spoken of as a blessing to a country. Gen. 27 : 28, 37 ; Deut. 7 : 13 ; 33 : 28 ; Hosea 2 : 8, 22. Our Saviour turned water into wine at a marriage feast, and directed it to be used in celebrating the Lord's supper. John 2 : 7-10; Matt. 26 : 27-29. The Bible represents wine as having intoxicating qualities, and it has many warnings in regard to its use. Noah was made drunk by it, and so was Lot. Gen. 9 : 26 ; 19 : 32-35. The ruler of the wedding feast where Jesus turned water into wine alluded to the intoxicating nature of wine. John 2 : 10. Drunkenness is condemned as a sin. 1 Cor. 5 : 11; 6 : 10. The common wine required to be "refined" or strained previous to being brought to the table. Isa. 25 : 6. Wine was also made from pomegranate as well as grape. Song of Sol. 8 : 2. In Palestine the vintage comes in September, and is celebrated with great rejoicings. The ripe fruit is gathered in baskets, Jer. 6 : 9, and carried to the wine-press. It is then placed in the upper one of the two vats or receptacles of the wine-press and is subjected to "treading," which has prevailed in all ages in oriental and south-European countries. Neh. 13:15; Job 24:11; Isa. 16:10; Jer. 25:30; 48:33; Amos 9:13; Rev. 19:15. A certain amount of juice exuded from the ripe fruit from its own pressure before the treading commenced. This appears to have been kept separate from the rest of the juice, and to have formed the "new" or "sweet wine" noticed in Acts 2:13. The "treading" was by men. They encouraged one another by shouts. Isa. 16:9, 10; Jer. 25:30; 48:33. Their legs and garments were dyed red with the juice. Gen. 49:11; Isa. 63:2, 3. The juice ran by an aperture into the lower vat, or was at once collected in vessels. Wine is said to produce different effects: as the "darkly flashing" or "red eye," Gen. 49:12, a mocker, Prov. 20:1, the unbridled tongue, Isa. 28:7, the excitement of the spirit, Prov. 31:6; Isa. 5:11; Zech. 9:15; 10:7, the enchained affections of its votaries, Hos. 4:11, the perverted judgment, Prov. 31:5; Isa. 28:7, the indecent exposure, Hab. 2:15, 16, and the sickness resulting from the heat (chemâh, A. V., "bottles") of wine. Hos. 7:5. The allusions to the effects of tirôsh are confined to a single passage, but this a most decisive one, viz., Hos. 4:11, "Whoredom and wine (yayin) and new wine (tirôsh) take away the heart," where tirôsh appears as the climax of engrossing influences, in immediate connection with yayin. It has been disputed whether the Hebrew wine was fermented: but the impression produced by a general review of the above notices is that the Hebrew words indicating wine refer to fermented, intoxicating wine. Mingled liquor was prepared for high festivals, Prov. 9:2, 5, and occasions of excess. Prov. 23:30; Isa. 5:22. The wine "mingled with myrrh," given to Jesus, was designed to deaden pain, Mark 15:23, and the spiced pomegranate wine prepared by the bride, Song of Sol. 8:2, may well have been of a mild character. In the New Testament the "new" or "sweet wine," noticed in Acts 2:13, could not be new wine in the proper sense of the term, inasmuch as about eight months must have elapsed between the vintage and the feast of Pentecost. It had also the power to make persons drunk, at least in public estimation. The only wines of which we have special notice belonged to Syria; these were the wine of Helbon, Ezek. 27:18, and the wine of Lebanon, famed for its aroma. Hos. 14:7. Wine was produced on occasions of ordinary hospitality, Gen. 14:18, and at festivals, such as marriages. John 2:3. Under the Mosaic law wine formed the usual drink offering that accompanied the daily sacrifice, Ex. 29:40, the presentation of the first-fruits, Lev. 23:13, and other offerings. Num. 15:5. Tithe was to be paid of wine, as of other products. The priest was also to receive first-fruits of wine, as of other articles. Deut. 18:4; comp. Ex. 22:29. The use of wine at the paschal feast was not enjoined by the law, but became an established custom, in the post-Babylonian period. Some Biblical scholars hold that the Bible mentions two kinds of wine, one unfermented and one fermented and intoxicating.

Wine-press. Num. 18:27; Deut. 15:14; Judg. 7:25; Hos. 9:2. The wine-presses of the Jews consisted of two receptacles or vats placed at different elevations, in the upper one of which the grapes were trodden, Isa. 63:3; Lam. 1:15; Job 24:11, while the lower one received the expressed juice. The two vats are mentioned together only in Joel 3:13: "The press is full: the fats overflow"—the upper vat being full of fruit, the lower one overflowing with the must. The two vats were usually hewn out of the solid rock. Isa. 5:2, margin; Matt. 21:33. Ancient wine-presses, so constructed, are still to be seen in Palestine.

Winter. In Palestine, part of autumn and the seasons of seed-time and cold, extending from the beginning of September to the beginning of March, were called "winter." Gen. 8:22; Ps. 74:17; Zech. 14:8; Jer. 36:22. The cold of winter is not usually very severe, though the north winds, from the middle of December to the middle of February, are sharp. Snow falls more or less, but seldom lies upon the ground except in the mountains. Ps. 147:17. In shady places the ice will occasionally bear a man's weight, but thaws as soon as the sun rises upon it. In the early part of April the spring may be said to have arrived. Song of Sol. 2:11.

Witch and Wizard. Exod. 22:18, in the R. V., "sorceress." Lev. 19:31; 20:6, 27; Deut. 18:11; 1 Sam. 28:3, 9; 2 Kings 23:24; 2 Chron. 33:6; Isa. 8:19; 19:3. The witch of Endor was widely known as "one that had a familiar spirit," and was thereby professedly able to consult souls from the spirit world. Witchcraft was therefore a pretended converse with demons and the spirits of the departed. To this the ancient witches joined the arts of fortune-telling and divining. Their unlawful arts were akin to the others forbidden in Deut. 18:10, 11: "There shall not be found among you any one that maketh his son or his daughter to pass through the fire, or that useth divination, or an observer of times or an enchanter or a witch [R. V. "sorcerer"] or a charmer or a consulter with familiar spirits or a wizard or a necromancer." Superstition was prevalent in the East in the days of Moses, and continues to be so now.

Wolf. The Hebrew zeeb, "wolf," was so called from its tawny color. It is the common Canis lupus, still found in some parts of Palestine. Isa. 11:6; 65:25; Jer. 5:6; Hab. 1:8. It is of an unsated appetite; and often indiscriminately killing sheep and goats, apparently rather to satisfy its fierce nature than its hunger. Zeph. 3:3; Matt. 7:15; John 10:12. Persecutors are compared to wolves. Matt. 10:16; Acts 20:29. The peaceful reign of the Messiah is spoken of under the metaphor of the wolf dwelling with the lamb. Isa. 11:6; 65:25.

Word (logos), **The,** is one of the titles of Jesus Christ. The term occurs only in the writings of John. John 1:1-14; 1 John 1:1; Rev. 19:13.

World. This word in the A. V. is the translation of five Hebrew and four Greek words. It is therefore not always plain in what sense it is used. The Hebrew terms have these literal meanings: "The earth," "rest," "the grave," Isa. 38:11; "the world," corresponding to *aion* in the New Testament, or that which is finite, temporary, Job 11:17; "the veiled," unlimited time, whether past or future; used very frequently, and generally translated "forever;" and, finally, the poetical term for "world," which occurs some 37 times, but in various meanings which are easily understood. When the Hebrews desired to express the universe they employed a phrase like "heaven and earth and the sea, and all that in them is." Ex. 20:11. In the New Testament the Greek words are equally diverse: 1. *Aion*, "duration," thus used of time past, Luke 1:70, of time present, with the idea of evil, both moral and physical, Mark 4:19. Hence "children of this world," or worldly men, Luke 16:8; and so Satan is called "the god of this world." 2 Cor. 4:4. *Aion* is also put for endless duration, eternity, 1 Tim. 6:16, to signify the material world as created by the deity, Heb. 11:3; also the world to come, the kingdom of the Messiah. 2. *Ge*, the earth, in contrast to the heavens. Rev. 13:3. 3. *Kosmos*, used in several senses: (a) the universe, the heavens, and the earth, Matt. 13:35, and thence for the inhabitants of the universe, 1 Cor. 4:9, and an aggregate. Jas. 3:6. (b) This lower world as the abode of man, John 16:18; the inhabitants of the earth or mankind. Matt. 5:14. (c) The present world, as opposed to the kingdom of Christ, John 12:25; specifically, the wealth and enjoyments and cares of this world, Matt. 16:26, and so for those who seek the opposite things to the kingdom of God, the worldlings. John 15:19. 4. *Oikoumene*, the inhabited earth, Matt. 24:14, the people of it, Acts 17:31, sometimes the Roman empire, the then civilized world, Acts 17:6, including Palestine and adjacent parts. Luke 2:1; Acts 11:28. The Jews distinguished two worlds, or æons, the present æon to the appearance of the Messiah, and the future æon, or the Messianic era, which is to last forever. The closing days of the present order of things were called "the last days." Isa. 2:2; Micah 4:1; Acts 2:17. The same phraseology is found in the New Testament, but the dividing-line is marked by the second instead of the first advent of the Messiah. Matt. 12:32; 1 Cor. 10:11; Gal. 4:3; Heb. 1:2; 6:5; 9:26.

Wormwood. At least five species of this plant (*Artemisia*) are found in the Holy Land, and are distinguished for intense bitterness. Hence this word is often joined with or used in the same sense as "gall" and "hemlock," to denote what is offensive and nauseous. Deut. 29:18; Prov. 5:4; Amos 5:7; 6:12. To be obliged to use it as food expresses the extreme of suffering. Jer. 9:15; 23:15; Lam. 3:15, 19.

Writing is either ideographic or phonetic. In ideographic writing the signs used represent the ideas themselves, either pictorially by direct imitation of the object, or symbolically, as when the picture of an eye is used to convey the idea of sight or knowledge, and the picture of a lion the idea of courage. In phonetic writing the signs simply represent the sounds of which a word is composed. Ideographic writing —that is, writing by pictures or in hieroglyphics—is an art of very ancient date. Through all the Mosaic history books and writing are mentioned as in familiar use. Ex. 17:14; 2 Sam. 11:14; 1 Kings 21:8, 9, 11; 2 Kings 10:1, 2, 6, 7. The alphabet which the Jews used was based upon the Phœnician, and that upon some earlier alphabet, and underwent various changes. The materials used in writing were tablets of stone, Ex. 31:18; 32:15, 16, 19; 34:1, 4, 28, 29, or boxwood and brass, or plaster, Deut. 27:2, 3; Josh. 8:32, or skin, which was made into the finest parchment or vellum. For hard materials an iron stylus or engraver's tool was used, Job 19:24; Ps. 45:1; Isa. 8:1; Jer. 8:8; 17:1, but for parchment a reed pen and ink. 2 Cor. 3:3; 2 John 12; 3 John 13. The parchment was not put in leaves, forming a book, but put together in long rolls. The practice of employing an amanuensis was quite common in ancient days as it is now. Hence Paul gives as an authentication of his letters a few words written with his own hand. 1 Cor. 16:21; Col. 4:18; 2 Thess. 3:17. This fact also explains Rom. 16:22. The size of the apostle's writing is indicated. Gal. 6:11. The ink of the ancients was made of pulverized charcoal or the black of burnt ivory and water, with the addition of some kind of gum. The ink of the East at the present day is a much thicker substance than ours, but is not permanent; a wet sponge will obliterate the finest of their writing. The inkhorn was, and is, a long tube containing the reed pens, with a little case fastened at the side to hold the ink. The whole is thrust into the girdle.

Y

Yarn. 1 Kings 10:28; 2 Chron. 1:16, A. V. The Hebrew received text is obscure. The R. V. reads, "And the king's merchants received them [the horses] in droves, each drove at a price."

Year. The Jewish year had two commencements. The religious year began with the month Abib—April; the civil with Tisri—October. The year was solar. There were two seasons, summer and winter. Ps. 74:17; Zech. 14:8; Jer. 36:22; Amos 3:15. The months were lunar, of 30 days each, and twelve in number, although a thirteenth was necessarily intercalated six times in every 19 years. It was called Ve-adar. The festivals, holy days, and fasts of the year were: 1. The feast of the Passover, the 14th day of the first month. 2. The feast of unleavened bread, in the same month, from the 15th to 21st, inclusive. 3. The feast of

Pentecost, called also feast of harvest and "day of first fruits," on the day which ended seven weeks, counted from the 16th of the first month, that day being excluded. 4. The feast of trumpets, on the first day of the seventh month. 5. The day of atonement, a fast, on the tenth day of the seventh month. 6. The feast of tabernacles, or of gathering, from the 15th to the 22d day, inclusive, of the seventh month. The post-Mosaic festivals are Purim, in the twelfth month of Adar, 13th to 15th day; Dedication, on the 25th day of the ninth month. See APPENDIX.

Year, Sabbatical. Every seventh year all agricultural labor was suspended, and spontaneous productions were left to the poor, the traveller, and the wild beasts. Lev. 25:1-7. This was (1) for the sake of the ground; (2) for the preservation of wild beasts; and (3) to make the people provident and sensible of dependence. The people could fish, hunt, take care of bees and flocks, repair buildings, manufacture clothes, and carry on commerce. This year was religiously observed. Deut. 31:10-13. There was, moreover, a general release; no debt to a Jew was allowed to stand, but must be forgiven. Deut. 15:1-11.

Yoke. It was much lighter and larger than ours, so that the cattle stood farther apart. It was simply a stick laid upon the necks of the cattle, to which it was held by thongs instead of wooden bows, and in a similar manner it was attached to the plough-beam. In modern Syria wooden pins are sometimes used instead of thongs, the lower ends of which are held by a parallel stick under the necks of the oxen. The yoke was an appropriate emblem of subjection and of slavery, while the removal of it indicated deliverance. Gen. 27:40; Jer. 2:20; Matt. 11:29, 30. Breaking the yoke also represents the rejection of authority. Nah. 1:13.

Z

Zaanaim (zā'a-nā'im), *removals*. The plain, or the oak where Heber the Kenite pitched his tent, Judg. 4:11, some 2 or 3 miles northwest of the Waters of Merom (Lake Huleh.) Conder suggests the identification of Zaanaim with Bessûm, east of Tabor. Same as Zaanannim.

Zacchæus, or **Zaccheus** (zak-kē'us). A Jew—a tax-collector at or near Jericho. When Jesus was passing through Jericho on his last journey to Jerusalem, Zacchæus was anxious to see him. Luke 19:1-27. Of Zacchæus nothing more is certainly known than is stated in Luke.

Zachariah (zak'a-rī'ah), *remembered by Jehovah*. 1. Son of Jeroboam II., fourteenth king of Israel, and the last of the house of Jehu. There is a difficulty about the date of his reign. Most chronologers assume an interregnum of eleven years between Jeroboam's death and Zachariah's accession. B. C. 772-1. His reign lasted only six months. He was killed in a conspiracy of which Shallum was the head, and by which the prophecy in 2 Kings 10:30 was fulfilled. 2. The father of Abi or Abijah, Hezekiah's mother. 2 Kings 18:2.

Zacharias (zak'a-rī'as). Greek form of Zachariah. 1. Father of John the Baptist. Luke 1:5, etc. He was a priest of the course of Abia, the eighth of the 24 courses who ministered at the temple in turn. 2. Son of Barachias, who, our Lord says, was slain by the Jews between the altar and the temple. Matt. 23:35; Luke 11:51. There has been much dispute who this Zacharias was, but there can be little or no doubt that the allusion is to Zechariah, the son of Jehoiada, 2 Chron. 24:20, 21; and he may have been called "the son" of Barachias from his grandfather. He is mentioned as being the martyr last recorded in the Hebrew Scriptures, as Abel was the first—2d Chronicles being placed last in their Old Testament Scriptures.

Zadok (zā'dok), *just*. Son of Ahitub, and one of the two high priests in the time of David, Abiathar being the other. 2 Sam. 8:17. He joined David at Hebron, 1 Chron. 12:28, and subsequently anointed Solomon king, 1 Kings 1:39, and was rewarded by Solomon for his faithful service by being made sole high priest. There are seven persons of this name mentioned in the Bible.

Zalmon (zăl'mon), *shady*, Mount, a hill near Shechem, Judg. 9:48, the same as Salmon. Ps. 68:14. R. V., "Zalmon."

Zamzummim (zam-zŭm'mim.) Deut. 2:20. The Ammonite name for the people who by others were called Rephaim.

Zanoah (za-nō'ah), *marsh, bog*. 1. A town in Judah, in the lowlands or "valley." Josh. 15:34; Neh. 3:13; 11:30. East of Beth-shemesh, at Zănûâ, 14 miles west-southwest of Jerusalem. 2. A town in the highlands of Judah. Josh. 15:56. Za'nutah, 10 miles south-southwest of Hebron.

Zarephath (zăr'e-phăth), *smelting-house*, and Sarepta (sa-rĕp'tah). Luke 4:26. A town of Phœnicia, on the Mediterranean, between Tyre and Sidon. At Zarephath, Elijah found shelter with a widow during the great famine in Israel. 1 Kings 17:8-24. The prophet Obadiah mentions it as marking the limits of Israel's victory. Obad. 20. Jesus made reference to this incident in Elijah's life. Luke 4:26. Now in ruins.

Zaretan (zăr'e-tăn). Josh. 3:16. R. V., "Zarethan." See Zereda.

Zebedee (zĕb'e-dee), *my gift*. Greek form of Zabdi. A fisherman of Galilee, the father of the apostles James and John, Matt. 4:21, and the husband of Salome. Matt. 27:56; Mark 15:40. He probably lived at Bethsaida. It has been inferred from the mention of his "hired servants," Mark 1:20, and from the acquaintance between the apostle John and Annas the high priest, John 18:15, that the family of Zebedee were in easy circumstances: comp. John 19:27; Matt. 4:21. He appears only twice in the Gospel narrative, namely, in Matt. 4:21, 22; Mark 1:19, 20, where he is seen in his boat with his two sons mending their nets.

Zeboim (ze-bō′im), *hyænas*. It was a gorge or ravine apparently east of Michmash, and mentioned only in 1 Sam. 13:18. The "wilderness" is the wild tract between the central hills and the valley of the Jordan.

Zebulun (zĕb′u-lŭn), *a habitation*. One of the sons of Jacob, and of Leah. Gen. 30:20; 35:23; 46:14; 1 Chron. 2:1. Of the individual Zebulun nothing is recorded. He had three sons, founders of the chief families of the tribe. Gen. 46, comp. Num. 26:26. The tribe is not recorded to have taken part in any of the events of the wandering or the conquest. Its territory was remote from the centre of government. The conduct of the tribe during the struggle with Sisera, when they fought with desperate valor, was such as to draw the special praise of Deborah. Judg. 5:18.

Zechariah (zĕk′a-rī′ah), *Jehovah remembers*. 1. The eleventh of the twelve minor prophets, of priestly descent, and a contemporary of Haggai. Ezra 5:1. He was born in Babylon, and was both a priest and a prophet. Scarcely anything is known of his life. His prophecies were about B. C. 520.

THE BOOK OF ZECHARIAH consists of two divisions: I. Chaps. 1-8; II. Chaps. 9-14. The first division contains visions and prophecies, exhortations to turn to Jehovah, and warnings against the enemies of the people of God. The second division gives a prophetic description of the future fortunes of the theocracy in conflict with the secular powers, the sufferings and death of the Messiah under the figure of the shepherd, the conversion of Israel to him, and the final glorification of the kingdom of God. Some have ascribed this part of the book to Jeremiah because in Matt. 27:9, 10 a passage is quoted under the name of Jeremiah, while others have put it at a much earlier or much later period on account of the peculiarities of the style. The book contains six specific references to Christ: 3:8; 6:12; 9:9; 11:12; 12:10; 13:7, representing him as a lowly servant, a priest and king building Jehovah's temple, the meek and peaceful but universal monarch, the shepherd betrayed for the price of a slave (thirty pieces of silver), the leader to repentance, and the Fellow of Jehovah smitten by Jehovah himself, at once the Redeemer and the Pattern of his flock. Besides the prophet, 27 other persons of the name Zechariah are mentioned in Scripture.

Zedekiah (zĕd′e-kī′ah), *justice of Jehovah*. 1. The last king of Judah, the son of Josiah, and the uncle of Jehoiachin. His proper name was Mattaniah, but Nebuchadnezzar changed it to Zedekiah when raising him to the throne. He commenced his reign at twenty-one, and reigned eleven years, 598-588 B. C. 2 Chron. 36:11. He was a weak man, and the people were completely demoralized. In the ninth year of his reign he revolted against Nebuchadnezzar, in consequence of which the Assyrian monarch marched his army into Judæa and took all the fortified places. In the eleventh year of his reign, on the ninth day of the fourth month (July), Jerusalem was taken. The king and his people endeavored to escape by night, but, the Chaldæan troops pursuing them, they were overtaken in the plain of Jericho. Zedekiah was seized and carried to Nebuchadnezzar, then at Riblah, in Syria, who reproached him with his perfidy, caused all his children to be slain before his face and his own eyes to be put out, and then, loading him with chains of brass, ordered him to be sent to Babylon. 2 Kings 25:1-11; 2 Chron. 36:12, 20. Thus the double prophecy concerning him—that he should be carried to Babylon, but never see it—was literally fulfilled. Jer. 32:4, 5; 34:3; comp. Ezek. 12:13. 2. A false prophet in the reign of Ahab. 1 Kings 22:11, 24, 25; 2 Chron. 18:10, 23, 24. There are four persons of this name mentioned in the Bible.

Zephaniah (zĕph′a-nī′ah), *Jehovah hides*. 1. One of the minor prophets, in the days of Josiah. His prophecy was uttered about B. C. 620 to 609. The description of the judgment in ch. 1:14, 15, "The great day of Jehovah is near" (in the Latin version *Dies iræ, dies illa*), has furnished the basis for the sublime hymn of the Middle Ages, the *Dies Iræ* ascribed to Thomas a Celano, and often translated. There are four persons of this name mentioned in the Bible.

Zerah (zē′rah), *a rising of light*. 1. An Ethiopian or Cushite king in the reign of Asa, routed at Mareshah, in the valley of Zephathah, 2 Chron. 14:9, 10. There are four persons of this name mentioned in the Bible.

Zereda (zĕr′e-dah), *cooling*. A place in Ephraim, in the plain of Jordan. 1 Kings 11:26. Possibly it is the same as Zaretan, Josh. 3:16; Zererath, Judg. 7:22, R. V., "Zererah;" Zartanah, 1 Kings 4:12, R. V., "Zarethan;" Zeredathah, 2 Chron. 4:17, R. V., "Zeredah;" and Zarthan, 1 Kings 7:46. There seems to be much confusion about these names, but the Pal. Memoirs suggest as the site of Zereda, *Surdah*, 2½ miles northwest of *Beitin* (Bethel).

Zeredathah (ze-rĕd′a-thah). 2 Chron. 4:17, A. V. See **Zereda**.

Zererath (zĕr′e-răth). Judg. 7:22, A. V. See **Zereda**.

Zerubbabel (ze-rŭb′ba-bĕl), *begotten in Babylon*, 1 Chron. 3:19, or **Zorobabel**, Matt. 1:12, A. V., was the leader of the first colony of Jews that returned from the captivity in Babylon, Ezra 2:2, and was of the family of David, a son of Salathiel or Shealtiel, Hag. 1:1; Matt. 1:12, but called a son of Pedaiah, the brother or son of Salathiel, in 1 Chron. 3:17-19. He laid the foundations of the temple, Zech. 4:6-10, and was chiefly instrumental in restoring the religious rites of the nation. Finally he succeeded in completing the building. Ezra 5:2; Hag. 1:12, 14; 2:2, 4; Zech. 4:6, 10. He was the governor of Judæa. Neh. 12:47.

Zidon (zī′don), *hunting*. Heb. *Tsidon*. "Sidon," the Greek form, is found in Gen. 10:15, 19, in the Apocrypha generally, and in the New Testament. Zidon was a rich and ancient Phœnician city. The city was 25 miles south of the modern Beirut. Zidon is one of the most ancient cities of the world. The person after whom it is named was the "first-born" of Canaan, the grandson of Noah. Gen. 10 : 15 ; 1 Chron. 1 : 13. This was B. C. 2218. In Joshua's time it was "great Zidon," Josh. 11 : 8 ; 19 : 28, and seems to have been the metropolis of Phœnicia. Zidon was one of the limits of the tribe of Asher, Josh. 19 : 28, but was never possessed by the Israelites. Judg. 1 : 31 ; 3 : 3. In fact, the Zidonians oppressed Israel, Judg. 10 : 12, seeming themselves to be secure from all attacks and living "careless." Judg. 18 : 7, 28. Tyre was one of the colonies—a "virgin daughter," Isa. 23 : 12—of Zidon, but subsequently became the more important town. The Zidonians were famous for commerce, manufactures, and arts. Their sailors and workmen were noted. Zidonians assisted in the work of building the temple. 1 Chron. 22 : 4 ; 1 Kings 5 : 6 ; Ezek. 27 : 8. From Zidon also came idolatrous abominations to corrupt Israel. 1 Kings 11 : 5, 33 ; 2 Kings 23 : 13. The city was mentioned frequently in prophetic threatenings, but with much less severity than Tyre. Isa. 23 : 2, 4, 12 ; Jer. 25 : 22 ; 27 : 3 ; 47 : 4 ; Ezek. 27 : 8 ; 28 : 21, 22 ; 32 : 30 ; Joel 3 : 4 ; Zech. 9 : 2. In New Testament times Zidon (called "Sidon") was visited by Jesus, Matt. 15 : 21 ; Mark 7 : 24 ; Luke 4 : 26, although the "coasts" of Tyre and Sidon denoted the adjacent region as well as the cities themselves, and some think that the Saviour did not enter the cities. Hearers from among those people were drawn to his preaching. Mark 3 : 8 ; Luke 6 : 17 ; comp. Matt. 11 : 22 ; Luke 10 : 14. Herod's displeasure with this region is noted. Acts 12 : 20. The apostle Paul touched at Zidon on his way to Rome, and visited the Christians there. Acts 27 : 3. The site of ancient Zidon is occupied by the modern Saida. The burying-grounds are extensive, and many curious sarcophagi have been discovered. One was the sarcophagus of king Ashmanezer ; it has been placed in the museum at Paris, and antiquarians fix its date at from B. C. 300 to B. C. 1000. The ancient ruins are few.

Ziklag (zĭk'lăg), *outpouring of a fountain?* A city in the south of Judah, Josh. 15 : 31 ; afterward given to Simeon. Josh. 19 : 5. It was at times held by the Philistines. Achish, king of Gath, gave it to David, and it subsequently belonged to Judah. Its chief interest is in connection with the life of David. 1 Sam. 27 : 6 ; 30 : 1, 14, 26 ; 2 Sam. 1 : 1 ; 4 : 10 ; 1 Chron. 4 : 30 ; 12 : 1-20. It was also inhabited after the return from the captivity. Neh. 11 : 28.

Zimri (zĭm'rī). 1. A Simeonite chieftain, slain by Phinehas. Num. 25 : 14. 2. Fifth king of the separate kingdom of Israel for seven days. He gained the crown by the murder of king Elah, but the army made Omri king, and Zimri retreated into the innermost part of the palace, set it on fire, and perished in the ruins. 1 Kings 16 : 9-20.

Zin (zĭn), *a low palm tree.* The wilderness of Zin was a part of the Arabian desert south of Palestine. Num. 13 : 21, 22 ; 34 : 3 ; Josh. 15 : 1, 3 ; Num. 20 : 1 ; 27 : 14 ; 33 : 36. Kadesh is sometimes spoken of as in the wilderness of Zin, Num. 33 : 36, and again as in the wilderness of Paran. Num. 13 : 26. This is explained by the fact that Paran was the general name for the whole desert, while Zin was the northeastern corner of that desert.

Zion (zī'on), and **Sion** (sī'on), *dry, sunny mount.* This hill in Jerusalem is first mentioned as a stronghold of the Jebusites. Josh. 15 : 63. It remained in their possession until captured by David, who made it "the city of David," the capital of his kingdom. He built there a citadel, his own palace, houses for the people, and a place for the ark of God. 2 Sam. 5 : 7 ; 1 Kings 8 : 1 ; 2 Kings 19 : 21, 31 ; 1 Chron. 11 : 5 ; 2 Chron. 5 : 2. In the prophetical and poetical books the name occurs no less than 148 times, viz., in Psalms 38 times, Song of Sol. 1, Isaiah 47, Jeremiah 17, Lamentations 15, Joel 7, Amos 2, Obadiah 2, Micah 9, Zephaniah 2, Zechariah 8. In the New Testament it occurs seven times as "Sion," making the total number of times the name occurs 161. It was in the later books no longer confined to the southwestern hill, but denoted sometimes Jerusalem in general, Ps. 149 : 2 ; 87 : 2 ; Isa. 33 : 14 ; Joel 2 : 1, etc. ; sometimes God's chosen people, Ps. 51 : 18 ; 87 : 5, etc. ; sometimes the church, Heb. 12 : 22, etc. ; and sometimes the heavenly city. Rev. 14 : 1, etc. Hence, Zion has passed into its present common use in religious literature to denote the aspirations and hopes of God's children. A part of the hill is cultivated, and thus the traveller is frequently reminded of the prophecy, "Zion shall be ploughed *like* a field." Jer. 26 : 18 ; Micah 3 : 12. See **Jerusalem**.

Ziph, *a flowing.* 1. A city in the south of Judah. Josh. 15 : 24. 2. A town in the highlands of Judah, Josh. 15 : 55 ; fortified by Rehoboam. 2 Chron. 11 : 8. When pursued by Saul, David hid himself "in the wilderness of Ziph." 1 Sam. 23 : 14, 15, 24 ; 26 : 2. The site is Tell es Zif, about four miles southeast of Hebron, on the road to En-gedi. Tristram says : "How far the forest of Ziph," see 1 Sam. 23 : 14, 15, "extended it is not easy to say, but there are traces of it in an occasional tree, and there seems no reason, from the nature of the soil, why the woods may not have stretched nearly to the barren, sandy marl which overlies the limestone for a few miles west of the Dead Sea." 3. A descendant of Judah. 1 Chron. 4 : 16.

Ziz (zĭz), **the Cliff of.** 2 Chron. 20 : 16. R. V., the ascent of Ziz. The pass was the ascent through which invaders from the south and east, after doubling the south end of the Dead Sea, entered the hill-country of Judæa. Ziz was the key of the pass.

Zoan (zō'an), *low region?* or *place of departure?* A city of lower Egypt ; called by the Greeks Tanis—now San. Zoan was an exceedingly ancient city, built seven years after Hebron. Num. 13 : 22. The "field of

Zoan" was the place of God's wonders. Ps. 78:12, 43. When Isaiah wrote, it would appear to have been one of the chief cities in Egypt, as he speaks of "the princes of Zoan." Isa. 19:11, 13; 30:4. Ezekiel foretells the fate of the city in the words: "I will set fire in Zoan." Ezek. 30:14. There are no other Scripture references to Zoan. Zoan has been satisfactorily identified with the ancient Avaris and Tanis and the modern San. Very interesting discoveries have been made there within a few years. Among the inscriptions has been found one with the expression *Sechet Tanel*, which exactly corresponds to the "field of Zoan." Ps. 78:43. The mounds which mark the site of the town are remarkable for their height and extent, and cover an area a mile in length by three-fourths of a mile in width. The sacred enclosure of the great temple was 1500 feet long and 1250 feet wide. This temple was adorned by Rameses II. There are some dozen obelisks of great size, all fallen and broken, with numerous statues. "The whole constitutes," says Macgregor, "one of the grandest and oldest ruins in the world."

Zoar (zō'ar), *smallness*. Gen. 19:22, 23, 30. One of the cities of Canaan. Its earlier name was Bela. Gen. 14:2, 8. In the general destruction of the cities of the plain, Zoar was spared to afford shelter to Lot. It was one of the landmarks which Moses saw from Pisgah, Deut. 34:3, and it appears to have been known in the time of Isaiah, Isa. 15:5, and Jeremiah, Jer. 48:34. It was situated in the same district with the four cities of the "plain" of the Jordan, and near to Sodom. Gen. 19:15, 23, 27. See Sodom.

Zobah (zō'bah), *station*. A Syrian kingdom, sometimes called Aram Zobah, and also written "Zoba," whose kings made war with Saul, 1 Sam. 14:47; with David, 2 Sam. 8:3; 10:6, 8; 1 Chron. 18:5, 9; and with Solomon, 2 Chron. 8:3. It was on the north of Damascus. 2 Sam. 8:3; 23:36; 1 Kings 11:23. Zobah is found on the Assyrian inscriptions.

Zoheleth (zō'he-lĕth), *serpent*. A stone by "En-rogel," by which Adonijah "slew sheep and oxen and fat cattle." 1 Kings 1:9.

Zophar (zō'phar). One of Job's three friends, Job 2:11, is called the Naamathite, probably because he belonged to Naamah, Josh. 15:41, a town assigned to Judah.

Zophim (zō'phim), *watchers*. The field of Zophim was the place on the "top of Pisgah" to which Balak brought Balaam. Num. 23:14. If the word rendered "field" be taken in its usual sense, then the "field of Zophim" was a cultivated spot high up on the top of Pisgah. See **Pisgah.**

Zorah (zō'rah), and Zoreah (zō're-ah), *hornet's town*, and Zareah (zā're-ah), Neh. 11:29, a town in the low country of Judah —afterward assigned to Dan, Josh. 15:33; 19:41; the birthplace and burialplace of Samson. Judg. 13:2, 25; 16:31. From Zorah the Danites sent spies to search the land for a place of inheritance. Judg. 18:2. Zorah was fortified by Rehoboam, 2 Chron. 11:10, and inhabited after the return from captivity. Neh. 11:29. The place still exists as Surah, 13 miles west of Jerusalem.

Zuph (zŭph), or Suph, R. V. text, *flag, sedge*, Deut. 1:1, margin. 1. From the Hebrew *Sûph*, signifying a kind of seaweed, and the Hebrew name for the Red Sea. 2. Name of a person. 1 Sam. 1:1.

Zuph, the Land of. 1 Sam. 9:5, 6. The whole of this journey of Saul has been a curious puzzle in Scripture topography. Neither the starting point, nor the point to which he returned, is known, and the places between them cannot be determined.

Zur, *rock*. 1. Son of the founder of Gibeon. 1 Chron. 8:30; 9:36. 2. A prince of Midian. Num. 25:15; Josh. 13:21. He was slain with others by the Israelites. Num. 25:18.

Zuzim (zŭ'zim). Gen. 14:5. The name of a people in Ham, who were defeated in the famous invasion of Chedorlaomer. The Zuzim are believed to be the same people that the Ammonites later called the Zamzummim, and that others called the Rephaim or giants. See Deut. 2:20, R. V.

INTERESTING FACTS ABOUT THE BIBLE.

	OLD TESTAMENT.	NEW TESTAMENT.	IN WHOLE BIBLE.
Number of books in	39	27	66
Number of chapters in	929	260	1,189
Number of verses in	23,214	7,959	31,173
Number of words in	592,439	181,253	773,692
Number of letters in	2,728,100	838,380	3,566,480
Middle book in	Proverbs.	2 Thess.	Micah and Nahum.
Middle chapter of	Job 29.	Romans 13 and 14.	Psalm 117.
Middle verse of	2 Chronicles 20:17.	Acts 17:17.	Psalm 118:8.
Shortest book in	Obadiah.	3 John.	3 John.
Shortest verse in	1 Chronicles 1:1.	John 11:35.	John 11:35.

Ezra 7:21 has all the letters of the alphabet except *j*.

Isaiah 37 and 2 Kings 19 are alike; so are the last verses of 2 Chron. and the opening verses of Ezra.

The word *Jehovah* occurs 6853 times in the Bible; the word *and* 35,543 times in the Old Testament, and 6853 times in the New Testament. The shortest chapter in the Bible is Ps. 117.

APPENDIX.

CHIEF PARABLES AND MIRACLES IN THE BIBLE.

By the REV. EDWIN W. RICE, D.D.

PARABLES IN OLD TESTAMENT.

Trees choosing a king. Judg. 9: 7-15.
Samson's riddle. Judg. 14: 14.
Nathan and the ewe lamb. 2 Sam. 12: 1-6.
Woman of Tekoah. 2 Sam. 14: 6-11.
Escaped prisoner. 1 Kings 20: 35-40.
Thistle and cedar. 2 Kings 14: 9.
The vine. Ps. 80: 8-16.
Vineyard. Is. 5: 1-7.
Eagle and vine. Eze. 17: 3-10.
Lion's whelps. Eze. 19: 2-9.
Boiling pot. Eze. 24: 3-5.
Cedar in Lebanon. Eze. 31: 3-18.

MIRACLES IN OLD TESTAMENT.

Enoch translated. Gen. 5: 24; Heb. 11: 5.
The flood. Gen. 7: 11-24.
Sodom and Gomorrah destroyed. Gen. 19: 24.
Lot's wife made a salt pillar. Gen. 19: 26.
Burning bush. Ex. 3: 2-4.
Aaron's rod. Ex. 7: 10-12.
Ten plagues of Egypt, Ex., chaps. 7 to 12:
  1. Waters turned to blood. 7: 19-25.
  2. Frogs. 8: 5-14.
  3. Lice. 8: 17, 18.
  4. Flies. 8: 24.
  5. Murrain, (cattle plague). 9: 3-6.
  6. Boils. 9: 8-11.
  7. Thunder, hail, etc. 9: 22-26.
  8. Locusts. 10: 12-19.
  9. Darkness. 10: 21-33.
  10. Death of the firstborn. 12: 29-30.
Crossing of the Red Sea. Ex. 14: 21-31.
Marah's waters sweetened. Ex. 15: 23-25.
Giving the manna. Ex. 16: 14-35.
Water from the rock at Horeb. Ex. 17: 5-7.
Nadab and Abihu. Lev. 10: 1, 2.
Part of Israel burned. Num. 11: 1-3.
Korah and his company. Num. 16: 32.
Aaron's rod budding. Num. 17: 1, etc.
Water from the rock, Meribah. Num. 20: 7-11.
Brazen serpent. Num. 21: 8, 9.
Balaam's ass speaks. Num. 22: 21-35.
River Jordan crossed. Josh. 3: 14-17.
Walls of Jericho fall. Josh. 6: 6-20.
Jeroboam's hand withered. 1 Kgs. 13: 4, 6.
Widow's meal and oil increased. 1 Kings 17: 14-16.
Widow's son raised. 1 Kings 17: 17-24.
Elijah calls fire from heaven. 1 Kings 18: 28.
Ahaziah's captains consumed by fire. 2 Kings 1: 10-12.
Jordan divided by Elijah and Elisha. 2 Kings 2: 7, 8, 14.
Elijah carried to heaven. 2 Kings 2: 11.
Waters of Jericho healed. 2 Kings 2: 21, 22.

The widow's oil multiplied. 2 Kings 4: 2-7.
Shunammite's son raised. 2 Kings 4: 32-37.
Naaman and Gehazi. 2 Kings 5: 10-27.
The iron axe-head swims. 2 Kings 6: 5-7.
Syrian army's blindness. 2 Kgs. 6: 18, 20.
Dead man raised. 2 Kings 13: 21.
Sennacherib's army destroyed. 2 Kings 19: 35.
Sun-dial of Ahaz. 2 Kings 20: 9-11.
Uzziah struck with leprosy. 2 Chron. 26: 16-21.
Shadrach, Meshach, Abednego in the furnace. Dan. 3: 19-27.
Daniel in the den of lions. Dan. 6: 16-23.
Jonah and a great fish. Jonah 2: 1-10.

PARABLES IN THE GOSPELS.

1. Found in Matthew only (and not found in any other Gospel).—11.

The tares. 13: 1-24.
Hid treasure. 13: 44.
Pearl of great price. 13: 46.
Drag net. 13: 47, 48.
Unmerciful servant. 18: 23-34.
Laborers in the vineyard. 20: 1-16.
The two sons. 21: 28-32.
Marriage of king's son. 22: 1-14.
Ten virgins. 25: 1-13.
Ten talents. 25: 14-30.
Sheep and goats. 25: 31-46.

2. Found in Mark only.—2.

The seed. 4: 26-29.
Householder. 13: 34-36.

3. Found in Luke only.—17.

Two debtors. 7: 41-43.
Good Samaritan. 10: 25-37.
Friend at midnight. 11: 5-8.
Rich fool. 12: 16-21.
Servants watching. 12: 35-40.
The servant on trial. 12: 42-48.
Barren fig tree. 13: 6-9.
Great supper. 14: 16-24.
Tower and warring king. 14: 28-33.
The lost silver. 15: 8-10.
Prodigal (lost) son. 15: 11-32.
The shrewd steward. 16: 1-8.
Rich man and Lazarus. 16: 19-31.
Unprofitable servants. 17: 7-10.
Unjust judge. 18: 1-8.
Pharisee and publican. 18: 9-14.
Ten pounds. 19: 12-27.

4. In Matthew and Luke only.—3.

House on rock and sand. Matt. 7: 24-27; Luke 6: 48, 49.
The leaven. Matt. 13: 33; Luke 13: 20.
Lost sheep. Matt. 18: 12; Luke 15: 3-7.

5. In Matthew, Mark and Luke only.—7.

Light under a bushel. Matt. 5:15; Mark 4:21; Luke 8:16.
Cloth and garment. Matt. 9:16; Mark 2:21; Luke 5:36.
Wine and bottles. Matt. 9:17; Mark 2:22; Luke 5:37.
The sower. Matt. 13; Mark 4; Luke 8.
Mustard seed. Matt. 13; Mark 4; Lk. 13.
Wicked husbandmen. Matt. 21; Mark 12; Luke 20.
The fig tree and the trees. Matt. 24; Mark 13; Luke 21.

MIRACLES IN THE NEW TESTAMENT.

A. In the Gospels.

1. Found in Matthew only (not in any other Gospel).—3.

Two blind men see. 9:27-31.
Dumb demoniac. 9:32, 33.
Money (shekel) in the fish. 17:24-27.

2. Found in Mark only.—2.

Deaf and dumb cured. 7:31-37.
Blind man made to see. 8:22-26.

3. Found in Luke only.—6.

Draught of fishes. 5:1-11.
Raising widow's son. 7:11-15.
Infirm woman healed. 13:11-15.
Dropsy cured. 14:1-6.
Ten lepers cleansed. 17:11-19.
Malchus' ear healed. 22:50, 51.

4. Found in John only.—6.

Water made wine at Cana. 2:1-11.
Nobleman's son healed. 4:46-54.
Impotent man at Bethesda. 5:1-9.
Sight to man born blind. 9:1-7.
Lazarus raised to life. 11:38-44.
Draught of 153 fishes. 21:1-14.

5. In Matthew and Mark only.—3.

Syrophœnician's daughter. Matt. 15; Mark 7.
Four thousand fed. Matt. 15; Mark 8.
Withered fig tree. Matt. 21; Mark 11.

6. In Matthew and Luke only.—2.

Centurion's servant. Matt. 8; Luke 7.
Blind and dumb demoniac. Matt. 12; Luke 11.

7. In Mark and Luke only.—2.

Demoniac in synagogue. Mark 1; Luke 4.
The ascension of Jesus. Mark 16:19; Luke 24:51; (Acts 1:9, 10.)

8. In Matthew, Mark and Luke only.—10.

Peter's mother-in-law. Matt. 8; Mark 1; Luke 4.
Storm stilled. Matt. 8; Mark 4; Luke 8.
Devils at Gadara. Matt. 8; Mark 5; Luke 8.
Leper cured. Matt. 8; Mark 2; Luke 5.
Jairus' daughter. Matt. 9; Mark 5; Luke 8.
Woman's issue of blood. Matt. 9; Mark 5; Luke 8.
Palsy cured. Matt. 9; Mark 2; Luke 5.
Withered hand. Matt. 12; Mark 3; Luke 6.
Demoniac child. Matt. 17; Mark 9; Luke 9.
Blind of Jericho. Matt. 20; Mark 10; Lk. 18.

9. In Matthew, Mark and John only.—1

Walking on the sea. Matt. 14; Mk. 6; John 6.

10. In all the Gospels.—2.

Five thousand fed. Matt. 14; Mark 6; Luke 9; John 6.
Jesus' resurrection. Matt. 28; Mark 16; Luke 24; John 20; (Acts 1).

B. Miracles in the Acts.—16.

Pentecostal tongues. 2:1-4.
Lame man healed. 3:2-10.
Ananias and Sapphira. 5:1-10.
Angel opens the prison. 5:19.
Unclean spirits cast out. 8:6, 7.
Saul's conversion. 9:3-18.
Eneas healed by Peter. 9:32-34.
Dorcas raised to life. 9:36-41.
Angel delivers Peter. 12:4-12.
Elymas struck blind. 13:8-11.
Lame man at Lystra. 14:8-10.
Evil spirit cast out. 16:16-18.
Prison opened at Philippi. 16:25-31.
Eutychus restored. 20:9-12.
Viper from Paul's hand. 28:3-6.
Father of Publius healed. 28:8, 9.

TABLE OF TIME.

Hebrew divisions of the day.

Civil day — from sunset one evening to sunset the next evening.

Night Watches (Ancient).

First watch (Lam. 2:19), to about 10 or 11 P.M.
Second watch (Judg. 7:19), to about 2 A.M.
Third (morning) watch (Ex. 14:24), to sunrise.

Night Watches (New Testament).

First watch (evening), sunset to 9 P.M.
Second watch (midnight), 9 to 12 P.M.
Third watch (cockcrowing), 12 to 3 A.M.
Fourth watch (morning), 3 to sunrise.

THE YEAR.

The Hebrew *sacred* year began with the Passover; the *civil* year with the Feast of Trumpets. (See page 158.)

DAY DIVISIONS.—ROMAN TIME.
(New Testament.)

The natural day (from sunrise to sunset), the Romans divided into twelve equal parts. The following table shows the approximate beginning of each of the twelve hours; equal in midsummer to 1¼, and in midwinter to ¾, of one of our hours.

ROMAN HOUR.	IN MIDSUMMER BEGAN	IN MIDWINTER BEGAN
1st hour,	about 4.30 A.M.	about 7.30 A.M.
2d "	" 5.45 "	" 8.15 "
3d "	" 7. "	" 9. "
4th "	" 8.15 "	" 9.45 "
5th "	" 9.30 "	" 10.30 "
6th "	" 10.45 "	" 11.15 "
7th "	" 12. M.	" 12. M.
8th "	" 1.15 P.M.	" 12.45 P.M.
9th "	" 2.30 "	" 1.30 "
10th "	" 3.45 "	" 2.15 "
11th "	" 5. "	" 3. "
12th "	" 6.15 "	" 3.45 "
Day ends,	" 7.30 "	" 4.30 "

TABLES OF MEASURES, WEIGHTS AND MONEY IN THE BIBLE.

These tables are based upon the latest and highest authorities, as Schrader, Brandis and F. W. Madden (Jewish Coinage and Money), Whitehouse and Bissell.

1. MEASURE OF LENGTH.

	ft.	in.
Digit, or finger. Jer. 52:21,		$\frac{73}{100}$
4 digits = 1 palm. Ex. 25:25,		$3\frac{3}{100}$
3 palms = 1 span. Ex. 28:16,		$9\frac{23}{100}$
2 spans = 1 cubit,[1] Gen. 6:15,	1	7
4 cubits = 1 fathom. Acts 27:28,	6	4
6 cubits = 1 reed. Eze. 40:3, 5,	9	6
1 Roman foot,		$11\frac{64}{100}$
5 Roman feet = 1 Roman pace,	4	$10\frac{1}{4}$
$6\frac{1}{4}$ Roman ft. = 6 Greek ft. = Greek fathom,	6	$\frac{81}{100}$
625 Roman ft. = 1 furlong (Greek stadium),	606	9
1 Roman mile[2] = about $\frac{9}{10}$ of an English mile,	4854	
15 furlongs = Sabbath day's journey. Compare John 11:18 with Acts 1:12.		

[1] The cubit varied in length. The short cubit was about 15 or 16 inches; then a cubit a handbreadth longer (see Eze. 40:5), or about 19 inches; the Babylonian cubit after the captivity, about 21 inches. The Greek cubit, and the Jewish cubit used in temple measurements, was about 18 to 19 inches.

[2] *Webster's International Dictionary* notes that a Roman mile equals 1000 paces = 1614 English yards, or 4842 feet; but others make it equal to 1618 English yards, or 4854 feet, as in the table. It was equal to 8 Greek *stadia*, or furlongs.

2. MEASURE OF CAPACITY (Dry).

	pks.	pts.
$1\frac{4}{5}$ kab (cab)[3] = 1 omer,[2]		5
6 " $3\frac{1}{3}$ omers = 1 seah,[3]	1	1
18 " 3 seah = 1 ephah,[4]	3	3
180 " 10 ephahs = 1 homer[5] or kor,[5]	32	

[1] 2 Kings 6:25. [2] Ex. 16:16. [3] Matt. 13:33. [4] Ex. 16:36. [5] Lev. 27:16. [6] Eze. 45:14. But Josephus gives the equivalent of the homer at about $10\frac{3}{4}$ bushels, or 43 pecks, while the rabbins give it at about $5\frac{1}{4}$ bushels, or 21 pecks.

3. MEASURE OF CAPACITY (Liquid).

	gals.	qts.	pts.
1 log. Lev. 14:10, about			$\frac{4}{5}$
4 logs = 1 cab (kab), "			$3\frac{1}{3}$
3 kabs = 1 hin. Ex. 30:24, "		5	
2 hins = 1 seah, "		10	
3 seahs = 1 bath or ephah, 1 Kings 7:26, "		30	1
10 ephahs = 1 kor or homer. Eze. 45:14, "	75		5

4. WEIGHT (Troy).

	lbs.	oz.	grs.
1 gerah. Ex. 30:13,			$12\frac{6}{10}$
10 gerahs = 1 bekah. Ex. 38:26,			$126\frac{1}{2}$
2 bekahs = 1 shekel. Gen. 23:15,		$\frac{1}{2}$	13
60 shekels = 1 maneh. Eze. 45:12,		2	7 300
60 manehs = *Kikkar* (Heb. Kikkar. Ex. 25:29); or king's talent,[1]	158	1	240

[1] There may have been a smaller talent of 50 manehs or minas, rather more than 125 pounds.

5. SILVER MONEY.

(According to Bissell's Bib. Antiq.)

	cents.
1 gerah =	$.03\frac{65}{100}$
10 gerahs = 1 bekah,	$.36\frac{1}{2}$
2 bekahs = 1 shekel,	.73
60 shekels = 1 maneh,	$43.80
50 manehs = 1 talent,	$2190.00

(According to Madden and Whitehouse. — Old Testament period.)

1 shekel (holy shekel),	.64
50 shekels = 1 maneh or mina,	$32.00
60 manehs or minas = 1 talent,	1920.00

6. GOLD MONEY (Troy oz. = $19.47 $\frac{1}{10}$).

According to Bissell.

1 shekel (gold),	$5.35
100 shekels = 1 maneh,	535.00
100 manehs = 1 talent,	53,500.00

(According to Madden and Whitehouse. — Old Testament period.)

1 shekel,	$9.60
50 shekels = 1 maneh or mina,	480.60
60 manehs or minas = 1 talent,	28,800.00

7. ROMAN COPPER MONEY.

(New Testament period, coins were:)

1 lepton = 1 mite,	about $\frac{1}{8}$ ct.
2 leptons or mites = 1 quadrans, (the farthing of Matt. 5:26),	" $\frac{1}{4}$ ct.
4 quadrans = 1 as, (the farthing of Matt. 10:29),	" 1 ct.

(The "as" of N. T. times was much reduced from the earlier coin of that denomination.)

8. SILVER GREEK AND ROMAN MONEY.

(According to Madden and Whitehouse. — New Testament Period.)

1 denarius = 1 "penny" (Matt. 22:16;) drachma[1] or 16 ases,	cents. about .16
2 denarii or drachmas = didrachma,[2]	" .32
4 drachmas = stater[3] or shekel,	.64
30 shekels (Attic) = 1 mina or pound,	$19.10
60 minas or shekels = 1 talent (Attic),	1,146.00

[1] Luke 15:8. [2] Matt. 17:24. [3] Matt. 17:27.

(According to Bissell.)

1 denarius "penny" = 1 drachma =	$.18\frac{3}{10}$
2 denarii = didrachma ($\frac{1}{2}$ shekel) =	$.36\frac{6}{10}$
4 " = 2 didrachma (shekel) =	$.73\frac{2}{10}$

LIST OF OBSOLETE OR OBSCURE WORDS IN THE ENGLISH (A. V.) BIBLE.

By the Rev. EDWIN W. RICE, D.D.

Abjects, Ps. 35: 15—low, despised persons.
Abomination, Deut. 7: 26—idol; polluted thing.
Addicted, 1 Cor. 16: 15—devoted; given to.
Affect, Gal. 4: 17—seek to win.
Aha, Ps. 35: 21—"hurrah."
Albeit, Eze. 13: 7—although it be.
Allow, Luke 11: 48—to praise; to approve.
All to brake, Judg. 9: 53—brake to pieces.
Amerce, Deut. 22: 19—punish by fire.
Ancients, Isa. 47: 6—aged persons.
Anon, Matt. 13: 20—quickly at once.
Apothecary, Ex. 30: 25—not a druggist, but "a maker of perfumes."
Artillery, 1 Sam. 20: 40—bows; arrows; sling.
Astonied, Job 17: 8—astonished.
At one, Acts 7: 26—in concord, or agreement.
Attent, 2 Chron. 6: 40—attentive.
Avoid, 1 Sam. 18: 11—to withdraw.
Away with, Isa. 1: 13—bear or endure.
Barbarian, 1 Cor. 14: 11—foreigner; not a Greek.
Beeves, Lev. 22: 21—(plural of beef) oxen; cows.
Bestead, Isa. 8: 21—placed.
Bewray, Matt. 26: 73—expose; betray.
Blains, Ex. 9: 9—blisters; pimples.
Bolled, Ex. 9: 31—gone to seed.
Bosses, Job 15: 26—stud; knob; buckle.
Botch, Deut. 28: 27—swelling; boil.
Bravery, Isa. 3: 18—fine dress; showy.
Bray, Prov. 27: 22—to beat; pound.
Brigandine, Jer. 46: 4—coat of armor.
Bruit, Jer. 10: 22—report; fame.
By, 1 Cor. 4: 4—against.
By and by, Matt. 13: 21—at once; immediately.
Calker, Eze. 27: 9—one who stops leaks of a ship.
Camphire, Song of Sol. 1: 14—refers to cypress, or to "henna-flowers."
Careful, Phil. 4: 6—anxious.
Carriage, 1 Sam. 17: 22—baggage; what is carried.
Caul, Isa. 3: 18—network for the head.
Champaign, Deut. 11: 30—level place.
Chapiter, Ex. 36: 38—capital of a pillar.
Chapmen, 2 Chron. 9: 14—traders; merchants.
Chapt, Jer. 14: 4—cracked open.
Charger, Matt. 14: 8—large dish.
Charges, to be at, Acts 21: 24—to pay expenses.
Charity, 1 Cor. 13—love to God and man.
Clouted, Josh. 9: 5—patched.
Cockle, Job 31: 40—refers to weed in grain.
Collops, Job 15: 27—slices of fat.
College, 2 Kings 22: 14—refers to "second ward," or port.
Comfort, 1 Thess. 4: 18—to strengthen.
Compass, Acts 28 13—to make a circuit; surround.
Concision, Phil. 3: 2—cutting off.
Confection, Ex. 30: 35—compound of various things.
Conscience, Heb. 10: 2—to have sense of.
Convenient, Acts 24: 25—seasonable; becoming.
Conversation—(never means "speech" in Scripture) but, (1) Phil. 1: 27—behavior; (2) Phil. 3: 20—citizenship; (3) Heb. 13: 5—disposition.
Countervail, Esther 7: 4—to compensate.
Cracknels, 1 Kings 14: 3—brittle cakes.
Crisping pins, Isa. 3: 22—irons for curling the hair.
Cumber, Luke 10: 40—to burden uselessly.
Curious arts, Acts 19: 19—magic.
Damnation, 1 Cor. 11: 29—condemnation.
Daysman, Job 9: 33—umpire; arbiter.
Deal, Ex. 29: 40—portion, or part.
Delicates, Jer. 51: 34—choice dainties.
Deputy, 1 Kings 22: 47—deputed to rule.
Disposition, Acts 7: 53—ordering.
Dote, Jer. 50: 36—become foolish.
Do you to wit, 2 Cor. 8: 1—make you to know.
Draught, Matt. 15: 17—drain.
Draught house, 2 Kings 10: 27—cesspool.
Ear, to, Isa. 30: 24—to plow.
Earing, Gen. 45: 6—plowing.
Earnest, 2 Cor. 1: 22—a pledge or token of what is to come.
Emerods, 1 Sam. 5: 6—hemorrhoids; piles.
Enlarge, 2 Sam. 22: 37—make free.
Ensample, 1 Cor. 10: 11—example.
Ensue, 1 Pet. 3: 11—to follow and overtake.
Eschew, 1 Pet. 3: 11—shun; flee from.
Exchangers, Matt. 25: 27—bankers; brokers.
Exorcists, Acts 19: 13—one who pretends to cast out evil spirits by magic.
Eyeservice, Eph. 6: 6—work done when watched.
Fain, Luke 15: 16—glad; gladly.
Fats, Joel 2: 24—vats.
Fenced, Num. 32: 17—walled (cities).
Flood, Josh. 24: 3—Euphrates river.
Fray, Deut. 28: 26—scare; frighten.
Fretting, Lev. 13: 51—corroding; eating as a moth.
Gainsay, Luke 21: 15—disprove; contradict.
Garner, Matt. 3: 12—storehouse for grain.
Gin, Amos 3: 5—trap or snare.
Glistering, Luke 9: 29—sparkling; glittering.
Greaves, 1 Sam. 17: 6—armor-plates for legs.
Grudge, Jas. 5: 9—grumble.
Habergeon, Job 41: 26—coat-of-mail.
Haft, Judg. 3: 22—handle of knife; dagger.
Hale, Luke 12: 58—forcibly drag.
Halt, Luke 14: 21—lame; crippled.
Harness, 1 Kings 22: 34—body-armor of a soldier.
Hoised, Acts 27: 40—hoisted.
Hold, Judg. 9: 46—stronghold; prison.
Honest, Rom. 12: 17—honorable.
Hosen, Dan. 3: 21—trowsers and stockings in one piece.
Hough, Josh. 11: 6—to hamstring.
Instant, Rom. 12: 12—pressing; urgent.
Instantly, Acts 26: 7—earnestly; at once.
Jeopard, Judg. 5: 18—hazard, or risk of life.
Kerchief, Eze.13: 21—covering for the head.
Kine, 1 Sam. 6: 7—cows; milch-kine = milking-cows.
Knop, Ex. 25: 33—knob; a bud-shaped carving.

Leasing, Ps. 4:2—lying; falsehood.
Let, 2 Thess. 2:7—hinder; prevent.
Lewdness, Acts 18:14—wickedness; crime.
Libertine, Acts 6:9—child of a freed slave.
Listeth, John 3:8—desireth; wills; chooseth; like.
Lust, Ex. 15:9—desire of any kind.
Lusty, Judg. 3:29—healthy; vigorous; strong.
Magnifical, 1 Chron. 22:5—grand; magnificent.
Marishes, Eze. 47:11—marshes; swampy ground.
Maw, Deut. 18:3—stomach.
Meat, Gen. 1:29—any kind of food.
Meet, Matt. 3:8—suitable; fitting.
Mete, Matt. 7:2—measure.
Meteyard, Lev. 19:35—measuring-rod; yard measure.
Mincing, Isa. 3:16—walking with short steps.
Minish, Ex. 5:19—diminish; lessen.
Minister, Luke 4:20—attendant; helper.
Munition, Nah. 2:1—fortifications; ramparts.
Murrain, Ex. 9:3—cattle-plague.
Naught, Prov. 20:14—bad; worthless.
Neesings, Job 41:18—old form of "sneezing."
Nephew, 1 Tim. 5:4—grandchild.
Nether, Deut. 24:6—lower.
Noisome, Ps. 91:3—noxious; hurtful.
Occupy, Luke 19:13—trade with.
Offence, Rom. 9:33—that against which one stumbles.
Offend, Matt. 18:9—stumble against; cause to stumble.
Or ever, Dan. 6:24—before.
Ouches, Ex. 28:11—sockets (of gold or silver).
Outlandish, Neh. 13:26—foreign; strange.
Painful, Ps. 73:16—hard to do.
Painfulness, 2 Cor. 11:27—painstaking.
Peeled, Isa. 18:2, 7—robbed; plundered.
Pilled, Gen. 30:37, 38—peel; strip off bark.
Poll, to, 2 Sam. 14:26—lop; cut off, *esp.* hair.
Pommel, 2 Chron. 4:12—globes; apple-shaped.
Potsherd, Ps. 22:15—fragment of broken pottery.
Pressfat, Hag. 2:16—vat to receive grape-juice from the winepress.
Prevent, 1 Thess. 4:15—come before; precede.
Proper, Heb. 11:23—fair; handsome.
Provoke, 2 Cor. 9:2—stimulate; challenge to action.
Publican, Luke 5:27—collector of public revenue.
Quick, Ps. 124:3—living; lively.
Quicken, Ps. 71:20—make alive.
Quit, 1 Cor. 16:13—acquit; act.
Ravening, Luke 11:39—greediness; rapacity.
Ravin, raven, Gen. 49:27—plunder; capture; spoil.
Reins, Ps. 7:9—kidneys, hence emotions; affections.
Rereward, Isa. 52:12; 58:8—rear-guard.
Ringstraked, Gen. 30:35—marked with circular bands or rings.
Savour, Matt. 16:23—taste; relish; relish in mind.

Scrabbled, 1 Sam. 21:13—scrawled; made unmeaning marks.
Scrip, Luke 22:36—small bag or wallet.
Seethe, Ex. 16:23—boil; *perf.* "sod," *part.* "sodden."
Servitor, 2 Kgs. 4:43—servant or attendant.
Sherd, Isa. 30:14—fragment; shred, as of pottery.
Shroud, Eze. 31:3—shelter; covering, as of a tree.
Silverling, Isa. 7:23—small silver coin.
Sith, Eze. 35:6—since; forasmuch as.
Sod, sodden, Ex. 12:9—boiled; from the *verb* "seethe."
Sojourn, Gen. 12:10—to dwell temporarily.
Sometimes, Eph. 2:13—once; formerly.
Speed, Gen. 24:12—*subst.* success.
Steads, 1 Chron. 5:22—(Sax. *stede*) places.
Straightway, Luke 5:39—immediately; at once.
Strain at, Matt. 23:24—as in swallowing, (probably a misprint for "strain out.")
Straitly, Mark 1:4—strictly; closely.
Straitness, Jer. 19:9—scarcity of food; famine.
Strake, Gen. 30:37—a streak.
Strake, Acts 27:17—past tense of the *verb* to "strike."
Strawed, Matt. 21:8—strewed or scattered.
Sundry, Heb. 1:1—several; various.
Tabering, Nah. 2:7—beating, as on a tabor-drum.
Taches, Ex. 26:6—catches or clasps; any fastening.
Tale, Ex. 5:8, 18—reckoning; appointed number.
Target, 1 Sam. 17:6—light shield; buckler.
Temperance, Gal. 5:23—moderation; sedateness; self-control.
Tempt, Gen. 22:1—test; try.
Thought, Matt. 6:25—worry; anxious care.
Tired, 2 Kings 9:30; Isa. 3:18—adorned, as the head.
Trow, Luke 17:9—think; imagine; suppose.
Turtle, Sol. Song 2:12—a dove; the turtle-dove.
Twain, Isa. 6:2—two.
Undergird, Acts 27:17—pass ropes round hull of a ship.
Undersetter, 1 Kings 7:30, 34—prop; support.
Vile, Jas. 2:2—plain; poor.
Ware, Acts 14:6—aware; to know.
Wax, Luke 1:80—grow or become.
Wench, 2 Sam. 17:17—maid-servant.
Whit, 2 Cor. 11:5—(Sax. *wiht*) a bit; atom.
Wimple, Isa. 3:22—veil; covering of head and neck.
Winefat—wine vat.
Wist, Mark 14:40—(Sax. *wiste*) knew.
Wit, to, 2 Cor. 8:1—(Sax. *witan*) to know.
Withs, Judg. 16:7—young twigs of a willow; osier.
Withal, Acts 25:27—with the same; therewith.
Wittingly, Gen. 48:14—intentionally; knowingly.
Woe worth, Eze. 30:2—woe be or become.
Wont, Matt. 27:15—accustomed.
Wot, Gen. 39:8; Ex. 32:1—know.
Wreathen, Ex. 28:14—twisted; turned; "wreathen work."

CONCISE CHRONOLOGICAL TABLE OF BIBLE HISTORY.

Compiled by Rev. Edwin W. Rice, D.D.

Note.—Most of the dates in Bible History, before the dedication of Solomon's temple, are very uncertain. There are two chief systems of chronology: one based upon the Hebrew text of the Old Testament, and the other upon the Septuagint, or Greek text, and called the "short" and the "long" chronology. The dates in the margin of our English Bibles were computed by Archbishop Ussher (born 1580, died 1656), and based on the Hebrew or short chronology. Hales made a similar computation, based on the Greek text. The Septuagint text appears to make the *patriarchal period* 1466 years longer than the computations based on the Hebrew text. The following table shows the different dates according to Ussher and to Hales:

Ussher, or Hebrew Dates.	Hales, or Greek Dates (nearly).	Events.
B.C.	B.C.	
4004	5411	Adam.
3874	5181	Birth of Seth.
3382	4289	" " Enoch.
3317	4124	" " Methuselah.
2948	3755	" " Noah.
2348	3155	The Flood.
2233	2554	Confusion of tongues.
2155	2362	Birth of Nahor.
2126	2283	" " Terah.
1996	2153	" " Abram.
1896	2053	" " Isaac.
1836	1993	" " Jacob.
1706	1863	Jacob moves to Egypt.
1571	1728	Birth of Moses.
1491	1648	The Exodus.[1]
1451	1608	Canaan entered.

[The best authorities now agree that The Exodus cannot be placed earlier than about 1320 B.C. The time thus apparently lost is regained by shortening the period of the Judges, as many of the judges ruled in different parts of Canaan at the same time.

The bondage in Egypt was about 400 years, according to Acts 7:6; or about 430 years from Abraham or Jacob to the giving of the law, according to Gal. 3:17. The latest conclusions from Egyptian and Assyrian records are in substantial accord with these passages.]

B.C.	Events.
1280	Settlement in Canaan under Joshua.
1258-1095	The Judges—to Samuel and Saul.
1095	Saul.
1055	David.
1007	Solomon's Temple. (For table of kings of Judah and Israel, and of prophets, see next page.)
722-721	Fall of Samaria.
606	Assyrian captivity began.
588-7	Jerusalem destroyed.

B.C.	Events.
536	First return of Jews—Zerubbabel.
516-5	Second temple completed.
478	Esther made queen by Xerxes I.
457	Return of Jews (second company) with Ezra.
444	Nehemiah appointed governor. Malachi, prophet.
432	Nehemiah again governor at Jerusalem.
425	Death of Artaxerxes, Xerxes II. (2 months). Sogdianus, his half brother (7 months).
424	Darius II. (Nothus, king).

End of Old Testament history.

CHRONOLOGY BETWEEN THE OLD AND NEW TESTAMENTS.

B.C.	Events.
405	Artaxerxes II. (Mnemon).
359	Artaxerxes III. (Ochus).
351-331	Jaddua high priest at J.
339	Arses (king).
336	Darius III. (Codomannus).
332	Alexander the Great.
323	Alexander's death.
320	Palestine under Ptolemy Soter.
314	" " Antigonus.
311	(Era of the Seleucidæ.)
301	Palestine under Ptolemies.
280	Hebrew O. T. translated into Greek about this time.
205	Palestine under Antiochus.
170	Temple plundered by Antiochus Epiphanes.
167	Mattathias, the Jewish patriot; father of the Maccabæans.
165	Judas Maccabæus recovers Jerusalem.
141	Simon Maccabæus frees the Jews.
63	Pompey conquers Judæa.
54	Temple plundered by Crassus.
47	Antipater made governor of Judæa by Cæsar.
40	Parthians capture Jerusalem.
37	Herod retakes Jerusalem.
17	Herod begins to rebuild the temple.
5	Birth of Christ. (The common Christian era was fixed four years too late.)

225

TABLE OF KINGS AND PROPHETS IN ISRAEL AND JUDAH.
(THE DATES APPLY TO THE KINGS.)

IN THE UNITED KINGDOM.

Prophets.	B.C.	Kings.	Time of Reign.
Samuel.	1095	Saul,	Reigned 40 years.
Gad.	1055	David,	Reigned 40 years.
Nathan.	1015	Solomon,	Reigned 40 years.

IN THE DIVIDED KINGDOM.

JUDAH.				ISRAEL.			
Began B.C.	Kings.	Reigned Years.	Prophets.	Began B.C.	Kings.	Reigned Years.	Prophets.
975	Rehoboam,	17	Shemaiah.	975	Jeroboam,	22	Ahijah.
958	Abijah,	3	Iddo.				
955	Asa,	41	Oded.				
			Azariah.	954	Nadab,	2	
			Hanani.	953	Baasha,	24	
				930	Elah,	2	
				929	Zimri,	7 dys.	
				929	Omri,	12	
				918	Ahab,	22	Elijah.
914	Jehoshaphat,	25	Jehu.				Micaiah.
			Jahaziel.	898	Ahaziah,	2	Elisha.
			Eliezer.	896	Joram,	12	
892	Jehoram,	8					
885	Ahaziah,	1					
884	Athaliah,	6		884	Jehu,	28	
878	Jehoash,	40					
			Zechariah, son of Jehoiada.	856	Jehoahaz,	17	Jonah. [?]
				841	Joash,	16	
839	Amaziah,	29					
				825	Jeroboam II.,	41	
							Hosea.
810	Uzziah,	52	Zechariah, 2 Chr. 26: 5.				Amos.
				784	*Interregnum*,	11	
				773	Zachariah,	6 mo.	
				772	Shallum,	1 mo.	
				772	Menahem,	10	
				761	Pekahiah,	2	
				759	Pekah,	20	
758	Jotham,	16	Isaiah.				
742	Ahaz,	16	Micah.				
				739	*Anarchy*,	9	Oded.
				730	Hoshea,	9	
726	Hezekiah,	29	Nahum.				
				721	The kingdom of Israel overthrown by the Assyrians and Samaria destroyed.		
698	Manasseh,	55	Joel.				
643	Amon,	2					
641	Josiah,	31	Jeremiah.				
610	Jehoahaz,	3 mos.	Habakkuk.				
610	Jehoiakim,	11	Zephaniah.				
599	Jehoiachin,	100 days.	Ezekiel. Daniel.				
599	Zedekiah,	11	Obadiah. [?]		*Persian Kings, after the Captivity.*		
588	Jerusalem destroyed.			536	First year of Cyrus.		
				529	Cambyses.		
	Governors after the Captivity.			521	Darius Hystaspes.		
				486	Xerxes I.		
536	Zerubbabel,		Haggai.	478	Esther Queen.		
457	Ezra,		Zechariah.	465	Artaxerxes-Longimanus.		
445	Nehemiah,		Malachi.	424	Darius Nothus.		

Contemporary with Rehoboam was Sesonchis of the 22d dynasty in Egypt; with Jehoshaphat, Nesha king of Moab, and Eth-baal king of Tyre; and with Athaliah, Dido, who founded Carthage. During Uzziah's long reign the First Olympiad takes its rise; and Rome was founded (753) in the reign of Jotham.

CHRONOLOGY OF THE NEW TESTAMENT.

B.C.
- 5   Birth of Jesus.
- 4 (April)   Death of Herod.
  [For Events in Life of Christ, see JESUS CHRIST, p. 124.]

A.D.
- 8   Jesus among the doctors.
- 27   Baptism of Jesus.
- 28   Ministry in Judæa and Galilee. Sermon on the mount.
- 29   Baptist beheaded. Five thousand fed. Tour to borders of Tyre and Sidon. The transfiguration. Feast of dedication. Part of Peræan ministry.
- 30   Lazarus raised to life. Peræan ministry.
- April 1   Supper at Bethany.
- " 2   Triumphal entry into Jerusalem.
- " 6   Last supper and Gethsemane.
- " 7   Crucifixion.
- " 9   Resurrection of Jesus.
- May 18   Ascension of Jesus.
- 37   Death of Stephen. Conversion of Saul.

B.C.
- 40   Saul's escape from Jerusalem. [For table, see PAUL, p. 173.]
- 44   James of Zebedee beheaded.
- 45   Paul's first missionary tour.
- 51   Paul's second missionary tour.
- 53   Epistles to *Thessalonians*, from Corinth.
- 54   Paul's third missionary tour.
- 56–8   Epistles to the *Galatians, Corinthians, and Romans*.
- 58   Paul before Felix.
- 60   Paul sent to Rome.
- 61   Paul arrives at Rome. Epistle of *James* (?).
- 61–63   Epistles to *Ephesians, Colossians, Philemon, and Philippians*.
- 63   Paul supposed to be set free.
- 64–67   Epistles to *Hebrews, 1st and 2d Peter, Jude, 1st and 2d Timothy, and Titus*.
- 67   Paul's martyrdom (?).
- 70   Jerusalem destroyed by Titus.
- 80–95   John's Gospel.
- 65–95   *Revelation* of St. John.
- 93–100   Death of John.

NAMES, TITLES AND OFFICES OF CHRIST.

Advocate, 1 John 2:1. *Almighty*, Rev. 1:8.
Alpha and Omega, Rev. 1:8; 22:13.
Amen, Rev. 3:14.
Anointed, Ps. 2:2; Acts 4:26.
Apostle, Heb. 3:1.
Author and Finisher of our faith, Heb. 12:2.
Beginning of the creation of God, Rev. 3:14.
Beloved Son, Matt. 17:5.
Blessed and only Potentate, 1 Tim. 6:15.
Branch, Zech. 3:8; 6:12.
Bread of life, John 6:35.
Bridegroom, Matt. 9:15.
Captain of salvation, Heb. 2:10.
Corner-stone, 1 Pet. 2:6.
David, Jer. 30:9; Eze. 34:23; Hos. 3:5.
Day-spring, Lk. 1:78. *Day-star*, 2 Pet. 1:19.
Deliverer, Rom. 11:26.
Desire of all nations, Hag. 2:7.
Emmanuel, Isa. 7:14; Matt. 1:23.
Everlasting Father, Isa. 9:6.
Faithful Witness, Rev. 1:5; 3:14.
First and Last, Rev. 1:17.
First begotten of the dead, Rev. 1:5.
God, Isa. 40:9; John 20:28; 1 John 5:20.
Good Shepherd, John 10:11.
Governor, Matt. 2:6.
Great High Priest, Heb. 4:14.
Holy One, Luke 4:34; Acts 3:14; Rev. 3:7.
Horn of salvation, Luke 1:69.
I AM, Ex. 3:14, with John 8:58.
Image of God, 2 Cor. 4:4.
Intercessor, Heb. 7:25. *Jehovah*, Isa. 26:4.
Jesus, Matt. 1:21; 1 Thess. 1:10.
Judge, Acts 17:31.
King, everlasting, Luke 1:33.
King of kings, Rev. 17:14; 19:16.
Lamb of God, John 1:29, 36.
Lawgiver, James 4:12.
Light of the world, John 8:12.
Light, True, John 1:8, 9; 3:19; 8:12; 9:5.
Lion of the tribe of Judah, Rev. 5:5.
Living bread, John 6:31.
Living stone, 1 Pet. 2:4.
Lord, Matt. 3:3; Mark 11:3.
Lord God, Rev. 15:3; 22:6.
Lord of all, Acts 10:36; *of glory*, 1 Cor. 2:8.
Lord of lords, Rev. 17:14; 19:16.
Lord our righteousness, Jer. 23:6.
Maker and Preserver of all things, John 1:3, 10; Col. 1:16; Heb. 1:2, 10; Rev. 4:11.
Mediator, 1 Tim. 2:5.
Mediator of the new covenant, Heb. 12:24.
Messiah, Dan. 9:25; John 1:41.
Mighty One of Jacob, Isa. 60:16.
Morning star, Rev. 22:16.
Nazarene, Matt. 2:23.
Our Passover, 1 Cor. 5:7.
Priest, High, Heb. 3:1.
Prince, Acts 5:31. *Prince of life*, Acts 3:15.
Prince of peace, Isa. 9:6.
Prince of the kings of the earth, Rev. 1:5.
Prophet, Deut. 18:15; Luke 24:19.
Redeemer, Job 19:25; Isa. 59:20.
Resurrection and life, John 11:25.
Rock, 1 Cor. 10:4.
Root and offspring of David, Rev. 22:16.
Root of David, Rev. 5:5.
Ruler of Israel, Micah 5:2.
Same yesterday, to-day, etc., Heb. 13:8.
Saviour, Luke 2:11; Acts 5:31.
Shepherd and Bishop of souls, 1 Pet. 2:25.
Shepherd in the land, Zech. 11:16.
Shepherd of the sheep, Great, Heb. 13:20.
Shiloh, Gen. 49:10.
Son of David, Matt. 9:27; 21:9.
Son of God, Luke 1:35; Matt. 3:17; 8:29.
Son of man, Matt. 8:20; John 1:51.
Son of the Highest, Luke 1:32.
Son, Only-begotten, John 1:14, 18; 3:16, 18.
Sun of righteousness, Mal. 4:2.
True Vine, John 15:1.
Way, Truth, and Life, John 14:6.
Witness, Faithful and true, Rev. 3:14.
Wonderful, Counsellor, Mighty God, Isa. 9:6.
Word, John 1:1.
Word of God, Rev. 19:13.

JOURNEYINGS OF ISRAEL FROM EGYPT TO CANAAN.
By Rev. EDWIN W. RICE, D.D.

STATIONS.	MODERN NAMES.	EVENTS.	RECORDED IN.
1. Rameses,	Tel el Kebir (?),	Starting for Canaan,	Num. 33 : 3, 5.
2. Succoth or Pithom,	Tel el Maskhuta,	First camping-place,	Ex. 12 : 37.
3. Etham,	Wady Tumeilat,	Pillar of fire and cloud,	Ex. 13 : 20.
4. Pi-habiroth,	Near Ismaileh,	Pursued by Pharaoh,	Ex. 14 : 29.
5. Red Sea (crossed),		Egyptians drowned,	Ex. 14 : 21-31.
6. Marah,	Ain Howarah (?),	Bitter water made sweet,	Ex. 15 : 23.
7. Elim,	Wady Gharandel,	12 wells of water,	Ex. 15 : 27.
8. By Red Sea (east side),	Near Wady Feiran,		Num. 33 : 10.
9. Wilderness of Sin,	el Markha,	Quails and manna,	Ex. 16 : 1-36.
10. Dophkah,	In Wady Feiran,		Num. 33 : 12.
11. Alush,	In Wady Feiran,		Num. 33 : 13.
12. Rephidim (Massah and Meribah),	In Wady Feiran,	Water from a rock, Battle with Amelek,	Ex. 17 : 1-16.
13. Sinai,	Ras-sufsafeh,	The law given,	Ex. 19 to 40.
14. Taberah ("burning"),		Slain by fire,	Num. 11 : 3.
15. Kibroth-hattavah ("graves of lusting"),		Smitten with plague,	Num. 11 : 30-34.
16. Hazeroth (Rithmah),	Ain Hudhera,	Leprosy of Miriam,	Num. 12 : 1-16.
17. Wilderness Paran,	et Tih,		Num. 12 : 16.
18. Kadesh Barnea,	Ain Qadis (?),	12 spies sent,	Num. 13 to 19.
19. Forty years' wandering,		People rebel; 14,700 die; Korah and his company slain.	

[The unbelief of the Israelites causes Jehovah to condemn them to wander for forty years in the wilderness. During this period they had their head-quarters or encampments at the following seventeen places, and then reassembled at Kadesh for a final departure from the wilderness to enter Canaan.]

20. Rimmon-perez,	Probably et Tih,		Num. 33 : 19.
21. Libnah,	Probably el Beyaneh,		Num. 33 : 20.
22. Rissah,	Rasa,		Num. 33 : 21.
23. Kehelathah,	(?)		Num. 33 : 22.
24. Mt. Shepher,	Jebel Sheraph,		Num. 33 : 23.
25. Haradah,	Aradeh,		Num. 33 : 24.
26. Makbeloth,	(?)		Num. 33 : 25.
27. Tahath,	Elt hi (?),		Num. 33 : 26.
28. Terah,	(?)		Num. 33 : 27.
29. Mithkah,	(?)		Num. 33 : 28.
30. Hashmonah,	Heshmon (?) Ain Hoch,		Num. 33 : 29.
31. Moseroth,	West of Arabah,		Num. 33 : 30.
32. Bene-jaakan,	(?)		Num. 33 : 31.
33. Hor-hagidgad,	(?)		Num. 33 : 32.
34. Jotbathah,	Wady Tabah (?),		Num. 33 : 33, 34; Deut. 10 : 7.
35. Ebronah,	On Elanitic Gulf,		Num. 33 : 34.
36. Ezion-geber,	Head of Elanitic Gulf,		Num. 33 : 35.
37. Kadesh (Wilderness of Zin),	Ain Qadis (?),	Miriam dies; water from rock, Meribah,	Num. 20 : 1-13; 33 : 36.
38. Mt. Hor,	(?)	Aaron dies, Num. 20 : 23-29; Deut. 33 : 50.	
39. Zalmonah,	Alem-maan (?),	Fiery serpents,	Num. 21 : 7; 33 : 41.
40. Punon,	Anezeh (?),		Num. 33 : 42.
41. Oboth,	el-Alsa,		Num. 21 : 11; 33 : 43, 44.
42. Ije-abarim,	East of Moab,		Num. 21 : 11; 33 : 45.
43. Dibon-gad (in Zared),	Dhiban,		Num. 33 : 45.
44. Almon-diblathaim,	(?)	Amorites defeated,	Num. 21 : 13; 33 : 46.
45. Nebo,	Mts. of Moab,		Num. 33 : 47.
46. Plains of Moab,	Valley of Jordan.	Balaam's prophecy,	Num. 22 to 24.
47. Shittim,	Valley of Jordan.	24,000 die of plague,	Num. 25 : 9.
48. Moab, Plains of,		People numbered; law repeated; Reuben and Gad's land east of Jordan; Moses dies; Joshua, leader,	Num. 26 to 36; Deut. 1 to 31.
49. Jordan (crossed),	Near Jericho,	Waters divided,	Josh. 3 : 1-17.
50. Gilgal,	Near Jericho,	Circumcision renewed,	Josh. 5 : 2-9.
51. Jericho, Fall of,		Rahab saved,	Josh. 6 : 1-27.
52. Ai, Defeat at,		Achan's sin,	Josh. 7 : 1-26.
53. Ai taken,		12,000 slain,	Josh. 8 : 1-29.
54. Shechem,		Altar built; law read; blessings and cursings from Ebal and Gerizim,	Josh. 8 : 30-35.
55. Gilgal, Return to,		[Gibeonites craft and punishment,	Josh. 9 : 1-27.
56. Gibeon rescued,		[Sun and moon stand still; five kings slain,	Josh. 10 : 1-27.
57. Makkedah, Libnah and Lachish destroyed,			Josh. 10 : 28, 29, 33.
58. Eglon, Hebron, and Debir taken,			Josh. 10 : 34-40.
59. Gilgal, Return again to,		[Southern Canaan conquered,	Josh. 10 : 40-43.
60. Merom,		[Great battle; northern Canaan conquered,	Josh. 11 : 1-23.
61. Shiloh,		[Tabernacle set up; land divided and settled,	Josh. 12 to 18.

www.ingramcontent.com/pod-product-compliance
Lightning Source LLC
Chambersburg PA
CBHW021843230426
43669CB00008B/1065